MYSTERIOUS WORLD

IRELAND

IAN MIDDLETON • DOUGLAS ELWELL
PHOTOGRAPHY BY IAN MIDDLETON
ILLUSTRATIONS BY JIM FITZPATRICK

MYSTERIOUS
WORLD
PRESS

WHEATON, ILLINOIS USA

Dedication

To my girlfriend, Nika.
You truly are a beautiful lady, whose continuing
love and support give added meaning to everything I do.
Ireland will always be our special place.

© 2006 Doug Elwell, Inc. All Rights Reserved.
Mysterious World Press™ is the print division of Mysterious World®
http://www.mysteriousworld.com
Mysterious World® is wholly owned and operated by Doug Elwell, Inc.™
http://www.dougelwell.com
Mysterious World Travel Guides™ design and layout style copyright © Doug Elwell, Inc.
All Rights Reserved. Printed in the United States of America.

Library of Congress Cataloging-in-Publication Data
Ian Middleton, Douglas Elwell
Mysterious World: Ireland
http://ireland.mysteriousworld.com
Bibliography: http://ireland.mysteriousworld.com/Bibliography/
No index included.
1. Travel. 2. History. 3. Ancient Mysteries.
ISBN 0-9760827-3-X

Table of Contents

THE HISTORY

THE JOURNEY

A complete bibliography can be found at http://ireland.mysteriousworld.com/Bibliography/

Foreword

"St. Columba at Iona" © 1999, Jim Fitzpatrick.

Welcome to *Mysterious World: Ireland*, the first in a series of travel guides to be published by Mysterious World Press™, a division of Mysterious World® (http://www.mysteriousworld.com). Mysterious World is an online travel site that has been in publication since 1998, offering a variety of travel and related information including a quarterly journal with articles about exotic travel destinations around the world. Our journal is by far the most popular part of our site, and since 1998 *Mysterious World Journal* has grown in size from a handful of travel articles generating a few dozen visitors per week to close to a hundred articles with thousands of visitors per *day* as the size and quality of our journal continues to grow. The combination of quality of research, writing and design to be found in *Mysterious World Journal* makes us stand out head and shoulders above the competition, and we are increasingly setting the standard for knowledge and innovation in the fields of travel, history and ancient mysteries for all others to follow.

Over the years, the quality of our articles has led many of our loyal readers to express an interest in subscribing to a print version of our magazine. However, I have found that print magazines have a shallow and transitory quality about them that makes them unsuitable as a serious publishing medium. Academic journals are somewhat better, as they are non-commercial in orientation, but precious few libraries keep many journals in storage, and as a result much knowledge has been lost to obscurity. My own experiences in performing research for many of our articles has forced me to explore many dusty, dungeonlike basements and decipher the labyrinthine coding systems of numerous libraries, cracking open countless books and bound journals, many of which had not seen the light of day since well before I was born. Moreover, with the advent of the Internet, printing magazines and journals has become an inefficient and redundant means of publishing, often requiring the same information to be processed and published in two entirely different (and expensive) media. For my part, I find leafing through stacks of magazines and journals to find "that one article" to be a time-consuming and unnecessary chore that the Internet was specifically designed to eliminate. To this end, we will continue to publish *Mysterious World Journal* as an online-only publication that can be easily accessed by absolutely anyone in the world who has an Internet connection, and an open mind.

However, though *Mysterious World Journal* covers a variety of subjects, some of which are only peripherally related to travel, it is still essentially a travel journal. As such, it occurred to us that our readers may have a need to take Mysterious World on the road with them — "off the beaten path" — where Internet connections and other aspects of postmodern civilization are few and far between. To this end, we have devised a means of putting Mysterious World in print in a format that is truly useful — as a new type of travel guide, the *Mysterious World Travel Guides* series. But our travel guides are not merely dispassionate listings of sights to see, places to eat, and so forth; i.e., "just another travel guide", though they will include a great deal of useful travel information. They will be more like a form of travel journal in that they will include not only useful travel information, but also the personal story of one man's journey throughout each country, written in a language and terminology that is readable and interesting to any reader, from the hard-core adventurer to the armchair traveler.

Also unlike most travel guides, the *Mysterious World Travel Guides* series offers an in-depth look into the history and ancient mysteries of every country that we will be exploring. From the most ancient historical and archaeological records we will explore the myths and legends, deities and demigods, kings, queens, warriors, wizards and creatures great and small that populate the histories and mythologies of each country and give it its distinctive character. As such, our travel guides should interest a wide variety of readers, particularly those interested in books on travel, history, and/or ancient mysteries, and those who like all three should find our books very satisfying indeed. That, combined with our unique, full-color format replete with hundreds of photographs and illustrations by top artists from around the world should make each *Mysterious World Travel Guide* something that you will use and cherish for years to come.

So kick back, relax and spend some quality time with *Mysterious World: Ireland*, the first in our *Mysterious World Travel Guides* series, and experience the ancient mysteries, history, and one man's journey to rediscover mysterious Ireland.

Doug Elwell, Publisher
Mysterious World

publisher@mysteriousworld.com
http://ireland.mysteriousworld.com
http://www.mysteriousworld.com

Introduction

"Tuan: The Coming of Nemed" © 1992, Jim Fitzpatrick.

I am Tuan
I am legend
I am memory turned myth.

I am the story teller. Warriors and young boys creep away from the hearths of wine halls to hear me. Greedy for tales of honor and history they watch my lips with bright eyes, for I give them what is more precious than gold: treasure unlocked from my heart. My words burn like flame in the darkness. I speak and hearts beat high, swords warm to the hand; under my spell boys become men.

But I know both the pain as well as the brightness of fire. I am the story teller who cannot find rest. The peace of death will never be mine. I am condemned to watch and to speak; my hand reaches in vain for the warrior's sword.

Once I, Tuan, was a man, the chieftain of a great race, the Cessair. My warriors sat on wolf skins; they raised golden goblets to me brimming with wine. Neither evil nor harm dared cross the threshold where I sat, my throne studded with jewels, inlaid with ivory.

But the gods envy the happiness of men; flood and sword combined to destroy my people. Now the wine hall stood empty, ruined; doorway and roof gaped wide to receive the beasts of the earth and the birds of the air. It was ordained that I alone should be saved to bear witness to my people's fate. I watched helpless while the fair land of Èireann was ravaged by the scavengers and foes. The golden cities I once loved lay fathoms deep beneath gray seas.

For many years I wandered as a man seeking shelter in caves and the depths of the forest; but when at last the noble race of Nemed came to reclaim their homeland I was barred from greeting them as either chieftain or warrior. Another fate was mine; to watch unseen, keeping the secrets of time close in heart and brain. The gods had singled me out for a strange fate, unfamiliar pains and pleasures, for as the years passed, they bound me within the bodies of beast and bird so that I might watch and keep the history of Èireann unnoticed by men.

The first transformation came upon me unaware. I had grown old as a man. The years had left my body naked and weak; my joints ached and my hair fell gray and matted over my bowed shoulders. One day a great weariness came upon me. I sought shelter in my cave certain that death had claimed me. For many days and nights I slept. Then at last I awoke to the sun. My limbs felt strong and free. My heart leapt up within me for I had been reborn as Tuan, the great-horned stag, King of the deer-herds of Èireann. The green hills were mine, the valleys and the streams.

As I ran free across the heather-covered plains, the children of Nemed were driven from their homeland. Only I remained, grown old as a stag, their story locked in my heart. Then the great heaviness of change again weighed me down; again I sought shelter in my cave. Wolves eager for my blood and sinewy flesh howled to the moon. But I slept, floating loose in dream-time. Through the heaviness of sleep I felt myself grow young again. When the low rays of sunrise touched me I awoke.

The wolves still sniffed about the entrance to my cave. But now I was young and strong; fit to face them. I, Tuan, with joyful heart, thrust my sharp tusks out of my lair and the wolves fled yelping like frightened dogs. I was fresh, lusty with life; I had been born again, a black boar bristling with power, thirsty for blood. Now I was a king of herds; my back was sharp with dark bristles; my teeth and tusks were ready to cut and kill. All creatures feared me.

"Tuan above Moy Tura" © 1977, Jim Fitzpatrick.

But while I had lain locked in dreams a new race of men had come to disturb the silence of mountain and valley. They were the Fir Bolg and they also belonged to the family of Nemed. These I did not chase and when they chased me I fled, for their blood was mine also. The Fir Bolg divided the island into five provinces and proclaimed the title *Ard-Rí*, that is High King, for the first time in Èire-ann.

As I roamed the purple hills I would often leave my herd and gaze across to the High King's hall and remember with sadness the time when I also had sat in council, with warriors at my feet, and felt the bright eyes of women gaze upon me.

Once again the ache of change drove me back to my lonely cave in Ulster. After three days fasting, another death floated me beyond dream-time. Nights circled from summer into winter until one morning I woke and soared high into the clear sky.

I was reborn
I was lord of the heavens
I was Tuan the great sea-eagle.

13

I, who had been king among the heather and scented woodlands, became lord of the heavens. From the highest mountain I could see the field-mouse gathering wheat husks — nothing escaped my sharp eye.

Motionless, feathering the air, riding the wind, I watched as another tribe of the children of Nemed came to Èireann. Known as the Tuatha dé Danann they sailed down over the mountains in a magic fleet of sky riding ships until they came to rest among the Red Hills of Rein led by Nuada, their king.

Rather than fight their own flesh and blood the Tuatha Dé offered to share the island with the tribes of the Fir Bolg. But on the advice of his elders Eochai, their High King refused, and the battle lines were drawn up.

I, Tuan the eagle, watched that fratricidal struggle; that terrible slaughter of kinsmen known as the First Battle of Moy Tura. I saw the same green plain across which I had, as a stag and boar, led my herd, drenched in blood. There I saw for the last time the Fir Bolg in their fullness and their pride, in their beauty and their youth, ranged against the glittering armies of the Tuatha Dé Danann. The battle was fierce and ebbed and flowed like waves on a sea of fortune and price.

The circles of my eyes were rimmed with bitter tears as I watched that dreadful carnage of kinsmen, for all who fought were bound by a common bond, the blood of Nemed the Great. The battle raged for many days; death cut down the flower of youth on both sides.

At last the Tuatha dé Danann took the sovereignty of Èireann from the Fir Bolg and their allies. But in that First Battle of Moy Tura, Nuada, King of the Tuatha Dé, had his arm struck off, and from that loss there came sorrow and trouble to his people. For it was a law with the Tuatha dé Danann that no man imperfect in form could be king. So it happened that Nuada, who had led his people to victory, had to abdicate his throne and hand the royal crown over to the elders of his race.

I, Tuan, the sea-eagle, wept secretly with Nuada over the loss of his crown, for he was a noble king and a just ruler who had won back the land of Èireann for his people. His mutilation and his loss were the result of his bravery in battle. For he was a great warrior, skilled and courageous and as one with his god, the sun.

When the noise of battle and the wailing of women had faded into silence, when the earth had soaked up the blood, when the plain of Moy Tura had become a sad, spirit-haunted place marked by pillars and cairns, I, Tuan, still sailed high above it. I knew that that same force of history that governed the fortunes of men had made me the winged bearer of myth. I knew that the pattern of change is never completed until the world's end. Still I would have to bear the burden of man's triumph and grief.

I am Tuan
I am Legend
I am memory turned myth.

I have lived through the ages
In the shape of man, beast and bird
Mute witness to great events,
Guardian of past deeds.[1]

On the surface, Tuan Mac Carrill appears to have been a very long-lived man indeed, a man whose life was mysterious beyond easy reckoning. However, Tuan was not a man, nor an eagle, but instead a very clever literary device that had been invented by the early Christian monks as a means to help them organize the ancient history of the land that they themselves would name "Ireland".

Using the "Tuan" narrative device, the Irish monks were able to knit together a comprehensive history of Ireland. Tuan, a mythical chieftain of the tribe of Cessair, the first known civilized people believed to have ever inhabited the lonely isle, starts his narrative with how he had seen his people destroyed by the Great Flood of Noah, and by the great world war that had immediately preceded it. Yet he himself was saved by God for greater things, to be a witness to the entire history of Ireland, even up to the present time.

The use of this narrative device was necessary because, before the Christian monks had intervened, there was no "Ireland" as we understand it today. The history of the land now known as Ireland up to that time had been, save for a few periods of relative stability, primarily a series of chaotic upheavals caused by the constant invasions of numerous peoples, some of whom were merely looking for plunder and conquest, and others who were sailing to the lonely isle of green west of civilization in hopes of finding a fresh start. In that sense Ireland was the first true "melting pot" of the ancient West, preceding America in that role by thousands of years.

In this isolated land each new wave of immigrants managed to hold on to their ancient customs and traditions, and many of the earliest invaders who had been defeated in battle by succeeding waves of invaders never left the island entirely, but instead were restricted to certain isolated sections of the country where they continued to worship their own tribal deities and develop their own unique histories and traditions. Christianity, which arrived over a thousand years after the Partholónians had first set foot on Ireland's Flood-washed virgin soil, came to be the first lasting, unifying force for the lonely isle, due largely to the Christian monks who worked tirelessly to preserve, organize and make sense of the vast amounts of ancient, and largely oral, traditions of the various ancient peoples that still populated the land. And contrary to the stereotype of Christian missionaries, these monks not only did not erase the ancient and typically pagan history of Ireland, but are, by their tireless work in preserving the old myths and legends, most likely the sole reason much of it still survives to the present day.

For this reason, to help preserve and defend the history and traditions of Ireland to pass on to future generations, we have chosen to follow in the footsteps of the ancient monastic traditions and take the same objective, unbiased look at all of Ireland's history, both pagan and Christian, in all its glory — and contradictions. Also like those ancient scholars, we will continue to employ Tuan the Eagle as a narrative device, setting him aflight once more to oversee and help explain all that Ireland has to offer to all who earnestly seek to explore her history, and her mysteries. To this end, we have developed a design that incorporates the image of an eagle adapted from the famous *Book of Kells* that we will use to represent "Tuan the Eagle" in the top outer corners of every page hereafter. In the third and largest section, "The Journey", there also will be a special section on every page: an emerald-green bar on the outer margins that will contain not only comprehensive and context-relevant travel information, but also special comments labeled "Tuan's Notes" that will refer the reader back to the first two sections, "The Mystery" and "The History", for more information on selected topics.

"The Journey" is also further divided into four major sections, one for each of the four ancient provinces — Leinster, Munster, Connaught and Ulster — that Ireland has been formally divided into since ancient times (now they are only informal, regional divisions). Each of these sections is indicated by characters adapted from each of the four Gospels in the Four Gospels page from *The Book of Kells*: the man, from the Book of Matthew, which is used for Leinster; the lion, from the Book of Mark, which is used for Munster; the bull, from the Book of Luke, which is used for Connaught, and the eagle, from the Book of John, which is used for Ulster (see p. 382 for the complete folio). These characters all appear in the emerald margin, and also serve as handy thumbmarks on the edge of the pages that allow you to locate the four subsections of The Journey more quickly.

So, now that we have set the context, let us take wing with Tuan and begin our journey to rediscover mysterious Ireland in Section I: The Mystery.

Notes

[1] Tuan narrative from Jim Fitzpatrick's *The Book of Conquests* (New York: E.P. Dutton, 1978).

PART I: TH

E MYSTERY

The Mystery

I am the wind upon the waves
I am the waves upon the ocean
I am the roaring of the sea!

I am the raging bull triumphant
I am the eagle plotting in its lair
I am the sunlight that creates the heavenly bow
I am the salmon that leaps from the waters.

I am the divine spark that brings life!

I am the spear that wins the battle
I am the wild boar that attacks without fear
I am the water that flows everlasting
I am the fountain of knowledge.

I am the god who stole fire from heaven!

Who understands the light of the sun?
Who can predict the path of the moon?
Who can read the secrets of the tree?

If not me?

These are the words spoken by Amergin, the Chief Poet of the Milesians, as he first set foot upon fair Èireann's shore. The Milesians were the first of the Gaelic peoples to invade the sacred isle, and Amergin's words are believed to be one of the greatest poems ever to be uttered in a land that has forever been known for its verse.

THE MYSTERY
THE MYSTERY

The Milesians had defeated the previous inhabitants of Ireland, the Tuatha dé Danann, in battle, and with his poems Amergin had defeated their magic. The Tuatha Dé were once mighty in magic, and had fought and won the land not once but twice against mighty opponents. But now, with the coming of the Milesians, it appeared that their time had come. The stars were now aligned in favor of the sons of Mil, and the gods had determined that the rulership over the land was to pass on to the Gaedel, that is, the Milesians and related peoples, better known to history as the Gaels.

The Sons of Magog

The Gaels were only the most recent of a series of peoples who had invaded the sacred island over the millennia. According to the primary ancient historical text of Ireland, the *Lebor Gabala Èrenn*, "The Book of the Invasions of Ireland", there were a total of 5 peoples who had invaded Ireland before the coming of the Gael: the Cessair, the Partholónians, the Nemedians, the Fir Bolg and the Tuatha dé Danann. The Milesians were the final invaders recorded in the *Lebor*, and are considered to be the first of the Gaelic peoples to inhabit Ireland. However, though only the Milesians were considered to be true Gaels, all of these invading peoples — save the Cessair — were related to the Milesians, as they were all descendants of Magog, the son of Japheth, the son of Noah. As it says in the *Lebor*,

> Magog, of him are the men of Scythia and the Goths, that is, the Gaedil. Magog had five sons, Baath, Ibath, Barachan, Emoth, Aithechta. As for Baath, his son was Feinius Farsaid, father of the Scythians. As for Feinius Farsaid, he was son of Baath s. Magog s. Iafeth [Japheth]. As for Ibath, one of the two sons of Magog, his son was Alainus. He had three sons, Airmen, Negua, Isicon. Airmen had five sons, Gotus, Uiligotus, Cebitus, Burgandus, Longbardus. Negua had four sons, Vandalus, Saxus, Bogardus, Longbardus. Isicon, the third son of Alainus, had [five] sons, Francus, Romanus, Albanus, a quo Albania in Asia Minor, and Albanactus ... a quo western Alba, and Britus, from whom are called the islands of Britain. Then was the world divided into three divisions: Europe, Africa, Asia. Seventeen years before the scattering of the languages there

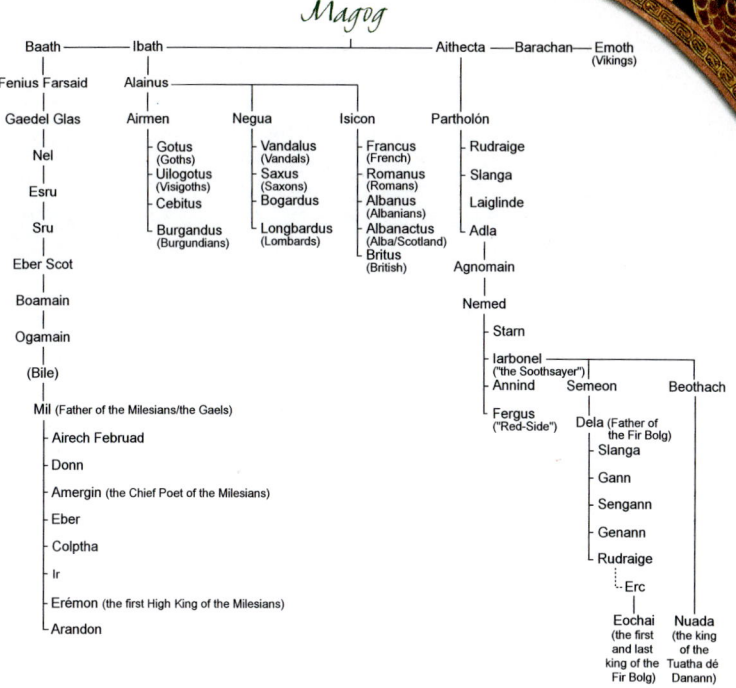

Figure 1: The most likely genealogy of the line of Magog, son of Japheth, son of Noah, according to the *Lebor,* with duplicates reconciled.

came the first man of the seed of Iafeth into Europe, Alainus s. Ibath s. Magog s. Iafeth s. Noe. Alainius, of him are the Franks and the Romans. And his three sons came with him, Armen, Negua, Isicon: so that on the hither side they begat those sons of whom we have heard: Saxus s. Negua s. Alainus s. Ibath s. Magog s. Iafeth s. Noe, of him are the Saxons. Emoth s. Magog, of him is the people of the north of the world. Barachan [was another son of Magog]. Aithechtaig s. Magog, of his progeny are the peoples who came into Ireland before the Gaedil — Partholón [was the first]. Nemed was of the family of the son whom Partholón left in the east, Adla s. Partholón. Also the children of Nemed, the Gaileoin and Fir Bolg and Fir Domnann and Tuatha dé Danann.[1]

23

Though after the the Flood the sons of Magog originally were allotted only the lands of what is now Central Asia, they became a wandering, conquering people, driving the sons of Gomer west into Central Europe, adding what is now southern Russia and Eastern Europe into their domain. They also invaded north, east and south, influencing the development of numerous Asian, Near Eastern and European cultures including parts of France, Spain and eventually Ireland, which they invaded from the sea via Spain. For more information on the Giants of Asia, see our groundbreaking essay on the subject at http://www.mysteriousworld.com/Journal/2003/Autumn/Giants/

The descendants of Magog, though not elucidated in Genesis 10, are fully laid out in the *Lebor Gabala Èrenn*, as the inhabitants of Ireland are primarily of Magogian ancestry. Magog, according to the *Lebor*, had five sons, from whom proceeded the Scythians, the Gaels, and numerous other Central Asian and European peoples of note whose allotted lands were originally what is now Central Asia. However, they had greatly increased their lands through conquest so that the descendants of Magog at their peak occupied a wide band of territory that bordered on the north with what is now Central Europe and Russia, on the south with what is now Italy, Greece, Turkey, Armenia, Iran, Afghanistan, Pakistan and India, on the east with what is now China and on the west with the Atlantic Ocean. It is in these lands where the sons of Magog finally settled.

The Scythians

The Irish are largely descended from the Scythians, a warlike people based in Central Asia who conquered much of the civilized world in ancient times, including parts of Asia, the Near East, Russia, and parts of Europe as far west as Ireland. Artwork by Angus McBride, from *MAA 137: The Scythians: 700-300 BC*, © Osprey Publishing (www.ospreypublishing.com)

Though the descendants of Magog included such prominent peoples as the French, the Romans and the Russians, most relevant to our present study were the Scythians — a magnificent race of tall, Caucasian, blonde and red-haired warriors who, along with their ancient ancestors, had dominated the Central Asian steppe for thousands of years. The Scythians were best known for being the first people to not only domesticate the horse, but also to use it effectively in battle, either under a saddle or pulling a chariot. They were also well known for their use of the composite bow, which they would shoot over the backs of their horses as they feigned retreat, much like the classic "Parthian Shot" maneuver of the later Parthians. In appearance the typical Scythian could easily pass for a typical Scot or Gael, except they were taller and broader, and wore lots of gold. Otherwise they were nearly identical, right down to the brightly colored tartan-style fabrics and use of breeches, an innovative trouser-like clothing style they themselves had invented to make riding on horseback easier. Most of all they loved their horses. And they had good reason to, as it was from horseback that the Scythians conquered far and wide, becoming the terror of the civilized world.

However, despite their barbaric tendencies, which included such practices as tattooing themselves from head to toe and using the gold-plated, hollowed-out skulls of their defeated enemies as drinking vessels, they were

THE MYSTERY
THE MYSTERY
THE SCYTHIANS

also capable of civilized behavior, having developed extensive trade networks stretching all the way from Europe to China. Basirov explains,

The Scythians were known by the Achaemenians as SAKA and SKUDRA, by the Greeks, SKYTHIA, by the Romans, SCYTHIAE (pron. SKITYAI), which has given us the English word SCYTHIAN; they lived in a wide area stretching from the south and west of the River Danube to the eastern and northeastern edges of the Taklamakan Desert in China; this vast territory includes now parts of Central Europe, the eastern half of the Balkans, the Ukraine, northern Caucasus, southern Russia, southern Siberia, Central Asia and western China. We know a great deal about their physical appearance; they were long-headed giants with blond hair and blue eyes; this well-known fact is attested by various classical sources, and by their skeletal and other remains in numerous archaeological excavations, which give a fairly detailed description of these ancient Iranians;

This mummy of a 40-year-old, tall, Caucasian red-headed woman was found in the Taklamakan Desert in western China in the late 1980s. Dressed in tartan plaid and displaying distinctly Caucasian features, the Taklamakan mummies reveal a missing link in our understanding of the history of the ancient Scythians, and of the Gaels. Image from *Nova*, "Mysterious Mummies of China". Copyright © 1998 WGBH/Boston.

recently, a large number of their mummified corpses were discovered in western China; these mummies, which are extremely well-preserved in the arid conditions of the Taklamakan desert, are now on display at the museums of Khotan, Urumchi, and Turfan in Sinkiang; they are dressed in Scythian costume, i.e., leather tunic and trousers, and are usually displayed in the sitting position, exactly as described by Herodotus; what is extraordinary apart from their northern European features, however, is their gigantic heights, well over two metres as they are now, in spite of the natural shrinkage expected during the past thousands of years.[2]

Though the contributions of these "giants in the Earth"[3] are routinely downplayed or even ignored by historians, the Scythians and related Magogian peoples in fact played a major role in the evolution of the histories of both Europe and Asia. Their invasions led them to conquer and rule over numerous nearby countries during various periods, including Eastern Europe, Egypt, Canaan, Babylon, Persia, Afghanistan, China and especially India, whose ancient history is full of stories of tall, blonde, Caucasian, chariot-riding giants conquering and forming ruling dynasties over the native populace. And though an analysis of the history and conquests of the Scythians could easily fill several volumes, most important to our present discussion is their conflict with their cousins to the west, the Gomerians, better known to history as the "Cimmerians".

Gog & Magog

According to Genesis 10:2, Magog had an older brother named "Gomer". Gomer's hordes initially occupied what is now Greece, Turkey, Armenia, and parts of the ancient Near East, eventually becoming known to history as the "Cimmerians". Like Magog's descendants, some of Gomer's descendants also migrated northward, occupying the lands west of Magog's lands in and around what is now known as the Ukraine. However, conflict arose between the descendants of the two brothers, the Gomerians and the Magogians, and the Magogians won, driving the northern branch of the Gomerians that had lived in the Ukraine further west into Central Europe where they later became known as the "Germans". There, the fierce "Germani" tribes and their Gallic cousins would eventually bring mighty Rome to her knees — but that is a story for another time.[4]

This conflict between the descendants of Gomer, or "Gog", and of Magog appears to have been the central conflict that set the tone for the history of Eurasia for thousands of years, a conflict that played itself out in numerous wars and rumors of wars throughout Asian and European history. This struggle between the two warring brothers, Gog and Magog, made itself known most clearly in the battles for the control of Ireland. There, the Gomerians would forever become enshrined in Irish legends as the "Fomorians", a race of giant, brutal barbarians based in what is now central and northern Europe that routinely invaded and plundered not only Ireland, but all of the British Isles.

The Partholónians, a tribe of Magogians listed in the *Lebor* as the second people to have invaded and settled Ireland in ancient times, are said to have had to drive out the Fomorians before they could do so. It is interesting to note that even though the Fomorians had in fact invaded and occupied Ireland for a time before the coming of the Partholónians, they were not given the same status of the other invaders that are listed in the *Lebor*, instead being denigrated to the level of a dark, dangerous, almost demonic infestation that the Partholónians had been sent by higher powers to cleanse the land of — an infestation that seems to have been considered to be the very antithesis of life, light and civilization. As Marie-Louise Sjoestedt explains in her critical work, *Celtic Gods & Heroes*,

> The race of Partholón fought the first battle of Ireland against the Fomorians. The name (Fomoire) is a compound of the preposition *fo* "under" and a root which appears in the German *Mahr*, name of a female demon who lies on the breast of people while they sleep (cf. Eng. "nightmare"), in the name *Morrígan* ("queen of demons"), and perhaps in the name of the formidable *Marats* of the Veda. The Irish form means "inferior" or "latent demons". The myth presents the Fomorians as native powers constantly driven back to the limits

"Fomor Shapechangers" © 1992, Jim Fitzpatrick. The Fomorians were the perennial antagonists in ancient Irish mythology, representing the powers of darkness, death and destruction.

of the world controlled by civilizing races, and always about to invade it and devour its produce. In Partholón's time they had lived for two hundred years in the islands near the coast, "having no other food". They fight against Partholón and his people "with one foot, one hand and one eye", a monstrous form, or a ritual posture (either interpretation seems possible), which has a magic value and a demonic significance. After seven days they are defeated and driven off. But we shall soon see them return, for the Fomorians never lay down their arms. They are like the powers of Chaos, ever latent and hostile to cosmic order.[5]

The Fomorians did in fact return again at least twice. The second time they were driven out by the Nemedians, another descendant of Magog. The third time the Fomorians came they were met by the legendary Tuatha dé Danann and once again the Fomorians, though powerful, were defeated by the superior might and magic of the sons of Magog.

29

"Lugh the Il-Dana" © 1979, Jim Fitzpatrick. Lugh, the greatest of the kings of the Tuatha dé Danann, was later deified as the god of life, light and civilization *par excellence* in Celtic myth.

The sons of Magog were consistently represented in the legends of the ancient Irish as representing the power of life, light and civilization. The Tuatha dé Danann, the gods of light *par excellence* in Irish myth and legend, were worshipers of light and of the sun, whereas the wicked Fomorians were portrayed as worshipers of the dark and of the moon. Fortunately, the power of the Tuatha Dé prevailed over the power of the Fomorians, and for a time kept the sacred isle free of the darkness, death and destruction that was the legacy of the sons of Gomer.

The Coming of the Gael

Though the Tuatha dé Danann had defeated the wicked Fomorians and driven them from Ireland, they too were eventually displaced by another group of Magogian descent, the Gaedelic Celts, or "Gaels", better known to Irish history as the Milesians. All of the previous invaders, from the Partholónians to the Tuatha dé Danann, had

THE MYSTERY
THE MYSTERY
THE COMING OF
THE GAEL

descended from Aithechta, the youngest son of Magog, but the Milesian Gaels, the last of the invaders recorded in the *Lebor*, were actually the descendants of Baath, the eldest son of Magog — specifically, from Gaidel Glas, their eponymous ancestor (see Figure 1).[6]

Though the *Lebor* states that the Scythians were descended from Baath, generally speaking all of the descendants of Magog who lived in and around Central Asia are usually broadly classified as Scythians, mostly because there are so few records from these highly nomadic peoples to help us distinguish one tribe from another. However, we do have one possible clue about the heritage of the Milesians — there was a group of Scythians who lived in the region of Margiana[7] (modern Uzbekistan) known as the "Amyrgian Scythians" that are mentioned by Herodotus.[8] This of course matches perfectly the name of the Milesian leader "Amergin", forming a strong, though not definitive, clue as to the exact origins of the Gaels.

As the rightful heir of Baath, the eldest son of Magog, Amergin and his people had the right of rulership over all the other descendants of Magog. Thus, when Amergin first stepped upon the shore of Ireland and uttered "The Mystery", he was not merely waxing poetic. Whether or not he realized it, he was exercising his rights as the rightful ruler of the house of Magog, which included rulership over not only the Tuatha dé Danann, but also all of the previous invaders of the sacred isle.[9] Thus Amergin's "magic" was superior to that of the Tuatha Dé, as by birth he had the divine right to rule Ireland.

The Fate of the Nations

But the Tuatha dé Danann initially refused to recognize the divine right of the Milesians to rule Ireland, instead opting to defend their failing rule over the sacred isle through force. Greatly compounding their error was the fact that the Tuatha Dé, once the champions of life, light and civilization, had over the centuries become decadent and wicked, descending to the same level of darkness and decay as had the Fomorians. In fact, their corruption had become so complete that they had turned to worshiping demons and summoning spirits of darkness which, according to the *Lebor*, they had caused to inhabit the bodies of

THE MYSTERY

THE MYSTERY

THE FATE OF THE NATIONS

31

an army of giants and other fell creatures that they had used to fight against the Milesians.[10]

Though the Tuatha dé Danann had originally come to the sacred isle as a force for life, light and civilization, they had abandoned their ancient mandate and had fallen into the same wickedness of the Fomorians whom they had formerly driven out. Now it was the Milesians who held the moral high ground, fighting "the battle of Life" against the now wicked and apparently unredeemable Tuatha dé Danann, who had descended to the level of openly using demonic forces to fight their battles. This of course, in a world where a God of order and light rules the nations, could not stand, and so the Milesians were sent by divine providence to break the power of the fallen Tuatha dé Danann just as the Tuatha Dé had been sent to break the power of the Fomorians. In that light, it would appear that Ireland's essential function in history has been as a place of judgment, wherein the forces of darkness and light have repeatedly fought to determine the destiny of the West. It is here, in the sacred isle, where the ancient mystery play of the battle between the forces of light and darkness, between civilization and savagery, has repeated itself countless times in countless ways over the millennia.

The Journey

In retrospect, it appears that each new invading people only successfully conquered and occupied Ireland if they abode by the rules of order and civilization. Those who abandoned those higher principles invariably were destroyed by flood, famine, pestilence, war and/or some other disaster, opening the way for the next invasion of a people who would, ideally, bring lasting order and civilization to the land. Amergin must have realized this, because his poem, "The Mystery", was essentially a résumé, a litany in verse of why he was best qualified to rule Ireland. In it he explained how he understood the principles of nature, of life and, most importantly, of how mankind fits into God's well-ordered cosmos.

THE MYSTERY
THE MYSTERY
THE JOURNEY

He must have recognized that it was ultimately his responsibility as a leader to keep his people on the straight and narrow path, to keep them from falling into darkness and error as had all the previous inhabitants of the sacred isle, the result of which was invariably an imbalance with the natural order that led to their inevitable destruction. As such, as it was with Moses and the Israelites, Amergin had to lay down the rules from the beginning in a way that was clear to all, expositing these universal principles of life in poetic verse.

Ultimately the Gaels have succeeded in Ireland because they, unlike the previous invaders, have held to their first principles, seeking light over darkness, civilization over savagery, and maintaining a balanced approach to life, walking in harmony between the world of the natural and the world of the divine. It is this balanced approach in the Irish worldview that has given them the ability to weather any storm, to overcome any difficulty. And though she has had her ups and downs, this philosophy of balance has kept Ireland from suffering the fate of other nations that have strayed off the path in recent centuries. And as long as they continue to walk in harmony with both the world of the natural and the world of the divine, respecting both their mysteries and their history, the journey of the Gael in the sacred isle will continue.

Notes

[1]R.A.S. Macalister, ed., *Lebor Gábala Èrenn: Vol. I* (London: The Irish Texts Society, 1941), 155-157. Magog is listed in Genesis 10, but his descendants are not. Unfortunately, there are several traditions interweaved into the *Lebor* with contradictory genealogies of the descendants of Magog, so the *Lebor* should not be taken as an authoritative document at the same level as the Bible. As such, the listing given in Figure 1 should be considered only the most likely of several possible variations.

[2]Dr. Oric Basirov, "The Origin of the Pre-Iranian Peoples" (Circle of Ancient Iranian Studies at the School of Oriental & African Studies (SOAS), University of London: http://home.btconnect.com/CAIS/Religions/iranian/Zarathushtrian/Oric.Basirov/origin_of_the_iranians.htm, or http://arizonapersian.com/iran/_disc4/0000075a.htm). Interestingly, the Scythians tended to call themselves "Saka" or "Skita", close to the term "Scot", which until recently was routinely used to describe the inhabitants of both Scotland and Ireland. For more information on the Scythians, visit http://www.silk-road.com/artl/scythian.shtml and http://www.geocities.com/amuse_amenace/scythia.htm. For more information on the Taklamakan Mummies, visit http://www.mysteriousworld.com/Journal/2002/Winter/Fragments/#WhiteMummies

[3]For more information on the origin and history of the giant sons of Magog, see http://www.mysteriousworld.com/Journal/2003/Autumn/Giants/

[4]For more information on the history of the giant descendants of Gomer and their later conflicts with Rome, see Part IV of our series on giants at http://www.mysterious world.com/Journal/2003/Winter/Giants/

[5]Marie-Louise Sjoestedt, *Celtic Gods & Heroes* (Mineola, NY: Dover Publications, 2000 [reprint of the 1949 edition]), 5-6. The reference to these men with one foot, one hand and one eye may be literal. The Scythians were at one time at war with an Amazonian tribe of female warriors who would actually remove a hand and/or leg from their male children in order to keep them submissive. The Fomorian males who fought the Parthólonians might literally have had only one foot, one hand and one eye, but had developed a fighting style that compensated for their mutilation. (Greek Mythology Link, "Scythia" (http://homepage.mac.com/cparada/GML/Scythia.html)). For more on the Morrígan, see The Mystery: Deities & Demigods, pp. 96-97.

[6]Macalister, *Lebor Gábala Èrenn: Vol. I*, 147.

[7]Margiana is a region in Central Asia roughly corresponding to modern Uzbekistan and/or Turkmenistan. For more information see http://www.livius.org/man-md/margiana/margiana.html.

[8]For more information on the Scythians, see http://www.livius.org/sao-sd/scythians/scythians.html and http://pakhtun.com/theSakas.htm. Herodotus is one of the few reliable sources on the Scythians, and he divided them up into "4 main branches known as the MassaGatae, Sacae, Alani, and Sarmatians, sharing a common language, ethnicity and culture." From G. Singh, "The Scythians — Sakas" (LeVanay's Site: http://pakhtun.com/theSakas.htm). The "Alani" are the Alans, which most likely correspond to Alainus, the son of Ibath. Singh corroborates the Central Asian origin of many Europeans, pointing out that "A branch of the Sakas known as the Alani reached regions of Europe, Asia Minor and the Middle East. They have been connected to the Goths of France/Spain, Saxons and the Juts of Denmark."" This lends great weight to the theory that the Celts, along with many other European peoples, originated from Central Asia in ancient times, and also supports the geneology of the sons of Magog as described in the *Lebor*.

[9]Save of course the Cessair, all but one of whom, according to legend, had been wiped out by Noah's Flood.

[10]R.A.S. Macalister, ed., *Lebor Gábala Èrenn: Vol. V* (London: The Irish Texts Society, 1941), 33-35.

Note: The Latin designation *op. cit.* (*opere citato*) is used in this book as "previously cited" and *q.v.* (*quod vide*) is used as "cited later".

THE MYSTERY
THE MYSTERY
NOTES

TUATHA DÉ DANANN

Battle of
Conan's Tower
Tory
Island
Creeslough
Aran
Island
Letterkenny • Londonderry
DONEGAL
Lifford
Battle of Mag Itha
Ardara
Donegal
Ballyshannon
Bangor
Erris
Ballina
Landing Place of
Genann and Rudraige
SLIGO
Second
Battle of Moy Tura
Charlestown
MAYO
Castlebar
Murrisk
Westport
Achill Island
Clare Island
Inishbofin
Battle of
Ros Fraechan
Claremorris
Clifden
Tuam
First Battle
of Moy Tura
Burial Place
of Cessair
Galway
GALWAY
Gorumna
Island
Galway Bay
Aran
Islands
Ennistimon
Ennis
CLARE
Kilkee
Mouth
of the Shannon
Limerick
LIMERICK
Tralee
Battle of
Slieve Mis,
Meeting with
Bambha
Dingle Bay
Mallow
Fermoy
KERRY
Killarney
CORK
Kenmare
Macroom
Donnemark
Bantry
Clear
Island
Saint Georges Channel

Rathlin
Island
North Channel

Coleraine
DERRY
ANTRIM
Ballymena
Larne
ULSTER
Antrim
Strabane
TYRONE
Bangor
Omagh
Belfast
Burial Place
of Macha
Burial Place
of Bith
Enniskillen
FERMANAGH
Monaghan
ARMAGH
Portadown
DOWN
Armagh
Banbridge
Downpatrick
MONAGHAN
Newry
Loch
Rudhraighei
Cavan
Slieve Donard,
Burial Place
of Slanga
son of Partholón
LEITRIM
Sligo
Slieve Anierin
Carrick on
Shannon
CAVAN
Dundalk
Dundalk
Bay
CONNAUGHT
ROSCOMMON
LONGFORD
MEATH
LOUTH
Roscommon
Longford
Drogheda
Meeting
with
Eriu
WESTMEATH
Trim
Mullingar
Hill of Uisneach
Athlone
LEINSTER
DUBLIN
Dublin
Dublin
Bay
OFFALY
Tullamore
Naas
Tallaght,
"Plague Grave"
Burial Place
of the
Partholónians
Port
Laoise
KILDARE
Slieve Felim
(Eblinne)
Meeting with
Fódhla
Roscrea
LAOIS
WICKLOW
Wicklow
Nenagh
Durrow
Carlow
Arklow
Kilkenny
CARLOW
TIPPERARY
KILKENNY
Tipperary
Clonmel
Landing Place
of Slanga
Cahir
WEXFORD
Waterford
Wexford
Rosslare
WATERFORD
Dungarvan
Youghal
Landing Place of
Gann & Sengann
Cork
Burial Place of Nemed
(Great Island)

NORTH

ATLANTIC

OCEAN

Irish

Sea

The Invasions
of Ireland
MODERN PROVINCE NAME
MODERN COUNTY NAME

------- Modern International Boundary
━━━━━ Modern Provincial Boundary
—·—·— Modern County Boundary
★ Modern National Capitol
◉ Modern County Seat
• Modern Major City

0 10 20 30 40   60   80 Kilometers
0 5 10 15 20 30   40   50 Miles

CESSAIR PARTHOLÓNIANS NEMEDIANS FIR BOLG MILESIANS

The Invasions

An explanation of the Takings of Ireland, and of her history, and of her royal roll, here below: The island of Ireland is situated in the west; as the Paradise of Adam is situated in the southern coast of the east, so Ireland is in the northern portion, toward the west. Those lands are as similar by nature, as they are similar by their positions on the earth: for as Paradise hath no noxious beast, so the learned testify that Ireland hath no serpent, lion, toad, injurious rat, dragon, scorpion, nor any hurtful beast, save only the wolf. And so Ireland is called "the island of the West".... It is called Scotia also, because it is inhabited by the nations of the Scots.... Moreover the country is called Èriu from the heroes.[1]

he history of Ireland is essentially a history of invasions. So, it was for good reason that the Irish monks who compiled the most ancient history of Ireland entitled their work *Lebor Gabala Èrenn*, "The Book of the Invasions of Ireland". As we have seen, the vast majority of the invaders were Scythians or related peoples, all of whom had emigrated from Central Asia in ancient times to battle for control of "the island of the West", the mysterious island that defined the furthest western extreme of the known world at that time.

However, the first people to invade the sacred island, according to the *Lebor*, were not of Magogian extraction, but were direct descendants of Noah through his son, Bith. Bith is not mentioned in the Bible, but the Irish monks, ever wanting to harmonize the native Irish legends with the biblical text, and not willing to expunge this important person from Irish tradition forever without some sort of mention, apparently accepted his existence as true history, even going so far as to raise him to the high status of being a previously unknown son of Noah.

Though it is unlikely that Noah actually had a son named Bith (and indeed, much of the extrabiblical information in the *Lebor* ranges from suspect to demonstrably incorrect), it is not impossible, so we will proceed for now on the assumption that the record of the invasions of Ireland as given in the *Lebor* is indeed what happened in history, and leave it to others more qualified to confirm or deny its veracity. Here now, then, is an exposition of the Takings of Ireland, beginning with the Cessair:

The Cessair

"The Arrival of Cessair" © 1992, Jim Fitzpatrick.

Of the Taking of Cessair here below, and of the tales told of her before the Flood. Who first took Ireland in the beginning, after the Creation of the World? Cessair, daughter of Bith, s. Noe s. Lamech…. Cessair came thereafter from the Island of Meröe, fleeing from the Flood: for she thought it probable that a place where men had never come till then, where no evil nor sin had been committed, and which was free from the reptiles and monsters of the world, that such a place should be exempt from a Flood. And her wizards, indeed, told her that Ireland was in that case, and that on that account she should come to Ireland. Wherefore Cessair arrived, in search of Ireland.[2]

38

Cessair, as described in the *Lebor,* was the daughter of Bith, son of Noah. In her almost certainly apocryphal story, Cessair desired to escape the Great Flood that her grandfather Noah was predicting would soon come upon the Earth, and so she consulted her "wizards", or advisors, on how to escape it. They advised her that the land of Ireland in the West should be far enough away to escape the Flood and, on account that it was a safe and peaceful island, it was good for living as well. So, Cessair, who lived on the island of Meröe on the Upper Nile in what is now Nubia, south of Egypt, left with three ships to escape the Flood. Their journey was long but uneventful, until they tried to land on Ireland's shore near *Corco Duibne* (Corkaguiney Peninsula, better known as Dingle Peninsula, in what is now County Kerry), losing two ships in the process. The remaining ship finally landed at *Dun na mBarc,* "Fort of the Ships" (modern Donamark, between Bantry and Ballylickey, in County Cork). All that were left of the original expedition were Cessair, fifty women, and three men: Bith, her father, Ladra the pilot of the surviving ship, and a mysterious man named Finntan.

It was decided then that the three men would have to divide all the women amongst themselves so as to continue to be fruitful and multiply, so they divided the women into three shares: Finntan took Cessair and 17 other women, Bith also took 17, including one named Barrind, and Ladra took sixteen, including one named Banba. Ladra was dissatisfied with his share, and took off without so much as a fare thee well, leaving Bith and Finntan with 25 each. Bith was already old, so he didn't last long, and it soon came down to Finntan, who fled and hid in a cave high in the mountains. And as there had been only 40 days left before the Flood when they had landed, Cessair and all the women were soon taken by the floodwaters, only Finntan, hidden away in his lofty eyrie, surviving to tell the tale. This Finntan was later known to Irish history as Tuan Mac Carrill who, as we have seen, was believed to have been spared by God to be a living witness to the entire history of Ireland through his various transformations.

Though the landing place of the Cessair was near Donamark in County Cork, they actually settled just north of Waterford Harbor, in County Waterford. The burial place of Bith is traditionally believed to be Slieve Beagh in County Tyrone, in Ulster province, and princess Cessair is believed to be buried at Knockmaa, in County Galway, in Connaught province.

THE MYSTERY
THE INVASIONS
THE CESSAIR

The Partholónians

Here is the taking of Partholón. Now Ireland was waste after the Flood for a space of three hundred and eleven years till Partholón reached it.... He came thereafter out of Mygdonia, that is, out of Graecia Parva [Sicily of the Greeks]. He had a voyage of a month to Aladacia. A voyage of nine days had he from Aladacia to Gothia. A voyage of another month had he from Gothia to Spain. A voyage of nine days had he from Spain to Ireland.[3]

"Greek Princess" © 1993, Jim Fitzpatrick.

The Partholónians were the first people to invade Ireland after the Flood, an invasion that took place under less-than-ideal circumstances. Partholón had been forced to flee his homeland, the island of Sicily, as he was being pursued in retribution for the murder of his own mother and father whom he had slain in order to make way for his brother to be king. Interestingly, it is implied in the *Lebor* that a great plague had been sent by the gods as punishment for his wickedness, and 9,000 people died as a result of this divine retribution. So, Partholón was essentially fleeing for his life not only from his fellow Greeks, but also from the wrath of heaven.

There were many "firsts" that the Partholónians did in Ireland, including the first guest house, the first duel, the first insurance policy, the first brewer, the first gold, the first cattle and the first religious practices, including the first druids. Partholón was also known for clearing four plains of trees in order to make them useful for agriculture.

The Partholónians soon came into conflict with the Fomorians, an ancient, wicked people who would become a byword for evil in Irish folklore. They were indeed a strange people, described as "demons" having only one arm, one leg and one eye:

> In the third year thereafter was the first battle of Ireland, in the princedom of Partholón, the Slemne of Mag Itha, against Cichol Clapperleg of the Fomoraig, namely, men with single legs and single arms; to wit, demons with the forms of men. They fought against him, and the battle broke before Partholón. A week were they fighting it, and not a man was slain there, for it was a magic battle. For that is the battle in which not one man received a mortal wound nor yet expulsion. According to another authority, it broke before Partholón, and there Cichol s. Nil was slain, and his people were hard pressed: and Partholón received a mortal wound. Also that it was of the gory darts of those wounds that he died, after a long time following the battle. [That is] the battle of Mag Itha; whence it is called Seven-Taking. Cichol was slain and the Fomoraig destroyed.[4]

The Partholónians had successfully wiped out the wicked Fomorians in the first of a series of battles between the sons of Gog and the sons of Magog for the control of Ireland. They then continued to live in the land for a total of 550 years, but at the end of their time there they were struck with a plague, and every single one of them died. And even though they were a relatively civilized, agrarian culture, it is said that the Partholónians failed because they were not a society based upon morals, ethics and justice. As a result, they inevitably began to stray off the straight and narrow path, became accursed, and were eventually destroyed out of the land which then lay fallow for 30 years.

Partholón and the remnant of his people were buried in the Plain of Elta, in an area southwest of Dublin called *Tallaght*, "plague grave".[5] There is also a *Loch Rudhraighei* (now named Dundrum Bay) in the city of Dundrum, County Down, in Ulster province. It originally was named after one of the sons of Partholón after the waters of the bay had risen up against him in anger and purposely drowned him. Another son of Partholón, Slánga, is believed to have been buried in a cairn on the summit of Slieve Donard, also located in County Down.

The Nemedians

Now Ireland was a waste thereafter, for a space of thirty years after Partholón, till Nemed son of Agnomain of the Greeks of Scythia came thither, with his four chieftains; [they were the four sons of Nemed]. Forty-four ships had he on the Caspian Sea for a year and a half, but his ship alone reached Ireland.[6]

The Nemedians, under the leadership of Nemed — the heir of Partholón — were the next descendants of Magog to invade the sacred isle. As the heir of Par-

"Macha and Nemed, King of Ireland"
© 1975, Jim Fitzpatrick.

tholón, Nemed had the right of kingship over Ireland, which he set out to enforce with a fleet of 32 ships carrying approximately 1,000 people. When Nemed reached Ireland's shore, however, much like the Cessair, all but one of the ships wrecked, and most of the people were lost.

Despite this, Nemed was still able to fight effectively against the Fomorians, who had once again invaded and infested the land with their wicked progeny, defeating them in four decisive victories. After pushing back the Fomorians and establishing a foothold for his people, Nemed then continued in his ancestor Partholón's tradition of clearing the land and making it ready for cultivation. He cleared 12 plains in total and also established two royal forts before he died of a plague that also carried off over 2,000 of his people.

The power of the Fomorians had not been broken by Nemed's initial assaults, however, and after his death they returned to heavily oppress the Nemedians with punitive taxes. Two-thirds of their wheat, milk and even their newborn children had to be brought to the plain of Mag Cetne on every *Samhain* eve (Halloween), or else the Fomor would come and take them by force.[7] This of course was unacceptable to anyone, and the Nemedians chose to fight to the death rather than live as slaves to the wicked, cannibal Fomors. They set themselves under three champions: Semeon, son of Iarbonel the Soothsayer, son of Nemed, Erglan, son of Beoan son of Starn son of Nemed, and Fergus Red-Side son of Nemed. Fergus then raised an army of 60,000 and led them into the last great battle that was intended to rid the land of the Fomorians once and for all.

The power base of the Fomor in Ireland at that time is believed to have been at what is now Tory Island, located off the northern coast of County Donegal. Seated there was the Tower of Conan, from which Tory Island derives its name — *Túr Rí*, or "Tower of the King". From there King Conan commanded the Fomorian forces, and gathered the tribute from all Ireland. To defeat the powerful King Conan, the Nemedians called for reinforcements from Greece, who sent several ships full of choice warriors, druids, and vicious and venomous animals to use against the Fomorians. By using the magic of their druids, and setting the poisonous creatures to creep within the Tower, the Nemedians were able to greatly weaken and demoralize the Fomorians and flush them out of their stronghold to do battle.

Fergus Red-Side then defeated King Conan in single combat, and the Nemedians wiped out the Fomorians. However, the battle was not yet over, as Morc, the leader of the Fomor navy, came upon them in a great fury, nearly matching that of the righteously indignant sons of Nemed. Such was the fury of that combat that neither side noticed when the tides rapidly came in, and almost all of the combatants were drowned while they grappled with each other, leaving only 30 to tell the tale.

Down to 30 men, the Nemedians realized that they were too few to hold Ireland, and decided to return to fight another day. Fergus Red-Side fled with his son, Britain Mael, to the land that would thereafter be known as Britain; Erglan fled with his two brothers to the land of Alba, that is, Scotland; and most importantly, Semeon, son of Iarbanel the Soothsayer, son of Nemed fled to Greece, where his progeny multiplied and became known as the Fir Bolg.

THE MYSTERY
THE INVASIONS
THE NEMEDIANS

The Fir Bolg

Next comes the taking of the Fir Bolg here below. Ireland was a waste for a space of two hundred years after the capture of Conaing's Tower, till the Fir Bolg came. From the lands of the Greeks they came, fleeing from the impost which the Greeks had laid upon them — carrying clay on to bare rock-flags and making them flowery plains. Those men made them long canoes of the bags in which they were wont to carry the clay, and they came to Ireland, in quest of their patrimony.[8]

"Eochai Foresees His Doom"
© 1977, Jim Fitzpatrick.

Though the sons of Fergus Red-Side and Erglan never returned, the sons of Semeon did, after eight generations in the lands of the Greeks. There, much like the ancient Israelites, the sons of Semeon had been taken into captivity and enslaved, forced to work for the Greeks as hard laborers landscaping large, barren regions of Greece. While in captivity, they had become divided into three groups: the first group, the *Fir Domnann* (lit., "men of the earth"), dug the earth; the *Fir Bolg* (lit., "men of the bags"), carried and spread the earth; and the third group, the *Gaileoin*, were named from the *gai lin*, or "javelins of wounding" that they carried about with them to help keep order.

Tired of their enslavement, the sons of Semeon made canoes out of the bags they used to carry their dirt, and escaped back to Ireland. The leaders

of the three groups were the sons of Dela, of the line of Semeon, and were named Slanga, Gann, Sengann, Genann and Rudraige. They each departed to different parts of the island, landing days apart from each other. Slanga, leader of the Gaileoin, landed at Inber Slaine, the mouth of the River Slaine, in County Wexford. Gann and Sengann, leaders of the Fir Bolg, landed at Inber Dubglaisi, the mouth of the Douglas (Blackwater) River in County Cork. Genann and Rudraige, the leaders of the Fir Domnann, landed at Inber Domnann, the mouth of the River Domnann, in County Mayo. Finding the land empty of opposition, the leadership then proceeded to divide Ireland into five provinces: Leinster, Munster, Connaught and Ulster, and a fifth, ruling province called *Mídhe* (literally, "middle"), centered on the Hill of Uísneach, located in what is now County Westmeath.

However, contention arose between the families over who was to rule the island, and much blood was shed until one man arose above the rest: Eochai, son of Erc. Eochai was the first High King of Ireland, and the first to institute a system of justice as the foundation of the first true civilization in Ireland. Sjoestedt explains,

> With the Fir Bolg we seem to emerge from the era of agrarian culture. No plains are said to have been cleared in their time, nor any lakes to have been formed. Their contribution is proper rather to a warlike aristocracy, for they introduced into Ireland the iron spear-head and the system of monarchy. It is said of their king Eochaid mac Eirc that "no rain fell during his reign, but only the dew; there was not a year without harvest. For falsehood was banished from Ireland in his time. He was the first to establish the rule of justice." Thus there appears with the establishment of the first Celtic communities in Ireland the principle of association between the king and the earth — the king's justice being a condition of the fertility of the soil — which is the very formula of the magic of kingship.[9]

However, though the Fir Bolg had achieved the justice necessary to live in harmony with the land — what Sjoestedt refers to as "the very formula of the magic of kingship" — they were not fated to rule over it for long. After 37 years of their rule, the relatively stable beginnings of civilization that the Fir Bolg had achieved were greatly shaken by the next, and most celebrated, people to invade the sacred isle: the Tuatha dé Danann.

THE MYSTERY
THE INVASIONS
THE FIR BOLG

45

"Nuada The High King", © 1978, Jim Fitzpatrick. Nuada was the King of the Tuatha dé Danann, who led them to victory over the Fir Bolg and rulership over all Ireland.

The Tuatha dé Danann

Thereafter the progeny of Beothach s. Iarbonel the Soothsayer s. Nemed were in the northern islands of the world, learning druidry and knowledge and prophecy and magic, till they were expert in the arts of pagan cunning…. Thereafter the Tuatha dé Danann came into Ireland. Their origin is uncertain, whether they were of demons or of men; but it is said that they were of the progeny of Beothach s. Iarbonel the Giant.

In this wise they came, without vessels or barks, in dark clouds over the air, by the might of druidry, and they landed on a mountain of Conmaicne Rein [Slieve Anierin] in Connachta. Another company says that the Tuatha dé Danann came in a sea-expedition, and that they burnt their ships thereafter. It was owing to the fog of smoke that rose from them as they were burning that others

THE MYSTERY
THE INVASIONS
THE TUATHA DÉ
DANANN

46

have said that they came from a fog of smoke…. These are the two reasons why they burnt their ships: that the Fomoraig should not find them, to rob them of them; and that they themselves should have no way of escape from Ireland, even though they should suffer rout before the Fir Bolg.

Thereafter, the Tuatha dé Danann brought a darkness over the sun, for a space of three days and three nights. They demanded battle or kingship of the Fir Bolg. A battle was fought between them, to wit the first battle of Mag Tuired, in which a hundred thousand of the Fir Bolg fell. Thereafter the Tuatha dé Danann took kingship of Ireland. Those are the Tuatha Dea — gods were their men of arts, non-gods their husbandmen.[10]

While the sons of Semeon, son of Iarbonel the Soothsayer, son of Nemed — the "Fir Bolg" — had retreated to the lands of Greece to escape the plagues and the revenge of the Fomorians after their pyrrhic victory at the Battle of Conan's Tower, another line of the descendants of Iarbonel, the sons of Beothach, had fled to "the northern islands of the world" in order to learn the martial and other skills that they realized would be necessary to not only retake Ireland from the Fomorians, but also to keep it for the long term. Stung by the slaughter at Conan's Tower, the descendants of Beothach — now known as the Tuatha dé Danann, "the tribe of the goddess Danu" — had resolved to do whatever it took to make sure that such an event never happened again. To this end, they journeyed to some mysterious cities in "the northern islands of the world", where they would learn to master the arts of life, and of death.

During their time in these mysterious (and yet to be discovered) cities of northern Europe, the Tuatha dé Danaan spent many generations learning "druidry and knowledge and prophecy and magic, till they were expert in the arts of pagan cunning".[11] The four cities in which they acquired their advanced knowledge of the arcane and "diabolic" arts and sciences were known as Failias, Goirias, Findias and Muirias. And from each of these cities they acquired an artifact of great power:

THE MYSTERY
THE INVASIONS
THE TUATHA DÉ DANANN

47

The Four Treasures of the Tuatha dé Danann

The Stone of Destiny

The Spear of Victory

The Sword of Light

The Cauldron of the Dagda

✛ *Lia Fail,* "The Stone of Destiny"

From the city of Failias the Tuatha Dé brought the *Lía Fail*, the great magical *omphalos* stone whose power was to identify the true king of Ireland by uttering a roar when he stood upon it at his coronation. This was usually done at the installment of each king to prove that he was indeed the one "chosen of the gods" to lead the people. These types of stones also typically were believed to have an oracular function, allowing the pagan priesthoods to communicate with their gods. The *Lía Fail*, currently sited at Tara, along with the *Clogh Óir* of Country Tyrone and the *Crom Cruach* of County Cavan, form a triad of oracular stones known as "The Three Magical Stones of Ireland".

✛ *Sleá Bua,* "The Spear of Victory"

From the city of Goirias was brought the *Sleá Bua*, the spear that Lugh used in the Second Battle of Moy Tura to destroy the great evil Eye of Balor. It is said that so great was its power that the battle would never go against the one who had it in hand. It was also believed that it would automatically return to the thrower's hand after it was thrown, and would automatically slay the target if the thrower uttered the word, *ibar* ("yew") as he threw it. Some traditions have it that the *Sleá Bua* was actually not a magical spear, but a magical slingstone. The terminology is so unclear, yet the weapon so powerful, that one wonders if it was not indeed some sort of high-tech weapon, the true nature of

THE MYSTERY
THE INVASIONS
THE TUATHA DÉ DANANN

which the ancient scribes could not fully comprehend. It was also known in some sources as the *Gáe Assail*.

48

⚜ Claímh Solais, "The Sword of Light"

From the city of Findias was brought the *Claímh Solais*, the powerful magical sword that Nuada, King of the Tuatha dé Danann, used in both battles of Moy Tura. It is said that when it was drawn from its battle scabbard, none could stand against it. Like the *Sleá Bua*, it may be that the *Claímh Solais* was also another technologically advanced weapon, much more powerful than a typical "sword".

⚜ The Cauldron of the Dagda

From the city of Muirias was brought the cauldron of the Dagda, a magical vessel from which none would depart unsatisfied, as it provided a limitless amount of food and drink of the highest quality.

Though the *Lía Fail* still resides in its place in Tara, the whereabouts of the rest of the four treasures are currently unknown.

THE FIRST BATTLE OF MOY TURA

After the Tuatha Dé had successfully landed and committed themselves to the conquest to the island, they then demanded the Fir Bolg either give them the kingship of Ireland, or give them combat, so that kingship could be decided by force of arms. Despite the fact that High King Eochai's druids warned him of certain defeat, the Fir Bolg chose combat, and they were to meet the Tuatha Dé on *Maigh Nia*, later called *Maigh Tureidh* (pronounced "Moy Tura"), which means "the Plain of the Towers" — so named after the many battle-pillars that were erected on the field. This plain is located near the village of Cong in County Mayo, and is to be distinguished from the plain of the same name to the north in County Sligo, on which the Second Battle of Moy Tura would later be fought between the Tuatha dé Danann and the Fomorians.

The Badb

Before the battle was joined, the Tuatha Dé began to employ the diabolical magic that they had learned during their time in northern Europe in order to weaken and demoralize the host of the Fir Bolg and their allies. They called upon the *Badb*, their three "war witches" skilled in the art of sorcery — Macha, Mórrigan and Nemain — and sent them to the Hill of Tara to curse the armies of the Fir Bolg that were assembling there.

With their diabolic sorceries the *Badb* were able to darken the skies where the Fir Bolg were gathering for war. They then caused the standing stones of the plain of Tara to wail and moan like banshees, while causing the illusions of dark, hulking shadows, huge, spectral warriors and horrid, ghoulish creatures to stalk the darkening skies. And for the terrifying climax, they conjured up the image of a great red dragon, which coiled and menaced throughout the sky over the heads of the terrified Fir Bolg before bursting into a horrid red rain of blood and fire that burned the skin and spoiled the hair and garments of the entire host.

César the Druid

All of this greatly terrified even the most seasoned warriors of the Fir Bolg, as the people of that time were very superstitious, so the psychological warfare that was being employed by these "war witches" proved to be highly destructive to their morale. Fortunately for the Fir Bolg, they too had a powerful druid, César, who immediately began to counteract the magic of the *Badb*. With a crash of lightning, César made his dramatic entrance upon the Hill of Tara. Seeing that the situation was grim, César immediately called upon one of the forbidden elder gods of his race, *Crom Cruach*, and then spent the next three days weaving spells and conjuring deities powerful and wicked in order to thwart the power of the *Badb*. Slowly but surely, he wove a fine web of sorcery throughout the wind, the water and the earth to hem in their wicked spells.

Finally, after three days of wailing stones, terrifying spectres and the rain of blood and fire, César once again called upon *Crom Cruach* — the god who should not be named — summoning him by incantations that should not be uttered. And Crom answered, the great power of the elder god snuffing out the powerful sorceries of the *Badb* like a candle in the wind, the shadows, blood and fire quitting the skies as if struck by a furious gale.

Heartened by the power of their wizard's magic, the host of the Fir Bolg and their allies let up a cheer and proceeded on to the plain of Moy Tura, ready for the battle that would decide the fate of Ireland. They had thought that their victory over the war witches of the Tuatha Dé was an omen of victory, but they were not aware of the terrible price they would have to pay for the intercession on their behalf by the terrible and wicked Crom Cruach, payment that could only be made in flesh, blood, and the souls of the damned.[12]

The Tuatha Dé Assemble

"The Tuatha Dé Assemble" — © 1979, Jim Fitzpatrick.

The Tuatha Dé then began to assemble on the plain of battle. As the nights passed, waiting for the Fir Bolg to arrive, they began to reminisce on how far they had come since their ancient ancestors had first left Scythia: about the rulers of Scythia who sought to enslave them with heavy taxes; their conflicts with the Assyrians and the Philistines as they journeyed west; the pyrrhic victory at the Tower and the flight of their ancestors; the long time of learning in the frozen lands of the north, where they learned the art of war in order to take revenge; and most importantly, the promise and the memory of fair Èireann that kept them going through it all. Thus heartened, the Tuatha Dé renewed their resolve to fight for the kingship of Ireland, even if it meant shedding the blood of the Fir Bolg, their kinsmen.

THE MYSTERY
THE INVASIONS
THE TUATHA DÉ
DANANN

The Battle Begins

The Tuatha Dé had tried once more to make peace with the Fir Bolg, their kindred, and partition the island into two parts, but the Fir Bolg were proud and arrogant, and chose combat over conciliation. Soon afterward the two armies took to the field. The Tuatha Dé were preceded by the *Badb* who, dressed in black robes and carrying fiery torches, hurled curses and foul imprecations at the Fir Bolg. Meanwhile Fáthach, poet of the Fir Bolg, rallied the spirits of his people with memories of their past victories, exhorting them to achieve even more glorious exploits.

The Dagda, High Chieftain of the Tuatha Dé, led the first charge against the Fir Bolg, but his charge was met by a countercharge by a tribe of hill giants led by their chieftain, Nert Chú. But the mighty Dagda hewed his way right through the giant hillmen until they were no more. In the meantime, however, the Fir Bolg army — led by Rúa, their commander — had broken the lines opposite the Dagda, and the Fir Bolg had wreaked havoc on the Tuatha Dé with their broad-pointed spears. The carnage they wrought forced the Tuatha Dé to flee the field, but the battle was yet to be decided.

On the second day, Breas, "the Beautiful", champion of the Tuatha Dé, was slated to lead them into combat. Though heroes were wounded on both sides, the battle that day went to the Tuatha Dé, and the score between the two armies was even. On the third day of battle, the Dagda once again led the Tuatha Dé into battle, and in a single combat, slew Cirb, one of the greatest heroes of the Fir Bolg. Then, outmaneuvering the Fir Bolg, the Dagda crushed their defensive positions, and the demoralized and badly beaten Fir Bolg once again retreated.

The fourth day of battle proved to be the last day, when Nuada, High King of the Tuatha dé Danann, took the field. Also, the *Badb* were back to their full strength once again, and began to plot powerful sorceries to use against the stubborn Fir Bolg. The Mórrigan, in her guise of the crow, told Nuada to throw his shield into the air, which she made to blot out the sun. After the sun had been eclipsed, once again the dark, terrifying phantoms appeared in the sky, led by the *Badb* who appeared to ride before them in a fiery chariot, showering the Fir Bolg with a rain of liquid fire from their blazing torches while moans and howls echoed throughout the valley. It was as if the dead themselves were rising from their graves!

Then the battle frenzy of his race seized Nuada, a magical warp spasm of berzerk fury that made him supremely powerful, fearless, and deadly in combat. Thus transformed, he led his personal guard and an army of *sídhe* ("sith")[13] warriors that he had summoned down from the sky against the Fir Bolg, slaughtering 300 of them while they stood trembling in fear at the terror of the *Badb*, the fell light that shone forth from Nuada, and the ghost riders of the *sídhe* that rode alongside him. So great was the terror of the onslaught of the Tuatha Dé that only Streng, the hero of the Fir Bolg, stood firm and repelled their attack, rallying the Fir Bolg to kill 150 of the Tuatha Dé and then dueling Nuada to a stalemate before withdrawing back to their lines.

Meanwhile, against the power of the *Badb*, Cesár had once again conjured the terrible worm god *Crom Cruach* to defeat their witchcraft. Crom sent a powerful demon, The Collector of Lost Souls, to soak the ground in blood and reap a harvest of souls in payment for Crom's favor. The spells of the *Badb*, and the *Badb* themselves, quickly fled away from the gigantic, horned, skeletal figure of the Collector, who reached high into the sky and waved away the powerful riders of the *sídhe* as if they were flies while he advanced upon Nuada to collect his first payment. Nuada, however, wielding the *Claímh Solais*, once again shook the Earth with his battle frenzy, and hurled the Sword of Light into the skull of the terrible Collector, who shrieked horribly and disappeared back into the bowels of the Earth. But payment still had to be made, and *Crom Cruach* knows no mercy. Crom's payment for his favor was in human souls, and César paid the debt of the Fir Bolg with his life as Crom devoured him horribly.

But the battle was not yet over. Streng still stood as the champion of the Fir Bolg, and Nuada, nearly spent by his battle with the Collector, was now forced to face him again in single combat. After numerous blows, each warrior wounding the other, the exhausted Nuada fell back

53

against his battle pillar. Streng then struck him a hard blow, severing Nuada's right, sword arm.

Enraged by the maiming of Nuada, the Dagda led the Tuatha Dé in a final assault on the Fir Bolg, who were led by their High King, Eochaí, his son Slaine, and Streng. Realizing that defeat was imminent, Eochaí fought hard, but became overcome with thirst, taking a troop of 100 with him to find water. But the Badb used their magic to hide all water from him, and a troop of 150 Dé Danann warriors led by the three young sons of Nuada found him by the Strand of Eochaill. There they engaged the Fir Bolg, slaying all, including Eochaí, who slew

"Streng, Champion of the Fir Bolg"
© 1977, Jim Fitzpatrick.

all three of Nuada's sons in his greatest and most heroic fight. He lies buried there even today, at *Cairn Eochaí*, the cairns of Nuada's three sons lying at the western end of the strand.

Demoralized by their great losses of numbers, and in leaders, both sides retired and prepared for a parley. Though the Tuatha Dé had won the battle, the Fir Bolg had won their respect by acquitting themselves well, and the greatest hero of the battle was Streng, champion of the Fir Bolg. Streng wished for peace and parley, but the rest of the warriors pressed for battle, and were defeated once again in a final, desperate combat with the Tuatha Dé. Finally they realized their defeat, and Streng sued for pardon, receiving an offer of a choice of provinces in which to live under the rulership of the Tuatha Dé. Streng chose Connaught for his people, and his ancestors live there to this day.

THE MYSTERY
THE INVASIONS
THE TUATHA DÉ
DANANN

Requiem

In hindsight, one wonders why the Tuatha Dé won over the Fir Bolg. They were no more moral, or just, than were the Fir Bolg, both sides relying on witchcraft and violence to impose their rule over the other. The Tuatha Dé were fewer in number, and were less familiar with the land than were the Fir Bolg. And the closeness of the battle and the losses that both sides endured makes it clear that neither side necessarily had "the favor of the gods". Perhaps it was the fact that the princes of the Fir Bolg had murdered each other so ruthlessly in their quest for the High Kingship that had caused the Fir Bolg to fall out of favor with the divine realm, their violent nature ultimately disqualifying them as viable candidates to rule the blessed land. Or perhaps it was their arrogance and unwillingness to share the land with their kindred, instead choosing war. The fact that the Fir Bolg were the first to bring kingship and justice to Ireland may have been the only reason why they were not destroyed and driven out by the Tuatha Dé altogether, as the Fomorians had been by the Partholónians and the Nemedians.

The answer may be that Nuada was given the divine right of kingship over Ireland simply because Beothach, son of Nemed, his ancestor, was elder to Semeon, son of Nemed, the ancestor of Eochaí. Thus, as the rightful heir of the line of Magog, Nuada had the right of rulership over the Fir Bolg by birth, a rule which they did not accept, even if it meant fighting against the will of the gods themselves. In either case, the First Battle of Moy Tura was not a battle of good against evil, between Magogian and Gomerian, as previous battles had been. It was now a battle to determine which of the sons of Magog would rule over Ireland, the mysterious island of the destiny of the West.

Though one could reasonably argue that the Fir Bolg — who were the first to bring justice to the land — did not deserve the punishment that they had received at the hands of their kinsmen, in the end the headship went to the strongest and the fittest by divine right of combat, which turned out to be the Tuatha dé Danann. And as it turns out, only the Tuatha Dé would have been able to defend fair Èireann against the next invasion of the Fomorians, so their victory in the end must have all been part of the divine plan.

THE MYSTERY
THE INVASIONS
THE TUATHA DÉ DANANN

The Kingship of Breas

Though the Tuatha Dé had bested the Fir Bolg and had taken the High Kingship of Ireland, Nuada, the High King of the Tuatha Dé had been mutilated in battle, his right arm cut off by Streng while he lay exhausted against his battle pillar. As a result of this mutilation, he was no longer able to be the High King, as the laws of their gods demanded that the king be whole in mind and body. It was decided instead that Breas the

"Breas the Beautiful" — © Jim Fitzpatrick.

Beautiful, a champion of the Tuatha Dé who had helped lead them to victory at the First Battle of Moy Tura, would be king in his stead. Moreover, since Breas was one-half Fomorian on his father's side, having him as High King might forestall the inevitable Fomorian invasion and instead allow the Tuatha Dé to have an extended peace. Since they had suffered great losses against their kindred, and the Fir Bolg were still mighty and might ally themselves with the Fomor if they invaded, in their weakened state the Tuatha Dé deemed the compromise a wise solution.

Unfortunately, though Breas was charismatic, in his heart he was arrogant, and he made a poor king, failing to take proper care of his people and to uphold their tra-

56

ditions. It is said that he did not "grease the knives" of his champions, a metaphor meaning that he did not give them rich rewards for their service, which was customary among the Celts. And this rudeness and lack of respect for traditions extended to every decision he made. In his court there were no jugglers nor fools, no music and dancing, no life and no light. He even went as far as to disrespect Ogma, the wisest man in the kingdom, debasing him by forcing him to collect firewood for the Royal Palace. Even the Dagda, the great chieftain and father of their race, was not given an adequate portion, instead forced to give his best food to lesser men who had gained favor with the king through flatteries.

One of the most famous anecdotes about the reign of Breas has to do with a famous poet who came to entertain him one day. But in return for his services he was offered neither bed nor fire, as was the custom, and for his sustenance he received only three dry biscuits on a small dish. Thereupon he pronounced the first *aer*, or satire, ever to be pronounced in Ireland, the first of those rhythmic maledictions by means of which the poets, masters of the power of the word, can bring blotches on the face of a prince or sterility upon a whole province:

> *Without food upon his dish,*
> *Without cow's milk upon which a calf grows,*
> *Without a man's abode under the gloom of night,*
> *Without enough to reward poets, may that be the fate of Bres!*[14]

Thus Breas began to lose favor with his people by disrespecting the elders of the tribe and failing to uphold the traditions of their culture. But the worst part of his reign was the fact that he failed to protect his people from the predations of the Fomor. Gradually, the Fomorians had threatened and cajoled Breas into giving them higher and higher tributes to keep them from attacking, until the Tuatha Dé were paying them the same 2/3 that their ancestors, the Nemedians, had fought and died to escape. However, unlike their Nemedian forebears, Breas did not lead them into an uprising against their now Fomorian masters — who had enslaved them bit by bit over time — but continued to indulge their lust for tribute in exchange for peace. As a result, the Tuatha Dé, once a mighty people, teetered on the brink of enslavement.

THE MYSTERY
THE INVASIONS
THE TUATHA DÉ DANANN

The Silver Arm

In the meantime, Nuada had begun to waste away along with his people, not with hunger but with the sickness and the grief brought about by the loss of his sword arm, and of his kingship. Nuada was a mighty warrior and one of the greatest kings of the ancient world, being the rightful heir of the line of Magog. Yet now he lay bedridden and in a deep depression, without his right arm and his right to rule those whom he had literally given his right arm to protect.

Seeing his plight, the great Tuatha Dé healer Dian Cécht devised a solution — he created for Nuada a silver arm that performed exactly as his former arm had, but with the greater strength, durability and unlimited endurance that are the advantages of the mechanical device. Heartened, he took his sword, the *Claímh Solais*, and cried out to the sun as it arose over the sacred hills of Èireann:

> *I am Nuada, son of the Sun!*
> *I am he of the Silver-Arm!*

And from that day forward, he was known as *Nuada Airged Lámh*, "Nuada of the Silver Arm". And as his strength was renewed, hope was rekindled in the hearts of his people, the sacred tribe of the goddess Danu.[15]

The Return of the King

As Nuada's health waxed, the favor of the people towards King Breas waned, so that even his own poets began to curse his name and rally the people towards reinstating Nuada. Soon the people began to pay little heed to him, and withheld the cruel taxes and levies for whom Breas had become little more than a collector for the Fomorians. The chieftains of the tribes then demanded that Nuada be reinstated as High King, allowing Breas to stay until the end of his seventh year so that he would not be ruined and in disgrace. In the meantime, Nuada began to rebuild the Tuatha Dé war machine back to its original strength, training them specifically to handle the brutal, blitzkrieg-style warfare that has always been the trademark of the Fomorian race.

But Breas was too proud to admit defeat, and he turned to his father's kin, the Fomorians, to help him to regain his throne. To this end, Breas traveled

58

to the land of the Fomor to visit with their Wizard-King, Balor of the Evil Eye, who lived in the mysterious Tower of Glass. Arriving there in secret, Breas promised to personally lead the armies of the Fomor against Balor's ancient enemy, Nuada of the Silver Arm.

"Lugh Rides to Battle",
© 1979, Jim Fitzpatrick.

THE COMING OF LUGH THE IL-DÁNA

However, while Breas was busy betraying his people, a mysterious figure named Lugh appeared to the Tuatha Dé, claiming kinship, lauding his superior skill in every art and science, and telling of his desire to help them free themselves from the Fomor yoke. He then told them of his origins, how he was the son of Cian, the son of Dian Cécht, the Chief Physician of the Tuatha Dé and of Ethne, the daughter of Balor, the Wizard-King of the Fomorians.

Lugh then told the story of how Balor's druids had prophesied that Balor, Lugh's grandfather, would one day be killed by his own grandson. In order to avoid this fate, Balor had ordered the infant Lugh drowned. But Eithne, Lugh's mother, had managed to fool her wicked father, and instead spirited young Lugh off to Spain to be raised by Tailltiu, daughter of the King of Spain and the Queen of the Fir Bolg. It was there that Lugh was taught all the arts and sciences, particularly the art of war, by both men, elves and even the great sea-god Manannan Mac Lir, who lent Lugh his magic horse, sword and armor. In time Lugh, fully equipped, trained and ready, returned to fulfill his destiny to lead the tribe of Danu to victory against the Fomorians.

THE MYSTERY
THE INVASIONS
THE TUATHA DÉ DANANN

The Wrath of Indignation

Just as Lugh was finishing his story, the tax collectors of the Fomor arrived, heavily armed and ready to take their tribute by force, if necessary. And while they were busy intimidating the unarmed Tuatha Dé into handing over their taxes, Cochpar, the leader of the Fomor, made the critical mistake of dishonoring Nuada by placing his hand on the breast of the Mórrigan, Nuada's fairy queen and lover. Enraged, Lugh exhorted Nuada to fight to defend her honor, but he refused as the Tuatha Dé had been caught by surprise and were unarmed. Lugh then summoned The Riders of the *Sídhe* and single-handedly slaughtered all of the Fomorian tax collectors, save nine whom he sent back to Balor as a warning. Thus the stage was set for the Second Battle of Moy Tura.

Balor did not need the warning, however, as he and his druids had been watching these events as they occured from afar through his crystal ball. Cathleann, Balor's wife and prophetess was also watching, and she paled when she saw Lugh, realizing that Lugh was the one whom it had been prophesied would kill Balor and end his reign of terror. Balor's arrogance overcame him, however, and he dismissed Lugh as a mere boy, sending Breas with a powerful army of Fomor to bring back Lugh's head. But Balor was cunning, as Breas was only a diversion to keep Lugh occupied while Balor's main force landed on the far western shore of the island.

When Nuada received word of the invasion, he chose wisely not to divide his forces, realizing correctly that Breas' assault was most likely a diversion. Instead he told Lugh that since he was the one who had provoked the Fomor, then he must face their wrath alone. Lugh departed in wrath from Nuada, and went to the house of his father, Cian to ask for help. There, he began to build an army of the faithful from among the people, and called upon his brothers to raise up the army of the *sídhe*, the fairy host, from the fairy mounds. Together with his father's army, the army of Bove the Red, ruler of Connaught, and the Riders of the *Sídhe*, Lugh crushed Breas' army. The arrogant Breas warned Lugh of the approaching Fomor invasion, but Lugh was unafraid, because he knew that Balor was destined to fall under his sword. The Fates had already decided in favor of the Tuatha Dé, and of Lugh the Il-Dana, their champion — the divine weapon whom they had forged in order to break the power of the wicked Fomorians.

THE MYSTERY
THE INVASIONS
THE TUATHA DÉ
DANANN

THE SECOND BATTLE OF MOY TURA

The Roll Call of Power

A "carnyx" war-horn of the type used by the Celts before battle to frighten and intimidate their enemies.†

Before the great battle with Balor's forces took place, the Tuatha Dé took stock of their magical inventory, the various healers, druids and artisans each stepping forward in turn, promising to do their part in winning the battle. Mórfhis the Druid promised to cause the twelve mountains of Eíreann to fall on the Fomor; the cup-bearers promised to place an unquenchable thirst on the Fomor, and then hide the 12 rivers and 12 lakes of Èireann from them. Figol the Wizard promised to cause three showers of fire to fall on the Fomorians, and to cause them to retain their water so that the poisons in their body would accumulate. The *Badb* promised to enchant the trees, rocks, and soil of Eíreann so that the Fomor would have no firm ground on which to stand. Goibhnu the Smith, Créidne the Craftsman and Lúchta the Carpenter promised to make every weapon of the Tuatha Dé hit its mark, and to quickly renew every shattered blade, spearhead, armor plate and shield so that they would be ready for battle the next day. Ogma promised to create a battle strategy that would cause 1/3 of the army of the Fomors to be captured. Dian Cécht, the Healer, promised to heal any man who had not been beheaded so that they could rejoin the battle the next day. And finally, Cairbre the Poet, the son of Ètain, promised to compose a satire, a song that would shame and humiliate the Fomorians and rob them of their fighting spirit.

However, when the time came for the wizards and druids to roll the mountains and cause fire to rain from the heavens and use all the rest of their magic to weaken the Fomorian host, Balor had three spells for every two of theirs, and their power was set to naught. The great magic of the Tuatha Dé was to no avail, because Balor was the greatest wizard of that age.

But Lugh spoke to the entire army and so encouraged them with his powerful words so that each of them felt like kings and heroes. The next day, as the

THE MYSTERY
THE INVASIONS
THE TUATHA DÉ DANANN

powerful, well-ordered host of the Tuatha Dé approached the field of battle, they began to shout, beat their shields and blow their boar-head carnyx horns in order to intimidate the Fomor. Their wizards and druids lit their fires, cast their war spells and chanted their battle incantations once again, while the *Badb* proceeded in front of the assembly, dressed as black witches carrying smoking torches and screaming foul imprecations at the Fomor. All together, though the Fomorians were indeed stout fighters, they grew fearful of the terrible *sturm und drang* coming from the people whom Balor had led them to believe would be like lambs led to the slaughter, and doubt began to grow in their hearts as to the rightness of their cause.

Sensing the fear and doubt in the hearts of his men, Indech, the great *Feldmarschall* of the Fomorians, spurred his steed and led a furious cavalry charge into the Dé Danann flanks, followed by a group of giant berzerkers. And though their furious charge weakened the Dé Danann flanks, the shield wall held, and the headstrong Fomorians were decimated by the Dé Danann javelins. Octriallach, the son of Indech, then called out Prince Cassmael of the Tuatha Dé for single combat, crushing him with his huge battle-axe while both armies stood still to witness the contest.

Thereafter, the battle raged for two whole days without victory for either side. But the Fomor noticed that the weapons and armor of the Tuatha Dé were newly forged every day, as if they were brand new. This is because though the war magic of the wizards and druids had been largely countered by Balor, the skill and magic of the craftsmen, Goibhnu, Créidne and Lúchta, had not been, and this gave the Tuatha Dé a tremendous advantage over the Fomor, whose weapons and armor were beginning to fail them. The Fomor also noticed that the Dé Danann casualties reappeared fresh and whole the next day, ready for battle, while their own were out for the duration. This was because the healer, Dian Cécht, had prepared a Well of Healing for them, in which he had immersed the bodies of the heroes and healed them of every wound. The Fomor soon learned their secrets, however, and though they were not successful in killing the Tuatha Dé craftsmen, they rendered the Well of Healing useless by covering it over with a huge pile of rocks, which can be seen to this day.

The Duel of the Fates

On the third day, the whole of the Dé Danann army took the field. Nuada arranged the Tuatha Dé into a block of nine squares, their magic number. The fierce, half-bestial Fomorians, however, stood in a concave, ragged mass at the northern end of Lough Arrow, ready to bring disorder to the well-ordered Dé Danann ranks. The dark crescent of the Fomorian forces stood in stark contrast to the glittering host of the Tuatha Dé, which shone brilliantly in the morning sun.

With a blast of brazen trumpets, the Fomorians suddenly raged across the plain with a terrible war whoop, flanked by their brutal cavalry. The Dagda signaled for the phalanx, and the army of the Tuatha Dé formed a near-impenetrable shield wall bristling with spears. The bodies of the berzerking Fomorians, impelled to self-destruction by the powerful thought-magic of

"The Single Combat of Nuada of the Silver Arm and Indech the Mighty, King of the Fomor", © 1979, Jim Fitzpatrick.

Balor, quickly piled up in front of the shield wall, which began to buckle under the sheer weight of flesh that pressed down on it.

Seeing the slaughter of his men, Indech made another furious charge at the Dé Danann center. Intent on breaking their front line, he finally managed

THE MYSTERY
THE INVASIONS
THE TUATHA DÉ
DANANN

to do so, but at great loss. But though his casualties were high, Indech had succeeded in breaking the Dé Danann line, and had even managed to kill Ogma, the great philosopher-priest of the Tuatha Dé, who would later be deified by their descendants as the god of wisdom.

Enraged at the loss of this great tribal chieftain, Nuada challenged Indech to single combat in order to even the score, and both armies stopped to watch the duel of the greatest champions on the field. Nuada, who was clearly superior to the hot-headed, overconfident Indech, quickly dehorsed him, and offered him mercy if his army quit the field and left Ireland to the Tuatha Dé. Indech refused, and the price of his refusal was his head.

Nuada was victorious, but his time on Earth was drawing to a close. Balor of the Evil Eye had yet to take the field, and he was the mightiest of all powers of that age. Balor had prepared a terrible spell for this day and hour to destroy his hated enemy, Nuada. Surrounded by countless candles and human sacrifices, Balor called upon the terrible *Crom Cruach*, who this time sent Death itself in order to take Nuada's life. The Demon of Death swiftly engulfed Nuada in a tangle of shadows, slowly draining his life force while Nuada stood helpless. Unsure how to defeat this greatest of all foes, Nuada attempted in vain to use the *Claímh Solais*, the Sword of Light, that he had used to destroy the Collector. But one cannot slay Death, and the demon finally claimed its prize.

Enraged by the cowardly way that Nuada was defeated, the Dagda then led the remnant of the Dé Danann army in a furious charge against the remnant of the Fomorian horde in order to crush and sweep it from the plain — just as he had done against the Fir Bolg seven years earlier. The brutality of the fighting that day was unparalleled in the annals of warfare, as the very forces of good and evil, of Gog and Magog, were dueling once again to determine the destiny of the West.

The Great Eye

Thus Nuada was taken away by Death itself, to the great halls of the Underworld to take his place beside his forefathers. But Balor's power was spent by summoning Death itself to do away with his ancient foe, and he slumped, exhausted, in the chair that sat beneath the Great Eye — the power weapon,

THE MYSTERY
THE INVASIONS
THE TUATHA DÉ
DANANN

so mighty in its sweep!

Suddenly Lugh appeared, his glittering armor reflecting the last rays of the sun that was setting on the West. Calling out a challenge to Balor, he hacked his way in glittering arcs through the remnant of the Fomor rabble that remained between him and his prize. In response, Balor bid his druids to raise the lid of the Great Eye, a massive apparatus of sinister origins that sat upon a tall, pyramidal tower of polished ebony. Upon its surface were carved arcane spells in a strange language of symbols from the distant south, from the land whence Cessair had come before the Flood had cleansed the world of darkness.

When Balor's druids had finally opened the Great Eye with their strange implements, the Eye seemed to come to life, moving of its own volition on its ebon base to catch the last rays of the setting sun. As it did so, it seemed to amplify them within its midst, looking as if it contained the living fire of life itself. Balor then opened a small golden scarab that sat fixed upon his forehead, revealing a thin point of red light that appeared to reach to infinity. As he tilted his head, the Great Eye tilted with it, as if following the thin beam. And as Balor gazed upon the clashing armies, so did the Great Eye. Suddenly, after a brief utterance from Balor, the power of life in the Great Eye turned to the power of death as an irresistible beam of blinding light lanced outward from it, instantly vaporizing everything it touched. Sword and armor, flesh and bone, none could withstand the power of the Great Eye.

The Spear of Destiny

Charging towards Balor on his magic white horse, Aonvarr, Lugh knew the time had come to use his most powerful weapon — the *Sleá Bua*, the Spear of Victory. From the most advanced druids in the world, the Persians who lived to the south of the lands of his ancestors, came the terrible *Sleá Bua* — a spear that throws itself! Lugh carefully reviewed the arcane script engraved on the haft of the spear, gripping the handle firmly as he lined it up for accurate throwing. Methodically performing the ritual of the spear, Lugh finished the incantation and pulled the trigger that sent it forth, "towards thy foe". Straight to its target it went with a trail of lightning, and a roar of thunder! The magic

THE MYSTERY
THE INVASIONS
THE TUATHA DÉ
DANANN

missile seemed to move of its own will, streaking straight towards its target, and in an instant it struck the center of the Great Eye, just as it was about to sweep away Lugh and the rest of the Tuatha Dé. Instantly, with a blinding flash and a terrible thunderclap, Balor fell dead, and the core of the Great Eye fell to Earth, blazing like a torch, crashing with a great explosion that carved out a massive crater. Thus ended Balor of the Evil Eye, and the power of the Fomorians, who never again invaded the sacred isle.

"Lugh faces the Evil Eye", © 1979, Jim Fitzpatrick.

Requiem

The myth of the battle between Lugh the Il-Dana and Balor of the Evil Eye is perhaps the most celebrated in all Irish mythology. After the defeat of Balor, Lugh went on to be the greatest king of the Tuatha dé Danann. After his death, Lugh was deified by his people, and continued to be venerated by the Irish well into the Christian period. Even as late as the 20th century, the Lughnasa assemblies, where the god of light and life was celebrated with music, dance, games and feats of strength,

THE MYSTERY
THE INVASIONS
THE TUATHA DÉ
DANANN

had continued on, though they were no longer religious festivals but merely social gatherings where the festivities continued on in a more secular spirit. It is these festivals and related social events that help give the Irish their unique character and culture, a tapestry of life woven from countless strands of heritage.

The story of the battle between Lugh and Balor has also had a powerful effect on Western popular culture. J.R.R. Tolkien quite clearly called upon the old myths and legends of the Tuatha Dé, the Fomorians, and other peoples from Celtic myth as inspiration for his tales of Middle Earth. In Tolkien's world, the Great Eye of Balor became the Great Eye of Sauron who, like Balor, wished to conquer and enslave the entire world. Within the character of Aragorn, the returning king, we see much of both Nuada and Lugh, including particularly the army of the dead which has a ready cognate with the Riders of the *Sídhe*.

Speaking of the *sídhe*, George Lucas also clearly drew upon Irish mythology as inspiration for his epic film, *Star Wars* (1977), where Darth Vader was known as "The Lord of the Sith™". And of course Lugh's destruction of Balor's evil Eye can clearly be seen in Luke's destruction of the "Death Star". Both of these modern myths struck deep chords in the popular imagination, and remain perennial favorites, because they both draw upon the same ancient, archetypal Celtic myths.

And as for the Tuatha Dé, though they held the land for many centuries, ruling it in the splendor of the kings of old, their time in the land was not to be forever. Eventually, like the Numenóreans of Tolkien's Middle Earth, they went into decline, becoming corrupt and worshiping the same forces of darkness that had led the Fomorians to their own destruction. At the height of their power and beauty, they became inwardly corrupt, appearing glorious and blessed on the outside, while on the inside they were full of avarice and unrighteous power. They had abandoned the ancient mandate to uphold the law of light and civilization, and thus lost the right of rulership over the sacred isle. As a result, it came time for another invasion of civilized peoples who would uphold the Law of Life and keep fair Èireann from falling into darkness. This time, destiny chose the Milesians, better known to history as the Gaels.

THE MYSTERY
THE INVASIONS
THE TUATHA DÉ
DANANN

The Milesians

The taking of the Gaedil and their synchronizing, here below. As for the Gaedil, we have given their adventures from Iafeth s. Noe onward, and from the Tower of Nemrod, till we have left them at Breogan's Tower in Spain; and how they came from Egypt, and out of Scythia to the Maeotic Marshes, and along the Tyrrhene Sea to Crete and to Sicily; and we have further related to you how they took Spain by force. We shall now tell you below simply, how they came to Ireland.[16]

The journey of the Milesians, also known as the Gaels, is perhaps the most interesting and convoluted tale of all of the invasions. As discussed previously, the Gaels were the eponymous ancestors of Gaidel Glas, the son of Feinius Farsaid, the son of Baath, the son of Magog. Much is written in the *Lebor* about the line of Baath, particularly about Feinius Farsaid, who is said to to have helped build the Tower of Nimrod.[17] As a result of the falling of the Tower, the one language that all the people of Earth had previously spoken became confused, and each of the 72 different nations fathered by Shem, Ham and Japheth began to speak in 72 different tongues. Not to be undone, Feinius is said to have then constructed the Gaelic language from parts of all 72 of the different languages that had come about as a result of the confusion of languages caused by the fall of the Tower:

> Now these three sons of Noe, Sem, Ham, Iafeth [Japheth] begat and fathered many numerous and various nations and progenies to wit, seventy-two peoples.... And there were seventy-two languages given to them after the confusion of Nemrod's Tower:[18] so that in the end of ten years after that, Feinius Farsaid extracted the speech of the Gaedil out of the seventy-two languages … and he gave it to Gaedil Glas son of Nel, and to his sons; so that from them is the language named.[19]

According to the *Lebor*, Feinius Farsaid had originally been a prince of Scythia before he had been called out by Ninus, the king of Assyria, to help build the great Tower that was designed to unite mankind. Ninus, the son of Belus, is described in the *Lebor* as an Assyrian king who had apparently declared himself "King of the World", being the first king since before the Flood to claim rulership over the world and all of its peoples.[20] However, because of Ninus' arrogant claim to be the ruler of the world, and because of the possibility that a united mankind could eventually mount an attack against heaven itself, God destroyed the Tower, scattered the peoples, and confused their languages so that there was no chance that mankind could mount another challenge to His authority again until the appointed time at the end of the age. After the destruction was over and the languages scattered, however, Feinius took it upon himself to reconstruct the pre-Tower global language from the 72 languages of the 72 nations. He then named it *Gaidelic*, or "Gaelic", after Gaedel Glas, his grandson.

THE HISTORY OF THE GAELS

Feinius had two sons, Nenual and Nel. He had left Nenual in charge of his princedom in Scythia when he had gone to help build the Tower. His second son, Nel, was born at the Tower, and because of his exceptional intelligence and ability, Nel was eventually wed to the daughter of Pharaoh Cincris of Egypt, who was named "Scota". Nel and Scota had a son, and his name was

THE MYSTERY
THE INVASIONS
THE MILESIANS

Gaedel Glas, after whom Feinius named the language of the Gaels.

As for Nel, the other son of Feinius, he lived southward in Egypt, and took Scota daughter of Pharaoh Cincris to wife: and there that Scota bore Gaedel Glas, from whom are the Gaedil, to Nel son of Feinius Farsaid. So from that Scota the Gaedil are called Scots, and the name Feni is given to them from Feinius, and Gaedil from Gaedil Glas, as the learned said,

> Feni are named from Feinius —
> A meaning without secretiveness
> Gaedil from comely Gaedel Glas,
> Scots from Scota.[21]

Gaedel Glas

Gaedel Glas' life story is particularly interesting, and includes an encounter with Moses himself. Nel, Gaedel and his wife all lived on an estate in northern Egypt that had been ceded them by the Pharaoh. According to the *Lebor*, their next-door neighbors were the Israelites, who also lived on the shores of the Red Sea around Pi-Hahiroth, in northeastern Egypt. In this improbable but interesting scenario, Nel and Gaedel Glas are said to have had a significant role in the Israelite exodus from Egypt:

Now it fell out that the Sons of Israel, in that flight, came to the estate where Nel was, and his son, Gaedel Glas. The Sons of Israel alighted and took camp at Pi-Hahiroth, on the border of the Red Sea. Then Nel son of Feinius came to converse with them, and there Aaron met with him, and told him tidings of the Sons of Israel, to wit, the marvels and miracles of Moses, and how the ten plagues — a clearness of testimony — were brought upon the people of Egypt, by reason of the Israelites' enslavement. And they ratified a treaty and friendship…. Now in that night a venomous poisonous serpent stung the little son whom Nel had, Gaedel Glas, and death was near to him. From that he received the addition to his name. His people said to Nel that he should carry the lad to Moses. The lad was brought to Moses, and Nel came with him. Moses made fervent prayer before God, and put the famous rod upon the place where the serpent stung the lad, so that he was cured. And he said: I command, and God commandeth, that no serpent harm this lad or any of his seed for ever: and that no serpent shall ever dwell in the homeland of his progeny. And, he said, there shall be kings and lords, saints and righteous, of the seed of that lad: and in a northern island of the world it is that the dwelling of his race shall be. This is the reason why there is no serpent in Ireland, and why no serpent or venomous reptile can do harm to any of the seed of Gaedel.[22]

It was from this encounter with the serpent that Gaedel became known as Gaedel Glas, *glas* being the Gaelic word for the color green, describing the color his skin turned where he had been bitten. As recounted in the Book of Exodus and corroborated in the *Lebor*, the host of Pharaoh was soon after drowned in the Red Sea, and Nel and Gaedel continued to live in Egypt for a time without fear of reprisal for having allied themselves with the Israelites. Nel lived out his years and died in Egypt, while Gaedel and Scota had a son, Esru, and a grandson, Sru.

Civil War & Exile

But a new Pharaoh later arose, and began to oppress the descendants of Feinius, who were now led by Sru. Sru and his son Eber Scot were then forced to leave Egypt, taking four ships with 24 wedded couples and three hirelings on each. From there they sailed to their native land of Scythia to rule with their close relatives, the sons of Nenual, Sru's great grand-uncle. Upon arriving in Scythia, however, Sru died, and Eber Scot seized the throne of Scythia by force, only to be assassinated later by Noemius, the son of Nenual. This fratricide continued for several generations until it came down to Mil, the descendant of Nel, and Refloir, the descendant of Nenual.

As a sign of peace, Refloir gave his daughter Seng in marriage to Mil, and they had two sons: Airech Februad and Donn. But Refloir did not trust Mil, and plotted to kill him. The two met on the field of battle, and Mil gave Refloir a mortal wound in his thigh. However, despite their victory, Mil and his progeny were not given the kingship of Scythia, but were instead sent into exile.

THE MYSTERY
THE INVASIONS
THE MILESIANS

The Sons of Mil

Mil left Scythia with four ships carrying fifteen wedded couples and 1 hireling each, arriving back in Egypt 914 years after the drowning of Pharaoh in the Red Sea, which would have been around 350-300 BC.[23] Upon arriving in Egypt, Mil took the daughter of Pharaoh (also named Scota) as a second wife, and she gave him two sons while they were in Egypt: Amergin and Eber. During their sojourn in Egypt, the Milesians also learned the principal arts of the Egyptians, including craftsmanship, druidry, law and warcraft.

The Island of Destiny

However, Pharaoh was later deposed by Alexander the Great, and their position was lessened. Mil then decided to leave, not so much because of Alexander, but because Caicher, his druid, had told him that it was his destiny to rule *Innisfáil*, the mysterious Island of Destiny. So, Mil took his wife and his people to sea in search of a new life in this mysterious island of the West. After a long and circuitous journey in search of the land of his ancestors, during which time Scota gave birth to two more sons, Colptha and Ir, the Milesians eventually arrived in Spain. There they tarried for a while, conquering the native Tuscan, Langobardi and Barchu peoples while Scota gave birth to the last of Mil's eight sons, Eremon and Arandan.

During their time in Spain, Breogan the son of Brath built a tower in the city of Braganza. On one *Samhain* eve, Íth, the son of Breogan, espied an island from afar and decided to check and see if it was indeed *Innisfáil*, the land of his ancestors:

> As for Íth, s. Breogan, it was he who found Ireland at the first. He came alone, on a clear winter's evening, on to the top of Breogan's Tower, and he began to spy out the sea far to the northeast, till he saw Ireland away from him. He goes round back thereafter to his other brethren, and tells them what he had seen. Brego s. Breogan said that what he had seen was no land at all, but a cloud of the sky, and he was for hindering him from going thither; but Íth he could in no wise hinder. Íth launched his ship on the sea and sailed to Ireland, with thrice fifty warriors; till they landed in the "Fetid Shore" of Mag Ítha, on the northern side of

Ireland. People came to hold converse with him on that strand, and each of them told their tidings mutually, through the Scotic language. Íth asked of them what was the name of this island. Inis Elga, said, they; Mac Cúill, Mac Cécht and Mac Gréine are its three kings. Íth gave them counsel, and said unto them: It is right for you to maintain good brotherhood; it is fitting for you to be of good disposition. Good is this your island, plenteous its honey, its harvest, and its wheat, its fish and its corn. Moderate is it in heat and in cold. Within it is all ye need. Íth bade them farewell, and made for his ship.[24]

Unfortunately, for Íth, the Tuatha Dé took his kind words about their island as an indication that he was a spy who was gathering information in preparation for an invasion, and they killed him. Ironically, the Milesians might have left the Tuatha Dé the rule of Ireland and stayed in Spain, but upon hearing word of Íth's death, the Milesians became hard set to take Ireland not only to fulfill the destiny of Mil, their father, but also to avenge the death of their brother.

Mil stayed in Spain, sending Èber Donn, Eremón and Amergin the Poet to lead the invasion force. When they reached the island, however, they found that every port they approached was blockaded, framed with long spears held by demons that the Tuatha dé Danann had summoned by means of druidry, and for a while it was impossible to dock. "Every time that the Sons of Míl came up with Ireland, the demons would frame that port with, as it were, a hog's back; whence Ireland is called "Hog Island". They skirted around Ireland three times, and landed at last at Inber Scéne."[25] It was there that Amergin uttered "The Mystery".

But the last invasion of Ireland was only beginning. The Tuatha Dé went to battle with the Milesians, using the full might of their dark magic to repel their divinely appointed replacements at the battle of Sliab Mis: "At the end of three days and nights thereafter the Sons of Míl broke the battle of Sliab Mis against demons and Fomoraig, that is, against the Tuatha dé Danann…. The sons of Mil fought the battle of Life; there were monsters in the shapes of giants which the Tuatha dé Danann summoned to themselves by druidry."[26]

THE MYSTERY

THE INVASIONS

THE MILESIANS

73

The Tuatha Dé had violated the divinely appointed division between the realm of the natural and the realm of the divine, summoning evil spirits to try to change the outcome of the battle that was meant to be won by the Milesians. However, it was to no avail, as the Sons of Mil were destined to rule Ireland, and after several defeats in battle, the Tuatha Dé were forced to parley with the Milesians.

The Sons of Mil first met with Queen Banbha, who ruled from Sliab Mis, promising to name the island after her if she surrendered peacefully. They then met with Queen Fódhla in Eblinne, and also promised to name the island after her. Finally, they met with Queen Èriu in Uisnech, and she too gave them leave to rule the island as long as they honored her by naming the island after her. And this is why Ireland has ever after had three names: Èriu, Banbha and Fódhla, Èiru being the principal. As it is said in the *Lebor*,

> They had colloquy with Èriu in Uisnech. She said unto them: Warriors, said she, welcome to you. Long have soothsayers had knowledge of your coming. Yours shall be the island for ever; and to the east of the world there shall not be a better island. No race shall there be, more numerous than yours. Good is that, said Amergin; good is the prophecy. Not right were it to thank her, said Èber Donn, eldest of the sons of Míl; thank our gods and our own might. To thee 'tis equal, said Èriu; thou shalt have no profit of this island, nor shall thy progeny. A gift to me, ye sons of Míl, and ye children of Breogan, said she: that my name shall be on this island. It shall be its principal name, said Amergin.[27]

The three queens of the Tuatha Dé had judged rightly that it was the divine destiny of the Milesians to rule Ireland, and that opposing them would lead only to their own destruction. But the three kings of the Tuatha Dé, Mac Cúill, Mac Cécht and Mac Gréine, foolishly challenged the divine right of the Milesians to rule Ireland. They demanded that Amergin take his forces out to sea again and, if they landed successfully once more, then that would be a sign that the gods had taken away the rule of Ireland from the Tuatha Dé and given it to the Sons of Míl. If that occurred, Kings Mac Cúill, Mac Cécht and Mac Gréine agreed to willingly hand over their crowns to the Milesians. Amergin agreed to sail their ships out as far as nine waves, and then return again as they requested. This agreement is believed to be the first judgment in Ireland.

However, the three kings of the fallen Tuatha Dé had dealt falsely, as they intended to misuse the power of their druids and poets to cause the ships of the Milesians to founder and sink. And as soon as Amergin had reached the ninth wave, every wizard, druid and poet in the island sang their songs and cast their spells so that there was a storm so great that it churned the sea from top to bottom, blowing the Milesians all the way to the west of Ireland. But Amergin knew in his heart that it was the destiny of the Sons of Mil to rule Ireland, so he sang a second poem to calm the waters:

> I seek the land of Ireland,
> Courséd be the fruitful sea,
> Fruitful the ranked highland,
> Ranked the showery wood,
> Showery the river of cataracts,
> Of cataracts the lake of pools,
> Of pools the hill of a well,
> Of a well of a people of assemblies,
> Of assemblies of the king of Temair;
> Temair, hill of peoples,
> Peoples of the Sons of Míl,
> Of Míl, of ships, of barks;
> The high ship Èriu,
> Èriu lofty, very green,
> An incantation very cunning,
> The great cunning of the wives of Bres,
> Of Bres, of the wives of Buaigne,
> The mighty lady Èriu,
> Erimón harried her,
> Ír, Eber sought for her —
> I seek the land of Ireland.[28]

And so the waters were calmed, and Amergin stepped onshore to rule Èriu, the island of the destiny of his fathers. But the remnant of the Tuatha dé Danann,

THE MYSTERY
THE INVASIONS
THE MILESIANS

75

though compliant with their agreement, remained unwilling to be ruled over by the Gaels, and instead retreated to the Underworld through the numerous raths, caves, standing stones and fairy trees throughout the land. There they are believed to live to this day, known now as the *sídhe*, ruled over by the Dagda, the immortal All-Father of the Tuatha Dé. And as long as the Gaels respect the *sídhe* and leave them in peace, it is said, the two worlds, the Upper World and the Underworld, will continue to live in harmony until the end of the age.

Notes

[1] R.A.S. Macalister, ed. *Lebor Gábala Èrenn: Vol. I* (London: The Irish Texts Society, 1941), 165.

[2] R.A.S. Macalister, ed. *Lebor Gábala Èrenn: Vol. II* (London: The Irish Texts Society, 1941), 187.

[3] R.A.S. Macalister, ed. *Lebor Gábala Èrenn: Vol. III* (London: The Irish Texts Society, 1941), 3-5.

[4] *Ibid.*, 13-15. The reference to these men with one foot and one hand and one eye may be literal. The ancient Scythians were at one time at war with an Amazonian tribe of female warriors who would actually remove a hand and/or leg from their male children in order to keep them submissive. Thus, the Fomorian males who fought the Partholónians might literally have had only one foot, one hand and one eye, but had developed a fighting style that compensated for their mutilation. (Greek Mythology Link, "Scythia" http://homepage.mac.com/cparada/GML/Scythia.html).

[5] Answers.com, "Lebor Gabála Érenn" (http://www.answers.com/topic/lebor-gab-la-renn). No word on who buried them if "everyone" died in the plague.

[6] Macalister, *Lebor Gábala Èrenn: Vol. III*, 121.

[7] This "treat or trick" concept may have been part of the cultural roots of the traditional Celtic Halloween.

[8] Macalister, *Lebor Gábala Èrenn: Vol. IV*, 15.

[9] Marie-Louise Sjoestedt, *Celtic Gods & Heroes* (Mineola, NY: Dover Publications, 2000 [reprint of the 1949 edition]), 7-8.

[10] Macalister, *Lebor Gábala Èrenn: Vol. IV*, 107-111.

[11] *Ibid.*, 107. Cf also T.W. Rolleston, *Celtic Myths & Legends* (Mineola, NY: Dover Publications, Inc., 1990 [Reprint of *Myths & Legends of the Celtic Race*, 2nd Rev. ed. (London: George G. Harrap & Company, 1917), 105-106, and Sjoestedt, *Celtic Gods & Heroes*, 7-8.

[12] For more of this excellent and highly entertaining interpretation of the First Battle of Moy Tura, see Jim Fitzpatrick's *The Book of Conquests* (New York: E.P. Dutton, 1978). Many images from this best-selling graphic novel also appear in this book.

[13]*Sídhe* can be pronounced either "shee" or "sith", the pronunciation apparently varying by region. Learn more about the *sídhe* in The Mystery: Creatures Great and Small: Fairies (pp. 149-165).

[14]Sjoestedt, *Celtic Gods & Heroes*, 7. For more about the famous poets of ancient Ireland, see The Mystery: Wizards, Druids & Poets: Poets (pp. 136-141).

[15]This interpretation of the story of Nuada's Silver Arm and subsequent restoration of the Tuatha Dé is based in part upon Jim Fitzpatrick's *The Silver Arm* (Limpsfield, Surry, UK: Dragon's World, 1981). Many images from this excellent second book in the series also appear in this book.

[16]Macalister, *Lebor Gábala Èrenn: Vol. V*, 11.

[17]Though some traditions hold that the Tower of Babel had been built by Nimrod, the Tower was most likely built around 2000 BC, over 1,500 years after the time of Pharaoh Narmer of Egypt, the most likely candidate for the mysterious Nimrod. For an expert analysis on the identity of Nimrod, see http://www.mysteriousworld.com/Journal/2003/Autumn/Osiria/

[18]This statement is based upon a conflation of the Nimrod account in Genesis 10:8-12 and the Tower of Babel account in Genesis 11:1-8. Though rabbinic and some church traditions hold that Nimrod was indeed the builder of the Tower of Babel, Nimrod was more likely Narmer, the first Pharaoh of the united Egypt, who lived around 3500 BC, preceding the Tower of Babel event by some 15 centuries. Learn more about Nimrod and Narmer at http://www.mysteriousworld.com/Journal/2003/Winter/Osiria/

[19]Macalister, *Lebor Gábala Èrenn: Vol. I*, 147. The *Lebor* gives the name of the language that all Earth spoke before the fall of the Tower as "Gorthigern" (II:57).

[20]Ninus ruled Assyria ca. 800 b.c., and was most likely not the builder of the Tower, which was probably built ca. 2000 b.c. The identity of the king who built the Tower is currently unknown, but may have been Amraphel, king of Shinar. See http://www.mysterious world.com/Journal/2003/Autumn/Osiria/#NimrodAsBabylonianKing for more information.

[21]Macalister, *Lebor Gábala Èrenn: Vol. II*, 53, 87.

[22]*Ibid.*

[23]*Ibid.*, 67. Dating the Exodus around 1250 BC, Mil probably arrived in Egypt around 350-300 BC. This dating is most likely correct, as the *Lebor* states that Alexander invaded soon after, as he did indeed do in 332 BC, though there was no "Pharaoh" by that time as the Persians had been in control of Egypt for about a decade. The king whom Alexander supplanted was actually a Persian by the name of Darius III Codomannus.

[24]R.A.S. Macalister, ed. *Lebor Gábala Èrenn: Vol. V* (London: The Irish Texts Society, 1941), 11-19.

[25]*Ibid.*, 31. *Inber Scéne*, "the Mouth of the Scéne River", was named after Amergin's wife, who died during the journey.

[26]Macalister, *Lebor Gábala Èrenn: Vol. V*, 33-35. It appears that the Tuatha Dé may have been resurrecting the ancient giants from before the Flood, those that were called "Rephaim" in the Bible. For more on this chilling possibility, see Part I on our series on Giants in the Earth at http://www.mysteriousworld.com/Journal/2003/Spring/Giants/#TheRephaim

[27]Ibid., 35-37.

[28]Ibid., 115-117.

Deities & Demigods

Though the Tuatha Dé had retreated into the Underworld, they remained very much alive in the myths and legends of the ancient Irish. Even today their names resound in myth and memory, kept alive by place names and storytellers who remember the glories of the days of old — before the coming of the dark times. Now, not only the gods of the Old World, but even the great God brought to the sacred isle by St. Patrick are being mercilessly trampled down and paved over by the beast of secular humanism. Relentless in its need to devour truth, life and light in favor of "progress", the modern world seems intent on replacing all the ancient holy sites — both pagan and Christian — with countless strip malls connected by endless superhighways, full of people in a hurry to go nowhere. Gradually forgetting their sacred past, the Irish — and all the peoples of the West — risk a head-on collision with the ancient powers of the world, who will not be forgotten.

The Milesians had conquered the land, but the Tuatha Dé controlled the Underworld, led there by the Dagda through the countless sacred mounds, raths, stone circles and fairy trees to be found throughout the sacred isle. Over time, their original giant stature shrank in the minds of the Gaels so that they eventually came to be known as "the little people", or "the fairies" — the actual Gaelic term being the *shí* ("she") or, more commonly, the *sídhe* ("sith"). From their Underworld abode they continue to control the natural forces of the land, of which the Milesians are merely the stewards. In that sense, the Tuatha Dé are still the rulers of Ireland, though they are restricted by their ancient covenant with the Milesians to remain in the Underworld. But if the descendants of the Gaels break this ancient covenant, the *sídhe* will no longer be restricted to their Underworld prison, and all hell will literally break loose on the land as the Riders of the *Sídhe* burst their ancient bonds and come forth to take their due.

In this section, we will do a review of all of the major deities of Ireland, all the primeval deities of

THE MYSTERY

DEITIES &
DEMIGODS

Ireland (ancient gods and goddesses who preceded those of the Tuatha Dé) and the demigods — exceptional people in Irish history who claimed partial divinity, and had exceptional abilities to prove it. First we will start with the Dagda, the All-Father of the Tuatha Dé, the recognized chief god of ancient, pre-Christian Ireland, and the legendary ruler of the Underworld:

Greater gods

"Dagda Finds His Mark", © 1977, Jim Fitzpatrick.

THE DAGDA

The Dagda, though he appeared with and fought alongside mortal men in the legends, was actually believed to be a god, specifically, the father god of the Tuatha dé Danann. The son of the god Beli and the goddess Danu, the Dagda — literally, "the good god" — was not good in the sense of moral goodness, but in the sense that he was good at everything. He was an excellent king, a powerful warrior, a wise counselor, a cunning magician, a jovial friend, an amusing clown and a general father figure in

80

whom can be found aspects of all of the other Celtic deities. Thus, he was referred to as the *Eochaid Ollathair*, "All-Father", the king of the gods, and in his original name, *Dagos Devos*, he is also akin to Deus, Zeus and other Indo-European sky-gods. The fact that the word *deva* that makes up the latter half of the Dagda's name is Hindu in origin also lends credence to the belief that the Tuatha Dé had indeed emigrated from Central Asia, which borders what is now India.

The Dagda is seen in the legends as a giant of a man, alternately described as immensely athletic, or immensely fat, depending upon the situation. And though he usually appears as a jovial and comical character, dressed as a peasant and often acting like a clown, he was in fact a figure of immense power. In battle he wielded a huge, magic club which he could use either to kill nine men with one blow, or to resurrect nine men by touching them with its handle. He also possessed a magic cup, "The Cauldron of the Dagda" (*q.v.*), which provided an infinite amount of food and drink for his immense appetite. The Dagda was also known for his magic harp *Uaithne* which, when played, could be used to produce not only sublimely beautiful music, but also rally and direct troops in battle, cause various emotions such as sorrow and laughter and even induce sleep.

Though the Dagda was married to the goddess Breg, he was also quite a womanizer, being associated with various other goddesses including Áine, Boann and the Mórrigan. He had several prominent children through both his wife and his lovers, including Ogma, Aenghus Óg, Bodb Derg, Aed Minbhrec (or Aed Cáem), Cermait Milbél and Mídir. He was also the father of two daughters, the goddesses Brigit and Ainge.

The Dagda's palace was the Palace of the Boyne, in County Meath, and his throne was what is now known as Newgrange. He was also associated with Mount Brandon in County Kerry, which was formerly known as *Slieve Dagda* where Lughnasa festivals were held before the coming of St. Brendan (*q.v.*). Some also connect the Dagda with the god Sucellos of Gaul, the Norse gods Thor and Odin, and with the Cerne Abbas giant in Dorchester County, England, which also has a huge club. And though his people were defeated by the Milesians, legends say, the Dagda continues to rule over the Tuatha dé Danann in the Underworld.

THE MYSTERY
DEITIES &
DEMIGODS
GREATER GODS

ÁINE

Áine, also known as "Anu" or "Danu", was the eponymous mother goddess of the Tuatha dé Danann. She was also either the mother, daughter, or wife of the Dagda, depending upon the tradition, as well as the mother of several other prominent Danann deities. One of the chief goddesses of ancient Ireland, Áine was considered to be both a fairy goddess and the goddess of love, desire and fertility, particularly in Munster province. She is also closely associated with the sky and the sun, and occasionally equated with the Mórrigan in the myths.

"Áine",
© 1975, Jim Fitzpatrick.

Áine had numerous husbands and lovers throughout Irish history, taking various forms in the various myths and legends wherein she makes an appearance. One of the most prominent is an affair she had with Manannan Mac Lir (*q.v.*), where Áine and Manannan traded their spouses (who were already secretly in love with each other) in order to be together. In another tale, "The Battle of Mag Mucrama", Áine was ravished by Ailill Olum, the King of Munster. Enraged, Áine bit off his ear and, thus maimed, Ailill lost the kingship. However, from this inappropriate union came one of the great kings of ancient Ireland: Eógan, the patriarch of the Eóganacht clan. The Eóganacht ruled Munster province for many centuries, and for a time — through their most famous descendant, Brian Boru — all of Ireland.

Another prominent legend involving Áine has her combing her hair on the bank of a river, when Maurice, the Earl of Desmond, happened by and became enraptured by her beauty. Maurice had better control of himself, however, and merely stole her magic cloak, refusing to return it to her unless she married him. Their son Gerald, the Earl of Desmond, according to the legend, still lives in Lough Gur, reappearing every seven years to ride around the surface of the lake on a white horse with silver horseshoes. Several aristocratic Munster families actually claim descent from Gerald, and thus from Áine. One tradition even has Áine having an affair with Finn McCool (*q.v.*).

Áine was celebrated throughout Ireland, and was particularly honored in Munster province, well into the modern period. As late as the twentieth century, festivals in a much reduced form were still held every Midsummer's Eve in County Limerick, where the locals carried torches of hay and straw around Knockainy at night, and then waved the torches over their cattle and crops in order to bring luck and a greater harvest for the coming year. One legend has it that once, when local farmers had omitted the ritual in deference to the death of a local man, torches and fairy lights were still seen on Knockainy, led by none other than Áine herself.

On another St. John's Night, (another name for Midsummer Eve), several young girls had come to the hill to watch the *cliars* (torches) and join in the games. Suddenly, Áine appeared to them and thanked them for honoring her, but asked them to have everyone leave the hill, as "they" wanted the hill to themselves. Inquiring as to the "they", Áine obliged the young girls by having them look at the hill through a magic ring, which allowed them to see that the hillside was indeed already filled to capacity by the *sídhe*. And though the religious elements in this ritual are long gone, in this practice we see a clear memory of the ancient fertility rituals that were once practiced by the ancient Irish, rituals that yet echo in many of the common agricultural practices and superstitions still prevalent in Ireland.

Áine is associated with a number of locations throughout Ireland, but is most closely associated with Knockainy, in County Limerick, and nearby Lough Gur. There is also another Knockainy in nearby Augher, in County Waterford. She is also associated with the Legananny Dolmen in County Down, Ulster province, and Knockaine and the well Tobar Áine near Lissan, in County Derry, also in Ulster province.

OGMA

Ogma was the Tuatha Dé god of wisdom and knowledge, having taught them all the arts and sciences including, most famously, the art of writing in ogham. Ogma is the son of the Dagda and either the goddess Danu (Anu/Áine), Boann or Brigit, depending upon the version of the myth one references. Also like the Dagda, it is not clear as to whether he was actually a "god", or merely a very intelligent man who became deified as a tribal deity over time, as is so often the case in ancient religion. Ogma was also a master strategist, having devised the strategy that the Tuatha Dé used to successfully defend against the invasion of the Fomorians in the Second Battle of Moy Tura. However, evidence against his deity lies in the fact that Ogma was killed in the Second Battle of Moy Tura by Indech, King of the Fomor.

Ogma was also known as "Ogmios" by the Celts of Gaul, known variously as *Ogmios Grianainech*, "Ogma the Sun-Faced" and *Ogmios Cermait*, "Ogma the Honey-Tongued", indicating his sunny disposition and great eloquence. The Celts even depicted him as having chains made of gold and amber that issued from his mouth that connected with the ears of his followers, indicating his powerful ability to use rhetoric to influence people. Though his association with knowledge and wisdom would typically make him cognate with such deities as the Roman god Mercury and the Egyptian god Thoth, due to his great strength and warrior abilities the Celts tended to associate him more with Hercules than with Mercury, much to the confusion of the Romans.

Ogma is the patron of druids, bards, and all who seek knowledge. He is represented as a strongly-built older man with a bald head, dressed in a lion skin and holding a staff.

AENGHUS ÓG

Aenghus Óg ("Aenghus the Young") was the Tuatha Dé god of love and youth, and one of the sons of the Dagda. The story of his birth is one of the more famous legends of the Tuatha dé Danann:

The Dagda fell in love with the goddess Boann, the mother goddess and protectress of the River Boyne, that runs through the Boyne Valley. Boann was also attracted to the Dagda, but feared the vengeance of her husband, Lord

Elcmar, should she start such an affair. To solve their problem, the Dagda sent Lord Elcmar on a mission to a faraway place, and while there he cast a spell upon Elcmar which made time stand still. With her husband out of the way, the Dagda and Boann embarked upon a love affair which bore them a child, Aenghus. The child was taken by the Dagda and given to someone else to raise in secret. When Lord Elcmar returned home he suspected nothing, because for him it had felt like he had been away for only a short time.

While Aenghus was a young boy, he learned of his real father. Deciding that the Dagda must acknowledge all his birthright and grant him his inheritance, he journeyed to seek the advice of Manannan Mac Lir, the sea god and master of trickery. Manannan advised Aenghus to approach his father on the eve of *Samhain*, for this was a magical time when great changes could occur. Aenghus agreed and when the time approached he went to the Dagda and asked him to hand over his palace at *Brú na Bóinne* (Newgrange, in the Boyne Valley) for a day and a night. The Dagda, unaware that the sea god had put him under a spell to help sway his decision, agreed to hand over his palace to the boy.

After the period allotted, the Dagda returned to Newgrange to reclaim his home, but Aenghus refused to leave, stating that the agreement was for a day and a night. And as there was no distinction made as to it being a single day and night, it could mean that he was now lord of *Brú na Bóinne* from that day forth. The Dagda, realizing he had been tricked, left the palace.

Another prominent legend, "The Dream of Aenghus", tells of how a vision of a beautiful woman surrounded by fifty maidens had come to haunt Aenghus in his dreams. He became so ill from the love of this woman that everyone around him became worried for his health. His mother, Boann, sent her armies out across the whole of Ireland in search of this woman, but she was not found. Eventually Aenghus sent for his brother, Bodb Derg, who was the king of all the *sídhe*. Bodb set out in search of this woman and eventually found her, discerning through his magic that her name was Caer Ibormeith, the daughter of Ethal Anbúail, the king of Connaught. Meeting her was not as simple as he might have imagined, however, because a spell had been cast upon Caer and her maidens that forced them to spend part of each year transformed into swans. Undismayed, Aenghus also turned himself into a swan and joined her. The two of them flew around the lake three times, then flew to his palace at Brú na Bóinne, chanting music so beautiful along the way that those who heard it could not sleep for three days and nights. They then lived out their lives in bliss.

Aenghus Óg figured prominently in several other legends, being the protector of several heroes including Diarmuid the *Fianna*, and Eochaid. He is also believed to be the father of Maga, from whom came the Knights of the Red Branch, and of Delbaeth, from whom came Èríu, Banbha and Fódhla, the last three queens of the Tuatha dé Danann.

Aenghus Óg also had a magic sword named *Móralltach* which he lent to Diarmuid, and a magic cloak that made him invisible. He was made immortal by drinking the Ale of Immortality, and it is said that four swans circled above his head wherever he traveled. Along with Manannan Mac Lir, he is also credited with bringing the first cows to Ireland from India. His primary function was as the god of love, however, and it is said that his kisses turned into singing birds, and his music was irresistible to all who heard it.

AED MINBHREC

Aed Minbhrec was one of the lesser-known sons of the Dagda. He appears in the myths as a prince of the Tuatha dé Danann who was wrongly accused of adultery and killed by a jealous husband. His *sídhe* is Ballyshannon, County Donegal, Ulster province.

AINGE

Ainge was another daughter of the Dagda. In one legend, she is seen gathering twigs that are then stolen by Gaible, son of Nuada. However, these twigs resent being stolen, and plant themselves, turning into a forest.

BODB DERG

Bodb Derg ("Bove the Red") was one of the sons of the Dagda, and served as king after he stepped down from the kingship of the Tuatha dé Danann. He was the god of poetry and wisdom, and was renowned for his good judgment.

Bodb shows up as a supporting character in several legends, including "The Dream of Aenghus", where he helped his brother Aenghus Óg by identifying the beautiful woman haunting him in his dreams. He is also mentioned in "The Destruction of Da Derga's Hostel". His gold-smith, Len, was renowned for his skill, having created the Magic "Spear of Len" later used by Finn McCool to slay Aillen, the Great Green Goblin. Len lived and worked near what was later named Lough Léin, modern Killarney, County Kerry. His most prominent appearance is in the Second Battle of Moy Tura where, as "Bove the Red", he assisted Lugh in defeating the Fomorian army led by Breas.

Bodb is described as living in several different places, including Slievenamon in County Tipperary, near Killaloe in County Clare, and of course Newgrange in the Boyne Valley, County Meath, after he took over the rule of the Tuatha dé Danann. Another prominent place that remembers his name is Lough Derg in County Donegal.

BRIGID

Brigid Bhoidheach, "Bride the Beautiful", was the tutelary goddess of the Gaelic peoples of the West. Brigid, one of the daughters of the Dagda, was the goddess of fire, arts and crafts, smithing, fertility, cattle and crops, poetry and, generally speaking, the creative impulse which was believed to be feminine in nature. She has many names, including "Lady of the Shores", as she also presides over magical, in-between, transitional places, such as that between the land and the sea, which so fascinated the religious imagination of the Celts. She also appears to have had aspects of a sun goddess. The worship of Brigid took place mainly on Imbolg, on February 1.

Brigid is also known as "the Two-Faced One", because in some legends her face is dark and ugly on one side, yet white and beautiful on the other. This was meant to symbolize the mystery of the turning of seasons from the *Cailleach*, the hag of winter, to the fair maiden of spring, as Brigid was seen as the creative force of fertility that came and went with the seasons — the eternal flame of femininity which is the basis of all life. Brigid's name originates from the Gaelic words *breo-saighit*, which means "fiery arrow", the flame being the fire of creativity that strikes craftsman and poet alike. As such, she was patronized by both poets, artisans and professionals of all kinds, all of whom drew heat, life and light from her divine forge.

Brigid was also believed to be the guardian of new-born infants, and women commonly hung rowan crosses over cradles and recited a prayer to Brigid to protect their children. Brigid was also the first to "keen" for the dead, a high, mourning wail also associated with banshees (q.v.). Brigid bore a child for King Breas of the Tuatha Dé, and their son, Rúadán, was the man who tried to kill the Tuatha Dé smith Goibniu at the Second Battle of Moy Tura. She was also believed to be the wife of the famous satirist Senchán Torpeist, thought by some to have been the author of the famous epic poem, *Táin Bó Cuailgne*. Brigid is remembered in several places in County Cavan, Ulster province, Brigid's worship most likely being centered at Corleck Hill near Drumleague, County Cavan.

Cermait

Cermait Milbél ("honey-mouthed") was another of the sons of the Dagda. Like Aed Minbhrec he was also killed by a jealous husband, Lugh. Cermait's son MacCuill took revenge on Lugh later by killing him with a spear.

Dian Cécht

Dian Cécht (lit., "swift rolling power") was the principal healing god and physician of the Tuatha dé Danann. With Danu/Aíne he fathered Étan and Cian, and was the grandfather of Lugh. For the Second Battle of Moy Tura, he constructed a special healing well wherein he could heal any wound short of decapitation simply by immersing the body of a warrior into its waters. Dian Cécht also made the magical silver arm for Nuada, but not before slaying his son Miach, who had upstaged him by restoring Nuada's original fleshly arm. After Miach was buried, 365 plants grew on his grave, which turned out to be the 365 healing herbs that are useful for medicinal purposes. Dian Cécht's daughter Airmid dutifully began to categorize and catalog this priceless medical information until, in another senseless, jealous rage, Dian Cécht purposely scattered the carefully ordered plants, effectively destroying a huge amount of useful medical information simply for spite. Dian Cécht's *sídhe* is likely Heapstown Cairn in County Sligo.

Donn

Donn, "The Dark One", was the Irish god of the dead and of the Otherworld, who is sometimes confused with the Dagda. He was a retiring, aloof deity, actually more similar in function to other classical Underworld gods such as Hades and Pluto, where the Underworld is perceived as a gloomy, even hellish place where the dead are kept until the final judgment. His name may be based upon Èber Donn, the eldest son of Mil, who had been cursed by Èriu that neither he nor his descendants would ever enjoy the fruits of their conquest. As a result of the curse (or the prophesy), Donn mac Míled ended up drowning off the west coast of County Cork near the Beara Peninsula, where he is believed to still reside in *Tech Duinn*, "The House of Donn". There, according to variations on the myth, the dead either live with Donn, or visit him as a waystation on their way to the Otherworld. Further legendary accretions actually have Donn as the cause of storms and shipwrecks. He may also be associated with the fairy king Donn Fírinne *(q.v.)*, who is believed to live in nearby County Limerick.

Donn is most closely associated with west Munster, the province that is most often linked with the dead in Irish mythology. Donn's House is located on a rocky islet near Dursey Island on the far western extreme of the Beara Peninsula.

Mídir

Mídir, "the Proud", was another of the sons of the prolific Dagda. He was the arrogant and haughty ruler of the Otherworldly dwelling of *Brí Léith*, also known as Slieve Callary, where he had his fairy palace. The legend he is most associated with is "The Wooing of Ètaín", wherein he took a second wife, Ètaín Óg (the appelation "Óg" indicating that she was a Danann *sídhe*). His first wife, Fuamnach, became jealous of course, and used her magic to turn Ètaín into a butterfly.

Mídir was also possessive, which turned out to be his undoing. The magic cauldron inherited from his father was stolen from him by Cú Chulainn, and his three cranes were stolen by the satirist Aithairne Ailgesach. Mídir had three daughters, Doirenn, Aife and Aillbe, whom he married to the sons of Lugaid: Menn (the Stammerer) Ruide, Fiacha and Eochaid. The placename story of Lough Ree, in County Roscommon, Connaught province, also involves Mídir, and a magical horse whose urine was the original source of the lake's waters. Mídir is most associated with Slieve Callary, near Ardagh in County Longford.

THE TRIPLE SOVEREIGNTY GODDESS

The goddess of sovereignty was the goddess of the land, and in order to rule the land, it was believed, kings had to ritually wed the goddess in the *hieros gamos*, a religious ritual that was ubiquitous throughout the ancient world. By so doing, the king was in effect married to the land, and the fertility of the land was thus assured for the coming year.

The triple sovereignty goddess appears to have varied in character throughout the centuries, the *Badb (q.v.)* perhaps having filled that role at one time. The most commonly known sovereignty goddess, however, was the one that greeted the Milesians at their conquest, made up of the three last queens of the Tuatha dé Danann — Èriu, Banbha, and Fódhla:

Èriu

Èriu, "one who is elevated", was the chief of the three sovereignty goddesses, and the eponymous queen of the land of Ireland ("Èriu's land"). When the Milesians landed, Amergin treated with all three sister-queens and promised all three that the land of Ireland would be named after them, but Èriu's name was to be the principal.

Èriu was married to Mac Gréine, one of the three last kings of the Tuatha dé Danann before the Milesians invaded Ireland, but she had been around a bit, having had a celebrated affair with Elatha, son of Delbáeth, giving birth to Breas, "the Beautiful", the ill-fated, half-Fomorian king of the Tuatha dé Danann. She was also Lugh's consort,

"Èriu",
© 1975, Jim Fitzpatrick.

a necessary relationship for the king as she was considered to be the land incarnate. Èriu, along with all of her sisters, was eventually killed at the Battle of Tailltiu.

Èriu is believed to have founded the festival at Uisnech, and is believed to be buried under the "cat stone" atop the Hill of Uisneach, in County Westmeath, Leinster province.

Banbha

Banbha, whose name means "woman of the cows" had, like Èriu, been promised by Amergin to have the land of Ireland named after her. However, the only regions that still retain her name are south Leinster and the plain of Meath containing Tara. She also met with the Milesians at Slieve Mis, County Kerry, in Munster province.

Banbha may be equated with Boann, the cow goddess (lit., "woman of the white cows"), who was also considered to be a sovereignty goddess, though a definitive association has never been made between the two. The term "woman of the white cows" refers to the fact that white cows were considered cows of the Otherworld.

"Boann, The Cow Goddess",
© 1976, Jim Fitzpatrick.

Assuming that Boann and Banbha were variant names of the same goddess, Banbha/Boann fulfilled several related roles, being a water goddess, a cow-goddess and a general fertility goddess. The association between Banbha and Boann is supported by the fact that the Boyne Valley wherein the Hill of Tara is situated was named after Boann, this same region also being referred to as "Banbha" in ancient times.

The birth of the River Boyne has its roots in an ancient legend known as "The Well of Sergais". It is said that a long time ago, when the gods walked the earth, there was a well shaded by magical hazel trees bearing crimson nuts. It was believed that whomever should eat these nuts would be graced with the knowledge of the world. The nuts fell off the trees and into the well, and were eaten by one of the vividly colored salmon who swam there, which then became known as The Salmon of Knowledge.

This well was owned by the god Nechtain, who was very possessive of it. Only he and his three cup bearers were allowed anywhere near it. But one day his wife, Boann, was overcome with curiosity, and went to the well without Nechtain's permission or knowledge. When she violated this *geas*, or prohibition, the well overflowed and gushed forth onto the surrounding countryside, forming the Boyne ("Boann") Valley and what was thereafter referred to as the Boyne River.

Fódhla

Fódhla, (lit., "under earth") was the third person of the threefold sovereignty goddess, and was particularly associated with agriculture. Her name is suggestive of the Underworld, and she may once have been the Queen of the Underworld, later relegated to the role of more of a generic fertility goddess in whose domain lay the fundamental power of the land to bring forth produce.

"Fódhla", © 1998, Jim Fitzpatrick.

Fódhla was married to Mac Cécht, the third of the last three kings of the Tuatha dé Danann before the coming of the Milesians. The exceptional High King Ollam Fódhla also bears her name, who was known for his laws, poetry and other significant accomplishments.

Fódhla had met with the Milesians at Slieve Felim, in County Limerick, which was likely also her *sídhe*.

The Badb: The Triple War Goddess

Just as the goddess of sovereignty is triple in aspect, so too is the goddess of war, a motif that was common among the ancient Celts. The *Badb*, (literally, "the crow"), was the great warrior goddess of the ancient Celts. The *Badb* was a triple goddess, made up of three distinct personages: Macha, Mórrigan and Nemain. The *Badb* are also sometimes referred to as the *Mórrigna*, as the Mórrigan appears to have been the dominant one of the three. The *Badb* could appear singly or in a group of three women, and was most frequently found haunting a

"*Mórrigan na Badb*", © 1979, Jim Fitzpatrick. The Mórrigan (foreground) is considered to be the most dominant of the three *Badb*.

battlefield before, during or after a battle. Like the Greek Furies, the Norse Valkyries and Norns, and the Fates of the Roman myths, the *Badb* appear to have been the goddesses of destiny, determining the fates of men from birth to death, and collecting their souls once their lifeline was complete. When the *Badb* appeared, either as a pretty young girl, a beautiful woman, an old hag, or in her classic crow form, it was an omen of certain doom for those who saw her. As the archetypal "Washer at the Ford", she is often seen washing the severed heads and limbs of the dead in river crossings just before or after a battle, making sure that someone sees her so that the horror of the moment is complete.

The *Badb* is decidedly evil, deriving great satisfaction in causing pain and suffering, and delighting in slaughter. For this reason, she would purposely fill opposing armies with great rage and battle fury in order to make the carnage all the more brutal in order to satisfy her

**THE MYSTERY
DEITIES &
DEMIGODS
GREATER GODS**

blood lust. The *Badb* appeared numerous times in various guises to many of the heroes in the myths, either as Macha, Mórrigan, Nemain and/or the ubiquitous crow, and may be remembered in the *badbh chaointe*, a banshee-like figure who in more recent times was believed to haunt battlefields and keen for the dead. She was also believed to be married to the war-god Neit. The Badb were commemorated in County Kerry, Munster province, in the townland of Lisbabe (*lios baidbhe*, "Badb's Fort") near Aghadoe.

The crow was the symbol of the *Badb* and an omen of evil to all who beheld it.†

The *Badb* made their most famous appearances at the First and Second Battles of Moy Tura, where they took on the role of the "war witches" of the Tuatha dé Danann, casting spells against their opponents in order to give the Tuatha Dé the advantage. But aside from their collective work, each of the three members of the *Badb* also had their own solo careers:

Macha

Macha, also known as *Mong Ruadh* ("the red-haired"), was the eldest of the three *Badb*, and a classic Celtic war goddess. She represented old age and the end of the life cycle, though she could also appear as a beautiful young woman if she so desired to achieve her ends. She appeared several times throughout Irish history in various guises, first as the wife of Nemed, the king of the Nemedians. She later appeared as a queen of Ulster who married her rival, King Cimbáeth.

"The Curse of Macha", 1910, Stephen Reid.†

However, this marriage did not guarantee her control of the throne of Ulster, which was instead to

THE MYSTERY
DEITIES &
DEMIGODS
GREATER GODS

pass to Cimbáeth's sons from his previous marriage. To solve this problem, she went to visit his sons in Connaught, disguised as a leper. Finding them roasting a pig outdoors near some woods, she doffed her disguise and feigned seduction of each son one by one, leading each into the forest, where she subdued and bound them. She then led them back to Ulster where she forced them to build her a fortress, which she named *Eomuin*. It is from this and other accounts that Macha took on the reputation of being a warrior goddess, the most martial of the three *Badb*.

Perhaps her most famous legend is "The Twins of Macha". In this story, Macha paid a mysterious visit to a nobleman of Ulster named Crunnchu. Instead of leaving after her visit, however, the beautiful Macha stayed with Crunnchu, gradually insinuating herself into his life. In time she married him, and she soon became pregnant.

Impressed with his goddess wife's supernatural strength and speed, one day Crunnchu, while attending the king's races, foolishly boasted that his wife could easily outrun the king's horses. Enraged, the king forced Crunnchu to have Macha race his horses, or be put to death. Forced to comply, Macha raced and won against the king's horses, but collapsed at the end of the race and gave birth prematurely to twins. She then uttered the famous Curse of Macha, wherein she said that for nine generations, the men of Ulster, when Ulster was at its greatest need, would feel the pains of childbirth for five days and four nights, and be unable to fight until the pains subsided.

This curse figured prominently in the famous Irish legend, *The Táin*, wherein Queen Maeve of Connaught attacked Ulster in order to steal the Brown Bull of Cooley. As a result of Macha's curse, however, the Ulstermen were unable to defend their lands for five days and four nights, forcing the famous hero Cú Chulainn to hold off Maeve's huge armies single-handedly until their pangs subsided.

Macha lent her name not only to Emain Macha, the capitol of Ulster, but also to Armagh (*Ard Macha*), the county of which Emain Macha is the seat. Her worship is not prominent in the major festivals, as she represents winter and undesirable old age, but she is nevertheless mentioned in the rituals of *Samhain*, or Halloween, as that is the time when the seasons begin to turn from fall to winter.

THE MYSTERY
DEITIES &
DEMIGODS
GREATER GODS

"The Morrigan", © 1992, Jim Fitzpatrick.

Mórrigan

Mórrigan, the "phantom queen", was the goddess of war fury whose legend stretches well into ancient times. As the middle sister of the *Badb*, she represented the flower of womanhood, the time when a woman is at the height of her beauty and fertility. As such, she is often compared to Danu/Áine and was perhaps a memory of an ancient fertility goddess that preceded them both. Usually referred to as "*the* Mórrigan", she appears to have been the most powerful and wicked of the three *Badb*, incorporating aspects of all three in her personality, having also the ability to shift her apparent age from young girl to mature woman to old hag at will. She, like the other *Badb*, could also appear as any person or animal as suits her wicked whim, using her powers most often to cause conflict and confusion, particularly conflict that was violent in nature, such as warfare. Then, when she had caused the armies to clash, she filled them with her battle-fury, delighting in the blood, slaughter and dying groans of the heroes whom she had manipulated into self-destruction.

The Mórrigan allied herself with the Tuatha dé Danann in both battles of Moy Tura, giving battle strategy to the Dagda in return for his favors in the first battle against the Fir Bolg, and working to drain the strength out of Indech, the Fomorian warrior-king, in the second. She also had a significant role in *The Táin* where, overcome with desire for Cú Chulainn, she appeared to him as a beautiful young girl. Cú rebuffed her, however, as he feared that she would drain away the strength that he would need to hold off the Connachtmen. Furious at his dismissal, the Mórrigan then proceeded to curse Cú Chulainn, appearing in various animal forms to attack him, breaking his chariot wheels, and causing various misfortunes that gradually took their toll on him. In the end, when Cú Chulainn had finally been defeated the Mórrigan, in the form of a crow, alighted on his shoulder, signaling his impending death.

Another prominent legend of the Mórrigan involves Finn McCool. One day the Fianna were hunting near the caves of Keshcorran, and the Mórrigan (the *Badb*) appeared to them as three hags winding wool. This is highly reminiscent of the Roman Fates, who also were believed to be three women who wind the thread of men's destinies: the youngest selects the thread, the mature woman measures it, and the eldest cuts it, determining when that man's "thread", or life, has run out. Thus the term, "fate".

The Mórrigan is perhaps the most ubiquitous female deity in Irish myth, appearing numerous times at various places throughout her history. She is remembered in half a dozen place names throughout Ireland, most prominently in *Dá Cich na Mórrigna* (The Paps of Mórrigan) near Newgrange in County Meath. Her *sídhe* is in the caves of Keshcorran, County Sligo, in Connaught province.

Nemain

Nemain, "battle frenzy" or "battle panic", is the third and youngest of the *Badb*. She was also a wife of the war god Neit. Not much is known of Nemain, but her name seems to suggest that it was she who caused warriors to panic and flee the battlefield. Alternatively, her powers may be the same as the Mórrigan's, able to bring blood lust into men so that they may slaughter each other all the more. Nemain may be cognate to Nemetona, the war goddess of the Continental and British Celts.

THE MYSTERY
DEITIES &
DEMIGODS
GREATER GODS

97

Elder gods

Though the primary gods of the ancient Irish were Dé Danann in origin, the elder gods of the peoples who had come before the Tuatha Dé were still widely worshiped throughout Ireland, and have been remembered even into modern times in numerous legends, artifacts and place names. Though generally wicked, and largely forgotten, these elder gods of the sacred isle still demand, and command, recognition.

"César the Druid", © 1977, Jim Fitzpatrick.
César is shown here summoning Crom Cruach during the First Battle of Moy Tura.

CROM CRUACH

Crom Cruach was one of the most wicked of the ancient fertility deities of ancient Ireland. His mysterious name can be translated several different ways: *crom* can mean crooked, bent, or crescent-shaped, and *cruach* can mean hill, mound, or head, in the sense of preeminence. *Cruach* could also be based upon the word *crú* ("blood").

Based upon these possible translations, Crom Cruach has been variously translated as "Bloody Crescent", referring probably to the moon, indicating that Crom was a god of death and the night; "Lord of the Mound",

98

possibly indicating his status as a chief god of the Irish pantheon at one time; "Bloody Head" and "Mound of the Gallows" are also sometimes used, indicating perhaps that the worship of Crom involved the worship of a severed head, not uncommon among the Celts, possibly even that of a prisoner that had been sacrificed to Crom.

Though Crom is never seen in the traditional legends, only showing up briefly in *The Book of Leinster*, *The Book of Ballymote*, and *The Yellow Book of Lecan*, in these histories Crom was described as "the chief idol" of ancient, pagan Ireland even into early Christian times. His appelation, "bloody crescent", may have been intended to mean that Crom was a god of the night, of the moon, and of blood sacrifices, perhaps even indicating that he was a sort of "grim reaper" character, the "bloody crescent" referring to his sickle blade. Crom was also a fertility god, as the sacrifices given to him were intended to propitiate his wrath and help ensure fertility of field and herd in the coming year. Unlike other Irish fertility deities, however, Crom Cruach apparently inspired great terror in his adherents, and the sacrifices his priests demanded were quite excessive by comparison.

Crom Cruach made a couple of prominent appearances in both the First and Second Battles of Moy Tura, having been summoned to aid the armies of both the Fir Bolg and the Fomorians, respectively. Crom was described as a great, primeval god, a "demiurge" whose power helped create the universe, a figure of extreme evil on par with the Satan of the Bible. As such, Crom's mighty favor required great sacrifices, which in ancient times apparently included humans. Every *Samhain* (Halloween), the ancient Celts would sacrifice 1/3 of their milk, corn, firstborn livestock and even their firstborn children to the idol. Crom's barbaric rituals also involved self-destructive practices such as self-laceration, which often resulted in the death of many worshipers. On one particularly horrid *Samhain* Tigernmas, the king who had reintroduced the worship of Crom to Ireland, actually died along with three-fourths of his people during the violent and blood-thirsty rituals that accompanied the worship of Crom.

The idol of Crom Cruach is believed to have been located at the Plain of Mag Slécht, "The Plain of Adoration", in County Cavan. The Crom Cruach stone is believed to be the same as the "Killycluggin Stone", which had been found buried near where the original Crom Cruach stone is

THE MYSTERY DEITIES & DEMIGODS ELDER GODS

believed to have been situated, in the town of Killycluggin. The stone is currently on display in the Cavan County Museum, on loan from The National Museum. The idol was described as being covered in gold and possibly silver as well, and unadorned with any carvings, though the Killycluggin stone is covered with Celtic-style artwork typical of the La Téne Period, and of course is not covered with gold. It was also described as being surrounded by twelve lesser stones that were similarly unadorned. St. Patrick himself finally put a stop to the sacrifices, smashing the idol of Crom and ending the barbaric practices forever. The broken idol can still be viewed today in the County Cavan Museum.

LIR

Lir was a very ancient deity who was a personification of the sea, as his name literally means "the sea". Though he made few if any appearances of note in the legends, his daughter, Sinann, and his son, Manannan Mac Lir, made significant contributions to Irish mythology.

MANANNAN MAC LIR

Manannan Mac Lir was the sea god of the ancient Irish, equivalent in many ways to the Greek Poseidon and the Roman Neptune. Manannan, along with his father, Lir (Mac Lir simply means "son of Lir"), appears to be a very ancient deity, predating even the gods of the Tuatha dé Danann. Manannan is believed to have once lived on the Isle of Man, a large island between Ireland and Scotland that takes its name from him, though he was believed to spend most of his time in

"Manannan Mac Lir Riding Aonvarr", © JJP.

an underwater palace called *Emain Ablach*, also sometimes referred to as *Tir Tairngire* or *Mag Mell*. All of these places are believed in various traditions to be part of the "Otherworld", also known as *Tir nan Óg*, "The Land of Eternal Youth", a paradise under the sea that mirrored life on the land except pain, age and death were forgotten.

Though as god of the sea Manannan was a major deity, his role in the myths was often more that of a trickster character, manipulating people and situations by casting spells on people, or lending aid to one side or another in order to achieve his goals. However, when he was forced to go to war he was quite capable, riding either his magical, self-propelled currack known as "Wave Sweeper" or a magic horse named *Aonvarr* that he could ride equally well on both land and water. He also carried an enchanted sword, *Frecraid*, "The Answerer", which could penetrate any armor and killed every time it struck. Manannan was the one who had trained Lugh *(q.v.)* in all the arts and sciences, and even lent him his sword, armor and steed to use against the Fomorians in the Second Battle of Moy Tura.

Manannan was also a very powerful druid, having taught the druids the art of druidry himself. He was able to cover himself with a mist to make himself invisible, and wore a great multicolored cloak that allowed him to cause forgetfulness or even change one's destiny with a single wave. He also had a special "crane bag" wherein he held all his treasures, including language, which he is believed to have given to mankind.

Manannan was married to the beautiful Fann, princess of the *Daione Shí (q.v.)*, with whom he ruled the undersea portion of the Underworld, the Dagda apparently ruling over the land portion. Also like the Dagda, he liked to spread it around a bit, and had several other wives and lovers, including Aife, Aíne, Caíntigern and an unrequited love for a woman named Tuag.

Manannan was venerated in the Isle of Man as late as the 19th century, when people were still bringing rushes and green meadow grass to the top of Mt. Barrule as payment for "rent" of the land from Manannan, who still was considered to be its divine lord. Manannan was generally venerated all around Ireland, Scotland, and wherever Celtic peoples lived in the ancient world, particularly along the coastlands, prayers usually being directed to him by fisherman who wished for a bountiful catch.

Demigods

Demigods are a class of beings that are part human, part divine, being the offspring of a god and a mortal. Demigods were the same "heroes of old, men of renown" mentioned in Genesis 6 and thereafter, and as such were indeed "giants in the Earth", usually described as being exceptionally tall, strong and intelligent, frequently manifesting abilities that can only be described as supernatural. Just as the Greek god Zeus was believed to have fathered many sons from mortal women, the most prominent of which was Heracles, so too the Dagda and other deities of the ancient Irish intermarried with mortal women, producing giants with exceptional strength and other abilities that made them stand literally head and shoulders above their peers. And the first of the demigods of ancient Ireland was *Nuada Airgetlámh*, "Nuada of the Silver Arm".

NUADA AIRGETLÁMH

Nuada Airgetlámh, better known to Irish history as "Nuada of the Silver Arm", is one of the most celebrated figures of Irish history and myth. A literal giant of a man, as the son of Beothach, the son of Iarbonel the son of Nemed, he was the rightful heir of the line of Magog, and the High King of the Tuatha dé Danann, the fifth people to invade Ireland. Nuada was a model for all of the great Irish kings and heroes for thousands of years.

Nuada made his first appearance in Irish mythology in *Cath Maige Tuired* "The Battle of Moy Tura", the most important document in the

"Nuada of the Silver Arm",
© 1980, Jim Fitzpatrick.

Mythological Cycle of Irish legends. According to the legend, his ancestor Beothach had led the Tuatha dé Danann to the four cities of northern Europe after their pyrrhic victory at Conan's Tower. There they learned the art of war in order to retake Ireland, which they did some time later, under the leadership of Nuada.

Nuada first led the Tuatha dé Danann against the Fir Bolg in the First Battle of Moy Tura, in which he first showed his exceptional skill, strength and supernatural abilities. Nuada's greatest power was his ability to manifest the *ríastrad*, the "battle fury" or "warp spasm", that was essentially a berzerk fury similar to that of the later Viking berserkers, where Nuada would fly into a rage and slaughter everything in sight, heedless of his own safety. He also possessed the powerful *Claímh Solais*, "The Sword of Light", against which none could stand. Though Nuada was unmarried, his lover was the Mórrigan, who protected him in battle and also gave him counsel on war strategy. Near the end of the battle, however, Nuada was confronted by Streng, the hero of the Fir Bolg who, in single combat, managed to beat back the exhausted Nuada and cut off his right, sword arm.

Thus mutilated, Nuada lost the kingship of the Tuatha dé Danann, as their rules stated that their king could have no serious blemishes, and Nuada fell into great sorrow and illness. However Dian Cécht, the great healer of the Tuatha dé Danann, fashioned a silver arm for him that worked even better than his original arm had. Thus restored, "Nuada of the Silver Arm" was healed, body and soul, and returned to the kingship of the Tuatha Dé.

However, Nuada was limited in his ability to rule over the Tuatha dé Danann due to the great power of the Fomorians, led by Balor of the Evil Eye *(q.v.)*. He made his final appearance in The Second Battle of Moy Tura, where he defeated the Fomorian general Indech, but was himself killed by a powerful demon summoned by Balor. After his death, the kingship over the Tuatha Dé was taken over by Lugh.

Nuada also appears in various myths and legends, believed to have been the consort of Boann under the psuedonym "Nechtan". He was also closely associated with the Eóganacht dynasty of Munster province, to the point that the leaders of the clan had the alternate title of *Mug Nuadat*, "the servant of Nuada". Nuada's burial place is believed to be in or near the Grianán of Aileach, in County Donegal.

**THE MYSTERY
DEITIES &
DEMIGODS
DEMIGODS**

LUGH

Lugh Lámfadha, ("Luke the Long-Armed") was the greatest hero of the ancient Irish and the central figure in the Irish Mythological Cycle. Superceding Nuada as High King of the Tuatha dé Danann, he also superceded him in the myths as the sun god *par excellence*, his very name *lugh* meaning "light". Commentators also have noted his many similarities with the Roman god Mercury. His surname, *lámfadha*, "long-armed", is descriptive of his ability to hurl his spear, the magical *Sleá Bua*, an extraordinarily long distance. In this way he was very similar to the Hindu god Savitar, who was known

"The Coming of Lugh the Il-Dana",
© 1979, Jim Fitzpatrick.

as "he of the wide hand", more evidence that the Tuatha Dé — and all of the descendants of Magog — had originally emigrated from Central Asia.

Lugh was also known as *Samildánach*, due to the fact that he was a man of many skills, the art of war being the preeminent. He was also known as "the Il-Dana", from *ildánach*, a word that indicates that he may have also been a druid and/or poet of the highest order. Another title he bore was *Maicnia* ("child-warrior") due to the fact that the precocious Lugh had become a warrior at a very early age.

Lugh was the son of Cian, the son of Dian Cécht and of Eithne, the daughter of Balor, the Witch-King of the Fomorians. Balor, fearing the prophecy that he would be killed by his grandson, had locked his daughter Eithne in a tower of glass in order to prevent conception. However, Cian, aided by the druidess Bírog, had broken into the tower and seduced Eithne, producing triplets. Balor drowned Lugh's two other siblings, but Eithne successfully fooled Balor into believing that the third, Lugh, had been drowned as well. Lugh, however, had actually been secreted off to

Spain to be raised by Tailltiu, the daughter of the King of Spain. During this time Lugh was also fostered by Manannan Mac Lir the sea god and by the *sídhe*, who taught Lugh all the arts and sciences. Manannan also lent Lugh his magical steed, *Aonvarr*, his magical sword *Frecraid*, "The Answerer", and a magical suit of armor that shone like the sun — thus Lugh's epithet, "The Shining One".

After his training had been completed, Lugh traveled to Tara, the then capitol of Ireland in County Meath, in order to offer his services to King Nuada to help free Ireland from the Fomorian yoke. He was initially rebuffed, however, as in order to enter Tara, one had to be the best person in Ireland in a particular skill or trade, and all the positions had been filled. Lugh pointed out that he was a skilled builder, smith, warrior, poet, magician, physician, scholar, and was accomplished in every other trade, but every skill he listed was already spoken for. But when he pointed out that he was the only one in Ireland who was skilled at *every* trade, the guard relented, and he was allowed into Tara. However, instead of having the guard open the gate after nightfall (which was forbidden), Lugh easily leapt over the gate and into the palace yard, saving him the trouble.

Lugh then encouraged Nuada to attack Balor and free Ireland from his yoke, but Nuada was fearful and cautious about making war with the powerful Balor and did nothing. Angered by Nuada's lack of leadership, Lugh killed a contingent of Fomorian tax collectors single-handedly, ensuring Balor's wrath. Nuada, however, upon hearing that the Fomorians were attacking in retaliation, refused to defend the island, instead telling Lugh that since he had killed the tax collectors, he could now fight off the invasion by himself. Enraged at Nuada's failure to defend the hard fought freedoms of the Tuatha Dé, Lugh effectively dismissed him as king, and rode off to fight off the Fomorian invasion with the help of his father Cian, Bobd Derg, and the Riders of the *Sídhe*.

After easily defeating Breas' army, Lugh rode off swiftly to fight off a second Fomorian invading force, this time led by Balor. Realizing that the Tuatha Dé would need more weapons to fight off the Fomorians, he sent his father, Cian, to Ulster to secure weapons and supplies. Unfortunately, along the way Cian met up with the sons of Turenn, who killed him as they were in a blood feud with Cian's clan. King Nuada learned of the

THE MYSTERY
DEITIES &
DEMIGODS
DEMIGODS

murder, and gave the sons of Turenn up for judgment to Lugh. However, instead of having them killed, Lugh instead chose the *eric*, or "blood money" option, where they would perform a service for him in lieu of execution. As repayment for their transgression, Lugh put a *geas* on them, a form of punishment that forced them to perform a series of tasks similar in scope to those fulfilled by Hercules. These tasks essentially had to do with gathering weapons and supplies for the Dé Danann army from very dangerous sources. They performed these tasks successfully, but later died of the wounds they had suffered in the process.

Lugh finally arrived at the scene of battle between the Tuatha Dé and the Fomorians several days later, by which time the battle had been nearly lost to the Fomorians. Nuada had been killed by the Demon of Death, and Balor was about to use his evil eye to destroy the Dé Danann army. Realizing the immediate peril to himself and to the Tuatha Dé, Lugh whipped out his magical spear, the *Sleá Bua*, and destroyed Balor's evil Eye with a single shot — perhaps the most famous single event in Irish mythology. After the battle, Lugh was made the High King of the Tuatha dé Danann, and ruled the land well for forty years. During this time he instituted many traditions, including the Tailltiu Festival, in honor of his foster mother. Though he was very long-lived, as were most giants, Lugh's reign was cut short when he was killed near the Hill of Uisneach by Mac Cuill, Mac Cécht and Mac Gréine — the last three kings of the Tuatha Dé — in revenge for the killing of their father, Cermait.

After his death Lugh was deified by the people to the level of a major deity, and is believed by some sources to have been buried at Newgrange. As late as the early twentieth century, he was remembered every August 1 in the *Lughnasa* festival *(q.v.)*, when the ripening of crops is celebrated. As such, he may have also had aspects of a fertility god. After the advent of Christianity, however, though the festivals continued until relatively recently, Lugh was replaced by St. Michael, who is remembered in the Michaelmas festival, popular throughout Ireland and the British Isles.

Lugh was believed to have had at least four wives and several children, and was also married to the sovereignty goddess Èriu, which was believed to be necessary in order to be the true king of Ireland. Lugh's most famous son was the legendary Cú Chulainn.

THE MYSTERY
DEITIES &
DEMIGODS
DEMIGODS

106

"Cú Chulainn", © 1984 Jim Fitzpatrick.

CÚ CHULAINN

Cú Chulainn, "the Hound of Culann", was born Sétanta, the son of Lugh and Dechtire. Dechtire was the daughter of the druid Cathbad, who was an advisor to Conchobar Mac Nessa, the ruler of Ulster. Cú was born in Muirthemne.

A precocious child like his father, Lugh, Cú became lonely growing up without friends, and insisted his mother let him go to Emain Macha, the capitol of Ulster province, where he could play with other boys closer to his age and ability. When he arrived, however, he entered the hurley field without asking permission, and was attacked by all 150 boys who were playing there. But Cú was such a powerful warrior even at the age of seven that he dodged or caught all 150 of the javelins they threw at him, and then proceeded to chase all 150 of them from the field, beating 50 of them unconscious with his hurley stick until he was finally stopped by King Conchobar himself.

Sétanta picked up his new name, "the Hound of Culann" one day when he went to meet King Conchobar at the fortress of Culann, the King's chief smith. Conchobar had forgotten to tell Sétanta about the powerful, fierce watchdog watching the gate, however, and the hound attacked him as soon as he entered. Unafraid of the powerful beast, Sétanta killed it with his bare hands, bashing its head against the doorpost. Apologetic to Culann the smith for killing his prize dog, Sétanta offered to take the place of Culann's hound as the guardian of the front gate. And from this incident, Sétanta was renamed *Cú Chulainn*, "the Hound of Culann".

One day Cú Chulainn heard his grandfather, Cathbad the druid, prophesy that if a man took up arms for the first time in his life on that day, he would have a short but glorious life. Wanting that short but glorious life, Cú went to Conchobar and demanded weapons and a chariot, but none of the weapons he was given would stand up to the great force of his blows or the fury of his combat. Finally, Conchobar gave him his own weapon, the *Claímh Solais*, handed down to him from Nuada and his specially reinforced chariot, which Cú used from thenceforth.

In order to prove himself, Cú immediately went out and killed three great champions, Foill, Fannell and Tuachell, who had been known for killing many men in Ulster. Although he was but a boy, he already had the strength of a strong man. Moreover, along with the *Claímh Solais*, Cú apparently also inherited the *ríastrad*, or "warp spasm" from his predecessor, Nuada. Angry at being dismissed as a mere boy by the three warriors, he manifested the *ríastrad* and slaughtered all three men with ease. Upon returning to King Conchobar's palace, the battle frenzy was still so powerful upon him that Queen Mughain and 150 women stripped bare to meet him, hoping to distract his mind from violence until they could calm him down from his battle fury. Effectively distracted, they then immersed him in three vats of cold water to cool him down. However, his fury was so great that the first vat exploded, and the second vat boiled, but the third vat merely became hot. Eventually, Cú cooled down and returned to his senses.

The precocious Cú quickly grew into a tall, powerful and handsome man. In the myths his appearance was greatly embellished, described as having hair of three colors: brown at the roots, red in the middle, and blonde at the tips. He is also described as having four dimples in each cheek, colored red, yellow, green and blue, respectively, as having seven pupils in each of

"Emer, Wife of Cú Chulainn",
© 1976, Jim Fitzpatrick.

his bright blue eyes, and as having seven fingers and toes. Despite this seemingly odd appearance, however, he was a favorite of the ladies, but he only had eyes for Emer, the daughter of Fogall Manach of Lusk, County Dublin. She was considered to be the most worthy maiden in Ireland, as she rated the best in the six gifts: beauty, voice, speech, needlework, wisdom and chastity.

Fogall told Cú that he was not yet tested as a warrior, and thus not yet fit to marry his daughter. He suggested that Cú train to be a warrior under Domnall Míldemail of Alba (Scotland). Domnall in turn told Cú that his training would best be completed by the warrior-goddess Scathach. From Scathach he received very advanced battle training and learned numerous battle maneuvers that would prove to be very useful, emerging from his training as quite probably the greatest warrior in the world at that time. He also received from her the fearsome *Gae Bolga*, a special spear that was thrown from the foot, and was thus very difficult to defend against. Cú also fought with Aífe, Scathach's twin sister and bitter enemy, and defeated her, Aífe later bearing him his first son. He also had affairs with Scathach and with Uathach, her daughter.

Returning from Alba, he went to Fogall's castle in Lusk in order to marry his true love, Emer, whose hand he believed he had now won. Fogall, however, still refused him. Cú then flew into a rage, leapt over the wall and slew 24 of his men before Fogall leapt from the wall to his death. Cú then took Emer, plundered the castle of its silver and gold, and returned to his castle at Dundalk, in what is now County Louth.

Cú was routinely unfaithful to Emer, but there was never any real threat to their love until his affair with Princess Fann of the *Daoine Shí*, the wife of Manannan Mac Lir. Emer discovered them together but, so impressed with Fann's love for Cú, she decided to let her have him for the greater good. Fann, also impressed with Emer's graciousness and genuine love for Cú, decided to leave them be and return to her husband, Manannan. Manannan then settled the affair with his magical cloak of forgetfulness, waving it between Fann and Cú so that they each forgot each other and returned to their spouses.

The seminal event in Cú Chulainn's life was his single-handed battle against the army of Queen Maeve in the central epic of the Ulster Cycle, *The Táin*. In this important story, Cú was forced to single-handedly hold off the forces of Queen Maeve of Connaught because the Ulstermen, the Knights of the Red Branch, were stricken with childbirth-like pains per The Curse of Macha (*op. cit.*). For the five days and four nights of the curse's duration, Cú kept the armies of Maeve at bay, systematically slaughtering dozens of heroes with his sword, short spear and the *Gae Bolga*, and hundreds of men-at-arms with his terrible sling. His critical error, however, was insulting the Mórrigan by spurning her offer to aid him, as well as her sexual advances. She then proceeded to wear him down with various curses, and attack him in the form of various animals.

The final blow came after Cú killed the druid Calatin and his 27 sons. To revenge their family, Calatin's three daughters feigned friendship with Cú and secretly fed him a stew made of dog, tricking him into breaking his *geas* (taboo), which was to never eat the flesh of a dog — his namesake. Half paralyzed from the curse of breaking his *geas*, he was then mortally wounded by a javelin thrown by Lugaid Mac Con Roí, the son of Cú Roí, the sorcerer. Realizing his short but glorious life was drawing to a close, he tied himself to a standing stone, turning it into a battle pillar so that he might die standing up, in combat. Lugaid then beheaded Cú at the pillar, but was in turn slain by Conall Cernach, one of Cú Chulainn's friends. Even then, none dared approach him until the Mórrigan alighted onto his shoulder in the form of a crow, proving that he was indeed truly, finally dead.

Cú Chulainn is widely regarded as the greatest hero of Irish myth. His name is remembered in numerous songs and legends, as well as place names, including Cú Chulainn's Leap, a sheer-sided rectangular rock at Loop Head on the northern end of the Shannon estuary in County Clare, a bed, a house and a grave near Anascaul on the Dingle Peninsula, in County Kerry, and the Cuchullin Hills in the south of the Isle of Skye, where it is believed he trained with Scathach. He is most closely associated with Dundalk, his fortress being located in County Louth, in Leinster. He was also associated with Ulster province, particularly with Emain Macha, the ancient capitol of Ulster, where he served as a champion of the Knights of the Red Branch.

The Knights of the Red Branch

The Knights of the Red Branch were the powerful guardians and protectors of Ulster, and were based at Emain Macha, County Armagh. They took their name from the assembly hall in Emain Macha named *Craebruad*, "red branch", where there was a large, red roof beam, or "branch" that stood in the midst of the hall. The house of the Red Branch were the descendants of Ross the Red, the King of Ulaid (Ulster), and were also known as *Clan Rury*, "Red Clan".

The Knights of the Red Branch were essentially a professional military order comprised of exceptional warriors who swore fealty to the king to protect him, Emain Macha, and Ulster from enemies both foreign and domestic. Their greatest champion was Cú Chulainn, but there were also many other capable warriors who were also legendary in their time, and afterwards:

♀ King Conchobar, the Founder:

Conchobar, the greatest king of Ulster, was the grandson of Ross the Red, and grandson of the giant Fachtna Fáthach. His uncle, Fergus Mac Roich, was to be king, but through the scheming machinations of Conchobar's mother, Ness, Conchobar was given the throne for one year. During that year Conchobar's rule was so excellent that the people of Ulster insisted that he remain as king. Fergus, equally impressed, agreed and abdicated his throne to his nephew. Conchobar later founded the Red Branch Knights, and was himself a capable warrior, possessing among other things a magical sword named *Gorm Glas* ("blue-green").

Conchobar was an excellent king, but his one failing was an incident where he broke his word and killed a man named Noísi, the husband of a woman named Deirdre, whom he had sworn to protect. He did this because he wanted the beautiful Deirdre for himself, though she had spurned him. This act of treachery, detailed in the legend, "Deirdre and the Sons of Uisneach", caused 3,000 Knights of the Red Branch, along with their leader, Fergus Mac Roich, and Conchobar's own son, Cormac Connloinges, to renounce their loyalty to him and instead ally themselves with Maeve, the Queen of Connacht, Conchobar's arch enemy.

✟ Fergus Mac Roich

Fergus Mac Roich was the greatest of all the Ulster heroes, second only to Cú Chulainn. Originally the heir to the throne, he temporarily ceded rule to Conchobar, later willingly giving up the throne to him as he had proved to be an excellent king. He regretted his decision later, however, after Conchobar broke his oath to the sons of Uisneach, killing Noísi and imprisoning Deirdre. As a result of this treachery, Fergus foreswore his oath of fealty to Conchobar, instead allying himself with Queen Maeve of Connaught. His sexual dalliances with her soon became legendary, which some believe is where he earned the title *Mac Roich*, "son of the great horse". They had a daughter together, Ciar, from whose name County Kerry was derived, and a son, Connmac, who founded Connemara.

Fergus also used his knowledge of The Red Branch and of Ulster to aid Queen Maeve in securing the Brown Bull of Cooley in *The Táin*, but was reluctant to kill his fellow Ulstermen until, at the final battle, he lost his temper with Conchobar and killed hundreds with his great sword, *Caladbolg*, nearly killing Conchobar himself until Conchobar's son, Cormac Connloinges, successfully pled for his father's life. Fergus had also been a tutor to Cú Chulainn, and might have killed him in the last battle of *The Táin* had he not sworn an oath to his former student not to fight against him.

Always a man of honor whose word was bond on the battlefield, Fergus was less honorable in the boudoir, being the favorite lover of Maeve who already was married to Aillil, king of Connaught. Unable or unwilling to kill Fergus, Aillil did nothing but make a sarcastic comment when he discovered them *flagrante delicto* in a lake. Lugaid the warrior-poet was not averse to avenging Aillil's honor, however, and he killed the naked Fergus with a javelin through his heart. Fergus is remembered in the town (and song) of Carrickfergus, County Mayo.

⚜ Conall Cernach
The son of Amergin the poet, Conall was a very powerful fighter second only to Cú Chulainn (Fergus was no longer counted as a Red Branch Knight after having allied himself with Maeve). He was Cú's foster brother and accompanied him on many adventures. He even avenged Cú's death, killing Lugaid, Cú's slayer. Conall was himself killed by three Connachtmen who were avenging Lugaid's death in the town of Ballyconnell, in County Cavan, that was named after him.

⚜ Leoghaire Buadach
Leoghaire "the victorious" was the third of the three great champions of the Red Branch, frequently contending with Cú Chulainn and Conall Cernach for the *curadmir*, or "champion's portion". Leoghaire's mantle is considered to be one of the three treasures of Ireland.

⚜ Cormac Connloinges
Cormac was the son of King Conchobar, but joined Fergus in voluntary exile after his father's treachery against the sons of Uisneach, also aiding Queen Maeve in her assault upon Ulster. He was also one of the champions of Conaire Mor, the High King of Ireland, and some traditions have him married to Niam, daughter of Celtchair, or even to the legendary Étain. Forgiven by his father on his deathbed, Cormac was killed by Connaught raiders while returning home to Ulster to assume the kingship.

⚜ Dubthach Dóeltenga
Dubthach Dóeltenga, "Dubthach the Insulting One", was known for his gruff and rude disposition He was a cunning warrior, but not well liked by the other knights, as he routinely insulted and disparaged them all. Dubthach joined Fergus and Cormac in exile, and makes appearances in all the major stories of the Ulster Cycle.

⚜ Celtchair
Celtchair was a powerful warrior, described as "huge and grey". He possessed a magic lance named *Luin* that lusted for blood so badly that if it was not stored in a vat containing black fluid or poison, it would burst into flames.

THE MYSTERY
DEITIES &
DEMIGODS
DEMIGODS

FIONN
MAC CUMHAIL

Fionn Mac Cumhail, or "Finn McCool", was a blonde giant who had been born in what is now County Meath around the time of Christ into the *Clanna Baioscne* of Leinster. Finn displayed characteristics of a hunter, warrior and seer in the myths of the Fenian Cycle (*q.v.*), wherein he was the head of his clan and of the *Fianna Èireann*, a military order based in Leinster province that was similar in function to The Knights of the Red Branch. So great was Finn's fame that

"Fionn Mac Cumhail", © 1993, Jim Fitzpatrick.

countless myths, folktales and placenames around Ireland and the British Isles still bear his name.

Finn had been born Demna Máel, a name that indicates that he may have had associations with druidry and the Otherworld from an early age. Not only was Finn exceptionally tall, strong, and charismatic, he was extremely long-lived, remaining the leader of the Fianna until the latter half of the third century AD when he died at the ripe old age of 230.

There are at least two variant, though similar, traditions regarding the birth and early history of Finn, which we will combine here for sake of brevity. Finn was the son of Cumhail, head of the High King's military forces, the Fianna, his mother being Muirne, the daughter of the High King, who at that time was the famous Conn of the Hundred Battles. It had been prophesied that if Cumhail ever married, he would meet death in his next battle, but Muirne was so beautiful that he could not resist, so he married her in secret.

Some time before, however, a druid had prophesied to the High King that the son of his daughter would take the kingdom from him. So, the High King

114

had kept Muirne locked up in order to avoid his fate. Cumhail had outwitted the king, however, and nine moons later Muirne gave birth to Finn.

In fulfillment of the druid's prophecy, Cumhail was killed by a rebel faction of the Fianna led by Goll Mac Morna. Fearing the prophecy of his own downfall, the High King threw the young Finn out of a window into a lake with the intention of drowning him. Finn survived, however, and in one variation of the story he arose to the surface with a salmon in his hand, foreshadowing "The Salmon of Knowledge" (*op. cit.*) that would become an important part of his story.

There are also at least two variant traditions on what happened next. In the "primary" tradition, Muirne saved Finn from the water and gave Finn to a local druidess to raise in secret. In another tradition, Finn's grandmother on his father's side grabbed him and ran into the wilderness to raise him in safety, going so far as to kill the man who had built their house for them to ensure its secrecy. The druidess (or his grandmother, depending upon the tradition) then proceeded to train the young Finn in feats of physical prowess from the first day he could walk. Soon he was as fleet and agile as a deer, and had become a superior athlete and warrior. And when she perceived he finally was ready, his foster mother then took young Demna to Tara so he could take his rightful place among the Fianna.

Along the way, they came upon a hurling match. Joining in, Finn easily defeated the other boys at hurling and, when they set upon him in a jealous rage, he easily defeated them in combat. The local chieftain, who had been watching the game, asked, *Cé hé an giolla fionn?* "Who is that fair boy?", the term "fair" referring to the color of his hair, which was apparently a very light platinum blonde. It was from that time on that "Demna" became known as "Finn", as *fionn* means "fair" in Gaelic.

Finn continued on his journey to Tara, and after a time came to the Well of Sergais, along the River Boyne. There he met Finnegas, a druid who had been waiting by the well for seven years to catch The Salmon of Knowledge, the flesh of which was said to give the one who ate of it supreme wisdom. The Salmon, it was believed, gained its knowledge from eating the hazel nuts that fell into the wells on the sacred hills.

THE MYSTERY DEITIES & DEMIGODS DEMIGODS

Finn, unlike Finnegas, easily caught the Salmon, which had appeared to him suddenly, as if it was his *destiny* to have the supreme wisdom. Furious, Finnegas ordered young Finn to roast it, warning him that there must not be a single blister on the fish from the cooking, or he would cut off Finn's head. However, as The Salmon of Knowledge was cooking, Finn noticed that a blister had started to erupt on its skin, which Finn pushed down with his finger. His finger was of course burned, and he placed it in his mouth to soothe the pain, taking a piece of the Salmon of Knowledge with it. After Finn had swallowed the morsel, Finnegas saw the light of wisdom shine forth from his eyes, and he realized that Finn had received the gift of supreme wisdom.

Finn eventually reached Tara and confronted King Conn of the Hundred Battles, proclaiming his rights as the son of Cumhail, the former head of the Fianna. Conn received him with gladness as an ally and placed him in his service, seating him next to his own son, Art. It was then that Finn learned of a great trouble that had come upon Tara — a goblin, one of the *sídhe* named Aillen of the Flaming Breath, had been destroying Tara every *Samhain* eve (Halloween). Aillen came forth from the Underworld on Halloween, as did the rest of the fairy host, according to Celtic tradition. However, unlike the rest of the *sídhe*, who contented themselves with minor mischiefs, Aillen made it a point every year to burn down the High King's palace at Tara with great balls of fire that came forth from his mouth. And no one, not even the Fianna, was able to stop him, because before he came to destroy he played a song on his silver harp so sweet that it placed all who heard it into a deep slumber. That year, Conn had decided to offer to anyone who could stop the goblin from destroying Tara, "whatever inheritance is right for him to have," a challenge that Finn, looking to make a name for himself, eagerly accepted.

It was here that the wisdom from the salmon first made itself useful. One other interesting difference between the two traditions is that in the primary tradition, the wisdom came upon Finn automatically, but in the variant tradition, Finn "bit his thumb to the marrow" in order to bring the wisdom forth. Another interesting variant tradition has Tara burned down not by a goblin, but by a hag who lived "on the eastern side of the world", who sent her sons to burn down Tara every *night*.

In both versions, Finn was given the wisdom of how to defeat the goblin. The "wisdom" came in the form of an aging Fianna named Fiacha. Fiacha gave Finn a magic spear called *The Spear of Len* that had been forged in the Otherworld, and advised Finn to place the tip of the spear against his forehead when the goblin played his music so as to ward off the magic. Finn did so, and only just managed, with the power of the spear, to stay awake. Then, after quenching the goblin's fire with his magic cloak, Finn used his magic spear to pierce Aillen through the heart, pinning him to a tree as he ran away.

Greatly pleased at finally being rid of the goblin, King Conn gave Finn his choice of rewards. Finn chose to be given his rightful place as the chief of the Fianna, and the king accepted, as did Goll Mac Morna, who had been the leader of the Fianna since Cumhail's death. Finn then led the Fianna through many adventures, his leadership — which lasted the lifetimes of three High Kings — marking the zenith of their fortunes.

In life, Finn's residence was the Hill of Allen in County Kildare. He is also sometimes linked to the *Dinn Rí* in County Carlow, the Giant's Causeway in Country Antrim and numerous other structures, both in Ireland and all around the British Isles.

The Fianna

The Fianna, or "Fenians", were a band of hunters and warriors that existed in Ireland for many centuries, possibly as early as the 3rd century BC and as late as the 10th century AD. Like the Knights of the Red Branch, the Fianna were a military order made up of volunteers who gave up their lands and titles in order to be part of an elite fighting unit that enjoyed a special status within ancient Irish society. The Fianna were led by a *rígfhéinnid* ("Fenian king"), and though they stood apart from the rest of society, their essential mission was to protect Ireland against foreign enemies, both natural and supernatural.

Though the Fianna are often compared to the English knightly orders, unlike other military orders, Fenian membership was not hereditary, but could only be achieved by rigorous initiation involving numerous physical and intellectual tests. One test involved the initiate standing in a waist-deep hole, given only a shield and a hazel stick to defend himself while nine warriors

117

threw their spears at him. If he was wounded even once, he failed the test. Among numerous other tests that required exceptional ability, the initiate was also required to leap over a branch as high as his forehead, to pass under a branch as low as his knee, and to be able to remove a thorn from his foot without missing a stride. On top of that, the would-be Fenian had to be intelligent and well-educated, probably the equivalent of at least a master's level of education in liberal arts.

The tales of the exploits of the Fianna are part of a larger body of knowledge known as "The Fenian Cycle" of ancient Irish mythology. For a long period, the history of the Fianna appears to have been divided between the Leinster Fianna and the Connaught Fianna. During the time of Finn McCool, the Leinster Fianna were led by Conn of the Hundred Battles, and the Connaught Fianna were led by Goll Mac Morna. But when Finn returned to Tara and killed Aillen the Green Goblin, he was rewarded with the leadership of all the Fianna, and the two branches were united as one under his leadership.

Though Finn was the leader of the Fianna during the zenith of their fortunes, there were many other powerful and colorful Fenian warriors worthy of mention:

✦ Caílte Mac Rónaín
Caílte Mac Rónaín was a nephew of Finn McCool, and was known for his fleetness of foot. He acted as Finn's steward, and was also known for his golden tongue, being an excellent orator and entertainer. He was also a giant killer, and later legends have him surviving until the Christian era where he argued with St. Patrick, defending the old, chivalrous, Fenian values. Known as Derglas in some Scottish lore, Caílte actually has much in common with the Roman god Mercury, also known for his fleetness of foot, and oratorical skills.

✦ Conan Mac Morna
Conan Mac Morna, who was portrayed as fat, bald and rather foolish, was the comic figure in the Fenian organization, much like the Red Branch Knight Dubthach Dóeltenga. Full of bluster and mischief, greed and meanness, Conan was also a capable warrior who occasionally teamed up with Finn on his many adventures.

✝ Diarmuid

Diarmuid Ó Duibne was the hero of the legend, "The Pursuit of Diarmuid and Gráinne", a leading member of the Fianna, and one of the great lovers of Irish legend. Soon after he was born, Diarmuid's father, Donn, took him to Newgrange to be fostered by Aenghus Óg. While there, Donn's wife committed adultery with Roc, Aenghus Óg's steward, and she gave birth to a child. Enraged, Donn slew the child, but Roc brought the child back to life as a huge, vicious boar, on which he laid a *geas* to hunt Diarmuid to death (though the boar usually roamed around Ben Bulben, in County Sligo). And at the end of the tale, "The Pursuit of Diarmuid and Gráinne", the "Boar of Ben-Bulben" did indeed finally kill Diarmuid.

Diarmuid had some magical items and abilities, including his sword, *Nóralltach* ("great fury"), a large spear, *Gáe Derg* ("red spear"), *Crann Buí* ("yellow shaft") and a smaller spear that he used for hunting small animals called *Gáe Buide*, ("yellow spear"). He was also known for his *ball seirce*, a "love spot" given to him by the goddess of youth that made him irresistible to women. Diarmuid was one of the most popular of the Fianna, and was featured in numerous folktales.

✝ Goll Mac Morna

Goll Mac Morna was the leader of the Connaught Fianna, and the one responsible for killing Cumall, Finn's father, at the Battle of Cnucha. Though he had lost one of his eyes in the battle, he gained control of the Fianna from Finn's father, but gave up the leadership willingly to Finn after he killed Aillen the Green Goblin. All was not always well, however, as conflicts occasionally broke out between Finn and Goll, as well as their descendants.

✝ Oisín

Oisín, also called "Ossian" in some contexts, was one of the greatest warriors of the Fianna, and a great poet, so renowned in the Fenian mythology that the Fenian Cycle is often referred to as "The Ossianic Cycle". Oisín was the offspring of the union between Finn McCool and the goddess Sadb, who had been transformed into a fawn by an evil druid. One day Finn's hounds Bran and Sceoland chased Sadb back to their

THE MYSTERY DEITIES & DEMIGODS
DEMIGODS

master, who lived on the Hill of Allen. As soon as Sadb reached the protection of that magical hill, however, she was transformed back into a beautiful woman. Taken with her beauty, Finn married her, but she was later lured out of the protective circle of the hill by the evil druid, transformed back into a fawn, and was never seen again. Seven years later, however, Finn found a naked boy under a rowan tree on Ben Bulben, a many-storied hill in County Sligo. This was Oisín, and the boy grew to be a powerful man and one of the greatest of the Fianna.

Oisín's greatest claim to fame is recounted in *Laoi Oisín id Tír nan Óg* ("The Lay of Oisín in the Land of Eternal Youth"). There Oisín, while hunting one day with the Fianna, was visited by a beautiful fairy woman named *Niamh Chinn Óir*, "Neve of the Golden Hair", who rode out from the Underworld under the sea on Aonvarr, the magical horse of Manannan Mac Lir, onto the land where they were hunting. Niamh then declared to the handsome young Oisín

"Oisín and Niamh", © 1990, Jim Fitzpatrick.

that she had been watching him for some time, had fallen in love with him, and wanted him to return with her to the land of *Tír nan Óg* to live together in paradise forever. Naturally he agreed, and they proceeded with 300 years of blissful lovemaking, producing two sons — one named Oscar —

and a daughter. Lonely for his old friends, however, and unaware in his bliss that 300 years had passed, Oisín decided to visit the Fianna. Niamh warned him to never dismount Aonvarr and touch the ground, though,

THE MYSTERY
DEITIES &
DEMIGODS
DEMIGODS

120

knowing that if he did, time would immediately catch up with him, and he would instantly wither and quickly die.

When Oisín reached the headquarters of the Fianna on the Hill of Allen, he was astonished to see how men had shrunk in stature and had become weaker than the Fianna he had known, who had been literally giants among men. But 300 years had passed and the Fianna had come and gone, a reality with which Oisín had yet to come to terms. Seeing these lesser men straining to lift a stone that even the least of the Fianna would be able to throw a mile with one hand, Oisín literally stooped to help them lift it. Unfortunately his stirrups broke under the strain, and he fell to the ground, aging 300 years in an instant.

Though some traditions have it that he died shortly thereafter of extreme old age, others have Oisín living on as an old man to argue the virtues of the old ways with St. Patrick, much like Caílte Mac Rónaín had done. These arguments became so popular that an enormous number of variations sprang up between the 13th and 18th centuries. Oisín's adventures are closely associated with the Hill of Allen, in County Kildare, and numerous other related locations.

♀ Oscar

Oscar (lit., "deer lover"), was the son of Oisín and Niamh. Often referred to as "The Galahad of the Cycle", Oscar was portrayed in the legends as a clumsy misfit who later excelled beyond all his peers to become one of the greatest of the Fianna. Whenever there was an exceptional challenge to be met, Oscar was called upon because he was the strongest, bravest, and best warrior of the Fianna of his time. Oscar defeated Goll Mac Morna, the hereditary enemy of his line for the rulership of the Fianna, and even defeated Cairbre Lifechair, the High King of Ireland who had allied himself with the Morna clan. However, though Oscar had mortally wounded Lifechair, the High King had also mortally wounded Oscar with a spear through his heart. Strangely enough, as Oscar was dying, he spent his last words telling a joke so poignant that it caused Finn McCool to weep. Oscar was buried under the great cairn at Benn Étair, also known as "Howth", in County Dublin.

THE MYSTERY
DEITIES &
DEMIGODS
DEMIGODS

Maeve

Maeve (lit., "she who intoxicates"), was the warrior queen of Connaught as portrayed in The Ulster Cycle of Irish mythology, and was perhaps the most powerful female figure in all of Irish history and myth. Though there actually may have been a Queen Maeve at one time, it is likely that the legends we have of her are greatly elaborated, possibly the accretions of several different regional, fertility and sovereignty goddesses. To top it off, Maeve was also described in some legends as a queen of the fairies.

As a demigoddess, Maeve's exceptional power lay in her excep-

© 1984, Jim Fitzpatrick.

tional beauty, charm and physical attributes. These attributes were described as being quite substantial, and she used them to manipulate men and events to great effect. Her sexual appetite was described as being so voracious that she was said to have lain with 30 men per day in order to quench it, Fergus Mac Roich *(op. cit.)* being the only man who could effectively satify her ravenous lusts.

This "great whore" played the role of the Queen of Connaught in the seminal Irish legend, *The Táin*. There she played a sort of anti-heroine, a woman drunk with power, abusing her authority and sacrificing the lives of thousands of men in order to quench her naked lusts. Willful, arrogant and domineering to the last, Maeve gambled the fortunes of both Connaught and Ulster on a mere whim, deciding to use her massive armies to steal the famous Brown Bull of Cooley from Ulster just so that she could say that she owned a bull that was greater than her husband's. In order to control her armies, she used their lust for her incredible beauty, earning the dubious title, "Maeve of the Friendly Thighs" through the unique reward system she employed in order to improve loyalty and raise morale.

Maeve had several husbands and countless lovers, her most famous husbands being King Conchobar of Ulster, and Ailill, King of Connaught. Her most famous lover was of course Fergus Mac Roich. She was spurned by Cú Chulainn, however, who was unimpressed with her methods of persuasion, forcing her instead to beg for her life when he caught her off guard during her attack on Ulster. Though she survived Cú's special attentions, Maeve's predations were finally put to an end after she killed her pregnant sister Clothra in order to make sure that there were no rival heirs to her throne. Clothra's child, Furbaide Ferbend was saved, however, and taken to live on an island in Lough Ree on the southeast border of County Roscommon called Inis Clothrand. Years later, Maeve traveled to Lough Ree in order to bathe, possibly as part of some sort of ritual. Furbaide, recognizing his mother's murderer, decided to take revenge. Taking a hardened piece of cheese that he was eating, Furbaide used it as a slingstone, hitting Maeve square in the forehead, killing her.

The highest point of the island, believed to be the place where Maeve finally got hers is called Greenan Hill, from *Grianán Meidbe*, "Maeve's sun porch". Maeve is also associated with numerous other places scattered around Connaught, particularly with Cruachain Aí in County Roscommon, where she had her palace, and The Táin Trail, a series of very famous places featured in *The Táin*, located mainly in Ulster and northern Leinster provinces. There are also some interesting, albeit tenuous links with Tara that indicate that Maeve may have actually originated from Leinster before effectively taking over the rule of Connaught province from the weak and indecisive King Aillil.

For more information on the Deities & Demigods of ancient Ireland, visit
http://ireland.mysteriousworld.com/Mystery/Deities/

THE MYSTERY
DEITIES &
DEMIGODS
DEMIGODS

Wizards, Druids & Poets

mong the greatest mysteries of ancient Ireland were the *druids*, a mysterious caste of Celtic society composed of wizards, philosophers, scientists, scholars, theologians, shamans, doctors, warriors, musicians, comedians and poets that formed a broad-based intellectual class whose exact function in Celtic society is still not fully understood.

Generally speaking, the druids were essentially a priestly class whose primary function was the acquisition, memorization and transmission of knowledge. However, just as in modern education one can choose a course of study from scores of different professions, so too the types of knowledge that the druids studied and taught to their followers also varied dramatically, from the sublime to the mundane, from the esoteric to the comic. As such, because the classification "druid" encompassed such a wide array of varying professions, the term is usually subdivided into three different subclasses: "wizards", "druids" and "poets".

Wizards

Wizards were a type of druid that sought to understand the more esoteric, "hidden" aspects of nature, what in later times would be described as "sorcery", "witchcraft" or "black magic". These types of druids were the most spectacular, using "the dark side" to conjure powerful demons and invoke terrible curses to destroy their enemies, the most powerful being able to subvert even the fundamental forces of nature itself in order to achieve their destructive goals. However, such power comes at a cost, and the druids who abused their power always came to a bitter end as the spiritual forces of good worked to subvert and destroy them in a way that reaffirmed the primacy of life, light and civilization. And though there were few of these wizards, they were often the most powerful, influential, and feared of all the druidic orders. And the greatest of these was the Witch-King of the Fomorians, Balor of the Evil Eye.

BALOR

Balor "of the Evil Eye" was the Witch-King of the Fomorians, and the arch-enemy of Nuada, King of the Tuatha dé Danann. He was an evil wizard of terrible power who had once lived in a tower of glass in the legendary island of Hy-Brasil, before his powerful sorceries brought about its destruction. Though not actually of Irish ancestry, he was considered in some myths to be the grandson of the Celtic war god Néit, and he also figured prominently in the myths and legends of ancient Ireland as the antagonist *par excellence*.

Balor actually made his first

"Balor of the Evil Eye"
© 1984, Jim Fitzpatrick.

appearance in Irish mythology as the enemy of the Milesians, who were apparently the only ones who could resist his power. He lived to the north of Ireland, possibly in Scotland, or perhaps an island between Scotland and Ireland, which some believe to have been Tory Island. There he also lived in a tower of glass, wherein he kept his daughter Eithne hidden away from men because of the prophecy that he would one day be killed by his grandson. However, in revenge for Balor's theft of his magical gray cow, *Glas Gaibhnenn*, Cian, the son of Dian Cécht, enlisted the help of a druidess named Bírog to help him gain entry to the tower. Eithne later gave birth to Lugh, who would kill Balor at the end of the Second Battle of Moy Tura, fulfilling the prophecy.

If not for Lugh's timely intervention, however, Balor most likely would have destroyed the Dé Danann army. The wizards, druids and poets of the Tuatha Dé were no match for Balor, who not only single-handedly counteracted all of their spells, but actually proved to be even more powerful than all of the Dé Danann druids combined.

THE MYSTERY
WIZARDS, DRUIDS
& POETS
WIZARDS

126

Moreover, he was able to call successfully upon the elder god Crom Cruach, who sent a powerful demon to destroy Nuada, Balor's arch enemy, a feat that had never before been successfully performed, at least not in legendary history.

Balor was also unusually powerful in that he appeared to be in posession of a very advanced form of technology that was referred to as "The Eye of Balor", "Balor's Evil Eye", or simply as "The Great Eye". Balor used this large, eye-shaped apparatus — that required several druid technicians to operate it — in the Second Battle of Moy Tura to destroy much of the army of the Tuatha Dé before Lugh finally destroyed it with the *Sleá Bua*. The eye apparently was able to shoot out some kind of magic fire, not unlike a "laser", which would instantly incinerate whatever it touched. As such, it appears that Balor was not only a very powerful sorcerer, but also a very advanced scientist, as we understand that term today.

Though Balor's homeland is uncertain, he is associated with numerous sites on Tory Island, off the northern shore of County Donegal, where folktales say he took the magical gray cow that he had stolen from Cian. Other islands between Ireland and Scotland may also contain clues regarding his mysterious origins, and fate.

Cú Roi

Cú Roi, (lit., "hound of god") was one of the more enigmatic figures of ancient Irish history. Variously categorized as wizard, king, warrior and world traveler, Cú Roi's motivation was his search for *fir fer*, "the truth of men", a sort of warrior code of honor which he sought to affirm and instill into the warriors of Ireland. In his search to affirm this warrior code, Cú Roi traveled the island with a battle axe in one hand and a huge rock in the other, challenging even Cú Chulainn himself to prove his warrior mettle.

Some scholars believe that Cú Roi actually stood at the center of a mythological cycle native to Munster province, now lost. However, Cú Roi still appears in a couple of legends of Cú Chulainn's, including one where he accompanies Cú Chulainn to the Otherworld, and actually defeats him in combat. In another folktale, "Briccriu's Feast", Cú Roi transforms himself into a giant troll-like creature called a *bachlach* (q.v.), and challenges Cú Chulainn, Conall and Leoghaire to a beheading contest in order to see

THE MYSTERY
WIZARDS, DRUIDS
& POETS
WIZARDS

who was the greatest warrior in Ireland. All three cut off his head, but he merely laughed after replacing it each time. Then, when it came time for Cú Roi to cut off *their* heads, Conall and Leoghaire refused to let him, but Cú Chulainn stood still, waiting for the fatal blow. Cú Roi then revealed himself to the heroes, and proclaimed Cú Chulainn the greatest hero of Ireland due to his honor and bravery. Interestingly, Cú Roi also shows up in *The Táin*, where he offers to kill Cú Chulainn for Queen Maeve, though Maeve turns down his offer. However, Cú Chulainn later kills Cú Roi by using his wife, Bláithne, to betray him. Bláithne was then killed by Cú Roi's poet, Ferchertne, in revenge for her betrayal.

Cú Roi appears to have been a sort of "mixed-class" character, a "warrior-wizard" whose intentions were not evil *per se*, portrayed instead as a man who followed his own rules regardless of the consequences. In that way, he was less of an evil character than a "trickster" character, keeping everyone on their toes by keeping things interesting. He was most closely associated with Munster province, particularly County Kerry, and the region around the Beara peninsula in County Cork. His legendary magical fortress is believed to actually be what is now the Iron Age ruin of Cahirconree on Sliab Mis, a mountain on the Dingle Peninsula in County Kerry. This fortress was believed to be impregnable, and to actually revolve on its axis every night so that the entrance could not be found after dark. Cú Roi could even make it rotate by means of a spell from very far away. Cú was also associated with Temair Luchra in County Kerry.

Fer Doirich

Fer Doirich, "The Dark Druid", made his lone appearance in a legend of Finn McCool as an evil, wizard-type druid who fell in love with the goddess Sadb. When Sadb spurned his love, he misused his power to transform her into a fawn. The power to transform others is a power commonly attributed to wizards, who usually misuse that power in order to take revenge, or simply for their own amusement. Interestingly, when Sadb entered the "magic circle" of Finn's home, the Dun of Allen, the magic was dispelled and, as long as she stayed within the dun, she retained her normal form. Unfortunately, when Finn was away one day, Fer Doirich lured Sadb away from the dun, and she transformed back into a fawn, after which Fer Doirich took her away with him forever.

Druids

Unlike the spectacular wizard types, most druids were content to serve more sedate roles as priests and oracles, acting as intermediaries between the affairs of the gods and men in order to make sure that their people remained in good standing with the divine realm. This class of druid might be more accurately described as a combination of priest and academic, as they most concerned themselves with the acquisition, memorization and transmission of information, particularly information that had to do with their religious beliefs.

"César, Druid of the Fir Bolg"
© Jim Fitzpatrick.

However, along with their priestly and academic interests, many druids also pursued the study of the liberal arts and sciences such as law, medicine, history, chemistry, geography, grammar, and all of the other arts and sciences we know today. But unlike modern academics, the druids never taught within hallowed halls, preferring secluded groves of trees hidden deep within the forests or similarly natural settings such as on the shores of sacred lakes. Also unlike modern academics, the druids rarely wrote down anything, instead relying purely on memorization and oral transmission of information. Another important difference between the druids and modern academe (which is based upon the linear Greco-Roman model) is the fact that the druids did not make distinctions between mythology and history, instead combining their teachings on history, theology, philosophy, mythology, astronomy and all other information they had to convey to their students in the form of stories. As such, they were less concerned with the memorization of names and dates than in conveying a general concept through the story, from which the facts and figures radiated like spokes from the hub of a wheel. Interestingly, druids sometimes even taught their students through the use of riddles, very much an "outside the box" method of teaching that modern education has only recently begun to rediscover.

Druids in ancient Celtic society, particularly in Ireland, occupied the upper class of society, being in some ways even more important than the king himself. For example, in solemn assemblies the druids always spoke first, even before the king, as their words were the words of the gods. And though as a protected class the druids were not required to join the army in times of war, they often fought anyway, indicating that some types of druids were more like warrior monks, "majoring" in martial skills as part of their education. One type of druid, known as the *brehon*, served as judges and arbiters, whose word was absolute. Generally speaking, the druids were essentially the intelligentsia class that ruled society from behind the scenes.

Here is a listing of the major druidic figures in Irish mythology. More information about druids can be found at http://ireland.mysterious world.com/Mystery/WDP/Druids/

BARACH

Barach was the chief druid of Ulster, who served King Conchobar during the latter part of his reign. Barach was best known for being the first to tell the king the story of the crucifixion of Christ. Upon hearing the news that the Son of God had been so cruelly mistreated, Conchobar flew into a rage and began to vent his anger by hacking away at a tree with his sword. Unfortunately, he became so enraged that a slingstone that had been lodged in his head suddenly became dislodged, and he died.

BÉ CHUILLE

Bé Chuille was one of the daughters of Flidais, goddess of the wild, and sister to the druidess Dianann. Bé Chuille, along with Dianann, served as a druidess for the Tuatha dé Danann. In the First Battle of Moy Tura, she used her power over plants and trees to create the illusion of large amounts of warriors in order to deceive the Fir Bolg. Bé Chuille also had the gift of divination, which allowed her to foretell the number of Dé Danann warriors who would die in the battle.

BIROG

Birog "of the Mountain" was a powerful druidess who helped Cian, the son of Dian Cécht, impregnate Eithne, daughter of Balor, who would later give birth to Lugh. She also rescued the young Lugh from being killed by Balor, who was afraid that one of Eithne's triplets would be the one who was fated to slay him. She then took the young Lugh to be fostered by Tailltiu, Queen of the Fir Bolg.

BODHMALL

Bodhmall was the daughter of the druid Tagh, and sister to Muirenn, the mother of Finn McCool. Finn was born in Bodhmall's house on Slieve Bloom, and his mother gave him to Bodhmall to raise and train in the druidic arts. Slieve Bloom is one of an extensive chain of mountains connecting Counties Laois and Offaly, Leinster province.

CAICHER

Caicher was a druid of the Milesians who told Amergin the Poet that his people would one day rule Ireland.

CAILITIN

Cailitin was the druid of Queen Maeve and King Allil in *The Táin*. He was the father of 28 children, also named Cailitin, as they all acted as one person and one body, the group sometimes being referred to as "Clan Cailitin". They studied the black arts in Scotland, and fought with poisoned javelins that always hit their target. In addition, all of Cailitin's children were purposely mutilated, their right feet and left hands removed, possibly as part of their martial training. This may help explain the origin of the one-armed, one-legged, dart-throwing Fomorians that the Partholónians met when they first arrived in Ireland — both may have been trained by the same people.

The Cailitin clan was sent by Queen Maeve to assassinate Cú Chulainn, but Cú caught all 29 of their javelins on his shield. Cú was also aided by the hero Fiachu Mac Fer Fhebe, who cut off all their right arms. Cailitin's widow later gave birth to sextuplets, three sons and three daughters, who used their black magic to fool Cú into eating dog meat, breaking his *geas* and marking the beginning of the end of his short but glorious career.

CATHBAD

Cathbad was the *Ard Druid*, or "High Druid" of Ulster during the reign of King Conchobar, and one of the leading figures of the Ulster Cycle of Irish mythology. His primary function was that of a seer, i.e., a prophet who predicts the future. Several of his progeny were also famous, his daughter Deichtine being the mother of Cú Chulainn, fathered by none other than Lugh himself. He also had two prominent foster sons named Crom Deroil and Crom Darail, both druids. Cathbad was the druid whom the young Sétanta (Cú Chulainn) overheard prophesying that the one who first took up arms on that day would have a short but glorious life. He was also the druid in the tale, "Deirdre and the Sons of Uisnech", who warned King Conchobar that if a king married the beautiful young Deirdre, it would lead to the destruction of the kingdom of Ulster.

CÉSAR

César was the druid of the Fir Bolg who made an appearance in Jim Fitzpatrick's interpretation of the First Battle of the Moy Tura, as laid out in his seminal work, *The Book of Conquests*. In the battle, César made his first appearance to counter the red rain and spectral warriors that had been conjured up by the *Badb* in order to demoralize the Fir Bolg and their allies. Initially calling upon their tribal gods for aid, as was normal for a typical druid, their tribal gods failed to stop the wicked magic of the *Badb*, so he made the fateful decision to call upon the wicked elder god Crom Cruach for aid. This of course was what Balor of the Evil Eye would also do at the Second Battle of Moy Tura. However, unlike Balor, César's attempt to use the elder god to defeat the Tuatha dé Danann failed, and César was horribly devoured by the god in payment for his services.

DIANANN

Dianann was the sister of the druidess Bé Chuille and the daughter of the woodland goddess Flidais. She was also the sister of Bé Téite, and possibly of Fann, wife of Manannán Mac Lir. Dianann also fought in both the First and Second Battles of Moy Tura along with Bé Chuille, using her sorcery in the second battle to create the illusion of a host of Dé Danann warriors using grass and leaves. Dianann was killed by the Fomorian warrior Dé Domnann during the fighting.

DUBH

Dubh, also known as Dubhlinn, was a legendary Irish druidess. Upon learning that her husband Énna had taken a second wife, Dubh drowned her and her entire family. In revenge, one of the family's servants killed Dubh with a sling stone, and her body fell into a large pool that once sat at the mouth of the Liffey. From that event, this pool became known as *Dubh-linn*, "Dub's Pool", from which came the name of the city of Dublin. Modern dredging has since eliminated the pool, but her name lives on as the largest city in Ireland.

FEDELM

Fedelm was the prophetess of Cruachain, the ancient seat of Connaught, where Queen Maeve and King Aillil reigned. At the beginning of *The Táin*, she appeared as a tall, beautiful woman with long, blond hair down to her knees, gold-clasped sandals, and three irises in each eye, riding in a chariot. In response to Maeve's request for an augury as to whether or not her invasion of Ulster would succeed, Fedelm correctly warned Maeve that if she attacked Ulster, she would be defeated.

FINNEGAS

Finnegas was a seer who lived for seven years upon the banks of the Boyne, watching for The Salmon of Knowledge to appear in the Well of Sergais, along the River Boyne (another tradition has him at *Linn Féic* (Fiac's Pool) near Rosnaree, County Meath). This pool was special as hazel nuts fell into it, giving wisdom to the salmon that lived there. Finnegas never saw the special Salmon of Knowledge until the young Finn McCool came by one day, and the Salmon suddenly appeared, as if it had been waiting for him. Finnegas then caught the fish and gave it to Finn to cook, warning Finn that if he ate any of the fish, or if even a single blister appeared on the fish while he was cooking it, he would kill him. Fearful for his life, Finn noticed a blister and pushed it down with his thumb. His thumb was burned as a result, and as he instinctively put it into his mouth, the wisdom of the salmon passed into him instead of Finnegas, who received only the flesh as his reward for his seven-year wait.

THE MYSTERY
WIZARDS, DRUIDS
& POETS
DRUIDS

133

THE FOUR DRUIDS OF THE TUATHA DÉ DANANN

When the Tuatha dé Danann returned from their time of learning in the four cities in the north, they brought with them four magical artifacts from each of the cities that would help them conquer and keep control over Ireland. Along with these artifacts came four druids who tended them, as follows:

✦ **Morfesa of Failias:** Morfesa was the instructor of learning in the city of Failias, and the keeper of the *Lia Fáil*, the great omphalos stone of the city of Failias.

✦ **Esras of Goirias:** Esras was the chief instructor in the city of Goirias, where he was the keeper of the *Sleá Bua*, "The Spear of Victory", that was given to Lugh.

✦ **Uiscias of Findias:** Uiscias was the chief instructor in the city of Findias, and the keeper of the *Claímh Solais*, "The Sword of Light", that was given to King Nuada of the Tuatha dé Danann.

✦ **Semias of Muirias:** Semias was the chief instructor in the city of Muirias, and the keeper of the magical Cauldron of the Dagda.

IARBONEL

Iarbonel was a literal giant of a man, the eldest son of Nemed and Macha, the High King of the Nemedians, and a powerful druid, whose specialty was prophecy and soothsaying, Iarbonel was one of the few descendants of Nemed to survive the battle of Conan's Tower. After the battle, his son Semeon went to Greece, whose progeny were the Fir Bolg. His son Beothach, however, went north to dwell in the four cities of Failias, Goirias, Findias and Muirias, his progeny returning to Ireland as the Tuatha dé Danann. Iarbonel is believed by some to have gone north with Beothach.

MIDE

In an alternative history of the naming of *Midhe* (Meath), the middle province of Ireland generally believed to have been created by the Fir Bolg, *Midhe* was named after a Nemedian druid named Mide who was the first druid to ever light a fire on the Hill of Uisnech. This fire burned for seven years, and from this fire every other fire in Ireland was lit. As a result, Mide and his successors were entitled to a pig and a sack of grain from every household in Ireland from thenceforth. When the other druids objected, Mide had their tongues cut out and burned in the fire at Uisnech.

MUG RUITH

Mug Ruith was a powerful druid of early Ireland much celebrated in myth, legend and festival. He is sometimes referred to as The Archdruid, and was believed to be either blind or one-eyed. Merely by blowing with his own breath he could dry up lakes and rivers, and raise storms. During the Christian period, Mug Ruith was resurrected by Christian monks for didactic purposes, and paired up with the wizard Simon Magus who appears in the biblical Book of Acts. Together, they were believed to have created a magical flying machine, the *roth rámach* ("rowing wheel"), which was thereafter displayed at the festival of Tlachtga, named after Mug Ruith's daughter. Interestingly, the legend also states that the *roth rámach* would reappear over Europe at the time of the end as an engine of destruction to punish the nations who gave disciples to Simon Magus. Mug Ruith is believed to have lived on Valencia Island, in County Kerry.

TADG MAC NUADAT

Tadg, the chief druid of Leinster, was the father of Muirenn, the mother of Finn McCool. Tadg was instrumental in the death of Finn's father, Cumhail, at the hands of Goll Mac Morna, as he did not approve of their marriage. However, Finn later killed Tadg, and took possession of the Hill of Allen for his own.

THE THREE DRUIDS OF THE PARTHOLÓNIANS

The Partholónians had three powerful druids, which are described as being three brothers who had three fathers and three mothers through joint parentage:

✛ **Eolas:** Eolas specialized in acquiring knowledge as learned from experience.

✛ **Fios:** Fios specialized in acquiring esoteric knowledge.

✛ **Fochmarc:** Fochmarc specialized in acquiring information through reading and research.

135

"Fáthach, Poet of the Fir Bolg", © 1977, Jim Fitzpatrick.

Poets

The poets, Gaelic *fili*, were the lowest of the three orders of druidry, but still part of the upper class of society. The *fili* class of druidry was further subdivided into seven levels, the highest of which was the *Ollam*.

The *fili* were essentially poets of an exalted status, and were generally considered to be the voices of the nation. They usually served kings, princes, and other exceptional people, the office being hereditary in nature, passed from father to son, mother to daughter. However, of the seven levels of *fili*, only three are still remembered: the Bard, the Brehon, and the Ollam:

BARD

The Bards were one of the lower orders of *fili*, but often the most popular, as they were the ones who told the tales around the fireside about kings and heroes, myths and monsters, and all the folktales and legends of the Irish. Bards were the keepers of the folktales, and were usually accomplished singers, musicians and/or poets. They held multiple roles in society, including lorekeeper, storyteller, comic, entertainer and, perhaps most importantly, communicator between the world of men and the Otherworld. Bards were sometimes also sorcerors, enchanters, and even herbalists, incorporating aspects of both wizardry and druidry into their array of talents. Bards were the interpreters of the mysteries, drawing upon the sacred power of *imbas forosnai*, the magic muse of inspiration that is the motivation behind all creativity. As such, they were very much "practical priests", bringing a love and understanding of the mysteries of myth, legend and life to the common man through the medium of music, song, dance and the spoken word.

BREHON

The Brehon were the legal authorities of ancient Ireland. Not judges *per se*, the typical Brehon was more of an interpreter and keeper of the law, more like a legal expert than a lawyer as we understand them today. The Brehon were the keepers and arbiters of the Brehon Laws, a collection of law records that stretch back to at least the 6th century AD. No decisions, specific case or statute laws are recorded, except for a very few famous ones. The Brehon Law was still in use in Ireland as late as the reign of James I (AD 1603-1625).

OLLAM

Ollam was an ancient designation for anyone who had achieved the highest possible degree of skill in any field, similar to the doctorate level in modern academe. In ancient Ireland, however, the designation *Ollam* usually referred to the highest level of *fili*. This was quite an accomplishment, as the rank of Ollam required 12 years of training and the memorization of 350 different tales. Moreover, the rank of Ollam required the student to be proficient in various forms of divination including *imbas forosnai*, the ability to discern spiritual things in order to prophesy future events; *dichetal do chennaib*, a form of divination that may have involved the fingertips, the message usually taking the form of quatrains or some other type of poetic verse; and *teinm laída*, "chewing the marrow", another form of divination perhaps akin to that practiced by Finn McCool, who was said to bite his thumb down to the marrow in order to magically find the answers to important questions.

Ollam were the equivalent of movie stars in their day, followed about by a coterie of 24 men and always given the red carpet treatment wherever they went. They were usually at the top of the food chain at the king's court, where the Ollam functioned as both a poet, historian and storyteller. They were also the keepers of the genealogies, so their services were central to the institution of kingship. Combining all the abilities of the Bard, the Brehon, and all other lower grades of *fili*, the Ollam was the master of all skills. However, his most feared skill was the power of satire, wherein Ollam were able to make or break careers and reputations with only a few well-chosen words. Thus the ultimate power of the Ollam, and all poets, lay in the spoken word.

Here is a listing of the major poetic figures in Irish mythology. Additional information can be found at http://ireland.mysterious world.com/Mystery/WDP/Poets/

AMERGIN

Amergin was the Chief Poet of the Milesians, the sixth and last of the Magogian peoples to invade the sacred isle. He is sometimes referred to as the first poet of Ireland, though that is more of an honorary title as we know for certain that poets of various types had accompanied previous invasions. Amergin, however, could well be considered the greatest poet of Irish history, or at least the most famous, as the first thing he spoke when he first set foot upon Irish soil was one of the most famous poems of Irish history: "The Mystery". And it was through another famous poem that Amergin was finally able to overcome the combined power of all the wizards, druids and poets of the Tuatha dé Danann, who had banded together in order to fend off the Milesian invasion, despite the fact that their conquest of the island had been divinely ordained.

After the Milesians had defeated the supernatural armies of the Tuatha Dé, it was Amergin who successfully parleyed with the three queens of the Tuatha Dé — Èriu, Banbha and Fódhla — and reached an agreement with them that the Milesians would rule the upper world, while the Tuatha Dé would retreat to the Underworld. Amergin also used his power of divination to determine who was to be the High King of Ireland, deciding in favor of his brother Eremón over his other brother, Èber Donn.

Èber Donn was not satisfied with this judgment, however, and threatened to go to war. Amergin, after already proving that he was a poet of the highest order, as well as a diviner, then also made clear his abilities as a judge by dividing Ireland into northern and southern principalities, Eremón ruling the north, and Èber Donn ruling the south. Èber Donn was still not satisfied with this, however, and went to war with his brother Eremón. Èber Donn was killed in the fighting, and as a result, Eremón became the High King of Ireland, fulfilling Amergin's prophecy.

Through the power of his spoken word, Amergin was able to calm even the fiercest winds, and in his poem, "The Mystery", he described himself as having an understanding of all aspects of nature, both individually and in their totality. Proving the power of the spoken word over nature, the world of the flesh and the world of the spirit, Amergin defined the office of the Ollam, and as such is justly remembered as the greatest poet in Irish history.

ABCAN MAC BICELMOIS

Abcan was a dwarf poet and harper of the Tuatha dé Danann, who lived by the River Erne near the falls of Assaroe, one mile west of Ballyshannon in County Donegal. He was known for his bronze boat with its tin sail, which he frequently used on the river.

CENN FÁELAD

Cenn Fáelad was a warrior-poet of the Uí Néill during the 7th-century AD, and was the first poet to be listed in the Annals. He is believed to have completed the compilation of the Brehon Laws, and is also believed to have written the *Auraicept na nÉces*, "The Scholar's Primer".

CRIDENBÉL

Cridenbél was a satirist of the court of Breas, king of the Tuatha Dé. Old, blind, and ugly, he stayed in Breas' good graces through flattery. He is best known for always demanding, and receiving, the three best bits of food from the Dagda's plate at every meal, leaving the Dagda near starvation. However, the Dagda took advantage of his blindness by giving him three gold coins instead of three bits of food, and Cridenbél choked to death on them.

CAIRBRE MAC ETAÍNE

Cairbre was the son of Etaíne, the daughter of Dian Cécht, his father possibly being Ogma. He was a very famous satirist, and also lived during the time of Breas. Very much the opposite of Cridenbél, however, Cairbre visited the court of Breas one day, and was appalled at the cheap and shabby way he was treated, given poor accomodation and only three dry biscuits to eat. Furious, he composed a bitter satire that was the beginning of the end of Breas' reputation as a competent king. In some versions of the story, the satire hit so close to the mark that red blotches broke out on the enraged Breas' face, a disfigurement that some used as an excuse to get rid of him.

Cairbre also composed a satire that he used to help break the morale of the Fomorians before the Second Battle of Moy Tura, and was also known for his ability to use the terrible *glám dicenn* against his enemies. This was a special form of poet's curse similar to a *geas* where he stood on one foot, closed one eye, and raised up one arm towards his target while he uttered the words of power. This curse could terribly disfigure the target's appearance, and even kill him. And even if he survived, he would thereafter be shunned and unable to function at any level in society.

CNU DEIREÓIL

Cnu Deireóil was a golden-haired dwarf who was a harper for Finn McCool. Standing at around 4 feet high, and said to be at least part fairy, Cnu was believed to be a son of Lugh. Cnu was usually associated with great happiness and delight in many stories of the Fenian Cycle, and was also known for the ability to use his magical harp to induce sleep.

DO DERA

Do Dera was Lugaid Mac Con's jester, a form of poet that specialized in comedy. Do Dera looked something like Lugaid, and when Lugaid was forced to flee the Battle of Cenn Abrat, Do Dera put on Lugaid's crown and pretended to be him until his master could escape. Unfortunately, though Lugaid successfully evaded capture, Do Dera was killed by Éogan, King of Munster, who was *not* amused.

FÁTHACH, POET OF THE FIR BOLG

Fáthach was the chief poet of the Fir Bolg during the time of King Eochaid. He embodied the function of the poet to rally the spirits of his people with stirring words remembering past deeds of courage and self-sacrifice. At the First Battle of Moy Tura, Fáthach made a great, stirring speech to the assembled Fir Bolg which greatly bolstered their morale. In order to watch the battle, he erected a pillar, now known as "Fáthach's Pillar", from which he lamented the destruction of the youth of the Fir Bolg in their defeat against the Tuatha dé Danann.

FEARFLATHA Ó GNIMH

The bard of the O'Neills of Clandeboye (ca. AD 1540-1640), Fearflatha was considered to be one of the last of the true bards, as he was the last to receive classical rather than vernacular training in the bardic arts.

LUGAID

Lugaid was a warrior poet of Aillil, king of Connaught, who was the husband of the famous Queen Maeve. Though blind, Lugaid's skill and accuracy with his spear was so great that when he heard the adulterous Maeve and Fergus swimming together in the lake, he threw his spear right through Fergus' heart.

SENCHA MAC AILELLA

Sencha Mac Ailella was the chief judge and poet in King Conchobar's court. He was known for his wisdom and his role as a peacemaker, and also helped to foster Cú Chulainn, whom he taught the art of eloquence.

SENCHÁN TORPÉIST

Senchán Torpéist (ca. 570-617) held for a time the title Chief Poet of Ireland. In this role he succeeded Dallán Forgaill. He is best known for having saved the epic poem, *The Táin*, from oblivion, claiming that the ghost of Fergus Mac Roich had appeared to him and laid out the poem in its entirety. Senchán also appears in a fanciful tale where he is carried off by Irusán, the King of the Cats (*q.v.*), who was angered by a satire that Senchán had written that made fun of cats.

Creatures Great & Small

long with the ancient gods, demigods, warriors, wizards, druids and poets, numerous creatures great and small shared the limelight in the myths and legends of ancient Ireland. Ranging from giants in the earth above, to fairies in the earth below — and everything in between — the fertile imaginations of the ancient Irish conjured up creatures to suit every fancy, and to explain every mystery that could not otherwise be explained away as "an act of the gods". And whether real or imagined, even the rumor of the possible existence of these creatures has had a tremendous impact on the worldview of the Irish, an impact that has left deep impressions in the myths, legends, and ancient monuments throughout the length and breadth of the blessed isle.

Giants

Giants are among the most common mythological beings to appear in the myths and legends of the ancient world, and Ireland is no exception. Numerous legends and folktales have a giant as the antagonist, the hero of the tale being the man who defeats the wicked giant and restores the community to order, whether by recapturing stolen treasure, rescuing the damsel in distress, avenging a murder or simply ridding the community of a source of fear that is keeping it from maintaining a peaceful, ordered existence.

Most giants by far were ruthless, greedy, cannibalistic monsters that thought only of their next plunder, or their next meal which, if cattle were not available, could well be human flesh. Every giant had a special sack that they carried with them wherever they went, so that they could all the more easily take whatever their eyes fancied. The things they loved to plunder the most were pretty, shiny things such as gold, silver, jewelry, gems and/or fair maidens, particularly those with blonde or red hair. And because of their exceptional size, strength, speed (some legends around the world describe giants running down deer and buffalo) and wicked intelligence, they usually got their way, unless a hero was there to stop them.

THE MYSTERY
CREATURES
GREAT & SMALL
GIANTS

However, though most giants in the myths and legends of ancient Ireland were rotten to the core, many heroes of Irish history, such as Nuada and Finn McCool, were also gigantic in stature, tall and powerful even by today's standards. Nuada, the descendant of Iarbonel the giant was, like all the royal line of Magog, exceptionally large and strong, and also manifested supernatural abilities. Finn McCool, a giant of a man in his own right, probably at least seven feet tall, was an almost supernaturally gifted athlete and warrior. Over time Finn grew to be so large and strong in the songs of the bards that huge rock formations, primarily in northeastern Ireland, were often attributed to Finn's failed attempts to hit an opponent with a boulder, the massive rock landing dozens, even hundreds of miles away. Another giant hero, Oisín, as we have seen, was shocked when he returned from the Otherworld to find that mankind had greatly shrunk in size since the time of the Fianna, indicating that not only Oisín, but all of the Fianna were also gigantic in stature — the main distinguishing characteristic of these men of renown.

© 1979 Julek Heller

The legends of the giants most likely came from the invasions of the Gaelic Celts and related peoples, who were described by Roman historians as being a tall, strongly built blond- and red-haired race who ranged from 7-9 feet tall, sometimes even taller. The Gaedelic Celts, or "Gaels", often fought naked, swinging huge, two-handed swords that were nearly as tall as they were. They were also madly fond of horses, being particularly well known for their use of chariots in battle long after they had fallen out of use in the more civilized countries of the Mediterranean and ancient Near East. Despite their superior size, strength, and numbers, however, superior Roman strategy and tactics led to the eventual defeat of the Continental Celts, and many of the giant Celts and their allies were driven far north into the forests of Germany and even as far as Scandinavia, where they entered into the mythology of the Vikings.

Other Celtic peoples, such as the Fir Bolg (lit., "men with bags") fled far west into the British Isles, many making their last stand in Ireland where they conquered and ruled over the native peoples. Another prominent people, the Fomorians, who were usually described in the myths as huge, wicked and cannibalistic giants that were possessed of strange powers and bizarre habits, were probably also among those giant peoples who invaded ancient Ireland. And the Fomorians were defeated by still more giants emigrating from Central Asia — the giant sons of Magog, the greatest of which were the Tuatha dé Danann.

Over time, particularly after the conquest of the emerald isle by the Milesians, the power of the formerly omnipotent giants began to wane to the point where they had degraded to the level of isolated bands of scavengers and plunderers who literally "sacked" towns and villages by burning them down and stuffing all the valuables into their ubiquitous sacks. It is likely that it was this chaotic period in Irish history, when giants roamed the land and terrorized the people, that inspired many of the folktales about the wicked, plundering giants and the heroes who arose to conquer them. Eventually the power of these ancient men of renown became degraded to the point where they had no choice but to make peace and integrate with the peoples over whom they had formerly ruled. Thus conquered, their reign of terror eventually ended, and the times of their glory faded into myth.

THE MYSTERY
CREATURES
GREAT & SMALL
GIANTS

For more information on the origin and history of the giants, start with Part I of our four-part series on Giants in the Earth at http://www.mysteriousworld.com/Journal/2003/Spring/Giants/ or visit http://ireland.mysteriousworld.com/Mystery/Creatures/Giants/

FAMOUS IRISH GIANTS:

✦ Áeda

Áeda was an ugly male giant of the Fenian Cycle who romantically pursued the beautiful giantess Bébinn. Enraged at her rejection, he pursued and eventually killed her.

✦ Bébinn

Bébinn was a beautiful giantess of noble mien who asked the *Fianna* for protection against the unwanted advances of Áeda. Enraged at being spurned, Áeda broke into their palace and killed her.

✦ Bachlach

A *bachlach* was a form of giant troll, or "churl", that usually worked as a herdsman or other type of menial laborer. The wizard Cú Roi appeared in the tale "Briccriu's Feast" (*q.v.*) as a bachlach in order to diguise his true identity.

✦ Goll Mac Carbada

Goll Mac Carbada was a huge, one-eyed giant who was the constant enemy of Cú Chulainn thoughout the Ulster Cycle, whom Cú killed in the end. Some scholars have noted that the conflict between Cú and Goll Mac Carbada may parallel the conflict between Lugh and Balor, and between Finn McCool and Goll Mac Morna, the conflict between hero and giant being a common motif in Irish myth.

✦ Ciudach

Ciudach was an amiable giant of good looks and disposition who hailed from the region of Roscommon, Connaught province. In one legend, while on the run with Diarmuid, Gráinne actually had an affair with Ciudach, indicating that he must have been very amiable indeed. In later stories, however, Ciudach appears to transform into a dark, evil creature or spirit that haunts caves and eats humans. The legend of the Ciudach actually appears to have extended across the western Celtic world, appearing on the Isle of Man and even as far as Inverness in Scotland.

✤ Fachtna Fáthach

Fachtna Fáthach was a wise, benevolent and civilized giant, the son of Cathbad the druid. Fachtna was the king of Ulster and with his wife, Ness, fathered the famous Conchobar Mac Nessa. After his death, Fachtna's brother Fergus Mac Roich married Ness and succeeded Fachtna as king until Ness maneuvered Conchobar, the rightful heir, into position as king.

✤ Fer Caille

Fer Caille (lit., "man of the woods") was the "churl", or giant, troll-like, herdsman figure that makes a prominent appearance in the influential myth, *Togail Bruidne Da Derga*, "The Destruction of Da Derga's Hostel" *(q.v.)*. Fer Caille is described as having only one eye, one hand, and one foot, just like the Fomorian giants whom the Partholónians had fought against. His hair is described as being very long, hard and spiky, sticking straight up like the bristles on a boar's back, and so stiff and sharp that if one poured out a bucket of apples onto his head, not a one would hit the ground. In the story he is accompanied by an extraordinarily ugly woman, and carries a live boar on his back for the main course in a feast. Fer Caille uses his magic to entice Conaire, the hero of the story, into staying a while and joining him in the feast, thus delaying him on his journey. The "churl" is an interesting recurrent motif that appears occasionally in Irish myth, introduced perhaps to inject the elements of danger and horror into the storyline, and whose presence may indicate that the Fomorians were never completely driven out of Ireland.

✤ Ingcél Caech

Ingcél Caech, (lit., "one-eyed") was another one-eyed giant whose eye was so huge that it was said to be as broad as an oxhide. His eye was also unusual in that it had three pupils, and was as black as a beetle.

Ingcél was also a pirate who hailed either from

THE MYSTERY
CREATURES
GREAT & SMALL
GIANTS

Britain or Cornwall, frequently leading his band of giant pirates to raid the coastlands of Ireland. Along with the sons of Donn Désa and the seven sons of Maeve (the "Maines"), Ingcél Caech was responsible for the destruction of Da Derga's hostel in the tale of the same name.

✦ Midchaín

Midchaín was a huge giant who lived in and protected a hill in northern Lochlann (Scotland). He rarely needed to fight, as his voice was so powerful and penetrating that he could actually kill men with a shout. In the epic *Oidheadh Chlainne Tuireann*, "The Fate of the Children of Tuireann", Lugh sent the sons of Tuireann on a *geas* to fulfill their blood money, part of the fulfillment of which involved being forced to endure hearing three shouts from Midchaín.

✦ Muircartach

Muircartach is the name of a monstrous, giant, evil sea hag of Irish and Scottish folklore, related to the *Cailleach Beara* of County Cork. She is hideously ugly, being bald with a black face and a single, huge eye protruding out from her forehead. When she rises from her watery home, she is believed to cause great storms, this belief perhaps being the basis of the "sea hag" myth that superstitious sailors blame for causing sudden, powerful storms. Occasionally she is seen in the myths as showing up at people's doors in the form of a dripping wet, pathetic old woman, begging for shelter. But only the foolish would let her inside, as once she was inside, she would swell up to her normal, huge size and wreak havoc. She could be friendly sometimes, however, healing the sick or wounded with her pot of balsam, and even raising the dead by poking her wizened finger into their mouths.

✦ Searbhan

Searbhan was a solitary Fomorian giant who figured prominently in the legend, "The Pursuit of Diarmuid and Gráinne". Also known as *Lochlannach*, "the Norseman", he lived in the forest of Dubros, County Sligo, where he protected the magical rowanberry trees with his powerful magic. Unable to overcome his magic, Diarmuid ended up having to use the giant's own magical club to defeat him.

Fairies

The fairies, known variously as the *shí* ("shee") or *sídhe* ("sith"), are the "little people" or nature spirits who are believed to live in an "Otherworld" that the ancient Irish and other Celtic peoples believed existed parallel to our own. The *sídhe* are so named due to the fact that they are believed to live in the mounds, raths, stone circles and various other prehistoric sacred spaces to be found throughout Ireland, the basic meaning of the word *sídhe* being "mound". Thus the appelation *Daoine Sídhe*, or

"Fann, Princess of the *Daoine Shí*", © 1984, Jim Fitzpatrick.

"People of the Mounds". The fairies are generally divided into two different classes: solitary fairies, such as the leprechaun, and the "trooping fairies", or *macara shí*, who are believed to come forth as a group from all of the raths, mounds, dolmens, stone circles, fairy trees, holy wells, and every other type of sacred place in Ireland twice per year: on Beltaine Eve (May 1st) and Samhain Eve (Halloween).

It was believed that during these times, the material and spiritual worlds came closest together, and as a result, spiritual "doorways" between the two worlds opened up, allowing the fairies easier access to the upper world. At those times, particularly on Samhain Eve, the Trooping Fairies were believed to flood out over all Ireland, harassing people foolish enough to be caught out after dark, and trying their best to scare and play tricks even on those wise enough to stay in. This belief, likely acted out by the people as part of their ritual celebrations, was the basis for the modern "Halloween" celebration, and the concept of "trick or treat" most likely came from the idea that if the spirits were not placated with small gifts, or at least treated with civility, they might

THE MYSTERY
CREATURES
GREAT & SMALL
FAIRIES

149

react violently and take revenge. This revenge might take the form of minor pranks such as curdling the milk, stealing food, or soiling laundry to major crimes such as burning down houses, stealing cattle or children, and perhaps even killing people if they felt the level of disrespect warranted it. It is for this reason that the fairies are always referred to as "the good people" or "the gentry" as an extra measure to help avoid offending them, and their sacred places are always given a wide berth. And of course purposely invading a fairy rath or cave, plowing over a fairy ring, cutting down a fairy tree or otherwise violating any other of their sacred places would invariably bring great wrath and ruin upon the offender, a belief that is widely prevalent even today.

However, if one stood in good stead with the fairies, they could also be friendly and helpful, keeping things clean, helping with small chores, giving money to the poor and toys to children, and even counteracting spells cast by witches or other, evil fairies. Fairies often consorted with various heroes of ancient Ireland, and were as likely as not seen to be benevolent, even openly friendly with humans, sometimes even cohabiting and raising families with mortal men and women. As such, just as in the world of humanity, there was both good and evil to be found in the world of the fairies, though that good and evil was relative.

THE ORIGINS OF THE FAIRIES

There are various theories on the origins of the fairies in Celtic folklore, including 1) the fairies were the remnant of the deities of previous inhabitants of the land who had been conquered, their deities shrunk down to a more manageable, less intimidating size; 2) the fairies were the conquered, aboriginal inhabitants themselves who, forced to live on the fringes of society, snuck about and took revenge in small ways, mostly at night; 3) the fairies are the personifications of the powers of nature; and 4) fairies are the spirits of the dead, who live on in a sort of eternal purgatory, neither in heaven, nor in hell. This gray, purgatory concept fits well with a fifth possible explanation first posited by Christian theologians that fairies are in fact a type of fallen angel, of an order that was not good enough for heaven, nor evil enough for hell.

According to the Mythological Cycle, however, the fairies are believed to be the descendants of the Tuatha dé Danann, with whom the Milesians had made a covenant. In this covenant, the Tuatha dé Danann agreed to emigrate to the Underworld and reign there, while the Milesians would retain the rule of the upper world. And though this is the most widely held explanation for the fairy superstition, it may be, however, that some of the other theories might also be at least partly true.

THE OTHERWORLD

The "Otherworld" or "Underworld", where the fairies were believed to live, was portrayed in the myths in several ways, the most common being:

✤ An underground realm that can only be accessed via caves and/or magical doorways that are located in megalithic monuments, fairy trees, holy wells, and other sacred places;

✤ A magical, underwater land believed to parallel the upper world in every respect, save that everyone there is eternally young and beautiful;

✤ A mysterious island paradise that can be seen only by the dead or those who have "the second sight".

These numerous Otherworld locations were known by various proper names, including *Tír nan Óg*, "The Land of Eternal Youth"; *Tír Tairngire*, "The Land of Promise", *Emain Ablach*, "The Place of the Twin Apple Trees", an island off the coast of Scotland whose name was no doubt influenced by the biblical Eden; *Hy Brasil*, a mysterious island where it is believed the heroes of old such as Cú Chulainn went to live in paradise; *Mag Mell*, a generic fairyland often cited in the myths, which may have been an island southwest of Ireland; *Roca Barraidh*, another mystical, enchanted, otherworldly island; *Tír fo Thuinn*, a submerged city under the sea where the Tuatha Dé are said to have fled in some legends; *Tír nam Ban*, yet another mystical island inhabited by beautiful women just waiting for Irish heroes to come and visit; and *Tír nam Béo*, "The Land of the Living", a place of eternal life and another of the places where the

THE MYSTERY CREATURES GREAT & SMALL FAIRIES

Tuatha dé Danann are believed to have fled. And though the names and the geographic characteristics often differed, all of the locations for the Otherworld shared the common aspect of being in a sort of "parallel dimension" or "higher frequency" wherein perceived time moved at a different rate than it did in the normal world. As a result, those mortals who were fortunate enough to be taken to the Otherworld often found out, to their chagrin, that they could not return to visit their families on the upper world. This was because, during the few years they had spent in the Otherworld, in the upper world many centuries had passed, and their family and friends had long passed on.

Tír nan Óg, "the Land of Eternal Youth", was the most commonly used name for the Otherworld. It was so named as it was believed to be a paradise where death, and even age, have no sting. Though it is always the abode of the fairies, *Tír nan Og* shows up in different contexts throughout Irish legend. Some see it as a place where the righteous dead go to live with the fairies in splendor, forever. Others have seen it as a place where victorious heroes go after death, where they continue to battle on gloriously, fighting, dying, and rising to fight again amidst scenes of luxury and splendor. Still others see it as an underwater kingdom that mirrors the world on the land, gifts of aquatic sheep and cows from the gods to earthbound mortals occasionally showing up in the legends to underlie this belief. More often, the Underworld is either one, two, or all three — myth, being in its very nature indistinct and subject to imaginative interpretation. The variant myth of *Hy-Brasil* has *Tír nan Óg* located far out in the Atlantic Ocean, where it occasionally rises, Atlantis-like, with tinkling bells to entice the adventurous to their doom. This myth may be a form of apocalyptic harbinger, where it was believed that the Underworld will rise again at the time of the end, and the two worlds, the upper world and the Underworld, will once again become one, to the ruin of us all.

THE ORIGINS OF THE *SÍDHE*

The term *sídhe* has an interesting pedigree, a study of which may shed some light — or darkness — upon our understanding of the religious

THE MYSTERY
CREATURES
GREAT & SMALL
FAIRIES

beliefs of the ancient Celts. As we have seen, all of the invaders save the Cessair were the descendants of Magog, most of whose descendants had settled in

Central Asia. There, the sons of Magog eventually became known as the "Scythians", a nomadic people who emigrated to Ireland (and other places) in several waves, as described in the *Lebor Gabala Èireann*. It may be that the term *sídhe* was derived from the word *scyth*, "sith", though in ancient times the name "Scythian" was also pronounced "skit-yai" or "scoti", leading some to believe that the general designation of all of the inhabitants of Ireland and Scotland as "Scots" may indicate Scythian origins.

Another explanation for the origin of the name *sídhe* may be *seid*, a form of shamanism commonly practiced by ancient, pre-Christian Celtic cultures, better known today as Wicca, or "witchcraft". In fact, both may be right, as the ancient Scythians were indeed known for their shamanic practices. The *fili* or poets of ancient Ireland were sometimes also known for practicing divination while wearing cloaks of bird feathers, the same way that Central Asian shamans communed with the spirits. Altogether, it is highly probable that the belief in the *sídhe*, or "fairies", was part of a very ancient pagan religious tradition that the Scythian ancestors of the ancient Irish had brought with them when they emigrated to Ireland from Central Asia.

THE REVENGE OF THE *SÍDHE*

The *sídhe* have also made their mark on popular culture, the most obvious being George Lucas' *Star Wars* films, where they appeared as the "Midichlorians", a symbiotic, sub-microscopic race believed to live in all things. This name is based no doubt upon "mitochondria", a scientific term designating that part of the cell that is responsible for producing energy. In this powerful modern myth, these tiny but formidable powers lay behind the mystical, all-pervading "Force" of the *Star Wars* mythos, in which the "Jedi" (a technologically savvy form of warrior wizard not unlike the wizard Cú Roi in abilities) were able to harness the power of "The Light Side" of the Force in order to help them maintain the balance of order and light in the galaxy.

However, just as there were good and evil fairies, there were also good and evil Jedi. Lucas, staying true to tradition, even went so far as to actually use the word *sídhe* to describe the practitioners of "The Dark Side of the

THE MYSTERY
CREATURES
GREAT & SMALL
FAIRIES

Force", naming them "The Sith" — those Jedi who used The Force to kill and enslave, rather than to help and heal. In this dualistic view of the universe, the Jedi and the Sith both drew upon the power of the supernatural, "fairy" realm in order to gain for themselves extraordinary powers. As a result, they got involved in the ongoing battle between the forces of light and of darkness that is taking place in the spiritual world behind the scenes — the Jedi following the light *seid*, and the Sith, the dark *seid*. However, though there are some superficial similarities, the "theology" presented in the *Star Wars* movies is not like the battle between the forces of God and of Satan — as it is understood in Christian theology — but between two different types of fallen spirits — one civilized, one savage. In that sense, the light side and the dark side are merely two sides of the same fallen coin.

At the time of the end, when the two worlds become one, some believe that the ancient battle between these spirits of light and darkness will break out upon the face of the Earth, with apocalyptic consequences for mankind. And when the war of the spirits of light and dark, of civilization and savagery, breaks forth upon the face of the Earth, it will do so because mankind has failed to properly respect God, nature and the *sídhe*, the spirits to whom God had, in ancient times, delegated the authority to oversee nature. It is at that time that the Ghost Riders of the *Sídhe* will come forth to take revenge upon the upper world — as described in Revelation 9 — to take payment from mankind for failing to live in harmony with God, nature, and their fellow men.

TERMS AND DEFINITIONS:

The fairy world is often seen interacting with the world of humanity in the myths, leaving behind an array of terms that have integrated themselves into everyday thought and language throughout Ireland. Here is a list of some of the most prominent terms, with their definitions:

⚜ Fairy Cat

Also known as *Cat Sith*, the fairy cat is as large as a dog and black in color, with a light spot on its breast. It is believed that these cats are actually transformed witches or fairies, traveling in disguise in order to spy on or protect someone, sneak in somewhere, or gather information.

⚜ Fairy Dart

The term *gáe sídhe*, or "fairy dart" is usually used to describe flint arrowheads that are sometimes found near mounds, raths, and various megalithic monuments that were built in prehistoric times. The term is also sometimes used to describe unexplained aches and pains, particularly the swelling of joints, feet and/or hands, that are believed by the superstitious to have been caused by spiritual "darts" or curses shot at them by malevolent fairies.

⚜ Fairy Dog

Also known as *Cú Sith*, the fairy dog is usually huge, the size of a cow. Its dark coat is usually either black or dark green and marked with white rings around the neck. Huge and vicious, this spirit animal is said to roam all around Ireland, particularly in County Galway.

⚜ Fairy Fire

Teine sídhe, "fairy fire", is common to bogs, marshlands, raths and other dark and mysterious places believed to be haunted by the fairy folk. Fairy fire, also known as *Teinne Sionniic* ("fox fire"), *Liam na Lasoige* ("William with the Little Flame") or "Will o' the Wisp" (in English folktales), is believed to be the manifestation of the spirits of fairies in their true form, that of a greenish-yellow ball of cool, lambent light approximately 1'–2' in diameter. These balls of light flit about just out of reach around 10 feet off of the ground and, according to legend, often purposely mislead travelers into following them into the marshlands and bogs. And though these people think that following the fairy fire will lead them to a secret fairy treasure, in reality these foolish individuals invariably come to a tragic end in the deeps of the perilous bogs. The evil fairy spirits then feed off of the

155

escaping life force of their hapless victims, and any personal wealth they had carried with them remains in the bog, adding all the more to the "fairy treasure" and making their allure all the more deadly.

Fairy fire is now believed to be what is now called *ignis fatuus*, or "false fire", that is caused by the spontaneous ignition of marsh gases — which explains why it is predominant near bogs and marshlands. Despite this, fairy fire remains a popular and celebrated folk belief worldwide.

✟ Fairy Grass

Féar Gortach, or "hungry grass", is an enchanted form of grass that curses those who tread upon it with a great hunger that cannot be sated, stealing the very life force from their bodies. Fairy grass is otherwise indistinguishable from normal grass except by those who have "the second sight".

✟ Fairy Herbs

Several types of herbs are believed, according to folklore, to be useful conduits of fairy magic. These include the dandelion, which is believed to fend off heart disease and illnesses caused by fairy curses; eyebright, a purplish flower believed to help cure diseases of the eye; foxglove — whose name means "fairy fingers" — though poisonous if swallowed, is believed to be useful externally to aid sprains, bruises and bone ailments; the yarrow, a plant with feathery leaves and pinkish-white flowers, is considered to be another powerful fairy herb, useful for healing and divination. Other herbs with links to the fairy world include ivy, plantain, polypody of oak and vervain.

✟ Fairy Lover

The *leanhaun sídhe* is a female fairy who falls in love with a mortal male and seduces him, usually with negative consequences for the man. This is because though she brings him great pleasure, and their affection for each other may be genuine, the fairy lover will drain the life force out of her hapless victim much like a vampire. In some traditions, the *leanhaun sídhe* is a kind of muse who attaches herself to artists and poets, giving them great inspiration and bursts of creativity, but burning them out quickly, her victims usually dying young, tragic deaths. Fairy lovers are believed to haunt wells and springs where poets purposely go to seek them out in order to gain inspiration.

✦ Fairy Mist

A magical mist that the fairies use to conceal themselves as they travel through forest and glen, this mist causes forgetfulness in those careless mortals who allow themselves to become engulfed in it. People so affected usually end up lost, sometimes never to return.

✦ Fairy Music

Fairies are particularly known for their sweet music, which they sometimes use to lure mortals to follow them into the Underworld in order to abduct them. Musicians were known for seeking out fairies, particularly leprechauns (*q.v.*), in order to steal a tune from them and become rich and famous. However, woe usually befell those who did, as the fairies usually took revenge for the theft of their heavenly music, the end of such musicians being much like those poets who sought out fairy lovers for inspiration.

✦ Fairy Palace

Known as a *bruig* or *bruiden*, the fairy palace was a royal residence that doubled as an doorway to the Underworld. The term *bruig* usually denotes the interior of a fairy mound, and is used in the name *Brú na Bóinne*, "the Palace of the Boyne", specifically Newgrange, which was believed to be the most important *sídhe* in Ireland. Usually fairy palaces were lavishly decorated in silver, gold, and precious gems, and were luxurious far beyond any earthly palace.

✦ Fairy Ring

The *fáinne sídhe*, or "fairy ring", is essentially what is now called a "crop circle". They are usually found in fields of crops, lawns with longish grass, or in other vegetation that is tall, pliable and regular enough to retain a coherent pattern. They may also appear as a depression in low grass, filled with sprouting mushrooms. Fairy rings are believed to be created by fairies dancing in circles, often creating unusual shapes and patterns, usually circular. If a mortal steps into the circle, they will be compelled to dance with the fairies for what seems like only a few minutes, but in actuality several years, decades or even centuries may go by unless a bystander pulls them out of the ring immediately.

THE MYSTERY
CREATURES
GREAT & SMALL
FAIRIES

✝ Fairy Sleep

Fairy sleep is an enchanted slumber, usually the result of a spell, from which one cannot awake until a certain predetermined time or event (such as a kiss by a handsome prince).

✝ Fairy Stroke

A fairy stroke is a sudden, dramatic change in one's personality, life and/or health that was once believed to be the result of a powerful fairy curse. Explanations born of fairy superstitions had it that the fairies had abducted the one afflicted with the fairy stroke and replaced them with a simulacrum that was much different in ability and personality, much like the "changeling" phenomenon, except the stroke only affected adults. The medical term "stroke" was actually taken from this Gaelic term, which ably describes the dramatic and often unpredictable changes in personality and physical ability that real strokes can have on people.

✝ Fairy Tree

Fairy trees, or "fairy thorns" were thought to be powerful centers of fairy magic and entrances to the Underworld. Cutting one down, or even removing a branch without the permission of the fairies, could incur great wrath upon those who commit such a sacreligious act. One such tree is the fairy tree of Clare in Munster province (q.v.) that is still believed by some to be the gathering place for the Munster fairies before they go to war with the Connaught fairies. Recently a great deal of money was spent to build a bypass around this fairy tree, proving that the old superstitions are still alive and kicking. Trees believed to have magical properties in descending order of power include oak, ash and thorn, followed by apple, hazel, alder, elder, holly and willow. Druids often used branches from different types of trees to create different types of magic wands, oak being the most potent.

✝ Fairy Wind

Also known as the "fairy blast", the fairy wind is a sudden gust of wind, or even a whirlwind such as a dust devil, that is believed to be caused by the fairies. The wind is believed to be caused by the passing of the fairy host, and upon seeing such a wind the superstitious usually genuflect in order to ward off the potentially destructive power of the fairies. The wind can do many things, including help (or hinder) farm work, bring illness, defend fairy treasure from would-be treasure hunters, and even silence a musician who has stolen a fairy tune.

Though the fairy host, both the solitary and the trooping fairies, are too numerous to count, several particular fairies and types of fairies stand out in Irish myth and legend. The following is a selection of the most prominent, in alphabetical order:

AILLEN, THE GREAT GREEN GOBLIN

Aillen, "The Great Green Goblin", also known as "Aillen of the Fiery Breath", was one of the most powerful and wicked of the *sídhe* who came forth from the Underworld on Samhain Eve (Halloween). Aillen's abode was in a fairy mound near Tara, probably in the region of the Boyne Valley, from whence he came forth every year to do mischief. However, unlike the rest of the fairy host, Aillen's mischief came not in the form of mere pranks and trickery, but massive destruction. When Aillen came forth from the Underworld every Samhain, he went directly to the High King's Palace at Tara, where he would proceed to play sweet music on his silver harp — music so sweet that all who heard it immediately fell into a deep, enchanted slumber from which they would not awake 'til morn. Having subdued all potential opposition, Aillen then proceeded to belch great balls of fire from his mouth, burning down the entire palace complex. This he did every year until he was slain by the magic *Spear of Len* thrown by the hero Finn McCool.

THE MYSTERY
CREATURES
GREAT & SMALL
FAIRIES

159

BANSHEE

The banshee or *bansídhe* (lit., "woman of the fairies") is not a true *sídhe*, but a type of family spirit, or "tribal angel", that in ancient times had attached itself to a particular Celtic family bloodline. Families so affected usually have names that start with either O' or Mac, though over 70 families are known to be affected. This is due to the fact that the spirits follow not the names, but the bloodlines — even overseas — as they have since ancient times.

Banshee are best known for their high, keening wail that presages the passing of a family member, a sound that has been variously described as an eldritch shriek, a blood-curdling wail and/or the sound of a woman sobbing in Gaelic, perhaps the most precise description being "a thin, high wail containing all the sorrows of the world." The sheer volume of the keening is tremendous, and has been compared to that of fighting cats, or the wailing of a vixen, but much louder and longer — far louder and longer than any mortal lungs could sustain. It also has a distinctive mournful character that only a human voice can generate. The banshee's wail can be heard day or night, in any weather, and can occur weeks, days, hours, or even minutes before the death occurs. Thorough searches have revealed no traces of a physical source, even while the wailing is ongoing. Usually the banshee positions itself near a window or in a doorway, where it proceeds to emit its bone-chilling howl. And though the listeners are usually chilled to the bone by the shrieking, if not fleeing in terror, those who hear the cry need not fear death for, as the saying goes, "Hearing the banshee guarantees your safety". This is because the one who does *not* hear the banshee cry is the one who is fated to die.

Usually banshee are invisible, but when they do make themselves visible they usually appear as either

1) a beautiful fairy woman with red hair (*roe bansídhe*) or pure, flowing white hair, or 2) as an exceedingly ugly, grey-haired old hag with glowing, red eyes set in hollow sockets peering out from beneath a grey, hooded cloak. Both kinds usually wear this grey cloak over a green dress, though they are sometimes dressed all in white. They also are sometimes reported as lively entities perched on a wall or gatepost, clapping and wringing their hands while mourning for the one who is to die. Some of the more gruesome reports describe visions of the banshee washing the severed heads and limbs of those who are about to die in a stream or river near a town just before a major battle. Banshee have even been known to appear in the form of a crow, loudly tapping three times on a window pane or sill in order to warn the family of the imminent death. It is in this form that they are closely related to the triple war goddess *badb*, whose symbol is also the crow. This association is further strengthened by the fact that banshee are referred to as *badbh* in County Waterford, *badhbh* in Counties Wexford, Kildare and Wicklow, and *badhbh chaointe* in Counties Kilkenny and Laois.

DONN FÍRINNE, KING OF THE MUNSTER FAIRIES

Donn Fírinne is the king of the fairies of Munster province, and is also believed to have been one of the six chiefs of the Tuatha dé Danann. Donn makes his home in the hill of Knockfierna, in County Limerick, where a small cave is believed to lead to his palace in the Underworld. Here, he constantly plots the overthrow of his rival Finvarra, King of the Connaught fairies (*q.v.*). Local tradition holds that Donn has power over the storm, able to gather storm clouds

THE MYSTERY
CREATURES
GREAT & SMALL
FAIRIES

around his hilltop and hold them for a while as a warning of impending rain. If the weather is bad, then Donn Fírinne is said to be in the clouds. As such, Donn may be related to "Donner", the Germanic god of thunder, who was also believed to be immanent in the power of the storm. Some believe he may have also been related to Donn, the ancient Irish god of the dead.

FINVARRA, KING OF THE CONNAUGHT FAIRIES

Finvarra is the king of the fairies of Connaught province. He makes his home in the hill of Knockmaa, in County Galway, where the remains of a ruined cairn mark the entrance to his palace in the Otherworld. There he holds court with his beautiful wife, Queen Oonagh, and plots against his rival Donn Fírinne, king of the Munster fairies. Together as king and queen, in some traditions, Finvarra and Oonagh reign over all the fairies of Ireland.

Finvarra is known for his benevolence towards humanity, and will give good harvests, purebred horses of the highest quality, and great riches to those humans who ally themselves with his cause. Finvarra's light side has a dark side however (as all fairies do), as he has a tendency to carry off any beautiful young woman who strikes his fancy to his Otherworld palace, where she will become one of his many wives. In "The Wooing of Étain" (*q.v.*), Finvarra even attempted to kidnap Étain herself, but after agreeing to return her, Finvarra became a guardian spirit for her family forever after.

Finvarra is extremely good at games, particularly hurling (a form of field hockey), chess, and games of chance. Many a foolish mortal has lost everything when gambling with Finvarra, who has never been beaten.

THE MYSTERY
CREATURES
GREAT & SMALL
FAIRIES

Leprechauns

The leprechaun (from the Gaelic *luchorpan*, "little body") is the most common and celebrated of all the fairy folk. The leprechaun is also known as the *lubricán*, *lubberkin*, *lochorpán*, *luchorpán* and *lupracán*, and also has region-specific names, being known as *luchramán* in Ulster, *luchragán*, *lurgadán* and *cluricán* in Munster; *lúracán* in south Leinster and Connaught, and *liomreachán* in east Leinster. Leprechauns also share similarities with the grogochs, pechts, brownies, dwarves, gnomes and other semi-human fairy creatures that infest Irish, Celtic and Norse folklore.

The leprechaun, a classic example of a solitary fairy, is often called "the fairy shoemaker" because in the folktales they are often discovered by the gentle tapping noise they make with the tiny hammers they use to make their tiny shoes. The one who discovers their hiding place usually finds only a few tiny tools and the tiny shoe that the leprechaun had been working on just before their discovery, however, as leprechauns usually manage to escape just in time before being spotted. But if one is "lucky" enough to actually spot a leprechaun, he can be forced to reveal the location of his treasure, which usually consists of not only the stereotypical "pot o' gold", but may also contain all kinds of ancient, magical items of great power and worth that the leprechaun has managed to acquire (steal) over the centuries. More likely than not, however, the leprechaun will find a clever way to

THE MYSTERY CREATURES GREAT & SMALL FAIRIES

keep the would-be treasure hunter from finding his treasure, usually doing so in a manner that makes them look foolish.

Sometimes leprechauns, particularly the type known as the "cluricaun", live inside people's houses and look after things while the owner is out, often making little repairs and, if they like the owner, even leaving behind small gifts or doing them special favors. The cluricaun particularly likes to haunt wine cellars and, though perpetually drunk as a result, will do the owners a favor in return by keeping the place clean and making sure that all the corks in the wine casks are set in tight. However, if the leprechaun or cluricaun does not like someone, or feels that they have been disrespected in even the slightest way, they may play pranks on them and commit random acts of destruction, such as curdling the milk, leaving the windows open overnight during the winter, and perhaps even setting small fires for their own amusement. For this reason it was once common for homeowners to leave out small gifts for the leprechauns, such as bowls of milk, cheese, or other natural foods (leprechauns won't eat processed foods) twists of tobacco, shots of liquor or other small gifts to keep them placated. And for good reason, as some tales have leprechauns doing some very bad things to people they don't like, up to and including abducting unbaptized human babies and replacing them with fairy changelings. After abducting a child, the leprechaun is believed to then transform into a dust devil and carry them off to the Underworld. Thus there arose the Irish tradition of genuflecting and saying "God bless me!" whenever a dust devil passes by, or throwing one's left shoe at it, because if one does that, it is said that the leprechaun will drop the baby or whatever else it is carrying, possibly even its treasure!

Despite this, most leprechauns are relativelely harmless, except for one type known as the *fir darrig*, or "red man", who lives only to torment humans. He appears in various different guises throughout Ireland, but he most often appears as a huge man with flaming red hair dressed all in red who delights in playing pranks and invoking evil hallucinations so as to entrap and enslave the unwary.

The Truth about the Leprechaun

The stereotypical image of the leprechaun is that of a jolly little man with a *shillelagh* capering about in a little green suit and high hat set with a gold buckle. In recent decades, popular interest in the leprechaun has grown significantly outside of Ireland proper, due largely to the influence of movies and television commercials where the leprechaun has been transformed into either a perpetually jovial, almost hyperactive character or a vicious, horrible mass murderer. The truth about the leprechaun, however, is that he is neither particularly jovial nor particularly violent, but has much more in common with a typical vagrant, usually being portrayed in the folktales as a solitary, sullen, unkempt character dressed in soiled clothing, smoking a pipe filled with whatever vile weeds he can dig up, and perpetually drunk on *potchín* ("potch-een"), a horrid brew distilled from whatever rotten old vegetables he can get his grubby little hands on. Leprechauns typically live in ramshackle huts in bogs made up of blocks of peat, or in mounds, raths, standing stones, caves or abandoned buildings where they while away the hours smoking, dancing, playing music, telling tall tales and drinking *potchín*.

Origins of the Leprechaun

One theory has it that leprechauns are the cast-off male offspring of fairies, some of whom turn out to be not stately and beautiful, as is the fairy ideal, but squat and ugly, and so are abandoned at birth to fend for themselves. (Female fairies are always born beautiful, accounting for why there are never any female leprechauns.) Another theory is that they are the offspring of unions between human men and fairy women, not able to fit into either world and thus forced to live between the worlds, not quite human and not quite fairy. This, and the fact that they tend to be larger than standard fairies and smaller than humans, may justify the use of the term "halfling" as another way to describe the leprechaun. As such, the leprechaun might be seen as forming a bridge between the world of humanity and the realm of the fairy in the myths and legends of ancient Ireland.

THE MYSTERY
CREATURES
GREAT & SMALL
FAIRIES

Mythical Beasts
ABC's (Alien Big Cats)

Alien big cats (ABCs) are basically large, wild cats that have been sighted in areas of the world where large, wild cats are otherwise unknown, such as Ireland. The most commonly sighted type of alien big cat in Ireland has been described as approximately twice the size of a feral cat (a normal-sized house cat that has been born in the wild), and are distinguished by their relatively short, thick, bushy tails that are banded like that of an American raccoon. Some have suggested that these large cats are the result of crossbreeding between big cats such as puma and lynx that have been lost or purposely released into the wild by irresponsible collectors, and large feral cats. Others believe that they might be sightings of the Irish version of the Scottish wildcat, a rare but documented large cat that lives in the Scottish highlands that matches many of the descriptions of the alien big cats reported in Ireland.

Ancient Irish legends also refer to Irusán, "The King of the Cats", who is described as being the size of an ox. Irusán lived in a huge cave in the mountains of Knowth, from where he regularly went forth and terrorized the countryside. According to the legend, Irusán had heard of how the poet Senchán Torpéist (*op. cit.*) had composed a satire making fun of cats, and came forth to take revenge against him. He caught Senchán, threw him upon his back, and then took him on a terrifying ride across the country before finishing him off. However, Senchán was saved from certain doom by Saint Ciarán, who killed Irusán by throwing a red-hot poker at him, thus saving the poet and forever ending the monster's predations.

THE MYSTERY
CREATURES
GREAT & SMALL
MYTHICAL BEASTS

Barnacle Goose

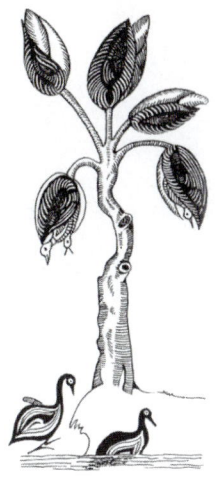

The Barnacle Goose is a real type of goose whose name comes from an ancient folktale. At one time it was widely believed that Barnacle Geese actually hatched from barnacles that can be found on ships' hulls, or on trees that are rooted near the sea shore. When they hatched, they immediately flew off or swam in the water, but if they landed on dry land, they would perish. So prevalent was this belief that Irish Catholics would eat Barnacle Goose on Lent, claiming that it was allowed because it was actually a form of fish! Barnacle Geese are also referred to as Bernicles, Barhatas, Clacuse and Clarkgeese.

Bledlochtana

Bledlochtana is a generic Gaelic term for "monster" that was first mentioned in the story, "The Battle of Moy Tura". On the fourth day of the battle, the *Bledlochtana* are said to have cried out so loud that their voices could be heard all over the world. It was once believed that the *Bledlochtana* rise every year on the anniversary of the battle and howl in commemoration for the many lives that were lost.

Bocanách

The Bocanách is a giant, evil, dark, supernatural goatlike being that stalks lonely roads late at night and waylays travelers. It is said that during the battle between Cú Chulainn and Ferdiad in *The Táin*, Bocanách flew around and shrieked in the air, indicating that they are actually a type of demon that sometimes takes corporeal form.

Cornu

Also known as the "Corra", the Cornu is a demon that St. Patrick turned into a monstrous black bird, banishing the beast to haunt St. Patrick's Purgatory in Lough Derg, in County Donegal. See also "Caoránach" (p. 179).

"Jormangund", © Bob Eggleton

DRAGONS

Dragon are the most popular and easily recognized mythical creatures in the world. In the West, the dragon is seen as an apocalyptic harbinger of evil, in appearance usually portrayed as a gigantic, lizardlike creature with huge, batlike wings, powerful claws, a venomous bite, and fiery breath. The original Greek word from which the term "dragon" was derived was *drakon*, which means "to protect", or "to guard". This is because dragons are often portrayed in the myths as guarding a fabulous treasure, of which they are very jealous and will go to almost any length to protect. Dragons are also to be distinguished from sea serpents which, though essentially the same as land dragons, usually live in the sea, large lakes or sometimes rivers.

Unlike the benevolent guardian dragon that is the symbol of Wales, Irish dragons are seen as thoroughly evil and destructive creatures who must be slain in order to restore peace to the land. Dragons in Irish mythology are less prominent than they are in English or Welsh literature, but they still make appearances in the myths. For example, in the tale *Táin Bó Fraích* ("The Cattle Raid of Fráech"), the hero Fráech is portrayed as slaying a dragon. Another myth in the Ulster Cycle has a dragon swallowing Dáire, a son of Finn McCool, though Dáire later escapes unharmed.

Dragons are also prominent in legends during the Christian Era, various saints coming into opposition with them on several occasions. One of the more famous legends of the dragon is of "St. Attracta's Monster", also known as *An Cathach* ("The Battler"), a dragon with a large, rounded body, a whale-like tail, iron talons that made sparks when it moved, a horselike mane and a single huge eye. This fearsome, fire-breathing monster lived on the island of Inis Cathaig (Scattery Island) in the Shannon Estuary south of Kilrush, County Clare, but it was banished in the 6th century by a bishop named St. Senan, who founded a monastery on the island after the beast was driven off. The dragon was later named for St. Attracta, who founded a safehouse nearby some time later.

Most fearsome of the dragons of Irish myth was the Dragon of the Apocalypse. The Dragon of the Apocalypse was an ancient beast unique to the folklore of Ireland that was believed to be part serpent, part salmon. And though it made its home in the murky depths of *Loch-Bél-Dracon*, "The Lake of the Dragon's Mouth", near Sídhe Uamain in Connaught province, it is believed that the Dragon of the Apocalypse will arise from the depths to signal the Day of Judgment and the Second Coming of Christ. The Dragon, it is believed, will judge Ireland for the death of John the Baptist by rising on St. John's Day (June 24th) during the time of the apocalypse, and lay waste to the land.

FACHAN

The Fachan are a type of troll similar to the Fomorians that fought with the Partholónians. They had one hand protruding from their chest, one leg, one eye, and one tuft of hair on their hideous heads, the whole covered with matted feathers. They inhabited lonely moors and desolate places and were very hostile to humans, who greatly feared them.

GABORCHEND

The Gaborchend were a race of humanoid monsters distinguished by the black fur on their bodies and their doglike heads, earning them the title, *Cynocephali* (lit., "dog-headed"). They were believed to be the earliest inhabitants of Ireland though, like the Fomorians and Fachan, they were considered to be a form of parasitic infestation and were destroyed by the various waves of Magogian invaders.

THE MYSTERY
CREATURES
GREAT & SMALL
MYTHICAL BEASTS

GRUAGACH

The Gruagach were a large-headed, soft, almost shapeless hairy ogre of Northern Ireland and Scotland that appear to have been aboriginal inhabitants of the isles that were defeated and driven to the fringes of society. For this reason they are sometime classed as a form of solitary fairy.

POOKA

The pooka was quite literally the Irish Nightmare, both in the sense of being like a bad dream, and because it had much in common with the Nightmare hell-horse that abounds in legend around the world. The pooka lived in solitary hills and mountains, old ruins and desolate places, but occasionally came forth from its lair in order to search for victims to first torment, and then devour. And though the pooka was actually a shape-shifter, able to take just about any form it chose in order to attract its prey, such as a goat, a bull or an eagle, it usually took the form of a tall, dark, magnificent steed dragging chains behind it as if it had escaped from hell itself.

This diabolical creature took great delight in its hunt for unsuspecting victims, and particularly favored children, for they are the most easily terrified, and the pooka loved most to feast on fear. The pooka hunted by offering someone a ride on its back or, if they refused, it would simply grab them with its powerful jaws and throw them on its back. There its powerful magic kept them irresistibly bound, and they were taken on a wild ride around the countryside that inevitably ended with the pooka either hurling itself off a cliff, or diving deep into a lake. It then horribly devoured its victim, both body and soul.

Though usually a terrifying creature, the pooka could be tamed and, to some extent, integrated into the community. One tale has a pooka actually working as a tame horse for a farmer, who had tricked him into servitude. Another tale describes another pooka that dwelt on a hill in Leinster that came forth on Samhain (November 1) every year to sit as an oracle, answering prophetic questions that people asked of him regarding their fate in the coming year. This continued until the coming of Patrick, who finally broke and brought to heel the power of the *sídhe*.

Pooka are equally at home on land or in the water, and most often frequent desolate places that are are nearby large, deep bodies of water.

TORC TRIATH, "THE KING OF THE BOARS"

Torc Triath was the first and greatest of all the boars of Ireland, having been brought to Ireland by Brigid the poetess, the daughter of the Dagda. Torc Triath is essentially a huge wild boar (5' at the shoulder) with massive, 12" long tusks and a nasty disposition. He gets along well enough with humans, however, as long as they stay out of his way.

In Welsh legends, Torc Triath (known in Wales as *Turch Trwyth*), was originally a king who had been turned into a huge boar as punishment for his wickedness. He had several sons, the two most prominent named Grugyn Silver Bristles and Llywdawg the Hewer. However, his transformation only further enabled his ability to do wickedness, as together with his sons he proceeded to lead an entire tribe of gigantic boars to ravage the whole of Ireland. Later they were driven out of Ireland by King Arthur and his knights, but they thwarted Arthur's plans by swimming across the Irish Sea to Wales, where they began the destruction anew. But Arthur and his knights caught up to them and, after a series of battles, managed to kill or drive off all of Twrch Trwyth's evil brood.

THE MYSTERY
CREATURES
GREAT & SMALL
MYTHICAL BEASTS

THE WILD HUNT

The Wild Hunt, also known as The Phantom Pack, The Hounds of Hell, The Irish Hounds and more generally as the *Coinn Iotair* ("Hounds of Rage"), was a pack of spectral hell hounds that occasionally appeared to ravage the Irish countryside. They appeared only when there was great evil in the land, such as the rule of an evil king, a great crime or injustice, a general disrespect for God/the gods (such as a failure to pray or make proper sacrifices) the worship of an evil deity, and so forth. The number of hounds that appeared and the amount of destruction that they caused was dependent upon the level of evil that had been done in the land.

The pack appeared as a group of huge, powerfully built hounds (4' at the shoulder) with flickering green eyes and green tongues of flame that proceeded from their cruelly fanged maws. Their bodies were jet black, ringed with a green glow, and were partly transparent, belying their spectral nature. They appeared to move as normal dogs, but as they were spiritual in nature they could move equally well over or through any medium, at any rate they wished. The most prominent (and most evil) hound of the pack was named *Saidthe Suaraigh*, ("Bitch of Evil"). It is she of all the pack who most relished collecting the souls of the damned and dragging them down to hell.

The pack was led by a dark master who some believe to have been Crom Dubh, a legendary pagan chieftain of pre-Christian Ireland whose power was later broken by St. Patrick himself. The master was known as "The Master of the Wild Hunt", appearing as a 7-foot-tall, powerfully built warrior carrying a huge, magical black spear. Like his pack he also had glowing green eyes, but he was dressed in jet black leather armor, and wore a helm crowned with the antlers of a mighty stag. Like his pack he was also a spectre, and appeared outlined in the same eerie green glow that outlined the pack.

The Master of the Wild Hunt directed the hounds to hunt down and destroy the source of evil in the land that was disrupting the natural order. The essential purpose of the pack was as "the avengers of the gods", collecting on the spiritual debt that had accumulated in the land as a result of the transgressions against the natural order, finding and devouring the transgressors and dragging their souls down to hell as repayment. The intent of the master was not to cause random chaos, but only to destroy the source of evil and restore the balance, and to achieve this end the Master would direct the pack to terrorize the people into turning away from their evil or, failing that, destroy the evil at its source. If this source was too powerful to kill directly, such as a wicked king or a powerful evil wizard, the Master would cause The Wild Hunt to continue to appear night after night until the fearful and superstitious peasantry sought out and overthrew the source of evil that was causing the pack to appear. Or, the Master might instead have the pack appear in the dreams of the powerful man (or woman) until they stopped their evil behavior. The power of the Master was irresistible, and once he selected his target, only a pardon from the divine realm could save the transgressor from certain doom.

The Wild Hunt might also appear during times of great distress, such as before a battle, where they could be seen chasing the souls of the damned through the skies. In this way they were similar to the Riders of the *Sídhe* who also sometimes appear in the skies before and during major battles. A later Christian variant of The Wild Hunt called The Hounds of Heaven had the hounds not dragging their victims down to hell, but howling with a bell-like sound that had the effect of bringing all who heard it to repentance.

THE MYSTERY
CREATURES
GREAT & SMALL
MYTHICAL BEASTS

Sea Monsters

Though mankind has mapped the entire surface of the Earth, and has even charted the depths of space millions of light years away, we have yet to fully explore the vast and mysterious world beneath the sea. And though in this watery Underworld the Irish imagination saw numerous creatures both fair and foul, the type of sea monster that most gripped the Celtic imagination were the mysterious sea serpents.

"Sea Serpent", © Bob Eggleton

SEA SERPENTS

Sea serpents are among the most common mythical creatures to be found in the myths and legends of the world, and Ireland is no exception. In fact, due to the large amount of lakes, rivers and shoreline, legends and sightings of sea serpents far exceed those of dragons. However, in Ireland the line between sea serpent and dragon is not at all clear, almost seeming at times to be a mere formality as both beasts, whether of sea or of land, typically are extremely greedy, ill-tempered and ruthless, concerned only about guarding their vast treasure hoards, or acquiring their next meal.

Sea serpents in appearance are basically like dragons, except they usually have smaller legs and claws, or flippers. Some types have no claws or flippers at all, being more like a giant sea snake with an attitude, moving through the water with a unique vertical undulating movement that is otherwise unknown in the animal kingdom. Sea serpents have actually been known to attack and sink even large ships, wrapping their bodies around the whole of the ship like a boa constrictor and dragging both ship and crew down to Davy Jones' locker for a quick meal, perhaps saving a bit for a snack later on.

Though sightings of sea serpents have been common in the seas around Ireland, most of the stories are actually about lake monsters, also known as "water horses", smaller versions of the mysterious sea serpents that inhabit freshwater lakes and rivers. Both, however, are equally ill tempered and, if they happen to be in a particularly foul mood, insulting. Here is a listing of the most commonly known sea serpents and lake monsters to be found around Ireland:

✝ Lig na Baste

The Lig na Baste was a sea serpent that was believed to once live in the caves off of Ballintoy Harbor in Country Antrim, Ulster province. According to the legend, the inhabitants of the harbor in ancient times were extremely wicked and disrespectful to God. As a result, He let loose a great serpent that routinely attacked and destroyed local shipping until they finally repented. The creature reappeared in the 1500s and started to wreak havoc with shipping once more, reaffirming this ancient legend.

✝ The Monster of Lough Ree

The Monster of Lough Ree in County Longford also has an interesting history, stretching back into early Irish myth. The first recorded sighting of the monster was in a book called *The Life of St. Mochua of Balla*, wherein is described an account of how a group of hunters had refused to follow a stag into the middle of the lake on account of the horrible monster that lived there. After a while, one of the hunters dared to swim out to the island, but on the way back, he was horribly devoured by the creature.

Information on the monster after that point is sketchy until another prominent sighting in the 20th century, on May 28, 1960, by three Catholic priests who were out fishing. Suddenly, they saw a strange beast with a 2-foot-long serpentine head raised 1½ feet out of the water, propelling itself in a vertical, undulating motion. Most of its body, except the head, part of the neck, and one looping coil of its body, remained under the water, so the precise size of the beast could not be measured.

THE MYSTERY
CREATURES
GREAT & SMALL
SEA MONSTERS

After these respected priests had brought forth their story, several other witnesses also brought forward sightings of the mysterious creature. In one instance two men recalled how they had once seen what they thought was a calf swimming in the lake, but when they went to save it, it immediately submerged. After they thought about it, they realized that calves did not swim with their noses pointed up at an angle, and realized that they had just sighted the monster. A cabin cruiser also reported hitting a "snag" in the middle of the Shannon River (which runs into

"Guardian of the Ruins", © Bob Eggleton

Lough Ree), but subsequent dredging revealed nothing, indicating that they had actually hit a large creature. Several other fishermen also came up with various reports of snagging something absolutely huge on their lines which was literally able to tow their boats around the lake before they were forced to cut their lines, some of which were the strongest available on the market. One fisherman who was using a net actually caught something so big that it left a nine-foot hole in the net.

In 2001 a three-man team from GUST (Global Underwater Search Team, http://user.bahnhof.se/~wizard/GUSTeng03/) underwent an expedition to locate the monster using visual surveillance and hydrophone equipment. They received some promising results, particularly one sighting of what they described as a dark, tube-shaped object swimming away from the island, propelled by something below the surface. Ancient legends also tell of a mysterious sunken city beneath the lake whose inhabitants were so wicked that the gods destroyed them. Could it be that the Monster of Lough Ree is guarding an ancient secret at the bottom of the lake?

✦ Muirdris

The Muirdris was a lake monster that was believed to haunt Lough Rudraige, in County Down. Fergus Mac Léti, a mythical king of Ulster, is said to have encountered the Muirdris one day while swimming, describing its motion as being like the expanding and contracting of a bellows. The sight of the monster was so fearsome that Fergus' mouth actually turned to the back of his head, and he immediately fled for the shore. Because of this deformity Fergus lost his kingship, and in revenge he returned to the lake and slew the monster. The battle took two days, and at the end of the battle, Fergus reemerged from the water and died from exhaustion.

✦ Olliphéist

The Olliphéist, literally, "great fabulous beast", was a dragonlike lake monster that was so huge that as it traveled, it carved a huge gouge out of the land that later became the Shannon River. When St. Patrick came to drive the Olliphéist from the land, the beast became so enraged that it swallowed a drunken piper whole. The piper was so drunk, however, that he did not realize that he had been eaten, and continued to play in the beast's belly. This so annoyed the Olliphéist that it spewed out the piper, who continued to go on playing as if nothing had happened.

✦ Píast

The *Píast*, (lit., "the Beast") also known as the *Biast* or the *Péiste*, was a huge, dragon-like sea serpent that had the aspects of both a classical dragon (*op. cit.*) and a monstrous fish. It is described as having a long, sinuous, reptilian body, four partially finned feet with large, protruding claws and a long, looping tail ending with either a fish tail or a poisonous barb (or both), the whole covered with fishlike scales. The head of this vile beast is particularly repellent, being on the end of a longish neck, with horns and a hideously humanlike face sporting red eyes and huge tusks. It is also reported to be able to breathe fire in some legends, and particularly enjoys feasting on human flesh.

One legend of the Píast has it terrorizing and even devouring some of the monks at Glendalough Monastery at Glendalough Lake, County Wicklow. This Píast, like all serpents of both land and water, was driven out eventually by St. Patrick, but it is said that the Píast and its horrid brood will return at the time of the end and ravage the countryside once more. It is for this reason that the Píast is often associated with the legendary "Dragon of the Apocalypse" (*op. cit.*) Interestingly, the Píast may be the same creature as the mysterious "Piasa" creature of North America. An image of the Piasa that is very similar in description to the Píast was painted in ancient times on the bluffs overlooking the Mississippi River near Alton, Illinois, the origin of which is uncertain. Could this have been a mark left behind by St. Brendan on his famous journey to the West, depicting the furthest extent of his travels? Or perhaps Brendan was designating America as the land of the dragon, the "apocalyptic beast" of the end times, with which the Píast is closely associated? For more on the mysterious Piasa creature visit http://www.mysteriousworld.com/Journal/2006/Spring/SpecialUpdate/

The Connemara region in County Galway, Connaught province is known for its numerous sightings of "water horses", a common term for serpentlike lake monsters, and would be an excellent place to start for would-be monster hunters. For more information about the mysterious sea serpents, start at the first in our series of articles at http://www.mysteriousworld.com/Journal/2002/Spring/SeaSerpents/

THE MYSTERY
CREATURES
GREAT & SMALL
SEA MONSTERS

CAORÁNACH

The Caoránach, also known as the Keeronagh, was a female, demonic monster that haunted County Donegal during the time of St. Patrick. Not much is known of this mysterious creature, save that it was a terrifying, devilish creature that filled the countryside with its equally devilish offspring. She was finally driven off by St. Patrick and banished to the bottom of Lough Derg, which it still haunts to this day.

DOBHAR CHÚ

The Dobhar Chú is a mysterious water creature, also known as the "Water Horse", "Horse Eel", "Irish Crocodile" or, most commonly, "Master Otter", that haunts the lakes of Ireland, particularly in Connaught province. It is given the latter name as it is, in appearance, essentially a huge otter with either a catlike or doglike head and vicious, sharp teeth. Typically they are reported as being slimy and very dark or black in color, and can be very long, up to twenty feet long or longer. Though they typically travel low to the ground, they can also rear themselves up to a terrifying height and use their terrible claws to slash their victims. Interestingly, one report described that, when the creature reared up to defend itself from several dogs, a large hump appeared upon its back, which might explain the prominent hump that is seen above the water during some lake monster sightings.

The Dobhar Chú appears to have an almost magical quality about it, one report stating that after they had killed one, the body would not burn or even rot after it had been left out for several weeks. Some scientists have speculated that the Dobhar Chú is actually a type of otter that has been isolated and inbred for many centuries, resulting in an unusually large, fierce, primitive form.

The creature has been known to attack and even kill people, so take precautions before you go out monster hunting. The Dobhar Chú is endemic to the west and parts of the Midlands, and there have been confirmed sightings in the city of Cartron, in County Mayo, on an overgrown ring fort at the top of the hill; Lough Mask in County Mayo; Glenade Lake in County Leitrim; Sraheens Lough, on Achill Island, off the coast of County Mayo; and Lough Brin, 10 miles west of the town of Kenmare, in County Kerry. However, sightings could occur at any isolated lake west of the Midlands.

THE MYSTERY
CREATURES
GREAT & SMALL
SEA MONSTERS

"Jasconius", © Bob Eggleton

JASCONIUS

Jasconius was the name of a giant aquatic creature that is featured in the legend, "The Voyage of St. Brendan". In the legend, the saint and his followers had gone to sail the great ocean of the West to find the Promised Land that Brendan had seen in a vision, and along the way arrived at an island whereon there was no beach sand, trees or grass. Brendan, concerned about the safety of this "island", decided to stay the night in their boat, while his followers made camp on the bare surface of the island. The next morning, the priests carried out the raw meat that they had brought with them to dry and salt it for the rest of the voyage. As soon as they built the fire, however, the island began to roll and shake, and the priests called out to God for help and ran for the boat that Brendan had wisely stayed in. As they pulled away from the island, the island began to pull away from them also. Brendan then explained that God had revealed to him in a dream that the island was actually a giant sea creature named Jasconius, the greatest of the ocean's creatures.

The description of Jasconius is that he is so huge, his total size might actually be the circumference of the earth, indicating that it may be an example of the old, universal Leviathan/Jormangund myth making an appearance in Irish legend. Bestiaries from the Middle Ages named the creature "Aspidochelone", describing it as a giant turtle on whose mossy back many sailors have mistakenly lit fires, only to be taken down with the creature, ship and all, to a watery grave. Later bestiaries, however, describe this legendary creature as a giant whale like the one that swallowed Jonah. In either case, if you go monster hunting out along the coast of Ireland, don't land on any uncharted islands. And definitely don't light any fires.

Kelpie

The Kelpie, or *Eich Uisge*, were powerful, evil sea *sídhe* who lived just off the shores of Ireland and Scotland, usually taking the form of horses, either as land horses or "merhorses". In the myths, the Kelpie abducted people and took them either

"Merhorse", © Bob Eggleton

to their Underworld palace to be their slaves or, in the worst cases, devour them. One way they would do this would be to appear as a beautiful white horse, whose appearance begged to be ridden. Once the victim was on their back, however, the Kelpie would take off, gallop from the land onto the water, and then descend into the water through a vast, magical whirlpool that led to their Underworld lair.

The other technique they used to entrap certain people was to appear as a very attractive person of the opposite sex who was the very embodiment of that person's romantic ideals. Then, after much charming and sweet talk, the Kelpie would shed a single tear, and ask the victim to wipe it away. If they did, the victim would become charmed by the Kelpie, and would willingly follow it to its lair to be its servant. Mortals could also willingly marry a Kelpie, but with the same result. So wicked were the Kelpie that just seeing one could be an omen of a drowning or some other maritime catastrophe.

181

MERMAIDS

Mermaids (and mermen) like the mysterious sea serpents, are one of the most common mythological figures around the world. In ancient Ireland they were referred to as the "Merrow", also known as the *Murdhuacha, Moruadh, Moruach, Muir-Gheilt, Samghuba,* or *Suire*. Merrow females appeared as typical mermaids, being beautiful, voluptous women from the waist up, and fish from the waist down. The male Merrow were ugly, however, with green hair, skin and teeth, beady, slanted eyes and a pointed, red nose.

"Mermaid",
© Bob Eggleton

Merrow maids, like all other mermaids, loved to sit out on rocks and comb their beautiful hair while singing with their heavenly voices in order to tease and torment sailors into coming towards them and crashing their ships on the rocks. Merrow maids were otherwise friendly to humans, however, and were able to polymorph themselves into complete human form by using their magic, red-feathered caps in order to take on mortal lovers. And if a man wanted to keep his beautiful Merrow maid, he could hide her feathered cap and keep her as his beautiful Merrow bride. Her aquatic ancestry could be betrayed by her children, however, who could have webbed feet and hands, scaly skin, and an unnatural affinity for the water.

The Merrow might still be found along any part of the shoreline around the sacred isle, but would be most common along the coast of Connaught province. A church founded by St. Brendan the Navigator in the city of Clonfert, County Galway named Clonfert Cathedral is famous for its carving of a mermaid just inside the doorway, which is often rubbed for good luck. This may be a representation of Liban, a daughter of Éochaid and Étain, who in the myths was transformed into a mermaid. She was later given a choice of 300 more years of life, or immediate entry into heaven, and she chose heaven. In her memory, her likeness can be found carved into the architecture of many churches.

Murrisk

"Murrisk", from the Gaelic *Muir Iasc*, is a huge fish that lives along the coastline of County Mayo, near Croagh Patrick, in Connaught province. The Murrisk is deadly poisonous, and if it vomits into the water, all of the sea life anywhere near it is instantly killed. Moreover, if it breathes into the air, the fumes from its rotten breath will kill any bird that comes near it, and will infect the entire region with disease.

The Salmon of Knowledge

The Salmon of Knowledge was a special, magical form of salmon that was said to give anyone who ate it supreme wisdom. The Salmon lived in the Well of Sergais near the River Boyne, and it gained its knowledge by eating the hazel nuts that fell into the wells on the sacred hills. One could tell how many hazel nuts it had eaten (and how wise the salmon was) by counting the number of spots on its back. There are at least two important myths involving the Salmon of Knowledge, whose well is guarded by the god Nechtan. Unfortunately, the exact location of this well remains a mystery.

Suileach

The Suileach was a huge, multi-eyed lake monster that lived in Lough Swilly in County Donegal. The monster was said to have plagued the entire region until it was finally slain by St. Colmcille.

Tarbhe Uisge

The *Tarbhe Uisge*, or "Water Bull", was an evil, black water *sídhe* like the Kelpie that appeared as a huge, black bull. It had fiery nostrils that were redder than lightning, a head as black as a thundercloud, and a great bull neck that it used to crash through the waves. The Tarbhe Uisge occasionally fathered calves by normal cows that were called *Corc-chluasask*, or "split ears". It was tradition, at least on the Isle of Skye, to kill such offspring immediately, or ill luck was sure to follow.

For more information on the mysterious creatures of ancient Ireland, visit http://ireland.mysteriousworld.com/Mystery/Creatures/

THE MYSTERY
CREATURES
GREAT & SMALL
SEA MONSTERS

Folklore & Mythology

nce upon a time, settling in after a hard day's work, they gathered around the turf-fire, passing the time chatting about the day's events while keeping their fingers busy weaving, whittling, spinning and sewing. The young boys would climb up wherever they could get a good view, while the young girls crouched between the knees of their fathers and brothers, all waiting anxiously for the *seanachie*, the local lay storyteller, to begin to tell his tales. The *seanachie* would take his time, however, easing back into his chair and reddening his pipe with an ember from the fire, waiting for the muse of inspiration to stir his soul into motion.

Then, all at once the storyteller, usually a man ancient of days and saintly in habit, began to speak, weaving a tale that those in attendance may never have heard, though they might have heard him tell his tales for many years — such was the size of his repertoire. Perhaps it was a pithy, local anecdote from the recent past, an adventure tale of Finn McCool and the Fianna, or maybe, in more recent centuries, a story about St. Patrick. Whatever the tale, however, the storyteller always had his audience's complete attention from the first word to the last.

Such was the way that the oral traditions of Irish folklore and mythology were passed down for countless generations. Not only were the poets, from the Bard to the Ollam, the inheritors of the myths and legends from ancient days. These stories circulated throughout all levels of society, kept sacred word for word by simple farmers and craftsmen who made it their duty to remember the old tales from days long ago, usually ending their soliloquey with a statement along the lines of, "That is my story! If there be a lie in it, be it so! It is not I who made or invented it." Rees and Rees give an example of a classic lay storyteller of this type named Seán Ó Conaill in their book, *Celtic Heritage*:

> His family had lived in the same place for at least five generations…. He had never left his native district except on the memorable occasion when he had gone by train to the famous fair at Killorglin, and had

THE MYSTERY FOLKLORE & MYTHOLOGY

walked home again! He had never been to school, was illiterate so far as unimaginative census-officials were concerned, and he could neither speak nor understand English. But he was one of the best-read men in the unwritten literature of the people whom I have ever known, his mind a storehouse of tradition of all kinds, pithy anecdotes, and intricate hero-tales, proverbs, rimes and riddles, and other features of the rich, orally preserved lore common to all Ireland three hundred years ago. He was a conscious literary artist. He took a deep pleasure in telling his tales; his language was clear and vigorous, and had in it the stuff of literature.[1]

Stories were mainly told around the turf-fire to pass the time during the long winter nights, but only rarely during the summer, except during special occasions, such as weddings and christenings. During these times all kinds of stories were told, including rhymes, songs, riddles, folk-prayers, genealogical lore, and local traditions. However, the stories that were given the greatest pride of place were the mythological tales, fairy tales and folktales.

Mythological Tales, Fairy Tales & Folktales

The preeminent 19th-century folklorist Douglas Hyde put together the first scientific analysis of Irish folktales in 1890. In the preface to his seminal work, *Beside the Fire*, he divided the folklore of Ireland into two classes: 1) mythological and adventure tales that usually have to do with mythical or semi-mythical characters such as Lugh, Cú Chulainn, and Finn McCool, and 2) the "wonder tales", usually referred to as "fairy tales", that typically involve the realm of the *sídhe*.[2] Also in circulation, however, was a mass of stories, riddles, rhymes and related information of a more ephemeral character that does not fit clearly into Hyde's dual classification, so we will add a third category and name it "folktales". Thus, for ease of understanding, we are dividing Irish folklore into three categories: 1) mythological tales, 2) fairy tales and 3) folktales. First, let us begin our review of Irish folklore and mythology with the most important

THE MYSTERY
FOLKLORE &
MYTHOLOGY

type of folklore, the mythological tales, or "cycles". It is with these cycles, the most important of ancient Irish folklore, that we will occupy most of our time here.

MYTHOLOGICAL TALES

When the Christian monks first began transcribing and compiling the ancient mythological tales from the numerous, and often conflicting, oral traditions of the ancient poets and lay storytellers of the early Christian period in Ireland, they were faced with an enormous task. In order to help organize this vast amount of material, they compiled the body of literature that they had gathered from the whole of Ireland and divided it into four mythological "cycles", or bodies of literature that represent complete, distinct mythic traditions. These cycles were distinguished by region and by type of material, whether primarily mythological, semi-historical, or historical, and were divided as follows:

✤ **The Mythological Cycle:** Mythological stories from Ireland's prehistoric period that may have been based upon historical events;

✤ **The Ulster Cycle:** Heroic stories that are semi-historical in character, centered around Ulster and Connaught provinces;

✤ **The Fenian Cycle:** Heroic stories that are semi-historical in character, centered around Leinster and Munster provinces;

✤ **The Cycle of Kings, or Historical Cycle:** Stories centered around the kings of Ireland that are primarily historical in character, some of which also contain mythical elements.

Naturally, printing the complete cycles here would be impossible, so instead we will provide summaries of some of the most famous myths and legends, those that have had the most influence on the worldview of the ancient Irish. The rest will be published regularly on our Ireland website, http://ireland.mysteriousworld.com. We will start first with the first and most important of the cycles, the Mythological Cycle.

The Mythological Cycle

Since we have already examined much of the Mythological Cycle in the early chapters of this book, we will provide only a brief review here. The primary sources from which we have acquired our understanding of the Mythological Cycle are primarily the *Lebor Gabala Èrenn*, or "The

THE MYSTERY
FOLKLORE &
MYTHOLOGY
MYTH TALES

Book of the Invasions of Ireland" and the *Metrical Dindshenchas*, or "The Lore of Places", a book that is comprised of 176 poems that provide a very thorough catalog of the major place names in Ireland, and their significance to Irish history. There are also a number of secondary sources that have provided more details into the ancient "Invasions" period of Irish history that we have not examined yet, the most prominent of which include *Cath Maige Tuireadh*, ("The Battle of Moy Tura"), *The Dream of Aenghus*, *The Tragedy of the Children of Lir and The Wooing Of Étain*.

✦ The Battle of Moy Tura

Cath Maige Tuireadh, "The Battle of Moy Tura" expands upon the information given in the *Lebor* regarding specifically the Second Battle of Moy Tura, wherein the Tuatha dé Danann fought off the final invasion of the Fomorians. Among the details it includes are how Nuada had lost the kingship after he had lost his arm, the birth, kingship and treachery of Breas, the coming of Lugh the Il-Dana, Nuada's recovery of his throne and his preparations for war, the Dagda's tryst with the Mórrigan and her pledge to help the Tuatha Dé win the battle, the Second Battle of Moy Tura and the final battle between Lugh and Balor of the Evil Eye.

✦ The Dream of Aenghus

Aenghus Óg, the son of the Dagda, began seeing a girl in his dreams with whom he fell in love. His mother, the goddess Boann, searched all of Ireland for her but could not find her. Bodb Derg, another son of the Dagda, finally found her at a lake called *Loch Beul Draguin*, "The Lake of the Dragon's Mouth", at the Harp of Cliach. There he discovered the girl of Aenghus' dreams, chained with a golden chain around her neck, surrounded by thrice-fifty maidens bound together in pairs with chains of silver. She was named Caer Ormaith, daughter of Ethal Anbual, from *Sídhe Uaman* in Connaught province. She was a princess, and the 150 maidens were her ladies in waiting.

However, her father refused to let his daughter go, even after the Dagda appealed to his king and queen (the famous Ailill and Maeve), because there was a spell on his daughter and her handmaidens that caused them to tranform into beautiful swans every other year. Unconcerned, Aenghus went to Caer, and also transformed himself into a swan when her time came. They then flew around the lake three times, and then flew off to Aenghus' home in *Brugh na Boinne* together, singing music so sweet that all who heard it fell fast asleep for three days and three nights.

"Children Lir Enchantment", © 1990, Jim Fitzpatrick.

✦ The Tragedy of the Children of Lir

Lir was a chieftain of the Tuatha dé Danann who fell in love with King Bodb Derg's daughter, Eve. They married and she bore him four beautiful children: a girl and three boys. But tragedy struck and Eve died. Lir was heartbroken and would have died too if not for the love of his children.

The King was saddened to see Lir so unhappy and the children without a mother, so he arranged for Lir to marry his other daughter, Aoife. For a while Aoife was a loving and attentive wife and mother. But soon she became jealous of the love Lir had for his children and this jealousy consumed her.

One day, while taking the children to the king's palace Aoife stopped the chariot at Lough Derravaragh. She then sent the children into the water to bathe, but then cast a terrible spell upon them while they were in the water, turning them into swans and sentencing them to spend 300 years on the lake, 300 years on the Sea of Moyle, and then 300 years on the cold and stormy Atlantic Ocean. The spell would only end upon the ringing of a Christian bell.

When the king heard of his daughter's deed, he turned her into a demon of the air for all eternity. He then built a castle beside the lake and lived there so he and Lir could be close to the children. For the first 300 years they lived happily as swans, and people would come from miles around to hear them sing their beautiful songs, so they were never lonely.

But the years they spent on the Sea of Moyle and the Atlantic were full of hardship and loneliness. When the years had passed they heard of a holy man named St. Patrick, and sought out one of his disciples. They were taken into the church where their beautiful white feathers fell away to reveal three withered old men and a frail old lady. Patrick's disciple baptized them before they died, and as he knelt by their grave he saw four beautiful white swans flying up to heaven.

✦ The Wooing Of Étain

Mídir, one of the sons of the Dagda, was visiting his foster son Aenghus one day when he fell in love with Ètaín, the beautiful daughter of the king of Ulster. With the help of Aenghus and the Dagda, Mídir was able to take Ètaín home with him, much to the anger of Mídir's wife, who cast a spell on Ètaín and turned her into a pool of water, Ètaín later turning into a purple dragonfly. For the next thousand years she had to live her life this way, until she arrived at the house of Ètar in Ulster, where she fell into Ètar's drink and was swallowed. Ètaín stayed in Ètar's belly, becoming a baby that was born nine months later. Once again Ètaín grew to be a beautiful woman, and got married to the High King of Ireland, but Mídir re-appeared from the Otherworld and ran off with her again. The two then turned into swans and flew off to his fairy home in *Bri Léith* (Ardagh Hill).

The Ulster Cycle

Set around the beginning of the Christian era, the Ulster Cycle, also known as the "Ulaid" or "Ultonian" Cycle, is a collection of stories that centers around the legendary King Conchobar Mac Nessa of Ulster, Cú Chulainn, his greatest champion, and their immediate family, friends and enemies. Though the action is set around Emain Macha, the capitol of Ulster, in what is now County Armagh, it includes characters from both Ulster and Connaught provinces.

The stories are essentially heroic tales from a time when warfare was often decided by single combats between champions, and wealth and personal prestige were measured in cattle. The centerpiece of the Ulster Cycle, and arguably the most famous of all Irish folktales, is the *Táin Bó Cúailnge*, "The Cattle Raid of Cooley", usually referred to simply as *The Táin*. Other important stories in this cycle include "The Twins of Macha", "Bricriu's Feast", "The Destruction of Da Derga's Hostel", "The Exile of the Sons of Uisneach" (also known as "Deirdre and the Sons of Uisneach"), "The Wooing of Emer" and "The Tragic Death of Aife's only Son". And though *The Táin* is the most important of the Ulster legends, some of the stories are in chronological order, so we will start with "The Twins of Macha" as it is the story of the founding of Emain Macha, the home of Cú Chulainn and The Knights of Red Branch.

✠ The Twins of Macha

One day an Ulster nobleman named Crunnchu was sitting and tending his fire at home when a mysterious and beautiful woman suddenly entered his home, took the turf from his hands, and began tending the fire for him. Instead of leaving, however, she began to tend to his house as if she was his wife and, soon afterwards, consummated their relationship by sleeping with him. Before the mysterious beauty had entered his life, Crunnchu had been widowed for some time, and had been left to look after the house and his two children alone so, needless to say, this new development was quite a blessing.

The mysterious lady remained with him, and he learned that her name was Macha (*op. cit.*). Soon they were married and she became pregnant. As the hour of birth drew near, Crunnchu went into town where a festival of

THE MYSTERY
FOLKLORE &
MYTHOLOGY
MYTH TALES

horseracing was taking place. He got drunk and began to boast to the king that his wife could run faster than all of his horses. To his surprise, however, the king became angry and demanded that this woman be brought before him, or else he would cut off Crunnchu's head!

Macha came before the king and pleaded with him to hold off on the race until after she had given birth, but he wouldn't budge. Stunned, she turned to all the men of Ulster who were standing around gaping at her and asked, "who among you will help me? Can't you see that I'm with child?" But no one would dare to defy the king's edict. Macha then had no choice but to race the horses. To everyone's astonishment, the very pregnant Macha actually beat the king's best horses, but at the end she fell to the ground and gave birth to twins.

After having recovered her prodigious strength, she looked up in fury at all the men around her and uttered the following curse: "You men of Ulster," she said, pointing her finger around. "For nine generations, at a time when Ulster needs you to defend it, will know the pain of child birth and be rendered weak and helpless at your hour of need." And the spot where she lay when she uttered the curse became known as *Emain Macha*, or "The Twins of Macha".

⚘ The Exile of the Sons of Uisnech

The story of The Exile of the Sons of Uisnech contains events that proved to be critical in the early history of the Kingdom of Ulster, setting the stage for the events portrayed in the seminal story of the Ulster Cycle, *The Táin*. The story centers around a young woman named Deirdre, who was the daughter of Fedlimid mac Daill, the chief storyteller of the court of King Conchobar. The king asked Cathbad the Druid (*op. cit.*) to divine her future, and Cathbad predicted that she would be very beautiful, but also that her love was dangerous, as kings would go to war over her. So, Conchobar had her raised secretly, grooming her as a future wife for him once she came of age. However, as she grew up, she fell in love with Naoise, King Conchobar's nephew, and they decided to run away together to Scotland, taking along Naoise's two brothers for protection. Unfortunately, every local petty king they sought refuge with tried to kill Naoise so as to have the beautiful Deirdre, so they were forced to leave Scotland as well. They eventually ended up on a remote island together, but King Conchobar found out where they were and sent Fergus Mac Roich (*op. cit.*) to fetch them hence, promising them safe passage home and a fair hearing.

However, while they were on the way back to Emain Macha, Conchobar sent assassins to waylay them, slaying Naoise and his brothers. Conchobar then forced Deirdre to marry him. Deirdre, heartbroken and forced into a loveless marriage to a liar and a murderer, killed herself by hurling herself from a speeding chariot. Fergus, outraged not only because he had been used by Conchobar to murder fellow Knights of the Red Branch, but also because the king had failed to keep a solemn oath of safe passage, renounced his oath of loyalty and, along with Conchobar's son and heir Cormac Connloinges and 3,000 Knights of the Red Branch, transferred his loyalty to King Ailill and Queen Maeve of Connaught, King Conchobar's sworn enemies. Thus the stage was set for the most famous of all of the Irish epics, *The Táin*.

✟ The *Táin Bó Cuailgne*

The Táin is essentially the story of a contest of wills between King Ailill and Queen Maeve of Connaught, and the consequences that can occur when there is competition between the king and the queen over who is truly the ruler. The story begins with a simple argument between Ailill and Maeve over who was the richest. While engaging in this "pillow talk", they began to compare each other's properties horse for horse, cow for cow, and goat for goat, until they realized that they were exactly equal in wealth, with one important exception.

There was one exceptionally large and strong bull named *Finnbennach* ("the Whitehorned"), of which there was no match in all the herds of Connaught. Finnbennach had originally belonged to Maeve, but the proud bull had decided that he did not want the dishonor of being part of a woman's herd, so he went over to dwell in Ailill's herd instead. So great was this loss to Maeve that it was as if she had nothing at all, and she purposed to find a bull that was better than Finnbennach so her wealth would be greater than that of Ailill's.

THE MYSTERY
FOLKLORE &
MYTHOLOGY
MYTH TALES

Maeve then heard that there was indeed a bull greater than Finnbennach: *Donn Cuailnge*, "the Brown Bull of Cooley", the champion bull of Ulster. And when she realized that having the Brown Bull was the only way she could best her husband, Maeve set her heart on acquiring it at any cost. To this end she sent messengers to Dáire mac Fiachna, an underking to King Conchobar of Ulster, with the pretense that she was merely borrowing the bull, but in her heart she purposed to keep it as her own. Unfortunately her messengers, during some drunken revelry in Dáire's court, let it go that Maeve intended to take the Brown Bull by force if Dáire did not lend it to her, so Dáire wisely decided against even lending it. Hearing the bad news, the enraged Maeve then mustered the armies of Connaught in order to take the Brown Bull by force.

As Maeve approached Ulster, however, she was stopped by the teenage warrior Cú Chulainn who, at only 17 years of age, was the only thing standing between her and the Brown Bull. This was because The Curse of Macha was upon The Knights of the Red Branch, and they were feeling terrible, searing birth pangs in their bellies that kept them from fighting. Seeing the hopeless situation, Cú cleverly demanded the right of single combat at fords, as Maeve's massive armies had to cross over several rivers in order to reach Ulster. Confident that her mighty warriors could easily best this young boy, Maeve sent warrior after warrior to their doom, as the young Cú was the mightiest warrior in Ireland. Frustrated, Maeve broke the rule of single combat and instead sent several warriors at a time to take him out, but Cú's exceptional athletic skills, combined with the special warrior "feats" that he had learned from Scathach and Aife, saved him from certain death.

After Maeve's treachery, Cú decided that he did not need to abide by the rules either, so he set out on a campaign of extermination against Maeve's forces, killing hundreds of her men sniper-style with his sling until Maeve sued for parley. But the tricksy Maeve again reneged on her oath, and sent assassins to kill Cú, whom he also easily dispatched. Finally she turned Cú's own best friend, Ferdiad, against him, and Cú was forced to kill him with the *Gae Bolga*. Mórrigan the witch-goddess then attempted to seduce Cú, but he refused her, and she proceeded to curse him and attack him in many forms. While he was preoccupied,

Maeve took the long way around, ravaging the Ulster country-side and capturing the Brown Bull.

Worn down but not defeated, Cú was saved by the arrival of King Conchobar and the Knights of the Red Branch, whose pangs had finally subsided. They quickly routed Maeve's demoralized forces, but not before she had acquired the Brown Bull. Taking the bull back to her palace, Cruachan Aí in what is now County Roscommon, she set the two bulls in a ring and let them fight each other to decide which was the best. After an epic struggle of several days, the Brown Bull of Cooley finally defeated the White Bull of Connaught and tore it to pieces. The Brown Bull then returned to Ulster, but all of the chaos had caused it to go insane, and it attacked and killed its former masters, as well as hundreds of people who had come to worship the sacred bull. Eventually the Brown Bull's mighty heart burst, and it lay down and died.

At the same time, perhaps symbolically, Cú also died. He had been gradually worn down, seriously injured by Maeve's warriors, cursed by the daughters of the druid Calatin, mortally wounded by a javelin thrown by Lugaid Mac Con Roí, and then beheaded by Lugaid while strapped to his battle-pillar. Thus the wages of Maeve's sin was death — the death of thousands of warriors, the death of the greatest hero of Irish myth, and the death of the very thing that she lusted to possess.

✟ Bricriu's Feast

Bricriu's Feast is about a wealthy and powerful man of Ulster named Bricriu, who was known as "Bricriu of the Venomous Tongue" due to the fact that he greatly enjoyed telling lies and purposely causing disputes in order to amuse himself. One day he decided that the ultimate amusement would be to put on a great feast for King Conchobar himself, and all the Knights of the Red Branch. To this end, he built an exact replica of the king's palace, the House of the Red Branch in Emain Macha, near his home at Dun Rudraige, filling it with all the finest food and furnishings available.

Bricriu then invited King Conchobar and the Red Branch Knights to the great feast he had prepared. Conchobar was initially interested, but his knights, knowing Bricriu's reputation, counseled him not to go. But Bricriu threatened to cause chaos if they didn't come, including setting fathers against sons, mothers against daughters, and even causing the breasts of every woman in Ireland to strike against each other until they were destroyed! Faced with such a horrible prospect, Conchobar decided it was best to go to the feast.

As they had predicted, Bricriu then began to plot ways to set the men of Ulster against each other for his own amusement. He first decided to let the three greatest champions of Ulster, Cú Chulainn, Conall Cernach and Loeghaire Buadhach, fight over the *curadhmhír*, or "champion's portion" — the largest, choicest cuts of meat, finest drink and best position at the table — which was a great honor. They then set against each other, causing great chaos and bringing Bricriu great amusement, until they were calmed down by a wise man named Sencha Mac Ailella.

In order to cause more chaos, Bricriu then told the wives of the three champions that the first of them that entered the main hall would one day become the Queen of Ulster. At first they approached the hall modestly, but then broke into an undignified run, making so much noise that those within the hall thought they were being attacked and shut the door in their faces. Eager to help their wives win, Conall and Leoghaire tore down the pillars of the house in order to allow their wives entrance to the hall, while Cú Chulainn actually lifted up the entire house to allow his wife Emer to enter. When he let the house fall again, Bricriu and his wife were thrown out into the courtyard by the crash, falling into the mud and filth. Bricriu then chastised the men of Ulster for destroying his house, and Cú and the rest of the knights made amends by putting everything back in order.

The question of who deserved the champion's portion still had not been settled, however, so King Ailill of Connaught was called upon to settle the dispute. He decided that Cú was the champion, but Connall and Leoghaire disputed that judgment. So, they traveled to visit the famous warrior-wizard Cú Roí Mac Dáire in the southwest of Ireland. But after putting them through many trials, Cú Roí also rewarded the champion's portion to Cú Chulainn.

Still not satisfied, the three returned to Emain Macha. Suddenly, a gigantic *bachlach*, or herder-troll, entered the great hall of the Red Branch and brought forth a challenge to the three warriors. If he allowed them to cut off his head that night, they would allow him to come back and cut off their heads the following night. They agreed, and Conall cut off the giant troll's head, but the churl simply placed it right back on his shoulders. Leoghaire did the same, but the troll simply replaced it again. Then Cú Chulainn did it for a third time, and the *bachlach* picked up his head and walked off, head in hand.

The next day the troll returned to chop off their heads, as they agreed. He told Conall to lay his head down on the chopping block so he could chop it off, but he would not. The churl then told Leoghaire to lay his head down on the block, but he would not either. The *bachlach* then told Cú to lay his head down on the block, and he complied, keeping his word. The gigantic troll then lifted up his huge axe to the rafters of the ceiling and brought it down on the back of Cú's neck, but stopped short and only tapped it gently.

The troll then revealed himself to be the wizard Cú Roi in disguise, who had followed after them in order to resolve their dispute. Cú Roí then declared that Cú Chulainn was indeed the greatest champion of Ireland, saying, "Rise up, Cú Chulainn, of all the heroes of Ulster, whatever may be their daring, there is not one to compare with you in courage and in bravery and in truth. The Championship of the heroes of Ireland is yours from this out, and the Champion's Portion with it, and to your wife the first place among all the women of Ulster."[3]

⊕ The Destruction of Da Derga's Hostel

There was once a great High King of Ireland named Eochaid Feidlech. One day while out walking about his lands, he beheld a very fine elf-woman named Ètain washing herself by a well in Bri Leith. Entranced by her unequalled beauty, the king approached her, and they were soon married. In time the *sídhe* woman gave birth to a very beautiful daughter, whom they also named Ètain. King Eochaid lived out his years and died, and his daughter Ètain got married to King Cormac of Ulster.

Young Ètain, however, was childless save one daughter. The king at first wanted to divorce young Ètain and remarry in hopes of having a son, but at the elder Ètain's request, he decided to keep trying with young Ètain. However,

THE MYSTERY
FOLKLORE &
MYTHOLOGY
MYTH TALES

197

he also decided to have the daughter he had with young Ètain killed so that there would be no contest for the throne. To this end his servants took his daughter to a deep pit to throw her in, but the child smiled at them so warmly that their hearts melted, and they decided instead to take her to be raised in secret by foster parents. They chose the cowherds of Eterscel, great-grandson of Iar, king of Tara, to be her foster-parents. In order to conceal her from the king's men, however, the cowherds constructed a special wicker house for her to stay in with no door, but with a window and a skylight. There she grew up to be a great embroideress, and a very beautiful young woman.

One day some of the King of Tara's men came by the house and, looking into the window, saw therein the most beautiful maiden they had ever seen. The King told them to bring her to him to be his wife, as his wizards had prophesied that the childless king would one day have a male heir by a woman of unknown race. But before the King's men retrieved her the next day, a spirit in the form of a bird perched on her windowsill and, exiting the body of the bird, entered into the young girl. As the bird-spirit passed into the girl's body, he told her that she would bear a son from him, and that she was to name him Conaire, son of *Mess Buachalla*, which means "Conaire, son of the Cowherd's Fosterchild". He also told her that Conaire's *geas*, or taboo, would be that he was never to hunt or harm birds in any way.

Mess Buachalla then married the King of Tara, fulfilling the prophecy. They had a son, and she named him Conaire as she had been instructed. Young Conaire grew up with three foster-brothers: Fer Le, Fer Gar and Fer Rogein, three great-grandsons of Donn Desa the champion, a military man of the army from Muc-lesi. Etercel, the King of Tara, died while Conaire was still young, and a bull-feast was gathered in order to determine who would be the next king. In this ritual, a specially prepared bull was slaughtered and a feast was laid out for a specially trained druid. In the ritual, the druid ate his fill of the meat, drank a broth of the animal's juices, and then retired for the night after a special spell had been chanted over him. Whomever he dreamt of during the night, it was believed, would be the next king. In his dream, the Druid saw a man passing along a road to Tara, stark naked, with a stone and a sling.

Meanwhile, Conaire and his foster brothers had been out in their chariots playing various sports when his brothers suggested that he return to Tara in order to see whom the druid had seen in his dream. On his way he passed through Dublin, where he saw many large, white, speckled birds of many colors and great beauty. He pursued the birds, but they always stayed just a spearcast ahead of him. He chased them until his horses were exhausted, and then he chased them on foot with his sling to the sea, where he attacked them. The birds, however, were actually spirits, and they transformed into men with swords and spears and started to attack *him*. One of the birds interceded on his behalf, however: Nemglan, the king of his father's birds, as his father had actually been a bird spirit. Nemglan then told him of his *geas*, that he was not allowed to shoot at birds, which he had not known before. He then told the young Conaire to walk to Tara naked with his sling, as it had been prophesied that the next King of Tara would approach Tara in such wise. He did so, and along the way he encountered three lesser kings waiting for him with raiment, in anticipation of the prophecy, to cover his nakedness. They then took him to Tara to be crowned. There they received him with gladness, as he was both the foster-son of the previous King, and a demigod, the semi-divine son of the spirits of the air. Upon his coronation, Conaire also was given eight *geas*:

1) Thou shalt not go righthandwise round Tara and lefthandwise round Bregia.
2) The evil-beasts of Cerna must not be hunted by thee.
3) And thou shalt not go out every ninth night beyond Tara.
4) Thou shalt not sleep in a house from which firelight is manifest outside, after sunset, and in which light is manifest from without.
5) And three Reds shall not go before thee to Red's house.
6) And no plunder or rapine shall be wrought in thy reign.
7) And after sunset a company of one woman or one man shall not enter the house in which thou art.
8) And thou shalt not settle the quarrel of thy two thralls.

Conaire's reign was very bountiful and peaceful for a long time.

But in time, his three foster-brothers, angry at not having been chosen for the kingship, joined forces with the dread pirate Ingcel, and began to pillage and plunder with them. Unfortunately, the people began to get angry with Conaire for not enforcing the king's justice against the pirates and, shortly thereafter, his reign began to go downhill. It was then that Conaire began to break his *geas*, which would lead to his eventual downfall.

Conaire had become aware of a war between two of the sons of Carbre, in Thomond, and he went there to negotiate a peace between them. Unfortunately, in doing so he broke *geas* #8, "thou shalt not settle the quarrel of thy two thralls". He also stayed with each of the quarreling brothers for five nights each, ten in total, breaking *geas* #3, that said that he could not stay away from Tara longer than nine nights.

Meanwhile, because he had failed to enforce the king's justice, and worse, had broken some of his own *geas*, King Conaire's authority had begun to unravel, and all four quarters of the land were in turmoil. To avoid the chaotic areas he was forced to travel righthandwise around Tara, and lefthandwise around Bregia, breaking *geas* #1. On the way he went hunting, but a fairy mist had come up. After the mist had broken, he realized that he had been hunting the evil beasts of Cerna, breaking *geas* #2. In need of shelter, one of Conaire's servants suggested Da Derga's Hostel, in Leinster province. On the Road of Cualu, on the way to Da Derga's Hostel, however, Conaire espied three riders dressed all in red. Conaire recognized that he should not follow these men, lest he break another of his *geas*, so his son, Le Fri Flaith, offered to follow them instead. But the men always stayed exactly one spearcast ahead of the boy, so he could not catch up to them. They instead called out to him, identifying themselves as exiled Riders of the *Sídhe*, and warned him in a song that great destruction was coming nigh to the house of Conaire. Conaire then realized that he had broken *geas* #5, as not only were these three fallen elves dressed in red, but the name of the hostel they were traveling to, *Derga*, means "red".

Along the way to Da Derga's Hostel, Conaire and his men were overtaken by a giant troll named Fer Caille (*op. cit.*). He was accompanied by a giantess who was so ugly, that it was said that her lower lip reached her kneecaps. Fer Caille carried on his back a huge boar that he had plundered, breaking *geas #6* which says that no plunder would be taken during Conaire's reign. While Conaire was in the hostel, the ugly, giant hag that had accompanied Fer Caille, Cichuil, came and prophecied doom to Conaire and his host. She then insisted on entering the hostel, breaking *geas #7*.

Meanwhile the seven Maines, the sons of Queen Maeve, had foresworn allegiance to Conaire and hooked up with Ingcel the pirate. As both had been exiled from their own countries, Ingcel from England and the Maines from Ireland, they agreed to plunder each other's countries. As Ingcel's fleet approached Dublin via Howth, they espied the light from Da Derga's Hostel, and Conaire's men also espied the lights from their ships, breaking the final *geas: #4*: "Thou shalt not sleep in a house from which firelight is manifest outside, after sunset, and in which light is manifest from without." Ingcel's men then raided the hostel, and Conaire and his men were defeated after a long struggle, all of his *geas* apparently having been prophecies of what would befall him just before his death.

Like Cú Chulainn, then, Conaire appears to have been blessed with a short but glorious life, and Ireland was, for a time, the better of it. But when his time of glory was over, it was *really* over, and the ending thereof was catastrophic. Such is the way of the fairies.

✦ The Wooing of Emer

Cú Chulainn was a man of exceptional skill and beauty, and the men of Ulster wanted him to have a wife so that his unmarried state might not be the occasion of sin with their wives. To this end they looked far and wide over the island in search of a suitable wife for him, but they could find none that pleased him more than a woman he had once seen from afar — Emer, the daughter of Forgall the Wily, who lived in Lusk in what is now County Dublin. Cú Chulainn went to Forgall to ask for Emer's hand in marriage, but he told Cú that he was too young and inexperienced to have his daughter. He suggested that Cú go to train in Alba (Scotland) with Domnall the Soldierly, and then he would be worthy of her. Domnall suggested that there was someone even better to train him, namely Scathach, who lived "eastward of Alba". After some interesting experiences there with Scathach, her daughter Uathach, and Aife, their rival, Cú Chulainn returned to Forgall to claim Emer as his wife. Forgall did not keep his word however, so Cú, enraged, manifested the *ríastrad* and performed his "salmon-leap" feat, clearing three ramparts and landing on the inside of the dun. He then killed 24 men with three blows and Forgall, seeing his doom, leapt from the rampart, dying from the fall. Cú then took Emer and her foster-sister and, along with two loads of gold and silver, leapt back across the ramparts and returned home with the booty.

✤ The Tragic Death of Aife's only Son

During his time training "east of Alba", Cú Chulainn had an affair with Aife, one of his teachers. Some time later, she gave birth to a son, named him Connla, and trained him in all the martial arts. Cú also left Aife his thumb ring as a sign that the boy was his son, so that no one would kill him accidentally. Later, when Connla was grown, he traveled to Ireland, presumably to meet his father.

When he landed, he was met by the Knights of the Red Branch who, along with Cú, were concerned about the unannounced approach of what appeared to be an exceptional warrior. Disrespectful of their demands to come under their protection, Connla defeated several of the Red Branch Knights, forcing Cú himself to take him on in single combat. Cú defeated Connla by treacherously using the *Gae Bolga*, a secret weapon that gave him an unfair advantage, only then learning as the boy died that he was his son.

The Fenian Cycle

The Fenian, or "Ossianic" Cycle is much like the Ulster Cycle in form, as it too is essentially a collection of heroic tales, except the Fenian Cycle revolves around the adventures of the legendary Finn McCool and his band of warrior-hunters, the Fianna (*op. cit.*). The Fenian Cycle is set around the third century AD, and most of the action takes place in the provinces of Leinster and Munster. The primary protagonist of the stories is Finn McCool, who is the leader of the Leinster Fianna, and the antagonist was one Goll Mac Morna, who was the leader of a rebel faction of the Fianna that was based in Connaught province. And though their battles primarily took place in Leinster, their influence was felt all over the island, as the Fianna were the guardians and knight protectors of Ireland.

Though there are countless tales of Finn and the Fianna not only from Ireland, but also from the British Isles, three stand out as being the best known and most influential: "Sadb and the Birth of Oisín", "The Lay of Oisín in the Land of Eternal Youth" and "The Pursuit of Diarmuid and Gráinne".

✦ Sadb and the Birth of Oisín

Oisín was perhaps the most important of the Fianna next only to Finn McCool himself. So important was he to the history of the Fianna that he was made the narrator of much of the cycle. His name, *Oisín*, means "little deer", and was derived from the unique circumstances of his birth.

The story of Oisín's birth starts when his mother, the goddess Sadb, had been turned into a doe by an evil druid named Fer Doirich whose love she had spurned. One day, while Sadb was cavorting in the forest near the Dun of Allen, Finn's hounds Bran and Sceoland chased her back to Finn's home. As soon as she reached the protection of the magic of the dun, the evil druid's magic curse was lifted, and she turned back into a beautiful woman.

"Sadb", © 2000 Jim Fitzpatrick.

Finn was smitten with her, and they were soon married. However, one day when Finn was out defending Ireland from an invading force, Fer Doirich took on Finn's likeness and lured her out of the dun. As soon as Sadb left the protection of the dun, she turned back into a doe, and the dark druid led her away forever.

Seven years later, Finn found a small boy under a rowan tree on Ben Bulben, a many-storied hill in County Sligo. The boy told him that he had been taken care of by a fawn all that time, until the evil druid finally took her away. That boy grew up to be Oisín, a great warrior and poet of the Fianna.

THE MYSTERY
FOLKLORE &
MYTHOLOGY
MYTH TALES

203

✿ The Lay of Oisín in the Land of Eternal Youth

Oisín's most famous tale is *Laoi Oisín id Tír nan Óg* ("The Lay of Oisín in the Land of Eternal Youth"). One day Oisín, while hunting with the Fianna, was visited by a beautiful fairy woman named *Niamh Chinn Óir*, "Niamh of the Golden Hair". Niamh had been watching and dreaming about Oisín for years, and finally she had decided to reveal herself and her love for him. She then offered to take him with her to the land of Tír nan Óg, to live with her in married bliss, forever.

After three years of wedded bliss, Oisín began to miss his companions, the Fianna, and decided to visit them. Niamh attempted to dissuade him, but finally she relented and lent him her steed, Aonvarr, a magic horse that could travel equally well on land or on water. She also gave him the warning that he must not under any circumstances allow any part of his body to touch the ground, or else great disaster would befall him.

When Oisín reached the Hill of Allen where the Fianna had been headquartered, he was shocked to find the place abandoned, and that the men who now lived in the area were much smaller and weaker than the mighty, giant heroes of the Fianna had been. Watching them straining to lift a rock that even the weakest of the Fianna could have easily thrown a mile, Oisín leaned over in his saddle to attempt to help them lift it. Unfortunately his stirrups broke in the process, and he fell to the ground. He then realized why Niamh had warned him not to touch the ground, because though it had felt like he had spent only three years in the Otherworld, in the world of men 300 years had actually passed. As a result, as Oisín fell to the ground, Niamh's fairy magic was broken, and Oisín aged 300 years in an instant. And though his powerful life force lingered long enough for him to tell his tale to the bewildered men whom he had tried to help, the mighty Oisín soon died.

✿ The Pursuit of Diarmuid and Gráinne

"The Pursuit of Diarmuid and Gráinne" was a romantic tale that was so famous, that some feel it may have been the inspiration of the Germanic tale of Tristan and Isolde. The story begins after the long-lived Finn McCool's most recent wife had died, and his men had asked him to marry again. It was suggested that Finn marry Gráinne, the beautiful daughter of King Cormac

Mac Art, the High King of Ireland. Cormac thoughtfully asked his daughter Gráinne if she wished to marry Finn. She agreed, thinking that her father meant that she would actually be marrying into Finn's family, not Finn himself, who by that time was very old.

When Gráinne arrived at the Dun of Allen, she looked around Finn's court, and found herself attracted to Finn's son Oisín, Finn's grandson Oscar, and Diarmuid O'Duibhne. Naturally Oisín and Oscar politely refused her advances in deference to their father, but when she saw the *ball seirce*, or "love spot" on Diarmuid's forehead, she instantly fell in love with him and placed a *geas* upon him, claiming that he must come with her, or she could never love another man again. Thus cursed, Diarmuid was forced to elope with Gráinne.

The result of this betrayal led to Finn McCool flying into a jealous rage, and demanding that the Fianna hunt down the pair and return them to him for judgment. Diarmuid and Gráinne evaded the Fianna for years, experiencing many adventures and hiding in places all over Ireland, many of which still bear their names. Eventually, Diarmuid met his fate at Ben Bulben, in County Sligo, where he killed, and was killed, by the Boar of Ben Bulben (*op. cit.*). Unlike the more famous tale of The Exile of the Sons of Uisneach, however, Gráinne did not end her own life, but finally consented to be wed to Finn.

The Cycle of Kings

The Cycle of Kings, also known as The Historical Cycle, is essentially a loose collection of stories about the life and times of many of the High Kings of Ireland during the Old and Middle Irish Period, between the fourth century BC and the eight century AD. The content of the Cycle of Kings is actually a compilation of several lesser cycles of the surviving genealogical, historical and legendary information that the official court poets of the various High Kings had handed down to the Christian monks who then, as with the rest of the Cycles, dutifully transcribed them into written form. Though the stories in the Cycle of Kings tend to be less heroic, and less fantastic, than the other three Cycles, the stories therein still incorporate numerous fantastic and legendary elements that inspire memories of an epic past. And though most of the informa-

THE MYSTERY
FOLKLORE &
MYTHOLOGY
MYTH TALES

tion is still largely historical, some of the stories have significant elements of fantasy, the two most prominent of that genre being *Buile Shuibne*, "The Frenzy of Sweeney" — generally considered to be the glory of the Cycle of Kings — and the well-known and oft-cited "The Legend of King Labhraidh Loingseach".

♦ *Buile Shuibhne* — "The Frenzy of Sweeney"

"The Frenzy of Sweeney", like many of the stories in the Cycle of Kings, is set during the early historical/Christian period of Irish history around the 6th century AD. The story, a mixture of poetry and prose, is about Sweeney, a legendary king of Ulster. The story begins when a bishop named Ronan Finn sets up a church in Sweeney's kingdom, the bell of which rang regularly to call the faithful to worship. King Sweeney, however, did not like the piercing sound of the bell, and attacked the bishop, throwing his psalter into the lake and threatening to kill him.

"The Battle of Moira", © 1979, Jim Fitzpatrick.

Sweeney then departed to take part in the Battle of Moira, an important

battle that took place in AD 637. Moira is a small town near Lisburn, in Country Antrim, Ulster province. The name "Moira" comes from *Magth Rath* or *Moirath*, which means, "The Plain of the Fort". The primary antagonists in the battle were Donal the High King of Ireland and Congal Claen, a powerful Ulster King. Donal was victorious, and Congal was slain. Sweeney was probably a lesser king in the army of Congal.

Just before the battle, Bishop Ronan had blessed Sweeney's troops, but Sweeney had mistaken it as mockery and killed one of Ronan's psalmists with a spear in revenge. He then threw another at Ronan, but it struck his bell instead, breaking it. Enraged, the bishop cursed Sweeney, cursing him to go mad whenever he heard a bell, or any loud noise. He also cursed Sweeney that he would one day die by the point of a spear.

And as soon as the battle commenced, when he heard the loud noise of the clash of arms, Sweeney went insane. He dropped his weapons and began flying like a bird, flitting from spot to spot, becoming fearful and skittish as birds are, avoiding any contact with humans. Like Nebuchadnezzar in the Book of Daniel, Sweeney then spent the next seven years living in the wild, naked and constantly hungry. After the seventh year, his kinsmen briefly managed to coax him back down to earth, but a "mill hag" challenged Sweeney to a leaping contest, and he soon reverted to his mad, birdlike self.

Sweeney ended up spending most of the rest of his life hopping and fluttering about throughout Ireland and even western England, composing poems about each place to which he traveled. Eventually, as an old man he settled down to rest with St. Moling, who put him into the care of one of the local women who worked at the parish. But the woman's husband grew jealous of Sweeney and killed him with a spear, fulfilling the curse. Fortunately, Sweeney received the holy sacrament before he died, and was thus reconciled with God.

In retrospect, the character of "Sweeney" may have actually been a literary device not unlike Tuan MacCarrill, a means though which the poets and monks who put the story together could weave together a mass of otherwise unrelated information. By having Sweeney hop and flutter about Ireland and western Britain, the authors (or redactors) were able to insert a great deal of placename information similar to that found in the *Dindschenchas (q.v.)* within the body of the story, retaining much information that might otherwise have been lost.

THE MYSTERY
FOLKLORE &
MYTHOLOGY
MYTH TALES

⚜ The Legend of King Labhraidh Loingseach

Another of the more colorful stories of the Cycle of Kings is "The Legend of King Labhraidh Loingseach". Labhraidh was a legendary High King of Ireland during the 6th century BC. It is believed that he was one of the ancestors of the *Laigin*, ("Lein") the people who early inhabited the province of Leinster, from whom its name was derived. It is believed that the Laigin may have been part of, or related to, the various peoples that accompanied the invasion of the Fir Bolg.

The background of the story is one of fratricide and brutish behavior amongst the Laigin royalty. King Leoghaire Lorc and his son Ailill Áine were both killed by the king's brother Cobhthach Cóel Breg, who then forced the young Labhraidh to drink their blood and eat their hearts. Struck dumb by the extreme trauma of the situation, the young Labhraidh refused to speak for a long time, and became known as Máel, or "speechless one". Some time later, however, during a game of hurling, he was hit on the shin and called out, "I am hurt!", from which he derived his adult name, *Labhraidh*, or "the one who speaks". The envious and fearful Cobhthach later exiled the popular prince Labhraidh to Gaul (modern France), from which he received his surname, *Loingseach*, "the exile".

While in Gaul the young Labhraidh had built a reputation as a very capable warrior along with the many other exiles who had come to serve him there, and he soon became renowned as a great warrior and protector of the French King. His reputation spread far and wide, eventually as far as Ireland where his exploits attracted the attention of Moiriath, the beautiful daughter of a Munster King.

Moiriath sent Craftine, her harpist to play Labhraidh a love song, which convinced him to return to Ireland and reclaim his rightful place on the throne. The King of Gaul equipped him with an army of 2,200 men armed with broad spears made of a special blue-gray iron called *Laigin*, from which the Laigin of Leinster derived their name. Labhraidh then landed at Loch Garman (Wexford) and journeyed back to the *Dinn Rí* ("The Palace of the King") where ruled the wicked King Cobhthach. He then launched a ferocious attack on Cobhthach, killed him and all his guards, and re-took the throne of Leinster.

Some versions of this tale continue on from here, revealing King Labhraidh's secret: that he had ears like a donkey. To hide this he grew his hair long, and only had it cut once a year. In order to keep his terrible secret he then would have each barber killed. One year a widow's son was chosen to cut the King's hair, and the widow pleaded with Labhraidh not to kill her son. Labhraidh actually sympathized with the widow and agreed to spare the boy, so long as he never told a soul about his affliction.

The boy became ill with the secret, and a local druid told the boy to go tell his secret to an oak tree, thus unburdening himself. He traveled deep into the forest and found a tree. It worked, and from that moment on the boy was healed. The next day the King's musician was looking to build a new harp, and coincidentally he had this particular oak tree cut down.

When the harp was finished the King called upon his musician to play his favorite song. But no matter how hard he tried, the only song that came out was: "Labhraidh Loingseach has donkey's ears! Labhraidh Loingseach has donkeys ears!" and soon everyone knew his terrible secret. It is said that once his secret was out, the King stopped killing his barbers and learned to be less sensitive about his ears.

For more analysis and publication of the complete, unedited mythological tales of Ireland, visit http://ireland.mysteriousworld.com/Mystery/Folklore/MythologicalTales/

FAIRY TALES

Second in importance to the great mythological epics of ancient Ireland were the "fairy tales" that had to do primarily with mankind's interaction with the mysterious Otherworld of fairies, leprechauns, mermaids (and men) banshees, hags, and evil and mischievious spirits and creatures of every description. And since the number and variation of stories is also far too numerous to mention here (and much has already been covered in previous chapters), we will instead quote here part of a single classic poem of the *sídhe* known as "The Leprechaun, or Fairy Shoemaker":

THE MYSTERY
FOLKLORE &
MYTHOLOGY
FAIRY TALES

THE LEPRECHAUN,
OR FAIRY SHOEMAKER

Little Cowboy, what have you heard,
Up on the lonely rath's green mound?
Only the plaintive yellow bird
Sighing in sultry fields around,
Chary, chary, chary, chee-ee! —
Only the grasshopper and the bee? —
"Tip-tap, rip-rap,
Tick-a-tack-too!
Scarlet leather sewn together,
This will make a shoe.
Left, right, pull it tight;
Summer days are warm;
Underground in winter,
Laughing at the storm!"
Lay your ear close to the hill.
Do you not catch the tiny clamour,
Busy click of an elfin hammer,
Voice of the Leprechaun singing shrill
As he merrily plies his trade?
He's a span
And a quarter in height.
Get him in sight, hold him tight,
And you're a made
Man![4]

(For more analysis and publication of the complete, unedited fairy tales of Ireland, visit http://ireland.mysterious world.com/Mystery/Folklore/FairyTales/)

FOLKTALES

Folktales, the third leg in our triad of folklore types, are essentially a boundless, informal collection of simple short stories, riddles, rhymes, anecdotes and genealogical lore of a more local flavor that has circulated throughout Ireland since her beginning. These are the types of stories that lay storytellers still tell today in their *ceili* houses and pubs, where the local wise man, or "historian", has taken up the responsibility of upholding the local stories and traditions. And though no folklore or mythology is outside the bounds of the storyteller, including the epic tales of the Fianna and the Tuatha dé Danann, more likely than not their stories will be about more mundane, scary or humorous topics such as "The Lawyer and the Devil", "The Banshee Calls for the O'Briens", "Never Ask a Cat a Question", or a very simple, but entertaining story about "A Big Potato". And though the storyteller's stories may seem frivolous, ranging from the sublime to the ridiculous, he once filled a real need in the hearts and minds of the ancient Irish for something more than the daily grind. Glassie explains in *Irish Folktales*,

> They cut turf in the spring, dig spuds in the fall. They have followed the cows into the sloughs and gotten drunk together in the town. Conversations too quickly find the old ruts and sail too swiftly to first principles so perfectly framed in words that there is no knowing whether they erupt from the depths or ride on the surface. So the ceiliers come and they sit and they wait, crying inwardly for someone gifted with wit to build a story in the place that lies between inescapable daily realities and inescapable philosophical propositions.[5]

The "tales around the turf-fire" once held the pride of place in the hearts and minds of the ancient Irish, a place that needed to be entertained with stories about daily life that was something more than mundane, told by a real human being who had experienced both the joys and sorrows of life. Today, the television set has all but erased the ancient seat of the storyteller, its pixels of red, green and blue now replacing the rolling red, green and blue flames of the turf fire — entertaining our minds, but not feeding our souls.

Again, for lack of space, we cannot even begin to print all the old folktales available, so we will instead publish them on a regular basis at http://ireland.mysteriousworld.com/Mystery/Folklore/ Folktales/. However, for your edification, here is one short tale[6] that is particularly appropriate to end this chapter, and section:

THE OLD TIMES IN IRELAND

Galway

Lady Gregory 1926

The first man ever lived in Ireland was Partholón, and he is buried and his greyhound along with him some place in Kerry. The Nemedians came after that and stopped for a while and then they all died of some disease. And then the Firbolgs came, the best men that ever were in Ireland, and they had no law but love, and there was never such peace and plenty in Ireland. What religion had they? None at all. And there was a low-sized race came and worked the land of Ireland a long time. They had their time like the others.

Tommy Niland was sitting beside me one time the same as yourself, and the day warm as this day, and he said, "In the old times you could buy a cow for one and sixpence, and a horse for two shillings. And if you had lived in those days, Padraic, you'd have your cow and your horse." For there was a man in those times bought a cow for one and sixpence, and when he was driving her home he sat down by the roadside crying, for fear he had given too little. And the man that sold him as he was going home he sat down by the roadside crying, for fear he had taken too much. For the people were very innocent at that time and very kind. But Colmcille laid it down in his prophecy that every generation would be getting smaller and more liary; and that was true enough.

And in the old days if there was a pig killed, it would never be sent to the saltery but everyone that came in would get a bit of it. But now, a pig to be killed, the door of the house would be closed, and no one to get a bit of it at all.

In the old times the people had no envy, and they would be writing down the stories and the songs for one another. But they are too venomous now to do that. And as to the people in the towns, they don't care for such things now, they are too corrupted with drink.

Aye.

Notes

[1] Alwyn and Brinley Rees, *Celtic Heritage: Ancient Tradition in Ireland and Wales* (New York: Thames & Hudson, 1998), 12-13.

[2] Paraphrased from Henry Glassie, *Irish Folktales* (New York: Pantheon Books, 1985), 23.

[3] Lady Augusta Gregory, ed., "The Championship of Ulster", in *Cuchulain of Muirthemne* (Internet Sacred Text Archive: http://www.sacred-texts.com), http://www.sacred-texts.com/neu/celt/cuch/lgc08.htm.◊◊

[4] W.B. Yeats, ed., *Fairy & Folk Tales of Ireland* (New York: Touchstone, 1998), 77.

[5] Glassie, *Irish Folktales*, 6.

[6] *Ibid.*, 207. Note that this folktale contains several factual errors. Lay folktales of this type were better known for their moral and ethical value rather than their factual accuracy.

Twilight of the gods

"Twilight of the Gods",
© 1992 Jim Fitzpatrick.

*The one God comes to drive out
the many gods,
The spirits of wood and stream
grow silent.*
Merlin, *Excalibur* (1981)

In the length of ages, the glory of the gods of Èireann faded into twilight, their power dimming into the dusk of night. Gone were the heroes of old, conquered were the giants, defended was the land of Èireann. No more mystery, no more tales of conquest, romance and plunder were heard, only the endless clamour of battle without honor, purpose or meaning.

Lesser men had taken the thrones of Ireland, men small in mind and in stature who did not respect the gods of their fathers, nor the values that they held dear. Instead they lusted after gold and plunder, after power raw and unglorious, appearing on the outside to be righteous, while on the inside they were full of darkness and corruption. Having abandoned the ancient principles of life, light and civilization, every man's hand was raised against his brother, the weak and helpless became a prey, and the blessed isle dissolved into chaos. Proud banners once swelled with courage now lay trampled into the dust. Having turned from the gods of their fathers to the worship of demons, the kings of old had led the sacred isle to the brink of ruin.

It was into this chaos that the first Christians arose in the East, bringing the light of salvation and the Good News of a new beginning for the island of the destiny of the West — a new, spiritual invasion bearing not tidings of war, but of peace.

THE MYSTERY
TWILIGHT OF
THE GODS

215

PART II: T

The Coming of Christianity

Into the darkness of the Gentiles came the light of Christianity. Seeing the dawning of a new light from the East, the old gods of Ireland fled away, diminishing and fading into the myths and legends of the sacred isle. The next great invasion was at hand. This invasion, however, was not one of conquering kings, giants and mighty men, but of men meager of stature and worldly import, whose message of love and self-sacrifice would turn the ancient world upside down.

The invasion of Christianity into Ireland came at first not as a flood, but as a trickle. Around the time of the fall of the Roman Empire, numerous waves of barbarian invasions – originally emanating from Central Asia – had gradually worn the mighty but increasingly idle and decadent Roman Empire down to the point where, in AD 410, Rome was finally conquered and occupied by the Visigoths under King Alaric. Her spoils plundered, her gods defiled, her people slaughtered, enslaved or scattered, the mighty Roman Empire, the light of Europe, ceased to exist, and the West was plunged into a prolonged Dark Age. Brown explains in *The Rise of Western Christendom*,

> The most striking, and decisive, feature of conventional narratives of the end of the Roman Empire and the early Middle Ages has been the insistence that the history of western Europe has always been characterized by a natural unity. This unity was regarded as the ideal. Departures from it were held to be a sign of decay and of aimless anarchy. It was assumed that the unity of western Europe had first come into existence under the Roman empire. From the north of Britain to North Africa, the charmed world enclosed within the Roman frontiers was the first Europe. In 1912, the author of a study of the Romanization of Roman Britain could write: "The safety of Rome was the safety of all civilization. Outside roared the wild chaos of barbarism." After the year AD 400 [however,] the frontiers of the empire collapsed, and the wild chaos of bar-

barism flooded into the empire from across the North Sea, the Rhine, and the Danube. The period of the "Barbarian Invasions" effectively destroyed the first unity of Europe. But all was not lost. Christianity had already spread widely in continental western Europe. It was through the insubstantial but tenacious bonds created by the Catholic Church that the broken unity of Roman Europe was recreated. All roads came to lead, yet again, to Rome, as the papacy established itself as the undisputed center of a new, Catholic West.[1]

Christianity had initially been violently repulsed by the Roman Empire, and Christians were at best tolerated for centuries afterwards. This persecution did not subside until Emperor Constantine beheld a vision of a cross in the heavens that inspired him to issue the famous *Edict of Milan* in AD 313, wherein Christianity was cited as the new official religion of the Roman Empire.[2] As a result, with the official *imprimatur* of the state, and with the help of the superior Roman communications and transportation systems, Christianity spread far and wide throughout the empire and beyond, trickling even as far west as Ireland.

The wheel of fate had been set in motion to allow Christendom to spread to the far corners of the empire because, a century later, the Roman Empire would cease to exist, and the light of Rome would be smashed into a thousand sparks, the sole remains of which remained smouldering on the outer rim of the old Republic. But it was from these embers that the fire of civilization would be slowly relit, a civilization based this time not upon paganism, but upon Christianity. And one of the brightest embers remaining from the Roman period was Irish Christianity.

Irish Christianity

St. Patrick was the first successful missionary to Ireland, though Christianity already had been filtering in to Ireland through informal channels for some time. As with Rome, the first Christian missionaries were initially repulsed by the Irish, but unlike Rome, there were no Christian martyrs. St. Patrick met with strenuous opposition from the druids at

Tara, opposition that included threats of violence and even spectacular feats of magic, but the response of the Druids was not openly violent as was that of the Romans. Instead, the Druids first attempted to discourage the Christians with sanctions, and then by well-reasoned arguments. But eventually the faith of the one God overrode that of the many gods, and one by one the Druids converted to the new monotheism. In practice, however, Druidism was not destroyed by Christianity but rather absorbed, its more practical elements retained, and the pagan elements removed, creating a form of Christianity that was uniquely Irish.

The Rise of Monasticism

What was truly unique about Irish Christianity, however, was its monastic character, a form of organization that had first been introduced by Patrick, though he had originally intended to impose an episcopal structure like that of Rome. And though it took a long time to take root, once it had settled in, the monastic structure fit so well into Irish culture that it remained entrenched for many centuries, becoming very closely integrated with Irish daily life.

> The early Irish monasteries were not like those we think of in medieval Britain and Ireland: rather they were little towns of streets of wooden huts and halls clustered round a church. Among the buildings were schools for teaching religion as well as many other things. The monastic domination of Irish Christianity was to last right into the twelfth century. For the most part the monastic orders and their houses remained native in structure and organization, unaffected by changes and improvements in the continental orders…. It is easy to see why the Irish church began and developed in such an individual manner. The lack of towns and urban communities, of road networks, the geographical remoteness, the political divisions … all conspired to produce an establishment that functioned as a series of monastic community centers, autonomous yet linked, operating in some respects like the *tuatha* themselves.[3]

The monasteries lived on the lands and the whims of the *tuatha*, tribal units that had ruled over the various regions of Ireland since ancient times. However, so well integrated were the monastic communities that some of the *tuatha* were actually headed by abbots or bishops. The integration of the *tuath*, or tribal "secular" areas of authority and the monastic authority was fairly deep, to the point that both monks, unreformed pagans and even druids worked side by side in the fields, schools, markets and workshops, each learning from the other the wisdom that each, the sacred, the secular, and the pagan, had to offer. In the end, what came out in the wash was a working combination of all three, the Irish church as it has come to be known in history.

In sum the early Irish church, unlike the Roman church, was based upon a more egalitarian structure that tended to integrate with society, rather than impose a rigid structure upon it. This was one of the primary reasons that Christianity succeeded in Ireland, much more so than its neighbors, because it acted as an integrated, supportive force, rather than a domineering one. As LaHane explains, "The monastic variety of the religion was quite different from the hierarchical, diocesan structure of the established Roman church. It kept more of the simple, explicit prescriptions, and more of its attractive, half-mythical content than the judicial hand of Rome enouraged. Moreover, monasteries did not obtrude on the lives of those who wanted no change".[4] In this way, Irish Christianity was more of a "grass roots" religion that, as the early Christians had done in the Roman Empire, eventually overcame paganism through patient, self-sacrificial acts over time. In that sense, by engaging in self-sacrificial activity rather than grasping for political power through the imposition of a hierarchical, ecclesiastical system, Irish Christianity was perhaps the one heir of Christendom that was most like the original.

WARRIOR MONKS

The ideal of self-sacrifice was indeed so strong in the early Irish church that some monks took the monastic concept to the extreme, leaving society and even monastic life to live alone in the wilderness. They took their example from the famous St. Antony of Egypt, the first true Christian monk, who had left society for a period of solitude in the desert of Sinai around AD 270, taking naught with him but bread, water and salt in order to purify himself from the decadence of society.[5] Added to this extreme example of "crucifying" one's own flesh in order to be more like Christ was the desire for martyrdom, the ultimate form of Christlikeness, which Irish Christians had never experienced during the evangelization of Ireland. Searching for a substitute for physical martyrdom, these young ascetics created alternative forms of martyrdom. Among these were "green martyrdom", where a monk would go off on his own and live in solitude in a relatively desolate area, and "white martyrdom", where a monk would go off on his own not only to a desolate area, but sail off to a completely different island, taking up residence on one of the small, uninhabited islands that dot Ireland's shore.

This type of martyrdom was the basis of the creation of the famous monastery of Skellig Michael, which had been founded by monks seeking white martyrdom, eventually growing from a group of isolated hermits into a full-blown monastery. The most extreme example of white martyrdom took place when a monk would simply set sail into the west, searching for the mythical "Promised Land" that many believed lay far away west, beyond the Atlantic. Very often this extreme form of white martyrdom would result in the better known "red" form of martyrdom, however, as many of these monks were never heard from again. These extreme, "warrior monks", in many ways, were very much carrying on the beliefs and practices of their Celtic warrior forebears, effectively fusing the warrior code of the ancient Celts with the Christian ethos of self-sacrifice to create a uniquely Irish form of extreme monasticism.

INTELLECTUAL GIANTS

This "rugged individualism" embodied in the character of the Irish warrior monks was not the only attraction that emergent Celtic Christianity had upon the ancient Irish. The advance of Christianity also was enhanced greatly by the Irish love of literature and story. The dramatic *sturm und drang* imagery to be found throughout the Bible greatly appealed to these ancient Celts, who were not only interested in the concept of heroic self-sacrifice, but were also possessed of a powerful intellectual curiosity that took great delight in both fantastical imagery and theological conjecture. In such an environment the Bible would of course become an immediate best-seller, and any religion based upon it would flourish, as the Bible presents a heady mixture of fantastic imagery and intellectual discourse that has obsessed countless minds for thousands of years.

> Memorizing and reciting legends had been the function of one of the highest classes in the land, and was imitated by others far away from the comfort and splendour of royal courts, the *seanachies*, who kept the imaginations of humble people awake and alive around the glowing embers of an evening fire. Now there was a new source of tales, the lore of the Old and New Testaments. And there were comments to make, and meanings to be dug, and subtleties to be explored and exploited by the burrowing minds of recruited monks. The race that had devised the exquisite complexity of the Brehon law and took an almost perverse delight in mental system and classification turned to Christian theology with refreshed vigour. Irishmen learned and recited the psalms with ease, took in and extended the tables and classes of saints with a mature aptitude, and through their trained awareness of the numinous powers of nature relished the symbols and mysteries of the new creed.... In these and other ways the new religion captured the people's imagination.[6]

HOW THE IRISH SAVED CIVILIZATION

Thus conquered by the latest of the invasions, Ireland then became known not for its wars, but for its piety. As a result, after the destruction of the ancient Christian centers of continental Europe by the barbarian invasions, Ireland, safe in its inobtrusive, "backwater" status, stood to literally rewrite the map of the entire western Christian world — and that's exactly what it did.

As Thomas Cahill comments pithily in his influential *How the Irish Saved Civilization*, "Ireland, at peace and furiously copying, thus stood in the position of becoming Europe's publisher."[7] The once-great libraries of Rome and continental Europe had been all but destroyed by the barbarian invasions, books and learning having been denigrated to the level of a specialty discipline exclusive to the few remaining elites. The Irish, however, absolutely obsessed with books and learning, had been furiously acquiring and copying every book they could get their hands on for the better part of a century, illuminating many of these documents with their characteristic gross capitals surrounded with red dots, a technique that had been adopted from Coptic Christians fleeing Muslim persecution in Egypt. And now, with their combination of Christian zeal and love of literature, the Irish monks set out to re-evangelize — and "re-literize" — the British Isles, continental Europe, and the entire Western world.

The re-evangelization of Europe was started by St. Columba (aka St. Colmcille). Columba, feeling guilty for having accidentally started a small war over the ownership of a copy of the Psalms, decided upon a self-imposed exile, never to set foot upon Ireland again. He then proceeded to the Isle of Iona, between Ireland and Scotland, where he built his first and greatest monastery: Iona. From there he proceeded to evangelize much of Scotland, only retiring after having founded over sixty monastic communities. But Columba's accomplishments were only the beginning. LaHane explains,

> Just as the unyielding warrior Cú Chulainn had served as the model of prehistoric Irish manhood, Colmcille now became the model for all who would earn the ultimate victory. Monks began to set off in every direction, bent on glorious and heroic exile for the sake of Christ. They were warrior-monks, of course, and certainly not afraid of whatever monsters they might meet. Some went north, like Colmcille. Others went northwest, like Brendan the Navigator, visiting Iceland, Greenland, and North America, and supping

on the back of a whale in mid-ocean. Some set out on boats without oars, putting their destination completely in the hands of God. Many of the exiles found their way to continental Europe, where they were more than a match for the barbarians they met. They, whom the Romans had never conquered … fearlessly brought the ancient civilization back to its ancient home.[8]

THE CREATION OF "IRELAND"

Though the Irish monks had saved western Christianity through their assiduous scholarship and evangelical zeal, they also had saved Irish history by obsessively collecting and transcribing all of the myths, legends and lore that remained in the oral traditions of the druids, bards and poets whose traditions had survived the ages. Several important collections of these ancient traditions still remain, one of the best being the famous *Book of Leinster*, one of the most important remaining sources of Irish genealogy, mythology and literature, from which we have the best copies of the *Lebor Gabála Èrenn*, the most complete version of the *Táin Bó Cuailnge*, the *Metrical Dindshenchas* and an Irish translation of the Latin epic, the *Aenid*. Without the early Christian monks' obsessive need to collect and store information, much of Ireland's ancient history – and particularly, its *mystery* – would surely have been lost.

From these collections of ancient texts, the Irish monks created the nation that we now know as Ireland. Before Christianity had come and unified the entire country under one symbol, the Cross, Ireland was essentially a collection of warring *tuatha*, large tribal groups that constantly vied with each other over control of the island. However, with the unification of the island under one faith, and the creation of a national identity through the collection, codification and transmission of all of the myths and legends of the sacred isle into a generic, "national" format, the seeds of what would one day become "Ireland" were sown.

CONCLUSIONS

The Irish, "Celtic" form of Christianity as it evolved in Ireland was unique in that it was both monastic and ruggedly individualistic in character. It also sought, instead of overruling and controlling, to integrate with the prevailing social, economic and political structures, thus creating a church that has lasted the centuries and left as its heritage a Christianity that is still deeply ingrained into the Irish national character. In many ways, Irish Christianity represents the most successful branch of Christianity ever to evolve in the Western world. As Bamford explains in *The Voice of the Eagle: The Heart of Celtic Christianity*,

> The Celtic Church stands for a purity, power and innocence that, at least in Christian history, have never been surpassed — a time when heaven and Earth, God and nature, humanity and the cosmos seemed more interdependent and interpenetrated than in other Christian ages. Everywhere in Celtic Christian Ireland — in the monasteries and hermitages, on the rocky promontories and steep hillsides, in the protected valleys … we find a unique "holy intimacy" of the human, the natural and the divine.[9]

Though Christianity was not the last force to invade Ireland, it was perhaps the single most powerful force for change in Irish history. And as it had been with the previous invasions, it appears that Christianity also had been sent to Ireland in order to maintain the primacy of civilization and light over the powers of chaos and evil that were once again threatening to undermine the sanctity of the island of destiny of the West. Before the coming of Patrick, license and immorality, chaos and civil war were the bywords for Irish daily life, a condition that would have kept the island of destiny from ever becoming one nation, from ever becoming "Ireland". But the great God of gods had mercy on the sacred isle, and sent His saints to sacrifice themselves in order to restore life, light and civilization to the land of Èiru. And the first, and greatest, of these saints was St. Patrick.

The Saints
ST. PATRICK

St. Patrick (AD 390-461) is the National Apostle and Saint of Ireland, and probably the most famous and celebrated person in Irish history. There are varying stories on his origins, but most believe that he was born a Romanized Briton either in Cumbria (Wales) or Scotland. The tradition has it that he was captured in a raid by the famous King *Niall Noígallach* (Niall of the Nine Hostages, *q.v.*), and was sold by the Irish raiders as a slave to a man named Milchu, a chieftain of Dalriada, in what is now County Antrim. There he was put to work as a shepherd for Milchu, who was also the local high druid.

"St Patrick Banishes the Serpents"
© 1998 Jim Fitzpatrick.

During his captivity, Patrick learned a great deal about the Irish language and customs, also learning a great deal about the Druidism that he was destined to banish from the sacred isle. After six years in captivity Patrick was visited by an angel, and to his surprise, the angel admonished Patrick for tarrying too long in Ireland, telling him to escape back to his family. This he did successfully, reuniting with his family and friends in Britain.

The Call

Feeling the call into ministry, Patrick later emigrated to France and joined the monastery at Tours. After his sojourn there, he spent some time at the renowned Abbey of Lérins, located on the island of the same name off the coast of Provence. Patrick was then taken as a student by the renowned St. Germain, who aided him in his entry into the

THE HISTORY
THE COMING OF
CHRISTIANITY
THE SAINTS

priesthood. The time he spent helping St. Germain battle the various heretical sects that had been springing up around Europe during that period gave him valuable experience that would prove helpful later in life. And all throughout his early ministry, Patrick continuously experienced visions of the children of Ireland calling out to him to return and evangelize the island. So to help him achieve his goal, Germain recommended Pope Celestine I commission Patrick to evangelize Ireland, replacing Palladius, who had been driven from the island by a fierce Wicklow chieftain.

The Return to Ireland

So, around 433, Patrick returned to the island of his captivity to liberate it from the bondage of the druids. Predictably, the druids resisted him fiercely, yet not with force of arms, but with slander and with magic. Patrick first rested for a time on an island off the Skerries coast now known as Inis Patrick, later moving to the mainland. He then proceeded to Dalriada — where he had spent six years of his childhood enslaved by the druid Milchu — with the intention of repaying his slave price and converting his former master to Christianity.

Along the way to Dalriada, however, Patrick was attacked by a local chieftain named Dichu. But as Dichu raised his sword arm to slay the saint, it was held frozen in place by the Holy Spirit until Dichu relented and agreed to help Patrick. Converted by this experience, Dichu gave Patrick a barn that the druids had previously used as a place of worship. This barn, "Saul" (Gaelic *sabhall*), is believed to be the first Christian church in Ireland, and it served Patrick as a retreat throughout his ministry.

As Patrick began to approach Dalriada, Milchu, hearing tell of Patrick's coming and of the miracles he had wrought, flew into a frenzy, set his house and all his possessions on fire, and threw himself onto the flames in order to escape the shame of being bested by his former slave. Disappointed but not disheartened, Patrick returned to Saul, hearing there about the sacred annual convocation that the High King Leoghaire ("Leary") had called at Tara. It was on March 26, Easter Sunday, AD 433, that the convocation was to take place, and Patrick saw it as an ideal opportunity to light the fire of Christianity in Ireland.

The demonic oracles of the fallen druids had warned them of the coming of Patrick and of Christianity, so they had summoned their full force at Tara to repel him. And though the king had decreed throughout the land that all fires were to be extinguished until a signal fire was lit at Tara, Patrick broke the decree by lighting the Paschal fire on the Hill of Slane. Infuriated, the druids demanded that the fire and he who lit it be extinguished, prophesying that if they were not, that this new "fire" would burn throughout Ireland forever. But once again God was with Patrick, and both the fire and Patrick were protected from the druids.

Patrick then marched forth upon Tara along with his retinue, sweeping aside with a prayer the deep darkness that the druids had summoned to oppose him. Then suddenly, the Arch-Druid Lochru took to the air, held aloft by demonic power like Simon Magus. But with another prayer from Patrick he was cast down and destroyed, with him going the morale of the druids and their will to resist.

Patrick then attempted to convert the High King Leary, but was initially rebuffed. The second time, however, after he had preached the doctrine of the Trinity using a shamrock, the king relented and allowed Patrick to preach the faith to the four corners of Ireland. As a result, the druidic prophecy that the fire that Patrick had lit would burn forever throughout Ireland began to come true. The spread of Christianity in Ireland is thus dated as having started on April 5, 433.

To the Four Corners

After successfully preaching the Gospel in Meath, Patrick turned west, towards Connaught. Unfortunately, as was so typical of the Irish monarchy, the *Ard Rí* was often High King in name only, as evidenced by the fact that the "High King" Leary could not guarantee Patrick safe passage to Connaught. Patrick was instead forced to pay the price of 15 slaves to guarantee his own safe passage. On the way, as he passed through Granard, in what is now County Longford, Patrick heard that the people in nearby Magh-Slecht (now Moysleet, County Cavan, in Ulster province) were worshiping the primeval pagan deity Crom Cruach (*op. cit.*). The idol of Crom Cruach was in the form of a "huge pillar-stone, covered with slabs of gold and silver, with a circle of twelve minor idols around it."[10]

Patrick immediately struck the false idol down with his crozier, and it instantly crumbled, along with the 12 lesser idols that surrounded it. He then had all the people of the area assemble, and that day the king, his six sons, and 12,000 of the people converted to Christianity. Patrick then spent the next seven years preaching throughout Connaught, founding churches, and dividing the land up into parishes and diocese.

The next notable event in Patrick's career occurred when he was visiting Rathcrogan, the seat of the kings of Connaught. Out one morning near the fountain of Clebech, singing praises to God, Patrick was confronted by the king's two daughters, Ethne the blonde, and Fedelm the redheaded, who had come forth to the fountain for their usual morning bath. Astonished by the presence of these men singing praises near their bath, the king's daughters queried as to why Patrick and his entourage were there. When Patrick responded that they were there to worship God, Ethne asked Patrick a series of theological questions regarding the nature of God, all of which Patrick responded to convincingly. Having assured them of the rightness of his faith, Patrick then converted and baptized the girls and, upon their insistence to see the face of their new spiritual "husband", Patrick is said to have given them the Eucharist to engage them in holy communion with the Church. Immediately upon receiving Communion, the story goes, they were taken by the Holy Spirit and died, laid out in fine linen, white and clean, to live with Christ, their new husband.

In AD 440, Patrick left his work in the hands of his capable protégés in Connaught and proceeded to evangelize Ulster province, where he met with great success. In 444 he came to Armagh, and decided to make it the central hub of his ministry. The local king even gave Patrick title to the hill on which the old cathedral of Armagh (rebuilt in the 13th century) still stands. However, there is also another, newer cathedral which has an interesting story behind it. It is said that, when Patrick was surveying his land, one of his companions spotted a doe with her fawn, and made to kill them for food. Patrick forbad him however and, taking the doe upon his shoulders, carried it to a neighboring hill. Laying down the fawn, he then proclaimed that in future times that hill would be a place where God would be given great glory. And in 1804, "by National subscription, *cum Gloire De agus Onorana h'Eireann* ('To the Glory of God and the Honour of Ireland'), and as a memorial to the National Apostle," the cornerstone for the new National Cathedral of St. Patrick was laid, the building being completed in 1904.[11] Having then made Ulster his apostolic seat, he began to set up his church hierarchy along a Roman model, appointing hundreds of bishops and priests, baptizing thousands of people, and building over 50 churches. He also founded a monastic system which, in later years, would actually come to define the Irish Catholic system much more than the episcopal (bishop-ruled) system he had intended.

Patrick then embarked on the final leg of his quest to evangelize the four corners of Ireland, proceeding south to Munster, where he focused upon converting the centers of authority, correctly ascertaining that the populace would imitate their leadership. One notable event that occurred during his time in Munster concerned the conversion of Prince Aenghus. While in the midst of the ceremony, Patrick accidentally planted his crozier onto the prince's foot and then leaned on it, piercing his foot. When Patrick noticed the blood, the prince remarked that he thought that the piercing was a part of the ceremony, that his foot should be pierced just as our Lord's had been on the cross. Impressed by the prince's faith, Patrick then inscribed a cross upon Aenghus' shield with the tip of his crozier, saying that his shield would become the source of many spiritual and temporal victories for the prince. Patrick then spent several years preaching and building churches in Munster province, greatly praising and blessing the people of Munster.

Eagle Mountain

Perhaps the most famous and important event of Patrick's career was his intercession on behalf of Ireland on Eagle Mountain in Connaught, County Mayo. Eagle Mountain, now known as Croagh Patrick, is now considered to be the holy hill, or "Mt. Sinai" of Ireland. This is due to the fact that, in imitation of Moses, St. Patrick spent 40 days and nights in prayer, fasting and penitential exercise on the mountain in order to plead the cause of Ireland before God. At the height of his ecstatic experience, he saw many forbidding visions and temptations. In his most trying experience, he saw a vision of all of the demons that ruled over Ireland gathering all their strength in order to tempt him away from his intercession. There were so many, that they appeared to be a huge flock of hideous, black birds of prey so huge that it covered both heaven and Earth, blocking his vision completely. All other attempts to escape this curse having failed, Patrick, sorely pressed by their attempts to sway him from his course, rang his bell among them, symbolizing his preaching of divine truth. He then cast his bell at them, and they fled immediately, casting themselves into the sea. So great was Patrick's victory that day that not one evil thing was to be found in Ireland for seven years.

Having thus vanquished the demons, Patrick then came before God Himself, and would not stop in his intercession until the following five demands were met:

- ♰ Many souls would be freed from the pains of purgatory through his intercession;

- ♰ Whoever in the spirit of penance would recite his hymn before death would attain the heavenly reward;

- ♰ Barbarian hordes would never obtain sway in his Church;

- ♰ Seven years before the Judgment Day, the sea would spread over Ireland to save its people from the temptations and terrors of the Antichrist; and

- ♰ Greatest blessing of all, Patrick himself should be deputed to judge the whole Irish race on the last day.[12]

Requiem

In 461, after having completed his semi-autobiographical work, the *Confessio*, Patrick died at his sanctuary at Saul, and is believed to have been buried at Armagh, close to Emain Macha. Having banished the "snakes", or Druidry, from Ireland and having replaced it with the light of Christianity, Patrick is still remembered in song, legend and festival throughout Ireland today, and is generally considered to be the most famous and celebrated person in Irish history.[13]

St. Brigid

St. Brigid, the second of the three great saints of Ireland, was born around AD 452 at Faughart, near Dundalk, County Louth. Later writers exclaimed that "a flame and fiery pillar" had hovered over the hut where she was to be born, though she was born a slave, the illegitimate daughter of Dubthach, a pagan chieftain of Faughart, and Brocessa, one of his slave girls. Her early life was characterized by an extreme generosity, always giving what she had to the poor, even if it made her even poorer than they.

One day the king of Leinster, a Christian, persuaded Dubthach

to free Brigid from slavery and accept her as legitimate. He did this and, as Brigid had grown to be an extremely beautiful young woman, he decided to arrange a marriage between her and a very famous poet in order to profit from her beauty. However, Brigid wanted to dedicate her life to God, and in order to avoid the marriage she decided to mar her famous beauty, some stories say, by actually plucking out one of her own eyes! Other accounts say that she developed a severe skin disease that made her unattractive, but most likely she simply refused to marry.

Brigid then followed through on her vow to serve God and became a nun. She took her vows on the Hill of Uisneach, from which the sacred fires of Ireland traditionally had been first lit since very ancient times. And ever since, St. Brigid has been associated with the eternal, sacred flame. She then set out to found various monasteries all over Ireland, the most famous of which was *Cill Dara*, "The Church of the Oak", in County Kildare. This monastery had in turn been named for the great oak under which the monastery had been built. This monastery eventually

THE HISTORY
THE COMING OF
CHRISTIANITY
THE SAINTS

grew to be a very great center of learning, where the perpetual flame burned for as long as the monastery was in use. It was also known as the first "double monastery", as it included facilities for both monks and nuns. Another of Cill Dara's lasting legacies was the school of art that Brigid founded. This exceptional school turned out some of the most magnificent bells, croziers, chalices and illuminated manuscripts ever created in Ireland. The greatest of these illuminated manuscripts was *The Book of Kildare*, which was described as being "the work of angelic, and not human skill".[14] Unfortunately, this manuscript has been lost since the time of the Reformation.

St. Brigid was an exceptional woman and servant of God, being both pious, beautiful, chaste, intelligent, talented, graceful, a visionary leader and an accomplished administrator. At the end of her exceptional life around AD 523, she was buried in an elaborate tomb at the right of the high altar at the Kildare Cathedral, her tomb becoming the object of veneration for pilgrims who journeyed to see it every February 1. This was of course the former feast day of the Celtic goddess Brigid, whom St. Brigid had replaced in the hearts and minds of the ancient Irish. Due to Viking raids in AD 878, however, her remains were moved to Downpatrick, where they were interred along with the remains of Sts. Patrick and Columba *(q.v.)*. Thus the remains of the three patron saints of Ireland, Patrick, Brigid and Columba, were given their final place of rest in Downpatrick Cathedral, where they reside to this day.[15]

The "St. Brigid's Cross" is a classic example of how Christianity adopted and modified the meanings of many of the pagan symbols that pre-existed Christianity, such as the "sun wheel", a symbol that originated with the ancient Celts who had brought it with them from Central Asia in ancient times.†

St. Brigid remains as one of the most popular and celebrated Irish saints, and her example of Godly service has served as a role model to generations of Christian women. Known affectionately as "the Mary of the Gael", St. Brigid worked hand in hand with St. Patrick to spread the Gospel to the four corners of the sacred isle, spreading the unforgettable fire that burns still in the hearts and minds of the Irish.

THE HISTORY
THE COMING OF
CHRISTIANITY
THE SAINTS

235

St. Columba

St. Columba (lit., "St. Dove"), also known as St. Colmcille, ("St. Dove of the Churches") or simply as St. Colum, was the third of the three great saints of Ireland. Columba was born *Crimthann*, "fox", on December 7, 521 into the Clan O'Donnell. He was of royal blood, being a descendant and potential heir of the famous King Niall of the Nine Hostages, the pirate-king whose raiders had kidnapped the young St. Patrick over a century before. Columba, however, turned down his chance to rule Ireland and instead decided to make himself a living sacri-

"St. Columba Of Iona"
© 1998 Jim Fitzpatrick.

fice to God, giving away earthly power and privilege for a life of study, evangelization and quiet contemplation as a Christian monk.

Seeming to have "taken up the mantle" from Sts. Patrick and Brigid, St. Columba became one of the most important and influential saints of Irish history, even during his own lifetime. Like Patrick, much legendary material has accreted around Columba's birth and life, his birth even being described as having been accompanied by "signs and wonders". It is even said that St. Patrick himself prophesied his coming while baptizing a chieftain of Columba's tribe:

> *A manchild shall be born of this family*
> *He will be a wise man, a prophet, a poet,*
> *A loveable lamp, pure, clear –*
> *There will not be a word of falsehood in him….*

His birth was accompanied by signs and wonders. While his mother, Eithne, was pregnant an angel came to her and showed her a mantle of exquisite beauty in which all the flowers of creation were woven in extraordinary colors. The angel gave it to her, but after a while asked for it back. Sadly, Eithne returned it. Then the angel raised it up, spread it out, and allowed it to fly through the air. As it dispersed over creation, Eithne protested its loss. The angel replied: "Do not grieve, for you shall bring forth a son, so beautiful in character that he shall be reckoned one of the prophets of God, predestined to lead innumerable souls to heaven now and always."[16]

St. Columba was baptized at *Tulach-Dubhglaise*, "Temple-Douglas", by a priest named Cruithnechan, who afterwards became his tutor, or "foster-father".[17] After completing his basic schooling, Columba began his monastic study under St. Finnian at the monastic school of Moville, where he is said to have performed numerous miracles, including turning water into wine. There he received his diaconate degree, the lowest of three levels of Christian authority at that time, the next higher ranks being priest and then bishop.

Columba then sought out Gemman, the Bard of Leinster, a master poet and bard who still taught the old ways. Under the instruction of Gemman, Columba learned the ways and traditions of the poets, and forever after the poetic muse influenced his rhetoric and made his ministrations all the more powerful. Columba then enrolled in the monastery of Finnian of Clonard, where he received the best education then available in Ireland, learning his Latin, his Scriptures, his history of Ireland, and further refining his art of poetry.[18] Graduating from Clonard he continued his studies at Glasnevin, outside of what is now Dublin, studying under St. Mobhi. But a plague of yellow fever swept through Glasnevin, to which St. Mobhi, the abbot, succumbed. Columba apparently took this as a sign that it was time for him to cease his studies, as he then immediately returned to Derry, the land of his nativity, where he began his apostolic work in earnest.

In order to help him start his ministry, Columba's family gave him a plot of land in County Derry near Lough Foyle, the estuary of the River Foyle where the

237

river connects to the sea between modern Counties Derry and Donegal. There he founded his first church but, like Patrick, Columba continued on to evangelize the entire island, leaving behind numerous churches, oratories, holy wells and other artifacts that still bear his name. Perhaps the most memorable of these churches was Durrow, "a noble monastery in Ireland known in the Scots [Irish] language as *Dearmach*, 'the Field of Oaks', because of the oak forest in which it stands".[19] This church, located in what is now County Offaly, Leinster province, is best known for *The Book of Durrow*, now on display at Trinity College, Dublin (*q.v.*). Another very famous monastery associated with St. Columba is Kells, in County Meath, where the famous *Book of Kells* is believed to have been created. And though up to 300 churches throughout Ireland have been ascribed to him, Columba's first church in Derry remained his favorite.

The Turning Point

The defining moment of St. Columba's life revolved around a copy of the Psalms — specifically, the psalter of St. Finnian. Desiring his own copy of Finnian's Latin Vulgate version of the Psalms (a translation of the Psalms into Latin), St. Columba copied Finnian's psalter down to the last detail. Finnian discovered the copy, however, and brought the matter to King Diarmuid mac Cearbhaill, the then High King of Ireland. Diarmuid found in favor of St. Finnian, judging "To every cow her calf, to every book its copy". It was history's first copyright case.[20]

St. Columba did not agree, however, and turned to his powerful family, the Uí Neills, to decide the matter by force. And though the Uí Neills defeated the King of Ireland at the Battle of Cooldrevny in 561, killing over 3,000 of the king's men, Columba felt such great remorse for causing so many deaths on account of a mere book that he decided that he must do penance. His confessor, St. Molaise, told him that his penance was to leave Ireland forever, and to save as many souls abroad as he had caused to be killed in the battle. Setting sail from Derry in his coracle with 12 companions for the Isle of Iona, Columba vowed never to return to Ireland again, remembering the poignant moment with a poem not unlike Amergin's "The Mystery":

Delightful to be on the Hill of Howth
Before going over the white-haired sea:
The dashing of the wave against its face,
The bareness of its shores and of its border....
Great is the speed of my coracle,
And its stern turned upon Derry:
Grievous is my errand over the main,
Traveling to Alba of the beetling brows....[21]

Exile on Iona

Arriving at the island of Iona on the eve of Whitsunday, 563, Columba and his companions began to immediately build Iona's first monastery, which would later become so famous that it would come to be known simply as "Iona". The first humble dwellings consisted of a church refectory and cells, constructed of wattle and rough planks.[22] From their ideal position situated on an island between Ireland and Scotland, they then proceeded to evangelize the Scottish peoples of *Dál Ríata* (Dalriada) along the western shores of Scotland, a region then controlled by the Irish clan of the same name. Columba then took it upon himself to convert the northern Pictish tribes, though Christianity had been on the island since the time of the Pictish St. Ninian some two centuries earlier. Nonplussed, and concerned about the clear relapse into paganism that he found throughout Scotland, Columba proceeded afresh.

Visiting King Brude, who lived near Inverness, St. Columba found the door barred against him. But with the sign of the cross, the door burst asunder, and they entered. So awed by this incredible display of spiritual power, the king listened, and was baptized into the faith. St. Columba then spent the remaining 32 years of his life preaching to the Picts and Scots of northern Scotland, founding numerous churches and monasteries and converting many thousands more than the original 3,000 that his penance demanded.

Return from Exile

The last major event in St. Columba's life was at the Council of Drumceat in his native Ireland, which he was called to attend in order to help make some major religious, social, economic and political decisions that would prove to be significant to the social evolution of Ireland. For one, his kinsman Conall, the king of the Dál Ríata had died, and he had been asked to crown the new king. Other important decisions included the colonial status of the Scottish colony of Dál Ríata, as well as the social status of the bards, whose bawdy wit, pagan stories and vicious satires were becoming an increasing problem in the new Christian order.

Naturally Columba, being of royal blood, a poet, and having lived in the Scottish colony of Dál Ríata for many years, was the ideal man to advise on these decisions. However, there was the matter of his self-imposed exile from Ireland, which would preclude his attendance at the convention. Some redactors believe this was circumvented by Columba being blindfolded, or by having Scottish turf strapped to the soles of his feet (or both), but others feel that Columba's self-imposed exile existed only in the minds of later writers who wished to romanticize his dramatic decision to leave Ireland. In either case Columba did indeed return to Ireland to attend the meeting, and did indeed crown the new king.

The council lasted for over a year, during which time Columba successfully argued for the independence of the Scottish Dál Ríata, pointing out that the Irish presence there was unnecessary and unwanted. The poet question, however, hit Columba closest to the heart, as he was both a Christian and a poet. The poets were the last bastion of the old pagan culture, as their traditions centered around the memorization and retelling of the old tales, and it would seem to be the natural decision for a Christian leader to use this opportunity to crush his ideological opponents once and for all. But by that time, Columba pointed out, most of the poets were actually Christian monks who had taken over many of the functions of the old poets. As such, Columba decided that it was best that the poets be allowed to continue to exist as a distinct social class, so long as they paid proper respect to the needs of the new order. Greatly relieved at hearing this, numerous poets and bards then entered the hall and serenaded St. Columba for his wise judgment in keeping the old traditions — and truly, the entire oral history of Ireland — from falling into oblivion.

Requiem

Perhaps the most perfect story of the life of St. Columba is the gentle way he passed into the next life. Columba had been granted the knowledge by God of how he would die, and when. On the day that he was to pass on he informed his fellow brothers, and then went for a walk in the fields nearby the monastery. As he returned to the road to the monastery, he was met by his faithful white horse, which was used to carry pails of milk. The horse approached him gingerly, and placed its head upon St. Columba's breast, whereupon it began to weep and mourn, sensing its master's passing. Columba blessed the horse, then passed over to the monastery, where he blessed the granary, blessed the animals, blessed the monks, and then retired for the night.

In the middle of the night he arose and went to the church, and fell down on his knees before the altar. Diarmuid, Columba's attendant, and some of the other monks found him there before the altar, the space around him filled with a blinding, angelic light. The brightly lit church suddenly went dark, however, and Diarmuid was forced to search for his master in the sudden blackness. Feeling their way in the dark, they finally found the old saint slumped against the altar, and in the dim light saw the look of ecstasy upon his face as he began to see his reward approaching near. Columba then arose and performed his last act on Earth, which was to bless the monks one last time. He then lay down beside the altar and, having fulfilled a lifetime of service to God, finally gave up the ghost.[23]

This great saint, Columba, was largely responsible for the retention of the ancient heritage of Ireland which, had he not existed, might have been lost forever. Unusually intelligent, tall, handsome and having a voice melodious and of extreme power, St. Columba towered over all of the saints of his time, standing in the gap at a time when the fate of Ireland was held in the balance.

THE HISTORY
THE COMING OF
CHRISTIANITY
THE SAINTS

"The Voyage of Brendan — The Crystal Columns" © 1992 Jim Fitzpatrick.

St. Brendan, "The Navigator"

St. Brendan was another prominent Irish saint, born into the Eóganacht clan of Loch Lein, in Ciarraighe Luachra, near the present-day city of Tralee in County Kerry, Munster province, around AD 484.[24] Like many early Irish saints, his birth was also said to be heralded with signs and wonders:

> One day in the year 484, a prosperous Kerry farmer saw a bright light shining in the sky over Fenit, a village on the coast a few miles west of Tralee. The same night thirty cows brought forth thirty calves in his barn. Next morning, guided by the light, he walked to the village, and found a new-born baby in a cottage. To the babe, St. Brendan, he offered the thirty calves. And so, in a manner suspiciously akin to the birth of Christ, St. Brendan was born.[25]

Early Years

Signs and wonders accompanied the saint throughout his early life, so when he was two his parents decided

242

to put the young Brendan under the care of a foster-mother: the abbess St. Ita of Kileedy. There he learned basic religious teachings, including the three things that most displease God: hating others, embracing evil, and trusting riches, as well as the three things that please God: steadfast faith, leading a simple life, and generous charity.[26] Five years later, at the age of seven, Brendan then returned to his family.

A local bishop named Erc, however, saw promise in the young lad, and decided to take him under his wing for more advanced training into the Christian faith. After five additional years of training under Erc's patronage, Brendan began to show some real promise, so St. Erc sent him north to Galway to study under a monk named St. Jarlath. There he began to learn the more formal rules of the monastic order, such as the rule of St. Ailbe, and even memorize all of the psalms. And after his education and ordination by St. Erc was completed in 512, he established his first monastery: Ardfert. And it was from this first monastery that he set out on his famous voyage to seek out the Promised Land of the West.

The Journey

Navigatio Sancti Brendani Abbatis, or "The Voyage of St. Brendan" was the very famous tale of St. Brendan's journey to visit the "Promised Land of the West" that he had heard was the land that God had promised to the saints to be their eternal inheritance, forever. In this classic tale of white martyrdom, some versions say, one day St. Brendan climbed nearby Slieve Dagda (later named Brandon Mountain after him), and fasted for forty days and forty nights, seeking God's will. It is said that an angel then came to him in a dream and promised to guide him to the Promised Land. Other accounts, most notably the *Navigatio* itself, say that Brendan learned of the mysterious Promised Land from one St. Barrind, who had sailed there himself. There he had found a great land of peace and plenty where the sun never set. This land was divided by a great river that ran east and west, and was guarded by an angel of the Lord. Yearning to see this "Promised Land of the Saints", Brendan purposed in his heart to sail there and see it for himself.

Taking 14 dedicated monks to help him on his journey, Brendan built a sturdy ship made of a wood frame covered with ox-hides smeared with fat, including oars, a rudder and a single large sail on a central mast. Then, after taking on provisions, and blessing the ship and its crew in the name of the Father, Son and Holy Spirit, they embarked on their quest to find the mysterious Promised Land of the West.

Their journey was initially made easy by a favorable wind that carried them for 15 days, but after that the wind dropped and they were forced to use the oars. Shortly thereafter, they became worn out and despairing. St. Brendan, however, told the brothers to have faith that God would send a wind to send them where He willed. And sure enough, when they had put up their oars and placed their trust in God, the wind returned and they were taken on their way.

The Patience and Faith of the Saints

After 40 days, when all their food and water had run out, they finally arrived at an island, but could not land as the cliffs were too sheer. St. Brendan once again reminded the starving monks to have faith, and after they had sailed around the island for three days, they finally found the perfect place to land. Moreover, when they landed, a friendly dog came to greet them, and led them to a place where meals sat prepared for them, enough for three days and nights — exactly what they needed.

They then departed again, and soon came upon another island — this time, an island of sheep. There they met a single monk, another white martyr who had preceded them by some years and had been living on that island as a hermit. The sheep on this island were bigger than cattle as no one took milk from them, and the climate was so ideal that grass grew year-round, so they were able to take on much provision.

After saying their goodbyes to their fellow brother, and thanking him for the meat for their journey, Brendan and his monks set off once more. The next island they saw, however, seemed peculiar, as it had no shoreline, no sand, and no grass, being completely hard and stony. Brendan realized what it was and said nothing, staying in the boat while the brothers camped out on the barren island for the night. In the morning, when they began to cook and preserve the meat that they had brought with them from The Island of Sheep, the barren island began to move and shake. They then ran for the boat, leaving all their food and possessions behind. And when they were a safe distance away, Brendan revealed the secret of the island: it was actually a giant sea creature named Jasconius *(op. cit.)*, who had grown angry at having a fire built on his back and had decided to evict his unwanted tenants.

The saints then continued on their journey, which eventually came to take seven years in total. Along the way they visited numerous other locations: an island populated by angelic birds who sang the praises of Christ continually; a monastic community run by St. Ailbe; a "soporific well" that caused them to go to sleep for as many days as the number of cups they had drunk from it; a "coagulated sea" that was as smooth as glass, where no wind blew for days; a "devouring beast" that breathed fire and nearly sank their ship; an island of three choirs, and an island of grapes.

Along the way a gryphon — a mythical creature that is part lion, part eagle — attacked them, but it was killed by a great eagle that had been sent by God to defend them. Next they encountered a clear sea, where they could see the fish all the way at the bottom. They then encountered a "crystal pillar", which some believe was an iceberg, that appeared to be wrapped in a net of silver. This was followed by an encounter with an Island of Smiths, where evil, giant smiths threw huge balls of fire at them, causing the sea all around them to boil. This island was then closely followed by an island with a fiery mountain, most likely a volcano.

America, the Promised Land

Finally, after some more interesting experiences, St. Brendan and company encountered the great region of fog through which they had to pass in order finally to reach the Promised Land of the Saints. The Promised Land appeared just as St. Barrind had said it would, and they too were met by a youth who blessed them, and bade them stay for a time, after which they were to return to their homeland with as many fruits and precious stones of the land as they could carry. This was the Promised Land of the Saints, he explained, which would be given to the saints at the end of time.

Though there have been many interpretations as to the many wonders that St. Brendan saw on his journey across the Atlantic, it seems likely that the saint may

**THE HISTORY
THE COMING OF
CHRISTIANITY
THE SAINTS**

indeed have discovered America nearly 1,000 years before Columbus. O'Meara explains,

Some recent books have suggested that Brendan did [reach America].... The Irish got to Greenland by 900 at the latest, and to the Sargasso Sea, well west of the Azores, about the same time. He suggests the identification, among other possibilities, of the Island of Sheep and the Paradise of Birds of the Voyage of Saint Brendan with the Faroes; the Island of Smiths with Iceland; the Island of Paul the Hermit with Rockall; the region of whales with Greenland; the region of fog with Newfoundland; the Island of the Community of Ailbe with Madeira; the Coagulated Sea with Sargasso; the Island of the Three Choirs with the Bahamas; and the Island of Grapes with, possibly, Jamaica.[27]

If so, the Promised Land of the Saints is, no doubt, North America, the river that divides the continent north and south being the St. Lawrence River, which is west of Newfoundland and north of Nova Scotia. But how far did St. Brendan travel to the interior of the country? If he did indeed travel as far as Jamaica, it would not have been difficult to proceed through the Gulf of Mexico to the Mississippi River and then into the interior of the country.

The Beast

Interestingly, as we have discussed previously, in 1673, midway up the Mississippi River near Alton, Illinois, the legendary explorers Jacques Marquette and Louis Joliet discovered a painting of a mysterious dragon-fish on a cliff known by the local Indians as the "Piasa".[28] This creature, as discussed previously, matches in both name and description almost exactly the mysterious "Piast" of ancient Ireland, which was also a combination of a dragon and a fish.[29] Could it be that St. Brendan marked the furthest extent of his travels into the mysterious "Promised Land" that would be given to the saints of the Most High at the time of the end with the mark of a dragon, or "beast"? And if so, why would he use the symbol of a dragon[30] to mark America as the Promised Land of the Saints, and tell the local Native Americans that its name was *Piasa*, literally, "the beast"? The answer to this question may lead us to some disturbing conclusions too complex to deal with here.[31]

Requiem

Not long after its publication, though it was initially intended to be mainly a story for the instruction and edification of the saints, the *Navigatio* ended up being one of the most famous and enduring stories of Western Christendom, becoming so wildly popular all over Europe that it is widely held to be one of the great stories of western literature.[32] And though St. Brendan was said to have died as soon as he returned to Ireland, in fact he went on to found several more monasteries, including Inis-da-druim (Coney Island in County Clare) in 550. He then went to visit Iona, doing missionary work in Britain for three years, later returning to Ireland to found several more monasteries, the most famous of which is Clonfert, which he founded in 557.[33]

Though not as famous as the three great saints of Ireland, St. Brendan was a very popular and well-respected saint. His most famous church, Clonfert in County Galway, is beautifully preserved, with stained glass and numerous ornate carvings, including even a perky mermaid. Brendan is remembered today as one of the great saints of Irish history, and as one of the great heroes of Western literature. Read more about all the great saints of Ireland at http://ireland.mysterious world.com/History/Christianity/Saints/

The Journey

So the journey of the Gael continued, this time in the form of Christianity, a journey that continues to this day. But the evangelization of pagan Ireland was no easy process — deep-rooted traditions die hard. And though the saints did not have to fear the red martyrdom during their journey to spread the Good News across the sacred isle, they did have to fear compromising their morals and ethics with the pagan value systems that they routinely encountered during their travels. Sex, violence, witchcraft and war still remained to be subdued before the four quarters of the sacred isle could become one land, before the land of Èiru could become Ireland.

To this end, as they traveled about the sacred isle evangelizing and converting the people to the new faith, the early Christian monks began to analyze and codify all aspects of ancient Irish life and literature, song and story. From the four quarters of the land they gathered together all of the traditions of ancient Ireland, keeping those that were edifying, editing those that were questionable, and ignoring those that were worthless. And from this analysis of the culture of ancient Ireland, the early monks, from Patrick onward, were much better able to communicate the message of the Gospel in a way that the Irish could understand and appreciate. As a result, Christianity spread like wildfire and, despite modern assaults from secularism, remains the dominant belief system in Ireland today.

Let us now take an "eagle's eye" view of the culture and traditions that the first Christians encountered, so that we may see ancient Ireland as Patrick, Brigid, Columba, Brendan and other Irish saints experienced it.

Notes

[1] Peter Brown, *The Rise of Western Christendom* 2nd ed. (Oxford: Blackwell Publishing, 2003), 4. The internal quote was taken from F. Haverfield, *The Romanization of Roman Britain*, (Oxford: 1912), p. 10.

[2] Charles G. Herbermann and Georg Grupp, "Constantine the Great" (The Catholic Encyclopedia Online: http://www.newadvent.org/cathen/), http://www.newadvent.org/cathen/04295c.htm.

[3] Peter and Fiona Somerset Fry, *A History of Ireland* 2nd ed. (New York: Barnes & Noble, 1993), 35.

[4] Brendan LaHane, *Early Celtic Christianity* 2nd ed. (New York: Continuum Books, 2005), 41.

[5] E.C. Grupp, "St. Anthony" (The Catholic Encyclopedia Online: http://www.newadvent.org/cathen/), http://www.newadvent.org/cathen/01553d.htm.

[6] LaHane, *Early Celtic Christianity*, 42.

[7] Thomas Cahill, *How the Irish Saved Civilization* (New York: Anchor Books, 1996), 183.

[8] *Ibid.*, 187-188.

[9] Christopher Bamford, trans., *The Voice of the Eagle: The Heart of Celtic Christianity* (Great Barrington, MA: Lindisfarne Books, 2000), 21-22.

[10] Patrick Frances Cardinal Moran, "St. Patrick" (The Catholic Encyclopedia Online: http://www.newadvent.org/cathen/), http://www.newadvent.org/cathen/11554a.htm.

[11] Charles D. Trimble, "County Armagh" (From Ireland: http://www.from-ireland.net), http://www.from-ireland.net/descrs/arm/coarmaghdes.htm.

[12] Moran, "St. Patrick", http://www.newadvent.org/cathen/11554a.htm.

[13] The life of Patrick summarized from Fry, *A History of Ireland*, 26, 33-35; Moran, "St. Patrick", http://www.newadvent.org/cathen/11554a.htm; Trimble, "County Armagh", http://www.from-ireland.net/descrs/arm/coarmaghdes.htm. For additional information on St. Patrick, check out the St. Patrick Center at http://www.saintpatrick-centre.com.

[14] W.H. Grattan-Flood, "St. Brigid of Ireland" (The Catholic Encyclopedia Online: http://www.newadvent.org/cathen/), http://www.newadvent.org/cathen/02784b.htm.

[15] For more information visit http://www.visitdownpatrick.com.

[16] Bamford, *The Voice of the Eagle*, 42.

[17] Columba Edmonds, "St. Columba" (The Catholic Encyclopedia Online: http://www.newadvent.org/cathen/), http://www.newadvent.org/cathen/04136a.htm.

[18] LaHane, *Early Celtic Christianity*, 113.

[19] *Ibid.*, 115.

[20] Cahill, *How the Irish Saved Civilization*, 170. Cf. also Mary Jones, ed., "An Cathach" (Jones' Celtic Encyclopedia: http://www.maryjones.us), http://www.maryjones.us/jce/cathach.html.

[21] LaHane, *Early Celtic Christianity*, 120.

[22] Edmonds, "St. Columba", http://www.newadvent.org/cathen/04136a.htm.

[23] Bamford, *The Voice of the Eagle*, 44-45.

[24] W.H. Grattan Flood, "St. Brendan" (The Catholic Encyclopedia Online: http://www.newadvent.org/cathen/), http://www.newadvent.org/cathen/02758c.htm.

[25] LaHane, *Early Celtic Christianity*, 53-54.

[26] *Ibid.*, 54-55.

[27] John J. O'Meara, trans., *The Voyage of St. Brendan: Journey to the Promised Land* (Dublin: The Dolmen Press, 1978), xii.

[28] For more information on the mysterious Piasa creature of Alton, Illinois, see http://www.mysteriousworld.com/Journal/1999/Spring/Piasa01/.

[29] Cf. The Mystery: Creatures Great & Small: Mythical Water Creatures: Sea Serpents: Piast (pp. 177-178).

[30] Cf. Revelation 12.

[31] For an in-depth analysis of the Piasa creature and its apocalyptic implications, go to http://www.mysteriousworld.com/Journal/2006/Spring/SpecialUpdate/.

[32] O'Meara, *The Voyage of St. Brendan*, xiv.

[33] John Healy, "Clonfert" (The Catholic Encyclopedia Online: http://www.newadvent.org/cathen/), http://www.newadvent.org/cathen/04064b.htm.

THE HISTORY
THE COMING OF
CHRISTIANITY
NOTES

Ancient Irish Culture

ncient Irish culture, as we have seen, was a patchwork of histories and traditions, myths and legends from the numerous invaders that have conquered the sacred isle throughout the millennia. From the tales of the powerful Fianna of Leinster province in the east, the myths and legends of the Tuatha dé Danann who held the south, the fierce Fir Bolg who made their stronghold in Connaught in the west, and the glorious tales of The Knights of the Red Branch who controlled Ulster in the north, each province of Ireland has its own histories and traditions that make each region unique. Yet unlike the British Isles, which have yet to fully integrate culturally Ireland, despite the recent troubles, remains a culturally cohesive unit, with religious, social, economic and political systems that are uniquely Irish.

In this chapter of The History, we will take a look at the ancient Irish culture that confronted the early Christian monks who were struggling to evangelize the sacred isle. In the process, we will attempt to summarize the major elements of ancient Irish culture that we have covered thus far, and look at them in some more detail in order to shed some more light on the specifics of daily life in ancient Ireland. In so doing we hope to provide a more solid understanding of the lifeways of the ancient Irish, including the religious beliefs, social folkways and mores, and the economic and political structures which, to some extent, still persist in the modern Irish worldview.

Ancient Irish Religion

The religion of the ancient Irish was, like all ancient, non-monotheistic religions, essentially the worship of the material world as the outward manifestation of deity. Outside of direct revelation from a divine being, as is typical of monotheistic religions, it is the predisposition of man to worship that which his five senses can perceive. And those things that hold the greatest power over him, such as the sun, moon, and stars, and natural forces such as the wind, the rain and the fertility of the land, were believed to be the

251

highest manifestation of the impersonal deity that they believed lay behind the powers of nature. As such, the sun, moon, stars and other natural forces stood at the center of the ancient pagan cosmogony, forming the absolute point of reference against which all things were measured. And over time, these beliefs became concretized in their myths, rituals and architecture.

The religion of the ancients revolved around the worship of the sun, moon and stars, beliefs that were reflected in their architecture.[†]

THE PAGAN WORLDVIEW

As a result of this five-sense-oriented mindset, the pagan mind developed a worldview that was relative to the environment in which it was situated, creating complex mythologies to explain the capricious actions of the natural forces that it encountered, and formulating "metaphoric" rituals specifically designed to control them. As Dáithí Ó hÓgáin explains in *The Sacred Isle: Belief and Religion in Pre-Christian Ireland*,

The human mind, in its attempt to unravel a mystery, tries to concretize and dramatize its components — in other words, to think metaphorically. It is this metaphoric mode of thinking which gives rise to the calcified imagery which we know as superstition, and we can be sure that the earliest inhabitants of Ireland were just as adept at developing and preserving such traditional beliefs and practices as has man in every other time and place. Antique peoples in general had the impression that hidden forces lay in the environment, and this was expressed in a belief that the landscape was inhabited by spirits of one sort or another. Considering that Ireland was thickly forested at the time, the mystery of the depths of these forests must have impressed itself on the incomers, and no doubt the precarious nature of their existence would have added to their sense of awe…. Therefore, they would have had a practical approach to the world of the unknown and have used elements of ritual to come to terms with it, and to placate and control it.[1]

The ancients developed their complex mythologies and rituals as a means of controlling nature — specifically, to ensure their continuance in accord with natural principles so that their lifeways would not come into conflict with the powerful natural forces that surrounded them. In order to achieve this goal, they created symbols — idols, as some have called them — that embodied the natural forces, and made sacrifices to these symbolic entities in which they believed the divine forces of the universe had become focused as a result of their rituals. By giving a form to these natural forces that they could understand, ancient man believed he had created a means to communicate with and placate these natural forces so as to ensure the fertility of land and womb and, by extension, their own continued existence in the land. As McCaffrey and Eaton neatly summarize in their popular work, *In Search of Ancient Ireland*, "In order to counter [their] fear, people would seek the protection of elemental gods who could command authority over nature and thereby make life safer. The gods and goddesses, with their various powers over the environment, made the forces of nature more controllable and consequently less frightening."[2]

THE HISTORY
ANCIENT IRISH
CULTURE
RELIGION

Sacred Architecture

Having successfully captured the divine essence of the natural forces into an object of adoration, an "idol", it stood to reason that in order to maximize their ability to sympathetically control the forces of nature, the idol had to be placed in a setting which magnified the immanent powers of nature into the idol most efficiently. Believing that the sun, moon and stars were the highest manifestations of the divine force immanent in nature, the ancient Irish — and pagans throughout the world — aligned their sacred architecture with the risings and settings of the sun, moon and certain stars in such a way that these sacred temples of nature could best draw upon their divine power. Thus we see even in the pagan mind a canny sort of logic that guided the development of their sacred architecture, the understanding of which we can use to better understand their motivations for creating the countless stone artifacts that remain as their ancient legacy.

The vast number of sacred artifacts left behind by the ancients is too large to enumerate here, but we can list the types of sacred architecture, a brief description of the purpose and use of each, and a listing of the best-known artifacts of each type to be found in Ireland:

✠ Barrows

Barrows are mounds of earth often found over ancient graves, and are either usually linear or circular ("round") in shape. See also "Mounds".

✠ Bullauns

Bullauns are typically round, flat stones that have a hemispherical depression in the middle that tends to collect rainwater over time. Usually located near holy wells and similar sacred places, it was believed even into modern times that drinking the water from such stones would cure various aches and pains, and improve one's general health. Though bullauns can be found all throughout Ireland, perhaps the most famous bullaun stone is St. Brigid's Stones in County Cavan. This bullaun stone is unique in that it is one large, star-shaped stone with several depressions, each of which contains a blessing/cursing stone. It was believed that if one turned the stone clockwise in its depression, it would bring a blessing, but if one turned it counterclockwise, it would bring a curse.

THE HISTORY
ANCIENT IRISH
CULTURE
RELIGION

✤ Cairns — Cairns are essentially huge piles of rocks usually used to mark important graves, historic locations and/or astronomical alignments. Loughcrew and Carnbane in County Meath, and Heapstown Cairn, Barroe North Round Cairn and Knocknarea in County Sligo are classic examples of cairns. Fourknocks Chambered Cairn in County Meath is a good example of a "chambered cairn", a cairn with a large internal space that can be entered. Ballybriest Court Cairn in County Derry and Ossian's Grave in County Antrim are interesting examples of the type of cairn known as a "court cairn", which is essentially a row of modest-sized stones surrounding a gravesite. Another type, the "portal" or "wedge", is essentially a combination of a cairn and a dolmen, with two portal stones supporting a large capstone, the rest covered with dirt and rocks creating a passage that becomes lower and narrower at the back — a "portal" that was no doubt intended to give worshipers the feeling that they were descending into the Underworld. A good example of a portal or wedge cairn is the Gleninsheen Wedge Grave in County Clare. See also "Passage Cairns".

✤ Cists

A cist is a grave that is lined with stone and/or wood, often also having a stone or wooden lid, usually used for people of some importance.

✤ Dolmens

Also known as "cromlechs", dolmens are monuments that are composed of two upright "portal" stones that support a third, usually very large, flat, "capstone". Dolmens, like many forms of ancient architecture, were believed to be portals to the Otherworld, doorways from the world of the physical to the world of the spiritual. They remain today as some of the most spectacular of ancient monuments, and can be found throughout Ireland. Prominent dolmens include the Proleek Dolmen in County Louth, Browne's Hill Dolmen in County Carlow, Harristown/Kilmogue Dolmen in County Kilkenny, Poulnabrone Dolmen in County Clare, Carrickglass Dolmen in County Sligo, Kilclooney Dolmen in County Donegal, Tirnony Dolmen in County Derry, Legananny Dolmen in County Down and Ballykeel Dolmen in County Armagh.

THE HISTORY
ANCIENT IRISH
CULTURE
RELIGION

✦ Hill-Forts

See "Stone Forts".

✦ Megaliths

Megaliths, literally, "big stones", are typically very large, upright stones that were usually used to mark certain places where important historical events took place. Sometimes these stones were purposely planted in preparation for a battle for warriors to use to lean against as they defended against their foes. Called "battle pillars", these types of stones were useful to guard one's back as well as to help defend against wide, swinging strokes from one's opponent, as there was a chance that their sword could strike the pillar and chip or even break. The Plains of Moy Tura (lit., "The Plains of the Pillars"), where the First and Second Battles of Moy Tura took place, both still have numerous battle and commemorative pillars. These battle-fields can be found in Counties Mayo and Sligo respectively (*q.v.*).

However, though these plains have numerous, famous pillars, probably the most famous megalithic stone pillar is Cú Chulainn's battle pillar in County Louth. The Cat Stone on the Hill of Uisneach in County Westmeath is another famous megalithic structure that is actually composed of several megalithic stones — one, it is believed, for each of the five ancient provinces of Ireland. The Turas Colmcille in County Donegal also contains numerous, beautifully carved standing stones, and the Doagh Hole Stone in County Antrim has a unique hole through its middle that will allow only a slim, feminine hand to pass through it.

✦ Holy Wells

Holy wells are essentially wells that have been set apart for sacred use. They are typically constructed from stone, and are sometimes underground, allowing worshipers in ancient times to symbolically pass into the Underworld as part of their rituals. Water from holy wells was of course believed to be holy and efficacious towards good health, a belief that continued well into the Christian period when Ireland's holy wells were repurposed for Christian use. Prominent holy wells include St. Movee's Well in County Dublin, Colmcille's Well and St. Ciaran's Well in County Meath, St. Brigid's Well in Westmeath, St. Gobnait's and St. Latieran's Wells in County Cork, Cormac's Well in County Sligo, St. Columb's Well in County Derry, St. Brigid's Well in Longford, Trinity Well and another St. Brigid's Well in County Kildare, St. Declan's Well in County Waterford, two more St. Brigid's Wells in Counties Clare and Roscommon, Struell Wells in County Down, and two St. Patrick's Wells in Counties Tyrone and Fermanagh.

✛ Mounds

Mounds are among the most common artifacts of the ancient world, and are to be found worldwide. Simply piles of compacted earth, mounds are usually the remnants of ancient earthworks, or of burial plots for persons of some import. Some of the most famous mounds include the Hill of Tara, Cormac's House and the Mound of the Hostages in County Meath, Rathcroghan Mound in County Roscommon, the Mound of Down in County Down, and of course Emain Macha in County Armagh.

✛ Ogham Stones

Ogham stones are simply large standing stones carved with Ogham writing, usually used to mark boundaries or commemorate certain events. There are numerous Ogham stones throughout Ireland, County Kerry's Dingle Peninsula alone having as many as sixty. Several excellent examples can also be seen in the National Museum. Perhaps the most spectacular, however, remains *in situ* in County Cork, and is known as the Ballycrovane/Faunkill Ogham Stone. This is believed to be the largest Ogham stone in Ireland, possibly the world.

✛ Passage Cairns

Passage cairns are typically very large structures made of a combination of earth and stone that are circular in construction. They receive their name from the fact that they have one long, central passage that usually leads to a broader chamber near the center of the structure. This chamber typically served as the seat of an idol — probably in the form of a sacred stone — and as such these cairns may have served as the center of worship for a given region, or even the entire country, as may have been the case for Newgrange, in County Meath. Burials and cremations are also occasionally found in passage cairns, though the function of these structures was more likely ritual in nature rather than funereal.

The most interesting characteristic about passage cairns is the fact that many of them are aligned with various solar events, particularly sunrises and sunsets on certain days of the year. The classic example, Newgrange, even has a special "roof box" that only lets the sun enter into the passageway on a certain day of the year: the winter solstice. On that day a shaft of light streams all the way back to the very end of the passage and illuminates a special stone (still there today) that is covered with spiral and zigzag patterns which some scientists now believe may have been a form of scientific notation used to track the movements of the sun. It may also be, as was the case in other parts of the world, that the sun illuminated an idol that once stood in its place at the end of the passage.

The three best examples of passage cairns in Ireland are to be found in the Boyne Valley — Newgrange, Knowth and Dowth — which are definite must-sees. Interestingly, Newgrange and Dowth form a synchronized pair. Whereas the rising sun illuminates the inner chamber of Newgrange on the winter solstice, it is the setting sun that illuminates the central chamber of Dowth at the end of that same day. Thus, the name Dowth, which means "darkness".

☩ Raths

Raths are circular remnants of the foundations of ancient fortifications, and were often considered to be the domains of fairies. Significant raths include The Rath of the Kings, The Rath of the Synods, Rath Gráinne and Rath Maeve in County Meath, and *Rath na dTarbhe*, "The Fort of the Bulls", in County Roscommon. The famous Ardagh Chalice was found buried in a rath near the village of Ardagh in County Limerick. See also "Mounds" and "Stone Forts".

☩ Stone Circles

Also known as stone "henges", stone circles are essentially rows of megalithic stones arranged in a circle, usually surrounded by a bank-and-ditch structure. They usually performed a ritual function, and are often aligned with the cardinal points of the compass, as well as major rising and setting points of the sun, moon and stars. Significant Irish stone circles include the Drumbeg, Cashel-keelty, Shronebirran, and Uragh stone circles in County Cork, Eightercua Stone Circle in County Kerry, Grange Stone Circle in County Limerick (the largest stone circle in Ireland), Beaghmore Stone Circle in County Tyrone and the Drumskinny Stone Circle in County Fermanagh.

✤ Sacred Stones

Sacred stones are essentially idols in the form of tall standing stones, usually 3-5 feet tall and covered in sacred carvings. The most famous sacred stones of Ireland are the *Lía Fail* at Tara, in County Meath, the *Clogh Óir* of County Tyrone and the *Crom Cruach* of County Cavan. Together, these three form "The Three Magical Stones of Ireland". These stones were believed to have an oracular function, in that it was believed that the local deity of the region spoke through the stone, and could answer questions (though the actual talking was probably done by one of the deity's druids who was hidden nearby). The *Lía Fail* was used in the coronation of the High Kings of ancient Ireland up to the time of Brian Boru, and it was actually believed to emit a roar when the king stood upon it. Other prominent sacred stones include the Turoe Stone, which may also have been an object of adoration, and the famous spiral-designed "kerbstones", 97 of which surround Newgrange, the purpose of which is still a mystery.

✤ Stone Forts

Ancient Irish stone forts were not like later medieval castles, but were instead composed of huge piles of loosely fitted rocks arranged to create massive walls that were so thick, several men could easily walk abreast atop them. Famous stone forts include Dun Aonghasa and Dun Eóghanacta in County Galway, and Doon Fort and the Grianán of Aileach in County Donegal. The Grianán of Aileach, however, despite its similarity to other stone forts, is now believed to actually have served as a "theater in the round", used possibly for sacred reasons rather than defensive, though it may have served as both.

THE DRUIDS

All ancient peoples had within their societies a class of individuals that were set apart for special service to be emissaries, or "go-betweens" between the realm of the flesh and the realm of the spirit. These ancient priests went by various titles such as "hierophant", "shaman", or even "witch-doctor", but regardless of their specific cultural customs and nomenclature, they all served the same function in each society: as interpreters of the mysteries of life, and of the afterlife. And the interpreters of the religious mysteries of the ancient Celts was the priestly caste that were referred to as the Druids. Ó hÓgáin explains,

> Although belief in spiritual or Otherworld forces is a general tendency in human culture, ancient and primitive peoples have generally relied on a small number of individuals to act as intermediaries between themselves and these powers. Such special individuals are marked out from their fellows by some extraordinary traits or abilities, and particularly by their mental powers. The selection of them to mediate on behalf of their community is a rather spontaneous process, and is studied by modern scholars under the heading "shamanism". There is abundant evidence for shamanism among the ancient Indo-European peoples, and the early Celts doubtlessly had such select personages among them also. A distinction can be made as to the degree to which such religious practice is institutionalized — for instance, societies with more general and structured organization would tend to regulate the role of the shaman with standardized training and with more systematic dogma. Such a development among the Celts is instanced by the phenomenon of Druidism.[3]

The druids were essentially the priestly class of the Celts. The term druid actually comes from a compound word comprised of two different terms: *dru*, "great", and *wid*, "knowledge". Thus, these "men of great knowledge", or "professors" to use a modern term, were essentially a combination of priest and academic, and were in charge of not only the religious rituals of the Celtic peoples, but also the sum total of their accumulated knowledge.

FAITH & WORSHIP

The faith of the ancient Irish was based upon several principles, including a distinction between the physical world and the spiritual world, and a belief in reincarnation. Their afterlife was very similar to that of the ancient Egyptians in that they believed that when people died, their lives contined on, but in a more idealized form, in a place where there was no sorrow or pain, and every day was a delight. However, they also believed in a hell, though the criteria for being sent to this hell is not clear — most likely only liars and cowards went there, those who did not follow the Celtic ethos of duty, honor and loyalty in life, finishing that honorable life with a glorious death on the battlefield.

In practice, the ancient Irish religion, unlike the later Christian religion, was more celebratory than obligatory. Having much more in common with the Greek *bacchanalia* than the Christian sabbath, the worship of the ancient Irish on the great holy days of the year essentially involved riotous revelry, feasting, and even drunken orgies. At these times of feasting, the Roman historians noted that the Celts tended to get into quarrels over the slightest insult, and they always fought to the death as their belief in reincarnation led them to the conclusion that the glory of victory was worth the risk of death.

FESTIVALS

There were four major festivals of the Celtic year, marking the four quarters of the Celtic calendar. These were, in order, *Samhain*, *Imbolg*, *Beltaine* and *Lughnasa*:

✦ *Samhain*

Samhain, the most important festival of the year, took place on November 1, the first day on the Celtic calendar. The festival also marked the beginning of winter and the symbolic "death" of the previous year, thus its association with the "hag" or witch that represented old age and death. *Oice Samhain*, or "Samhain Eve", took place the previous evening, and it was believed to be one of the two times in the year when the physical world and the spiritual world came closest together. At these times, spiritual "doorways" between the physical and spiritual world were believed to open up, and the *sídhe* marched out across all of Ireland playing tricks on people. If someone had done wickedly that year, the dead and the *sídhe* (the distinction was not always clear) would come after him and play vicious pranks on that person, sometimes physically harming or even killing them. To avoid this "spiritual revenge", people would often leave out little gifts of food or liquor to placate them, and sometimes even dressed up in order to fool the spirits and keep them off their trail. Others dressed up specifically to be able to play pranks on people and maintain their anonymity in order to avoid reprisals from the world of the living. These pranks were an effective way of "letting off steam", and helped to maintain communal order.

On the national level, great rituals were held at the major religious centers around Ireland, and included sacrifices of animals — and in elder times, humans. In more recent times most people merely gave blood to be offered to their pagan gods, but the Samhain festival of the god Crom Cruach (*op. cit.*) actually required the people to sacrifice 1/3 of their milk, corn and even their children to this bloodthirsty devil-god. This occurred even up to the time of St. Patrick, when Patrick finally stopped the bloody ritual after King Tigernmas and three-quarters of his subjects had died in the horrible, bloody orgiastic ritual that surrounded this wicked idol. Not all Samhain festivals were this violent, of course, but during certain periods of Irish history Samhain was definitely a time of great wickedness and blood-letting around all of Ireland.

During the Christian era, Samhain Eve was replaced by the Christian festival of "All Hallows Eve" in order to help ease the transition from paganism to Christianity. This of course has come to be known as "Halloween" in modern times, where the costumes, tricks, and treats of the ancient Irish have been adapted into mainstream popular culture, particularly in America.

✟ Imbolg

Imbolg, which was celebrated on February 1, marked the beginning of spring and the return of the fertility of the land. It was particularly associated with the goddess Brigid, later "St. Brigid". Not much is known of what actually occurred at these festivals, but recently people have begun to develop what are called "green man" festivals, where a man dresses up in leaves and dances around a field, symbolically representing the returning of the fertility of the land after winter. These impromptu festivals usually finish with a storyteller telling tales of Brigid around a bonfire.

✦ Beltaine

The festival of *Beltaine*, which occurred on May 1, was the second time in the Celtic calendar when it was believed that the doors between the physical and spiritual realms opened up and the *sídhe* flooded out across all Ireland. The name Beltaine comes from the words *bel*, or "bright light", and *tine*, which means "fire". The Celts also worshiped a sungod named "Belenus", who may have been worshiped as part of the ritual in some quarters. In the evening, fires were lit all over Ireland, traditionally starting with a fire on the Hill of Uisneach in what is now County Westmeath, and then spread out over all of Ireland from there. However, it was most likely that most of the ritual fires were lit in a local holy place and then distributed out to various hilltops. And since it was said that every hilltop across Ireland had a blazing bonfire on Beltaine, the ritual may have been a way of symbolically drawing upon the light of the sun in order to drive away the evil spirits of darkness and help ensure the coming of summer.

Beltaine was also the time when farmers started to pasture their cattle, and on that night they would create two parallel rows of fire and drive their cattle between them in order to drive away evil spirits and help insure health and fertility for the year. Drunken revelry was also in order for that evening, which probably made the process fairly interesting.

✦ Lughnasa

Lughnasa, named after the Celtic god Lugh (*op. cit.*), marked the end of summer and the beginning of autumn in the Irish calendar. Lughnasa was essentially a harvest festival, and took place over a period of weeks, but was usually marked most especially on August 1. The festival was kept particularly well at Tailtain near Tara, where the "Tailltiu Festival", held in honor of Lugh's foster mother, was also celebrated. This festival

THE HISTORY
ANCIENT IRISH
CULTURE
RELIGION

included not only foot races and feats of strength, but also horse racing, athletic contests, philosophical debates and courtships.

Though these four most important festivals marked the four quarters of the Celtic calendar year, there was another interesting and little known festival called "The Wren Festival" which persists to this day. This ancient holiday, which still takes place on the day after Christmas, is known as "Wren Day". The festival still takes place in County Kerry in the town of Dingle, during which time the "Dingle Wren" is celebrated.

"Tailltiu", © 1977, Jim Fitzpatrick.

The origin of this ancient festival is unknown, though it may be a remnant of an old druidic festival, as the wren was believed to be "the king of all birds", the cleverest and most wise. As Ó hÓgáin explains, "The wren has been thought to have a special connection with druids. This springs from a fanciful etymology of the bird's name, *drean an druí-én* ('druid-bird'), which one glossarian explains as 'a bird who makes prophesies'. A medieval text gives detailed prognostications from the directions from which the wren is heard to call."[4] Thus, the wren is probably still celebrated as part of a modified, but still ongoing, ancient tradition.

The Wren Festival has some similarities to the Samhain festival, where people also dress up in costumes and get a little rowdy. It is different, however, in that it is much more positive and upbeat, with people dancing in the streets to the sound of music while the "wren boys",

a group of singers and musicians, frequent houses and pubs singing songs in return for small gifts. At the end of the festival, everyone ends up at the pub, pretty much like every other festival.

Ancient Irish Society
STRUCTURE

Ancient Irish society was composed of groups of various sizes, the most basic unit being the family:

✦ The Family

The Irish family unit was the same as it is today, made up of the parents, their children and often the grandparents, who usually lived together as an extended family unit.

✦ The *Sept*

The *sept* was the extended family, including all of the near relatives such as aunts, uncles, cousins, and so forth. All of the family members of the *sept* may or may not have lived in the same town, but they were more likely than not to have kept in relatively close proximity.

✦ The *Clan*

The *clan*, which means "children" or "house", was a term that included all of the relatives of the oldest ancestor that can be accounted for. "Clan O'Reilly", for example, would include all the descendants of the original O'Reilly, though most in the O'Reilly clan may never have met each other, nor even known of each other's existence, due to geographical distance.

✦ The *Finna*

The *finna*, or *fine*, was a term used to denote a grouping of people somewhere between clan and tribe that were genetically related but not necessarily intermarried. The *Fianna* of Finn McCool may have been derived from this word, though they were more of a military order.

✦ The *Tuath*

The *tuath*, or "tribe", was made up of several *septs* or clans, all of whom were descended from a prominent ancestor or small group of ancestors. However, due to the fact that oftentimes strangers were adopted into the *tuath*, and intermarriage between different clans and *tuath* often took place, the *tuath* was not nearly as homogeneous as the family or the *sept*, except for the royalty who were very stringent about maintaining genetic purity within the royal line.

THE HISTORY
ANCIENT IRISH
CULTURE
SOCIETY

265

Ancient Irish society, then, was based upon the family as the most basic unit, and upon the *tuath* as its largest. Patterson describes the inner workings of the *tuath* in her excellent *Cattle Lords & Clansmen: The Social Structure of Early Ireland*, "Tuath society was internally divided into different social ranks based upon control of productive property, and on social standing; each of these influenced the other, but social standing was also affected by the community's perceptions of the morality, lawfulness, prestige, and even the stylishness of an individual's behavior, and that of his/her kin."[5] So, though even the peoples within the *tuath* may have been closely related, social stratification existed even within that unit, indicating that each *tuath* probably constituted a complete society that could exist independently within the larger national framework. As such ancient Ireland, before the advent of Christianity, was not yet a unified nation, but rather more of a collection of *tuatha* competing for national hegemony.

LAWS

Brehon Law, or "The Brehon Code", was the basis of the ancient Irish legal system which, as we have seen, was administered by a special class of druid known as the *brehon*. Though the term "Brehon Law" is the most widely known designation for this ancient body of law, its true name is "the law of the *Féine* or *Féne*, or free land-tillers".[6] Joyce explains the law code thusly:

> The Brehon Code forms a great body of civil, military, and criminal law. It regulates the various ranks of society, from the king down to the slave, and enumerates their several rights and privileges. There are minute rules for the management of property, for the several industries — building, brewing, mills, watercourses, fishing-weirs, bees and honey — for distress or seizure of goods, for tithes, trespass, and evidence. The relations of landlord and tenant, the fees of professional men — doctors, judges, teachers, builders, artificers — the mutual duties of father and son, of foster-parents and foster-children, of master and servant, all are carefully regulated. In that portion corresponding to what is now known as criminal law, the various offences

are minutely distinguished — murder, manslaughter, assaults, wounding, thefts, and all sorts of willful damage; and accidental injuries from flails, sledgehammers, machines, and weapons of all kinds; and the amount of compensation is laid down in detail for almost every possible variety of injury.[7]

The Law of Compensation

In many ancient countries, the basis of the law was *lex talionis*, or "an eye for an eye" where, if there was no effective justice system available, people often took justice into their own hands in order to right a wrong done to them. But in ancient Celtic society, the Brehon "law of compensation" usually replaced the *lex talionis*, where a monetary fine was usually paid in lieu of physical punishment.

If the convicted person did not pay the fine, however, there were some procedures that the plaintiff could use in order to be compensated for their loss: 1) procedure by distress where, with the permission of the court, and in the view of several witnesses, the property of the offender was taken in payment, and 2) procedure by fasting, where the aggrieved party would sit on the doorstep of the offender in order to shame them into paying. The latter was far more dangerous to the livelihood of the offender, as failure to honor the fast would cause them to greatly lose face, be subject to universal boycott, and perhaps even force them to flee the village.

Offenses that involved physical injury or death involved payment of the *eric*, or "blood money". The amount of money depended upon the type of injury done, and the social class of the injured, the greater the injury and the higher the social class, the higher the amount of the *eric*. The Brehon Laws were actually fairly thorough on this point, but the cost of injuries to a person could never exceed the amount of the *eric* that would be incurred if that person were killed. Interestingly, the brehon never sentenced anyone to death, they only dealt out fines, leaving capital punishment to the family of the person who had been killed if the murderer failed to pay the *eric*. The king, however, could order someone to be executed if he deemed the crime grievous enough, the form of execution usually being by hanging, or by drowning. The drowning was done either by tying the criminal inside a sack, or by tying a stone around their neck.

CUSTOMS & SUPERSTITIONS

Though the majority of the folklore and mythology of ancient Ireland was kept by the poets, there was also, circulating at the lay level, a body of more informal folklore that took the form of various customs and superstitions. These customs and superstitions grew out of the worldview of the ancient Celts, and were based upon the day-to-day observations of the workings of nature, and of man's place within it. And unlike the great epic literature kept by the poets, this information was common to the people at all levels of society, being integral to their daily lives. And an understanding of these customs and superstitions, many of which survive to this day, should lend additional insight into the minds of the ancient Irish.

Since there is such a wide variety of information available on this subject, and its matter often complex, we will provide only a brief summary of the most common beliefs, using the categories provided by Seán Ó Súilleabháin[8] in his classic, *Irish Folk Custom and Belief*:

House and Home

The belief in the fairies, and the spirit world in general, was paramount in the minds of the ancient Irish. It affected many parts of their daily lives, and the home was no exception. Great care was taken to make sure that a home was not built near a fairy fort, or *lios*, particularly not on any of the "paths" that the fairies would walk to and from their various *lios*, and especially not on a *lios* itself. And if one was so foolish to do such a thing, the fairies would certainly curse the home, haunt it, drive off the livestock, make the crops fail, dry up the well, or even burn down the house. Many houses have been abandoned for this reason over the centuries, some of which still stand today, because local traditions regarding haunted houses still die hard.

Precautions were often taken to avoid picking an unlucky site to build a house. The most common was to enquire of a local "wise" person who was aware of where the local "ley lines" were, lines of energetic force that were believed to network the entire island (and the world), and along which the fairies were believed to travel. Another method was to leave four stones or sticks at the four corners of where the house was to be built. If these markers were left in place overnight, it was believed, the fairies were not offended, and the location was safe to build on. If the house was haunted and had to be abandoned, it was believed to be unlucky to rebuild another house across the street. It was even believed that it was unlucky to build an extension west of a house.

Even if a good location was chosen, it was thought wise to bury objects such as the skulls of animals, empty vessels, coins or other ritual objects under the foundation of the house in order to placate the local spirits, or perhaps even give the house a resident "protective spirit". One could not reuse stones from abandoned houses in the building of new houses, however, lest the ill luck of the previous house pass on to the next. Coals of fire from the previous house could be taken, but the *croch*, or the chimney pot along with its utensils, was left with the previous house. Taking coals from the fire was very important, as the turf fire was the spiritual heart of the home, and the prosperity of house, farm and human life was thought to be closely linked with it. Thus the fire had to be carefully kept and guarded from evil-minded people, lest they take the "luck" from the home by taking some of the fire away with them.

Farmer, Fisher and Craftsman

The fertility of the land was of paramount importance to our ancient ancestors, and very many customs and superstitions surrounded it. We have seen that though building a house on a fairy fort or on a fairy trail was considered to be unlucky, for farmers it was considered lucky to have a fairy fort somewhere in their field, as it was believed to enhance the fertility of the land. It was also believed that a small amount of salt sprinkled on the fields before the crop was sown kept the fertility, or "luck", from escaping. During the Christian era, this was replaced by the sprinkling of holy water.

Another common way to "bless" the land was through the use of fire. On May Eve, when the bonfires were lit all around Ireland, farmers would either encircle the fields with fire taken from the sacred bonfires, or actually throw some of the fire into the fields. This was possible as Ireland has a naturally moist climate, so forest fires are rarely a problem. When the harvest

THE HISTORY
ANCIENT IRISH
CULTURE
SOCIETY

269

was completed, the spade was ceremonially placed in the fire to emphasize that the year's work was indeed over, then it was rescued from the flames by the woman of the house who then prepared a feast for the men. This feast was known as the *féil searra* or *clabhsúr* ("closure"), an informal celebration that included feasting, drinking, singing, dancing and storytelling.

The last sheaf of the grain crop was given special attention, and was known by various names, including the "churn", the "granny", *an chailleach* ("the old woman"), and *an luchtar*, (the "bunch" or "sheaf"). The last sheaf was usually taken home to great acclaim, placed in the ceiling beams of the kitchen during the feast, and was later used to weave "harvest knots" for the children to wear.

The fertility of the livestock was also of primary importance, as the Irish economy was primarily based upon cattle. As such, the greatest amount of customs and superstitions revolved around cows, around whom were woven a web of beliefs nearly as complex as those surrounding the home. The cow-house, or byre, was built using the same rules as the main house, keeping in mind the *lios* and the fairy trails between them. Red ribbons were also wrapped around the necks and/or tails of cows to provide additional protection from harm or disease, as well as rings made of rowan branches. On May Eve, the cattle were also made to pass through the fire in order to ward off ill-luck and evil spirits, walking between two parallel lines of fire. For the same reason they were also made to swim through certain sacred lakes or rivers at certain times of the year.

Many customs were specifically designed to protect cows from direct attack from the fairies. Sometimes cows were found ailing, with holes in their hides, near places where small, stone arrowheads littered the ground. Such cows were believed to be "elf-shot", the cure for which was to give them water in which the arrowheads had been boiled. To placate the fairies, a small amount of milk was allowed to fall on the ground, "for those who might need it".

And as with all aspects of Irish superstition, much care was taken to make sure the "luck", in this case, the "milk-luck", was not stolen from the farm, which might lead to disaster for the farm. For this reason, the milk was very carefully guarded, and no milk was given away on May Day or New Year's Day, lest the year's luck go with it. Also, milk could not be given away on a Monday or a Friday, milk vessels could not be lent, vessels which were milk-stained could not be taken to a well, and if the milk-stained vessel was cleaned, the water could not be poured into a river or stream. Milk also could not be given to a neighbor unless some salt had been put into it, and milk could not leave the house at all if someone there was ill.

The fertility of the land, variously termed "luck" or "profit", could not only be lost, it could also be stolen by evil "hags", or witches. It was believed that a hag could steal one's "profit" by bailing out their well or dragging a cloth over the dew of their fields on the morning of May Day while chanting, "Come All to Me!" For this reason, people usually sat up all night on May Eve to guard their fields and wells against the spells of these wicked hags. The butter churn was considered to be the most vulnerable spot from where the profit could be stolen, and much effort was put into protecting it, including putting a live cinder under it, as well as a horseshoe. Or, perhaps, iron nails would be driven into the wood, or a withy of a rowan tree would be wrapped around it. And even the fire could be a source of losing one's profit, so if someone tried to take some fire out of the house, by "reddening" their pipe or for some other reason, they were kept from doing so, and then forced to take a brash, or "hand" at the churn to make up for it.

Almost as important as the fertility of the land was the fertility of the sea, as fish typically were used to supplement the diet, particularly along the coasts. Many taboos were set before fishermen could set out for the catch, particularly surrounding the journey from the land to the sea. For example, if a fisherman met with a red-haired, barefoot and/or whistling woman, a woman in a red garment, a crowing hen, a rabbit, a priest or a fox while on his way to the sea, he would immediately turn back, as it was generally believed that seeing one of these things meant that there would be no luck, and thus no catch that day. Thus the curse, *Sionnach ar do dhubhán, girrfhia ar do bhaoite's nár mharbha' tu aon bhreac, Go Lá Fhéile Bríde!*: "May there be a fox on your fishing-hook and a hare on your bait, and may you kill no fish until St. Brigid's Day!"

Travel, Trade and Communication

Similar to the fears of the fisherman, if one saw a red-haired, bare-foot and/or whistling woman, a white button, a rabbit or a weasel as one set out on a journey, one needed to turn back or else suffer ill-luck on the journey. However, one was otherwise to continue on their journey even if they forgot something, as turning back to retrieve it would also cause bad luck. Travelers were advised to take either salt, a fire-ember, soot or a sprig of hazel or sally with them in order to protect them from ill-luck, usually brought on by evil spirits. If one encountered a funeral along the way, one was expected to take three steps of mercy (*trí choiscéim na trócaire*) with it, even if you have to walk backwards.

There were also certain rules about even which direction one should and should not travel on certain days. As the saying went, *Luan soir agus Máirt agus Máirt siar* — "Travel towards the east on Monday, towards the west on Tuesday". Small cairns were once to be found along road-sides where people had died during their journeys, the custom being to throw an additional stone on the cairn and say a small prayer while passing. Crossroads were a particularly important part of the journey, and were the center of a fair amount of customs and even social activities. Funeral processions often stopped there and the coffins laid down briefly before continuing. Unlucky animals and objects were often abandoned at crossroads, and some stories even have people selling their souls to the devil at crossroads. And until recently, dances were typically held at crossroads on Sunday evenings.

Mass media communications were of course not available in ancient times, but there were other methods of spreading news relatively quickly. Messengers on horseback, fire, smoke, light and/or sound could also be utilized to signal over large distances. It was even said at one time that all of Ireland could be roused by the passing of *sifíní*, or straws, from house to house.

The Community

Social relations within the community were of course the subject of many customs and taboos. One of the more pleasant customs was the *comhar na gcomharsan*, "mutual help given by neighbors", not unlike the Amish "barn-raising" custom where the neighborhood came together to help someone with a large, difficult task that they might not have been able to do themselves, such as turf-cutting, or bringing in the harvest. The only charge was that they would have to provide food and entertainment after the work was done for all those involved.

In ancient Ireland, life was lived mainly in the country which, despite its limitations compared to our modern times and its conveniences, was very satisfying and culturally rich. In fact, it was in many ways superior to modern life, as people were much closer and communicated much more easily with each other. The native culture was also much stronger than today, with storytelling, singing and dancing in houses and at crossroads being commonplace, self-consciousness being abandoned in favor of becoming a healthy, lively member of the larger community.

Game playing was also much more common, hurling and bowling being the most popular pastimes. It was much more common to make surprise house-calls on one's neighbors, and stay up sometimes very late drinking, smoking and telling tall tales. Public houses such as the local pub were also very popular gathering places. Weddings, wakes, funerals, fairs, sports and related events were also very popular places where social relationships were created and maintained.

Generally speaking, though life in ancient Ireland could at times be hard, and of course was without the conveniences of modern life, it was in many ways superior, as one was a member of a much more closely-knit community that was there to help in times of need.

Human Life

The ancient Celts, like most ancient peoples, believed in the existence of the soul as the source of human life. They also believed, however, that it was a concrete entity that existed independent of the body, and could move and act independently of it. Dreams were considered to be the soul traveling independent of the body while it was asleep, and events that occurred while one was asleep were believed to have actually happened in some way. The soul was believed to be in the blood, manifested in the breath, discernible by the body's shadow, and was sometimes believed to be bound up with something else, such as a tree that was planted

THE HISTORY
ANCIENT IRISH
CULTURE
SOCIETY

at the same time that one was born. Ghosts were actually believed to be the detached souls of the dead who remained tied to the earth.

Relations between men and women were strictly regulated, and many taboos surrounded the division between the sexes. We have already seen how it was considered bad luck to see a red-haired woman at the beginning of a journey, but there were also many other limitations to the role of women and men, what they could do, where, and when. One story tells how the building of a castle was halted simply because a woman stopped to observe the masons at work. Another story of Cú Chulainn tells of how Cú stopped telling a tale when he discovered that a woman had been smuggled into the forge where he and his audience were sitting, even after he had specifically told them not to bring in any women. Women also could not visit certain holy wells, or even cut a young boy's hair.

Women also had their own arenas of life where men were not allowed, however, the most important of these being childbirth. Pregnant women also had certain taboos. For example, if a pregnant woman met with a hare along the way, she had to either tear the ear of the hare, or part of her garment, or her child might be born with a harelip. A pregnant woman also should not enter a graveyard lest she turn her foot on a stone, which would cause her child to be born with a club foot. Pregnant women should also not abide in a house with a corpse therein, nor be part of a bridal party. If she visited a forge, however, she was always asked to blow the bellows in order to bring the smith good luck.

Newborn children were also similarly hedged about with numerous customs and superstitions. The ancient Celts held strongly to astrological beliefs, and also believed that the day and even the time of day the child was born would have an effect on their destiny. A child born at night would be able to see ghosts and fairies, whereas one born during the day, at exactly 12 midnight or on a Sunday, would not. Both children and animals born on May 1 (Beltaine) were believed to have good luck. Many superstitions were put into place to guard the newborn from being abducted by the fairies, who would abduct the children and replace them with a sickly, weak simulacra referred to as a "changeling".

In order to combat this, several things could be done: wrap the child with a *Brat Bhríde*, "Brigid's Cloak", a cloth that had been exposed on the eve of Brigid's feast; feed oatmeal to the mother just after the baby is born; sprinkle a small amount of urine in the room; conceal a piece of iron or a cinder in the baby's clothing; place a pair of tongs across the cradle; place unsalted butter in the baby's mouth; tie a red ribbon across the cradle, and countless other talismans.[9]

Marriage was another major source of custom and lay ritual. Most marriages were made by a local matchmaker, or *spéicéirí*, who arranged the match, the dowry, and all the other arrangements. Despite this, elopements still occasionally occurred, and the forcible abduction of brides was also considered a socially acceptable form of marriage, though this was likely done as a result of a secret agreement between the potential suitor, the father of the bride and, hopefully, the bride herself. One of the most prevalent traditions surrounding the wedding is "the race for the bottle", which took place right after the ceremony ended. In this race, all the husbands and wives rode on horseback, the wife riding "pillion" on a seat behind her husband, racing to the house where the wedding feast, or *bainis*, was being held. There, a bottle of whiskey had been placed near the house, and the first to get the bottle won. Another prevalent custom was the *geamari*, or *buachaillí tuí*, the "straw-boys", who were dressed in suits and hats made of straw. They were welcomed into the feast, their leader took the bride to dance, and then they spent the rest of the night in feasting and revelry, though always careful to keep their identities a secret. However, if they were not welcomed at the feast, they would play a "trick" on the wedding party. In this way, some of the customs surrounding the wedding festival were not unlike the customs surrounding the Samhain festival, the strawboys perhaps representing the local *sídhe*, whose approval of the marriage may have been considered to be required by the superstitious Celts in order for the marriage to succeed.

There were even amusing customs surrounding the unmarried. Perhaps the most prominent existed only in southwestern Ireland, during the Christian era, and was called the "Skellig Lists". Everyone, including bachelors and spinsters, enjoyed being invited to weddings, but some

THE HISTORY
ANCIENT IRISH
CULTURE
SOCIETY

never showed signs of ever getting married. So on Shrove Tuesday Night, when the traditional marriage season had passed, young people would play pranks on the bachelors and spinsters, including painting their walls with graffiti, taking their gates off of their hinges, stuffing their chimneys so their houses would fill with smoke, loosing their cows from their byres, taking the wheels off their carts, and so forth. The unfortunate unmarried would then be treated to a symphony of rude horns made from empty bottles with their bottoms cut off, intended to be a summons to the unattached to "travel to the Skelligs", or Skellig Michael, an ancient monastery on an island off the coast of County Kerry. This location was chosen because the monks on the island marked Easter later than those on the mainland, and thus the traditional, pre-Lent period, when most marriage ceremonies were performed, had yet to expire. The "Skellig Lists", then, were essentially comic poems about the various mismatches that could be achieved from the pool of available singles, and how comical some of those pairings would be.

Illness and Death

In ancient times, before the advent of medical science resolved many of the mysteries of life, illness and death were believed to be caused primarily by evil spirits. "Fairy blasts" and "fairy strokes" (op. cit.) were usually cited as the reason that people suddenly fell ill, and attempts were made to placate the spirit world in the hopes that the fairies would release their hold on the stricken one and allow them to heal. There were also available simple, local cures created by local herbalists and "wise people", some of which actually worked. For example, salicyl, used by the ancients as a curative, was derived from the bark of some types of willow. A derivative of salicyl, acetylsalicylic acid, is better known today as "aspirin". An extract of the foxglove plant, digitalin, was also used by the ancient Irish as a remedy for heart ailments since ancient times, and remains in use by modern science to fight heart disease even today. Penicillin, which had been used to cure infections long before it was rediscovered by Alexander Fleming, has been in use since ancient times also. And even simple country folk knew that leaving a loaf of white bread or a piece of bacon in a damp part of the house would result in a mold that could help infected wounds heal, making penicillin a classic example of a "folk remedy".

These ancient Irish "medicine men", in fact, appear to have been the inheritors of a significant body of legitimate medical knowledge, as studies have revealed that as much as 25% of their remedies actually have been proven effective. More interesting from the cultural perspective are the "magical" practices that often accompanied the application of these often effective medical cures. These Irish medicine men (and women) usually recited a "spell" when applying the medicine called an *ortha*, which was usually accompanied by some complicated ritual acts and gestures. These arcane rituals of course had no direct effect upon the illness of the patient, but they did have a powerful psychological effect upon them, with the result that the patient invariably felt much better after the ritual component of the cure had been completed. Interestingly, studies today have revealed that the mere presence of a doctor can have a powerful, positive psychological effect upon a patient, to the point that the administration of a placebo can often be as effective as real medicine. Perhaps then we can see in the seemingly bizarre antics of these ancient medicine men the fragmentary, degraded remnants of an advanced, ancient form of medicine that recognized and took seriously the power of psychology upon the health and recovery of the patient.

Recovery from illness also had its own specific taboos. If one's health began to improve on Sunday, it was regarded as an ill-omen, and sending for a doctor even in more modern times was believed to be a very grave sign — thus the saying, *Dearbhráthair don Bhás fios a chur ar an dochtúir*, "Sending for the doctor is brother to death". It was also considered incorrect to visit a sick person after having attended a funeral, and it was also considered wrong to allow fire or milk out of a house where someone was sick, lest the "luck", or power of life in the house, leak out and reduce the ill person's chance of surviving. For this reason the turf fire was kept well stoked so as to symbolically/magically increase the energy in the house and, by extension, the life-force of the sick so as to aid them in their recovery.

When a person was particularly ill, family and friends kept close by and were "on edge", during which time they would look for certain omens that

THE HISTORY
ANCIENT IRISH
CULTURE
SOCIETY

might indicate an imminent death. The most obvious omen might be the wail of a banshee, though the wail typically came to a relative of the dying, and was never heard by the dying themselves. Another powerful omen was if a raven or a crow perched on the windowsill, reminiscent of the *Badb*, or if a dog howled outside the window at night.

When a person was dying, it was common Celtic custom to make a hole in the wall or in the ceiling to allow the soul to more easily pass on into the afterlife. Doors and windows were also opened to ease the passage, and sometime the dying body was placed upon a straw mat, lest even a feather from their mattress impede their progress to the next life. Many believed that the soul then traveled to the halls of waiting in the *Tech Duinn*, "The House of Donn", located on the Beara Peninsula in County Cork. When someone died, their death was often signalled to their neighbors by the burning of a bundle of straw, or perhaps their mattress, if it was made of straw. The clock also was stopped at the moment of death, the mirrors were veiled, and loved ones and beloved pets were comforted.

The Celts commonly held a wake that was boisterous in character in honor of the deceased so the dead would not become jealous of those who inherited their property. Thus, stories, jokes, singing, dancing, drinking and various amusements were all done in honor of the deceased, to let them know that they were still considered a part of the community. Upon burial, the deceased was buried with many of the accoutrements that surrounded them in life, reflecting the Celtic view of the afterlife that was so similar to the Egyptian. The funeral procession was of course surrounded by very many taboos, as one might expect, including what time to bury the dead, in what part of the graveyard, how to dig the grave, what route the procession should take to the graveyard, appropriate dress for the funeral, and so forth. Another ancient custom was the hiring of professional keeners, who composed lamentations for the dead, should the near relatives be unable (or unwilling) to do so. Poets were also often hired to compose *caointe* or *mairbhní*, "dirges", in memory of the dead, particularly those who had died tragically or whose passing was a great loss to the community.

Ancient Irish Economy

The economy of ancient Ireland was based upon a mixed-farming system in which livestock predominated.[10] This was due to the fact that though Ireland has large areas of open land, and more than enough precipitation, there are also large areas of rocky and hilly areas and extensive forested regions. Moreover, much of the open land is filled with extensive boglands that are unsuitable for cultivation, or has poor drainage, making truly useful land somewhat scarce. The best land is scattered around the outside edges of the island, the majority of which is to be found in the eastern part of the country, in the Shannon River Valley, in Leinster province. Nerys explains, "This verdant landscape was deceptively promising. In his *Topographia Hiberniae* (1185-8 A.D.), the Norman-Welsh cleric, Giraldus Cambrensis, wrote,

> The island is, however, richer in pastures than crops, and in grass than in grain. The crops give great promise in the blade, even more in the straw, but less in the ear. For here the grains of wheat are shrivelled and small, and can scarcely be separated from the chaff by any winnowing fan. The plains are well-clothed with grass, and the haggards are bursting with straw. Only the granaries are without their wealth. What is born and comes forth in the spring and is nourished in the summer and advanced, can scarcely be reaped in the harvest because of unceasing rain.

Irish tradition itself associates strong rain-storms and flooding with Lugnasad, the festival which opened the harvest season in early August. But while wheat cultivation tended to languish, stock production was stimulated by the virtually perennial growth of forest browse and natural grass."[11]

THE AGRICULTURAL ECONOMY

Though the Irish agricultural areas provided only a modest return, the rich and perennial grasslands provided a constant, year-round supply of lush foliage for cattle to graze upon. For this reason, Ireland's economy came to be based more on cattle than on farming, as raising cat-

279

tle was simply more profitable. The Irish diet as a whole consisted primarily of oats, barley, wheat, and rye, in the form of bread, porridge and alcohol. Dairy products from cows and sheep included cheese, butter, curds and milk. Meat products included beef, pork, mutton and wild game, supplemented with fish and shellfish. Fruits and vegetables included fruit, nuts and berries, watercress, garlic, leeks, and seaweed, which was also commonly used as fertilizer along the coastlands. Peas and beans were also introduced into the Irish diet during the Middle Ages.

Cows have been and continue to be the backbone of the Irish cattle economy, and have even played an important role in Irish religion, society and polity.

THE CATTLE ECONOMY

Even though the cow was by far the most valued form of cattle, Irish farmers tended to keep a mixture of animals including, in order of importance, cows, sheep, chickens, goats and pigs. Riding horses were also kept, being even more highly prized than cows, as they brought prestige to their owners just as a new sportscar does today. However, donkeys were actually treated with suspicion and even contempt, and dogs were considered even lower than pigs. Personal prestige was closely associated with the type and amount of cattle one owned, and farmers tended to avoid low-prestige animals for that reason.

The remainder of the ancient Irish economy was composed of artisans and craftsmen, who produced little surplus for export, only enough to serve the immediate needs of their local clients. The few exceptions to this rule include quality leather, which was available in abundance, and the classic Irish woolen cloaks which, in the form of the famous Aran sweater, remain one of the most popular exports even today.

Ancient Irish Polity

Like all political structures, the ancient Irish polity was based upon a combination of ethnic and economic factors. As we have seen, the cow was considered to be the most valuable form of livestock in the country. So valuable was the cow, in fact, that it was used as a standard unit of currency, forming the basis of the "cattle-loans and clientship" system that formed the basis of the Irish political economy. This system integrated and supported a somewhat feudal social structure wherein the *bóaire*, or cattle-lords, lent farmers the use of their cattle in return for agricultural produce. Beneath these two levels of society were the *ceíle* and serfs, and above them the king, nobles, druids and warriors.

This stratified social structure was typical of the Indo-European "caste" system. This makes sense because, as we have seen, the ancient Irish were Indo-European in origin, having emigrated in several waves from central Asia, from lands immediately adjacent to India, where the caste system still predominates. Ellis explains in *The Celts: A History*,

> Like most early Indo-European peoples, early Celtic society was based on a caste system. At the bottom end there were the menials and producers equivalent to the *sudra* and the *vaishya* in Hindu society. Next came the warrior caste, equivalent to the Hindu *kshatriya*. Then came the intellectual caste, which included all the "professional" functions — judges, lawyers, doctors, historians, bards and priests of religion, the Druids. These were equivalent to the Hindu *Brahmin*. Similar caste divisions are found in

Greek and Roman society. When we get our first glimpse of Irish society, the Celtic structure had not greatly changed. There was a menial caste which was divided into several sub-classes ranging from prisoners to herdsmen and house servants. The *ceile* was the producer, the basis of the entire society. Above them came the warriors and nobles, the *flaith*, often coming under the title of *aire* (noble), which is cognate with the Sanskrit word *arya*, freeman. Then came the professional class, originally the Druids. At the top of society … came the kings and queens; indeed, there was a whole range of kings from minor kings who paid allegiance to more powerful kings, to overkings or High Kings.[12]

STRUCTURE

In ancient Ireland there were seven main classes of people, which in a society based upon kingship, also formed the political structure. The social hierarchy was basically pyramidal in shape, with the king at the top, the serf at the bottom and grades of classes in between that were defined by their nobility, property, function and free status within society.

✦ *Rí* — Kings

The kings occupied the highest level of society, and were the chief of the *arra*, or ruling elite. There were kings of several grades from the petty king, the *rí tuath*, which might rule over one *tuath* or *cantred* — the cantred being a designation for a region that contains approximately 100 villages. Above the *rí tuath* was the *ruiri*, whose dominion covered a region that today would be referred to as a "county". Above the *ruiri* was the *rí ruirech*, who ruled over entire provinces, and above them all was the *Ard Rí*, or High King, who ruled the whole island, though his control over the island was often in name only. Kings were always taken from a noble bloodline, each king having a poet in residence whose responsibility, among other things, was to keep the official genealogical records that showed who was officially in line for the throne.

✦ *Flaith* — Nobles

The *flaith*, or "noble" class of *arra* were just beneath the king, and included various lesser tribal or war leaders who actually performed the day-to-day governance of their territories and dispensed the king's justice. Nobles were usually also of royal blood, and could be in line for the kingship should the king die without an heir. The relative level of importance of the *flaith* depended essentially upon the amount of land he controlled.

✦ *Druids* — The Intelligentsia

Between the true nobles and the wealthy cattle lords sat the Druids, the intellectual class of ancient Ireland. As we have seen, the term *druid* means "man of knowledge". The druids were essentially a priestly class whose primary function was the acquisition, memorization, and transmission of knowledge, including religious, legal and intellectual matters. As such, they were in many ways the true rulers behind the political scenes.

✦ *Fianna* — Warriors

The warrior caste of ancient Ireland was, like the druidic caste, a special subculture that was set apart from the rest of society, and which enjoyed special privileges that were restricted from other classes, even nobility. Membership in the warrior class was not hereditary, as was the nobility, and was not restricted to the upper classes. Membership instead required rigorous testing, and successful applicants were required to leave behind land, title and property as a prerequisite for entry. In return, those who were successful enjoyed the privileges that only military service could provide, including complete provision, arms, training, and special access to king and court. The two warrior classes of ancient Ireland included the Fianna, headquartered in Leinster province, and the Knights of the Red Branch, headquartered in Ulster province.

✦ *Bóaire* — Cattle-Lords

The third of the three ruling classes, the non-noble propertied freemen, the *bóaire*, formed the middle and upper-middle class of society. Though they did not own land, paying rent to the nobles for use of their land, they usually owned large amounts of "movable" property, usually cattle. For this reason they were often referred to as *bóaire*, or "cattle-lords", though there were different types of this class.[13] This class enjoyed a privileged status similar to that of the nobility, but they were not eligible for rulership due to the fact that they were not of royal blood. However, those propertied freemen who were particularly wealthy could sometimes be endowed with the rank of petty nobility. This was essentially a nominal title that conferred no real status, being sought after primarily for the purpose of increasing one's social status relative to other propertied freemen.

✢ Ceíle — Non-Propertied Freemen

The non-propertied freemen, or *ceíle*, formed the middle and lower-middle class of society. This class was made up largely of farmers and tradesmen, those who did not own land or a significant amount of property, but who had useful skills. The *ceile* existed in a co-dependent relationship with the *bóaire*, where they "rented" cattle from the *bóaire*, paying them in agricultural produce. In Brehon Law (*op. cit.*), this class was considered to be the backbone of society, the status of the *ceile* being considered to be the ultimate source of law and authority. Particularly skilled tradesmen of this class could be raised in social status, especially those who served the nobility.

✢ *Senchleithe* — Serfs

Serfs were essentially poor farmers and landless agricultural laborers who lived on and tilled land owned by nobles and propertied freemen, paying the landlord rent in return for use of their land. Not quite as servile as a slave, serfs were still required to perform certain duties for their landlords in order to be accorded certain rights and social privileges. The social rank of serf no longer has an equivalent social class within Western society.

Though there was a degree of social fluidity within ancient Irish society, only talented people of impeccable character had a chance of rising up the social ladder. Some land was hereditary in nature, owned by the king or the nobility, but most of the land was held by the tribe and available for free use by farmers of the non-propertied classes. Moreover, the rights of the farmers were held in very high esteem, and their land was never taken away from them, at least not without suitable compensation and a new farm to go to elsewhere. Thus the fact that the lower classes did not own land does not mean that they were mere slaves, just not as rich as the nobility.[14]

In sum, though the culture of ancient Ireland was largely the same as the Central Asian culture from which the Irish had originally emigrated, the society that developed in Ireland was much more egalitarian in character than their cousins on the Indian subcontinent, possessing a degree of social fluidity and genuine concern for the rights of the common man that is not dissimilar to that present in Ireland today. In all other ways, however, religious, social, economic and political, a review of ancient Irish culture shows its clear antecedents to its roots in Central Asia, most aspects of which did not change until well into the Christian era, and some of which survive to this day.

Notes

[1] Dáithí Ó hÓgáin, *The Sacred Isle: Belief and Religion in Pre-Christian Ireland* (Wilton, Cork: The Collins Press, 1999), 3.

[2] Carmel McCaffrey and Leo Eaton, *In Search of Ancient Ireland: The Origins of the Irish from Neolithic Times to the Coming of the English* (Chicago: New Amsterdam Books, 2002), 78.

[3] Ó hÓgáin, *The Sacred Isle*, 63.

[4] *Ibid.*, 75.

[5] Nerys Patterson, *Cattle Lords & Clansmen: The Social Structure of Early Ireland* (Notre Dame, IN: University of Notre Dame Press, 1994), 150.

[6] Joyce, *A Smaller Social History of Ireland* (Tir nan Og: The Virtuality of Ancient Ireland, http://www.alia.ie/tirnanog/), http://www.alia.ie/tirnanog/sochis/iv.html.

[7] *Ibid.*

[8] Seán Ó Súilleabháin, *Irish Folk Custom and Belief* (Dublin: Three Candles, Ltd., 1967). All the information in this section, "Customs and Superstitions", is paraphrased from this book.

[9] *Ibid.*, 42-43.

[10] Patterson, *Cattle Lords & Clansmen*, 62.

[11] *Ibid.*, 64.

[12] Peter Berresford Ellis, *The Celts: A History* (New York: Carroll Graf Publishers, 2004), 27-28.

[13] Patterson, *Cattle Lords & Clansmen*, 196.

[14] Summarized from Joyce, *A Smaller Social History of Ireland*, http://www.alia.ie/tirnanog/sochis/iv.html.

THE HISTORY
ANCIENT IRISH
CULTURE
NOTES

A Short History of Ireland

ith the advent of Christianity, the history of Ireland began to come into sharper focus. No longer the province of oral tradition, with its distressing tendency to glorify the past in order to make it more "entertaining", history finally became the province of true historians, whose medium was no longer the capricious oral folktale, but the reliable written word. And with its history now literally written down in black and white, Ireland began to awake from its long, dark dream of myth to a new dawn of rationalism, where reason ruled over emotion, and the Word triumphed over the image.

War of the Worldviews

The effect of the evangelization of Ireland was not merely that of changing the religious beliefs of the ancient Irish, however, but also of changing their fundamental worldview, the very way they perceived reality. For example, as we have seen, the ancient Celts routinely fought to the death over even the slightest insult, secure in the belief that if they died, they would be reincarnated, given multiple chances to try again, like some absurd, cosmic video game. According to the Bible, however, life comes only once, and thence the judgment, so the Irish now had to live their lives according to strict moral and ethical standards, or risk eternal damnation. This of course had an immediate chilling effect on the warlike mindset of the ancient Celts, and the broiling disputes that had dominated the sacred isle slowly began to simmer down. This concept, along with the essential Christian concept of forgiveness, was the key that broke the cycle of violence that had held the sacred island enthralled. Over time, the ability to forgive one's neighbor brought about the stability that was necessary for old grudges to be forgotten, new alliances to be forged, regional governments to be established and, eventually, one king to rule over the land. Thus, where force of arms had failed, in time — through *forgiveness* — Ireland was finally conquered.

THE HISTORY
A SHORT HISTORY
OF IRELAND

THE WORD AND THE IMAGE

And whereas forgiveness was the message that eventually transformed Ireland from dozens of petty despots into one nation, the written word was the medium through which that concept was transmitted. Books were, and still are, a superior medium for transmitting information accurately over time, as opposed to the Celtic oral traditions that often varied by the telling. And though the Celts took to the new "books" like bees to honey, as well as the moral and ethical lessons contained therein, they still retained their great love for color and imagery. Small wonder, then, that they chose to lavishly illustrate their books with fantastic illuminations of a quality that amazes us even today. And though they became Christianized and literate, the Celts never completely lost their love of glorious imagery. As a result, their books overflowed with color and imaginative illustration like a wine press overflowing with new wine, resulting in a near-perfect "marriage" of word and image. It is in this reliable, illustrated form, as typified by *The Book of Kells*, that we have received the history of ancient Ireland.

THE CREATION OF "IRELAND"

As we have seen, before the coming of Christianity, there was no "Ireland" *per se*. The Ireland encountered by Patrick was a collection of warring *tuaths*, with a High King whose authority was nominal at best. Each province, Leinster, Munster, Connaught and Ulster, was more or less autonomous, and each of those provinces were in turn divided up into dozens of petty kingdoms that were locked in a constant struggle with each other for control of territories whose boundaries were in constant flux.

However, the coming of Christianity began to override this chaos by creating the first real sense of national unity, of a belief and culture that transcended political and cultural boundaries. Fry explains, "If anything held the Irish together at all, it was Christianity and culture: the abbots, bishops, priests, scholars and artists were not confined by being members of one *tuath* or another from crossing borders and wandering freely about the whole country. Monasteries flourished in all parts, and in many instances, played the composite roles of town, hostel, penitentiary, school, university, religious centre and sanctuary."[1] In time, Christianity spread like a blanket across the entire island, homogenizing the culture from that of many gods, many kings and many faiths, to that of one God, one King, one faith and, eventually, one nation.

This process was not instantaneous, however, and it took several centuries before a king would arise that could be considered a true *Ard Rí*, or "High King", whose authority actually extended throughout the four corners of the sacred isle. Ironically, Patrick may have come to Ireland at a time that was quite possibly the most politically fragmented situation Ireland had experienced in its long history, perhaps even as politically fragmented as it could possibly get. In Ireland's most ancient past, when her political history was primarily defined by the great invasions of the Magogian peoples, disputes over territory were decided by single, cataclysmic battles of epic proportions that decided once and for all who would rule over the entire island. By the time of Patrick, however, the time of the great invasions had long passed, and the rule of Ireland had descended into the hands of a mass of petty kinglets, none of whom were able to fill the boots of their mighty forebears. It is into this world of total war that Patrick returned, as the vanguard of the great spiritual invasion that would eventually conquer the entire island.

The Early Christian Period (AD 433-794)

Fry comments succinctly on this period, "At the beginning of the fifth century, history begins to become disentangled from legend in Ireland, and it is possible, by using a variety of sources — such as *The Táin*, other sagas, inscriptions and so on — to start building up a patchwork of key names and occasional rough dates."[2] The first true, reliable history of Ireland was not available until the introduction of writing, and written records in turn did not exist until the first Christians had begun to emigrate to the sacred isle during the fifth century AD. It was the Christians who zealously recorded all the myths, legends, and real history that they could get their hands on, their obsession with books and documentation being the only reason we know anything at all about this period of Irish history. And though Christianity had spread in small ways in the sacred isle for some time before the coming of Patrick, it had not made a significant impact upon early Irish life and thought

THE HISTORY
A SHORT HISTORY
OF IRELAND
AD 433-794

289

until the conversion of King Leoghaire by St. Patrick on April 5, 433. After that time, the early Christians began to take down written records of the situation then extant in Ireland, records that are now our only window into the religious, social, economic and political conditions of the time.

PATRICK'S IRELAND

The Ireland of Patrick's day was controlled principally by three major *tuatha*: the Uí Neill in the north, the Laigin in the southeast, and the Eóganacht in the south. At the same time, there were numerous, petty kingdoms throughout the island vying for independence. King Leoghaire, though his title was *Ard Rí*, or High King of Ireland, was actually only the High King of the Uí Neill, the most powerful tribe in Ireland that, by the time of Patrick, had forged for itself a mini-empire out of the northern half of Ireland.

THE RISE OF THE UÍ NEILL

Niall Noígallach ("Niall of the Nine Hostages") is the first king whose existence can be verified historically (i.e., by written records). Niall, who ruled over most of the northern half of Ireland from approximately AD 400-430, originated from Connacht province, claiming descent from the famous King Cormac Mac Art, founder of the Connachta dynasty (named after the legendary King Conn Cétchathach, "Conn of the Hundred Battles"). In order to achieve this position of prominence, Niall had to defeat the powerful Ulaid (Ulster) dynasty that had controlled the north — and dominated the entire island — for many centuries. And with the downfall of the Ulstermen, from which the famous King Conchobar, Cú Chulainn, Fergus Mac Róich and many other heroes of old had come, so too fell the fear of the men of Ulster which had no doubt held the island together politically to some extent. As a result, after the downfall of the Ulaid, the sacred isle dissolved into chaos as every regional, local and petty king began to maneuver for a dominant position in the emerging new order.

This new order took the form of the Uí Neill (O'Neill) dynasty, named after its founder, Niall Noígallach. At its peak, the Uí Neill ruled over all of Connacht province, most of Ulster, and the northern part of Leinster. Niall's sons had significantly expanded his initial conquests, driving the remnants of the Ulaid peoples to the far northeastern corner of the island, their last, tenuous hold on the island being centered in what is now County Antrim, where they founded a lesser kingdom called Dal Riata *(op. cit.)*. Fortunately for them, the Dal Riata were able to expand their diminished holdings by conquering the lesser kingdom of Argyll on the western coast of Scotland. Some of the conquered people of Argyll apparently then emigrated to Ireland to Emain Macha, the old capitol of the Ulaid, where they became known as the *Argialla* (lit., "givers of hostages"), indicating that they were a people who were willingly subservient to the dominant Uí Neill. This may also explain Niall's surname, "of the Nine Hostages", alluding to the old Celtic custom of taking hostages from a conquered people as a surety of obedience to the established order. As such, it may be that the Argialla were perhaps composed of nine different lesser tribal groups, or *finna*, who were subservient to the Uí Neill though, like most aspects of this period, the exact political situation is not certain.

Niall lived until around AD 450, though he apparently was superceded as ruler around 430 by his son, Leoghaire, who took over the throne of the Uí Neills at Tara, the ancient capitol of Ireland, in that year. *Tara* (lit., "place of the wide-ranging view"), which has a commanding view of all four provinces, was chosen by the Uí Neill as their principal ruling seat, though the Uí Neill were actually divided into northern and southern Uí Neill by the Argialla (along with the stubborn remnants of the Dal Riata) who still held, albeit in subservience, the center of old Ulster. It was into this political situation that Patrick returned to Ireland, meeting with King Leoghaire of the Uí Neill, whom he would convert to become the first Christian High King of Ireland.

The Laigin

Though the Uí Neills were the dominant force in fifth century Ireland, they were by no means without rival. The southern Uí Neill had carved out their territory at the expense not only of the Ulaid, but also of the *Laigin*, or "Lein" people, the people after whom the province of Leinster was later named. The Laigin were descendants of the Fir Bolg, who had controlled

THE HISTORY
A SHORT HISTORY
OF IRELAND
AD 433–794

Tara, the ancient capitol of Ireland, before its conquest by the Uí Neill. And whereas the Laigin were able to leverage their control of Tara for propagandistic purposes in their own bid to rule the sacred isle, after driving out the Laigin the Uí Neill were able to do the same, and did so with great gusto.[3]

After seeing the Uí Neill drive the Laigin out of Meath and northern Leinster, in the minds of the pagan Irish the Uí Neill were seen as being "favored of the gods", as it was believed in ancient, pre-Christian Ireland that the gods determined who would rule over Tara. Interestingly, by defeating the druids at Tara and converting the divinely appointed High King to Christianity, Patrick's timing was uniquely well suited to make it clear to all the Irish that his God was greater than even the gods of the powerful Uí Neills, who had so recently taken control of Tara. This would — and no doubt did — help Christianity spread all the more quickly.

Not much is known of the Laigin, except that they were divided into two main groups: the northern Laigin and the southern Laigin. The northern Laigin came to be ruled by the Uí Cheinnselaig dynasty, who were able to adequately defend against further Uí Neill incursions. But because the southern Laigin were never in conflict with the Uí Neills, they do not appear in the annals, remaining as a minor, unknown people. One thing is known, however – due to their good relations with the peoples of Connaught and Munster, the southern Laigin enjoyed an almost unparalleled level of peace and prosperity during this period.

The Eóganacht

Munster, the province that takes up most of the southern half of Ireland, was a fairly chaotic collection of rival factions during this period. One of the strongest of these factions was the Eóganacht dynasty, ruled over by the descendants of Eógan, who was believed to be a descendant of the legendary King Nuada of the Tuatha dé Danann. Fry explains the situation in Munster during this period thusly:

Munster in the fifth and sixth centuries was a collection of southern kingdoms with fluid boundaries, and the same sort of rivalries as Connacht and Ulster; most of the Munster kingdoms were ruled by members of the Eóganacht dynasty, descended from Eógan…. One of the leading members of the dynasty was Conall Corc who founded the kingdom of Cashel in County Tipperary, which was to become the dominant kingdom among several that emerged in Munster, whose stories are very vague indeed. Kings of Cashel claimed to be overlords of all the others. Corc's grandson may have been Aenghus, who ruled Cashel from the mid-fifth century to his death in c. 490. He is noted for having been defeated in thirty battles in a vain attempt to enlarge his territory at the expense of his neighbors. Among the Munster kingdoms were groups of vassal people known as the Déisi, and they are interesting as having been semi-independent allies of the Eóganacht rulers and having assisted them in border wars with Connacht. Some of the Déisi were given lands taken from the southern end of Connacht, approximately what is now County Clare, and these folks came to be called the Dál Cais people and their kingdom Dál Cais.[4]

Though the Eóganacht were relatively strong compared to the other petty kingdoms of the south, they were not nearly powerful enough to challenge the power of the Uí Neills in the north. So, in order to make up for this weakness, the Eóganacht painted themselves as peaceful and egalitarian rulers, as opposed to the hostile and warlike Uí Neills of the north. It was from this propagandistic dichotomy of peaceful and dictatorial rule that arose the idea during that period that Ireland was effectively divided into two halves — the northern half being referred to as *Leith Cuinn*, "Conn's half" (named after Conn of the Hundred Battles) and the southern half being referred to as *Leith Mug*, "Mug's half" (named after Mug Nuada, "the servant of Nuada", a hereditary title of the Eóganacht kings who claimed descent from King Nuada of the Tuatha dé Danann).[5]

The Dal Cais, though a minor player during this period, would eventually rise to be the most powerful dynasty of all, producing the famous Brian Boru, the first true High King of Ireland since the time of the Invasions. It was the Dál Cais, particularly Brian Boru, who would, for a time, unite all of Ireland under one banner, and fend off the next invaders of the sacred isle: the Vikings.

THE HISTORY
A SHORT HISTORY
OF IRELAND
AD 433-794

The Viking Invasion (AD 795-1014)

During the 8th century, for reasons unknown, there was a population explosion in Scandinavia that resulted in a mass migration. Too many people and not enough land forced countless Norwegians, Danes, Swedes and Finns to emigrate west. The first waves of Vikings landed upon the Shetland and Orkney Islands north of what is now Scotland, as well as England and Wales, also landing in Iceland, Greenland, and even the Hebrides. There they founded communities from which they proceeded to conquer even more territories. And it was from the settlements in the islands of Orkney, Shetland, the Hebrides and the Isle of Man that came the Vikings who would figure so prominently in the history of Ireland.

The first recorded Viking raid on Ireland took place in AD 795, when the church on Lambay Island, near modern Dublin, was burned and pillaged. Numerous other monasteries were also targeted, including Inismurray and Inisbofin on the west coast, indicating the broad extent of the raids. St. Columba's famous monastery of Iona, off the west coast of Scotland was not spared the sword either, and was pillaged so many times that, in 807, it was abandoned, the abbot Cellach moving the surviving monks to Kells, in County Meath, where they established a new monastery. It was there, in Kells, that the famous *Book of Kells* was finally completed.

Starting in the 830s, the raids changed in character from random pillaging to organized assaults with the intent of founding large-scale communities — a true "invasion". These raids, formerly restricted to the coastlines, now penetrated deep into the countryside, again focusing on the monasteries that had by that time become fairly wealthy – such as the famous monasteries of Clonfert, Lorrha, Terryglass and even Clonmacnoise. After pillaging to their heart's content, the Vikings then founded military bases and fortified port cities they called *longphorts*, the most famous of these being *Dubh Linn*, "black pool", referring to a tidal pool off the River Poddle, a tributary of the Liffey, now known as "Dublin".

At first, because of the divided nature of the country, the Irish were unable to organize a competent defense against the Viking incursions. However, when the Vikings starting founding cities, they became involved in the Irish political situation, and became subject to looting themselves — and to intrigues. The Irish even began to create their own navy, and attacked the Vikings at sea fairly effectively. By 848, King Máel Sechnaill I of Tara was able to defeat a large force of Vikings, killing 700 and then pillaging and burning their settlement at Dublin. Improvements in building design also had begun to make pillaging much more difficult for the Vikings, the old wooden church buildings having been replaced by new stone buildings. Innovations such as the invention of the round tower also created an easily defensible place of refuge that proved very effective against the lightly armed Vikings, making small-scale pillaging much less profitable. Many of these round towers remain as some of the most spectacular works of architecture to be found throughout Ireland.

In time, the Vikings abandoned pillaging and began intermarrying with the local peoples, learning to speak Gaelic (adding many Scandinavian loan words that are still in use today, such as *margad*, "market") and even converting to Christianity. Their *longphorts* became world-renowned trading ports, bringing much trade, money, and culture into Ireland, the word *phort*, "ford" being remembered in the names of many of these port cities even today, such as Waterford and Wexford. Other major cities founded by the Vikings include Wicklow, Limerick, Cork, Carlingford and, of course, Dublin. And though the Vikings had quickly become Irish, they still retained enough of their distinctive character to remain a threat to the established (dis)order.

THE RISE OF THE DÁL CAIS

In the latter half of the 10th century, a small kingdom arose in the Shannon River valley in County Clare, control of which was routinely disputed by the kingdoms of both Munster and Connacht. This was the petty kingdom of the Dál Cais clan, who were a part of the Eóganacht dynasty. King Mathghamain ("Mahon") was the first to make significant steps towards improving their situation, defeating King Cellachán of Cashel to take the overlordship of the Eóganacht. He then led the Eóganacht to a stunning victory over the Vikings of Limerick, plundering the city of its vast wealth and then burning it to the ground. He was later killed as the result of intrigue between the Vikings and rival Irish kings, however, being succeeded by his brother, the famous Brian Boru.

THE HISTORY
A SHORT HISTORY
OF IRELAND
AD 795-1014

Brian Boru

Brian Boru was born around AD 942 in Munster province, in what is now County Clare, as one of the sons of King Cennedig (Kennedy) of the Dál Cais clan. When Brian was a young boy, Viking raiders had murdered his mother, and so he grew up determined to drive them out of Ireland. To this end, Brian had decided to take the fight directly to the enemy, ignoring the more timid approach of the other Dál Cais kings, particularly his brother, Mahon. To achieve his goal, he hand-picked an elite force of fighters from among the Dál Cais army and proceeded to wage a very successful guerrilla war against the

"Brian Boru"
© 1987 Jim Fitzpatrick.

Viking King Ivar. Brian was so successful at this that fear of his small army spread throughout the whole region, attracting many volunteers to his cause. So great was his renown that even his brother, King Mahon reconciled with him, joining forces with him to destroy the Viking dominance of the region forever. The Viking King Ivar was not through, however, and had Mahon assassinated soon afterwards. Wishing to avoid a bloodbath, Brian challenged Ivar to single combat, and defeated him.

Now the king of the Dál Cais clan, Brian aggressively carried out his plan to place all of Munster under his sway. By defeating the king of Cashel in 978, thereby displacing the last of the Eóganacht kings, he took lordship over all of Munster. The following years then saw a dramatic rise in the power of Brian, which in turn led to a rise in the fortunes of Munster province and, eventually, all of Ireland.

But while Brian had taken control of the south, Máel Sechnaill II (Malachy), the high king of the Uí

Néill, still ruled the north from Tara. The Uí Néill claimed nominal rule over all Ireland, no doubt legitimized in their minds by their control of Tara, the ancient spiritual heartland of Ireland. As such, perhaps seeing the need to not be bested by this southern upstart, Malachy attacked and defeated the Vikings of Dublin. Then, still alarmed at the growth of his rival, Malachy attacked Brian directly. In response, over the next ten years Brian's armies and fleets systematically ravaged both Connaught and Meath itself, making it clear that Brian had the intent to become *Ard Rí*, or High King of Ireland, displacing the Uí Néill clan from their nominal hold on that title.

Seeing that their forces were evenly matched, Brian and Malachy met in 997 and divided Ireland between them — Malachy over the north, and Brian over the south. Though this treaty held firm enough for a few years, allowing their combined forces to subdue the Dublin Vikings and the recalcitrant Leinster kings, Brian determined again to become High King and, after a series of political maneuvers, persuaded Malachy to peacably yield the title at a symbolic ceremony that took place at Tara in 1002. Brian officially had become the *Ard Rí* – the first to do so since the time of the Milesians.

Brian then spent the next four years touring the country, consolidating his rule over the notoriously rebellious kings of Leinster and Connaught, though Ulster, under the rulership of the compliant Malachy, was of less trouble to him. Nevertheless, he made his rounds through Ulster as well, endorsing the Bishop of Armagh as the Archbishop of the Church of Ireland. While there he made sure that his name was added to *The Book of Armagh* as *Imperator Scottorum*, "Emperor of the Irish", *Scottorum* being the ancient Roman designation for the peoples of both Scotland and Ireland, the designation "Irish" being a later invention, derived from the name of the Tuatha Dé goddess Èriu.

Under Brian's rule, there was the beginnings of a renaissance of arts and letters; the economy and communications throughout the country greatly improved, as did the standard of living for many. The island had been united, the Vikings subdued, and the warring kings of the four provinces had at last been brought to heel under one sovereign King.

Alas, this *Pax Scottorum* lasted but ten years, at the end of which, in 1012, the northern kings of Ulster and the Viking Dubliners had started to strain at the leash, threatening to imbalance the tenuous peace that Brian had constructed. Malachy had requested help from Brian to put down the Viking Dubliners, who in an unorthodox move had allied themselves with Máel Mórda, the king of Leinster province. In 1013 Brian and Malachy laid siege to Dublin, with limited success. The Vikings, at an impasse, successfully appealed to their kinsmen from the Isle of Man and Orkney, a string of islands off the northeast coast of Scotland. Thus reinforced, in April of 1014, the Vikings and their Leinster allies attacked the Irish forces led by Brian Boru.

Meanwhile, while the Vikings were busy building their strength in a bid to retake the island, Malachy had abandoned Brian and his armies to bear the brunt of the Viking onslaught alone. Having lost a substantial portion of his army, Brian bravely stood his ground, and faced off with the Vikings in the city of Clontarf, on the north side of Dublin Bay, the battle being joined on Good Friday, April the 23rd, 1014.

Brian, believed to be 72 at the time, was too old to lead the army, delegating that responsibility to his son, Murchad while he himself watched from a guarded enclosure from the sidelines. The battle was a bloody scrum, a war of annihilation between two of the most capable infantry types of the time, between two of the largest armies ever assembled on the island. Murchad was unfortunately killed, but both the Vikings and the Leinstermen lost their kings, including Máel Morda of Leinster, Sigurd of Orkney and Brodar of the Isle of Man, and both sides lost many nobles. The war, believed by some to be the greatest ever fought on Irish soil, lasted the day, and ended with a decisive victory for the Irish. Unfortunately, a group of Vikings fleeing the field happened upon Brian Boru's tent, and fought their way through the guard to kill Brian as he knelt in prayer.

Brian Boru left behind a magnificent legacy that none of his surviving sons was able to uphold. After his death, Ireland once again became fragmented, his brief *Pax Scottorum* being only a brief twinkle in God's eye before the sacred island fell back into chaos. But though his kingship was brief, it was still largely a success, as the power of the Vikings had been subdued forever, and Ireland had at last had, if only for a brief shining moment, one, true King.

Historians have a tendency to distinguish the Viking invasions from the invasions elucidated in the *Lebor* perhaps mainly because the Viking invasions are a proven historical fact, whereas the invasions of the Cessair, the Partholónians, the Nemedians, the Fir Bolg, the Tuatha dé Danann and the Milesians are not. But in reality, the Viking invasions were typical of a land whose history was a history of invasions. Thus, despite the terror of their onslaught, the Vikings had only a moderate effect on the daily life of the Irish. Ireland's worst enemy, in fact, did not come from without, but from within.

An Age of Chaos (AD 1015-1166)

After the death of Brian Boru, Ireland fell back into anarchy. For around a century and a half, the Irish languished under the burden of constant skirmishing between the various factions who once again tried in vain to assert overlordship over the rest of the island. During this age of chaos, the Irish church went into great decline, leading the famous St. Malachy to tell St. Bernard, the abbot of Clairvaux, France that Ireland was "Christian in name but in reality, heathen."[6] Many of the monks were married, or had concubines. The monasteries had become so closely involved with local politics that the local rulers now controlled them directly, and even quartered troops there. Church attendance had dropped dramatically, and the quality of the worship and teaching had dropped so precipitously that the laity were ignorant of the most basic tenets of the faith. As a result, they had begun to slip back into their old pagan ways, and the church was in danger of losing its grip completely.

In response, Malachy sent monks to Clairvaux in order to relearn the Cistercian rules, and Bernard also sent monks to Ireland to begin reforms. In 1142 they began construction of a Cistercian-style abbey at Mellifont, and their order began to grow rapidly. Malachy, meanwhile, began to reinstitute the old episcopal system, organizing bishoprics and parishes, and reintroducing true Christian worship services including singing, chanting, and proper teaching. Exhausted, Malachy died at the relatively young age of 54. But his work was not in vain, because in 1152, the Synod of Kells was convened at Mellifont, the largest and most important gathering of the Irish church yet. The pope even sent a legate, who invested several top church officials with the *pallium*, the official wool collar that designated their office — the first time in the Irish church's history since Patrick for an Irish Catholic priest to be officially recognized by the Vatican.

Unfortunately, though the Irish Church was finally beginning to get its act together, politically speaking, Ireland had fallen back into anarchy. Worse than ever, the Irish chieftains had begun to adopt the Viking custom of blinding their opponents. This cruel practice allowed them to eliminate their rivals, yet avoid the guilt of having murder on their conscience. And as usual, kidnappings and ransoms once again became commonplace. But there was one kidnapping in particular that led to a disaster that the Irish still rue to this day.

The English Invasion (AD 1167-1851)
THE COMING OF THE NORMANS (AD 1167-1485)

In 1151, Diarmuid Mac Murchada (aka Dermot Mac Murrough), the king of Leinster, carried off the wife of his rival, Tigernán Ua Ruairk, the king of Bréifne (modern Counties Cavan and Leitrim). And though Tigernán's wife was returned to him a year later, he still carried a bitter hatred for Diarmuid. Tigernán then worked hard to destroy Diarmuid, turning even Diarmuid's own allies against him, and in 1166, Tigernán attacked Diarmuid with a large coalition of forces, dethroning him and forcing him to flee. Desperate, Diarmuid turned to his only remaining ally: the King of England, Henry II — an act that has given him perhaps the blackest name in all of Irish history.

The Treason of Diarmuid

In 1066, exactly 100 years previously, the Normans had successfully invaded England, displacing and subjugating the Anglo-Saxons for hegemony over the Isle of the Mighty. The ancestors of the Normans had been Vikings who had invaded France centuries earlier, taking on French titles and customs, but retaining their essential Viking heritage, their name "Norman" being a derivation of "Norseman" or "Northman" which simply means "Men from the North". After they had established their military ports and fortifications on the French coast the Normans, like their Viking cousins on the Isles of Shetland, Orkney and Man, then set out for additional conquests, focusing their initial attention on southern England.

A century later, the Norman king Henry II was beginning to think about embarking upon further conquest. Having already greatly expanded the English holdings on the Continent to the point that the English now controlled more of France than did the French, he had also entertained the thought of conquering Ireland. Thus, the coming of the desperate, throneless Diarmuid presented Henry with a unique opportunity to not only conquer Ireland but, through his puppet Diarmuid, effectively annex the entire island in one swift stroke.

The Coming of Strongbow

Henry cleverly suggested to Diarmuid to go to his barons and raise support directly, thereby avoiding the appearance of actively supporting an invasion of Ireland. Among the barons, Diarmuid managed to get the attention of one Richard Fitzgilbert de Clare, who was out of favor at court and looking for a way to get some positive press. De Clare, better known to history as "Strongbow", recruited some additional help from some of his family members and, with the help of Diarmuid's forces, took Dublin with little trouble in 1171. Conveniently, after having betrothed his daughter Aífe in marriage to Strongbow, Diarmuid then died in May of that same year. Terrified at the prospect of losing their most important port city to the Normans, the Irish rallied to retake Dublin. Playing on this fear, King Muirchertach of Leinster was thus able to muster a force of 30,000 men from all over Ireland.

THE HISTORY
A SHORT HISTORY
OF IRELAND
AD 1167-1851

The Irish were brave, but poorly trained and equipped compared to the Norman knights who, besides having been hardened by decades of battle, had the best weapons, armor, training, and leadership then available in the western world. The Irish by contrast had little or no armor, were still using spears, throwing darts, short bows and slings, and were poorly led, fighting as a large, disorganized rabble. So, even though Strongbow had a fraction of the forces as the Irish, including 200 mounted, heavily armored knights, 400 light cavalry, and 1,500 excellent archers and foot soldiers, in real terms the war was the Normans' to lose. And they proved this, when after two months of being sieged by the Irish in Dublin, 600 knights led a charge against the unsuspecting besiegers. Caught by surprise and leaderless, as the High King and his entourage were taking baths in the river at the time, the Irish fled in terror, the risky charge of the Normans leading to a total rout of a magnitude rarely seen in the annals of Western warfare.

Two Nations

The Normans then proceeded to systematically conquer almost all of Ireland, their superior weapons and tactics consistently leading them to lopsided victories. And in order to protect themselves from the marauding Irish raiders and keep their captured territories, they built numerous stone castles, many of which can still be seen today. However, the Irish were never truly beaten, simply displaced, moving like water around an oar. They moved up into the highlands, leaving the lowlands to the Normans, their day-to-day life being disrupted very little. And the Normans found it impossible to eradicate the Irish royal houses in order to replace them with Norman royalty, as was their practice, because the Celtic custom of having numerous wives and concubines made it so that each king had literally dozens of potential heirs. Fry explains,

In the struggle with the Normans, the Irish lack of unity turned from a weakness into a strength. There were so many Irish kings, fluidly combining and recombining, that they were impossible to defeat. As soon as one Irish king, or combina-

THE HISTORY
A SHORT HISTORY
OF IRELAND
AD 1167-1851

tion of kings, went down, others appeared. To attempt to catch them was like bobbing for apples at Halloween. Irish princely families were in no danger of dying out, as the leading Norman families were; due to the laxity of Irish marriage customs, chieftains often had enormous families. Pilib Mág Uidhir, the lord of Fir Manach, had twenty sons by eight different mothers and at least fifty grandsons, and Toirrdhelbach Ua Domnaill, the lord of Tír Conaill, had eighteen sons by ten different mothers and fifty-nine grandsons![7]

The initial, brilliant Norman victories were gradually offset by the numerous lesser defeats that took place over time. And after the defeat of the Normans by the Scots at the Battle of Bannockburn, the fortunes of the Celts of Ireland and Scotland began to rise. Supplemented by a new form of heavily armored Celtic knight called the *gallowglass* (from *gall-oglach*, "foreign fighter"), the Celtic armies began to be able to make a competent showing on the battlefield, defeating the formerly invincible Norman knights on more than one occasion. Moreover, the Irish began to adapt themselves to the Norman tactics, and an attempt was even made by King Edward Bruce of Scotland to create a sort of pan-Celtic union to resist the Norman intrusion into Scotland and Ireland. And though this union failed to come about, more and more the Normans began to wear down and soften. Like a rock slowly eroded by water, the Norman strength gradually declined over the three centuries of their dominion, until they, like the Vikings, became isolated into several small enclaves.

The Statutes of Kilkenny

The Normans then began to become so closely integrated with Irish society, adapting their language, dress, and culture, that it was becoming increasingly difficult to distinguish the rulers from the ruled. This trend forced the English crown to act in order to keep from losing control over their Irish colonies. Brendan Ó hEithir explains in *A Pocket History of Ireland*,

So successful was this cultural assimilation that two hundred years after the first invaders arrived the English crown was forced to take severe measures at a parliament which assembled in Kilkenny, the heartland of Norman Ireland, in 1366. Its purpose was to preserve the racial purity and cultural separateness of the colonizers, thereby enabling the English crown to retain control over them.... Their purpose was to prevent further assimilation, by legal and religious penalties. The settlers were forbidden to use the Irish language. They were also forbidden to use Irish names, marry into Irish families, use the Irish mode of dress, adopt any Irish laws and play the Irish game hurling. The measures were a failure. Gaelicisation had gone too far and by now the native population, having failed to beat the invaders on the field of battle, was in league militarily with the conquerors. By the end of the fifteenth century the English crown ruled only a small area around Dublin, known from its fortifications of earth and wood as "The Pale" (meaning a fence or boundary).[8]

Despite their failed attempt at Kilkenny to enforce English rule over the Norman settlers, England still retained control over Dublin and a substantial region around it known as "the Pale", named after a dividing fence that separated the "civilized" area around Dublin from the savage areas outside it.[9] And though they continued to have control over Dublin, by the end of the 15th century, England had effectively lost control of the lion's share of her former holdings. So different were these two Irelands, the Ireland within the fence, and the one without, that "Beyond the Pale" became an metaphor in the English language for something that is unusual, outrageous, and/or unacceptable, in memory of the anarchic conditions that existed outside of English control during this period. But the English adventure in Ireland was only just beginning, as more and more the fortunes of both England and Ireland had begun to become more and more intertwined.

THE TUDOR PERIOD (AD 1485-1603)
The War of the Roses

In 15th century England, there was a struggle for power that erupted into a vicious civil war, known to history as "The War of the Roses". Gormley explains,

> The Wars of the Roses were a series of civil wars fought in medieval England from 1455 to 1487 between the House of Lancaster and the House of York. The name Wars of the Roses is based on the badges used by the two sides, the red rose for the Lancastrians and the white rose for the Yorkists. Major causes of the conflict include: 1) both houses were direct descendants of king Edward III; 2) the ruling Lancastrian king, Henry VI, surrounded himself with unpopular nobles; 3) the civil unrest of much of the population; 4) the availability of many powerful lords with their own private armies; and 5) the untimely episodes of mental illness by King Henry VI.[10]

Finally, in 1487, the Lancastrians defeated the Yorkist faction, and the leader of the Welsh Lancastrians took power over all of England. The Lancastrian leader was then crowned King Henry VII, and the royal house he founded became known as The House of Tudor. This highly successful dynasty lasted for 118 years and produced some of the most famous monarchs of English history, including Henry VIII, Edward VI, Mary I and Elizabeth I, under whose management England flourished.[11]

The Protestant Reformation

To complicate matters, by the time of the Tudors, the Protestant Reformation had begun to make significant progress. The seeds of the Reformation had been planted by Oxford Professor John Wycliffe[12] during the 14th century, which were followed up by the Bohemian Priest Jan Hus[13] and by Martin Luther, who posted his 95 theses on the Wittenburg door in 1517.[14] Protestantism's central thesis was that the church was becoming too corrupt and worldly, and should abandon involvement in politics as well as its rigid episcopal system in favor of promoting the idea that each individual believer is a priest of God. To this end, like Wycliffe, who had

THE HISTORY
A SHORT HISTORY
OF IRELAND
AD 1167-1851

translated the Bible into English so that the common man could read it, Luther translated the Bible into German to help individual believers bypass the clergy and have a personal, one-to-one relationship with God. These concepts, which were truly revolutionary, led to civil war all over Europe, a conflict that would come to figure prominently in the history of Ireland right down to the present day.

The Wheel of Fate

Clearly, the wheel of fate was turning once again. King Henry the VIII was having a hard time creating a male heir to continue his line. His wife, Catherine of Aragon, produced only daughters or stillborn males, so Henry was desperate to marry another woman to replace the aging Catherine who would provide him with the sons he needed to carry on his lineage. The pope had denied him an annulment, so Henry was forced to choose between denying the pope, which could result in his excommunication, or fail to produce another male heir, which would lead to the end of his line and, most likely, another bloody civil war. It was in a third way, Protestantism, that Henry, quite literally, found his salvation.

In 1533, King Henry appointed Thomas Cranmer, a Protestant-leaning priest, to be the Archbishop of Canterbury. His reasons for doing so were not so much due to his love for Protestantism, but because Cranmer was willing to give Henry the annulment he so desperately needed. Archbishop Cranmer then crowned Henry's lover, Ann Boleyn, as Queen of England, after first performing a secretive annulment and a hasty remarriage. Their first child was a girl, however (Elizabeth I) but there was no going back. Henry ended up renouncing the authority of the papacy, instead proclaiming himself "The Supreme Head of the Church of England", in so doing officially breaking with Rome and founding the Church of England.[15]

DECLINE AND FALL (AD 1603-1851)

The rule of The Pale, which covered most of what is now Counties Dublin, Meath and Louth, was from 1515 onward controlled by The Irish Council, headed by a deputy of English descent. The council sent regular reports to King Henry as to conditions there, which were noticeably in decline. A strategy of military conquest of Ireland was considered, but would have been far too costly, so it was abandoned. However, Henry's daughter,

Queen Elizabeth, had no such concerns, and made it her goal to extend English rule to all of Ireland by force of arms. This policy came to a head in 1601, when the Earls of Tyrone and Tirconnell, Hugh O'Neill and Hugh O'Donnell, allied themselves with the Spanish in a final attempt to throw off the English yoke. They were defeated that year at The Battle of Kinsale, however, and both earls ending up fleeing the country, an event so infamous that it came to be remembered as "The Flight of the Earls". The result was a savage reprisal from the English that remains in the history of both peoples as the blackest period of Anglo-Irish relations.

The Coming of Cromwell

In order to ameliorate the threat of civil disorder caused by the emerging schism between Protestantism and Catholicism in England, Elizabeth wisely decided upon a policy of accomodation and compromise — a policy that was, on the whole, successful. However, her attempt to impose the same policy upon Catholic Ireland met with disastrous results, the repercussions of which still affect Ireland today.

Elizabeth's plan was to import Scottish Protestants into what is now Northern Ireland, giving them lands in the richest parts of Counties Tyrone, Donegal, Derry, Armagh and Antrim, divided into large estates into which the Protestants were "planted". These "plantations", as they came to be known, were built at the expense of the Irish, who were brutally forced off the land. This naturally built up a great deal of resentment, and the dispossessed Irish formed a rival faction, The Confederation of Kilkenny.

Oliver Cromwell, however, the Lord Protector of England who had been sent to Ireland in 1649 to place the Irish under the British heel, was a Protestant absolutist who had no patience with civil disorder of any kind, particularly Catholic disorder. In order to reinstate order in Ulster, he marshaled his huge military force and crushed the rebellion ruthlessly, driving out the survivors and giving their lands to the Protestant settlers. "To Hell or to Connacht" then became a popular phrase among these settlers, a warning to the native Irish Catholics that if they did not leave Ulster and emigrate to the lands in Connacht province, west of the Shannon River, they would be put to the sword.

THE HISTORY
A SHORT HISTORY
OF IRELAND
AD 1167-1851

Not satisfied with merely driving out the native Irish, however, Cromwell embarked upon a ruthless policy of ethnic cleansing throughout the Ulster region, reducing the Irish Catholic population of Ulster to 500,000 through famine, plague and systematic butchery — in the process earning for himself "a permanent place in the folk-memory of hate."[16]

The Penal Laws and The Treaty of Limerick

Adding insult to injury, in 1691 the Irish Council in English-ruled Dublin passed what are now infamously remembered as The Penal Laws, laws that were specifically designed to favor Protestants over Catholics. The intent of these laws was to encourage the Catholic Irish to convert to Protestantism, but the effect was only to create more resentment.

In 1685, there was another struggle for control of the English throne, this time between the Catholic King James II, and William of Orange, who was Protestant. The Irish Catholics backed King James, hoping to have the penal laws removed, whereas the Ulster Protestants backed William, hoping to be given even more land and power. In 1690, the two kings finally met at The Battle of the Boyne, where William of Orange was victorious, becoming the King of both England, Scotland and Ireland. This is where the term "Protestant Orange" came from, the Battle of the Boyne still being celebrated annually by some Ulster Protestants.[17]

After the successful sieging of Limerick by King William, the Treaty of Limerick was signed, where the Irish Catholic forces agreed to surrender in return for the abolition of the Penal Laws. William signed the treaty, but the Protestant parliament in Dublin would not ratify it, instead impressing even more laws upon the increasingly beleaguered Irish Catholics.

Revolution

In 1782, inspired — or perhaps intimidated — by the successful American Revolution in her former American colonies, the English granted the Dublin parliament near-total autonomy, though the administration was still appointed by the English crown. As a result of this newly invigorated parliament, led by the charismatic Henry Grattan (whose statue can still be seen today in College Green in Dublin, near the modern Bank of Ireland), many of the anti-Catholic and anti-Presbyterian penal laws were abolished.

However, the repeal of these laws was too little, too late for many. In 1791, a man named Theobald Wolfe Tone founded a society he called the "United Irishmen", with the intent of breaking ties completely with England and uniting "Protestant, Catholic and Dissenter" under the common name of "Irishman".[18] Tone gained the help of the French and led a coup in 1798, which was unsuccessful. Tone himself was captured and sent to prison, where he committed suicide. Despite his failure, however, he remains one of the most revered of Irish republican saints, a martyr for the cause of Irish independence.

As a result of this failed coup, in 1800 England decided to remove the measure of independence that they had formerly ceded to Ireland, "for good behavior", as it were, and once again imposed direct rule upon the island via Dublin. This rule was based upon the policy of the British Prime Minister William Pitt (the Younger)[19], and became known as The Act of Union. This act also promised Catholic equality, which once again was never implemented. The result of this move was of course, predictable: increased agitiation for revolution. Ó hEithir explains,

> For the remainder of the century, Irish nationalist politicians and agitators campaigned for three main objectives: Catholic emancipation, which meant equal rights with Protestants in all respects; Home Rule, meaning the re-establishment of a parliament for the whole of Ireland with a relationship — not clearly defined — with the English crown; and the ownership of the land for the people who worked it, which would be a reversal of the feudalism introduced by the Normans.[20]

Several more prominent revolutionaries appeared during this period, including the famous Robert Emmett, a Dublin Protestant who was remembered not so much for his unsuccessful 1803 uprising but for his eloquent last words, where he refused to have an epitaph written on his gravestone until Ireland was truly and completely free from foreign rule. Another prominent revolutionary who arose during the 19th century was Daniel O'Connell, who made his mark by finally achieving Catholic emancipation in 1823. He also agitated against the Act of Union, but when confronted with possible military force, O'Connell, pacifistic by nature, immedi-

THE HISTORY
A SHORT HISTORY
OF IRELAND
AD 1167-1851

ately backed down and, as a result, lost his credibility and political viability. Another movement called Young Ireland was formed in 1848 by a group of young idealists, but their attempt at revolution was weak almost to the point of being comical. Generally speaking, the attempts at fomenting revolution in Ireland generated a great deal of heat, but precious little light and, in the end, only made matters worse.

Disaster

Capping off this period of disastrous setbacks and failed coups for Irish Catholics was the infamous Irish Potato Famine, usually simply referred to as "The Famine". The stage was set for the famine at the beginning of the 19th century, when Irish Catholics had adopted the practice of tillage farming in order to produce potatoes to help supply Napoleon's armies. Though this improved their income for a time, it also reduced the amount of land available for pasturing livestock. As a result, the Irish became more dependent upon potatoes for nourishment than cattle, their traditional mainstay. The trouble started when the demand for potatoes dried up in 1815, after the final defeat of Napoleon at Waterloo, and the Irish were left with a large amount of potatoes, but with no market. This led to widespread unemployment, and the unemployed were forced to live on small plots of land where they subsisted on the small amount of potatoes they could grow for themselves.

Then, in 1845, the potato blight came. It was caused by a form of fungus called *Phytophthora Infestans*, which caused the potatoes to rot while in the ground and become inedible. And they also smelled bad — so bad, in fact, that one could walk by a field and tell if the blight was on it by the smell. The Irish shrugged it off as a one-off and replanted, but the blight returned a second year – and a third. In the third year there was also a cholera epidemic, greatly compounding the misery, and the death toll by both disease and starvation was beginning to rise. The blight finally began to tail off in 1850, 1851 being the last year that the blight hit heavily, but the damage had been done. The estimates from those who had died of starvation and disease, or had fled to America, were upwards of 1.5 million — an estimated 15-20% of the entire population of Catholic Ireland at that time.

The Road to Freedom (AD 1852-1998)

After the famine, the Irish had nowhere to go but up. So great was that disaster that it rivaled (and in sheer numbers far exceeded) even the slaughter at Conan's Tower that had forced the ancient Nemedians to abandon the sacred isle altogether. And like the Nemedians, whose descendants regrouped, retrained and reinvaded the sacred isle as the Fir Bolg and the Tuatha dé Danann, the Irish *diaspora* — those Irish that had fled to England and America to escape the famine — also regrouped in the lands of their captivity in an effort to retake their native land.

THE FENIANS

Though the Irish had fled to both England and America in order to survive the ravages of the famine, it was the Irish in America who were most instrumental in fomenting political change in Ireland. Ó hEithir explains:

> The Irish in America were quick to organize and become a force in American politics. Many of them also remained involved in Irish affairs, at one remove, determined to aid any attempt to overthrow British rule in the country they and their ancestors had to leave. The Irish in America were instrumental in founding the most persistent revolutionary organization of all, the Fenian Brotherhood, which became the Irish Republican Brotherhood (IRB), from which grew the Irish Republican Army (IRA). The Fenian Brotherhood, which was named after a band of mythical heroic warriors, was founded in a Dublin timber-yard on St. Patrick's Day 1858, with 400 American dollars to sustain it. Like the United Irishmen, its members were bound by oath to secrecy and loyalty to the Irish Republic.[21]

The objectives of the Fenians[22] were simple: they wanted the British out of Ireland, an Irish-controlled government that presided over all 32 counties, and a secular emphasis, to the point of including a "separation of church and state" clause in their proposed constitution. As a result they came into bitter conflict with the Catholic Church but, as

THE HISTORY
A SHORT HISTORY
OF IRELAND
AD 1852-1998

they were a secret society, they could not be easily stamped out. And though the Fenians did not succeed initially as a political movement, their network of members grew through the years to reach into every aspect of society, including the military and even the church.

HOME RULE

Though the Fenians were ineffective as a political party, they proved to be very effective in agitating for grass-roots rebellion. One of their most effective movements was the development of The Land League, which successfully returned control of the land in many parts of the country to the native Irish. They achieved this not so much through violence (though some definitely did occur), but primarily through the use of the boycott. The term "boycott" came from a man named Captain Boycott who, during this time of grass-roots rebellion, had successfully employed the technique of refusing to have any social or business contacts with anyone who was not loyal to the cause of Republicanism, in order to enact political change.

The most effective of the Fenians, however, was one Charles Stewart Parnell who, after successfully agitating to return the land to the native Irish, began to fight the much larger struggle concerning home rule. Parnell became so powerful that at the peak of his career, he was known as "the uncrowned king of Ireland". Parnell was disgraced after his affair with a married woman was discovered, however, and he died under mysterious circumstances in 1891 — another martyr to the cause of Irish independence.

THE GAELIC REVIVAL

After the death of Parnell, for a time political activity receded and the Irish began to express their Irishness through a cultural renaissance known as "The Gaelic Revival". Also called "The Celtic Revival", during this time the cultural grass roots that had been cultivated by the Fenians began to flourish, and Celtica became all the rage. In 1884 the Gaelic Athletic Association was founded in order to promote Irish forms of sport, specifically, hurling and Gaelic football. In 1893 The Gaelic League was formed, with the intent of reviving Gaelic as a living language, with limited success. Soon afterwards, the Irish National Theatre was established in Dublin with the intent of helping build a modern popular culture that was distinctly Irish. The major movers and shakers who helped to rebuild Gaelic culture through more modern art forms and media were Lady Gregory and W.B. Yeats, who were also instrumental in recording much of the mythology and fairy lore that still circulated throughout the countryside at that time.[23] Their collection and codification of the mythological and fairy lore that still circulated around the turf-fires at the end of the 18th century was legendary in and of itself, and the books that resulted from this fertile period are still considered classics in the field of folklore and mythology.

THE 1916 RISING

All together, the Celtic revival had had the effect of uniting the Irish culturally, but they were still disunited politically. Several new political movements began to grow in the early 20th century, however, most notably the Ulster Volunteer Force (UVF) that fought against Irish home rule and for independence for Ulster, and the Irish Volunteers, who were fighting for home rule, and a united Ireland. *Sinn Féin* ("We Ourselves") appeared as more of a philosophical movement in 1908, but would later evolve into a much more potent force. The most potent force in 1916, however, was a militant group called the Irish Citizen Army.

The 1916 Rising was led by the socialist leader of the Irish Citizen Army, James Connolly. This movement was made up not of a seasoned, professional military, but by normal citizens who were idealists of the same mold as Tone — teachers, authors, workers and tradesmen. Moreover, the rising was not coordinated with, or even approved by, the Irish Volunteers, who were allied with the Irish Citizen Army. To complicate matters, the shipment of munitions that was intended to arm many of the volunteers in the countryside was intercepted, so the coup, which took place on Easter Sunday, 1916, lasted only a few days, and failed with little struggle.

Though the coup was a failure, with little public sympathy or support, it did raise worldwide attention to the cause of Irish independence. Moreover, after the British made the mistake of killing 16 of the ringleaders, including

Connolly, who was essentially a harmless intellectual, the public mood swung back strongly in favor of home rule, and the Rising, though ineffective militarily, proved to be very effective politically.

THE DÁIL EIREANN

The English made the critical mistake of martyring the insurgents, and the nation, previously shocked and disgusted by their actions, embraced them as heroes. The result was a sweeping sense of national pride that changed the political course of Irish history, and the formation of the first independent Irish national congress, known as the Dáil Eireann, "the Assembly of Ireland":

> In the aftermath of the rising, a wave of nationalistic fervour swept the country and, in a general election held in 1918, Sinn Féin completely eclipsed the Irish Party. Then its elected members, instead of going to Westminster, set up an illegal assembly in Dublin called Dáil Eireann (assembly or parliament of Ireland). Some of those elected were still in jail after the rising and on their release they returned home to be met by cheering crowds.[24]

THE WAR OF INDEPENDENCE

On the first day that the Dáil convened in January of 1919, two men stole some explosives from a storage depot in County Tipperary, killing two police officers in the process. Though this action had not been approved (or even known) by the members of the Dáil, it was to be the first "shot" in the Irish War of Independence.

The War of Independence was essentially a guerrilla war on both the political and military fronts. Incapable of defeating the English on the battlefield, the Irish Catholics instead formed an organized terrorist force called the Irish Republican Army, or IRA, led by the legendary Michael Collins, that used ambush and subversive tactics to gradually undermine the enemy and their will to continue. The war gradually devolved into a struggle between terror and counter-terror, the British army developing a paramilitary force known as "The Black and Tans" that was specifically designed to terrorize the IRA into submission.

THE HISTORY
A SHORT HISTORY
OF IRELAND
AD 1852-1998

As this cold, bitter war continued, the English began to become more and more cruel, shooting civilians indiscriminately and even burning down whole city blocks. The English did not factor in the propaganda element, however, and soon found that their brutal tactics were not playing well either at home or abroad. Even loyal Irish police forces began to resign in protest, and the Lord Mayor of Cork, Terence MacSwiney, went on a hunger strike. And though he died after a 73-day fast, his use of the old Brehon method of "procedure by fasting" (*op. cit.*) in order to redress a grievance made him legendary throughout the world, influencing even a relatively unknown figure of Indian politics at the time — Mahatma Gandhi — to do the same.

The Anglo-Irish Treaty of 1922

Though Britain won the battles, they lost the propaganda war, and were forced to come to terms with the Irish separatists. A truce was agreed upon in 1921, and in 1922 a delegation put together by Eamon de Valera, led by Arthur Griffith and Michael Collins, met with a British delegation, led by David Lloyd George, who was accompanied by a young Winston Churchill. The treaty was signed under the threat of total war from the English, but it proved to be disastrous for both parties. It was at this time that the independent state of Northern Ireland began to emerge, carved from 6 of the 9 counties of Ulster that were predominantly Protestant, which was to remain a part of the British Empire. Under this plan, the remaining 26 counties would become part of an Irish republic, made into a mostly independent country that would be still nominally ruled by England, much like Canada and Australia had been.

However, civil war broke out once again between the newly formed Protestant "free state" in the north and the Irish republic in the south. Though outnumbered, the northern forces had superior equipment and organization. After only a year, the war was won by the Free State forces over the Republicans, and the Catholic Irish settled into another period of second-class status within their own country.

The 1937 Constitution

By 1937, after another period of political anarchy, the Dáil Eireann finally had enough support to put together a competent constitution that the majority

THE HISTORY
A SHORT HISTORY
OF IRELAND
AD 1852-1998

could agree upon, declaring Ireland to be a sovereign, free, democratic state made up of the same 26 counties that the Anglo-Irish treaty had ceded to them. However, this constitution made it clear that England no longer had control over Irish politics, at least not in the 26 counties. The northern 6 counties that were predominantly Protestant then became known as Northern Ireland. The southern 26 counties, however, did not officially become a republic until 1949 and the passing of The Republic of Ireland Act, though the 1937 constitution otherwise remains largely unchanged, to this day.

IRELAND & THE WORLD

The next major step in the political evolution of the Republic of Ireland was their entry into the European Union in 1973, a giant step toward international recognition as a legitimate, sovereign state.[25] And though the Protestant/Catholic schism in the north continued on for some time, with the signing of the Good Friday Agreement in 1998, relations have dramatically improved. And though the schism will likely never completely go away, socio-economic trends in Ireland seem to be moving more and more towards reconciliation, homogenization, secularization and globalization, with the effect that all Irish, north and south, are viewing themselves less and less as the inheritors of a bitter and pointless struggle over land and religion, and more and more as citizens of the world.

Notes

[1] Peter and Fiona Somerset Fry, A History of Ireland 2nd ed. (New York: Barnes & Noble, 1993), 43.

[2] Fry, A History of Ireland, 26.

[3] Michael Richter, Medieval Ireland: The Enduring Tradition (New York: St. Martin's Press, 1995), 36.

[4] Fry and Fry, A History of Ireland, 27-28.

[5] Richter, Medieval Ireland, 37-38.

[6] Fry and Fry, A History of Ireland, 60.

[7] Ibid., 83.

[8] Brendan Ó hEithir, A Pocket History of Ireland (Dublin: The O'Brien Press, 2001), 26-27.

THE HISTORY
A SHORT HISTORY
OF IRELAND
NOTES

[9] The stakes used to make up the fence were called "pales", as in *im*pale. They are better known today as "pickets".

[10] Larry Gormley, "Wars of the Roses" (Wars of the Roses: http://www.warsoftheroses.com).

[11] The House of Windsor, "The Tudors" (The Official Website of the British Monarchy: http://www.royal.gov.uk), http://www.royal.gov.uk/output/Page11.asp.

[12] Wycliffe Bible Translators, "John Wycliffe: Ahead of His Time" (Wycliffe: http://www.wycliffe.org), http://www.wycliffe.org/history/JWycliff.htm. Also see http://www.greatsite.com/timeline-english-bible-history/john-wycliffe.html.

[13] J. Wilhelm, "Jan Hus" (The Catholic Encyclopedia: http://www.newadvent.org/cathen/), http://www.newadvent.org/cathen/07584b.htm.

[14] For more information on Martin Luther and his 95 theses, see http://www.educ.msu.edu/homepages/laurence/reformation/Luther/Luther.htm.

[15] Fry and Fry, *A History of Ireland*, 105-106.

[16] Brendan Ó hEithir, *A Pocket History of Ireland* (Dublin: The O'Brien Press, 2001), 30-31. For more on the life and times of Oliver Cromwell, visit http://www.olivercromwell.org.

[17] Please note that this subject is still taboo, and should be avoided, especially when visiting Ulster province. For more information, see http://en.wikipedia.org/wiki/Orange_Order.

[18] Ó hEithir, *A Pocket History of Ireland*, 34-35.

[19] For more on the influential Prime Minister Pitt the Younger, see http://www.britannia.com/gov/primes/prime16.html.

[20] Ó hEithir, *A Pocket History of Ireland*, 37.

[21] *Ibid.*, 42-43.

[22] The Fenians were of course named after the *Fianna*, an ancient warrior order led by Finn McCool that protected Ireland from external invasion. See The Mystery: Deities & Demigods: Demigods: Finn McCool: The Fianna (pp. 117-121) for more information on the ancient Fenians.

[23] Much of the work of these two important turn-of-the-century authors is reflected in our detailed analysis of fairy lore in The Mystery: Creatures Great & Small: Fairies. All of their accumulated research will be published regularly at http://ireland.mysteriousworld.com.

[24] Ó hEithir, *A Pocket History of Ireland*, 58.

[25] See http://www.eu2004.ie or http://foreignaffairs.gov.ie/eu/ for more information.

Ireland Today

"County Limerick from Heaven" – © Barrie Maguire.

Ireland today is a land steeped in tradition, but with her face firmly set towards the future. In the last several decades, Ireland has transformed itself from a bitterly divided, introverted, protectionist state to one of the brighter stars of the European Union. The Irish themselves are becoming increasingly well-educated, well traveled, and cultured, easily the equal of their British and American counterparts. And the Irish quality of life has steadily improved to the point where there are now many more people emigrating to Ireland than leaving.

Both the Republic of Ireland and Northern Ireland are clean, friendly, well-managed countries where tourism — and tourists — are taken seriously. Relations between the two countries have also improved steadily, to the point where safety is no longer an issue, except in isolated sections of some of the larger cities, but this is typical of any Western country. In many ways, Ireland is the ideal tourist destination, particularly for those who are interested in Celtic tradition, history, and ancient mysteries.

Culture

Though relatively progressive, Ireland still remains a deeply religious country where the people take their faith seriously. The average pace is still a bit slower than neighboring countries, to the point where Ireland has often been accused of having a *mañana* culture (a Spanish loan word, used

THE HISTORY
IRELAND TODAY
CULTURE

in the sense of "I'll do it tomorrow") particularly when it comes to customer service. However, this too has been improving as Ireland strives to keep pace with its neighbors. Economically the island retains a vibrant economy, creating a general feeling of prosperity that has helped to soften the old ideological hard lines that have polarized the nation for centuries. All together, the future of Ireland looks bright indeed.

THE IRISH WORLDVIEW

✝ **Religious:** The Republic of Ireland is overwhelmingly (90%) Catholic, with a small but active Protestant minority, as well as small but growing Jewish and Muslim communities and a number of other nationalities in the larger cities, particularly in Dublin. Northern Ireland, by contrast, is majority Protestant, with approximately 60% Protestant and 40% Catholic. Partisan lines based upon the old Protestant-Catholic schism still exist in the north, but recent trends in popular youth culture have resulted in a reduction of church attendance and, by extension, religious dogmatism. And though there is a small but vocal minority of Protestants in the Republic of Ireland, the tensions that exist between Protestant and Catholic in the north are not shared in the south.

Colorful, public religious ceremonies are still held on major religious holidays not only on St. Patrick's Day (March 17), but also on Easter, Pentecost (fifty days after Easter), Trinity Sunday (the first Sunday after Pentecost) the Feast of Corpus Christi (the first Thursday after Trinity Sunday), and numerous other holidays throughout the calendar year. First Communions are also lavish affairs where young girls are actually dressed like little brides, and funerals remain as major community events where pretty much everyone attends, even if they did not know the deceased personally.

✝ **Social:** Social folkways and mores are essentially the same as that found in other western countries, with the exception that Irish customs tend to be a little more flexible regarding social interaction, but a little more rigid as regarding moral issues. Handshakes and hellos are the norm, but don't expect a hug unless you know someone well. It is okay, even expected, to be a little late to social functions, but it is considered rude to leave a party early, as the Irish (at least those who like to party) like to stay up late into the early morning hours. When visiting friends, you don't need to call ahead, you can just stop by and say hello and expect to share a beer or some food. However, calling ahead can't hurt, particularly if you would like to stay for a while.

When conversing, you may note an accent that you have never heard before. These accents vary from region to region, but all are intelligible. Don't try to imitate the accent, though, or you may cause offense, or just look foolish. However, it is a good idea to toast to their health by saying *Slainte* ("slawnt-sha") before drinking. Sports are a very popular topic of conversation, particularly Gaelic football and hurling in the south, and soccer and rugby in the north. Rugby tends to be more of a white collar sport, watched by a relatively small percentage of viewers mainly in the north, so keep the tacit religio-political distinctions in mind when choosing what to say about what sport. Golf is huge in Ireland and a safe topic, and tennis and horse racing are also popular throughout the island.

Generally speaking, Irish society is fairly open and friendly, and tolerant of outsiders, who are more likely to be seen as a source of interesting conversation rather than as an annoyance. As in most countries, it is usually best to avoid talk about hot religious and political issues, however, unless you know the mind of the person you are talking to — and of those who might overhear you. Islandwide, the general sentiment tends to be more on the egalitarian side, where there is usually little distinction between city and country folk. One of the few exceptions is perhaps in the area in Dublin known colloquially as "Dublin 4", a noted bastion of intellectual elitism.

What social status there is to be had in Ireland is usually defined either by wealth or artistic achievement. If you need help, people may well go out of their way to help you, or they may not. But if you are lost and/or in need of aid and no one is around, seek out the *Garda Síochána*, Ireland's national police force, and they will be happy to help. But don't forget to drive on the left side of the road, or the *Garda* will remind you.

✤ **Economic:** Since the tech revolution of the 1990's, Ireland has become known as the "Celtic Tiger" from its explosive expansion into the tech sector, where it is now one of the top exporters of computer software in the world. Ireland still has a substantial agrarian base, however, with one in seven workers

THE HISTORY
IRELAND TODAY
CULTURE

employed in that sector. The *mañana* culture definitely does not extend to the business world here, however, as those who held to that ethic have long since been weeded out by fierce international competition. If you are visiting Ireland on business, confirm the meeting time, plan to be punctual to business meetings and dress well, but don't except a difficult, tense meeting. Rather, your meeting will more likely be a pleasant time out, where useful work was accomplished, and fun was had by all.

It is important to remember that Northern Ireland still uses the British pound (£), while the Republic of Ireland is part of the European Union and uses the Euro (€). Working hours throughout the island are typically within 9-6, sometimes 9:00-5:30, 9:30-6, and so forth, and stores are open Monday through Saturday. Essential services and restaurants are open on Sunday, as are specialty shopping marts, as Ireland is not as rigidly sabbatarian as it once was. Ireland has a very up-to-date telecommunications system (more so than the U.S., in many respects), so phone and Internet connectivity are relatively easy to acquire, and Internet cafés abound in the major urban centers.

⚘ Political: The political situation in Ireland has progressively lost its harsh ideological edge, ruling parties having been replaced by a series of coalition governments made up of numerous special interest groups. Women have also been elected President of Ireland more than once, indicating a softening of the rigid patriarchal culture as well. And whereas a move away from rigid sectarianism is evident amongst the young, an ongoing interest in the Celtic Revival movement has created and sustained special, "English-free" zones where Gaelic is the primary language. These special areas, comprising several small, isolated areas in the far west of Ireland, are known collectively as the *Gaeltacht*, and may present some special challenges for the traveler. Moreover, even strictly English-speaking Irish people outside of the Gaeltacht areas will occasionally season their English with florid Gaelicisms to spice things up a bit, so patience may be the order of the day as someone may throw a few curve balls your way. We have listed some common Gaelic words on the inside back cover of this book, along with some useful information, which may help you out of a tight situation.

Literature

Irish literature is world-renowned, and its greatest works are required reading for any student of English. The Irish love of books and words became evident once again during the literary revival that took place during the 18th – 20th centuries, when the increasingly common use of the English language began to give a new generation of writers new ways to express themselves.

The Irish love of writing and story has been evident since very ancient times, and the ancient epics of Ireland have even reappeared in various forms in modern Irish literature. But the mod-

"James Joyce" – © Barrie Maguire.

erns stand very well on their own, to the point where, in Dublin, there have evolved "summer schools" that are devoted purely to literary pursuits, usually located around the former haunting grounds of the numerous luminaries in the field, of which there are many:

JONATHAN SWIFT (1667-1745)

Political satirist Jonathan Swift was born in Dublin, Ireland on November 30, 1667. He is believed to be the first Irish author to make a significant contribution to English literature with his most famous work, *Gulliver's Travels*, first published in 1726. Though usually labeled a children's book, *Gulliver's Travels* is actually a very clever political satire that provides us with some very detailed and cogent insights into the socio-economic and political conditions of the time.

In 1729 Swift followed up his first successful novel with *A Modest Proposal*, a darkly humorous piece written during lean times in Ireland where Swift, posing as a "political arithmetician" coolly suggested to

THE HISTORY
IRELAND TODAY
LITERATURE

the Irish public that the problems of hunger and overpopulation could be solved by simply eating all of the poor, homeless children that abounded during that time.

Swift died in 1745, but not before taking one last jab at his Dublin homeland by including in his last will and testament some funds to establish in Dublin a hospital especially for the treatment of idiots and lunatics as, he believed, "no nation needed it as much."

BRAM STOKER (1847-1912)

Abraham "Bram" Stoker was born in Clontarf, northern Dublin in 1847. His father was a civil servant who worked in Dublin Castle, while his mother was a writer who often told the young Bram horror stories. Bram was bedridden by a mysterious illness until he was seven years old, which caused him to be shy and bookish in his early years. In college, however, he flourished as an athlete, receiving numerous awards for his athletic prowess. But the young Bram's experience of being bedridden for many years, during which time his mother had regularly told him numerous horror stories, remained a dominant influence on him throughout his life.

The young Bram dreamed of becoming a writer, but he followed his father's wishes to go into civil service and acquired a job working in Dublin Castle. Bored with his rather tedious civil service job, Bram then began to write short stories, including "The Crystal Cup" (1872), and a four-part serial called "The Chain of Destiny" (1875). During this time he also did *gratis* work as the theatre critic for Dublin's *Evening Mail*, later becoming the editor of *The Irish Echo*.

In 1878 Bram was offered the job of actor-manager at the Lyceum Theater in London, which he gratefully accepted. It was during this time in London that he began to write books, his first being *Under the Sunset* (1882), a collection of eight horror/fairy tales for children. His first full-length novel was *The Snake's Pass*, which was published in 1890, the same year that he began to do research for his masterpiece, *Dracula* (1897). And though Stoker remained a prolific author until dying of exhaustion in 1912, having written numerous books, short stories and essays, he remains best known for *Dracula*, which remains a highly influential work to this day.

Oscar Wilde (1854-1900)

The next major Irish author to make a name for himself was the famous but controversial Dubliner Oscar Wilde. Wilde was mainly known for his plays, short stories and poems, and one successful novel: *The Picture of Dorian Gray*. His most memorable plays include *Lady Windemere's Fan* (1892), *A Woman of No Importance* (1893), *An Ideal Husband* (1895) and *The Importance of Being Earnest* (1895). Though he was married with two children, in 1895 Wilde was convicted of committing homosexual acts and was sentenced to two years of hard labor. His wife died in 1898, and Wilde, a broken man, died in 1900. Wilde was a celebrity in his own time, and his works remain a powerful influence in the worlds of drama and literature.

G.B. Shaw (1856-1950)

George Bernard Shaw was another prominent Dublin playwright. Shaw began writing plays in his teens, including "Misalliance", a play about difficult parent-child relationships that reflected his real life problems with his divorced parents. In 1876 Shaw left Dublin to live with his mother and sister, where he began his career in journalism and writing. There he wrote five novels before publishing any of them, including the novel, *Immaturity*. It was during this time that Shaw began to get involved in the growing socialist movement, speaking at socialist rallies at the Speaker's Corner in London's Hyde Park, where he developed an aggressive speaking style that was reflected in his later writing. He also founded the Fabian Society, an organization devoted to the incremental socialization of Britain through legislation, higher education and media propaganda, forming the ideological basis of what would later become Britain's Labour Party.

Shaw then began to write plays again, including *The Perfect Wagnerite*, about the Ring Cycle of the famed composer Richard Wagner, and *The Quintessence of Ibsenism*, about the Norwegian playwright Henrik Ibsen. From 1895-1898, Shaw worked as an art and theater critic, during this time also writing the plays *Arms and the Man*, and *Mrs. Warren's Profession*, the latter of which was censored by the British government. Shaw ended up writing over two dozen plays during his long and prolific career, winning the Nobel Prize in Literature in 1925. His most famous work was the play *Pygmalion*, upon which the movie *My Fair Lady* was based.

THE HISTORY
IRELAND TODAY
LITERATURE

W.B. YEATS (1865-1939)

William Butler Yeats was probably the greatest Irish poet of modern times. Born in Dublin, he spent much of his early years in London and Sligo, the latter of which came to be his favorite and most inspirational place to visit. His first volume of poetry, *Mosada: A Dramatic Poem*, was published in 1886, followed by *The Wanderings of Oisín* in 1889, which followed the adventures of the famous Fianna warrior Oisín. *The Celtic Twilight* followed in 1893, during the height of the Celtic Revival, inspiring an entire school of poetic thought that came to be known for its melancholy, dream-like style. In 1894, Yeats gained a sponsor in the person of Lady Gregory, the leading light in the Celtic Revival movement, who helped Yeats to continue examining his own Celtic roots.

Yeats published several other books of poetry during his prolific career, including *The Wind among the Reeds* (1899), *The Wild Swans at Coole* (1919), *A Vision* (1925), *The Tower* (1929), *The Winding Stair and Other Poems* (1933) and *Last Poems* (1939). From the 1920s on, Yeats' reputation as an exceptional poet had reached world-class status, and in 1923 he received the Nobel prize in literature. He even had a seat awarded him in the newly formed Irish Senate.

Yeats died in France in 1939, and his remains were returned to his beloved Sligo in 1948, under Ben Bulben's head in Drumcliff churchyard, as he had requested.

JAMES JOYCE (1882-1941)

James Joyce is generally considered to be the greatest Irish author of modern times. He was born into a chaotic situation, to a family that was originally well-to-do, but his father had lost his full-time job and had systematically misspent the family fortune. As a result, the young Joyce ended up spending most of his young life in poverty, being moved from temporary lodging to temporary lodging throughout Dublin as his family climbed their way down the ladder into poverty. As a result, he spent most of his young life wandering the streets, and saw everything — both good and evil — that Dublin had to offer.

The brilliant young Joyce was able to escape crushing poverty through a scholarship to University College, Dublin, where he flourished, taking a course of study in English literature and foreign languages. He also studied music, specifically, voice and piano, briefly considered pursuing a career as an Irish tenor, and even had an interest in drama.

Despite these side interests, Joyce decided to pursue a career in literature. Finding the atmosphere of the Irish literary revival to be stifling and introverted, however, Joyce decided to move to Paris, where he found what he felt to be an environment that was truly liberating. He would then spend the majority of his life in Paris, Trieste and Zurich, Switzerland with his wife, Nora, who provided much inspiration to his writing.

Joyce's first work, *Dubliners*, had originally been set to be published in 1912 by a Dublin publisher, but there had been such an uproar about the book that the publisher ended up destroying the entire first edition. This traumatic event caused Joyce — not unlike St. Columba centuries earlier — to leave Ireland forever. *Dubliners*, which was later published in London in 1914, was essentially a collection of short stories about real Dublin life as Joyce had experienced it, a gritty, no-holds-barred account that stood as a brutal indictment of Dublin life. His next work, *A Portrait of the Artist As a Young Man*, was an autobiographical work written in a stream-of-consciousness style through a proxy figure named Stephen Dedalus, through whom Joyce discussed religious parochialism, Dublin life, his love-hate relationship with his clinging, suffering family, and his adoption of art and literature as the highest form of religious devotion.

Though excellent, *Portrait* was merely to set the context for Joyce's masterpiece, *Ulysses*. *Ulysses* had originally been serialized in a Paris journal, but had been halted from publication in book form due to explicit sexual imagery. Also written in a stream-of consciousness style, *Ulysses*, set in 1904, follows a day in the life of a Dublin Jew named Leopold Bloom. Based upon the Greek poem *The Odyssey* (Ulysses being the Roman form of Odysseus), in *Ulysses*, Joyce raises Dublin from its dim perception as a minor city in an unimportant country to the center of all life and culture in the world, "the theater of all history", raising an otherwise banal day in the life of an average Dubliner to an event of epic proportions. Though initially banned in Britain and the United States, *Ulysses* was published in 1922 to international acclaim, and still stands today as the greatest work of literature in modern Irish history.

Joyce then remained in Paris for the next 19 years, bathed in the spotlight of international acclaim. There, in a circle of select acquaintances, he worked on his final novel, *Finnegans Wake* for 17 years, finally publishing it in 1939. Described by some as a "labyrinth" of complex, arcane references and literary devices, *Finnegans Wake* plays with the very concept of language, inventing its own "meta-language" that combines languages and worldviews from all over the world. Less a novel than an experience, *Finnegans Wake* may well be Joyce's attempt to fully explore the inductive method of thought, an experiential/emotional form of thinking where the strict linearity of words is deconstructed down to emotive meanings, from which perhaps Joyce was attempting to deduce the primal, structural basis of language. In this way he may have been trying to rediscover the original Druidic/Celtic way of thinking of his ancestors, which was non-linear in nature, and completely free of the restrictions of the written word.

Joyce's health had been failing during this period, particularly his eyesight, which made his work nearly impossible and may have accounted for much of the long period it took to write *Finnegans Wake*. Driven from France by the Nazis in 1940, Joyce and his wife left for Zurich, where Joyce would die a month later, on January 13, 1941. He was an international literary superstar for most of life, and remains today as the brightest star in the constellation of Irish literary genius.

SAMUEL BECKETT (1906-1989)

Samuel Barclay Beckett was born at Cooldrinach in Foxrock, County Dublin in 1906, the son of a middle-class Protestant couple. He went to school at Earlsfort House in Dublin, and then at Portora Royal School in Enniskillen, where Oscar Wilde had attended. At age 17 he matric-

ulated at Trinity College, Dublin, studying French and Italian. In his free time he reveled in the burgeoning independent theater, being particularly interested in the plays of J.M. Synge. He was also heavily influenced by the silent comedy of Buster Keaton and Charlie Chaplin.

After graduation, Beckett traveled to Paris, where he became an assistant to James Joyce *(op. cit.)*, becoming one of Joyce's favorite assistants on the "Work in Progress" that would later become *Finnegans Wake*. Similarly inspired by the French literary atmosphere, Beckett began his own writing, publishing the poem "Whoroscope" in 1930. In 1931 he published a short but groundbreaking study on the recently deceased French author Proust, simply titled, *Proust*. He then returned to Dublin to lecture at Trinity College, his *alma mater*, during which time he wrote some short stories that would later be used as the basis of his novel, *More Pricks than Kicks* (1934).

Restless, Beckett returned to Paris in 1932, where he published his first novel, *Dream of Fair to Middling Women*, the publication of which evidenced that he was emerging from Joyce's shadow. Still struggling with money, Beckett moved several times, returning to Dublin, then moving to London and finally settling in Paris in 1937, during this time working on his next novel, *Murphy* (1938). In 1941, Beckett and his wife, Suzanne, joined the French resistance, where they were nearly captured by the Gestapo after their cell had been betrayed. After the war, he wrote some of his finest work, including the trilogy *Molloy*, *Malone Dies* and *The Unnamable*.

Beckett then turned towards playwriting, writing his most famous work, *Waiting for Godot* in 1949. This was followed by several other brilliant plays, most notably *Endgame*, *Krapp's Last Tape*, and *Happy Days*. At the peak of his brilliant career, Beckett received the Nobel Prize in 1969, and continued writing books and plays until his death in 1989.

Ireland's authors, poets and playwrights stand tall as among the best in their respective fields, with four of her literati having been awarded the Nobel Prize in Literature in the 20th century alone (the fourth being awarded to Northern Irish poet Seamus Heaney in 1995). Ireland continues today as a great contributor to the ongoing literary legacy of the West.

THE HISTORY
IRELAND TODAY
LITERATURE

Music & Dance

Just as Ireland's plethora of historical and mythological traditions reflects the island's history of invasions, so too does its music and dance. Scholars who have studied the roots of modern Irish music and dance have revealed a panoply of

"The Bodhrán Player" – © Barrie Maguire. The ancient bodhrán is the only type of drum still in use today in traditional Irish music.

varying traditions coming not only from Ireland's ancient invaders, but also from cultural contacts from numerous other countries, forming a musical heritage that is truly a melting pot of Western tradition. In many ways, just as Ireland was the savior of Christendom and of the written word, so too it has served as the repository of music and dance traditions from all over the Western world, possibly also from Africa and even Asia, much of which would otherwise have been lost.

MUSIC

Ireland has had a rich musical tradition since ancient times. Brehon law actually identifies musicians as a specific subclass of bard (*op. cit.*), with harp players, or *cruitire*, being at the top of the musical hierarchy. Beneath harp players were various unfree, lower caste musicians, or *crónán*, followed by jugglers, mimes, and clowns, who rounded out the bottom rungs of society. Though as part of the bardic class of *fili* harpers were socially inferior to poets, they were still free, enjoying the same social status as *ceíle*, or non-propertied freemen, the broad middle and lower-middle class of Ireland that formed the backbone of society. Those who taught instruments such as the

harp and the *timpán* (a form of stringed instrument that was played with a bow) were even more highly esteemed, being considered equal to a *boaire*, or cattle lord, equivalent to our modern upper middle class.

The earliest known references to music can be found in the myths and legends of the Tuatha dé Danann, specifically the *Cath Maige Tuireadh*, "The Battle of Moy Tura", the most important document in the Mythological Cycle of Irish legends. In the story, the Dagda's magic harp, *Uaithne*, was stolen by the Fomorians. Tracking them back to their camp, the Dagda summoned his magic harp back to his hand, and it obeyed its master, killing nine Fomorians along the way. The Dagda then played three types of music in order to defeat the Fomorians: *goltraí*, which caused them to weep, *geantraí*, which caused them to laugh and *suantraí*, which caused them to sleep. These ancient forms of Irish music, unfortunately, have long since been lost.

Traditional Irish Music

Traditional Irish music, though old, is relatively modern considering the extensive ancient musical history of the sacred isle, most of which has long been lost. Though "traditional" Irish music tends to resist classification, as it is more of an interweaving of various different traditions from many different times and cultures, past and present, it is usually defined as music that has not been commercially produced, but has been passed down through "oral" (or perhaps, "aural" tradition is a more accurate term), where players merely listen to previous musicians and learn the music "by ear". Irish musicians have also picked up tunes through sheet music, recordings and even from the fairies, by some accounts, but generally speaking, Irish traditional music is considered to be that which has been passed on from player to player and singer to singer via direct, one-to-one transmission. And the most common venue in which traditional Irish musicians have carried on the Irish musical tradition has been through informal musical gatherings at home or at pub, typically referred to as *céilí*.

The Céilí

The general definition of *céilí* ("kay-lee") means simply a social gathering, usually of neighbors, and is most closely cognate to the English word "party". *Céilí*, however, can also be used to describe any kind of party-like occasion, such as a dance, a feast or,

THE HISTORY
IRELAND TODAY
MUSIC & DANCE

most relevant here, a concert. Also known as *seisun*, "sessions", these musical gatherings now typically take place in the local pub, and tend to be more low-key events, where the session serves mainly as background music for the conversation. Generations of players often hail from the same pub, players often becoming locally famous for having spent most of their lives doing *céilí* every Saturday or Sunday night, some of the older pubs able to boast dozens of local celebrities.

Song Types

Most of the types of traditional Irish music are directly related to the types of dances that accompany the music, such as jigs, reels, hornpipes and polkas, as music and dance were rarely separated in traditional Irish music. Some forms of music were so closely coordinated with their corresponding dances that they formed a "set" piece, where the dance could not be performed without the music, and vice versa. Other types of songs include slides, mazourkas, highlands and slow airs. The latter are usually instrumental versions of *sean nós* songs, a form of solo, *a cappella* singing, described as "old style", that is done in Gaelic with a particular lilting emphasis that is archetypally Irish in character. There are also other musical traditions and modern variations too numerous and complex to get into here.

Instruments

Irish traditional music tends to eschew percussion instruments in favor of string and wind instruments. Many of the ancient instruments used in Irish music, such as the *timpán* and the *corn* have long since been abandoned in favor of more modern instruments, such as the fiddle and the flute. Here is a listing of both the ancient and modern instruments typical of Irish music:

Ancient Instruments:
⚜ **The Cruit:** The *cruit* was the classical harp that is still in use today. Considered to be the premier instrument of ancient Ireland, it is better known today as the *cláirseach*. Irish harps were known for their sound construction, the sound box made from a single block of

wood, usually willow or sally. The neck was thick and heavy and bound with a metal band, while the fore-pillar curved outward, like the classic "Brian Boru" harp on display at Trinity College (*q.v.*).

⚜ **The *Timpán*:** Though it sounds like it should be a form of timpany, or drum (from the Latin *tympanum*, "drum"), the *timpán* was actually a form of string instrument played with a bow.

⚜ **The *Fidil*:** The *fidil* was another stringed instrument perhaps similar to the violin, but is not believed to be the violin as we know it, as the violin was not invented until the 16th century.

⚜ **The *Buinn*:** The *buinn* was most likely a horn, like a trumpet, possibly used in battle.

⚜ **The *Corn*:** A horn like the *buinn* except curved, which also may have been used in battle. This is probably the same as the *carnyx* war horn, which was often designed in the shape of a boar's head or some other fierce animal, a tongue-like apparatus being placed in the horn's mouth to provide an unnerving razzing sound.

⚜ **The *Cuiseach*:** A primitive flute made from corn stalks and reeds. Possibly the earliest type of musical instrument.

⚜ **The *Cuisle Cheoil*:** A slightly more refined version of the *cuiseach*.

⚜ **The *Feadán*:** Also known as the *foghurbhinn*, a sweet-sounding whistle, possibly the forerunner of the penny whistle.

⚜ **The *Píopaí*:** Probably an ancient form of bagpipes.

Though most of these instruments have long fallen into disuse, more and more Irish musicians are looking to the past to discover their musical roots and more fully explore the musical potential of these ancient instruments.

THE HISTORY
IRELAND TODAY
MUSIC & DANCE

Traditional Instruments:

✦ **The Fiddle:** "Fiddle" is a more colloquial term for violin, the first of which were made in Italy in 1549. The fiddle entered the Irish musical scene in the 18th century, where it has remained as a mainstay of Irish traditional music ever since, considered by most to be the best instrument on which to play traditional Irish music.

✦ **The Uillean (Union) Pipes:** The bagpipe is a very ancient musical instrument, known throughout the world in various forms. The Irish developed their own form of bagpipes in the 18th century, referring to them as *uillean* ("elbow") pipes, as the Irish bagpipe is filled with air via a bellows held under the elbow. They are also called "union" pipes, some believe, because they unite the unique sound created by the chanter, drones and regulators, though it may be that "union" is merely a corruption of "uillean". The uillean pipes are otherwise fairly similar to Scottish bagpipes, except they are said to have a sweeter sound, and are always played sitting down.

✦ **The Accordion:** Developed in the 19th century, there are three different types of accordion used to play Irish traditional music: the melodeon, the button accordion and the piano-keyed accordion. The oldest is the melodeon, which has ten buttons for the melody, and two for the bass notes. The button accordion was developed with two rows of buttons to provide a wider variety of melody notes, as well as several more buttons for bass notes. This form of accordion is the most popular, and there are two different styles of playing: the "push and pull", and a more smooth, flowing style. The piano-keyed accordion is mainly used by informal céilí bands.

✦ **The Flute:** A flute is simply a long, hollow tube with holes cut in it to produce notes of various pitches. Flutes were originally produced out of wood, but most professional musicians abandoned the wooden flutes for the metal as soon as they became available. As a result, many wooden flutes came onto the market, and were quickly picked up by lay musicians, and the flute has remained a mainstay of Irish traditional music ever since.

🜚 **The Tin Whistle:** One of the most ancient instruments remaining in the modern Irish repertoire, ancient forms of the tin whistle made of bone have been found as early as the 12th century in Dublin. The tin whistle is also called the "penny whistle", ironically, as it is surprisingly expensive. Unlike the flute, the tin whistle is blown from one end instead of the side. Though an easy instrument to learn how to play, it is difficult to learn how to play it *well*.

🜚 **The Concertina:** The concertina is composed of two hexagonal blocks with keys on one side, connected to each other by a bellows. It is essentially the same as a harmonica, except notes are determined by pressing keys, and the bellows provides the air.

🜚 **Accompaniment:** Besides these mainstays, there are numerous other ancient and modern instruments that have made their way into Irish traditional music, including: the piano, the guitar, the harmonica, the jaw harp, the banjo, the bazouki — a 19th century Greek instrument introduced into Ireland in the 1960s — the bodhrán, an ancient form of drum still in use today, and the bones, essentially old cow bones used to rattle together to create loud, castanet-like sounds.

Irish Music Today

The best known Irish music worldwide is that played by such rock bands as U2, Van Morrison, Thin Lizzy, The Pogues, Sinead O'Connor, The Corrs and The Cranberries, mystical, "New Age" groups such as Clannad, Altan and Dervish, solo artists such as Enya, and many more. As popular as these groups are both in Ireland and abroad, however, there is also a powerful undercurrent of homegrown bands that are more closely tied to Irish traditional music, such as The Chieftains, The Irish Rovers, The Dubliners, Christy Moore and, most recently, Celtic Woman. The most accessible and satisfying musical experience, however, may still be found at the local pub.

DANCE

The ancient Irish word for "dance" is not known. The Irish words used for dance in recent centuries include *damhsa* and *rince*, both of which are derived from the English loan words "dance" and "rink", respectively. The English word "dance" originally came from the French word *danse*, which in turn may have come from even earlier German antecedents. The English word "rink", even in ancient times, was used in the sense of a skating rink, referring possibly to the smooth, sliding steps to be found in certain dances, and/or the fact that dances, like skating, takes place within a defined space. Other loan words include "jig", which comes from the English word *jigeannai* (which in turn came from the Italian term *giga*), and the word "reel", which comes from the English word *rílleana*, in turn derived from the Anglo-Saxon word *rulla*, "to whirl".

Many of these dances, particularly the round, "reel" dances and the carol — originally a form of mating ritual dance that was performed on May 1st (Beltaine) — came with the Norman invasions, as did probably the ancient English names from which the modern terms "dance", "rink", "jig" and "reel" were originally derived. Other words that refer to specific reels and jigs, including *coir* and *port*, actually refer to the harp melody that accompanies those particular dances, underlining the fact that Irish traditional music was usually accompanied by dancing.

The Irish dances that are today considered to be traditional mostly came into existence in their present form during the latter half of the eighteenth century. During that time, men of the ancient bardic tradition known as "dance masters" were still common throughout Ireland, being a form of traveling dance teacher who taught people how to dance in return for money. Socially, the dance masters were a step above the typical traveling musician, affecting a jaunty appearance much more like that of the educated upper classes, though they typically lacked a formal education.

However, it is largely because of these dance masters, who memorized countless dances as part of their repertoire, that much of the ancient dancing traditions are still with us today.

It was during the fertile period at the end of the 19th century, when the Celtic Revival was at its peak, that many of the ancient dances to be found around the land were collected and memorized by these masters. The dances that are still remembered today are the solo or "step" dances, *céilí* dancing, Cotillion and Quadrille dances and, most recently, polkas and waltzes.

Solo or "Step" Dances

The step dances comprise the most commonly recognized forms of Irish dancing. They are usually performed by at least one couple, except for the hornpipe, which is always performed by a single male.

✦ **The Jig:** There are three types of jigs: the double jig, the single jig, and the "hop" jig. The double jig is the most popular form of jig, where the dancer throws the right foot forward about a foot above the floor, and then withdraws his right foot and taps the floor with his or her right toes, while hopping on his left foot. The dancer then switches feet three times, tapping the floor with his left toes, his right toes, and then his left toes once more. This sequence repeated a total of four times, except instead of tapping his left toe for the last time in the sequence, he performs a grinding step with the toes of his left foot if the dancer is male, or a light shuffling step if female. The last step, called the "battering" step, is the only point of difference between the double and single jig. In the double jig, the dancer hops on the right foot, while "battering" the floor with the ball of his left foot once as he kicks forward, and then a second time as he bring his foot back. In the single jig, the dancer batters the floor only once, as he kicks his foot out, but not on the return. Again this "battering" is only performed by the men, as it is considered too rough and unladylike for women. The third type of jig, the "hop" or "slip" jig, is similar to the reel, in that only the alternate parts of the tune are stepped. The slip jig is done in 9/8 time, and is distinguished most from the other type of jigs in that it consists primarily of sliding, tripping and hopping movements. It is usually danced by two or more couples, and the dancers promenade around the room before returning to their places.

✦ **The Reel:** The reel is considered to be the next most popular form of dancing after the double jig. It is most like the slip jig, except the steps of the dance alternate with a promenade movement. Sometimes, however, a sidestep is substituted in place of the promenade.

✦ **The Hornpipe:** The hornpipe is a vigorous solo dance that is danced exclusively by men. That is because it includes a lot of heavy battering and grinding foot movements that are considered to be unladylike. In that sense, it appears to be a more masculine, solo form of the jig.

Cotillion & Quadrilles

As we have seen, many of the dances that are still danced today in Ireland were collected by the various dance masters who roamed throughout the land. However, what is not more commonly known is that many of the dances that they taught were actually French in origin, such as the Cotillion and the Quadrille. The Cotillion is danced by four couples facing each other, forming a square. The similar Quadrille was named after the Italian word *quadriglia*, a cavalry formation that was square in layout. The Quadrilles are also danced by four couples set in a square, a formation that is referred to as a "set". There were six variations on the set known as "figures", each of which lasted three or four minutes. Modern set dancing was based upon the Quadrille form, which was popular during the first half of the 18th century, later modified into set dancing by the dance masters.

Céilí Dances

As we have seen, the term *céilí* has come to mean "social gathering" in the sense of a party. At a *céilí*, music is usually played, and dances almost always accompany the music. Thus, *céilí* is also sometimes used to refer to what others might simply refer to as a "dance". *Céilí* of this type began to emerge in the beginning of the 18th century with the popularity of the country dances such as the jig and the reel. These early *céilí* dances took the form of a "reel of three", where three couples danced, a reel of four, where four couples danced, going up to as many as eight or even 16 couples (the eight-hand and sixteen-hand reels, respectively), though theoretically, any amount of people could dance at one time. Over time, other forms of dance, such as polkas and waltzes, began to infiltrate the *céilí*, though they were usually altered to a form that was better suited to the Irish style of dancing. *Céilí* continue to this day as general gatherings where music, dance, storytelling and social interaction are evenly blended, taking place either at a private home or, more often, the local pub.

Riverdance

Since the 1980s, the trend in Irish dance has been to repackage traditional Irish dance into a more marketable form that is more accessible to the world market. Riverdance, and its followup act, The Lord of the Dance, originated as a seven-minute interlude between acts for the 1994 Eurovision Song Contest, held in Dublin and watched by over 3 million viewers throughout Europe. It was originally meant to be only a set piece between acts intended to showcase the best of Irish music, song and dance in a chorus-line type format, but the relatively short set piece received a huge response. A single then was released that ended up on the top of the pop charts for months, followed by a video that sold over a million copies in only a few years.

This huge and unexpected response led the founders, Moya Doherty and Bill Whelan, to develop a full-length show that also included musicians, singers and dancers from other musical traditions from around the world. Still going strong, the Riverdance troupe has toured the world several times since its debut in 1995, its combination of traditional and modern cultural forms and iconography symbolizing in many ways Ireland's emerging role as a bastion of traditional Celtic culture in the modern world.

THE HISTORY
IRELAND TODAY
MUSIC & DANCE

Traveling to Ireland

Ireland is one of the most popular tourist destinations in the world. Over six million Irish of the *diaspora*, as well as Celtophiles, lovers of ancient history, religion and mythology, or just people enamoured of the mystery that is Ireland visit every year, a number that has experienced a significant net growth over the past decade. According to the

"The Tackled Pony" – © Barrie Maguire.

World Travel Organization (WTO), over four million visitors to Ireland come from the UK, almost twice as many as come from all other countries combined, including America. Around 900,000 visitors came from the U.S. and Canada in 2004, up over 5% from 2003, and over 130,000 came from Asia, including Australia and New Zealand – both, like the U.S., also significant repositories of the Irish diaspora.

TRAVEL TIPS

Traveling to Ireland is surprisingly simple, especially when coming from other western countries such as the United States. This is particularly true of visitors from the UK, where the British tourist will find little difference in the quality of basic services. As always you will need a passport, but a visa is not required when coming from the UK, US, Canada, Mexico, any European Union country, and numerous other countries all over the world (see http://www.tourismireland.com for the latest information). Make sure to check with your health care provider to see if you are covered when traveling overseas, or else you may be in for a difficult time if there is an accident. If you are not covered, consult your travel agent on purchasing traveler's insurance, both for yourself, those with you, and for your possessions.

Money & Exchange Rates

It is advisable to carry some cash with you at all times, as not all hotels and restaurants take credit cards or traveler's checks, particularly those in the countryside. It is best to have all three of course, and to save your cash for emergencies. Also, don't keep all of your money in one place — divide it between your wallet, a money belt, and perhaps some hidden in your luggage as a backup.

If you are out of cash, ATMs can be found all over the island, though there are of course service fees. Cards accepted around the island include Master Card/Maestro, Visa/Electron, American Express, and Diners Club, though AmEx and Diner's will have more limited acceptance. If your card is lost or stolen, from Ireland call 1-800-558-002 (VISA), 1-800-557-378 (Master Card), 1-800-282-728 or call collect 336-393-1111 (AmEx) and 1-800-709-944 (Diner's). From Northern Ireland call 0800-895-082 or 0800-891-725 (VISA), 0800-964-767 (MasterCard), 01237-696933 and 0800-460-800 (Diner's). 800 numbers are free at payphones throughout the island and do not require coins or a calling card. These numbers may change, so be sure to verify these emergency numbers with your credit card providers before departure.

Most currencies can be exchanged at a local bank, as well as some post offices and tourist centers, but doing so will also incur service fees. Normal bank hours are 9:30 a.m.-4:30 p.m. Monday through Friday. Some of the larger banks may be open on Saturday, but all are closed on Sundays and bank holidays (see "Holidays").

It is important to note that the Republic of Ireland, as part of the European Union, is now on the Euro (€), whereas Northern Ireland is a part of the United Kingdom, and thus still uses the British Pound Sterling (£). In the Republic, the Euro is divided into 100 cents, with coins valuing 1, 2, 5, 10, 20 and 50 cents, 1 Euro (EUR 1) and 2 Euros (EUR 2), and notes valuing 5, 10, 20, 50, 100, 200 and 500 Euros. In Northern Ireland the pound sterling is divided into 100 pence, with coins valuing 1p, 2p, 5p, 10p, 20p, 50p and 1 pound, and notes valued at 5, 10, 20, 50 and 100 pounds. As of the date of this writing (May 2006), $1 US = €.79 = £.54. (For the latest exchange rate, visit XE.com's Universal Currency Converter® at http://www.xe.com/ucc/). Euros and pounds sterling

THE HISTORY
IRELAND TODAY
TRAVELING TO
IRELAND

are not interchangable, so you will need to make an exchange if you will be crossing between Northern Ireland and the Republic, though some merchants on the border areas may make exceptions. The best answer is of course to just keep some of both on hand.

Holidays

It is important to remember Ireland's major holidays, not only because certain facilities may be closed on those days, but so you can plan to attend one or more of the festivals that often accompany those holidays. However, though most of the major holidays are the same for both Northern Ireland and the Republic, many others are not, which needs to be remembered both for planning your itinerary and to avoid making embarrassing gaffes in polite conversation.

Public Holidays in the Republic of Ireland:
- ✝ New Year's Day: January 1
- ✝ St Patrick's Day: March 17
- ✝ Good Friday: date varies (though observed as a holiday by schools, banks, public offices, it is not an official public holiday)
- ✝ Easter Monday: Date varies
- ✝ First Monday of May
- ✝ First Monday of June (formerly observed on Whit Monday)
- ✝ First Monday of August
- ✝ Last Monday of October (commonly called the Halloween holiday)
- ✝ December 25: Christmas Day
- ✝ December 26: St. Stephen's Day, known as Boxing Day in Britain, Australia, New Zealand and Canada

Public Holidays in Northern Ireland:
- ✝ New Year's Day: January 1
- ✝ Bank Holiday in lieu of New Year's Day: The following Monday for weekend holidays
- ✝ St Patrick's Day: March 17
- ✝ Good Friday: Date varies
- ✝ Easter Monday: Date varies
- ✝ Early May Bank Holiday: First Monday of May
- ✝ Spring Bank Holiday: Last Monday of May
- ✝ Battle of the Boyne (Orangeman's Day): July 12
- ✝ Summer Bank Holiday: Last Monday of August
- ✝ Christmas Day: December 25
- ✝ Boxing Day: December 26
- ✝ December 27: Bank Holiday in lieu of Christmas Day (if either Christmas or Boxing Day falls on a weekend day).

What to Pack

Ireland is as (or more) civilized than even the best-managed Western countries, so you needn't go overboard on your packing and preparation. However, travelers to Ireland have noted a number of things that should and should not be packed, and have offered some good general travel advice, as follows:

- **Pack Light:** Pack enough clothes for a week. After the first week (if you stay that long), take your clothes to a local laundrette, who will clean and press your clothes for a very reasonable price. Do not bring food except a small amount of packaged snacks, preferable healthy ones such as energy bars, for emergencies, and most importantly, some bottled water. Keep it simple.

- **Pack Smart:** Make sure that you buy quality baggage, as it does make a difference in its survivability. Also make sure to place your name and complete contact information both outside and inside every bag, including carry-ons. Another good idea is to place some sort of identifying mark on your baggage, such as a sticker, a colorful baggage strap (also useful to make sure your bag does not come open), or something similarly distinguishing so someone else doesn't walk off with your luggage by accident. Also make sure to allow for some shifting during transit. Most suitcases have compartments and dividers for that purpose — make good use of them.

- **Pack Safe:** Use common sense when packing — do you really need to bring a knife, a lighter, a gun? Though this might seem like common sense, some people still pack these things, and worse. Due to the recent increase in security due to the increased terrorist threat, the U.S. in particular has become much more restrictive on what you can pack. The Department of Homeland Security has some useful data for American travelers (http://www.dhs.gov/dhspublic/theme_home3.jsp), but the best site to visit is the Transportation Security Association (TSA) website's special "Travelers & Consumers: Prohibited Items"

THE HISTORY
IRELAND TODAY
TRAVELING TO IRELAND

page at http://www.tsa.gov/public/interapp/editorial/editorial_1012.xml, which has links to downloadable documents that give complete listings on what you can and cannot bring. You can also get information on what not to pack by calling 1-866-289-9673 toll-free, or e-mailing them at TSA-ContactCenter@dhs.gov. Generally speaking, do not bring knives or scissors (except plastic or dull, rounded, non-serrated ones); weapons or realistic toy weapons of any kind, including flare guns or even BB guns; box cutters, ice picks, or any kind of sharp or pointed object; sports equipment such as bats, hockey sticks, or anything else that can be used as a weapon; screwdrivers or any kind of tools longer than 7 inches; any kind of martial arts or self-defense item; more than a four-ounce container of pepper spray or mace that does not have a locking safety feature to prevent accidental discharge; stun guns; and explosive or flammable items of any kind, including lighters (with fuel in them). This list is not comprehensive, so please check before packing. Note that some of these items are prohibited in carry-on baggage, but allowed as checked baggage. If in doubt, refer to the lists provided online, or check with your airline or travel agent. Better yet, just don't bring it, or mail it instead, if allowed by your postal system.

♦ **Bring Personal Identification:** Write down your complete name and contact information, and keep copies on your self, and in your luggage. Also include your blood type, immunizations, doctor and health insurance contact information, outstanding health issues, medications you are on, allergies, glasses or contact lens prescriptions, and contact information for next of kin.

♦ **Take Your Medicine:** Always bring any special medicines that you must have with you. For general needs, the local chemist (drugstore) can help you. Special vaccinations are not required, but always a good idea when going abroad. It is also a good idea to bring some medication for treating motion sickness and diarrhea, two of the most common travel ailments.

- **Dress for Cool, Wet Weather:** The most important article of clothing you should pack after the basics is a raincoat. Ireland is known for its wet weather, with rain showers that can come up on you out of the blue. Layers of clothing are also recommended so you can add or take away layers as needed. For your raincoat, a waterproof windbreaker should be adequate for most conditions, an umbrella and waterproof walking shoes or boots are also good ideas.

- **Avoid Bringing Electrical Equipment:** Try to avoid bringing anything that needs to be plugged in if you can avoid it, unless your home country has the same voltage/amperage as Ireland. The standard electric power outlet in the Republic of Ireland supplies 230 (+/-10) volts @ 50 Hz., and in Northern Ireland it is 240 volts @ 50 Hz. This should be okay if you come from the UK and most parts of Europe. However, if you try to plug in your appliance from the U.S., it will probably burn out and possibly start a fire, as the standard U.S. power supply is only 110 volts @ 60 Hz — roughly half as much as the Irish power outlet will supply. If you must bring AC electrical appliances, be sure to bring a tranformer or converter as appropriate, which are sold at most major department stores, electronics stores such as Radio Shack®, and travel stores. Some specialty appliances may need a heavy-duty transformer, so be sure to check with your travel agent before bringing any large appliances, or perhaps consider leasing it while you are there. Better still, rely on electronics that use batteries, but make sure to buy your batteries at home, as they may be more expensive and less reliable if you buy them abroad. Best of all would be to bring rechargeable batteries with a battery charger (with the appropriate converter). If you absolutely must bring that 1000-watt hair dryer, make sure that you have the appropriate converter or transformer, or you may end up burning down the hotel you are staying in (that *has* happened). Some hotels provide hair dryers and

THE HISTORY
IRELAND TODAY
TRAVELING TO
IRELAND

other appliances to their guests, so be sure to check before you risk it all for fashion. Note also that clocks and clock radios from the U.S. will not keep proper time in Europe, so bring a battery-operated travel alarm instead. Above all, unplug all appliances after use.

✤ **Good General Travel Advice:** The best time to visit Ireland is during the summer, when it is warmest and there is less rain. However, spring or fall may be better if you wish to avoid the peak tourist period. If you are seriously ill, hurt and/or in trouble and no one is around to help, dial **999** in both Northern Ireland and the Republic, and the *Garda Síochána* (pronounced "gar-dah she-ah-ken-uh" will come to your aid). When calling from outside Ireland, first dial your country's international access code (011 from the U.S.) then 353 for the country code, and then remove the 0 at the beginning of the regular number before dialing. When calling from within Ireland, pay phones are common, and phone cards can be purchased at reasonable rates. You can also purchase a SIM card for your existing cell phone, or rent a cell phone for your trip (see p. 351).

WHEN IN IRELAND

Once you have finally arrived, don't forget to enjoy yourself! Good preparation is insurance, not a substitute, for a good time. Set your cares aside and get out and meet people, visit places, and see as much as you can while you are there, as the few days or weeks you have scheduled for your vacation will pass more quickly than you think.

When you reach the next and final section of this guide, The Journey, you will find that each page in that section has a special, emerald-green bar on the outside margin of each page. This bar is filled with specific, context-sensitive information on Things to Do & Places to See, where to Eat & Drink, getting There & Back Again and Places to Stay while on your journey. It is thorough but not comprehensive, presenting a "best of" of things to do and see, eat and drink, transportation and accomodation throughout the sacred isle. The following is a brief overview of all of the travel-specific information provided in The Journey:

THE HISTORY
IRELAND TODAY
TRAVELING TO
IRELAND

346

Things to Do & Places to See

The majority of The Journey is taken up with a thorough but non-comprehensive review of the most popular and mysterious things to do and places to see around the sacred isle. From the most ancient Neolithic sites, to archaeological artifacts left over from the Viking invasions (with a smattering of the most popular modern things to do and places to see, such as the Temple Bar area in Dublin, and the Dinn Rí in County Carlow), as well as information on tours and tourist offices specific to each of the 32 counties, Things to Do & Places to See will give you an eagle's eye view of the best tourist activities and destinations that Ireland has to offer.

Eating & Drinking

The three basic types of eateries available are restaurants, cafés, and pubs. Restaurants run the gamut from family restaurants that offer good, basic fare to high-end hot spots offering exotic, upscale cuisine, many restaurants also having specialties such as seafood or local brews. Cafés tend to be more specialized, offering light meals throughout the day, and perhaps some local delicacy, unique dessert or special connection with Irish history as part of their story. Coffee shops are a common form of café, and Internet cafés can be found in every major city and most larger cities throughout the island. Pubs are of course among the most popular tourist destinations because of the great *craic* and exceptional quality of the local brews sometimes only available in certain parts of the country (as beers and stouts do not always travel well). Most pubs also offer "pub grub", normally a hearty (but fatty) meal that should do adequately for most people.

Irish cuisine has greatly improved over the last few decades, as the Irish have become increasingly concerned about their culinary reputation. The favored beverage is Guinness Stout, always a good decision when unsure of what to order. Murphy's Stout, brewed in County Cork, is another favorite. There are many other types of beers, so don't be afraid to experiment with some of the best brews in the world. When dining out, the normal courtesies apply, but tipping is not required, though a gratuity might be included in the bill. When eating, the knife goes in the right hand, and the fork in the left, where it stays, unlike the American habit of switching the fork to the right hand to eat. Normal table manners also apply.

THE HISTORY
IRELAND TODAY
TRAVELING TO
IRELAND

Pub etiquette is a bit different, as tipping is not required, but conversation is. Expect to be caught up in a friendly conversation about the news or the weather if you go into a pub. You may even be called upon to sing a tune in an impromptu *céilí*, though it won't be considered rude if you don't. Note that in the pub, good *craic* means having a good time, and not an invitation to use drugs, an important bit of information that can save you some embarassment. Also, if someone buys a round of beer and you partake, then you will be expected to reciprocate.

There & Back Again

Most tour packages include air, hotel, and local travel as part of the deal, but it is still a good idea to get familiar with the Irish transportation systems in case something goes wrong. Aer Lingus is the national airline, RyanAir being the other major airline among several others. There are three international airports: Dublin International Airport, Shannon International Airport, and Cork International Airport. Dublin mostly handles internal flights, as well as flights to Britain and Europe, Shannon International Airport handles mainly transatlantic flights and flights to Britain, and Cork handles mainly chartered and cargo flights, though all three handle international flights as needed.

Ireland also has excellent ground transportation throughout the island, the most popular being Bus Éireann, which covers the entire country. Ferries are a very popular way to travel to and from Ireland from Britain and western Europe, the Stena Line and Irish Ferries being the biggest. Cars are typically rented at airports or ferry crossings, but car rental companies are fairly common throughout the island, including both local and international "name" companies. Taxis are a good option, and provide the advantage of having a cabbie who can (and will) regale you with interesting local stories and gossip. Bikes are very popular to rent, but walking may be your best bet when possible.

Places to Stay

Hotels in Ireland are of a generally good quality, but not always, so it is a good idea to check with your travel agent to make sure, and perhaps pay a little extra for quality accomodations. Bed and breakfasts are a very popular and slightly less expensive option, some people enjoying

THE HISTORY
IRELAND TODAY
TRAVELING TO
IRELAND

"B&B-ing" across the island. Hostels are reasonably good, cheap alternatives to hotels, but you get what you pay for. Self-catering homes allow you to rent a home for a few weeks or months, if you plan an extended stay. Camping is another option, and an excellent way to see the Irish countryside.

FOR MORE INFORMATION:

There is no shortage of online information available for researching your trip to Ireland. Here is a sampling of some of the most popular websites:

General Information:

Official Tourist Board	www.ireland.ie
Tourism Ireland	www.tourismireland.com
All Ireland Travel	www.all-ireland.com
Go Ireland	www.goireland.com
1 2 Travel.com	www.12travel.com
IrishTourism.com	www.irishtourism.com
Ireland On-Line	home.iol.ie
Ireland Yes!	www.irelandyes.com
EnchantingIreland.com	www.enchantingireland.com
Travel-Ireland.com	www.travel-ireland.com
Heritage Island	www.heritageisland.com
Heritage Ireland	www.heritageireland.com
Heritage Towns of Ireland	www.heritagetowns.com
Ireland Event Guide	www.eventguide.ie
Education Ireland	www.educationireland.ie
Met Éireann: Weather Forecasts	www.met.ie/forecasts/regional.asp

Transportation:

Air:

Aer Lingus: Ireland's Official Airline	www.aerlingus.com
RyanAir	www.ryanair.com
Dublin International Airport	www.dublin-airport.com
Cork International Airport	www.cork-airport.com
Shannon International Airport	www.shannonairport.com
Air Coach	www.aircoach.ie

Ferries:

Stena Line	www.stenaline.com
IrishFerries.com	www.irishferries.ie
Swansea Cork Ferries	www.swanseacorkferries.com
Brittany Ferries	www.brittany-ferries.fr
Shannon Ferries (Ireland only)	www.shannonferries.com

THE HISTORY
IRELAND TODAY
TRAVELING TO
IRELAND

Mass Transit Systems:

Irish Rail . . . . .www.irishrail.ie
. . . . .www.iarnrodeireann.ie
DART (Dublin Area Transport System) . . . . . . .www.iarnrodeireann.ie/dart/
Translink . . . . .www.translink.co.uk

Car Rental:

Irish Car Rentals: . . . . .www.irishcarrentals.com
Autohire Ireland . . . . .www.autohire-ireland.com
Car-Rentals-In-Ireland.com . . . . .www.car-rentals-in-ireland.com
County Car Rentals . . . . .www.countycar.ie
Budget Car Rental . . . . .www.budget.ie
. . . . .www.budget-ireland.com
O'Malley Car Rental Ireland . . . . .www.omalley-car-rentals-ireland.com
Argus Car Hire . . . . .www.arguscarrentals.com
Motorhome Ireland . . . . .www.motorhome.ie
AA Roadwatch . . . . .www.aaroadwatch.ie

Buses:

Bus Éireann . . . . .www.buseireann.ie
J.J. Kavanagh & Sons . . . . .www.jjkavanagh.ie
Flexibus . . . . .www.translink.co.uk/flexibus.asp

Other:

Bicycle Hire . . . . .www.raleigh.ie
Walking . . . . .www.walkireland.ie

Accomodation

Hotels:

CMV Hotels . . . . .www.cmvhotels.com
Ireland-Hotels.com . . . . .www.irelandhotels.com
Hotel-Ireland.com . . . . .www.hotel-ireland.com
Select Hotels of Ireland . . . . .www.selecthotelsireland.com
Ireland's Best Hotels . . . . .www.irelandsbesthotels.net
IrelandIn1.com www.irelandin1.com
Stay In Ireland.com . . . . .www.stayinireland.com
Gulliver Ireland: Online Reservations . . . . .www.gulliver.ie
EBookIreland . . . . .www.ebookireland.com
Ireland View . . . . .www.irelandview.com
Roomex.com . . . . .www.roomex.com

Bed & Breakfasts:

Bord Failte approved: . . . . .www.townandcountry.ie
. . . . .www.irishfarmholidays.com
Ireland Bed & Breakfast Network . . .www.ireland-bnb.net
Bed & Breakfast Ireland . . .www.bedandbreakfastireland.net

THE HISTORY
IRELAND TODAY
TRAVELING TO
IRELAND

Hostels:
An Óige: Irish Youth Hostel Association . . . . .www.anoige.ie
IHO (Independent Hostel Organization) . . .www.holidayhound.com/ihi/
IHH (Independent Holiday Hostels) . . . . .www.hostels-ireland.com
Hostel International Northern Ireland . . . . .www.hini.org.uk

Self-Catering:
Irish Self-Catering Guide . . . . .www.selfcateringguide.com
Dream Ireland . . . . .www.dreamireland.com
Self-Catering Ireland . . . . .www.selfcatering-ireland.com

Camping:
Camping Ireland . . . . .www.camping-ireland.ie

Cell-Phone Rental:
RentAPhone-Ireland.com . . . . .www.rentaphone-ireland.com
IrishTourism.com . . . . .www.irishtourism.com/cell-phone-rental/

Regional/City Sites:
Northern Ireland . . . . .www.discovernorthernireland.com
Cork . . . . .www.corkkerry.ie
. . . . .www.cork-guide.ie
Kerry . . . . .www.kerry-tourism.com
Galway . . . . .www.countygalway.com
Shannon . . . . .www.shannonregiontourism.ie
Western Ireland . . . . .www.irelandwest.ie
Dublin:
Visit Dublin . . . . .www.visitdublin.com
Dublin Links . . . . .www.dublinks.com
Dublin Uncovered . . . . .www.dublinuncovered.net
Dublin Bus . . . . .www.dublinbus.ie
Dublin-Car-Hire.com . . . . .www.dublin-car-hire.com
DublinHotels.com . . . . .www.dublinhotels.com
Accomodation-Dublin.com . . . . .www.accomodationdublin.com

Further Information:
Hot-Footing around the Emerald Isle . . . . .www.ian-middleton.co.uk/
travelwriting/hotfooting.html
Photos of Ireland . . . . .www.ianmiddletonphotography.co.uk/Ireland/

Note: These websites are presented for your convenience only.
No endorsement is implied in their inclusion. Sites also may
change content or URLs. For more information see Part III:
The Journey, or go to http://ireland.mysteriousworld.com for
the latest information.

THE HISTORY
IRELAND TODAY
TRAVELING TO
IRELAND

The Journey

"I Will Give You Ireland" – © Barrie Maguire.

I f Tuan the eagle took wing over Ireland once more, he would see that Ireland remains today as a tapestry of traditions, woven with patience over thousands of years, that vividly illustrates in its ancient monuments and epic tales, its rolling hills and peaceful valleys, the sacred journey of the Irish. Tuan would also see that Ireland still retains much of its essential "Irishness", despite the slouching beast of secularism that lies crouching at the gate, corrupting and destroying all that it touches. This is due to the fact that the tapestry of Irish tradition is a weave of many layers that, like a cord of many strands, is not easily broken. And if the West continues to fail in its responsibility to uphold the ancient mandate of life, light and civilization, Ireland, who remains as the sole protector of the ancient traditions, may have the torch passed to her once more. Once again, the fate of the nations may be decided in the verdant green fields of the island of destiny. Once more, the smoldering embers of sacred history may rekindle the flame of the West.

As Professor Indiana Jones said in the classic archaeology/adventure movie *Indiana Jones and the Last Crusade*, "Seventy percent of all archaeology is done in the library. Research. Reading." Books and research are good ways to study the history and mystery of any given travel destination, as we have discovered, but in order to gain a complete understanding of any country, you need to get "boots on the ground" and see the places, meet the people, and do the things that the natives do. And in the next section, The Journey, that is exactly what we will do.

PART III: T

HE JOURNEY

Ireland

Country Name
PROVINCE NAME
COUNTY NAME

--- · --- · --- International Boundary
——————— Provincial Boundary
— · — · — County Boundary
——————— Major Highway
- - - - - - - Major Railway
★ National Capitol
◉ County Seat
• Major City

Introduction

ello, my name is Ian Middleton. Here's me standing outside of my favorite place to stay when in Ireland: Kirwan House in Wexford, County Wexford. I am a travel writer based in southern England, but I have traveled the world, writing travel books and articles about my many adventures. However, my favorite place to visit, and write about, is Ireland — my home away from home.

One fateful day two years ago whilst surfing the Internet looking for travel sites and related things of interest, I stumbled across this amazing website called Mysterious World (http://www.mysteriousworld.com). Ostensibly a travel site, it actually includes a great deal more historical and mythological information than I am used to seeing in a travel site. I found the site fascinating and, as a travel writer always on the lookout for someone to write for, I contacted the publisher straightaway with an idea I had about writing a series of articles on traveling in Ireland.

Doug Elwell, the publisher, got back to me fairly quickly, reacting to my initial email enquiry with some interest. However, instead of just a series of articles on Ireland, he suggested that we make an entire book out of it, and call it *Mysterious World: Ireland*, the first in a series of travel guides. "That's a great idea!" I replied, and a book was born.

Ireland

Tours

Enchanted Ireland
Gothic Image Tours
7 High St.
Glastonbury, Somerset
BA6 9DP, UK
Tel: + 44 (0) 1458 833385
Web: www.gothic imagetours.co.uk
Email: tours@ gothicimage.co.uk

Celtic Ways
'Murhy', Keash
Ballymote
Co. Sligo
Tel: (071) 9189377
Web: www.celticways.com
Email: john@celticways.com
A variety of day tours specializing in ancient and sacred Ireland.

Railtours Ireland
Run by Irish Rail and offers a variety of tours around the country all leaving from Dublin City. See Dublin chapter for more info.

Mind you I had already written a pretty good book about some of my travel adventures in Ireland (*Hot-Footing It around the Emerald Isle*, available at http://www.schmetterlingpro ductions.co.uk), but what Doug had in mind was not a simple travelogue, but a huge, rollercoaster of a travel guide, covering the entire island, crammed with all types of travel, historical

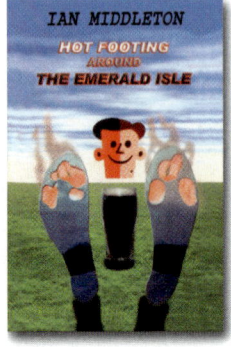

and mythological information, with some hot gypsies thrown in (well, maybe not so many gypsies). He wanted to cover not only the superficial, touristy side of Ireland (as other travel guides do), but explore absolutely everything to do with Irish history, religion and mythology — everything that makes Ireland *Ireland*. My contribution to the project would be the travelogue & travel info portion, covering all 32 counties and several islands, that would make up the lion's share of the book. However, like Mysterious World's online journal (http://www.mysteriousworld.com/Journal/), the book would also include some very substantial sections that Doug would write on the historical and mythological backgrounds of the many places that I would be visiting throughout the island (that's the less well-written stuff you just finished reading ;).

When Doug gave me my itinerary, I noticed that he had retained the old practice of dividing Ireland into four provinces — Leinster, Munster, Connaught and Ulster — in his planning. Though only used informally now, the use of the four ancient provinces into which Ireland originally had been divided by the Fir Bolg in ancient times helped to recall the ancient past that we were attempting to rediscover, as many of the stories behind these locations are still inextricably tied to the provinces in which they occurred. Interestingly, he also pointed out that I needed to travel clockwise around the island, as the ancient Irish believed that moving in that direction brought good luck. Moreover, moving anti-clockwise would actually bring bad luck. Why not? I thought, thinking that perhaps Doug was a little superstitious himself.

My part of the book was to be called "The Journey", which was about my journey to rediscover the ancient, mysterious side of Ireland that has slowly but surely been disappearing in the face of encroaching modernization. And in my research I discovered that numerous ancient archaeological sites and even Tara, the heart of ancient Ireland, are right now in real danger of being seriously compromised, damaged, or even destroyed to make way for such things as superhighways. As such, the current government of Ireland's legacy to future generations may well be the obliteration of their ancient past, just so commuters can shave a few minutes off their morning drive.

I then realized that the real importance on this project was not only to create a travel guide that actually had some depth to it, but to draw attention to the plight of that part of Ireland that is slowly disappearing — the raths, the stone circles, the megaliths — the very history of the land itself. Ireland is not just about leprechauns and pots o' gold — it is a country with an ancient history richer than most in the civilized West, a history that needs to be cherished and protected.

359

J.J. Kavanagh & Sons
Main Street
Urlingford,
Co. Kilkenny.
Tel: (056) 8831106
Web:
www.jjkavanagh.ie
Email:
info@jjkavanagh.ie

CAR HIRE
Many options — see relevant chapters for more info (p. 350).

BIKE HIRE
Eurotrek Raleigh Ireland
Unit 1, Finches Park
Long Mile Road
Dublin 12
Tel: 353 01 465 9659
Fax: 353 01 460 3096
Web: www.raleigh.ie
Email: info@raleigh.ie

WALKING
Ireland has an excellent network of way-marked walking trails.
Web:
www.walkireland.ie

Eastwest Mapping
Clonegal, Enniscorthy
Co. Wexford
Excellent selection of materials on the walking trails of Ireland.

Tel:
054 77835
Fax:
054 77835
Web: homepage
.eircom.net/
~eastwest
Email:
eastwest@eircom.net

Places to Stay

HOTELS
Irish Hotels
Federation
Tel: (01) 4976459
Web: www.
irelandhotels.com

B & B S
Family Homes of
Ireland
Tel: (091) 552000
Web: www.
familyhomes.ie
Email: bnb@
familyhomes.ie

Town & Country
Homes
Tel: (071) 9822222
Web: www.
townandcountry.ie
Email: admin@
townandcountry.ie

Irish Farmhouse
Accommodation
Tel: (061) 400700
Web: www.irish
farmholidays.com
Email: info@irish
farmholidays.com

THE JOURNEY
IRELAND
INTRODUCTION

Here's me standing by the side of the Scooby Van, but you can still see the front.

With this in mind I piled all my usual travel gear into the "Mystery Machine" (aka, the "Scooby Van", my name for a well-used Bedford Midi camper conversion that I have been using for the last couple of years for trips like this) and headed for Fishguard on the west coast of Wales to cross the Irish Sea on the ferry, arriving in Rosslare, southeast Ireland after only a few hours. The great thing about the ferry is that I can take my camper and everything across, saving the hassle (and cost) of flying, and of renting a car (which can get expensive). I can even use it to sleep in when funds are low, which I did frequently, as we shall see.

I finally made my way to Kirwan House in Wexford Town, "the last homely house" as I like to call it, from where I have begun many adventures. The year was 2004, and it was the fifth year I had been to Ireland. In that time I must have notched up over two years spent traveling or living in this country. I knew it well, or so I thought.

As I sat resting in the TV room, I picked up a copy of the *South East Voice* newspaper sitting nearby, and this headline jumped out at me: "Mysterious Circle Appears in Joe 'Boy' Conboy's Back Garden". I read on. It told how local man Joe had awoken one morning to find this mysterious circle. Many theories were suggested by other locals, (the most comical being from a farmer who claimed to have been abducted by Martians for eleven hours, warning that "they" were up to their old tricks again. Part of me couldn't help wondering if this was inspired by one too many pints of Guinness.) However, one quote really caught my eye: "It was the work of the fairies".

As I sipped my coffee I began to think more about this side of Ireland. It's a land aglow with stories, ancient myths and legends: from fairies to leprechauns, from the ancient gods to the legendary giants. Many stories of great battles and magical tales have their origins here, and many are famous around the world. It was becoming evident that I had experienced many wonderful things in this green land, yet this, the most significant part of Ireland, I had overlooked. It was time to put that right.

HOSTELS
IHH
57, Lower
Gardners St.
Dublin
Tel: (01) 8364700
Web: www.
hostels-ireland.com
Email: info@hostels-ireland.com

IHO
Dooey Hostel
Glencolmcille
Co. Donegal
Web: www.
holidayhound.com/ihi/
Email: info
@holidayhound.com
Tel: (074) 9730130

An Óige
Tel: (01) 8304555
Web: www.anoige.ie
Email:
mailbox@anoige.ie

HINI
Tel: (028) 9032 4733
(from ROI exchange
028 for 048)
Web:
www.hini.org.uk
Email:
info@hini.org.uk

CAMPING
Web: www.
camping-ireland.ie

THE JOURNEY
IRELAND
INTRODUCTION

Places to See Key for Leinster Province

Here is a list of the icons used in the county maps in this section:

☀ Multiple sites near each other

⚲ Ancient pagan, pre-Christian sites, often of unknown origin

☥ Christian sites

🏛 Historical sites, heritage centres

🦕 Cryptid sightings (mysterious, unknown and/or legendary creatures)

🏔 Scenic views and museums

❶ Nightlife and popular hangouts

🏚 Haunted houses and areas

✈ Major airports

🚆 Major train stations

🚈 Major DART stations

🚌 Major bus stations

Leinster Province

einster province is the easternmost of the four provinces, and contains two of the most popular counties to visit: Dublin and Meath. Leinster derives its name from the *Laigin*, an ancient people related to the Fir Bolg, who have lived in this region since the time of the invasions.

Leinster has a broad variety of places to visit, both very ancient and very modern. Dublin is both the modern political and cultural capitol of Ireland, and contains many places that should be considered must-sees for those seriously interested in learning about both ancient and modern Ireland. The National Museum is a good place to start to get a feel for the depth and breadth of the ancient pagan, Christian and historical sites that can be seen throughout the island. Conveniently nearby is Trinity College, current home of *The Book of Kells* and several other ancient books, another definite must-see. And when you are ready to take a break from sight-seeing, be sure to visit the Temple Bar area in downtown Dublin, where you will find some of the finest drinking and dining in the world.

Next to Dublin is Meath, the ancient religious and political seat of Ireland, which contains the oldest and most spectacular archaeological sites not only in the country, but in the world. Westmeath, Louth and the rest of the counties contain numerous hidden treasures often overlooked by the casual traveler, and County Offaly has the famous monastery, Clonmacnoise. And even Laois, though it is one of the least visited of all the 32 counties, also has a few surprises of its own.

Leinster
General Information

Dublin Tourist Office
Suffolk St.
Co. Dublin
Tel: (01) 6057700
Web: www.visit dublin.com
Also at:
Arrivals Hall
Dublin Airport
14 Upper
O'Connell

Brú na Bóinne Visitor Centre
Donore
Co. Meath
Tel: (041) 9880300
Entrance to Newgrange and Knowth is only via the tours from this centre.

Kells Heritage Centre
Headfort Place
Kells
Co. Meath
Tel: (046) 9247840
Web: homepage. eircom.net/~kellsnet/ heritage_centre.htm
Email: kellsheritage centre@eircom.net

THE JOURNEY
LEINSTER PROVINCE

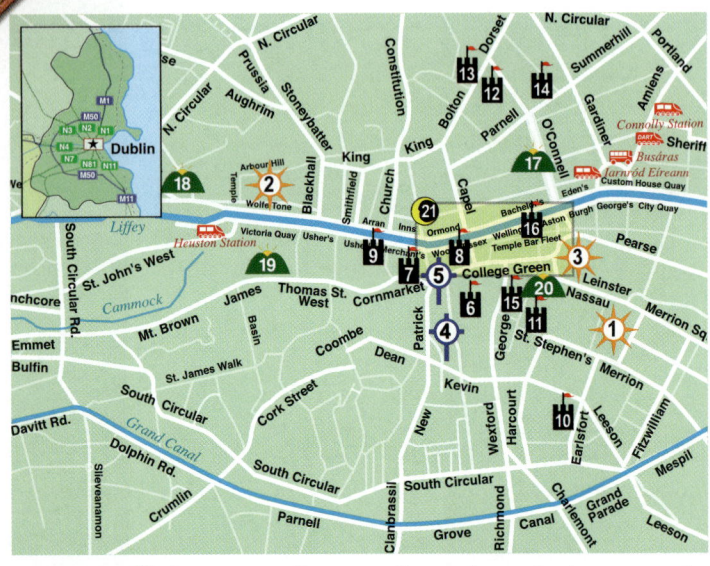

Places to See in Dublin City

Dublin
The National Museum of Ireland

Image courtesy National Museum of Ireland.

 y journey in search of mysterious Ireland took me first to the current seat of Ireland: Dublin, in County Dublin, in Leinster province. Naturally this was the best place to start my journey, or so I had thought.

I had decided to start at the National Museum of Ireland in order to get a good overview of Irish history

365

Dublin
Things to Do & Places to See

National Museum of Ireland
Kildare St.
Tel: (01) 6777444
Web: www.museum.ie
Entrance is free of charge, and the museum is located between Trinity College and St Stephen's Green. Open Tues-Sat, 10-5. Sun, 2-5.

St Patrick's Cathedral
St Patrick's Close, Patrick St.
Tel: (01) 4754817
Web: www.stpatrickscathedral.ie
There is a charge for entry. The site of the ancient well is located to the left just inside the garden gates.

Christ Church Cathedral
Christ Church Place

THE JOURNEY
LEINSTER
COUNTY
DUBLIN

Tel:
(01)
6778099
Web:
www.cccdub.ie
Email:
welcome@cccdub.ie
There is a €5
charge for entry.

Dublin Literary Pub Crawl

37 Exchequer St
Dublin 2
Tel: (01) 6705602
Web: www.dublinpub
crawl.com
Email: info@
dublinpub
crawl.com
This is a guid-
ed tour by two
actors who
performs comical
excerpts from
Dublin's best-known
writers. They visit
four pubs over 2
hours 15 mins. The
tour starts in the
Duke pub, Duke
Street at 7.30pm
nightly and there is
also an afternoon
one on Sunday at
12.00 pm. Bookings
can be made at the
Tourism Centre,
Suffolk St.

THE JOURNEY

LEINSTER

COUNTY
DUBLIN

and culture. This well-maintained building proved to be an excellent start in my journey, if only to point out how little I truly knew about the history of the island I had come to love. As I wandered through the echoing halls, I was greeted by row after row of sacred history laid out in neatly defined spaces, each room full of ancient artifacts yearning to tell me their secrets.

Caught in the moment, I had nearly forgotten that I had come here on a mission. Fumbling with my camera in front of one of the more impressive displays full of golden treasure, I was startled by an odd little man who suddenly sprung out from behind one of the displays, almost as if he had come out of nowhere.

"I'm terribly sorry, you can't take photos of the artifacts," said the little man, who turned out merely to be a short, rather rotund security guard. Then, as if sensing my discomfort, he peered upwards at me apologetically through his large glasses. Disappointed, I replied, "But I'm doing research for a travel guide to Ireland about the myths and legends and ancient history of the country." I secretly hoped this would appease him so I wouldn't be forced to overpower him and stuff his unconscious body inside the replica of the passage cairn we were standing next to.

"Well, the problem is there *is* a copyright on the artifacts and you will need permission. If you give me a moment, I'll see if we can get it." With a twinkle in his eyes, he then scuttled off to parts unknown, return-ing almost as soon as he had left. Unfortunately he said I could not have the special permission, so I put away my camera and continued the tour. As I stood in front of the Tara exhibit the security guard walked up and apologized once again. Though I hadn't thought of it at the time, he had really gone out of his way to help me, but I wouldn't realize until later why.

The museum is actually divided up into four facilities, three of which, the Decorative Arts & History Museum, the Archaeology & History Museum, and the Natural History Museum are in Dublin town and the fourth, the Country Life Museum, is in Castlebar, County Mayo, far off into the west. Today I was in the Archaeology & History Museum, which hosts an impressive array of artifacts from all periods. In the corner was a 15-meter dugout canoe found in a bog near Tuam, County Galway. It's one of the longest found in Europe and made from a hollowed-out oak tree. Dated around 2500 BC, it illustrates how Ireland's first inhabitants lived and moved around the waterways. Next to this was an example of how the next wave of inhabitants, the Neolithic people, left behind a legacy of megalithic tombs which feature largely in Ireland's legends and folklore. But what intrigued me most was a display of the pivotal point of Ireland's mysterious and spiritual past: The Hill of Tara. I realized then and there that this was to be where my journey would truly begin.

The display is a scale model of Tara's two main hills and of the surrounding hillsides. It is said that the site was abandoned in the 6th century AD, but up until then it had been the seat of the High Kings of Ireland and the location for some of Ireland's most famous battles. And though the political seat of Ireland is now Dublin, Ireland's ancient, spiritual seat was, is and always will be Tara — the heart of Ireland's mysterious past.

Before my journey to rediscover mysterious Ireland had begun, I had only been aware of the tales of fairies, leprechauns and the other superficial silliness normally portrayed in movies and TV. I had no idea that tales of warrior races with magical powers, cataclysmic battles between good and evil and tribes of giants roaming the land were also an important part of Ireland's legendary past. It seems that there is much more to this island's history than just funny little men guarding pots of gold.

Dublinia
Christ
Church Place
Tel (01)
6794611
Web:
www.dublinia.ie
Lying inside the old synod hall of Christ Church Cathedral, Dublinia is a recreation of medieval Dublin. Entrance fee also includes entrance into the church.

Dublin Castle
Cork Hill,
Dame St.
Tel: (01)
6777129
Web:
www.dublincastle.ie
Email:
info@dublincastle.ie
Tours are available daily.

Traditional Irish Musical Pub Crawl
Led by two professional musicians who perform songs while telling the story of Irish music. Lasts about 2 hrs.
Tel: (01) 4753313
Web:
www.discoverdublin.ie

THE JOURNEY
LEINSTER
COUNTY
DUBLIN

Dublin
Tourist
Office
Suffolk St.
Tel: (01)
6057700
Web: www.visit
dublin.com
Also at:
Arrivals Hall
Dublin Airport
14 Upper O'Connell

Gaiety Theatre
King St. South
Dublin 2
Tel:
(01)6771717
Web:
www.gaiety
theatre.com
Email:
boxoffice@
gaietytheatre.com

Festivals
St. Patrick's Festival
St. Stephen's Green
House
Earlsfort Terrace
Dublin 2
Tel: (01)676 3205
Web: www.
stpatricksfestival.ie
Email: info@
stpatricksfestival.ie
Office opening
hours: 9am-6pm
Monday to Friday

The "Ardagh Chalice," the crown jewel of the National Museum of Ireland. Image courtesy National Museum of Ireland.

THE ARDAGH CHALICE

The large quantities of Bronze Age weapons on display were recovered from lakes and rivers across the country, suggesting that they were offerings to the gods. Along with it are hoards of gold and silver brooches and many silver chalices, the most magnificent being the Ardagh Chalice from the 8th century. The chalice had been discovered around 1868, buried in the southwestern side of a *rath* (ring fort) near the village of Ardagh in County Limerick. It was found by a young man digging for potatoes, believing that the ring was magical and therefore protected from the potato blight that had caused the Great Famine. Dated to the 9th century AD, the chalice is considered to be the finest example of Celtic craftsmanship in existence today. The chalice is bronze, overlaid with gold and silver, and carved with *La Tène*-inspired Celtic ornamentation highly reminiscent of *The Book of Kells*. The techniques employed to create this magnificent chalice include engraving, casting, filigree, cloisonné and enameling, indicating a level of artisanship rarely seen in the ancient world. In other words, this pot of gold is truly worth guarding.

368

The next room was the treasury, housing a collection of clothing, jewelry and musical instruments from the Bronze Age. Horns are considered to be the oldest musical instruments in the country, and there is one called "The Loughnashade Trumpet" that was found close to the royal seat of the Ulster Kings at Emain Macha. This huge instrument was found in Loughnashade (Lake of the Treasures) in County Armagh and could have been a ritual offering to the Celtic deities. Musical instruments here were used in fertility rites, which were often associated with a bull. A plaque on the wall said that the most famous of these rites is told in the tale of the *Táin Bó Cuailgne*, "The Cattle Raid of Cooley" (or *The Táin* as it's more commonly known). *The Táin* is an ancient saga that played out across Ulster, concluding up on the Cooley Peninsula in County Louth. The story of The *Táin* is about how Queen Maeve of Connaught, in a fit of jealousy, had decided that she had to have a bull that was better than her husband's, her quest to acquire that bull forming the basis of a saga that is one of the most celebrated in Irish history.

The next exhibit was of the Altartate Cauldron, found in a bog near Clones, County Monaghan. This was from the Bronze Age, but the earliest ones date from 1000 BC and were carved from poplar or alder. It's believed that meals prepared in these cauldrons were used for rituals and some give rise to tales of magical cauldrons, like that of the Dagda, that provided an endless supply of food, or were used to rejuvenate dead warriors. Further along was a collection of ancient weapons and shields that could well have belonged to any of Ireland's ancient, mysterious races.

Ireland's ancient history was not all pagan, however. Much of it has been Christian, ever since Patrick single-handedly invaded and conquered Ireland, spreading the Gospel of Christ to the four corners of the island.

Trinity College
College Green
Dublin 2
Tel: (01)6081000
Web: www.tcd.ie
Email: info@tcd.ie

✤ *The Book of Kells*
The Old Library is open 7 days a week. Admission from 9:30 a.m.-5 p.m. Monday to Saturday, 9:30 a.m. to 4:30 p.m. on Sunday (June-Sept.) and 12:30-4:30 p.m. on Sunday (Oct.-May).

✤ *The Dublin Experience* operates from mid-May until the end of September, 7 days a week with shows on the hour every hour 10 a.m. to 5 p.m.

✤ *Walking Tours of the Campus* Student-run tours run from mid-April until early October from inside the front gate of the college. Tours commence every 40 minutes from 10:15 a.m. There are generally 9 tours a day.

THE JOURNEY
LEINSTER
COUNTY
DUBLIN

Dublin Ghost Bus Tours
59 Upper O'Connell Street
Dublin 1
Telephone (01) 873 4222
Web: www.dublinbus
.ie/your_journey/
ghost_bus_tour.asp

This nightly tour of Dublin's darker side starts and ends at the Dublin Bus office.

Tir Na Nog Tours
57, Lr. Gardner St
Dublin 1
Tel: (01) 8364684
Freephone Ireland: 1800 226242

Small group tours aimed at the backpacker market mostly, but open to anyone. There are tours to Newgrange, the Boyne Valley and the Wicklow Mountains. All leave from Dublin.

THE CROSS OF CONG

The medieval exhibition included a wonderful display of early Christian Ireland, with various enshrined bells, croziers and relics of Ireland's three patron saints: St. Patrick, St. Colmcille and St. Brigid. These three missionaries were very busy people during the coming of Christianity in Ireland, and the country is absolutely littered with relics, wells and churches blessed by them, as we shall see.

The Cross of Cong. Image courtesy National Museum of Ireland.

The most famous Christian relic on display is The Cross of Cong. This cross is composed of solid oak, 30 inches tall and 19 inches wide, covered with plates of bronze and silver. Parts of the cross are also covered with gold, including gold filigree work of a superlative quality. The Cross of Cong had been commissioned by King Turlough O'Connor of Connaught, and it is believed to have been completed and presented to the king in 1123. It is believed that the cross was later donated to Cong Abbey by the O'Duffy clan, where it was put on display during Christmas and Easter for many years. It is also believed that a piece of The True Cross is contained within this sacred artifact.

Another famous Christian artifact is The Tully Lough Cross. The Tully Lough Cross is an Irish altar cross believed to date back as early as the 8th century. The cross was originally found in pieces close to the edge of a crannog (artificial island) in Tully Lake, County Roscommon, and is the only known Irish example of an encased wooden cross.

OGHAM STONES & SHEELA-NA-GIGS

Nearby was an Ogham stone. Ogham is the earliest known form of writing in Ireland. The term "ogham" comes from "Ogma", the name of one of the tribal deities of the Tuatha dé Danann, whom they credited with teaching them the skill of writing, as well as all the other arts and sciences. *The Book of Ballymote*, compiled in AD 1300 records this, and over 300 Ogham inscriptions can still be found all over the country, mostly in the south. In fact, there are over eighty of them in County Kerry alone.

Most of these stones are simply inscribed with personal names and are believed to be either commemorative or boundary markers. There is even mention in *The Táin* saga of Cú Chulainn, the hero of the tale, using Ogham stones to mark his boundaries during battle.

There were many other carved stones on display, some with Celtic artwork from a period in the Iron Age known as the *La Téne* Period, which is generally dated from 600-100 BC. Other carvings include statues and faces, but two of the strangest were the Sheela-na-Gigs in the corner. A Sheela-na-Gig is a statue depicting a woman with her legs open and her hands exposing her genitalia. What was so strange is that this statue is commonly found above ancient church doorways. I couldn't help thinking that such a figure wasn't really in keeping with the religious faith, and hoped to learn more about this particular mystery along the way.

Disappointingly, the museum didn't mention much about the **ancient races** that the legends describe as being the first inhabitants of Ireland. There was a lot of information on the Viking invasions, however, whose influence on the history of Ireland was all too real. And though the rage of the Vikings is spent, their influence on Irish culture continues to this day.

Irish City Tours
Desk 1 Tourism Centre Suffolk Centre Dublin 2
Tel: (01) 6057705
Web: www.irishcitytours.com
Email: info@irishcitytours.com
There are 2 tours of Dublin City and Dublin Bay. Tours to Newgrange and Wicklow are also available.

Vagabond Tours
Tel: (01) 6607399
Web: www.vagabond-ireland.com
Email: info@vagabond-ireland.com
Four-wheel drive tours to the west of Ireland.

Tuan's Notes
The Ancient Races of Ireland
Learn more about the ancient races of Ireland in The Mystery: The Invasions (pp. 37-77).

THE JOURNEY
LEINSTER
COUNTY
DUBLIN

Eat & Drink

La Paloma
17B Temple Bar,
Asdills Row,
Dublin 2
Tel: (01) 6777392
This great little
Spanish restaurant
has brilliant food,
good service and a
lovely atmosphere.
The old wooden
décor, and candlelit
atmosphere is per-
fect for a
romantic
evening. I
especially rec-
ommend the
paella.

Tuan's Notes

The Vikings
*Discover more about
the Vikings in The
History: A Short
History of Ireland: The
Viking Invasions (pp.
294-299).*

**Brazen Head
Restaurant**
20 Bridge St.
Tel: (01) 6779549
Web: www.brazen
head.com

THE JOURNEY

LEINSTER

COUNTY
DUBLIN

THE VIKING INVASIONS

Upstairs I found a Viking exhibition. On display were the remains of a Viking warrior buried with his sword, and a vast collection of Viking weapons, pottery and coins with the image of a Viking king named Sitric.

There were various clashes between **the Vikings** and the kings of Ireland, which led me on to the medieval exhibition. In ancient times Ireland had been divided into five separate kingdoms: Meath, Leinster, Munster, Connaught and Ulster. Nowadays they form the four provinces, with Meath (from the Gaelic *Midhe*, meaning "middle") having become part of Leinster. Each province was ruled by a provincial king, who answered to the High King who ruled from Meath for most of Ireland's known history. The last High King of Ireland was Ruaidhri Ó Conchobhair, who died in 1183. After this, only the provincial kings and petty kings remained until kingship was finally wiped out. Petty kings, or tribal chieftains as they were often referred to, ruled over small settlements or clusters of agricultural land.

This explained another mystery that had been in the back of my mind for some time. Traveling Ireland years before, I had chanced to visit Tory Island — a tiny patch of tenuous land off the north coast of County Donegal — where the tradition of the petty king still remained. I even got to meet the king, a rather down-to-earth chap named Patsy. I remember at the time being confused as to why this humble man was called the "king", but now it all made sense. He truly was one of the last "kings" of Ireland.

The rest of the museum was dedicated to the years of English rule and Irish rebellion. I had a quick look around this, but I wasn't that interested, as my mission was to explore ancient Ireland, when times were less troubled.

Four Courts and the O'Donovan Rossa Bridge in Dublin. Dublin has superb restaurants, bars and nightlife, set in a romantic Old World milieu. Image © Doug McKinlay/Lonely Planet Images.

Dublin Town

The first time I had visited Dublin was in 1999. After having spent five weeks traveling up the west coast, the moment I got off the bus I took an instant dislike to the place. People pushed past me as I leafed through my guidebook to find the address of the hostel I'd been told about. I had left the peace, tranquility and easy pace of rural Ireland behind me and was back in the big city. It took a bit of getting used to. I'm still not a great lover of Dublin, mainly because I'm not a great lover of big cities. But as big cities go, Dublin is one of the best.

It was evening and the museum was closing, so I took a leisurely stroll along the Liffey. Before crossing over from Wales on the ferry, I'd stayed at the Hamilton Backpackers in Fishguard, a lovely little Welsh town from which the ferry crosses to Rosslare in County Wexford. I'd got chatting to Sean, from Cardiff and over a few beers in the pub next door (I was getting in practice for Ireland) I told him that I was about to go traveling around Ireland in search of its ancient legends and history.

Email:
info@
brazen
head.com
Dublin's oldest pub also has a good restaurant, with the original writing desk of Irish rebel, Robert Emmet.

Trocadero
3 St Andrew's St
Dublin 2
Tel: (01) 6775545
Web: www.
trocadero.ie
This lovely little restaurant comes highly recommended by the staff at *Backpacker World Magazine*. Situated in the heart of Dublin's theatrical section, the restaurant is frequented by all the actors once the shows are over. The walls are filled with pictures of past diners.

Beshoff Traditional Fish & Chips Restaurant
Dublin 7
Upper O'Connell St.
The story behind this great little place

"Ever heard of *The Mabinogion?*" asked Sean.

"No, I haven't," I replied.

"It's a book of famous Welsh legends, and some of them talk about clashes with the people from Ireland." Upon leaving Fishguard, I popped into the bookshop and bought a copy.

The Mabinogion is possibly the only ancient saga that relates to the Dublin area, largely because Dublin is a relatively recent settlement. It actually began as two Gaelic settlements, later being expanded into a major port city by the Vikings. Its original name was *Átha Cliath*, "The Ford of the Hurdle Work", named after an ancient ford that once crossed the River Liffey. The city's modern Irish name is *Baile Átha Cliath*. It's believed that a settlement here goes back to prehistoric times, but it was first documented in the 5th century. "Hurdle work" probably refers to wooden wattles that were once used to cross the river at low tide.

The early settlement was on a ridge overlooking the river crossing, and a monastery was founded near the tidal pool of the River Poddle, a tributary of the Liffey. The area around the monastery thus was named *Dubh Linn*, "Black Pool". Much of Dublin's history is actually based around the time of the Vikings, who apparently had changed the pronunciation from *Dubh Linn* into *Dyflinn*, as this is the name found in the Viking sagas wherever "Dublin" is meant.

THE BRAZEN HEAD PUB

I wandered along the Liffey to an area called the Merchant's Quay, and spot-ted the Brazen Head pub, with a sign underneath that said it was the oldest pub in Ireland. Inside, the barman explained that the area around Merchant Quay and Wood Quay is the site of

374

the original settlement established by King Turgesius.

"Is this really the oldest pub in Ireland?" I asked.

"Yes." he replied, and went on to explain that the Brazen Head was an old coaching inn from 1688, and it actually stands on the site of a 12th-century tavern. Nowadays they no longer do accommodation, but they have a restaurant and two bars: old and new. The old bar was once used as an escape route for Robert Emmet, who planned the 1803 rising while staying here. It's said that the bar could be moved back to allow him escape through a tunnel underneath. He took me upstairs and showed me the original writing desk used by Robert Emmet, situated in what is now the restaurant, and also some engraving on the window said to have been done by him also.

Dublinia

I finished my drink and wandered up the road. On the way I passed Dublinia, which was created by the Medieval Trust as a sort of living museum to Dublin's medieval history. The name "Dublinia" comes from a Latin derivation of the city's name after the Anglo-Norman invasion.

The *Dyflin*, a reconstructed Viking ship based upon the "Gokstad ship", a Viking burial ship found in 1880 in Sandefjorde in Norway. The Gokstad ship, which has been dated to AD 850, was probably the tomb of the Westfold King Olav Gierstada, the Westfold possibly being an ancient Viking designation for Ireland. The *Dyflin*, named after the old Norse name for Dublin is seaworthy, and may be seen in and around Dublin harbor. The *Dyflin* was prominently featured in the documentary, *In Search of Ancient Ireland*.†

a book off the shelf, sit and eat or drink while you read it and decide if you want to buy it or not.

Butlers Chocolate Café
24 Wicklow St.
Web: www. butlerschocolates.com
A must for the chocoholics, blends of hot drinks and assorted luxury chocolates.

Il Baccaro
Meeting House Sq.
Tel: (01)714597
Lying just off Eustace St. Although in the Temple Bar region, this nice little restaurant is tucked away in a quiet spot, and serves good Italian food.

Gruel
68a Dame St.
Tel: (01) 6707119
Good value food near Dublin Castle.

PUBS
Brazen Head
20 Bridge St,
Merchant Quay,
Dublin 8
Tel: (01) 6795186
Web: www.
brazenhead.com
Email:
info@brazenhead.com
Claims to be the
oldest pub in town.
This is a great place
with a nice historic
bar and
another more
contemporary
bar, along
with a good
beer garden.
The old bar
holds traditional
Irish music sessions
nightly, with a
Sunday afternoon
session being the
best as it's an open
session and anyone
can play. The modern bar holds contemporary music sessions.

O'Donaghues
Merrion Row
This pub is where
the Dubliners first
started out. Irish
music 7 nights a

St. Patrick's Cathedral, Dublin

ST. PATRICK'S CATHEDRAL

St. Patrick's Cathedral was just up the road. This is one name that was familiar to me. You would have to be deaf, dumb and foolish to have traveled Ireland and not heard of St. Patrick. He is Ireland's Patron Saint, and credited with just about everything associated with the coming of Christianity in Ireland. It is said that St. Patrick himself converted the local chieftain, MacEchold, to Christianity. Many monasteries and schools were set up around what was then a relatively unimposing cluster of settlements, and the town began to grow from there. Patrick used to baptize Christian converts at a well on the site where the cathedral now stands. The present cathedral dates from the 12th century, but there has been a monastery on this spot as early as the 5th century.

I had read that there is a cross carved into a stone at the northwest corner of the cathedral, which marks the site of the well, but I couldn't see anything around the walls. I found the main entrance around the corner and wandered in. There is a small charge for entry, but when I arrived a service was due to begin shortly. As I poked my head through the door, a man came over.

"Are you here for the service?" he asked.

"No, I'm writing a guide to ancient Ireland and I've heard about a cross-inscribed stone here that marks the spot of St. Patrick's Well. Could you tell me where it is?"

He directed me inside to the northwest corner, explaining that there were two ancient stones there. "But please be quick, the service will begin shortly," he said.

I tiptoed over. Two large, granite slabs lay horizontally on stands. The larger of the two is engraved with two crosses, the top being a large, encircled Celtic cross. A sign nearby explained that this stone was found buried nine feet beneath the ground at the site of St. Patrick's Well. So, it appeared my information was wrong. The second carved stone was slightly smaller, and also was unearthed in the grounds. It is believed to have marked the grave of one of the earliest Irish Christians. Both stones were found in 1901, and in all there are six of these stones inside the cathedral. A total of thirty-two of these stones have been found in Dublin, and it's believed that they were carved sometime between AD 800 and 1100.

I began to take a couple of photos when all of a sudden I heard a terrific voice booming behind me: "Sir, would you please refrain from flash photography!"

I turned to see a very irate priest in long, black robes thundering towards me.

"Are you here for the service?" he asked.

I apologized and explained myself. "I'm sorry, I didn't know the service had already started," I added. "The man at the door said I could get a quick look before it began."

"Well, we haven't started yet, but we like to give people some time to settle, and we have to calm down the tourists, so please, no more flash photography."

377

week. It's a great little old fashioned pub with lots of old photos of the band.

JJ's
Aungier St.
Great jazz sessions.

O'Shea's Bar & Restaurant
12, Bridge St Lower, Merchant Quay
Tel: (01) 6793797
Has Irish music all year round.

M.J. O'Neill Pub
2 Suffolk St.
Traditional Irish music every Monday night, and bar food served daily 4-10 p.m.

The Celt
81 Talbot St
North of the river near the train and bus station, this great little pub offers good *craic*, great music and local characters.

THE JOURNEY
LEINSTER
COUNTY
DUBLIN

*There &
Back Again*

A I R
Dublin Airport
Dublin Airport is
north of the city
just past the M50 on
the N1.
Tel: (01) 8141111
Web: www.
dublinairport.com

Ryanair
Ryanair offer very
cheap deals to
Ireland from
most destina-
tions in
Europe.
Web: www.
ryanair.com

Aer Lingus
Aer Lingus fly daily
to and from the US.
www.aerlingus.ie

F E R R I E S
There are two ferry
terminals in Dublin,
one on the northern
side of Dublin Bay
and the other in Dun
Laoghaire, just a few
miles south of the city
centre. Irish Ferries
operate from Dublin
Port and Stena Line
operates services daily.

THE JOURNEY
L E I N S T E R
C O U N T Y
D U B L I N

I put my camera away and then had a quick look at two of the other stones before heading for the door.

"Did the Reverend tell you off?" asked the doorman.

"Yes, I thought I could get away with shooting a couple of quick photos, but he was too quick." I replied.

I asked him where the well was originally sited, and he directed me to the main gate to the cathedral gardens. The site is located to the left, just inside. A stone plaque marks the spot and is surrounded by a crescent of flowers. I then took a short stroll around the rest of the lovely gardens and enjoyed the peace and quiet away from the hustle and bustle of the city for a while.

DUBLIN CASTLE

A short walk from the cathedral is Dublin Castle, which actually sits on the site of the original pre-historic settlement of Dubh Linn. The River Poddle now flows underground. The junction of this and the River Liffey forms a natural boundary

Dublin Castle

on two sides, and it's believed that a Gaelic ringfort was originally here to defend the settlement. King Turgesius and his settlers were expelled by the local Irish, but seventeen years later a much larger force came led by King Olaf the White. He established a settlement on the site of Dublin Castle, and built a great fortress and palace. The area from here down to Merchants Quay became a huge Viking settlement, which they used as a base for raids and for trading their plunder. It was from this point on that the city began to grow significantly and became known as the Viking kingdom of Dyflinn, which stretched all along this coastline from present day north County Dublin through to County Wicklow. The Vikings were eventually defeated in The Battle of Clontarf on Good Friday 1014. They remained in the area until finally being driven out completely by the invasion of the Normans, who built a wooden Motte that was the predecessor of Dublin Castle.

It wasn't until the 13th century that a stronger castle was built by the King of England. The only remnant of this medieval castle, however, is the Record Tower, which now houses the museum of the *Garda Síochána*. The rest of the building looks more like a child's play castle, having been painted in vibrant blue, red and yellow colors. The old coach house nearby is set in the lovely *Dubh Linn* gardens beside the rear of the castle. The building has a stone gothic-style façade and the grass out front contains a long, swirling pavement in the shape of two long snakes, whose heads both seem to guard the entrance to the gardens. The building was erected in 1835 to house the horses and carriage of the Lord Lieutenant.

Dublin Port
Terminal Road South, Ferryport, Dublin 1
Tel: (01) 855 2296

Stena Line
Tel: (01) 2047777 or book online at www.stenaline.ie

Irish Ferries
Tel: 0818 300 400
Web: www.irishferries.ie

Dublin Reservations
2-4 Merrion Row, Dublin 2
Tel: +353 818 300 400

TRAINS
The DART
The DART (Dublin Area Rapid Transport) system runs between Howth as far as Greystones in Co. Wicklow. There are also several commuter trains serving the north and south of the city from Connolly Station.

Irish Rail
Connolly Station
Tel: (01) 8363333
Web: www.irishrail.ie
North of the Liffey,

this station serves the north and south of the country.

Heuston Station
Tel: (01) 8365421
South of the Liffey, this station serves the west of the country.

Iarnród Èireann
Tel: (01) 8366222
Iarnród Èireann has a travel centre at 35 Lower Abbey St which opens from 9am to 5pm Mon-Fri and 9am to 1pm Sat.

Railtours Ireland
Run by Irish Rail and offers a variety of tours around the country all leaving from Dublin City. Railtours Desk, Dublin Tourism Centre, Suffolk St, Dublin 2. Open 8-6 (Sat 8-2 Sun 12-6) Tel: (01) 8560045 Web: www.irishrail tours.com Email: railtour@iol.ie

THE JOURNEY
LEINSTER
COUNTY
DUBLIN

Temple Bar

This area of Dublin is by far the most interesting to walk around in. The tourist office has a leaflet that outlines three good walks around Medieval Dublin, taking in all of this. This area is also great for eating and drinking. There is a wealth of good pubs and restaurants. The most popular section, which is hailed as the cultural capitol of Dublin, is Temple Bar.

Nowadays it is mostly a haunt for stag parties, and much of the culture is now just a case of getting as drunk as possible. It is also extortionately expensive. However, there is a great little Spanish restaurant called *La Paloma* here where I ate with my girlfriend a couple of years back. After the meal though, we elected to get out of Temple Bar and go find a more traditional spot. We passed a little pub called The Celt Bar, and decided to pop in there for a drink. The beer was good and the place was quite lively. "Good enough," I thought. And it was.

The Temple Bar area of Dublin is loaded with great restaurants, music and nightlife of a more modern flavor.

The magnificent façade of Regent House, which presides over the west entrance of the Trinity College campus.

Trinity College

Next to the National Museum and St. Patrick's Cathedral, Trinity College rounds out the trinity of "must-see" destinations in County Dublin. Trinity College lies south of the center of Dublin, just south of the Liffey and just west of the Pearce and Tara Street train stations. The college, besides being a major university of international renown, with over 13,000 faculty and staff, is also a major tourist attraction with over half a million visitors per year. And though it offers much to the visitor, including a special walking tour of Dublin and a major multimedia presentation known as "The Dublin Experience", by far the most well-known and celebrated feature of the Trinity College experience is the famed *Book of Kells*.

THE BOOK OF KELLS

The tiny island of Iona, which lies off the west coast of Scotland amongst the Inner Hebrides, is the birthplace of one of Christianity's most famous artifacts: *The Book of Kells*. Now kept in the Trinity College library along with a host of other ancient manu-

TRAMS
LUAS is a new tramline in Dublin. Two lines are open:
✦ **The Green Line:** Connecting Sandyford to St. Stephen's Green, ETA 22 minutes.
✦ **The Red Line:** Connecting Tallaght to Connolly, ETA 48 minutes.
Web: www.luas.ie

BUSES
Busáras
Store St.
Tel: (01) 8366111
Web: www. buseireann.ie
Naturally, being that Dublin is the nation's capital, the hub of the Bus Éireann network comes together here. Busáras is the central bus station, which lies just a short walk from the centre on the northern side of the Liffey. It's also close to the Connolly train station.

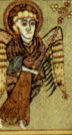

scripts, *The Book of Kells* is a lavishly illustrated, illuminated manuscript containing the four Gospels of Matthew, Mark, Luke and John that was written around AD 800. However, this is not just any religious book — it is also an incredible example of Celtic art, and a truly stunning piece of work by any measure. It is written on vellum and contains a Latin

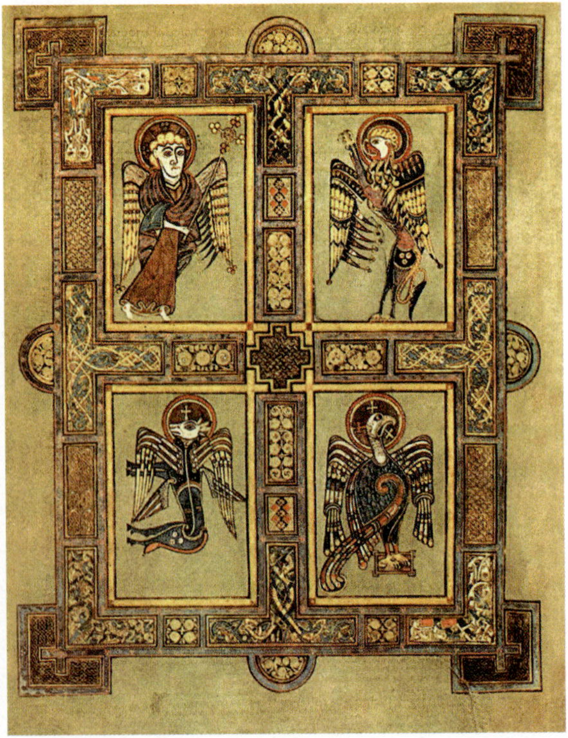

"The Four Evangelists" (folio 27v) from *The Book of Kells*. The book is on display year-round in the Old Library at Trinity College, though only two Gospels are available for viewing at any given time, and only one page of each is on display on any given month—one to display a major illuminated page, and the other to show two pages of script. Image courtesy Trinity College.

Dublin Bus
Head Office
59 Upper O'Connell St.
Tel: (01) 8734222
Web: www.dublinbus.ie
Dublin bus offers an extensive service that covers the whole of County Dublin.

DRIVING

All main roads lead to Dublin.

Car Hire
There are car hire offices at the ferry ports and airport. Or you can go to the following places:

Car Rental in Ireland.com
Old Airport Road
Swords
Tel: (046) 918832
Web: www.car-rentals-in-ireland.com
Email: help@car-rentals-in-ireland.com
This company has offices all around Ireland. Check the website for more details. Opening Hours: 9am-6pm Monday-Friday.

text of the Gospels in insular majuscule script accompanied by numerous, full-page decorative panels with smaller painted decorations appearing throughout the text.

The Old Library is also home to an exhibition with *The Book of Kells* as its centerpiece, along with other ancient manuscripts obtained by the college over the years. I picked my way through all the students sitting on the large, green lawn outside the building and made my way to the entrance. Two large banners advertised the exhibition: "The Book of Kells: Turning Darkness into Light." The reception area also has a souvenir shop with an interesting selection of books on ancient and Celtic Ireland. I joined the very long queue to the reception desk where you can buy your tickets. Then I was directed into the first room, where pictures and words charted the history of the various books owned by the library.

The Book of Mullins

The first was *The Book of Mullins*, an 8th century "pocket gospel". It was found in the monastery of St. Mullins, southern County Carlow. I had walked through there the year before on a 280-mile hike across Ireland for charity. St. Mullins is the starting point for the Barrow Way, a walking trail that follows the towpaths of the Barrow navigation. I distinctly remembered seeing the large monastic settlement there intertwined with the modern church and graveyard. It sits upon a hill overlooking the Barrow Valley. Unfortunately, due to a lack of available accommodation I was forced to walk on to the next town without having time to look around. I made a mental note to return there this time and see it properly.

The pocket gospel was an essential tool for traveling missionaries. Because it was so lightweight and

Budget Car Rental Ireland
Web: www.budget.ie
Email: reservations @budget.ie

Dublin Airport
Budget Desk
Arrivals Hall.
Tel: (01) 8445150

Dublin City
151 Lower
Drumcondra Road
Tel: (01) 8379611

O'Malley Car Rental Ireland
26 Lombard
Street East
Dublin 2
Tel: (01) 670 7890
Web: www.omalley-car-rentals-ireland.com
Email: help@omalley-car-rentals-ireland.com

Dublin Car Hire
Belgard Motors,
Belgard Road,
Tallaght
Dublin 24
Tel: (01) 4049999
Web: www.dublin-car-hire.com
Email: info@dublin-car-hire.com

THE JOURNEY
LEINSTER
COUNTY
DUBLIN

THE JOURNEY
L E I N S T E R
COUNTY
DUBLIN

easy to carry, the missionary could haul them around on their journeys and hand them out to Christian converts.

THE BOOK OF DURROW

The Book of Durrow was written 100 years before *The Book of Kells* at a monastery founded by St. Colmcille, in Durrow, County Offaly. It was encased in a shrine by Fiann Mac Mael Sechnail, then High King of Ireland. The book and the shrine were obtained by the college, but the shrine went missing in 1689 while the college was occupied by troops.

THE BOOK OF ARMAGH

The Book of Armagh is another famous manuscript obtained by the college. It was written in 807 and is a complete New Testament written in Latin. Interestingly there are several dossiers of texts relating to St. Patrick, and during the Middle Ages it was revered in Armagh, one of the nine counties of Ulster, as a relic of the saint.

All of these smaller manuscripts contain wonderful artistic writing and artwork, but they all pale in comparison to *The Book of Kells*. A large, illuminated display board shows an elaborate and colorful portrait of St. John, said to be one of the book's authors. Other displays show illustrations of "The Four Evangelists" and "The Virgin and Child". Other complex illustrations have wonderful patterns interwoven with scenes and images from the Bible. You would have to stare at them for hours to make out everything. Several other sections tell how the book was written on calfskin. In its original condition the book would have used the skins of 185 calves.

From the main exhibition area I made my way through a doorway and into the main exhibit, the actual book itself.

Nothing can prepare you for the spectacle of actually gazing down upon this masterpiece that is over 1,200 years old. The book was donated to Trinity College in the 17th century, and then was repaired and rebound into four volumes by Roger Powell in 1953 for easier display and maintenance, though it has been on display in the Old Library since the 19th century. In a cabinet there are always two Gospels on display, and the other two are kept elsewhere for safe keeping. When I was there, the book was open at the portrait of St. John. It shows him sitting on a throne, book in one hand and writing quill dipped in ink in the other. The other volume was open at a page of text, with distinctive rounded letters. The first letter of a paragraph is often interlaced with smaller illustrations. There are 340 pages in total, and all but two of the surviving pages contain elaborate illustrations. Thirty-one of these pages are fully illustrated in red, purple and emerald-green color. The exquisite rareness (and expense) of the inks used in the manuscript have, by their very existence in the text, proven that Ireland must have had trade links that spanned most of the known world at that time. It's believed that several artists worked on these, and it was possibly completed over a long period of time.

Tradition says that the manuscript was begun on the Scottish isle of Iona, where St. Colmcille lived during his exile from Ireland in the 6th century. Historians date the book to the 8th century, but some believe that it was as early as the 7th. Some believe that St. Colmcille himself had a hand in producing the book, but it's more likely that the monastery he set up in Iona and his tireless missionary work was the inspiration for the book.

THE JOURNEY

LEINSTER

COUNTY
DUBLIN

In the 9th century Iona was subject to frequent Viking raids and so the book was moved to Colmcille's monastery in Kells, and production was completed there. Given the incredible detail involved I could well believe that it might have taken two or three centuries to complete.

Much of this is speculation, however, as there is not a lot of hard evidence regarding the book's creation and history. The first-ever recorded mention of the manuscript was in *The Annals of Ulster*, wherein it describes how in the year 1007 "the great Gospel of Colmcille" was stolen during the night from the great stone church in Kells. It was missing for nearly three months when it was eventually found buried in a bog. The thieves it seems were only after the gold cover. This cover had been ripped from the manuscript and the rest thrown in a ditch. The cover was never found and much of the manuscript was damaged by water. It was returned to Kells where it remained until the 17th century when it was sent to Trinity College by the Bishop of Meath for safety during this troubled Cromwellian period.

The book that held me in such awe is now incomplete, but what there is has been expertly restored. How wonderful it must have been in its original glory! Also on display beside *The Book of Kells* were *The Book of Mullins* and *The Book of Durrow*. The former was quite faded, but you could still see quite clearly the elaborate writing style with images painted into the letters beginning each paragraph, just like *The Book of Kells*.

Originally all of these manuscripts were encased in silver or gold shrines in order to preserve them from damage. Most of these shrines have now disappeared, having been the target of raids due to their value.

The Long Room

The magnificent "Long Room" of the Old Library at Trinity College. The Long Room is full of irreplaceable books and artifacts.†

From the display room I ventured up a flight of stairs and emerged through a door to the breathtaking sight of the Long Room. This is the heart of the great library, and is like something out of an old movie. A narrow, polished wooden floor stretches out before you into the distance with recesses sectioned off either side. Each section contains bookshelves twice the height of the average person. There are two levels, and an arched, wood-beamed ceiling emphasizes the height of the room. As I walked, intimidated as my footsteps echoed throughout the cavernous hall, I half expected to see a huge letter "X" emblazoned on a tile in the center of the floor.

Brian Boru's Harp

Access to the bookshelves is forbidden, but along the center is a display of some of the library's best and most treasured books. Most prominently on display is Brian Boru's Harp, a magnificent wooden harp given to the college in the 18th century. Legend has it that this harp belonged to the High King Brian Boru, who apparently died during The

Email:
info@
fourcourts
hostel.com

B & B s
There are a number of B&Bs and hotels on Gardiner St. Lower, around the junction with Talbot St.

The Celtic Lodge
81-82 Talbot St., Dublin 1
Tel: (01) 6779955
North of the river, near to the bus and train station.

O'Shea's
12, Bridge St Lower Merchant Quay
Tel: (01) 6793797
South of the river in the old Viking area of the city.

AshleyLodge
4 Herbert Pk, Morehampton Rd, Donnybrook
Tel (01) 6683004
Email:
ashleylodge@
eircom.net
Just south of the city

Battle of Clontarf in 1014. However, the harp has since been dated to the 15th century, some 400 years after the time of **Brian Boru**.

Since its creation, the harp is believed to have had quite an interesting history. It had traveled to Rome where it had been preserved by the Popes for a number of years, and then back again, passing through many hands until it was sold to one Lady Henley "for twenty lambs and as many ewes". It then passed though more hands until it ended up under the care and protection of Trinity College around 1760. There it has been ever since, given the proper care and respect it deserves.

I had learned that Clontarf lies in the north of County Dublin, and planned to head up there to find out more about this man Brian Boru, whose name seemed to keep popping up. A plaque next to the harp claimed that there was no evidence linking this harp to the king, but that it was at least 500 years old. Wherever it came from, it certainly was a beautiful piece of woodwork, and I found it the most interesting exhibit in the room.

Back downstairs in the reception area I browsed through the bookshop before heading off on the next leg of my journey: North Dublin.

"Brian Boru's Harp". This harp, believed to have once belonged to Brian Boru, is the highlight of the Long Room collection. It has since become Ireland's national symbol.†

388

Brian Boru, "The Emperor of the Irish", AD 942-1014.
Brian Boru is considered to be the greatest king in Irish history.
© 1987 Jim Fitzpatrick.

Tuan's Notes

Brian Boru
(AD 942-1014) was born into the *Dál Cais* clan who ruled over County Clare, in Munster. After his elder brother's death, Brian became king, and aggressively brought all of Munster province under his sway, later coming into conflict with King Malachy of the O'Neill clan, who ruled the north. In 1002, Brian became the first true High King of Ireland since the Milesians, but was killed by Vikings at the Battle of Clontarf as he knelt in prayer — a fitting end for Ireland's one, true King.

Discover more about Brian Boru in The History (pp. 296-299), and The Journey (pp. 391-392, 562-563, 607-609, 739-742).

THE JOURNEY
LEINSTER
COUNTY
DUBLIN

Places to See in North Dublin

☀ Multi-Sites

1. Clontarf 🛍 🐚
   - Clontarf Castle 391-392
   - The Bram Stoker Dracula
   Experience 392-394
2. Howth Peninsula 🚴 ⚜ 🏔
   - Drumleck Point 394
   - Baily Lighthouse 395
   - Howth Castle 396-397
   - Deer Park Gardens . . 398-399
   - Deer Park Dolmen . . 400-401
   - The Cave of Diarmuid &
   Gráinne 402-403
   - St. Mary's Abbey 393
   - King Sitric Restaurant . . . 393
3. Skerries ⚜
   - St. Patrick's Footprint . . . 395

   - Swords Church 405
   - St. Movee's Well 406-407

⚜ Christian Sites

4. St. Patrick's Island 395, 405
5. Lusk Church 395, 404

🛍 Historical Sites

6. Lusk Heritage Centre
7. Argillan Castle

🏔 Scenic Views

8. Ireland's Eye 393
9. Fry Model Railway

Transportation

✈ Dublin Airport 397
🚢 Dublin Port 378-379

Driving Directions: See pp. 394-396, 403-404, 407

North of Dublin
Howth and Around
VAMPIRES AND VIKING KINGS

Clontarf Castle. Photo courtesy Clontarf Castle Hotel.

ave you been to the new Dracula Museum yet?"

"No," I replied. "Where's that?"

"It's just beyond the bridge there."

I was talking to a local man about things to see here in Clontarf, on the north side of Dublin. It's just a few minutes ride on the DART and the area is steeped in history. Upon arrival I had spotted a sign for Clontarf Castle Hotel and had gone to check it out.

Clontarf Castle
The original castle was built in 1172 but more than a century before that the area became a landmark during the famous Battle of Clontarf on Good Friday, 23rd April 1014.

North of Dublin
Things to Do & Places to See

Clontarf Castle Hotel
Castle Ave, Clontarf
Tel: (01) 8332321
Web:
www.clontarfcastle.ie
Email:
info@clontarfcastle.ie

Though technically a hotel, Clontarf Castle is also a great tourist destination as, unlike many other castle hotels, much of the medieval features of this castle remain intact, including knights' suits of armor adorning the hallways. Clontarf Castle is the perfect place from which to explore mysterious northern Dublin, and even further afield. Legend even says that the High King Brian Boru was killed on the site where this castle's reception area now stands.

know that Bram Stoker was born in this little suburb of Dublin? This is not for the faint-hearted, but is an experience you will never forget. Brilliantly put together, with incredible attention to detail, this shrine to Bram's creation is a journey into the world of the author and tells how the legends of the Clontarf area, along with the stories and

THE JOURNEY
LEINSTER
COUNTY
DUBLIN

Back then Clontarf was all woods with a great river flowing through it. The High King at the time was the famous Brian Boru. The Vikings had a stronghold in Dublin City then, ruled over by the Viking King Sitric. There are even old coins in the National Museum which have King Sitric's profile engraved upon them. They were found on a site near Christchurch Cathedral in Dublin. Battle began with the treachery of the provincial king of Leinster, Máel Mórda, who formed an alliance with Sitric.

Brian, enraged by this treachery, marched against them all, and a great battle was fought at Clontarf. His armies were victorious, but his victory was short-lived. He had set up his tent on the site where Clontarf Castle now stands, guarded by five of his soldiers. A few of the Vikings retreating from the battle chanced upon the tent and, knowing who was inside, killed the guards and slew the King as he prayed. Brian Boru was 72 years old.

Inside the hotel, the guy at reception told me that the stone pillar in the main reception area is the exact site of the killing. It was nice to see that much of the castle's medieval décor had remained. A knight's suit of armor guards each hallway, while hanging tapestries, nooks and crannies and little doorways add to the mystery of the castle. I had a coffee in the bar while I read the story of Clontarf. I took another wander around the place and then headed off before security became too concerned.

The Bram Stoker Dracula Experience

Back out on the street I'd got talking to this local man who told me about the Dracula Museum. Apparently, Bram Stoker was born right here in Clontarf. I must confess that I'd had no idea he was even Irish, let alone from Dublin. So I decided to go and check it out.

From the DART station you just have to turn left and go under the bridge and there is a small entertainment complex. I was told the Dracula Museum was inside the Bar Code building. This place was huge, and a sign directed me down a long corridor past a big swimming pool and into a large bar and restaurant area. There was no one around. I was a bit confused as I couldn't see any more signs. I spotted some steps going up into an amusement arcade and tried that. The museum reception was there.

It was after 12.00, yet no one seemed to be around. The museum only opens from midday to late evening on Friday, Saturday and Sunday. Though it was after midday on Saturday, the place seemed strangely devoid of life. The game machines around me were flashing and beeping, yet no one was playing them. I felt like I was in one of those movies where the apocalypse had happened and no one had told me, and that I was the only man left alive on earth. I wondered if this was part of the museum experience.

A while later a man came up to reception and informed me that the museum was indeed open. He led me through a long hallway to a set of double doors, and explained that guided tours are available on the hour, or I could go through alone. I opted for the latter.

He gave me a rough description of the museum and then left me to it. Through the double doors I found myself in a long, dimly-lit corridor with plaques on the left wall that took you through the whole of Bram Stoker's life. On the other wall was a history of all vampire movies inspired by Dracula.

Bram was born here in Clontarf in 1847 and from an early age suffered from illness. He had a fascination with the legends of the area, such as the bloody battle between

influences from the people around him, fired his imagination to create a number of brilliant novels, including his most legendary: *Dracula*.

Ireland's Eye
During the summer months boat trips to the island leave from the pier at Howth. Tel: (01) 8314200 or Mob: (087) 2678211. It was here that a prince of the royal house of Leinster established the first church. In the 8th or 9th century The Garland of Howth, an illuminated copy of the four gospels, was penned here. The book is now among the collection in the great library of Trinity College.

St. Mary's Abbey
A 14th-century abbey sitting on a hill overlooking the harbor and Ireland's Eye.

THE JOURNEY
LEINSTER
COUNTY
DUBLIN

Baily Lighthouse

From Howth take the turning just before the end car park by the pier. Drive up the hill and keep left of the church as the road forks. When you come to the pub on the left, the Summit Inn, take the road up the hill beside the pub. This leads to a car park where you can view the lighthouse. There is a network of walking trails along the coastline, that you can follow all the way to and from Howth village.

Drumleck Point

From Baily Lighthouse go back to the main road and turn left. Follow this road until you come to Ceannchor Road on the left (the turning is identified by a triangle of grass at the entrance. Follow this road to the end, keeping to the left. At the end of the road is a

Bram Stoker (himself) as Dracula. Bram spent much of his childhood bedridden as an invalid, much as his character, Dracula, was bound to his coffin. An artist's best work is often inspired by his own life experience. Image © The Bram Stoker Dracula Experience (www.thebramstoker draculaexperience.com).

Brian Boru's armies and the Vikings, and of his mother's stories of the famine in Sligo. It seemed that he drew largely upon Irish folklore for the inspiration behind his writing.

As I stood reading the plaques, teenagers came running past me screaming. No, this wasn't part of the exhibit, they had just come from inside. At the end of the corridor you cross a bridge through a tunnel of revolving lights. This is considered to be the portal between your world and the world of Count Dracula. What follows next is a fascinating recreation of Dracula's world of monsters. I soon found out that this was not for the faint-hearted. Things moved unexpectedly, vampires jumped out of walls and hissed at me. Devilish sounds followed me wherever I went, and figures rushed past me in dark rooms. It was brilliant.

The experience ended with two documentaries in the graveyard, if you dare stay long enough. Somehow after all that, being back in the deserted arcade didn't seem so eerie.

The Peninsula of Howth

Back outside I wandered onto Clontarf's very long pier. The harbor here at Clontarf was designed from a suggestion by none other than Captain William Bligh, of *Mutiny of the Bounty* fame. A wall was built to prevent silting on the estuary and allow large ships into the bay. I walked out along the path of this wall, lined with separate male and female bathing shelters. I wondered if this was a remnant of the older days. The men were out swimming in the cold sea, but there was no sign of any women. To my right was the unwelcome sight of industrial Dublin. To my left, however, was a large, golden, sandy beach and a coastline stretching right around the peninsula of Howth.

Dublin Bay forms a crescent shape, the northern section ending with a peninsula that was once an island. From here I could clearly make out the high cliffs and lighthouse, and decided to go see what it was like close up.

The northern end of Dublin Bay is defined by the peninsula of Howth, which is capped off by a quaint little lighthouse known as the "Baily Lighthouse".

path, follow this and turn right, following the trail until you come to an old telegraph pole.

St. Patrick's Island
Just off the coast of Skerries.

Lusk Church
In the center of the village of Lusk. Follow the R127 just north of Swords on the N1.

Howth Castle & Deer Park Dolmen
Lying in the grounds behind the Deer Park Hotel (see pp. 396-401 for detailed directions).

St. Patrick's Footprint
Red Island Skerries
On the rocks near the springboards, the tidal bathing place.

St. Movee's Well
Skerries, beside the road on Killalane St.

Eat & Drink

King Sitric Fish Restaurant
East Pier, Howth
Tel: (01) 8325235
Web:
www.kingsitric.ie
Email:
info@kingsitric.ie
Fine wine, high quality seafood and a great view. You'll need deep pockets for this one, but the food comes highly recommended.

Maud's Café
Harbor Rd.
Howth
Tel: (01) 8395450
Great little café that is also famous for its ice cream. I especially recommend the seafood chowder.

Big Blue
30 Church St,
Howth
Tel: (01) 8320565
Web: www.vinnys.ie
Email: info@bigblue.ie
Perched on the hill above the abbey, this Old World restaurant has good food with a good view.

From the Clontarf road I drove northwards until eventually coming into the village of Howth. It was mid-afternoon, so the first thing on the agenda was food. The seafront was lined with restaurants and cafés, so I was spoiled for choice. I eventually decided on Maud's Café. Maud is more famous for her ice creams, but this café also serves hot meals. I ordered a bowl of seafood chowder and a coffee and then leafed through a leaflet I'd picked up off the front desk entitled, "Howth is Magic."

Howth Castle

Howth Castle's towers are decorated with windows shaped like medieval-style crosses, giving the castle a romantic, Old World look

The leaflet mentioned Howth Castle, just on the outskirts of the village, which has been owned by the St. Lawrence family since the 1400s. It claimed that local legend tells of a 400-year-old elm tree that stands beside the castle, and if this tree should fall it will spell the end of the St. Lawrence family line. I had to check this out.

The turning to the castle isn't signed, but there was a sign pointing to the Deer Park Hotel, which is further up along the same road. I drove to the castle, which is still inhabited by the family. It's an interesting castle with much of it still remaining. The front tower and sides were decorated with medieval crosses. I could picture knights guarding the entrance while great medieval banquets were held inside.

Norman forces led by a man named Almeric stormed the peninsula in 1177. Tradition says that on St. Lawrence's Day, 10th August, they overcame the locals to take command of the area. Legend has it that Almeric's original name was Tristram and that he vowed after the battle to change it to that of St. Lawrence. Following the battle, Almeric was granted possession of the lands of Howth.

The Book of Howth, compiled in the 16th century, tells the full history and legend of the area, and credits Almeric with many a heroic battle against armies ten times stronger than his. Almeric died in battle in 1189 while fighting Cathal O'Connor, the King of Connaught.

I searched all over for the elm tree, which is said to have branches that are supported by large, wooden sticks, but I couldn't find it anywhere. I then drove on up the hill to the hotel, and asked in there. They handed me a pamphlet outlining the history of the area, while one of them got on the phone to a colleague.

"She says the elm tree has gone now," he said, after a bit of chat.

"So that's the end of that legend," I replied.

"And the family still lives on!" he said, with a hint of sarcasm.

Well that was true, but the legend did state that it would be the end of the family line, not their immediate deaths, so I guess time will tell.

PUBS
The Abbey Tavern
Howth
Tel: (01) 8390307/8390282
Web: www.abbeytavern.ie
Email: info@abbeytavern.ie
Also offers an evening of Irish food, music and dance.

There & Back Again

AIR
Dublin Airport
Just past the M50 on the N1.
Tel: (01) 8141111
Web: www.dublinairport.com

TRAINS
The DART runs regularly to Howth, and also stops at Clontarf Road. Another line of the DART takes you to Portmarnock and Malahide. The Northern commuter train will take you to all other villages along the coast including Rush, Lusk and Skerries. There is also a shuttle bus service between Howth

Junction DART station and Dublin Airport every 15 minutes.

BUSES
Bus 31 or 31B from Lower Abbey St, just off O'Connell St. in the city center, goes to Howth. Bus 33 from Eden Quay in the city center goes to Balbriggan and stops at Rush, Lusk, Swords and Skerries. Bus 33A travels between Balbriggan and Rush and stops at Lusk, Swords and Skerries.

DRIVING
Take the R105 from the city center towards Clontarf and through to Howth, or follow the M50 northbound and onwards through towards Baldoyle. From Howth take the R106 coast road for a lovely scenic drive through Portmarnock and Malahide to Swords.

THE JOURNEY
LEINSTER
COUNTY
DUBLIN

Deer Park Gardens

Located nearby on the grounds of Howth Castle is the Deer Park Hotel. And behind the Deer Park Hotel is Deer Park Gardens, a stunning vista studded with rhododendrons and criss-crossed by walking paths through quiet glades and scenes of sylvan beauty. The pamphlet mentioned a dolmen somewhere at the foot of this hill, so I left the van in the car park and ventured out in search of it.

The weather was beautiful, the soft light from the evening sun illuminating the purple, red and white hillside. I was directed to follow a path to the right of the hotel, and then branch off right and follow that trail, which then, allegedly, led straight to the dolmen. It sounded simple, but years of traveling have taught me that nothing is ever as simple as it appears.

I trudged along the muddy footpath which led into the undergrowth. There wasn't simply one trail, but many different tracks all branching off from one another. At a loss, I decided to choose my paths randomly. Soon I found myself in a magical wonderland of moss-covered woodland and rich green foliage. The soft sunlight filtered through the gaps in the bushes and sparsely illuminated the muddy paths scattered with fallen rhododendrons of all colors. I felt like I'd been transported into a magical, mythical world. I half-expected (or half-wished) for a beautiful fairy princess to come strolling around the corner. We would fall instantly in love and she would whisk me off to **Tír nan Óg**, The Land of Eternal Youth. But my dreams were as delusional as the belief that I knew where I was going.

Finally, I emerged from the undergrowth to find myself on a rocky outcrop at the top of the hill. The castle grounds and coastline formed a magnificent view below. A receding tide revealed vast, sandy beaches glistening in the sunlight. I found a good rock and perched myself upon it so as to enjoy the sights and sounds for a while, and to catch my breath.

It seemed that I had taken a wrong turn in search of the dolmen, because this certainly wasn't the foot of the hill. After soaking up the views for a while I decided to head back the way I came and see where I went wrong. As I made my way over the rocks and back into the undergrowth, I found a mountaineer's helmet lying on the ground, but no sign of a mountaineer. Perhaps he was the lucky one to have met this fairy princess before me — or perhaps an angry leprechaun.

Deer Park Gardens offers sylvan settings that rival even those described in fairy tales.

Tuan's Notes

Tír nan Óg
When the Milesians conquered the Tuatha dé Danann, a deal was made so that the Milesians would rule over the upper world, and the Tuatha Dé would rule over the "Underworld" beneath the Earth. Tír nan Óg is so named because it is believed to be an underworld paradise where death has no sting, where the righteous dead go to live with the fairies in splendor, forever. Any dolmen, rath, fairy tree, and sylvan glade can and often is identified as a doorway to the Underworld, and as such, is to be treated with respect.

Learn more about Tír nan Óg in The Mystery: Creatures Great & Small: Fairies (pp. 151-152).

THE JOURNEY
LEINSTER
COUNTY
DUBLIN

The Deer Park Dolmen

The Deer Park Dolmen. One can easily see how this dark, enigmatic structure could have been seen by the superstitious as an entrance to the Underworld.

Back down the hill I found myself getting even more lost. The sun was setting behind the hill and the flower-strewn, illuminated paths gave way to a deeper, darker forest. In Irish folklore the *sídhe*, or fairy folk are not all cute and cuddly — some are quite sinister and malevolent. I didn't fancy being abducted by the darker side of the fairy kingdom, so I turned back and found myself on the hill again. I followed another path that went in the direction of the hotel and soon found myself back at the entrance once again.

I re-read the directions. It said to keep to the right at all times, so I did. After clambering over the roots of large trees and wading through muddy puddles, I spotted a narrow lane to the right. I followed this across a muddy trail that was lined with wooden planks and soon emerged to the sight of a forbidding stone portal.

The massive capstone weighs 70 tons and measures 17ft long, 12ft wide and 6ft thick. It had fallen off its supports and one side lay resting on the ground.

Modern archaeology has dated it at around 1500 BC.

Local legend says two things about it. One is that it's part of the many rocks thrown by an Irish giant named Finn McCool from his home in the Bog of Allen. Finn McCool was the legendary leader of the mythical band of warriors known as the Fianna, who protected Ireland from its enemies in ancient times. It's said that from his home in County Kildare he would pitch giant rocks into Dublin Bay to help build a harbor. I guess his aim wasn't too good with this one.

The second legend relates to a woman called Aideen, who died of grief following the death of her husband, Oscar, at the battle of Garva in AD 284. This famous battle is where Finn McCool and the Fianna suffered a crushing defeat.

The Irish name for Howth is Bin Èadair and the name relates to the wife of Gann, a chieftain of an ancient race called the Fir Bolg. Her name was Etar. However, a conflicting view is that it takes its name from Èadair, a chieftain of another tribe called the Tuatha dé Danann.

It's said that the peninsula was home to a great king known as Crimthann, who was a very wealthy man due to many successful overseas raids. He is believed to be buried at the site where Baily Lighthouse now stands.

There are tales of another mythical warrior called Cú Chulainn, who is the hero of the *Táin* saga. A hill in the nearby village of Dunboe is supposedly where one of his epic battles, the Siege of Etar, took place.

I had no idea where Dunboe was, but whilst up at the viewpoint for Baily Lighthouse, I got talking to an old bloke sitting in his car listening in on the coast guard's radio frequency. Two other old women were inside, each with a snow-white French Poodle on her lap. He told me that the police station in Howth was originally Dunboe village, but was now part of Howth.

two tennis courts and a large golf course. There is also a bar and a bistro.

B&BS
King Sitric
Restaurant &
Accommodation
East Pier
Howth
Tel: (01) 8325235/
8326729
Web: www.
kingsitric.ie
Email: info@
kingsitric.ie
Named after the famous Viking King of the area, this excellent restaurant is also a four-star guesthouse that offers 8 luxury rooms all with stunning views of the harbor and Ireland's Eye. The restaurant also overlooks all this and serves up an array of local high quality seafood, as well as offering fine wines from the large wine cellar.

THE JOURNEY
LEINSTER
COUNTY
DUBLIN

The Cave of Diarmuid and Gráinne

Diarmuid and Gráinne's cave is
believed to be located somewhere
along the Howth coastline

The area seemed lit-
tered with stories. A
cave near Drumleck
Point, a little further
along the coast from
the lighthouse, is
believed to be one of
the hiding places of
the legendary flee-
ing lovers, Diarmuid
and Gráinne. It's
possible to walk all
around this coast-
line via the network
of walking paths
that encircle the
southern side of the
peninsula, so finding the cave may only take a bit of
luck, and a bit of pluck. I could have easily walked the
distance, but I was feeling lazy. The old man directed
me to the closest spot and told me to look out for an
old wooden telegraph pole. This was Drumleck Point.

Diarmuid and Gráinne are ancient Ireland's most
traveled couple. The story goes that Gráinne was
betrothed to **Finn McCool** by the High King, but
Finn was old, and Gráinne felt no desire to marry
him. However, in honor of her father she agreed to his
request. A great feast was held to celebrate the
impending marriage, and during the celebration
Gráinne met Diarmuid, one of the bravest warriors of
the Fianna. The two fell in love, but Diarmuid was
loyal to his master Finn and wouldn't dare take his
woman. So during the feast Gráinne concocted a
scheme. She drugged all the men's drinks except Diar-

muid's, and when they all fell asleep she convinced Diarmuid to run away with her.

When Finn awoke and realized that he had been betrayed, such was his fury that he chased the two lovers all over Ireland for the next seven years. The couple never spent more than one night in the same place for the whole of these seven years. Many sites around Ireland are said to be where

Drumleck Point is marked by an old-fashioned telegraph pole. The cave of Diarmuid and Gráinne is believed to be nearby, and you may find it if you are not too lazy.

they slept for a night, and this cave is one of them.

The coastline around here was rugged, and from the telegraph pole I could make out a large cave in the distance. I couldn't get to it though. Instead, I contented myself with sitting on the cliff looking out into the Dublin Bay, thinking about how many events this silent, peaceful stretch of water had seen over the thousands of years it has been here. Only it knew the truth.

From Howth I headed north along the coast road, which winds along a lovely scenic drive through the seaside villages of Baldoyle, Portmarnock and Malahide until rejoining the N1 at Swords. I followed this for a while before turning off for Lusk.

Tuan's Notes

Finn McCool was born in Meath into the Clanna Baioscne of Leinster around the time of Christ. Not only was Finn exceptionally tall, strong, and charismatic, he was extremely long-lived, remaining the leader of the Fianna until his death at the age of 230. Finn, who got his name from his bright, blond hair, was an exceptional athlete and warrior, but was best known for two things: his great wisdom, which he had derived from eating the "Salmon of Knowledge", and his defeat of the goblin king Aille, saving Tara from destruction.

Learn more about Finn McCool and the Fianna in The Mystery: Deities & Demigods (pp. 114-117).

THE JOURNEY
LEINSTER
COUNTY
DUBLIN

Tuan's Notes
Learn more about Diarmuid & Gráinne in The Mystery: Folklore & Mythology (pp. 204-205).

Lusk Church

Lusk Church may be one of the oldest churches in Ireland.

In the center of the village of Lusk is a very interesting old church. The earliest settlement here was in the 5th century. A round tower, without its conical roof, is all that remains of the old monastery. The church had been plundered and burnt several times by both Vikings and Irish by the 12th century. A square tower was built onto the round tower in the 15th century, and the rest of the current church was added over the following centuries. Lusk Church remains today as a history of Irish sacred architecture set in stone.

The name "Lusk" may derive from the Gaelic *losca*, "cave", which may refer to the same cave wherein **Diarmuid and Gráinne** had hidden nearby. Some believe that Lusk Church may be one of the oldest churches in Ireland, dating back to the time of St. Patrick. In either case, its architectural style is definitely ancient. Lusk is also the setting for the legend, "The Wooing of Emer".

I drove on to Rush, where I spent the night in a lovely campsite beside the beach. The view from the back of the Scooby Van was magnificent, and to the north I could quite clearly see my next destination: Skerries.

Skerries

St. Patrick's Island lies off the coast of Skerries, and it's said that this was his first landing point upon returning to Ireland as a missionary. The island is now named in his honor.

I drove through the town and onto Red Island, which is no longer an island, now joined to the mainland by a road. A car park in the center provides a great panoramic view, so I parked alongside the others and shared the view.

A local legend tells of how **St. Patrick** had come to Red Island to convert the local people, and while here his prize goat was stolen by the people of Skerries. He discovered this upon returning, and it is said that he took two giant steps back to Red Island and confronted the local people, demanding the return of his goat. The locals attempted to deny what they had done, but found they were unable to speak unless they told the truth. Thus they confessed that they had killed and eaten the goat.

St. Patrick's Island is also known as Church Island, and soon after Patrick's arrival a monastery was founded there. It was frequently plundered and burned by the Vikings over the years. In 1120, the Viking King Sitric re-established a mo-

Swords Church, near Skerries.

Tuan's Notes
St. Patrick
(AD 390-461) is the National Apostle and Saint of Ireland, and probably the most famous and celebrated person in Irish history. Born in Britain and enslaved by Irish raiders, Patrick escaped but felt God's call to ministry, and was sent back to Ireland by the Pope to convert the Irish. The Druids resisted him, but they were easily swept aside by the power of God. The High King then gave Patrick leave to preach the Gospel to the four corners of Ireland, driving away the serpents and the idols they worshiped.

Learn more about St. Patrick and the coming of Christianity in The History: The Coming of Christianity (pp. 219-233).

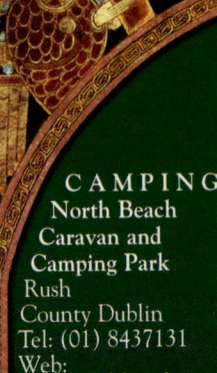
nastery on the spot. However, as King Sitric was also said to be ruler at the time of the Battle of Clontarf, 1014, I guess he was either very old, or this was his son. A century later the monks abandoned the monastery and moved to Holmpatrick on the mainland. The remains of the old monastery can still be seen on the island.

St. Movee's Well

Back in Skerries, beside Killalane Street, there is a holy well dedicated to a **Christian saint** named St. Movee, a hermit who lived in the area during the early 7th century. Local legend tells of how he had his hermitage in the old churchyard. One day his neighbor decided to take Movee's land for himself and proceeded to plow the land with his plow and horses. St. Movee asked him to stop, but the neighbor uttered the following:

"Saint Movee or Saint Movoo, I'll plow this furrow before I go!"

Suddenly the ground opened up and swallowed the plowman and his horses. Only a young boy remained to tell the tale.

Most holy wells have curative properties and the water from St. Movee's Well is said to cure eye problems. It's also said that the well itself will grant one wish to anyone who performs the follow ritual:

Pick a laurel leaf upon arrival and then walk around the well three times in a counter-clockwise direction.

Then go down the steps to the water, and put some water on the leaf.

Make your wish as you drink it, then throw the leaf into the well.

Another legend associated with the well is of Finn McCool. One of the large stones on the well has five finger marks in it. Some believe that these are the imprints made by Finn McCool as he tossed the stone from Lusk.

The weather was gorgeous and I almost drifted off to sleep as I sat overlooking the sea. I pulled myself together and turned the Mystery Machine south, to south Dublin, to search out the rest of the mysteries that County Dublin has to offer.

Places to See in South Dublin

South of Dublin
Dun Laoghaire and Around

WISHING I COULD FIND THE DRUID'S CHAIR

"Is there any significance to the name of this pub, The Druid's Chair?" I asked the barman.

"Yes, it's named after the nearby dolmen called The Druid's Chair. You'll find it at the bottom of the hill there, in the shape of a druid's throne. People say that if you sit in it you'll get sick. But you don't."

I was sitting at the bar having a drink and reading up on some literature I'd obtained. A meeting with the marketing manager of the Fitzpatrick Castle Hotel on Killiney Hill had once again brought me back to this area. I had wanted to know if there were any legends surrounding the castle. She said there was talk of secret tunnels leading from under the castle's dungeons to hidden coves along the coast, used by a family of smugglers who once owned the castle.

A lovely view of Dublin Bay from Fitzpatrick Castle Hotel

South of Dublin
Things to Do & Places to See

Dalkey Castle & Heritage Center
Castle St, Dalkey.
Tel: (01) 2858366
Web:
www.dalkeycastle.com
Email:
diht@indigo.ie
Open Mon-Fri
9:30-5 (April to December)
Weekends
11-5 (All year)

Dalkey Island
Aidan Fennel runs boat trips out to the island daily. He is licensed to carry up to 12 people and will drop you off and pick you up whenever you want. You can find him at the harbor just south of Dalkey Village. Just follow the signs for the coastal road. Coliemore Harbor, Coliemore Rd. Tel: (01) 2834298

THE JOURNEY
LEINSTER
COUNTY
DUBLIN

The literature hadn't mentioned any of this. However, it *had* mentioned a wishing stone at the summit of Killiney Hill Park, but said nothing more. Inside the pub I'd got talking to a couple of local men. I'd talked to the first man for about ten minutes about this, then he turned to his friend sitting next to him and asked,

"Have you heard of a wishing stone on the hill?"

"Oh yes," he replied. "It's up by The Witch's Hat.

It seemed he'd been so absorbed in his pint that he hadn't been listening to us.

"The Witch's Hat is the Obelisk," he explained.

"What do you know about it?" I asked.

"Well now, you walk around it three times and make a wish, of course."

"Do you know anything about the origin of the stone?"

He thought for a moment. "No." he replied. He then returned to his pint.

The other man turned to me and said, "Ask the barman. He's only a young fella but he knows a lot about the area."

So I did, and he replied that he knew nothing about the stone. But he did mention The Druid's Chair. I began to regret not stopping in here a few days ago when the weather was sunny. It had begun to rain outside, the first in two weeks, and the windscreen wipers on my van had stopped working. (How's that for timing?) But the worst thing was that I had explored this area before and had somehow missed all this.

For two years I'd been traveling in a little Bedford Midi camper conversion that I affectionately refer to as "The Scooby Van". This is because when I first bought it I couldn't help thinking it looked like just like "The Mystery Machine" from the children's cartoon *Scooby Doo*, only not as vividly colored. Now that I had gone on this trip to rediscover Ireland's ancient mysteries, that nickname seemed particularly appropriate.

I was originally here after stopping off at the Heritage Center in the nearby village of Dalkey. It is believed that in medieval times there were seven castles in Dalkey, back in the time when Dalkey was an important port for Dublin. Only two remain today, one of which now houses the heritage center. Human settlement here goes back to prehistoric times, and many Mesolithic artifacts have been excavated around the area, most prominent of which was the Dalkey Hoard.

Around 1838, an ancient gatepost was demolished in the village and a hoard of 10th-century silver coins were found buried underneath. None of the coins date after AD 975, so it is believed that they may have been stolen by the Vikings and possibly hidden there during the Battle of Tara in AD 980. The coins are now in the British Museum, as there was no National Museum in Ireland at the time.

Dalkey Island

On Dalkey Island, just off the coast here, lies one of the earliest stone churches built in Ireland around the 10th century. There is also a holy well.

Dalkey Island, just off the coast of south Dublin. Dalkey is believed to have hosted as many as seven castles and numerous other structures, some of which survive to this day.

Druid's Chair Pub and turn right at Killiney Avenue. At the next right you'll see a crude pathway going into a clearing between the two houses on the corner. The monument is inside there. You might have to beat your way through the overgrown grass, depending on the time of year and current state of upkeep by the locals.

Tully Church & Crosses
Lehaunstown Rd.
Cabinteely
Set in a remote part of the countryside on top of a hill, the church itself is 12th century and not much is left. What is far more interesting is the high Celtic cross nearby. The top of the cross has been carved into the shape of a roof, and it sits high upon a stone structure overlooking what is now

modern
Ireland.
To get there
take the turn-
ing off the N11
for Cabinteely
and follow
Brenanstown Road.
A little way you'll
see a sign pointing
left for the Tully
Church and Cross.

Killiney Church
(*Cill Iníon Léinin* —
the Church of
the Daughters
of Léinin)
Marino
Avenue West
Killiney
Open June,
July and August on
Sundays only
10 am-6 pm
Directly opposite
the DART station.
It was originally a
6th-century nun's
church. Léinin was a
local chieftain who
was converted to
Christianity along
with his seven
daughters. The
name of the town,
Killiney, comes from
this.

There is a set of rocks nearby Dalkey Island called "The Muglins". A local story says that a band of mutinous pirates who had taken over a ship called *The Earl of Sandwich* had set sail from the Canaries in 1765, later arriving on the Waterford coast where they hid their stolen treasure. A while later they were arrested and executed. Their bodies were originally displayed in St. Stephen's Green and Dublin Quay as a warning to all pirates, but the smell of their decomposing flesh was too much, and their bodies were moved and chained to the Muglins rocks near Dalkey Island. The treasure was never recovered, and must still be hidden along the Waterford coast.

The Heritage Center has a great leaflet listing all the local dolmens, and also shows a video presentation. Unfortunately, The Druid's Chair was not on that list.

And so it was I found myself trotting down the road in my raincoat in search of this Druid's Chair. I passed The Druid Lodge, a B&B the barman had also told me about, and wandered up to the front door, closely followed by a barking dog. There was no one home. The next turning to the right was Killiney Avenue. I tried in vain to remember the barman's directions exactly, but couldn't. I just remembered him saying it was at the end of the avenue, but I couldn't find it. I wandered up every turning, but to no avail. Further back up Killiney Hill Road I asked a man waiting for a lift.

"It's actually behind a high wall on private land, between two houses. It's very hard to see. I was shown it once when I was working there, but you'll have to get permission from the landowner."

I decided to head back up the hill and find the Wishing Stone. Perhaps it would help guide me.

The heart of Killiney Village is centered on a small

412

roundabout, where there is the pub and a small shop. Killiney takes its name from the Irish, *Cill Iníon Léinin*, meaning, "The Church of the Daughters of Léinin." Léinin was a local chieftain (or petty king) who is said to have been converted to Christianity in the 6th century by the monastic settlement at nearby Tully. Along with his seven daughters he founded a monastery on the site of the present day remains. Celtic churches back then were usually simple, wooden huts and called *cills* (pronounced "kills"), hence many place names in Ireland beginning with "Cill". The original church was built on the site of an ancient rath (an earthen mound used for fortification). The remains of the present church are 11th century, and from here Gaelic, Viking and Norman settlers practiced Christianity.

The Obelisk

Bus 59 from Dun Laoghaire stops at the roundabout and directly opposite are steps that lead up into Killiney Hill Park. My friend Paul had told me about The Obelisk a few days ago, saying that it lies at the summit of the hill and offers a fantastic view of Dublin Bay. I had come up here back then when the weather was sunny and warm, and the view was indeed stunning. South Dublin really doesn't feel like a suburb of a city. These little coastal villages are still just that — villages. But it does have the advantage of having a good transport system linking it with the city.

Today however was a different story. The wind howled across the open landscape and brought with it rain, and I fought to keep my umbrella from lifting me up and sweeping me into the air like Mary Poppins.

The Obelisk isn't that old. It was erected in 1742 by Colonel John Mapas, the landowner at the time. Just across from The Obelisk I saw a small, stone structure

Pavilion Theatre
Marine Rd. Dun Laoghaire Tel: (01) 231 2929
The Pavilion Theatre has regular music concerts and shows with artists such as Christy Moore.

Tourist Office
The Ferry Terminal Dun Laoghaire Open Monday-Saturday

Eat & Drink

The Dungeon Bar & Grill
Fitzpatrick Castle Dublin, Killiney Tel: (01) 2305400
Situated in the old castle dungeons, this excellent bar & grill serves up a great selection of dishes at very reasonable prices, given its location. The bar also has a huge television in a cosy little snug just before the restaurant. Highly recommended.

CAFÈS
Most of the cafes and restaurants in Dun Laoghaire are situated along Georges Street. Here are a few examples:

The World Café
56 Lower Georges St.
Harry's Café Bar, Opposite the AIB Bank.

Scott's Upstairs
17 Georges St. Tel: (01) 2802657/ 2808758

Country Bake
35 Castle St.
Tel: (01) 2852009
A lovely little café and cake shop with good food and friendly service.

Mia Cuchina
107 Lower Georges St.
Tel: (01) 2805318

Also in Dun Laoghaire, along the waterfront on Queen's Road, are a few recently opened cafés on the front of the

THE JOURNEY
LEINSTER
COUNTY DUBLIN

"The Obelisk"—or, as it is known locally, "The Witch's Hat". The peakéd cap and the somewhat anthropomorphic look of the monument does beg the question as to which name is more accurate. Conical hats of this type were indeed used in some types of pagan religions, so there may be an unsolved mystery here waiting to be uncovered by future generations of intrepid explorers—possibly an unsolved mystery of *occult* dimensions.

in the shape of a Mayan pyramid. I wondered if that was the wishing stone, but there was no indication upon it. I continued further along the hill in search of anything else that it could be, and was greeted by a middle-aged couple coming up the other way. We got talking.

Gerry English and his wife were actually from the north side of Dublin, but Gerry had grown up here. "I used to play here as a child and we always thought it was the pyramid," he said. So we wandered back up for a better look.

A little bit further down the hill was another small structure, but upon further investigation I found this to be a smaller obelisk that was dedicated to John Mapas. Back up at the pyramid Gerry's wife waved to us from the top of the hill. She was standing next to an old man and his little dog. "This fella knows all about the area," she shouted, her voice barely registering above the howling wind.

I introduced myself and shook his hand. He had a funny left eye and gaunt features. A raincoat and an old

414

baseball cap were all that protected him from the rain. His little dog, with matted white fur, stood beside him wagging its tail. He introduced himself as Ron and proceeded to explain all about the history of this area, waving his walking stick around to indicate specific places.

The Wishing Stone

Ron explained that the pyramid structure was indeed The Wishing Stone. "What you do," he said, "is walk around each level one at a time until you reach the top level. Then you must walk around the top stone three times and sit on it to make your wish."

Ron went on to explain how the landowner John Mapas would give relief work to local people during famine times and had them building all these structures, and also a number of stone seats that can still be found in the area.

Dalkey Island can be seen perfectly from the hill, and Ron explained that families from the Wicklow Mountains built a tunnel to the island to hide stolen cattle. "The goats that once lived on the island had been brought over to the mainland and all died. It

"The Wishing Stone" of South Dublin. Though it is a relatively modern creation, its construction reaches back to Mayan architectural principles for its inspiration, adding all the more to the mystery.

Pavilion building. All have tables outside as well as inside. Try any of the following:

Itsa Bagel (as the name suggests it offers mostly coffee and bagels)

Mao Café/Bar (offering a good selection of Asian food)

Roly @ The Pavilion (offers dinners mostly)

Kaffe Moka (a nice little café offering snacks and sandwiches)

West Coast Coffee (a good cheaper option)

There are also a couple of Internet cafés along Georges Street:

U-Surf
68B Georges St.
Tel: (01) 2311186

Net Café
Opposite the Post Office. This café has connections for your laptop also.

PUBS
Johnnie Fox's
(The highest
pub in Ireland)
Glencullen
Tel: (01) 2955647
Web: www.jfp.ie
Email: info@jfp.ie
Being the highest
pub in the country,
it's become one of
the most famous in
the country. There
is music and danc-
ing here 7
nights a
week. The
food comes
highly recom-
mended. The
only downside
might be the influx
of tour groups. It's in
a little village in the
Dublin Mountains,
so getting there
could be a problem.
You'll either have to
join a bus tour, get a
taxi or drive. Dublin
bus does run a serv-
ice to the village.
Check with them
for details: tel: (01)
8734222, web: www.
dublinbus.ie.

THE JOURNEY

LEINSTER

**COUNTY
DUBLIN**

seemed they could only live on the island. There is also a story of a stone that turns around with the incoming tide, but I haven't managed to find it."

We stood there for ages listening to Ron, blissfully unaware that we were getting soaked. Finally Gerry and his wife announced they were heading back down, and blamed me for the soaking. I pointed out that I was equally sodden, but it was hopeless.

THE SMALL OBELISK

Ron followed me round to the smaller obelisk and showed me the inscription on the front dedicating it to John Mapas. It's assumed this was a shrine to his life. In the pouring rain I decided it would be a good shelter in which to make a few notes.

"Be careful where you tread," advised Ron.

The "Small Obelisk". This structure, unlike the others, has an
inscription attributing its construction to one Colonel John Mapas.
It might also serve as a temporary
shelter against Ireland's precipitous
climate.

"Nowadays it's used for less ceremonial pur-poses." As if to illustrate this, his dog trotted in and cocked its leg.

"Come on Scruff," he called. "We'd best be off."

"Is that his name?" I asked.

"Yes, you just have to look at him to see why."

The poor little thing's fur was soaked and matted.

"He's a cross between a poodle and a terrier," Ron explained. "He can't help getting scruffy."

I shook Ron's hand and thanked him for imparting his incredible wealth of knowledge to me, and then watched as he hobbled off up the hill with his walking stick, Scruff faithfully trotting along by his side.

I made a few notes, then took my umbrella and made my way to the pyramid. A set of steps led up to the top stone, which was square and had the year 1840 inscribed upon it in Roman numerals. I alighted the first step and began walking around on the structure in a clockwise direction, stepping up a level after each circuit. As I walked around each ledge, I must have looked like a maniac attempting an old-time musical dance as I swung my umbrella back and forth across my shoulders to make sure it remained against the fierce wind blowing in from the sea. Upon reaching the top I circled three times and sat down on the wet stone.

"I wish it would stop bloody raining!" was my first wish. Not sure if I was allowed two wishes or not, I opted for a second wish:

"I wish I could find the Druid's Chair."

It couldn't hurt to try.

The summit of the pyramid lay at 170 meters above sea level, and from its peak I could clearly see the church on Dalkey Island. I could also see the network of walking paths that is all along this rugged section of the park. On a clear day it's said you can even see Wales east across St. George's Channel and the Mourne Mountains in County Down to the north. The port at Dun Laoghaire harbor is clearly visible as well, while to the west are spectacular views of the Dublin and Wicklow Mountains.

Walking here the other day I had seen many locals walking their children and their dogs, or sitting on the many rocky outcrops staring out to sea. You would never believe that such a peaceful, natural setting could be in the suburb of a city.

Taylors Three Rock Pub, Irish Night
Grange Rd.
Rathfarnham
Dublin 16
Tel: (01) 4942999
Web: www.taylorsirishnight.com
Email: info@taylorsirishnight.com
Located 6 miles south of the city centre, just off the M50, this pub hosts a night of Irish entertainment. The Merry Ploughboys provide the music and a hand-picked group of dancers perform a specially choreographed show. Runs all year round and bookings are essential. Another Druid's Chair dolmen is also nearby, but permission is required to view it.

The Druid's Chair
Killiney Hill Rd,
Killiney
Tel: (01) 2857297
A nice pub perched

on the hill by the round-about that also serves food.

McDonagh's Pub
Castle St., Dalkey
A modern pub in the lovely little village of Dalkey. Serves a good pint of Guinness.

There & Back Again

FERRIES
There are 3 sailings a day with Stena Line to and from Holyhead to the harbor here. Call Dublin (01) 2047777 or book online at Head Office: **The Ferry Terminal** Dun Laoghaire.

TRAINS
The DART (Dublin Area Rapid Transport) system runs between Howth as far as Greystones in County Wicklow and stops all along this coastline. There

THE JOURNEY
LEINSTER
COUNTY DUBLIN

One night in 1843 a woman named Etty Scott, who was said to be a visionary, claimed she had a dream about a Viking hoard of treasure buried beneath the White Rock along the Killiney coastline. This sparked a mini gold rush as workers from the nearby quarry abandoned their jobs and set out to help Etty find this treasure. It was never found.

The Druid's Chair

Back down the hill I decided to give finding The Druid's Chair one more try. I remembered the old man on the road saying that it was behind a wall just beyond the wooden gates of Druid Hill house. At the corner of the house and an adjacent road. I found a muddy path lined with rocks, and I followed it up to an opening in a small metal fence, but beyond this it was overgrown and seemingly inaccessible. I gave up.

Back out on Killiney Hill Road I tried The Druid Lodge once again, and found this time that the lady owner was at home. Seeing my condition, she very graciously invited me into the warmth of her B&B. Grateful, I put down my umbrella and followed her into the front room. A little cat was curled up asleep on a nearby sofa. "Ah, look!" I exclaimed, and walked over to stroke it. To my horror the whole cat was stiff and solid. "It's dead!" I thought. "Should I tell her?" I felt it again and then realized, to my embarrassment, that it was actually a fake sleeping cat.

"That's very good," I said, in an attempt to conceal my stupidity. "It almost looks real."

Cynthia smiled at me sympathetically. "It's made from rabbit's fur. It's not stuffed."

After gathering all the information on the B&B, I then asked her what if anything she knew about The Druid's Chair.

"It's behind the house, but you can't get to it from

418

here because we have a big wall at the back of the garden. But there is public access round the side via a little path on the corner."

"I saw that, but the field is overgrown," I said.

"That's where it is. The problem is it's a disturbed monument and so the council won't invest in its upkeep. Some of the locals look after it though, and occasionally cut back the grass. It's long now because of the winter, but you can beat your way through it and get to the dolmen."

We got talking about the area, and Cynthia showed that she too was full of local information. I asked about the tunnel to the island.

"Oh yes, it exists. It starts here." She pointed at Loreto Abbey in Dalkey on the map. "The entrance is closed off because of the children playing around there. It's considered very dangerous. They also discovered a tunnel leading from the hills to Dun Laoghaire harbor a while back, while doing some construction work."

Out on the road I wandered once again back round to find this dolmen. I returned to the path and stood staring at the thick, wet grass in front of me. It came up to my chest. I zipped up my raincoat as far as it would go and fought my way through it. I then made my way to a small clearing, about 20-foot square, emerging on the other side with wet trousers. There I saw three large stones. I looked at each one in turn and then, when I came to the last one, there it was — The Druid's Chair.

The rock was about five foot high, the side facing the wall cut out into the exact shape of a throne. I could have sat in it, but heeded the barman's warning. I felt wretched enough as it was, without adding to it. The throne was actually facing the ocean, which seemed fitting as the druids worshipped the water — specifically, the god Lir and, later, Manannan mac Lir.

are regular services throughout the day stopping all along the south coast. It also stops at Connolly Station. There are stations at Dun Laoghaire, Dalkey and Killiney.

BUSES
Dublin bus serves the area well, Bus 59 stopping at Killiney Hill Road. Check with Dublin Bus for details: tel: (01) 8734222, web: www. dublinbus.ie.

DRIVING
To get here from the city just take the N11 southwards to Wexford and follow the signs from there. For a more interesting route follow the coastal road southwards, which will take you through all the suburbs and the coastal villages that make up this really attractive part of Dublin.

THE JOURNEY

LEINSTER

COUNTY DUBLIN

Places to Stay

HOTELS

Fitzpatrick Castle Hotel
Killiney
Tel: (01) 2305400
Web: www.fitzpatrickcastle.com
Email: info@fitzpatricks.com
A lovely, luxurious hotel, part of the Fitzpatrick chain. Set in a castle, the hotel boasts a wealth of amenities.

Portview Hotel
Marine Rd.
Dun Laoghaire
Tel: (01) 2801663/2844260

The Kingston Hotel
Adelaide St,
Dun Laoghaire
Tel (01) 2801810
Web: www.kingstonhotel.com
An upper-range hotel over the €100 a night mark. This hotel overlooks the waterfront and many of the 53 en-suite rooms have great views.

"The Druid's Chair." Hewn out of solid rock, this ancient throne was likely the seat from which the local High Druid held court and gave counsel. Today, it is a disturbed monument and difficult to reach, but a fascinating part of Ireland's mysterious past nonetheless.

Was it actually possible this was once the seat of a High Druid? Or is it just coincidence that the rock became shaped like this? The leaflet I had also mentioned another dolmen called The Druid's Chair up at Taylor's Grange by the southern end of the M50, but when I went there I found that a private housing estate had been built around the site and a set of locked gates prevented the public from getting in to view it. It seemed highly unlikely that two dolmens could have been randomly carved out like this.

It was a pity the Dalkey Island tunnel was closed. I intended to drive by there on the way back to Dun Laoghaire. Unfortunately the rain had become heavier and, as I drove down the road struggling to see out the front window, I felt I shouldn't push my luck too far. After all, I had forgotten to wish for a safe journey home.

Though Dublin had been interesting, it was becoming increasingly clear that Meath, the ancient spiritual heart of Ireland, was where my journey to rediscover ancient Ireland would truly begin.

JIM FITZPATRICK

B & B S
The Druid Lodge
Killiney Hill Rd., Killiney
Tel: (01) 2851632
This is a lovely old historic house, overlooking Killiney Bay and Dalkey Island.

Tara Hall
24 Sandycove Rd, Dun Laoghaire
Tel: (01) 2805120
Mob: (087) 2025933
Old regency-style house built in 1780.

Hillbrook
6 Burdett Ave. Sandycove
Dun Laoghaire
Tel (01) 2300522
Mob: (086) 8509150
Open all year, this little B&B has 3 rooms.

For more information visit ireland.mysteriousworld.com/Journey/Counties/Dublin/

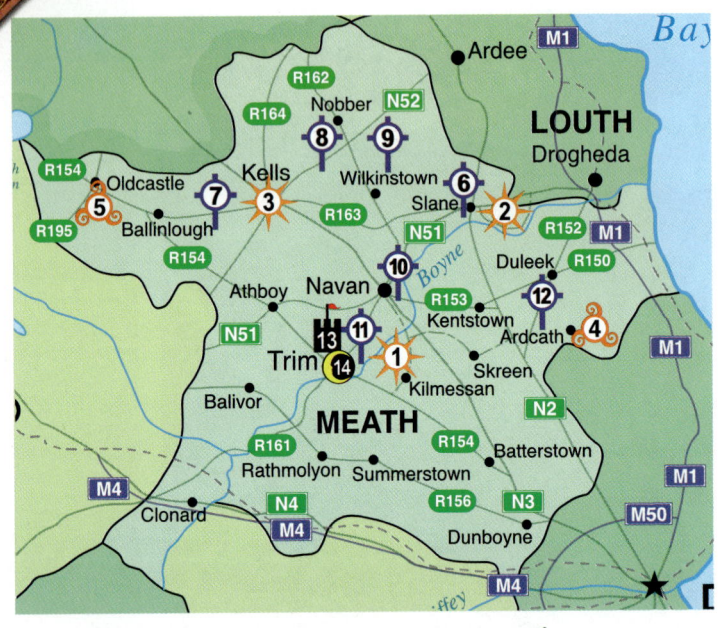

Places to See in Meath

Meath
Into the Heart of the Old Republic

The Hill of Tara, the Royal Seat of ancient Ireland.
Image courtesy SaveTaraValley.com.

uring my experience in searching County Dublin, I had noticed that, though it had much to offer in terms of history, in terms of *ancient* history, there was relatively little. Dublin, though now the capitol of Ireland, in ancient times was little more than a modest port surrounded by a small village, whereas County Meath boasted Tara, the very center of the Irish religious, political, historical and mythological universe. I was now heading into the center of that ancient universe, into the spiritual heart of Ireland, where my quest to rediscover mysterious Ireland would truly begin.

Meath and Dublin form a duality of opposites — ancient vs. modern, natural vs. artificial, traditional vs. progressive. "Beyond the Pale" is how the English described the area outside of the "civilized" area in and around what is now County Dublin. This was the *Gaeltacht*, where Gaelic was once proudly spoken,

Meath
Things to Do & Places to See

Summer Solstice Festival at Tara
Every year on the day of the summer solstice there is a festival which starts at sunrise and finishes at sunset. Throughout the day there is storytelling, walks and more.

Kells Heritage Festival
Festival Office, John St, Kells.
Tel: (046) 9240555
The first weekend of July.

The Friends of Tara
These folks look after the hill, keep it clean and generally tend to the well-being of the area. They hold regular meetings. They also arrange other celebrations such as *Lughnasa*. Check out the website for info on all these events.
Web: www. savetaravalley.com

THE JOURNEY
LEINSTER
COUNTY
MEATH

where even the might of the English was not sufficient to tame the savage Celtic chieftains who doggedly held on to the old ways. Today, however, the *Gaeltacht* survives only in small, isolated patches scattered throughout the country, the vast majority of Ireland having long since succumbed to creeping modernity. Where brute force had failed, popular "world culture" has succeeded in subverting the old order. And now, even Tara itself is threatened by the creation of a new highway that threatens to darken the heart of the old Republic. It was into this heart of darkness that I now headed — into the heart of the conflict between the ancient and the modern, between the sacred and the secular. Into the duel of the fates. Into the jaws of the dragon.

It was very late by the time I arrived in Slane, County Meath. Slane is a little village I have visited many times. Despite Slane being a name that most people would recognize, it's nothing more than a crossroads with a few pubs, B&Bs and shops. Its name has been made famous by Slane Castle, host to the annual Slane rock concerts.

I was first invited here by Joanne Macken, who I met at the Independent Traveller's World show in London. Joanne is the owner of the Slane Farm Hostel. The hostel is in an old converted coach house and stables, and as disconcerting as that may sound let me reassure you that any remnants of its prior usage have been well and truly dissipated — except of course that the exterior still retains its historic look and you wake up to the sound of cows in the fields out back. It's still a working farm, and lies just up the road from Slane Castle. As well as dorm and private rooms, there are now self-catering cottages. There is also a well-equipped kitchen, and in the cozy lounge Joanne has supplied a wealth of literature on the history and folklore of the County Meath area.

The Druid School
Contact:
Con Conner
Tel: (01) 4578343
Email: info@druidschool.com
Web: www.druidschool.com

The Convocation of Druids in Ireland
The first official organization of Irish Druidry.
Web: www.irish-druids.org

General Information:
✤ Info on the wells of Ireland and the Slaine restoration projects can be found at www.slaine.ie

✤ More info on the *Brú na Bóinne* complex can be found at www.knowth.com

✤ Information on the network of roads depicting a giant sword-wielding warrior visit www.mythicalireland.com

THE JOURNEY
LEINSTER
COUNTY MEATH

Brú na Bóinne

Brú na Bóinne, or "Palace of the Boyne", is generally considered to be the most important archaeological and historical region in all of Ireland. The principal attractions still lying here today include the magnificent passage tombs of Newgrange, Knowth and Dowth (just a few miles from Slane) and, most importantly, the Hill of Tara, ancient seat of the High Kings, which lies just south of Navan. With over 5,000 years of known history in the Boyne Valley, you could find things to keep you busy here for weeks. It's even possible to get involved with an archaeological dig in the area. This time, however, I opted to head straight to to Tara, hoping to find some answers there.

The Hill of Tara

To get to Tara from Slane I just had to head off to Navan on the N51 that follows the River Boyne, then head south on the N3 for a few miles until I saw a signpost for Tara and turned right. The Hill of Tara was just a short way up this road. I pulled up in the car park and wandered in. At the entrance is a Protestant

The Hill of Tara as seen from the ground.

425

St. Ciarán's Well, Kells: The Rosary is recited the first Sunday in August.

Save the Tara-Skryne Valley! Visit www.savetaravalley.com for information on the fight to save Tara.

Brighid's Academy of Healing Arts Gina McGarry Tel: (044) 85872 Web: www.brighidsacadamy.com Email: brighid9@iolfree.ie Offers guided ritual tours, courses, workshops, aromatherapy and health consultations.

Tree Wheel Crafts Adge offers custom-carved druid staves. Email: fluiddruid@eircom.net

Navan Tourist Information Centre 21 Ludlow St., Navan Tel: (046) 9073426 Email: info@meathtourism.ie

The Book of Invasions

According to the *Lebor Gabala Erenn*, "The Book of the Invasions of Ireland", the most ancient history of Ireland was essentially a series of invasions. For over a thousand years, wave after wave of Scythian immigrants had come from the far-away East to battle for dominion over the sacred isle. First came the Cessair, followed by the Partholónians, the Nemedians, the Fir Bolg, the Tuatha dé Danann and, finally, the Milesians, who continue to rule the sacred isle to this day.

Learn more about the Invasions and the earliest history of Ireland in The Mystery: The Invasions (pp. 37-77).

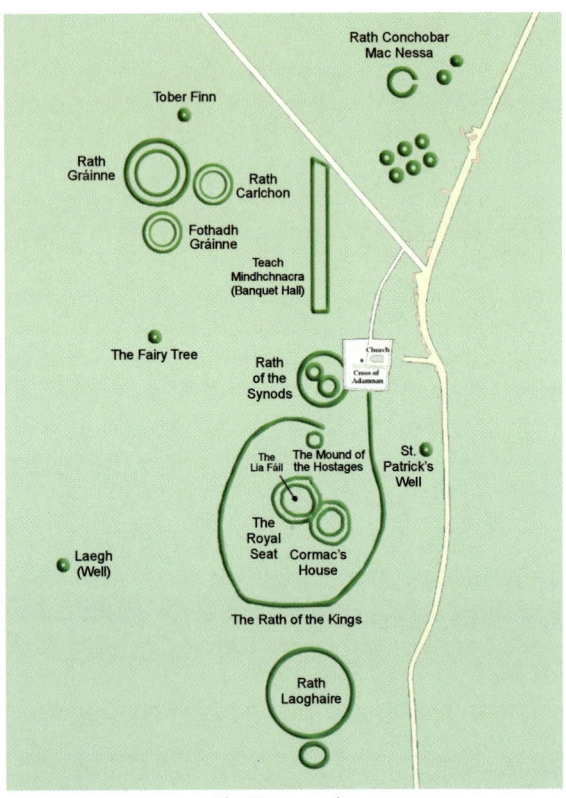

The Tara complex

church. I noticed a sign indicating a price, and feared for a moment that I would have to pay to enter the grounds. I paused briefly, hand clutching my heart, the other clutching my wallet. Fortunately, this was not the case. Further investigation proved this to be the cost of the visual presentation being shown in the church itself. I wiped my brow in relief and continued up the steps and through the stile, and soon found myself standing on a green hill seriously devoid of monuments.

Although only 155 meters in altitude, Tara dominates the Meath lowlands and overlooks much of Ireland. Its strategic position made it the Royal Seat for the High Kings who ruled over Ireland. Tara is the focal point of Ireland's story, her shaping and her national symbols, the harp and the shamrock, all have their origins here. Looking at these low, unassuming mounds, however, you would hardly believe this to be true. Yet, Tara is the setting for a series of legends that chart the successive invasions of Ireland, as recounted in **The Book of Invasions**.

The Royal Seat

The two most distinctive earthworks on the hill are The Royal Seat and *Teach Chormac* (Cormac's House). Both sit just beyond The Mound of the Hostages, are about 152 meters in diameter and are circular hills enclosed by an inner ditch, which marks it as a ritual enclosure rather than a defensive fortification. Another story says that the Milesian Queen Tea is buried underneath one of these mounds.

THE LIA FÁIL

I wandered over to The Royal Seat and climbed to the *Lia Fáil* at the top. This is the magical "Stone of Destiny" brought to Ireland by the Tuatha dé Danann. In total the stone is 10 feet long, but only half the stone protrudes from the ground. This was the

The *Lía Fail*, the sacred stone of the Tuatha dé Danann. It is believed to emit a roaring noise when touched by the true King of Ireland.

Trim Visitor Centre & Tourist Office
Castle St., Trim
Tel: (046) 9437227
Email: trimvisitorcentre@eircom.net
Web: www.meathtourism.ie
The visitor centre has a good audio-visual presentation telling the fascinating history of the town.

Brú na Bóinne Visitor Centre
Donore
Tel: (041) 9880300
Entrance to Newgrange and Knowth is only via the tours from this centre.

Kells Heritage Centre
Headfort Place, Kells
Tel: (046) 9247840
Email: kellsheritagecentre@eircom.net

The Lia Fáil
Learn more about the Lia Fáil in The Mystery: The Invasions (p. 48).

TOURS

Celtic Experience
Daily tours from Dublin Central to the Boyne Valley areas.
Tel: (01) 8386128
Mob: (087) 2593467
Freephone (Reservations only)
1-800 424252
Email: info@over thetoptours.com
Web: www.overthe toptours.com

Day Tours Unplugged
1 Fairway Green
Griffith Rd.
Dublin 11
Tel: (01) 8340941
Email: info@ daytoursunplugged.ie
Web: www. daytoursunplugged.ie
This company offers a tour of Newgrange leaving from Dublin.

Clonard, Duleek, Fourknocks and Loughcrew: See driving sections for info on how to get there.

coronation stone of the High King. It's said that the stone would roar when the rightful king placed his hands upon it. I stood beside it and placed my hands either side and held them there for a moment. Not a sound could be heard, so I crossed being High King of Ireland off my list of potential destinies.

The author of a 10th-century topographical guide places the *Lia Fáil* beside The Mound of the Hostages. The stone was moved to this mound after the 1798 rebellion. The stone itself is comprised of granular lime-stone, and experts say it is certainly not from this area. Its origins are a complete mystery. Long after Tara was abandoned in the 6th century, High King Brian Boru chose to adopt these ancient traditions during his inauguration ceremony, and this included the ritual marriage with the earth goddess and touching the *Lia Fáil*. Legend says that a great sound was heard all across Ireland when he did this — the last time that the stone has sounded, to this day.

Cormac's House

Cormac's House is named after Cormac Mac Art, a High King who features prominently in the legends

Cormac's House

associated with Tara. Even historians accept that Cormac was a real King at Tara, even though his birth and life are enshrouded in mystery. Archaeologists have dated these two mounds to around the time of Cormac's reign, so it's widely believed that these were built by his people, possibly on top of previous earthworks. It must have been a quite a task for people with none of the modern machines that we have today.

The Mound of the Hostages

I returned to the hill marked "Mound of the Hostages" that I had passed on the way in for another look. One story credits the Mound of the Hostages as the spiritual home of the Milesian Queen Tea. The Irish name for Tara is *Teamhair*, which is said to come from *Tea Mhur*, meaning "Tea's Ground". Queen Tea had asked Amergin to find her the most beautiful hill in Ireland on which she should be buried upon her death. Amergin chose *Druim Cain*, and renamed it *Teamhair*. The queen said that all the Kings of Ireland would rule from this hill from that point on. High Kings still

The Mound of the Hostages

Tuan's Notes
The Festivals
Ancient Irish festivals were more celebratory than obligatory, having more in common with the Greek *bacchanalia* than the Christian sabbath, often involving riotous revelry, feasting and even drunken orgies. There were four major festivals that marked the four quarters of the Celtic calendar, Samhain, Imbolg, Beltaine and Lughnasa, which divided the year evenly between the solstices and the equinoxes. The festivals were believed to help keep the world of man in balance with nature.

Learn more about the festivals and related aspects of ancient Celtic religion in The Mystery: Ancient Irish Culture (pp. 261-264).

Eat & Drink

Adam and Eve's Restaurant
18 Ludlow St.
Navan
Tel: (046) 9071444
Email: adamandeves
@eircom.net
Modern Irish cuisine.

Maguires
Hill of Tara
A nice little café
with good food at
reasonable
prices with a
great view of
the Hill of
Slane.

**Bennini's
Café and Patisserie**
French's Lane
Trim
Tel: (046) 9431002
Open 7 days, 9-5.

**The Hard Boiled
Egg Café**
Newmarket St., Kells
Tel: (46) 9293686
Good food at reasonable prices.

**Loughcrew Historic
Gardens Coffee Shop**
Oldcastle
Tel: (049) 8541356

ruled over Ireland after Tara was abandoned, and according to ancient bardic listings there were 188 High Kings in total.

The name "Mound of the Hostages" comes from Niall of the Nine Hostages (*op. cit.*), one of the 142 High Kings said to have ruled from Tara. Modern archaeology credits these man-made mounds as passage tombs, built by the Neolithic people in order to bury their dead. They consist of a stone passage with a chamber inside, built using slabs of rock. The stone section is then covered over with earth to form a small, round hill. The Mound of the Hostages is 70 feet in diameter and 9 feet high.

These tombs are significantly placed in order to coincide with the rising of the sun and the full moons of the ancient festival times. The inner chamber of The Mound of the Hostages, for example, was constructed so that it is illuminated by the full moon on August 1st, during the Lughnasa festival, as well as by the rising sun during the festivals of Samhain (All Saint's Day) on November 1st, and Imbolc (Candlemas) on February 1st — the "cross-quarter" day between the winter solstice and the spring equinox.

As I wandered over to the mound a group of children came running past, the little girl shouting, "Mummy, I want to see the fairies!" Once the children had been dragged away by their mothers, I took a look inside through the locked gate. Entry was forbidden. Inside was a small passage measuring seven feet long. On the left side I noticed a large stone slab decorated with swirling, concentric circles that have become synonymous with the Boyne Valley. Dating to 3000 BC, this is the oldest mound at Tara. When it was excavated, the remnants of over 100 burials were found.

The Rath of the Kings

The Royal Seat, Cormac's House and The Mound of the Hostages are all enclosed by a wider enclosure called The Rath of the Kings. The rath encircles an area of 70,000 square meters and has been dated at around 200-300 BC. Once again an inner ditch has been identified, making it a ritual enclosure rather than defensive. Some believe it may have been to keep out evil spirits.

To the south of Cormac's House is Rath Laoghaire, a ring fort 130 meters in diameter, and said to have belonged to King Laoghaire. Laoghaire was High King around the time of St. Patrick. Legend says that he was buried standing up with his sword in his hand, facing his enemies.

The Rath of the Synods

I wandered back towards the churchyard where just outside the cemetery wall lies The Rath of the Synods. This enclosure was ruined in 1899 by a group of British Israelites who excavated the mound in search of the Ark of the Covenant. In Ireland at that time there was no public body to prevent them from doing so.

The Rath of the Synods was excavated properly in 1952, and many discoveries were made which seemed to point to the site being used for many purposes. It's been dated between AD 100-300. Post holes were discovered which revealed that there were once round houses on the site. Roman pottery was also found, linking the inhabitants with the Romans, or at the very least showing they were in contact. Three church synods were believed to have been held here, the third being the most well-known: the Synod of Adamnán. St. Adamnán was a powerful cleric in the area around this time, and many objects are associated with him. One of these, the Cross of Adamnán, is believed to be the

PUBS

The Village Inn
Main St., Slane
Serves bar food and also has traditional Irish music every Friday.

The Boyne Valley Inn
Main St., Slane

Brady's Pub
11 Ludlow St., Navan
Nice old-style pub with stone and wooden décor.

Bounty Bar
Bridge St., Trim
Excellent pub with regular traditional Irish music at weekends, including some famous names.

Sally Rogers Bar
Bridge St., Trim
Modern pub with a nice terrace overlooking the river Boyne.

The Judge and Jury
Market St., Trim
In the centre of town. More spirited drinking spot with loud rock music.

THE JOURNEY
LEINSTER
COUNTY
MEATH

**Smiths
of Kells**
John St., Kells
Nice old pub in
the centre of
town, also does
accommodation.

Brady's Pub
Maudlin St., Kells
Typical old Irish pub
with a stone façade.

Tuan's Notes

Raths
Raths are circular remnants of the foundations of ancient fortifications, and were often considered to be enchanted, even to be the domains of fairies. The famous Ardagh Chalice was found buried in a rath near the village of Ardagh in County Limerick.

Learn more about raths, mounds, and other ancient earthworks in The History: Ancient Irish Culture (pp. 254-259).

standing stone lying beside the path in the cemetery. On the stone is the carving said by Michael Slavin in his *The Book of Tara* to be that of a sitting child, and that some say the stone is the shaft of a cross. Others say that this is the image of the Celtic deity Cernunnos. It is very faded, but it looked more like the Sheela-na-Gig I'd seen in the National Museum.

There is another standing stone in the cemetery, laying open the claim that the two stones are the sacred stones, *Bloc* and *Bluicne*. These two stones were part of the High King's inauguration ceremony. The prospective king would have to drive his chariot between these stones, and if he was worthy the stones would part to allow him through to the *Lia Fáil*. These two stones, along with another sacred stone called the *Moel*, were named after three druids.

To the northeast is a deep trench 200 meters long enclosed by parallel hills either side. This is said to have been the banqueting halls and is referred to in *The Book of Leinster*.

Rath Gráinne

Just beyond this lies Rath Gráinne, the home of Gráinne, daughter of Cormac Mac Art. This is the same Gráinne in the Diarmuid and Gráinne story I learned of in Howth. It was here that Finn McCool was betrothed to the beautiful Gráinne by the king, and I assume that the banqueting hall nearby was host to the great celebration during which Gráinne drugged all the guests.

The **rath** measures 60 meters in diameter with an external bank. Two smaller raths sit beside it. This was far more peaceful than The Rath of the Kings, and I had left behind the crowds. Obviously Tara is a hugely popular tourist attraction, but it seemed that most people congregated around that area, and possibly didn't know about this.

The Fairy Tree at Tara

Back on the road outside the entrance to Tara I saw a small building with a sign out front that read "Maguires". I wandered in to find a souvenir and bookshop with a small café out back. I browsed in the bookshop and bought a small booklet called *The Druids at Tara* by Michael Slavin. As I wandered outside I turned to the back and saw a black and white illustration of a tree with the following caption underneath: "The Fairy Tree at Tara".

That explained why the children I had seen earlier had been so excited about "the fairies". Immediately I wandered back in and asked the lady at the counter where it is. She directed me to walk up to just before the entrance to the church grounds and then turn right and walk over the hill to the other side.

Far over the hill I found a single hawthorn tree at the bottom. There was no sign indicating it was a fairy tree. I wandered around looking at other areas but still found nothing. I then returned to the first tree and compared it with the illustration. It seemed to fit. Upon returning to Maguires the lady asked me if I'd found it.

There & Back Again

TRAINS
There are no trains to anywhere in Meath. The closest you can get by train is Drogheda, County Louth from Dublin. See County Louth chapter.

BUSES
✠ Slane is on the Dublin to Derry route. The bus stops just across the river outside the village. There are several buses a day leaving from Dublin starting at 6.30 am.
✠ Trim & Athboy are on the Dublin to Granard route, which stops in both towns. Bus Èireann No 111 runs several buses daily.
✠ Bus Èireann No: 163 goes from Drogheda to Donore several times a day, just a short walk to the Newgrange visitor centre.

The fairies, or *sídhe* ("sith"), are the "little people" or nature spirits who are believed to live in an "Otherworld" that the ancient Irish and other Celtic peoples believed existed parallel to our own. The *sídhe* are so named due to the fact that they are believed to live in the mounds, raths, fairy trees, stone circles and various other prehistoric sacred spaces to be found throughout Ireland, the basic meaning of the word *sídhe* being "mound". Thus the appelation *Daoine Sídhe*, or "People of the Mounds".

Learn more about The Fairies in The Mystery: Creatures Great & Small (pp. 149-165).

"I think so," I said. "Was it the one sitting at the bottom of the hill?"

"That's the one," she replied.

"But there was no sign indicating it's a fairy tree."

"Oh no, there wouldn't be."

"How do you know it's a fairy tree then?"

"Well, you know, it's just one of them things that the locals have always known," she said. "Was there anything hanging from the tree?"

"Like what?"

"Like pieces torn from people's clothing, or coins stuck in the wood. The fairy trees are associated with healing. If you have an ailment then you are supposed to leave a personal item or a gift for the fairies and in return they will heal your affliction."

"There was nothing on it when I looked at it."

"Ah, they must have cleared them all off then." She turned to the guy working next to her. "Did you hear that? **The fairies** are after cleaning up the tree again."

Further reading had given me a deeper insight into the folklore of the fairy tree. Every lone hawthorn tree in Ireland is considered to be a fairy tree. When the Tuatha dé Danann retreated into the Otherworld, they used a variety of sites as their portals, and the hawthorn tree was one of them. The Irish people consider it extremely bad luck to cut one down, as doing so would invoke the wrath of the tree's inhabitants. Instead, these trees are traditionally used for cleansing or healing. In order to have your affliction healed you must tie a rag to its branches, from your own clothing, and as the rag rots away so does the affliction. In order to have the fairies grant you a wish, you must walk around the tree three times in a clockwise direction (Just

434

like I did at the wishing stone in Killiney, in South Dublin), then make your wish. You can also leave the fairies a gift of flowers or money.

It was the middle of June and the tree was beginning to flower. I sat beneath the tree to shelter from the light rain and the wind blew the soft white buds over me like a shower — or was it the fairies sprinkling me with their fairy dust? This is a common belief, along with the belief that if you are extremely lucky you may be allowed to see the fairies dancing around the tree at dusk.

St. Patrick's Well

Just south of Maguires is St. Patrick's Well, which was formerly known as The Well of the White Cow. This is one of two wells at Tara, the other is just south of Rath Laoghaire. These are said to be the two wells of the goddess Boann, who is the embodiment of the River Boyne. They run in opposite directions and are fed by two rivers that eventually run into the Boyne. Entrance from the road is via a stile, and a path leads up to the well, which has been enclosed by a stone structure and a gate.

Water from the well is still used by the local people. Along the path just before the main well, there is a small pool of water with coins at the bottom. This appears to be a tradition similar to that of the fairy tree, where people would leave a gift for the spirits before taking a sip of the water. Many of the wells around Ireland were sacred wells in the pagan religion, but when the Christian missionaries came they blessed the well, claiming to have driven out the evil spirits. After this they were usually renamed after the saint who was said to have blessed them.

⚜ Bus 103 from Dublin Lwr Abbey St. goes to Duleek
⚜ Regular buses go between Drogheda, Duleek and Slane.
⚜ Bus 188 goes between Drogheda, Slane, Navan, Kells & Oldcastle. You will have to change at Navan for Kells and again for Oldcastle.

For information on all buses originating from Drogheda Tel: (041) 9835023

FLEXIBUS
A local, daily service between Navan and Trim with 2 buses each way. There is also a weekly service to Duleek.
Tel (046) 9074830
Email: meathtransport@eircom.net
Web: http://community.meath.ie/flexibus

THE JOURNEY
LEINSTER
COUNTY MEATH

TAXI
Navan
Taxis
Tel: (046)
9072266

Kells Cabs
(Cumiskey)
Tel: (087) 2504242

DRIVING
✠ From Dublin take
the N2 straight into
Slane. From
Drogheda or Navan
take the N51.

✠ To get to
Tara go to
Navan and
take the N3
south towards
Dublin until
you see a sign indi-
cating a right turn to
Tara.
✠ To get to
Newgrange take the
N2 south from Slane
towards Dublin, cross
the river and take a
left turn a few miles
onwards (It is signed)
and follow for a few
miles until you come
across the Visitor
Centre on the left.
✠ For Duleek con-
tinue on to Donore
from Newgrange and
turn southward.

THE JOURNEY
LEINSTER
COUNTY
MEATH

Rath Maeve

I drove on down the road to the nearby village of Belper, which isn't really a village but rather a small scattering of houses. At a T-junction is a sign pointing right to Rath Maeve. I parked the van at the roadside and climbed over the gate into the site. Rath Maeve is 229 meters in diameter, so it was hard to actually make it out. It's about a mile from the main site of Tara and surrounded by trees. It's nice and secluded and I imagine that not many people visit it, or even know it's there.

One theory has it that Maeve was a warrior and sovereignty goddess of the Celts. In their mythology their gods were often represented as real people, queens or princesses like Gráinne. A fine example of Maeve as the warrior goddess is told in the *Táin* saga. When the Milesians came they adopted a tradition of ritual marriage between the High King and the sovereignty goddess Maeve.

Back at Maguires I learned about the upcoming solstice festival at Tara. This day wasn't far off, so I decided to attend it and experience what I thought would merely be a re-enactment of the old Celtic rituals.

Today's ritual re-enactments are serious affairs put on by practicing druids

The Solstice Festival at Tara

A thick, eerie mist had rolled in from the west and engulfed the whole of the Hill of Tara in what seemed like just a few minutes. I yawned as my tired, bleary eyes struggled to see what was happening through this preternatural mist. It was four-thirty in the morning and I was still trying to convince myself that I wasn't mad getting up at this ungodly hour.

I'd returned the night before, parked the Scooby Van in the car park and slept the night. Obviously, given the fact the festival was on, the only two B&Bs here were full. Many other people were camping in and around the car park, so I just joined them.

When my alarm went off I peeked out the window and saw a lovely light blue sky with a few stars still twinkling on the dawn horizon. The first event of the day was to be the re-enactment of the ancient pagan celebration of the sunrise. It looked to me like it would be a good sunrise. I was wrong.

✤ For Fourknocks continue south from Duleek past Ardcath and turn left for Clonalvy and follow signs. If coming from Drogheda take the R108 south and turn right at the sign for Clonalvy. Fourknocks is signed on the left.
✤ For Trim head back to Navan and take the R161 southwards.
✤ Clonard is on the N4 just before the Meath/Westmeath border.
✤ Kells is north of Navan on the N3
✤ For Loughcrew take the R163, Oldcastle Road beside the church out of Kells and follow this road until you see the signs for the cairns.

BIKE HIRE
Newgrange Bike Hire
Nr Newgrange Visitor Centre
Tel: (086) 0695771

THE JOURNEY
LEINSTER
COUNTY
MEATH

THE CEREMONY OF THE SUNRISE

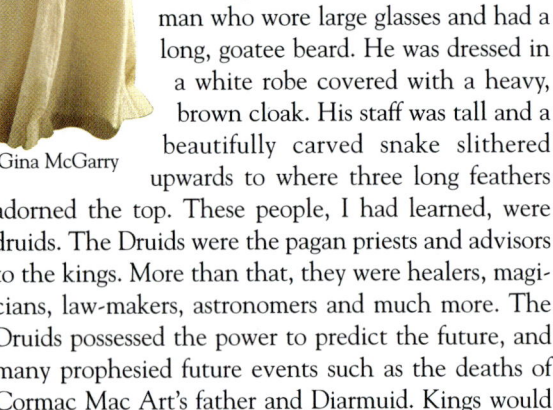

Gina McGarry

When I'd arrived at the mound of Cormac's House, I found everyone standing around the rim of the enclosure. In the center was a woman with fiery-red hair and wearing a long, golden-yellow dress. Standing around her were men and women dressed in robes and cloaks, each carrying a long, wooden staff. One man in particular stood out — a tall man who wore large glasses and had a long, goatee beard. He was dressed in a white robe covered with a heavy, brown cloak. His staff was tall and a beautifully carved snake slithered upwards to where three long feathers adorned the top. These people, I had learned, were druids. The Druids were the pagan priests and advisors to the kings. More than that, they were healers, magicians, law-makers, astronomers and much more. The Druids possessed the power to predict the future, and many prophesied future events such as the deaths of Cormac Mac Art's father and Diarmuid. Kings would consult their druids before going into battle. Druidry had died out with the coming of Christianity, so what I saw now I had assumed to simply be a re-enactment. But I was soon to learn otherwise.

The mist had now engulfed the whole of the mound. The woman at the center was Gina McGarry, the facilitator of the ceremony, and the high priestess. She had arrived swathed in black, representing the night. But at the moment of sunrise, she had doffed her black garment and revealed a bright yellow dress, representing the sun. While I watched Gina recite the sunrise ritual, a woman in blue wandered around the crowd and handed out

438

flowers. We were then invited to throw them at Gina's feet as a ritual offering to the sun. I followed everyone else as they walked clockwise around her before throwing the flowers. It seems that everything associated with a blessing or wish has a clockwise direction.

When the ceremony ended everyone dispersed in many directions. I got talking to a guy with scruffy hair and glasses walking his dog around. He said he was here last year and the dog kept upsetting the druids by jumping up at them as they performed the ceremonies.

"They take all this very seriously," he said.

"I thought it was just a re-enactment," I replied.

"Oh no, these people are serious about all this."

Beside him stood a plump man wearing a large raincoat. "There's a fella lives down in Johnstown, near here," he said. "In his field a fairy ring has appeared and he simply refuses to plow it. The old superstitions are still prevalent." I returned to the van and had breakfast before heading off to the next ceremony. The mist had cleared and the sun was shining once again.

THE CEREMONY OF WATER

At six o'clock I headed off to St. Patrick's Well for the Ceremony of Water. The old pagan beliefs were always

The Ceremony of Water

B & B S
There are a number of B&Bs on the N2 approach road to Slane from Dublin.

The Failte B&B
Main St.
Slane
Tel: (041) 9824760
Mob: (086) 3984260
Email: thefailtebandb @eircom.net
On the road to Slane castle, this B&B has 6 rooms.

Mattock House
Newgrange
Tel: (041) 9824592
Close to Newgrange just off the N51. Open all year and has 3 rooms.

Boyne View
Dublin Rd.
Tel: (041) 9824121
Lovely Georgian Guesthouse overlooking the Boyne Valley.

Navan:
There are a few B&Bs on the N51 Slane Rd.

The Druids
The Druids were the intelligentsia of ancient Celtic society, best described as a combination of priest and academic, as they most concerned themselves with the acquisition, memorization and transmission of information, particularly such information as has to do with their religious beliefs. They generally served as priests and oracles, acting as intermediaries between the affairs of the gods and men in order to make sure that their people remained in good standing with the divine realm.

Learn more about The Druids in The Mystery: Wizards, Druids & Poets (pp. 129-135, 260).

associated with the elements. They worshiped the things that visibly give us life. Water is one of these.

I arrived at the well to find yet again another large crowd of people gathered around. It was good to see the festival had a good turn out. Yamann Brady was facilitator and once again he was surrounded by **the druids**. Yamann gave a speech about how we as humans are comprised largely of water and how water is the giver of life. Without it we cannot survive. Yamann explained that he was part of an organization called *Slaine*, which is dedicated to relocating all the sacred wells of Ireland and cleaning and reclaiming them for the people. Each well would have a keeper, just like in the pagan days, who would assume responsibility for the well's upkeep. The keeper of St. Patrick's Well was an old man from the Seamrog B&B across the road.

Yamann then invited people to say a prayer or recite poetry, and to my surprise the chubby guy I met earlier stepped forward and recited a poem he had written himself. He didn't look the type to be a poet. He looked just like an ordinary farmer. But he recited a lovely poem that showed he was certainly a lot more than that. Other people stepped forward and recited poetry, sang songs and offered prayers. One girl offered a prayer for the goddess Brigid. Finally, water was passed around for everyone to drink.

THE CEREMONY OF EARTH

After the ceremony I was introduced to Adge, the druid with the goatee I had first seen at the Ceremony of the Sunrise. A newspaper sat on the table with a photo of Adge in front of the *Lia Fáil*. The first

Adge

line stated that Adge was a 21st-century druid. He was originally from Cornwall and came to Ireland during a troubled time in his life, when he was looking for a direction. Soon he met a group of people who belonged to a druidic grove in Leitrim and thus began his journey into the world of Druidism.

Adge explained to me, in his thick Cornish accent, that this was more than a re-enactment. Many of the people here are part of real druidic groves across Ireland and other countries around the world. They are trying to revive the old pagan ways and beliefs. Obviously this doesn't include ritual sacrifices anymore, but is now more about learning the ways of being connected with the earth and all its elements, such as air and water.

"I hate what they have done to Newgrange and Stonehenge," he said. "It's too commercial."

"How long has this festival been going on?" I asked.

"This is the second year. Obviously we want to promote it, but we want people who respect the ceremonies, not people just coming to party."

Adge then bade me farewell and wished me luck before heading off to prepare for another ceremony. He'd been involved in every ceremony so far. During

The Ceremony of Earth

Boyne Dale B&B
Donaghmore
Navan
Tel: (046) 9028015
Situated in full view of the Donaghmore round tower, this country house has 4 rooms and lies on the N51 road to Slane.

Seamrog
Hill of Tara
Tel: (046) 9025296
Situated right across the road from Tara, this little B&B offers 3 rooms (2 en-suite) at very good prices. (Open 1st May to 1st Oct)

Highfield House
Maudlins Rd.
Trim
Tel: (046) 9436386
Web: www. stayathighfield.com
A lovely period guesthouse two mins walk from town and overlooking Trim Castle.

THE JOURNEY
LEINSTER
COUNTY
MEATH

the Ceremony of the Earth he'd held up two branches, one from a holly tree and the other from the oak tree. He'd recited a ritual that explained how the two symbolized the coming of winter and summer.

THE CEREMONY OF AIR

It was midday and I headed off for The Ceremony of Air being performed at the *Lia Fáil* by Michael Gorman, an American druid who wore a long, purple cloak over white robes covering a well-rounded stomach. His fiery-red hair was swept into a center parting and hung to just above his shoulders. He wore small, round glasses and his grey goatee beard contrasted with his red hair. Michael talked about the air being another giver of life, like water. Mika stood behind him providing music on the *bodhrán*, an Irish drum that is held in one hand and beaten by the other hand with a stick. Michael led the crowd in songs and various wailing noises.

The sun was still shining. I looked around me at the other mound and it seemed more radiant. I don't know what it was, but the contour of the enclosure was more defined. I looked around at the rest of Tara and it seemed to be more illuminated than usual. Or perhaps I was getting a little carried away with these ceremonies?

The Ceremony of Air

The Save Tara Campaign: **www.savetaravalley.com**

THE SAVE TARA CAMPAIGN

On my way back to Maguires I met another druid who was taking part in the Save Tara Campaign. He explained that the government had approved plans for a motorway that would run beside the N3 and very close to Tara, bisecting the Tara-Skryne valley and greatly increasing noise, air and light pollution. The pristine mounds of Tara and its surrounds would also be profaned by cheap, touristy elements that would degrade the peaceful dignity of the mounds.

He then went on to explain that he runs a Druid School in Dublin dedicated to teaching people the art of Druidry and offering workshops for healing and spiritual awareness. Later on he showed me a drawing that linked the rising sun with all the ancient monuments in Counties Meath and Louth at various times of the year associated with pagan festivals. What was really interesting was that a line had been drawn at each of the associated times between the sun and the monument, and every time the line intersected with Lambay Island in Dublin Bay. How is it that such a so-called primitive race of people could have mapped this so precisely?

HOSTELS
Slane Farm Hostel
Harlinstown House
Slane
(041) 9884985.
Web:
www.slanefarmhostel.ie
Email: info@
slanefarmhostel.ie
Highly recommended
Slane hostel offers dorm, private and family rooms. Or you can enjoy your own space in their self-catering cottages.

Bridge House Hostel
Bridge St.
Trim
Tel: (046) 9431848
Email: npe@indigo.ie
Excellent hostel in a 600 year old building right beside the Boyne River. All the rooms have a view and are named after this view.

Kells Hostel
The Carrick Kells
Tel: (046) 9249995.
Email: hostels@iol.ie

THE FAIRIES

Outside the window I spotted a couple of teenage girls and a young girl dressed as fairies. It seemed that the fairy storytelling was about to begin, led by Janet Farrar, who is a well-known author on the legends of the fairies. Everyone followed her into the graveyard where she and her fairies sat beneath a tree and recited fairy

Janet Farrar's fairy stories are a perennial favorite for children and adults alike.

stories for the children, as well for the adults who, I must admit, enjoyed them just as much.

After the morning ceremonies I was introduced to Gina McGarry, the facilitator of the Sunrise Ceremony. Gina's American accent betrayed the fact she wasn't a local. She was, however, an Irish-American who held her Sligo ancestors in high regard and was grateful to them for instilling in her a passion for the land and all things Irish. Gina said she would be reciting the stories of the goddesses later that day.

Now, after Janet's wonderful stories, everyone gathered at Rath Gráinne for Gina's goddess walk. Despite the clouds rolling in and threatening rain, we all followed and listened intently as Gina brought the stories of Gráinne, Macha, Boann, and other female Celtic deities to vivid life. I watched the faces in the crowd as they hung upon her every word. She has a real gift for storytelling.

ORION RISING

After dinner I went to the church where two guys gave an astronomy talk which related interesting theories of a link between the constellations and the Irish legends. In particular they showed how the constellation of Orion resembled a warrior in battle and that the sun at the time of the solstice is in the hand of this warrior. They also mentioned a network of ancient roads around Tara that mirrored Orion and also formed the shape of a sword-wielding giant. The Milesian warrior Amergin described himself as a sword-wielding giant, and these guys have developed a theory that this ancient network of roads could be linked to him. The giant figure has his legs planted in the Boyne Valley and the rest stretches over counties Meath and Louth, intersecting at various important mythological and historical places.

It was almost eight by this time and my eyelids felt like lead weights had been tied to them. I attempted to get back to the van for a nap, but it was lashing down with rain and I was also talked into staying for the music by Yamann. I was glad I did because renowned harpist and singer Claire Roche provided some beautiful harp music, followed by more great Irish music.

THE CELEBRATION OF FIRE

At sundown everyone gathered in the churchyard for the Celebration of Fire. This was led by all the druids carrying banners and flags for all the nations joining in the festival. Fire torches were lit and people sang as they made their way to the intersection point of Tara's two main mounds, where everyone formed a large circle. Rituals were performed, a torch was lit in the center of the circle, and each druidic grove announced the country they were

Annual Events Calendar
All events are held once per year unless otherwise noted, and dates will most likely change from year to year. For future dates, visit www.festivals.ireland.ie, email Fáilte Ireland at festivals@failteireland.ie or visit http://ireland.mysteriousworld.com/Journey/ThingsToDo/Festivals/ Festivals are arranged as follows:
✦ Cultural: 445-454
✦ Music: 455-459
✦ Fine Arts: 460-465
✦ Food: 466-469
✦ Sports: 469-473

CULTURAL
Summer Solstice Festival at Tara
Every summer solstice day there is a festival which starts at sunrise and finishes at sunset. Throughout the day there is storytelling, walks and more. See pp. 437-443 for details.

THE JOURNEY
LEINSTER
COUNTY
MEATH

The Celebration of Fire

from, gave thanks and recited a ritual of their own. Michael Gorman then announced that a similar ceremony was being performed in California to coincide with this one.

Once the ceremony was over I gratefully crawled back to the cozy bed in the back of my van. With the setting of the sun it had turned very cold. It would have been nice to have said that the day had led me down the path of true enlightenment. I also would like to have avoided stepping in the ritual offerings of the sheep that roam freely over Tara. I couldn't quite figure out if these people were mad or not, but who is to say who is mad, and who isn't?

All things said and done, it was nice to see that Ireland's ancient traditions were being revived. Personally I felt that this festival is a brilliant way of illustrating Tara's importance in Irish history. Tara was the ancient capitol of Ireland, and this festival can help visitors to understand that Tara is more than just a green hill with lumps upon it. It certainly opened my eyes, and I hoped that The Friends of Tara would be able to stop the government from building a motorway through the area, and retain Tara as a peaceful, spiritual place where visitors can come and revel in the stories and secrets that it holds.

The Hill of Slane

Around ten miles northeast of Tara, off the N51, there is a church on a hill called The Hill of Slane. The hill lies just to the north of the Slane cross roads, and is visible from The Hill of Tara. Legend says that St. Patrick angered the High King Leoghaire by lighting the paschal fire on

The Hill of Slane, where St. Patrick lit the Paschal fire in opposition to druidic tradition.

the Hill of Slane prior to the time set by the Druids at Tara for the start of the pagan festival of Beltaine. This led to a supernatural showdown between the Druids and St. Patrick, which Patrick won easily.

Later, St. Patrick used a shamrock to explain the

St. Patrick

union of the Father, the Son and the Holy Ghost to King Leoghaire while on The Hill of Slane, the shamrock later becoming a national symbol. There are the ruins of a church and 16th-century Franciscan Friary on the hill now, along with a statue of St. Patrick. Slane actually takes its name from Sláine, a king of the Fir Bolg. Legend says that he is buried on that hill.

Email:
info@
dublinpub
crawl.com
This is a guided tour by two actors who performs comical excerpts from Dublin's best-known writers. They visit four pubs over 2 hours 15 mins. The tour starts in the Duke pub, Duke Street. Bookings can be made at the Tourism Centre, Suffolk St.

When:
✛ **Summer** (April – November) Nightly at 7.30 pm Sundays: 12 noon & 7.30 pm
✛ **Winter** (December – March) Thursday, Friday, Saturday, Sunday at 7.30pm. (Also 12 Noon on Sundays)

Dublinia
Christ Church Place Tel (01) 6794611 Web: www.dublinia.ie Lying inside the old synod hall of Christ Church Cathedral, Dublinia is a recreation of medieval

THE JOURNEY
LEINSTER
COUNTY
MEATH

Dublin.
Entrance
fee also
includes
entrance into
the church.
When: Open daily
except Dec. 23-26
& March 17.

**Traditional Irish
Musical Pub Crawl**
Led by two profes-
sional musicians who
perform songs while
telling the story of
Irish music.
Lasts about 2
hrs.
Tel: (01)
4753313
Web: www.
discover
dublin.ie/musicalpub
crawl.html
When: Year-round,
call or see website.

St. Patrick's Festival
St. Stephen's Green
House
Earlsfort Terrace
Dublin 2
Tel: (01)676 3205
Web: www.
stpatricksfestival.ie
Email: info@
stpatricksfestival.ie
When: Annual, dur-
ing week of March 17.

THE JOURNEY
LEINSTER
COUNTY
MEATH

Newgrange

From the *Lia Fáil* at Tara I began my spiral journey outward to the rest of the important archaeological sites of the Brú na Bóinne, and thence to all Ireland. My first stop was the Brú na Bóinne Visitor Centre where I joined a tour group for Newgrange. *Brú na Bóinne* is the Gaelic name given to the area that is home to the three most famous burial mounds in Ireland, and means "Valley of the Boyne". The three burial mounds, or passage cairns, are: Newgrange, Knowth and Dowth. The first two are the most visit-ed, mainly because entrance to Dowth is forbidden, though you can drive yourself to it and walk around and over it — you just cannot enter the chambers.

Against my better judgment I'd had to pay just over €5 for this tour, but as it turned out, it was well worth the money. The group was relatively small and had to be split into two when the tour entered the chamber. Our tour guide gave quite a detailed lecture that lasted nearly half an hour.

Covering an area of one acre, this magnificent monument was built around 3200 BC — over 500 years before the accepted dates for The Great Pyramid of Giza and about the same time as Stonehenge. The façade is decorated with white quartz from as far away as the Wicklow Mountains. But what's even more impressive are the giant kerbstones, of which 97 mark the perimeter. They weigh anywhere from one to twelve tons, and in all 400 were used in the mound's construction. It's been estimated that it would take eighty men three days to move one stone three miles. Many of the kerbstones have been ornately decorated with what is now known as Boyne Valley art. So the question remains, why would anyone go to such great lengths in order to build this mound?

It's widely assumed that Newgrange was built by the Neolithic people, and one would also assume that these people were primitive and lacked the intelligence of modern engineers. But these monuments are a testament to the contrary.

The entrance is blocked by a huge kerbstone that is intricately carved with the images like those I observed inside The Mound of the Hostages. When Newgrange was first built people had to climb over the stone to gain access. When reconstructing the façade during the excavation in the 1960s a decision was reached to alter the entrance slightly to allow steps to be put in for visitors to enter the passage. Otherwise the tomb has been exactly restored to its former glory.

Not only was this burial mound an incredible feat of engineering, but it was also an incredible feat of ingenuity. The entrance is precisely aligned with the rising of the sun at the winter solstice; the sun would align with the entrance to the mound at Dowth (*q.v.*). But its designers were also clever enough to realize it would have to be local dawn, and thus calculate where the sun would rise and how high. In the case of the Boyne Valley the sun would rise over the distant hills. A special "roof box" also was fitted above the en-

Puck Fair
Killorglin
Co. Kerry
One of Ireland's oldest festivals, a traditional horse fair, which includes open air concerts, parades and fireworks.
Tel: 066 9762366
Web:
www.puckfair.ie
E-mail:
info@puckfair.ie
When:
Annual, every August 10-12.

Heritage Week
Tel: 56 777 0777
Web:
www.heritagecouncil.ie
E-mail: mail@heritagecouncil.com
When: Annual, call or email for more details.

The Táin Walking Festival
Take a weekend to explore the spectacular landscape of the Cooley mountains. Virtually undiscovered the weekend will expose you to different walks at all levels.

THE JOURNEY
LEINSTER
COUNTY MEATH

The entrance to the Newgrange complex. In the upper center, above the main entrance, can be seen the "roof box", which lower center can be seen one of the 97 "kerbstones" that surround the monument. This kerbstone is covered with spiral designs whose meaning can only be speculated upon. Image © Nigel Callaghan.

trance for the light to shine through. The main entrance below then takes you through a narrow passageway that leads uphill to an elevation of two meters higher than when you entered. The passageway is 19 meters long, and the floor of the inner chamber is exactly level with the roof box. On the morning of the solstice, sunlight shines through the roof box and travels along the overhead passage, illuminating the inner chamber.

Once our group was assembled in the inner chamber, our guide then turned off the internal lighting. Then, by use of a spotlight from the roof box, he demonstrated how the light would illuminate the chamber. When the lights were turned back on he indicated the corbelled roof. No cement or binding agents were used to fix the stones in place — they had all been stacked like a house of cards. These ancient builders clearly realized that this was the most efficient and best form of support. The capstone is the lightest at two tons. Above that lie four meters of loose rock, then earth and grass. All this was to ensure the watertight integrity of the chamber, and to make sure that moisture would not loosen the rocks in place. All this points to the fact that these so-called primitive people really knew what they were doing.

Inside the chamber there are three recesses wherein cremated remains were found. In all probability the bodies were cremated outside and then the ashes placed inside the chamber. What this was for, no one really knows. There are many theories, but we may never know for sure as these people never left any written history. Stories of occupancy do exist though, and in keeping with the legends of the *sídhe*, the story of Newgrange is that it was once the home of the Dagda, the father god of the Tuatha dé Danann. The Dagda took as his home Newgrange, the greatest of all the fairy mounds. There in his fairy palace he kept his magic harp, *Uaithne*, which would fly into his arms upon command. Visitors could feast from the cauldron with a never-ending supply of food, which could be washed down with the ale that would render the drinker immune to all sickness.

Light from the sun passes directly through the roof box over the entrance to the end of the passage only on the winter solstice. Perhaps the patterns on this kerbstone were meant to mark other times of the year? Image © Knowth.com.

Viking Festival
Athlone
Contact:
Michael
McDonnell
Tel: (090)
6473383/6473392
Mob: (086) 2621136
This festival recaptures the plundering of Clonmacnois and the capture of the Viking King Olaf Scabbyhead. There are re-enactments, music and drinking all weekend. The festival is free.
When: First weekend in July.

Fleadh Nua
Ennis
This colorful traditional Irish festival includes outdoor street entertainment, céilí, set dancing, music and dance workshops, concerts and more
Tel: 065 6840406
Web:
www.fleadhnua.com
Email: ceoltrad@fleadhnua.com
When: Dates vary, see website for latest schedule.

THE JOURNEY
LEINSTER
COUNTY
MEATH

Knowth

Knowth is actually comprised of one large passage tomb surrounded by 18 smaller tombs. Image © Knowth.com.

After the tour we were returned to the Visitor Centre where I boarded a bus for the Knowth tour. Although Newgrange is the most famous and the oldest, Knowth is more impressive in that its large passage tomb is surrounded by 18 smaller tombs. The main tomb covers an area of one acre and has two passageways aligned with the rising and the setting of the sun at the equinoxes. The other difference here is that unlike Newgrange, Knowth was used for centuries after its usage as a passage tomb as a settlement right up until the arrival of the Milesians, whose local chieftain lived upon the main mound in a purpose-built enclosure. Even the Normans used this spot until integrating with the local people and moving into the towns. I wonder if they really knew what it was they were camped upon. By that time the entrances were completely covered over, so it must have simply appeared as a mound of earth

Unfortunately you cannot enter the main chamber as it is not safe, and the west passage is actually blocked by years of excavation. Excavations of Knowth began in 1962 and lasted for 40 years, believe it or not. One of the discoveries was that during the Iron Age the tradition of cremation burials changed to actual body burials. Thirty-five bodies have been found in the area, mostly of women. This gives the impression that it was a matriarchal society around this time.

There are 127 megalithic stones that surround the main mound, acting as a protective barrier. Over the years only three have been lost. Many have carvings similar to the kerbstone at Newgrange, and others like those in The Mound of the Hostages at Tara. A kerbstone on the main mound in Knowth is also known as The Calendar Stone. This beautifully carved stone, seemingly depicting the transition of the moon, illustrates that the builders were great astronomers and well aware of the lunar cycle.

The main mound at Knowth is actually bigger than the Newgrange mound. Yet despite this there isn't as much folklore surrounding it as with Newgrange. The only known mythological association is that it was the home of Englec, the daughter of Lord Elcmar, husband to the goddess Boann.

The eastern passageway in the Great Mound at Knowth. At 40 meters long, it is the longest megalithic passage in western Europe. Image © Knowth.com.

Dancing with Lunasa
Kinnitty
Co. Offaly
This 3-day revival of an ancient Celtic festival celebrating art, music, dance and poetry takes place at Kinnitty Castle on the weekend closest to the ancient Lunasa harvest celebration.
Tel: 0509 37299
Web: www.slievebloom.ie
Email: info@slievebloom.ie
When: Call or see website.

Celtic Spirit Culture Week
Inishmore, Aran Islands, Co. Galway
Cultural week on Celtic Heritage: Holy places, ancient rituals, old myths and legends, early Celtic church etc. with recognised scholars on Celtic heritage.
Tel: 099 61424
Web: www.irish-culture.ch
Email: info@irish-culture.ch
When: Last week of May.

THE JOURNEY
L E I N S T E R
C O U N T Y
M E A T H

Dowth

Dowth isn't open to the public. It's only possible to view it from the outside. But it is possible to drive there yourself and enter the grounds for free, so I did just that.

Although you cannot enter the chamber, it is still possible to wander around the area. I must admit this mound isn't as impressive as the others. It stands 50 feet high. The mound was badly damaged by an excavation in the late 1800s and part of it has collapsed.

This cairn also has two passages at the north and south. The north passage is the longest at 14 meters, but the south passage is only 3.5 meters. More interestingly, the south passage is illuminated by the setting sun on the Winter Solstice, after having illuminated the passage at Newgrange at sunrise.

Dowth means "darkness", which seems to reflect the fact that it is aligned with the setting sun at the winter solstice, and hence the beginning of the longest night of the year. The legends associated with this say that it was built by the druid Bressan, who wanted to build a tower that would reach the sky. His intention was to build it in a day, but obviously this wasn't enough time so he got his sister to cast a spell that stopped time and would allow them to complete the job before sunset. Bressan, obviously very pleased with his sister's work, thanked her in a way that was deemed inappropriate by the gods, and thus the spell was broken. The sun set and the tower was thus never completed. It was then given the name Dowth.

It's worth visiting this mound despite its damage, because you will more than likely be here on your own and not with a group. Also, you won't be rushed out to catch the bus back like I was in Knowth.

Fourknocks Chambered Cairn

Fourknocks Chambered Cairn is a reconstructed cairn with a huge inner chamber that includes unusual carvings.

After a quick visit to the church and high cross at Duleek I headed towards Ardcath and followed the signs to Fourknocks. At the beginning of the pathway was a sign directing you to the house where the key was kept. I was too tired to go searching for a key and decided to just view the cairn through the gate. Unfortunately, this time the gate was solid metal. I was in two minds whether to go get the key or continue on to Trim. In the end I decided to get the key. And I'm glad I did.

The key was available from Mr. Fintan White in a village a mile or so away from the monument. I paid a €20 deposit and returned to the cairn. Once inside I was glad I had made the effort to get the key. Fourknocks, which is dated to around 2000 BC, has a short passage with a huge chamber measuring 18 by 21 feet. It was magnificent. The roof was originally made from timber that rotted away long ago. After its excavation in the 1950s, the cairn was rebuilt with a metal roof, and grass was re-grown on the outside. There are three recesses, and above these are large

MUSIC

Fleadh Cheoil na hÈireann

In 1951, traditional musicians from Dublin met with traditional musicians from Westmeath to start the first annual *fleadh choil*, or national music festival. Today, musicians from the *Fleadh Cheoil na hÈireann* tour worldwide.
Tel: 01 2800295
Web: www.comhaltas.com
Email: enquiries@comhaltas.com
When: Call or see website for details.

Limerick International Band Competition

A truly memorable event where marching/concert bands, choirs and drill teams from Ireland and around the world converge on Limerick City.
Tel: (0)61 209173
Web: www.limerickspringfest.com/comp.htm

THE JOURNEY
LEINSTER
COUNTY
MEATH

stones with zigzags carved into them. This is different from the carvings of the mounds at Newgrange, and are said to resemble patterns on Native American Sioux Indian blankets. Human remains were found here, some cremated and some not. There are twelve carved stones in all, and one of the most interesting is at the right of the passage as you face outwards. Just before the passage begins is a carving said to depict a human face, but it was hard to see in the darkness.

Trim — Heritage Town

The town of Trim lies a few miles west of Navan, on the R161. As I drove into town I was astounded by the views of ruined medieval castles everywhere. I pulled up at the Bridge House Hostel, which sits right beside the River Boyne. Views from my room were spectacular. The owner, Frank, was a comical character whom I began to suspect was a leprechaun. He was short with a slight stoop, a mop of grey hair and a scruffy grey beard. As he giggled I suddenly imagined him with a pipe in his mouth and it all seemed to fit.

Frank pointed me across the road to a pub called Bounty Bar, where he said many famous Irish musicians play. Dermot O'Brien, a famous accordion player, was due to play there the following weekend. Frank also said that one of The Dubliners is from the area and a frequent visitor to the pub and the hostel. He then let me listen to a voicemail that he had left on Frank's phone.

The pub life in Trim is quite lively. There are a couple of modern pubs with contemporary music, one just across the bridge overlooking the river. I decided to stick to the nice traditional Bounty Bar across the road, which had an Irish music session. It was the first year of the smoking ban in places of work, which included pubs and restaurants. The government had brought in the ban at the beginning of the summer, so the smokers were going

Trim Castle is the largest medieval castle in Europe, and was a setting for the movie *Braveheart*.

outside and beer gardens were becoming very popular. It's typical of the Irish to find something good in something bad, and in this case they were saying that since the ban they are congregating outside and making new friends that inside they would probably never have thought of speaking to. However, I wondered if this positive attitude would continue when the winter sets in and going out in the cold and the rain to smoke would still be fun. After a few pints of Guinness the music was in full swing. The great thing about traditional sessions is that it is so informal. The musicians sit around the bar tables just like everyone else, drink beer and play their music. It's one of the reasons I love coming back to Ireland.

One of the highlights of Trim town is Trim Castle, which was founded in 1173 by Hugh de Lacy. It's the largest Norman castle in Europe and has been fully restored, and has even made an appearance in a movie: *Braveheart*. Entrance is available by guided tour. The original motte and bailey was destroyed by Rory O'Conner (*Ruaidhri ó Conchobhair*), the last High King of Ireland. The castle was then rebuilt by De Lacy's grandson-in-law around 1200, and has remained as you see it today. Just south in the village of Clonard there is another good example of a Norman motte built under the direction of Hugh de Lacy and standing 50 feet high, and a nearby church was built upon a 6th century monastic settlement established by St. Finian.

Waterford Int'l Festival of Light Opera
Waterford City
Co. Waterford
Competitive musical festival for amateur musical societies.
Tel: 051 375437
Web: www.waterfordfestival.com
E-mail: seandower@eircom.net
When: Starts in late September every year. call or see website for details.

Cork Int'l Choral Festival
Programme includes the Fleischmann International trophy competition, a full range of national competition's for schools, youth and adult choirs. A seminar on contemporary choral music and extensive fringe events.
Tel: 021 4223535
Web: www.corkchoral.ie
Email: chorfest@iol.ie
When: Last week of April, call or see website for latest info.

Wexford Festival Opera
Wexford City
Co. Wexford
The Wexford Festival specializes in the production of rare operas and also features a range of other cultural activities.
Tel: 053 22400
Web: www.wexfordopera.com
E-mail: info@wexfordopera.com
When: Call or see website for details.

Cork Jazz Festival
Cork City
A four-day jazz music festival with a variety of well known international jazz artists.
Tel: 01 6375219
Web: www.corkjazzfestival.com
E-mail: jazz@questcom.iol.ie
When: Last weekend in October every year.

THE JOURNEY
LEINSTER
COUNTY
MEATH

Kells

The Market Cross at Kells, now in front of the Kells Heritage Center.

"The ancestors of the family who donated *The Book of Kells* to Trinity College now want it back here in the Heritage Centre," said the lady behind the counter at the Kells Heritage Centre.

"Won't the college release it to you?" I asked.

"No, they say it will not be safe enough, but we have made all the necessary security precautions."

I suspected it was more a case of Trinity College not wanting to part with its most prized possession and largest tourist attraction. It must make them a lot of money each year.

She went on to explain that Kells is unusual in that it had five high crosses, while most towns have four. "High crosses were used to mark the entrances to the market towns in ancient times," she said.

The Market Cross sits outside the centre, covered over with a Perspex roof to protect it from the elements. I was directed inside where I watched an audiovisual on the town's history, while a group of noisy children ran about upstairs, then wandered into the next room where there was a replica of the Market Cross, despite the fact that the real one is just outside. The real cross was originally located in Cross

Street, but was moved and repaired after being damaged by a car. Upstairs there are replicas of artifacts found in the area on display. The real ones are in the National Museum.

Back outside I got talking to a man named Willie, who was quite active with the town's historical society.

"You know, everyone thinks that these passage tombs, ancient crosses and sites are all a mystery, but it's all quite simple really. These people were just telling their stories, or making their mark on the world just like we do, but in different ways," he said.

An interesting point.

Willie went on to explain the origins of the town's name: "The Irish name for Kells is *Ceanannus Mór*. But the original name was *Cul Dun Silbrinne*, which literally translates as 'The Corner of the House of the Adultress'."

"Do you know of any early legends here?" I asked.

"Well, the earliest account of this area is of a great warrior known as Nemedius who settled here in 2500 BC. The ancient district of Kells was known then as the Plain of Magh-Seredh. There is also an interesting legend called the Puck of Lloyd."

"Oh, what's that then?"

"The Puck of Lloyd was a half-man, half-goat who terrorized the community. In 1798 Captain Malloy led a cavalry charge against the Irish rebels and was killed. He was buried on the Hill of Lloyd, just outside town but it is said that his tortured soul created this monster. Eventually his body was moved to town and the monster was seen no more. The hill is just outside of town on the Oldcastle Road. Clyte is the ancient name for the Hill of Lloyd, and there is a mock lighthouse on the hill built in 1798 by the first Earl of Bective in memory of his father."

459

Willie Clancy Summer School
Miltown Malbay
Co. Clare
Summer school of traditional music.
Tel: 065 7084148/ 065 7084281
Web: www.setdancing news.net/wcss/
E-mail: angleann @oceanfree.net
When: Every July.

All Ireland Busking Festival
Dundrum
Street circus, children's shows, Viking longboats and a prize for the best buskers.
Tel: (028) 4375 1528
Web: www.allireland buskingcompetition .com
When: Every August.

Blackstairs Blues Festival
Tel.: 054-35364
Web: www.black stairsblues.com
email: enquiry@ blackstairsblues.com
When: Every Sept.

THE JOURNEY
LEINSTER
COUNTY
MEATH

FINE ARTS

Dublin Theatre Festival

Various venues in Dublin: www.dublin theatrefestival.com/venues/

An annual festival of *avant-garde* theatre productions, includes world premieres of Irish and international playwrights.

Tel: 01 6778439

Web: www.dublintheatre festival.com

E-mail: info@dublin theatrefestival.com

When: Every October. Call or see website for latest info.

Bloomsday Festival

James Joyce Centre and various venues in Dublin. A festival to celebrate Joyce and his masterpiece, *Ulysses*. Includes readings, re-enactments and street theatre.

Tel: 01 8788547

Web: www.jamesjoyce.ie

THE JOURNEY

LEINSTER

COUNTY MEATH

The Hill of Lloyd

I made notes of all this and then headed off as the centre was about to close. I drove out of town and parked up on the Hill of Lloyd, where there is a lovely view of the town. Queen Maeve camped here in Kells during her journey to the Cooley Peninsula during the *Táin Bó Cuailgne*.

COLMCILLE'S CHURCH

I stayed the night in the Kells Holiday Hostel and in the morning headed out to see the Kells Church beside the Oldcastle Road, which is a Protestant church standing on the site of the original monastic site established by St. Colmcille. Around the 6th century Kells was owned by the High King Diarmuid Mac Fergusso Cerrbheoil of the Uí Neill clan, that ruled Ireland for many centuries. Diarmuid was apparently a cousin of St. Colmcille. They weren't the best of friends, but in the end Diarmuid gave Colmcille the palace at Kells in compensation for some of the bad things he'd done to him over the years. Straightaway Colmcille marked out his area and established his monastery there.

In *The Annals of Ulster* it is recorded that a new church was established in the 9th century for the monks of Iona to flee to. Here they completed *The Book of Kells*, but still they were subjected to frequent Viking attacks. The core of this monastery is located in the present day church grounds.

Beside the side gate is a 1000-year-old round tower with its conical roof missing. Beside this is The Cross of Patrick and Columba, which is the oldest of the five that once stood here and stands 11 feet high. It actually has an inscription dedicating it to the two saints. Just along from this is the shaft of a cross, and also the base of another. Beside the church is an unfinished cross with the top half of its head missing. All of these crosses are beautifully inscribed with biblical scenes from both the Old and New Testaments. The unfinished cross depicts the crucifixion on the center of the unfinished head. It seemed that Willie was right in that the people who carved these crosses simply wanted to leave their mark — in this case, the mark of Christianity. Upstairs inside the church is a display explaining all the carvings of each cross.

Colmcille's Church is surrounded by several high crosses and a round tower.

Email: info@ jamesjoyce.ie
When: Week of June 16th.

Yeats Winter & Summer Schools
Sligo Park Hotel
Pearse Road, Sligo
The Winter School is a weekend of lectures and a tour of Yeats country. The Summer School is a much more elaborate affair, lasting for 12 days and running concurrently with the Yeats Festival.
Tel: 071 91 42693
Web: www.yeats-sligo.com
Email: info@ yeats-sligo.com
When: Call or see website for schedule.

St. Patrick's Festival & Cross Community Carnival Parade
Downpatrick, Co. Down & Armagh, Co. Armagh
Tel: 028 4461 9000
Web: www.st-patricks dayfestival.com
When: Week of March 17.

THE JOURNEY
LEINSTER
COUNTY
MEATH

COLMCILLE'S HOUSE

Beyond the other side of the church wall, on the north side, is Colmcille's House. I wandered out the other gate in the southwest corner of the churchyard, and walked up the road to it. Colmcille's House is 1,200 years old and not only is it built entirely of stone, even the steep, sloping roof is built of stone. It sits on a residential street among all the modern houses and stands out like a giant at a leprechaun convention.

A sign on the gate said that the key can be obtained from Mrs. Carpenter at Lower Church View. I wandered the entire length of the street looking for this house, but couldn't see a sign anywhere. Finally — possibly concerned as to why this strange man was studying all the houses in the street — a lady popped her head out of the window.

"Are you looking for something?" she asked.

"Yes, I'm looking for Mrs. Carpenter at Lower Church View," I replied.

"Oh you want the key to Colmcille's House!" she exclaimed.

I nodded.

"It's the house at the bottom with the brown door."

I thanked her and wandered back down the street.

There was only one house with an old brown front and a brand-new brown door. This had to be it. I knocked, and after a few minutes a tiny old lady opened the door.

"I understand you have the key to Colmcille's House," I said.

"If you wait up there I'll be up in a minute," she replied.

So I wandered back up and took some photos while I waited. When Mrs. Carpenter came she unlocked the door and we went inside. It was completely empty except for a tall metal ladder that led up to a small hole in the roof. I climbed the ladder but found I couldn't get through with my backpack on. The ladder was so steep that I didn't dare try to take it off while up there, so I came back down and took it off. Back at the top I was able to get through and found a stone attic. It was wedged right at the top of the sloping roof. There wasn't enough room to stand up, but I was able to crawl along and look through the small windows at each end.

The house was built in the 9th century, 300 years after Colmcille lived. It was obvious that the house wasn't built for him, but was more likely a small church or oratory. Perhaps this was where *The Book of Kells* was written, up in this tiny attic away from the sight of invading Vikings.

Cork Int'l Film Festival
An eight-day festival of Irish and international films, workshops, seminars and book launches.
Tel: 021 4271711
Web:
www.corkfilmfest.org
E-mail:
info@corkfilmfest.org
When: Every first Sunday in October.

Waterford Spraoi
Multi arts festival that features a program of international street theatre and music. Most events are held outdoors and are free of charge.
Tel: 051 841808
Web:
www.spraoi.com
E-mail:
info@spraoi.com
When: Every August Bank Holiday weekend (first Monday in August).

Galway International Arts Festival
Ireland's premier multidisciplinary arts festival.

THE JOURNEY
LEINSTER
COUNTY
MEATH

Tel: 091 509700
Web:
www.galway
artsfestival.ie
E-mail: info@
galwayartsfestival.ie
When: Every July.
Call or see website
for latest info.

Earagail Arts Festival
100 events through-
out Donegal —
music, drama, art,
readings, chil-
dren's event
and open air
celebrations.
Tel: 074
9168800

Web: www.
earagailartsfestival.ie
Email: info@eaf.ie
When: Every July.
Call or see website
for latest info.

**Dancing Thru' The
Ages — The Show**
Hall Arts Centre
Youghal, East Cork
A fresh and exciting
show that intends to
capture the culture
of Irish music, song
and dance.
Tel: 024 92571

Outskirts of Kells

Colmcille's Well

On the way back to the van I bumped into Willie and a friend of his.

"How's it going?" he asked.

"Great," I replied. "I've just been inside Colmcille's House. It's amazing to think that the monks might have worked on *The Book of Kells* in that tiny attic."

Willie lit a cigarette and sat down beside the church wall. "Well, I'll tell you something else," he said. "We've recently discovered a new souterrain nearby. It's not open to the public yet as it's still too danger-ous. But when I crawled down inside I found the most amazing thing. Inside the tunnel there is a small recess just large enough for someone to sit in. I sat in it, and directly opposite is another recess the exact shape and size of a book. It almost looks as if it was built for someone to flee with a book, place it in the recess and then sit and guard it."

This was interesting. It could have been the hiding spot for *The Book of Kells*.

"Where are you headed to now?" asked Willie.

"I'm going to St. Ciarán's Well and then heading to Loughcrew."

"Colmcille's Well is just outside of town here," said

Willie. "The town gathered there recently to recite the Rosary." Willie then gave me directions, and then I bade them both farewell.

COLMCILLE'S WELL

I continued up the Oldcastle Road and as I hit the outskirts of town, I spotted the small lane on the left beside the last house on the row. As Willie had said, there was a wooden pallet sitting at the entrance. I parked the van and headed down the lane, which took me down beside the field and eventually ended at the well. It was a lovely well with a small stone shelter erected over it, and the water was clean. I took a drink and sat there for a while to let the sun warm my face.

CASTLEKEERAN HIGH CROSSES

I returned to the van and continued along the Oldcastle Road for a few miles before coming to a sign pointing right for Castlekeeran High Crosses. I followed this country road for a few miles and eventually came to a sign beside a farmhouse on the right pointing into a field for the high crosses. I parked outside the house and climbed over the gate.

Castlekeeran High Crosses

Web:
www.
dancingthru
theages.com
Email:
info@dancingthru
theages.com
When: July – Aug., every Wed. and Thurs.

Cahersiveen Celtic Festival of Music and The Arts
Co. Kerry
Musical entertainment, art exhibitions, workshops in Irish music, dance and language, children's entertainment and walks.
Tel: 066 9472043
Web: www.
celticmusicfestival.com
When: Call or see website for latest info.

Sligo Live
Sligo City
Annual concerts and sessions w/big-name acts and pub ceílíers.
Tel: 086 8197929
Web: www.sligolive.ie
Email:
info@sligolive.ie
When: Call or see website for latest info.

THE JOURNEY
LEINSTER
COUNTY
MEATH

THE JOURNEY
L E I N S T E R
C O U N T Y
M E A T H

In the middle of the field, close to a river, is a small graveyard enshrouded by trees. There was a monastery set up here by St. Ciarán in 770. It was plundered by Vikings in 949 and burned down by Dermot MacMurrough in 1170. Nothing really remains of the monastery now, but there are a few damaged and undecorated, but interesting high cross-es. There is also an Ogham stone in the middle bear-ing the inscription, *Covagni Maqi Mucoi Luguni* (I know, I couldn't pronounce it either). A nearby plaque says it translates as "C. Descendant (?) of L". I wasn't sure if that was the full translation or only part. There is also said to be another high cross in the river, believed to have been stolen by Colmcille and then thrown in the river when chased by Ciarán. I wan-dered along the river beside the grounds, but I could-n't find it.

St. Ciaran's Well

St. Ciaran's Well

I drove on a little further down the road until I came to St. Ciarán's Well on the right. This was without doubt the most beautiful well I'd seen yet. It sits beside a flowing river at the foot of a small green hill. At the top of the hill is an oratory built in the 1900s, full of statues of the Vir-gin Mary and other

St. Ciaran's Well has a special recess in the rock which is believed to help cure back problems.

gifts and personal effects left there to cure an ailment. The sun was still shining, and once the teenagers went, the scene was very peaceful.

Nearby the well is a small, rounded recess in the limestone rock, which is said to cure back problems. So I thought I'd give it a go. I sat down. It wasn't very comfortable. Still, as the saying goes, "no pain, no gain". Once again I let the sun warm my face as I listened to river running, crows cawing and the birds singing.

The story is that the well was produced by a miracle of St. Ciarán's. There are actually several sections around the main well where water rises up from the ground among the limestone outcrops. Different sections have different curative properties. The water was cold and beautifully clear, and tasted delicious. I then lay down on the grass and enjoyed the sun and the tranquility of the area for a while. When traveling we are often in such a hurry that we forget to just stop and enjoy the simple beauty of places like this.

E-mail: festival@irishcoffeefestival.com
When: Call or see website for latest info.

Bantry Mussel Fair Seafood Festival
Bantry, Co. Cork
Open air free concert at Wolfe Tone Square. Special family events.
Tel: 027 50360
Web: www.bantry.ie
Email: mycommunity@bantry.ie
When: During the second week of May.

Galway Oyster Festival
A food festival, the highlight of which is the Guinness "World Oyster Opening Championship".
Tel: 091 522066
Web: www.galwayoysterfest.com
E-mail: info@galwayoysterfest.com
When: The last weekend of September.

THE JOURNEY
LEINSTER
COUNTY
MEATH

Fethard
Street
Party and
Seafood
Festival
Fethard on Sea
Co. Wexford
Tel.: 051-397502 /
051-397611

**Wicklow County
Gardens Festival**
Forty gardens large
and small throughout
Co. Wicklow open
their doors to the
public.
Tel:
0404 20070
Web: www.
visitwicklow.ie/
Gardens.htm
Email:
info@visitwicklow.ie
When: April-August,
call or see website for
latest info.

Strawberry Fair
Enniscorthy
Co. Wexford
Ten days of fun,
music and craic to
celebrate the annual
Strawberry harvest.
Tel: 054-33256
Web: www.
strawberryfestival.ie
When: Call or see
website for latest info.

THE JOURNEY
LEINSTER
COUNTY
MEATH

Loughcrew

Cairn T, the main mound at Carnbane East, atop *Slieve na Calliagh* at Loughcrew. Cairn T is surrounded by six smaller cairns. The backstone of the main passage in Cairn T is lit by the sun only two days per year, on the vernal and autumnal equinoxes. This is similar to Newgrange, except there the backstone is illuminated only one day of the year, during the winter solstice.

The old man stood in his garden, shotgun in hand and face staring at me with a fixed smile. I had pulled over the van outside a house to clear up some stuff that had fallen out the back cupboard after a very sharp turn. When I got back in the front seat I spotted him. I waved, and he waved back and continued to stare and smile. I wasn't sure if he was sizing me up as a potential target, or waiting for me to leave so he could shoot the crows in his garden. I didn't wait around to find out.

CARNBANE EAST

I was en-route to Loughcrew, and in particular, *Slieve na Caillaigh* ("The Hill of the Witch"), located just south of Oldcastle. It lies at the highest point in County Meath and contains in all 25 passage cairns spread over three hills. I followed the R163 and then followed the Loughcrew signs until I came across a car park. A sign said that the key to the main cairn is available from Loughcrew Gardens. So I headed back down the hill, turned right and soon found them on the left.

"I'm afraid a woman already has them," said the lady behind the counter.

So, I got in the van and drove back to the car park. As I set foot on the base of the hill I saw two women coming down. I waited and then asked if they had the key. They did, but unfortunately they couldn't simply give me the key because they had left a large deposit at the gardens. So I had to follow them back in order to have the key transferred to me.

Back at the car park once again I walked up to the main cairn on Carnbane East, closely followed by an English couple who had come for the key just after. This is The Hill of the Witch, and the main cairn on top is surrounded by six other smaller cairns, much like Knowth. The cairns on these hills are imaginatively labeled with letters of the alphabet. The main mound here is Cairn T. It's 113 meters in diameter and the entrance is aligned with the rising sun at the equinoxes. What I found great about these monuments is that they had remained untouched by tourism. You didn't have to pay and join a tour group to see them. The panoramic view from the top was of rolling, green valleys. The other cairns on Carnbane West are also visible.

I unlocked the gate and we each crawled down the narrow passage until we reached the chamber. There were three recesses, and the recess opposite the entrance contained a beautiful backstone carved with an array of artwork similar to those at Knowth. It must look fantastic when the sun hits it. This is just one of 27 decorated stones within the chamber itself.

The chamber was similar to that at Newgrange,

All
Ireland
Football Final
Dublin
The annual
National Gaelic
Football
Championship Final.
Tel: 01 8363222
Web: www.gaa.ie
Email: queries@gaa.ie
When: Call or see
website for latest info.

**Dublin City
Marathon**
A marathon
through the
historic streets
and scenic
suburbs of
Ireland's capitol city.
Tel: 01 6232250
Web: www.dublincity
marathon.ie
Email:
bhaa@eircom.net
When: Call or see
website for latest info.

**Galway Races
Summer Festival**
Ireland's most illus-
trious racing event.
Tel: 091 753870
Web:
www.galwayraces.com
Email: information
@galwayraces.com

The "Equinox Stone" of Cairn T that is lit by the sun every equinox.
The exact meaning of its symbols is still a mystery.

with a corbelled roof, which was re-roofed back in the 1960s. Despite having to crawl along the passage, once inside the chamber we could stand up complete-ly. Along with the keys, the lady at the gardens had also provided a large torch so we could see all around and inside the recesses.

The name "Carnbane" comes from *Carnbán*, which means "White Cairn". This seems to refer to the white quartz crystal that surrounds an inner layer of the cairn and its kerbstones. Cairn T is surrounded by 37 kerb-stones and the two largest sit either side of the entrance. To the right a little is another large kerbstone with a cut-out on the top. This is known as The Hag's Chair.

This chair has several legends attached to it. The first is of Queen Tailltiu or Queen Maeve having sat in this chair and proclaimed the laws to the people. But the more poignant and interesting is that of the *Cailleach Bhéarra*. The *cailleach*, which is Irish for "witch" or "hag", used to sit in this chair and smoke her pipe and survey her land. Another story tells of how the witch collected stones inside her apron and leapt onto each hill dropping stones as she landed,

Slieve na Callaigh ("The Hill of the Witch") features a druid's chair-like cut kerbstone believed to have been used by a local witch.

which created the cairns. Local folklore says that if you sit in the chair and make a wish, it will come true.

The smaller cairns around it aren't as intact as the main one. But they are interesting nonetheless. The main difference between Loughcrew and the *Brú na Bóinne* complex is that the cairns are covered with grey rocks and earth. Newgrange and Knowth are smooth with grassy tops.

I had to return the keys to the Loughcrew Gardens before closing time, so reluctantly I headed off. At the gardens I had a drink and a bite to eat in the coffee shop. I also bought a book called *Loughcrew, the Cairns* by Jean McMann. It was a good book and mentioned that nearby the car park is a gate where you can access the field and walk up to Carnbane West. I asked the lady behind the counter if there was a key to the cairn here, but there wasn't. "It's on private land," she said.

I drove back up the hill and just before the car park spotted the double gate on the left. I parked the van and climbed over. The cairn was visible on the distant hill so I walked over to it, keeping an eye out for the smiling farmer with a shotgun.

When: Call or see website for latest info.

Clifden Connemara Pony Show
Clifden
Co. Galway
World's largest showing of the Connemara Pony.
Tel: 095 21863
Web: www.cpbs.ie
Email: enquiries @cpbs.ie
When: Every year in August — call or see website for latest info.

Tralee Races
Tralee
Co. Kerry
The Tralee August meeting is the centerpiece of the International Rose of Tralee Festival (see p. 452).
Tel: 066 7126490
Web: www.traleehorseracing.com
E-mail: traleeraces @hotmail.com
When: Call or see website for latest info.

THE JOURNEY
LEINSTER
COUNTY
MEATH

Carnbane West is comprised of two large cairns surrounded by ten smaller cairns. And lots of sheep.

CARNBANE WEST

There are two large cairns here surrounded by ten smaller satellites. Cairn L, which is the one that is visible from the road, is magnificent. It is aligned to the November and February cross-quarter days (Samhain and Imbolg). It has a diameter of 133 meters and the entrance is tall enough to walk into without having to crouch. The interior is much larger than the one in Cairn T. Forty-one kerbstones surround the mound. I was so disappointed that you couldn't gain access anymore. This was by far the more interesting of the two. According to the book the chamber has 7 burial recesses.

Cairn D is the larger mound to the west, with a diameter of 163 meters. It has partially collapsed and according to the book there is no actual chamber, which begs the question, what was it used for? Some say it was a ceremonial mound to honor the memory of someone important, but whose body was not buried there.

Many of the other ten cairns were damaged, but some magnificent kerbstones and chamber stones still remained. I was saddened by the fact that the landowner allowed his sheep to roam freely over these ancient

monuments, and cause even more damage to them.

It really is a mystery as to the reason these monuments were built. It's clear that the builders worshiped the sun, or believed that the sun had the power to regenerate. Were these cairns simply put there for burials? Did the people believe that the sun would regenerate the souls of the dead, or transport them to the next life? Or were they used for a deeper purpose?

Cairn L at Carnbane West is aligned to the November and February cross-quarter days, one of the deeper mysteries of Celtic ritual.

THE JOURNEY
LEINSTER
COUNTY
MEATH

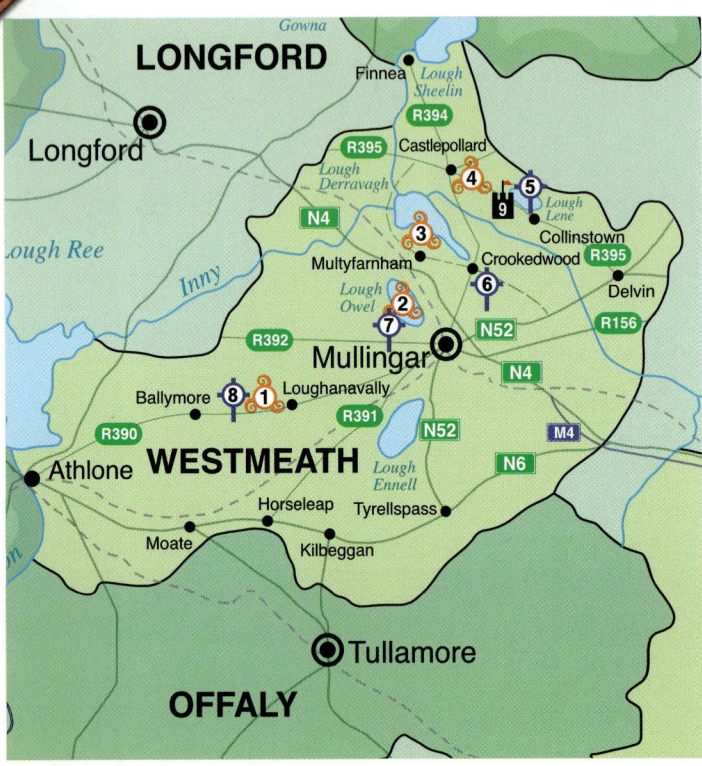

Places to See in Westmeath

Driving Directions: Instructions for driving to Fore Valley, Lough Derravagh, the Hill of Uisneach and St. Brigid's Well are given on pp. 475, 477

Westmeath
The Seven Wonders of Fore

St. Fechin's Monastery, Fore Valley

In the tiny village of Fore, just across the border with Meath, is the small monastic settlement established by St. Fechin in AD 630. Sitting on the hill above the valley are the remains of his church. This is different from most other monastic settlements in that it is said that the saint performed many supernatural wonders during its construction, giving rise to the legend of The Seven Wonders of Fore:

1. The Stone Raised by St. Fechin's Prayers
2. The Anchorite in a Stone
3. The Tree that won't Burn
4. The Water that won't Boil
5. The Mill without a Race
6. The Water that Flows Uphill
7. The Monastery in a Bog

Westmeath
Things to Do & Places to See

Fore Valley
Just right off the R195 from Castlepollard to Oldcastle. For the key to the Anchorite's Church ask at the Seven Wonders Pub.

The Hill of Uisneach
Just before Killare village as you travel the R390 between Mullingar and Athlone. Look for the brown sign in a lay-by on the left. The hill of is on the right of the road though, and not the left as the sign would indicate.

St. Brigid's Well
Killare
Just beyond the Uisneach Inn on the right. A lovely place in the grounds of a ruined church.

Mullingar Tourist Office
Market House
Tel: (044) 48650
Web: www.west
meathtourism.com
Email: info@west
meathtourism.com

Athlone Castle Visitor Centre
St. Peter's Square.
Tel: (090) 6494630

Lough Derravaragh Boat Hire Donore Shore
Tel: (044) 71500
Mob: (086) 8230363
Contact: Paul Smith
Email: camping@iol.ie
Located at the campsite, here you can hire a rowing boat or motor boat for anywhere between two hours to the whole day and explore this legendary lake. Packed lunches, hot food and fishing equipment are also available.

1. The Stone Raised by St. Fechin's Prayers

A massive, solid-stone lintel with a Greek cross inside a circle inscribed upon it tops the entrance to the ruined church on this hill. Local legend says that St. Fechin used the power of prayer to supernaturally lift the lintel onto its two supporting stones to form the doorway, thus creating the first wonder. The walls of the church are three feet thick.

2. The Anchorite in a Stone

Nearby is the Anchorite Church, which was built upon an original cell for hermits. It was used right up until the 17th century. The church was locked, but apparently the key is available from the nearby Seven Wonders Pub. To be honest I couldn't be bothered to climb back up the hill once down there, so I would advise anyone wanting to see inside to get the key first. The Anchorite in a Stone is said to be the second wonder, and I assumed it was inside the church.

3. The Tree that Won't Burn

Beside the road is a tree next to a holy well. The original tree is dead, but the stump remains next to the newer tree that had been planted to replace it. The tree usually has "clooties" tied to it for healing, as well as coins pushed into its bark for good luck. Clooties are special rags that you must rub across the infected part of your body, then tie to the tree near a holy well to effect a cure. I imagined this was done instead of having to damage a piece of your own clothing. It is also believed that the wood from this tree will never burn. I was very tempted to test this belief, but feared the wrath of the locals should I find otherwise.

4. The Water that Won't Boil

Next to the tree is a holy well. Not only is the water believed to have curative properties, it is also believed that the water from the holy well won't boil.

5 & 6. The Mill without a Race & the Water that Flows Uphill

A path leads down to a field and runs alongside the remains of the old mill. The story goes that the original mill on this site was built by St. Fechin, who then performed yet another miracle causing water to flow underground from Lough Lene, a mile away, and uphill to this mill. This formed wonders five and six.

Further down the path is an old ash tree with a small, square, stone structure. St. Fechin is said to have built it and back then it was filled with water. Through the power of prayer he would immerse the children in the water to cure their ailments.

7. The Monastery in a Bog

The final and more recent wonder is the Benedictine Priory built on a bog. It's by far the biggest structure in the area and was built around the 13th century by the De Lacy family.

Land of Lake & Legend

Lough Derravagh is shaped like a swan in flight, and is the setting for the legend of The Children of Lir.

It was evening when I arrived at the shores of Lough Derravaragh. I had followed signs from Multyfarnham to a campsite next to the lake.

Lough Ennell Lilliput Boat Hire Jonathan Swift Park, Lilliput
Tel: (044) 9226167
Mob: (086) 8286849
Web: www.lilliputboathire.com
Email: lilliputboathire@ireland.com

M.V. Ross
Jolly Mariner Marina Athlone
Tel: (090) 6472892
A ninety minute cruise on the Shannon River.

Viking Tours
7 St. Mary's Place Athlone
Tel: (090) 6473383/6473392
Mob: (086) 2621136
Web: www.iol.ie/wmeathtc/viking/
Email: vikingtours@ireland.com
Daily trips on Lough Ree and along the River Shannon to Clonmacnois. Live commentary on ancient battles and tales of buried treasure.

**Lough
Derravaragh
Caravan and
Camping Park**
Multifarnham
Mullingar
Tel: (044) 71500
Mob: (086) 8230363

The Wry Mil
9, Oliver Plunkett St.
Tel: (044)
49544/48635
Nice little
café that also
does B&B.

**Bam Bou
Café & Asian
Restaurant**
Church St.
Athlone
Tel: (090) 6491715
Great little place
opposite the
church, offering tra-
ditional Chinese
and Thai food.

The Riverside Inn
4/5 Castle St.
Athlone
Tel: (090) 6494981
Nice pub in the cen-
tre of town, also has
a restaurant and
carvery.

At the front of the campsite was a little café that also serves as the reception for the campground. It was late when I arrived and thankfully the friendly owners allowed me to squeeze in.

"We have very little room for tourers," explained the man. "The site is mostly full of private caravans."

"Do you not normally take them, then?" I asked.

"Well, we do take some, but we have limited space. It's best to phone ahead first to see if we can fit you in. But if people like yourself turn up late we'll try to squeeze you in. We wouldn't want to see anyone stranded."

I shook his hand and thanked him. He only charged me €5 for the night. "When I stayed in the site south of Mullingar last year, they charged me €15," I told him.

He shook his head in disgust. "That's daylight robbery," he said.

He directed me to an area where I could find a spot overlooking the lake, then explained where all the facilities were. I thanked him, parked the van and cooked some dinner. There is nothing better after a long day than arriving somewhere where you instantly feel welcome, rather than somewhere that just takes your money.

After dinner I wandered down to the shore. The sun had gone down and a milky twilight partially lit the lake. I wandered to the end of the wooden pier and sat down. The only sounds that could be heard was the lapping of the water against the nearby boats, the beating wings of the bats flying over my head, and the singing of a small group of swans whose silhouettes were just visible in the distance. Lough Derravaragh is 8 kms. long and shaped like a swan in flight, so it is quite fitting that one of Ireland's most beautiful but tragic tales should have its origins here: the Children of Lir (*op. cit.*).

In the morning I headed off into Mullingar. On the way I pulled off the N4 into a car park beside another great lake, Lough Owel. At four miles long and two miles wide, it's not as big as Derravaragh, but just as beautiful. Like Derravaragh, Lough Owel is believed to be a magical lake, and is rich in folklore. The lake has four islands and one of them is Church Island, where there are remains of a small oratory called St. Loman's Church. *Lughnasa* assemblies were often held here in ancient times. This involved immersing cattle in the water to ensure health and well being for the year to come.

The Hill of Uisneach

The Hill of Uisneach is the symbolic center of Ireland and has played host to many major historical and legendary events.

The first battle fought between the Milesians and the Tuatha dé Danann was led by Èriu, wife of the Tuatha Dé King Mac Gréine. She was defeated and mortally wounded in the battle, but Amergin granted her a dying wish: He promised her that the island would bear her name forever, a promise that was fulfilled. The Gaelic name Èriu was later changed by the Vikings into "Èriu's Land", or "Ireland".

Grogans Bar and Restaurant
Glasson, Nr Athlone
Tel: (090) 6485158/ 6485770
Open Mon-Sat 12-9 pm, Sun 1-8 pm.
Just north of Athlone, comes highly recommended by locals.

Fore Abbey Coffee Shop
Tel: 044 61780

PUBS
Sean's Bar
Main St. Athlone
Tel: (090) 6492358
Claims to be the oldest bar in Ireland, and they argue this out on radio with the Brazen Head in Dublin.

The Uisneach Inn
Killare
Uisneach
Tel: (044) 56215
A great little pub on the R390 road between Athlone and Mullingar just past the Hill of Uisneach. Also serves bar food.

TRAINS
Mullingar Station
10 minutes walk
from town centre.
Tel: 044-48274
Athlone Station
Tel: (090) 6473300

BUSES
Athlone Bus Station
Tel: (090)
6473300

DRIVING
Mullingar sits
in the centre
of Ireland just
off the N4. From
Kells take the N52.
From Navan take
the N51 and join
the N52. From
Oldcastle take the
R195 to Castlepollard
and around Lough
Derravaragh.

CAR HIRE
Hamills Rent-A-Car
Dublin Road,
Mullingar. Co.
Westmeath
Tel: (044) 44500

THE JOURNEY
LEINSTER
COUNTY
WESTMEATH

I was sitting next to The Cat Stone on The Hill of Uisneach, which lies beside the R390 between Mullingar and Athlone. According to legend, this great rock is said to be the burial spot of Queen Èriu, after whom this country takes its name. You would think that such a place of prime importance in Irish history would have been clearly marked and easily accessible. But getting here wasn't as easy as it should have been.

Mullingar is a vibrant, busy town in the heart of Westmeath, and also of Ireland. I had passed through here the year before on a 280-mile hike across Ireland for charity, and spent the weekend at the Railway B&B. I was lucky to get accommodation as everything fills up at weekends. The town straddles the Royal Canal, which I had been following. On the way in I had met Nuala, a local woman who invited me for dinner with her family and friends that night, after just talking with me for about ten minutes. I soon found this sort of kindness and friendliness in many more of the people of Mullingar. The memories of this all came flooding back as I drove into town.

The town takes its name from the Irish *An Muileann Cearr* ("Left Hand Mill"). Legend says that a local miller refused to grind barley for St. Colman, as he was busy grinding wheat for the crown. St. Colman created a miracle which got the mill to turn forwards and backwards at the same time, and proceeded to grind both grains simultaneously.

From Mullingar I crossed the bridge and followed the signs for Athlone. Just before the village of Killare I spotted a brown sign in a lay-by on the left saying, "Hill of Uisneach". I pulled over and read the sign, which explained that pagan fires were lit on the hill and that St. Patrick had visited it. The sign was parallel to the fence, which would make you assume that the hill behind, to the left of the road, is The Hill of Uisneach. So I found a gate, climbed over it and headed up the hill via a muddy path.

I had with me a book called *The Traveller's Guide to Sacred Ireland* (*Sacred Ireland* for short) by Cary Meehan, which is a brilliant and incredibly comprehensive guide to Ireland's sacred sites. The book mentioned that there is a great rock called The Cat Stone, several other megalithic monuments and evidence of fires having been lit here for centuries. I couldn't for the life of me see any of this. I wandered the hills for ages, climbing fences, dodging sheep and cows and their ritual offerings, but simply became more and more frustrated.

An hour passed and still there was nothing. I was about to give up when I emerged upon a hill overlooking the road and the lay-by where I had parked the van. Something caught the corner of my eye and as I looked up, I saw a large pile of rocks sitting just behind a tree. I jumped for joy as I realized that this must be what I was looking for. Then my mouth dropped open as the realization sunk in that what I was looking at lay high up on the hill on the other side of the road. I had just spent the last hour walking around the completely wrong hill.

Back down by the van I looked for ways up, but each gate stated that entry was prohibited. I drove a little way up the road and stopped at The Uisneach Inn in Killare village for a drink and some local information.

"What do you know about The Hill of Uisneach?" I asked the barman.

"Not a lot," he replied.

Many people might think that asking local people for information is the best thing to do, but in most cases people don't really take any notice of what is

Places to Stay

HOTELS

Newbury Hotel
Dominick St.
Mullingar
Tel: (044) 42888
Web: www.thenewburyhotel.com
Email: info@thenewburyhotel.com
This family-run hotel next to the train station.

Shamrock Lodge
Clonown Rd.
Athlone
Tel: (090) 6492601
Web: www.shamrocklodgehotel.ie
Email: info@shamrocklodgehotel.ie

HISTORIC HOMES

Mornington House
Multyfarnham
Mullingar
Tel: (044) 72191
Web: www.mornington.ie
Email: stay@mornington.ie
A lovely 18th-century manor house near Lough Derravaragh.

THE JOURNEY
LEINSTER
COUNTY
WESTMEATH

around them. They just take it for granted.

"Well, do you know how I can get up there?"

"The only way is over the fields," he said.

"But all the signs on the gates say you cannot enter."

"Ah don't worry, the landowner just puts that there for insurance purposes, so if you do go in you do so at your own risk. He doesn't mind if you do go up there."

There is a common problem over Ireland at the moment where landowners are cutting off access to their land because of a recent spate of compensation claims. It seems the "it's not my fault, give me lots of money in compensation" culture has hit Ireland. Apparently there have been a number of people claiming compensation for injuries obtained while walking over "private" farm land. And the sad thing is that they are winning. Because of this, landowners are now having to pay extortionate fees for Public Liability Insurance, even though the public are on private land.

I finished my drink and drove back to the lay-by. A bit further up on the other side of the road I found a gate without a sign on, so I climbed over. Just in case the landowner had changed his mind about letting people in, I could claim I didn't see the sign. However, if possible, you should obtain permission from the landowner first.

And so that is how I ended up sitting next to the Cat Stone, and I was very tired by that time. This 30-ton stone looks more like a giant bolder that has been cracked into several pieces. Meehan says the splits represent the ancient divisions of Ireland. A book called *Beneath the Shadow of Uisneach*, says that it was from here that the five ancient provinces of Ireland met, making this stone the symbolic center of Ireland.

The stone's Irish name depicts this: *Ail na Mireann* ("Stone of the Divisions"). The divisions were first made by the Fir Bolg.

The stone sits on a sloping hillside, but where it lies is a dugout that has flattened the area around the stone. Archaeologists admit it's a prehistoric barrow and therefore almost certainly a burial spot. This would seem to point to the stone being a monument to the life of the person buried here. So in this case the legend could well be true.

The "Cat Stone" on The Hill of Uisneach. The Cat Stone is believed to have been broken into five pieces by the Fir Bolg to symbolize the five divisions of Ireland that they had ordained: Meath (the "middle" or ruling province), Leinster, Munster, Connaught and Ulster).

It is on this hill that the fires were lit for the ancient festival of Beltaine. It was said that a fire lit at the summit here could be seen all over Ireland, and that all fires were lit from this one. This hill was also the gathering place of the kings of Ireland. Perhaps this was where the High King would meet with his provincial kings. Legend also says that Lugh came here to rescue his mother from the tyranny of the Fomorians. After saving the Tuatha dé Danann from the Formorians Lugh became King. It is on this hill that he was eventually killed and buried somewhere close to the summit.

St. Patrick also came here. At the highest point of the hill, 600 meters, lies a bed of stones called St. Patrick's Bed. Patrick is said to have met two broth-

The Wry Mill
9, Oliver Plunkett St.
Tel: (044) 49544

Roncalli B&B
St. Francis Terrace
Athlone
Tel: (090) 6474204
En-Suite rooms with cable TV. Close to town, bus and train station.

Inny River Lodge
Ballycorkey
Ballynacargy
Tel: (044) 73259
Mob: 086 8310857
Web: www.innyriverlodge.com
Email: info@innyriverlodge.com
Highly recommended
A lovely family-run farmhouse B&B. I stayed here after leaving Mullingar on my charity walk, and arrived soaking wet. Rooms are spacious and beautifully decorated. The friendly children and Anne's home cooked evening meal make this place feel more like home than a B&B.

Kinnegad
Erris House
18 Kingsbury,
Kinnegad
Tel: (044) 75667
Great little B&B,
with en-suite rooms
at excellent prices.

H O S T E L S
Lough Ree Lodge
Dublin Rd.
Athlone
Tel: (0) 902 89214
Web:
www.loughree
lodge.com
Email: booking
@loughrea
lodge.com
Despite its
name, it not any-
where near the lake
but on the Dublin
road about a mile
out of town. But it
does have a good
range of facilities
and accommodation.

Tuan's Notes
St. Brigid
*Learn more St. Brigid
in The History: The
Saints (pp. 234-235).*

ers, Enda and Fiach, who owned Uisneach at the time. He attempted to have a church built on the hill, but was rejected by the locals. It's believed he spent the night on the hill.

I headed up the hill and over a fence. At the crest of the hill I spotted the ordinance survey triangulation pillar that the book says marks the spot. Getting to it involved a detoured route because laying beside it was a bull and a calf, who upon my appearance had stood up and stared at me. I didn't fancy a painful and quick ejection off the hill, so I took a circular route around. Patrick's Bed is a mound of earth and rocks that was disfigured when the pillar was put in its place.

A very interesting story mentioned in *Sacred Ireland* tells of how, according to Geoffrey of Monmouth in his book, *The History of the Kings of Britain*, Uisneach is said to have been the original site for the stone circle of Stonehenge, in England. I became very interested in this, as I grew up very close to Stonehenge and as local people do, never really gave it a second thought, until recently.

Geoffrey says that when the Saxons were defeated in England, the king collected all the stone masons

St. Brigid's Well, Westmeath

from around the country and demanded they find a fitting monument to the brave men killed in this great battle. No one could come up with anything good enough, so Merlin was sent for. Merlin told the king about The Giant's Ring on Mount Killaraus (Uisneach) in Ireland. He said that the stones had been taken there by giants from Africa, who laid out the stones in a circle. In times of illness they poured water over a stone into a bath, which would then cure the illness. Different stones contained different cures. The king's brother led a band of 15,000 warriors to Ireland at the king's request to bring these stones back to England. Their army easily defeated the Irish army, because the Irish found it hard to believe that a king would invade a country just for a few rocks. Merlin was then called for to move the stones to Salisbury Plain.

St. Brigid's Well

Just down the road beyond The Uisneach Inn lie the ruins of an old church with **St. Brigid's** Well beside it. It's a large circular pool decorated with statues and candles. On a nearby tree is St. Brigid's cross, a unique version of the cross woven from wicker wood.

CAMPING
Derravaragh
Caravan and
Camping Park
Mullingar Lough
Multyfarnham
Tel: (044) 71500
Mob: (086) 8230363
Email:
camping@iol.ie
Located north of
Mullingar near the
legendary Lough
Derravaragh.
This lovely
campsite with
friendly staff is
located on the
shores of the
lake. Unfortunately
most of the spaces are
taken up with private
caravans, so there are
a limited number of
spaces for tourers.

For more information
visit ireland.
mysteriousworld.com/
Journey/Counties/
Westmeath/

A St. Brigid's Cross, a form of the cross unique to Ireland

Places to See in Longford

⚜ ANCIENT SITES

1. Aughnacliff Dolmen
2. Hill of Mídir
3. Greenan Hill (aka *Grianán Meidbe*, "Maeve's sun porch") (on Inis Clothrand/Inchleraun)

✟ CHRISTIAN SITES

4. Ardagh Heritage Village . . . 487
   - St. Mel's Cathedral
   - St. Brigid's Well

5. St. Diarmaid's Monastery (on Inis Clothrand/Inchleraun)
6. St. Rioch's Monastery (on Inis Bofin/Inchbofin)
7. St. Liobán's Monastery (on Inis More/Inchmore)
8. St. Ciarán's Monastery (on Hare Island)

⚔ CRYPTID SIGHTINGS

9. Monster of Lough Ree/Sunken City 490-491

Driving Directions: See p. 489. Boats to explore Lough Ree can be found in Athlone city, and can also be hired at Lough Ree House, west of the N55 at The Pigeons.

Longford

St. Brigid's Well, Longford

o you know how to get to St. Brigid's Well?" I asked the old man sitting on the wall beside his house.

He remained there for a moment, looking pensive, then removed his gloves and climbed down the ladder. "I'll take you there meself," he said.

"That's very kind of you," I replied.

"Ah, not at all. It's not that easy to find."

I was in Ardagh, a little village in County Longford. The nearby hill is said to be the legendary home of Mídir, a king of the Tuatha dé Danann. It ties in with an ancient and complex tale called **The Wooing of Ètaín**.

Ardagh

Ardagh is a heritage village filled with lovely old houses. In the center of the village, beside the T-junction, are the ruins of St. Mel's Cathedral. During an excavation traces of a wooden church were found on

Longford
Things to Do & Places to See
Ardagh
Heritage Village
Visit St. Brigid's Well and St. Mel's Cathedral. To get to St. Brigid's Well, ask at the house opposite the clock tower at the T-junction for permission.

Tuan's Notes
The Wooing of Ètaín
This legend involves Mídir, one of the sons of the Dagda and Ètaín, the beautiful daughter of the king of Ulster. Mídir was so taken with Ètaín that he took her, much to the chagrin of Mídir's wife, who cast a spell on her.
Learn more about The Wooing of Ètaín in The Mystery: Folklore & Mythology (p. 190).

THE JOURNEY
LEINSTER
COUNTY
LONGFORD

Eat & Drink

Market Bar
Cnr Ballymahon
Longford Town
St./Market Sq.
Tel: (043) 41806

PUBS
Seasons Restaurant & Steakhouse
Market Square
Longford Town
Tel: (043) 50430
Dinner Mon-Sat 6-
10 pm
Sunday Lunch
1-4 pm
Upstairs from
Market Bar.

Tuan's Notes
St. Mel
St. Mel was the
nephew of St. Patrick,
who put him in
charge of the cathe-
dral at Ardagh. He
was also believed to
be the bishop who
professed St. Brigid
into the ministry.

*Learn more about
Christian saints in The
History: The Saints
(pp. 228-249).*

THE JOURNEY
LEINSTER
COUNTY
LONGFORD

St. Mel's Cathedral

the site, which is said to have been the original church established by St. Patrick and left in the care of **St. Mel**. Local folklore says that Mel is actually buried within its walls.

At the post office I had asked for directions to the well, and they told me to go ask at this house on the corner next to the clock tower. And so it was I found myself trudging through a wet field with an old fella called Tom in search of this well.

"Where are you from?" asked Tom.

"Hampshire, in the south of England," I replied.

"Ah yes, I know it well. I lived in England for a long time."

It's amazing how many people I meet who have lived in England. Especially the older people, because back when they were young you either went to England for work, or the U.S. The people who went to England mostly came back when they retired.

We finally found the well through a small gate at the back of a field. We had to cross two fields to get here. Through the gate we made our way down a nar-row, overgrown lane to the well with a thorn tree beside it. A circular wall had been built to contain the well, but unfortunately the water had all dried up. According to *Sacred Ireland* the well is still visited at the beginning of February in honor of St. Brigid. Brigid joined St. Mel's monastery and is said to have spent her early years here as a nun. The nearby Church of Ireland is also referred to as St. Brigid's Church. Her saint's day is 1st February, which I assume is when the locals visit the well.

We waited out the short rain shower, then made our way back across the field. Fortunately for Tom, he wore his Wellington boots, while my feet got soaked. We took a detour through a different field to avoid the long grass and, much to my concern, attracted the attention of a herd of bulls.

"Ah, don't worry," reassured Tom. "They are just curious."

"Just so long as they don't get *too* curious," I replied.

Tom picked up a stick.

"I thought you said they were just curious," I said nervously.

"They are. It's always best to have a stick in your hand, though."

I began to suspect that Tom was just playing it cool, but in reality he was as concerned as me.

"When they are grouped together you don't have to worry," added Tom, as he waved his stick. "It's when one is on his own you should be careful."

Well, that's comforting then!

Fortunately, we made it back to the road and the safety of the gate without the help of an angry bull. Back in the village, Tom invited me inside to meet his wife, who proceeded to make us tea and biscuits. I filled up, as I knew I would need the strength — after all, I *was* going monster hunting the next day.

There & Back Again

TRAINS
Longford is on the Dublin to Sligo line. There are four trains a day each way. The train stops at Mullingar, just outside town center. Tel: 043-45208

BUSES
✠ Bus Éireann Nos: 22, 23 from Dublin to Ballina and Sligo stop at Mullingar and Longford.
✠ Bus No 119 goes to Ardagh on Saturdays only from Longford or from Dublin and Mullingar.

DRIVING
✠ Longford is off the N4, about half hour from Mullingar.
✠ Ardagh is off the R393 going south from Longford.

BOATING
Hire boats to explore the isles of Lough Ree in Athlone.

THE JOURNEY
LEINSTER
COUNTY
LONGFORD

TAXI
Nevins
Taxis
20 Ward's Tce
Longford
(043) 46549

T C Cabs
Lamagh
Newtownforbes
(043) 47500

Tuan's Notes

Sea Serpents

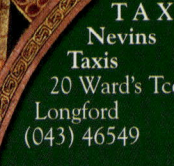

Sea serpents are among the most common mythical creatures to be found in the myths and legends of the ancient world, and Ireland is no exception.

Learn more about The Monster of Lough Ree and other mysterious creatures of Ireland in The Mystery: Creatures Great & Small (pp. 175-176).
Note: Travel information for Lough Ree is in the chapter on Westmeath.

THE JOURNEY

LEINSTER

COUNTY
LONGFORD

The Monster of Lough Ree

"What do you know about a drowned city in Lough Ree?" I asked.

I was sitting in the office of the librarian at Athlone Library.

"I've never heard of such a thing," he admitted.

I showed him the piece in *Sacred Ireland* that talked about this. He shook his head and once again said he had never heard of such a story. "There was a story about a giant **sea serpent** in the lake," he added.

"Oh, tell me about that then."

"Well, three local priests said they saw a giant creature emerge from the lake while fishing. Many of us are convinced that it was the work of two local men, who put them up to it."

"Are they still around?"

"No, they died sometime ago."

"But did they admit to putting the priests up to this?" I asked.

"No, they took it to their graves."

He led me upstairs and supplied a wealth of literature on the area, including an Irish report on the sighting and subsequent sightings of this monster called *Expanding Ripples*. Inside were excerpts from a report submitted to the Inland Fisheries Trust by three Dublin clergymen. It describes two sightings of a strange object moving slowly along the calm surface of the water about 80 yards away from their boat. They described a serpent-like head with a hump behind it.

This report was made in 1960. According to this book, there are many other tales of a strange creature having torn the nets of fishermen or run off with their lines. Three stories of similarity are recorded. These all state how something snagged one of the fishermen's lines and ran off with it, dragging the boat into the lake in the process before the line was cut. One incident tells of how the creature took the line and then proceeded to dive down into the depths of the lake, breaking the line after about 70 feet had reeled off.

The librarian then produced a copy of an *Irish Times* report from June 2001. It tells of how three cryptozoologists came to Lough Ree with the latest in underwater tracking equipment, devised from technology used to track Soviet submarines during the Cold War. They would go out onto the lake late at night, and while out there detected the movement of a large, unrecognized animal. The organization, which was called GUST (Global Underwater Search Team), actually received some promising results, and even spotted a long, tubelike object moving out from the shoreline of an island.

So, it seems that Ireland has a Loch Ness monster of its own. I spent the night in the Lough Ree campsite, which sits on the shore of the lake. After sundown I sat for a while looking out into the lake in the hope of sighting the monster, but the lake was guarding its secret very well.

Places to Stay

B & B S
Cunard B&B
Dublin St.
Longford Town
Tel: (043) 41890
Pub accommodation right in the center of town. Also serves bar food.

Ardken B&B
Ardagh Village
Tel: (043) 75029
Email: ardken @iol.ie
In the village, has 3 en-suite rooms.

C A M P I N G
Newtownforbes Camping
Kilmacannon
Longford
Tel: (043) 45503
Situated just a few miles north of Longford town on the N4. Signed on the right.

For more information visit ireland. mysteriousworld.com/ Journey/Counties/ Longford/

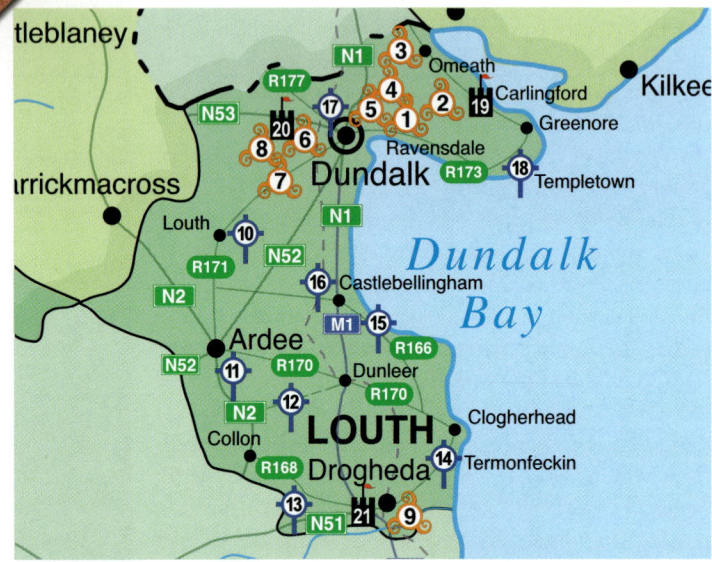

Places to See in Louth

⚔ ANCIENT SITES

⚜ CHRISTIAN SITES

⚑ HISTORICAL SITES

Driving Directions: See 493, 501-502. Cooley Peninsula map: 495.

Louth

A view of the Mourne Mountains, and of the Mystery Machine.

one with monster hunting for the time being, I continued on with the intention of getting to the Cooley Peninsula in County Louth. Louth is known as "The Wee County", as it's the smallest. Having been there before I already knew of one very strange phenomenon. I had seen signs indicating I was on The Táin Trail. Further reading had proved this to be a very famous legend in the Ulster Cycle, and not just a cycling trail, as I had previously suspected.

The plan was quite simple: I would drive to the peninsula and stop in a campsite along the coast. Unfortunately, my simple plan was thwarted by mechanical means. Five miles from Dundalk the van began to cough, splutter and generally emit

Louth
Things to Do & Places to See

Proleek Dolmen
This interesting dolmen is situated behind the Ballymascanlon Hotel. Go into the car park and then follow the path behind the hotel and it is signed.

Magic Hill
Gives the illusion that you are rolling uphill! (See pp. 496-500 for directions.)

Faughart, northeast of Dundalk
Birthplace of St. Brigit and Cú Chulainn.

Lady Well
Follow the sign off the R173 to Templetown. It lies after the turnoff for Templetown beach on the right.

The Táin Trail
An excellent map on the 25 mile cycling route is available from

some worrying sounds not conducive to a healthy engine. Fortunately, I just managed to make it to town.

I figured it was too late to find a mechanic, so I wandered around the town trying to locate one for the morning. None were to be seen anywhere. In frustration I wandered into a take-away and asked the guy behind the counter. To my surprise he got on the phone to a mechanic he knew named Christy.

With a bit of luck, Christy got the Mystery Machine running again. We stayed there for a while, smoking cigarettes and chatting while the engine ran. I gave Christy copies of two of my previous books as a small thank you for his help. He said he would give them to his son, in the hope it would inspire him to do well in school.

It was gone one in the morning by this time, and so Christy gave me his mobile number and said to call him in the morning if the problem returns. He then took me to a part of town where he said it would be safe to park up and sleep for the night.

Christy had been there for 2 hours, in the dead of night, and when I asked him how much I owed him, he refused to take any money. Despite my insistence that I pay him something, he simply wouldn't budge. I thanked him for his generosity and bade him good-bye.

As I drifted off to sleep I realized that I loved Dundalk. The first time I ever came here I found the people so friendly and helpful. My second time here had shown that this wasn't a one-off, and that this town, which is the border town to the north, is a shining example of how the north really is.

The Cooley Peninsula

This small peninsula lies just north of Dundalk. Half of it lies in County Louth, and the other half lies in County Down, Northern Ireland. It separates Dundalk Bay from Carlingford Lough, a flooded valley in the Mourne Mountains. It was morning as I drove along the R173 enjoying the wonderful sight of the low, green Cooley Mountains shimmering in the cool morning sunlight.

It's actually possible to drive around this peninsula in just a couple of hours, but as the saying goes, "good things come in small packages." The Cooley Peninsula is not only a place of stunning coastline, low mountains, forests and small villages, but it is also host to a wealth of Ireland's most famous legends and folklore.

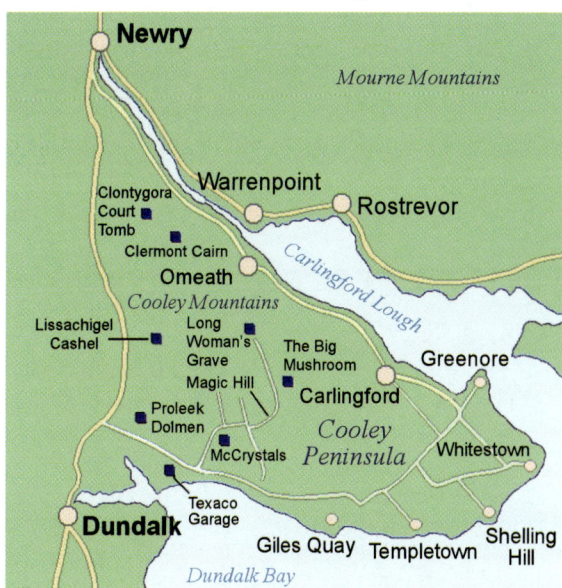

The Cooley Peninsula in County Louth, the setting for numerous myths and legends, including many important scenes from *The Táin*.

Festivals

The Táin Walking Festival
Take a weekend to explore the spectacular landscape of the Cooley mountains. Virtually undiscovered the weekend will expose you to different walks at all levels. Booking advisable.
Tel: 42 937 3033
Web: www.carlingford.ie/events.htm

Tain Rhythm & Roots Festival
Dundalk
Co. Louth
This popular festival has an eclectic range of folk, traditional and leftfield rock.
Tel: 042 9329649
Web: www.tainfestival.com

Tours

Sevens Coaches & Cab Hire
Tel: (042) 937 7777
Mob: (087) 937 7777
Offers tours to Carlingford and the Cooley Peninsula.

Dundalk Tourist Office
Joceyln St.
Dundalk
Tel: (042) 9335484
Web: www.eastcoast
midlands.ie
Email: info@
eastcoastmidlands.ie

Drogheda on the Boyne
Tel:
041 98 37070
Web: www.
drogheda.ie
Email:
tourism@
drogheda.ie

Carlingford Tourist Office
Old Dispensary
Tel: (042) 937 3033
Web:
www.carlingford.ie
Email:
info@carlingford.ie

FOR MORE INFORMATION
Visit www.
countylouth.com

Magic Hill

"Magic Hill" appears to be an incline, but it is actually a decline. Though officially dismissed as an optical illusion, local folklore still holds that this hill is the domain of powerful fairy magic.

The peninsula was actually part of the historical province of Ulster, before the treaty divided the country into two. I first came here two years ago in search of a mystery told to me by my friend Eilish, who worked at the hostel in Carlow. As I drove back to the hill the memory of my first visit came flooding back.

Upon learning I was a travel writer she immediately asked, "Have you been to the road where things go backwards?"

"The what?" I replied, not sure I'd heard right.

"The road where things go backwards. Daddy took some Americans there last year. What you do is drive to the bottom of the hill, put the car in neutral and take your foot off the brake. The car will roll back up the hill."

I must admit I thought I was the butt of an Irish joke. I mean, come on. It's always been the old joke about the Irish doing things backwards. They even say it about themselves, which is a clear example of just how fun-loving and laid back the Irish are.

Before I knew it Eilish had got her father on the phone and he was giving me detailed directions to this place. For the next few days I was waiting to be told the truth, but Eilish insisted it was real.

At the time I was traveling around Ireland promoting my book, *Hot Footing around the Emerald Isle*. My girlfriend Nika was with me, and the two of us decided to head up here and search out this interesting phenomenon. I had to pay a visit to a local paper in Dundalk first, where I met Joe Carroll, an enthusiastic man with a big grin. Joe knew all about Magic Hill, as some people call it, and he gave Nika and I some fruit for the journey.

Just north of Dundalk I took the turn off for Carlingford. The town sits in the shadow of Slieve Foy. It is said that Finn McCool laid down to rest on this mountain after his epic battle with a Scottish giant named Ruiscare. The locals say you can still see his imprint on the mountain if you fly over, and that late at night when all is silent, you can hear the echoes of his snoring across the town.

I had been instructed to turn off at the sign for McCrystals foodstore, but I'd missed it, possibly due to admiring the beautiful scenery. I pulled up next to an old man digging his front garden, and asked for directions to Magic Hill.

"Ah!" he grinned. "You are the second people to ask me that today! Go back out to the Dundalk Road and turn off just before the Texaco garage. Follow the road around to McCrystals foodstore, and ask there."

At McCrystals I bought an ice cream and asked for the directions.

Eat & Drink

Magee's Bistro
Thosel St.
Carlingford
Tel: (042) 9373751
Has a patio section out front.

Capitanos Corelli's Italian Restaurant
Newry St.
Tel: (042) 9383848
Web: www.belvedere house.ie
Email: info@ belvedere house.ie
Part of the Belvedere House chain.

Millmount
Drogheda
Tel: (041) 98344759
There is a restaurant next to the museum, serving a range of pizza, pasta and steak.

PUBS

P.J. O'Hare
Thosel St.
Carlingford
A nice old pub that doubles as a grocery shop. It was also once home to a leprechaun named Sean Óg, until he escaped....

THE JOURNEY

LEINSTER

COUNTY
LOUTH

A Shortcut to Mushroom

"If you go east from here to the end of the road you'll come to a T-junction. Take a right and then an immediate left. Follow the road to the top of the hill, then down into a dip where you'll see a big mushroom. Stop there, put the car in neutral and release the brake. You'll roll backwards up the hill."

A *big mushroom!* I thought. This phenomenon has obviously messed with the minds of the local people.

We continued on, passing signs for The Táin Trail, the legendary route carved out thousands of years ago through the entire midlands that was recounted in the epic saga, *Táin Bó Cuailgne* (The Cattle Raid of Cooley). The Cooley Peninsula is the focal point of the story. This is a 25-mile section of the trail that takes you on a circular route around the peninsula, along surfaced roads, old forest tracks and paths.

At the turn off the road followed a steep incline, and at the brow of the hill the road drops down into a dip. At the bottom of the dip I suddenly spotted a large, circular storage hut, which, if you imagined hard enough — or were very medicated — could well have been a large mushroom. I slammed on the brakes and almost sent Nika hurtling through the front window.

'What are you doing?' she asked.

"I think this is it," I replied excitedly. "Look! There's the mushroom!"

Nika remained quiet, possibly wondering if this obsession was beginning to affect my sanity. We were at the very base of the hill, so I put the van in neutral and took my foot off the brake.

"Bloody hell!" I cried. "Look, we're rolling uphill!"

And we were, we were rolling up the hill. It was amazing. No, it was astounding! The hill slanted upwards slightly then became steeper halfway up. At the steeper point we picked up speed, until finally reaching the brow of the hill and then beginning to roll down the big hill. I braked, put the van in gear and drove down the hill again to the mushroom. Once again we rolled back up the hill. I felt like a child who'd just watched a magician for the first time. I couldn't believe what was happening. I rode up and down that hill for the next half an hour, as traffic passed cautiously. The local people watched with amusement, obviously knowing exactly what I was up to. You could tell when the passing car contained tourists because they looked on with complete bewilderment at this deranged man driving up and down the hill. I drove up the other side and

*There &
Back Again*

T R A I N S

Drogheda Station
Trains run from Dublin Connolly station and travel north along the coast through Drogheda and Dundalk on the Belfast line. Drogheda train station is just off the Dublin Road, south of the river.
Tel: (041) 9838749.
Trains run roughly every half an hour.

Dundalk Station
Dundalk train station is on Carrickmacross Road.
Tel: (042) 9335521.
There are about 13 trains a day from Dublin, and quite a few going north to Belfast.

Like the trains, there is a main bus line from Dublin (Busáras) to Belfast.

Drogheda Bus Station
Corner of John St. & Donore St.
Tel: (041) 9835023.
There are plenty of buses from Dublin roughly every half hour throughout the whole day and evening.

Dundalk Bus Station
Next to the Long Walk Shopping Center.
Tel: (042) 9334075
There are hourly buses from Dublin.

✦ Bus 161 to Carlingford from Dundalk. There are several buses throughout the day.

✦ Buses 32, 33 & 36 Dublin to Letterkenny, Derry & Portrush all stop at Ardee.

THE JOURNEY
LEINSTER
COUNTY LOUTH

turned around. A man was building a wall in front of his house, and watched us with a smile.

Eventually I pulled the van over to the side and studied the road from there. From the ground it looked like the road actually slanted down and that it was the funny angle of the hill creating this illusion. The official line for this phenomenon is that it is an illusion. But when I returned a year later the woman in the tourist office said it was the work of the fairies. On their map of the peninsula, it was listed as "Fairy Hill".

But what I liked most about it was that no queues of tourists were paying to try it. There wasn't even a sign to indicate what it was. It hadn't been exploited one bit, and was just a piece of country road with a hidden secret.

THE LONG WOMAN'S GRAVE

Eventually I managed to tear myself away. We decided to continue up the road to The Long Woman's Grave. Once again we passed the man building his wall and waved. He waved back, took one look at our huge grins, and burst out laughing. I guess this was a familiar sight for him.

"Long Woman's Grave". It's name comes from a legend of how a man of the Uí Meath Mara clan had met a lovely, tall Spanish lady during his travels, and had brought her back to live with him as his wife. Mortified that the man's lands were not as vast and rich as she had been led to believe, she died on the spot.

PROLEEK DOLMEN

In the middle of a golf course behind the Ballymascanlon Hotel lies the Proleek Dolmen. This magnificent monument is said to have been placed here by a Scottish giant during his legendary battle with Finn McCool. It has just three stones supporting its 30-ton capstone, which lies 13 feet above the ground at roughly a 45-degree angle. Local folklore says that if you throw a stone up on top of the capstone you will be married within a year. I figured I'd give that one a miss.

Nearby is a long wedge grave, said to be the burial place of the giant after losing his battle with Finn McCool. Many of the capstones were missing.

The little village of Carlingford is a lovely medieval town with narrow streets and a great base from which to explore these legends. It sits in the shadow of Slieve Foy, and lies beside the beautiful, if somewhat haunting, Carlingford Lough. There is a hostel and a few B&Bs in town, and a good choice of pubs in which to mix with the locals. Upon my second arrival here I was directed to H. O'Hare. This little pub is typical of many old Irish pubs, in as much as it is also the local grocer's. The first time I ever entered one I thought I had gone in the wrong door. The front of the building is a shop, with shelves filled with condiments and various edibles. But venture a bit further towards the back and you'll find a

DRIVING
Drogheda is north of Dublin on the N1.

✝ From here take the N1 north and follow signs to Monasterboice.

✝ Continue on the N1 and then take the R170 across to Ardee. The jumping church is signed off the N2 just south of town.

✝ Take the N52 towards Dundalk and turn left for Knockbridge just before town. At the crossroads turn right and stop at sign for Cúchulainn's Stone.

✝ Go back through Knockbridge to the village of Louth for St. Mochta's House.

✝ Head into Dundalk and follow signs for the N53 to Castleblaney. From the start of the N53 turn left at the first crossroads for Cú Chulainn's home. Signed Castletown Motte.

✠ Go back to the N1 and cross the bridge. Where the road forks left is a sign for St. Brigid's Shrine and Faughart. From the shrine continue up the road and take the first right. Follow this road up to the car park on the left.

✠ Go back to the N1 and head north. At the roundabout follow signs for Carlingford. Just past the roundabout is the Bally-mascanlon Hotel, behind which is the Proleek Dolmen.

✠ Follow the R173 into Carlingford and around the entire peninsula. This is a lovely scenic drive. A map of The Táin Trail is available at the tourist office.

H. O.Hare's grocery and pub.

barman waiting to pour you a pint of your choosing. This pub also has another unusual attraction: locals say the original owner used to hunt **leprechauns** in the nearby Cooley Mountains. It's said that one of the captives, Sean Og, lived in the pub for 55 years and escaped Easter Weekend, 2001. A display on the wall offers a reward for his capture. Looking at his picture, I couldn't help but thinking that he looked oddly familiar.

The belongings Sean Óg the leprechaun (inset) left behind when he fled 55 years of captivity in O'Hara's Pub on Easter Sunday, 2001. There is a £50,000 reward for his recapture. Leprechauns can assume many forms, however, including people and animals, so be wary....

Dundalk, Home of Cú Chulainn

Cú Chulainn was the hero of *The Táin*. He is described in the saga as a mighty warrior who single-handedly held off the massive armies of Queen Maeve of Connaught. He was alone because the men of Ulster were under a curse that had rendered them weak and useless in their hour of need. Fantastic tales of him killing hundreds of men with slingstones, and how he defeated every man who came to battle him at the river-crossing he defended, are prevalent in this saga. But as well as being a great and apparently invincible foe, Cú Chulainn was also a husband to Emer, and they lived together here in Dún Dealgan (Dundalk).

On the N53 out of town I turned left at the first crossroads and parked the van beside the entrance to Castletown Motte. A lane led up to a Norman Motte with the old bailey walls still surrounding it, and the remains of an 18th-century castle in the middle. The views are spectacular. From the hill I spotted a single stone in the nearby field.

I couldn't get to it from the Motte because of a fence, so I walked back out to the road and entered via a nearby house. This standing stone is only a few feet high and is said to mark the home and burial spot of Cú Chulainn.

I headed back into town and then took the R171 to the village of Knockbridge. Just before it was a sign pointing left for Cú Chulainn's Stone. This tall standing stone is said to be the very stone that Cú Chulainn had strapped himself to in his last battle. Finally overcome by magic and trickery, and an epic battle with his foster brother, this seemingly invincible man dragged himself to this spot and tied himself to the stone in order to face his enemies standing up.

TAXIS

Clarkes Cabs
Drogheda
Tel: (041) 9837890
Mob: (087) 2472635

Harrys Hackney Hire
Carlingford
Tel: (087)769 3660

Skytes Taxi Service
Tel: 086/087 822 0562
Cooley's official taxi service.

A 1 Cabs
9 Crowe Street
Dundalk
Tel: (042) 9326666

Mr Kevin Gorman
Hale Street
Ardee
Tel: (041) 6853317

Tuan's Notes
Leprechauns
Learn more about leprechauns and other fairy folk in The Mystery: Creatures Great & Small: Fairies (pp. 163-165).

Cú Chulainn, "the Hound of Culann", was originally named Sétanta. He picked up his new name one day when he went to meet King Conchobar at the fortress of Culann, the King's chief smith. There was a fierce watchdog at the gate, however, that attacked him. Unafraid of the powerful beast, Sétanta killed it with his bare hands. Sétanta then offered to take the place of Culann's hound as the guardian of the front gate, and was thus renamed *Cú Chulainn*, "the Hound of Culann".

Learn more about Cú Chulainn and other ancient Celtic heroes in The Mystery: Deities & Demigods (pp. 107-111).

Cú Chulainn's Stone

Still, no one dared approach him, until the Mórrigan turned herself into a crow and alighted upon his shoulder. When he didn't move, Maeve's army knew for sure he was dead.

The stone stands 7 to 8 feet tall. It's at the back of the field, and is indeed characteristic of a warrior's stone. I noticed that it was leaning backward, almost as if it had buckled under the fury of **Cú Chulainn**'s last mortal combat.

St. Brigid's Shrine and Birthplace

I returned to Dundalk and took the N1 north across the bridge. Just before the roundabout there was a fork in the road. A sign pointed left to St. Brigid's Shrine. I followed the signs until I came to the car park.

St. Brigid's Shrine is located around a small, wooded stream where the saint was said to have worked as a young girl. Brigid was the daughter of a chieftain. It's said that in order to escape the confines of an arranged marriage, she plucked out one of her eyes so her would-be husband would no longer find her attractive and cancel the marriage. Surely there could have been an easier way?

This shrine was erected in 1934. It sits beside the stream, which is said to have curative powers. Annual pilgrimages have been performed here for centuries. A series of stones alongside the stream tell the saint's story. A water shrine sits near the car park and a number of statues depicting the saint are scattered around the area.

I continued up the road and took the first turning on the right. A country road twisted up a hill until I came to a car park. The view across the bay and of the Mourne Mountains was magnificent. This was once the main pass between Leinster and Ulster known as The Gap of the North. Whoever controlled this hill controlled the pass. At one time this was the main road through to the rest of Ulster.

I arrived at Faughart Hill, an ancient hill-fort and the place where St. Brigid was born in AD 454. The remains of a church and a graveyard sit beside the car park. Inside the graveyard, on the right-hand side behind a large tree, is St. Brigid's Well. Some steps lead down to the well, which is surrounded by a stone bee-hive structure. Unfortunately the well was in bad conditions when I arrived. Hopefully it will get cleaned up. It is also said that Cú Chulainn was born here.

KILDEMOCK — THE JUMPING CHURCH

As I pulled up in the narrow lay-by alongside the church, I noticed an odd-looking man with a heavy stoop dashing back and forth in front of the ruins clutching a lump of grass. He wore brown corduroy trousers a size too big for him, and a red lumberjack-style shirt that hung down the back of his trousers. His wild hair was black and grey and flapped about in the wind. As I wandered into the graveyard he noticed me and came over.

"A lovely day, isn't it?" he spluttered.

"It's beautiful," I replied.

It was difficult to understand him at first. He stood in front of me, stooped right over, hair over his eyes and a face tilted upwards looking up at me. His smile revealed a set of teeth that looked older than some of the mega-

THE JOURNEY

LEINSTER

COUNTY
LOUTH

Kildemock Graveyard and its keeper.

lithic stones I'd visited, The skin around his squinting eyes was old and withered. For some reason, I couldn't help thinking of Gollum from *The Lord of the Rings*.

"What are you doing?" I asked.

"The fifty-year clean-up."

"Oh…." Fifty years seemed rather a long gap between clean-ups for the graveyard.

…

"What does that mean, then?" I replied cautiously.

"Fifty years ago today my father first cleaned up this graveyard, and then did it every year afterwards. It was passed on to me when he died," he said.

I could think of better inheritances.

He introduced himself as Paddy, and proceeded to take me on a tour of the ruins and the graveyard.

The current 14th-century church stands on the site of a 5th-century church founded by St. Patrick and left in the care of one of his disciples, Diomoc. All that remains of the church are the foundations of the walls, and the high wall at the west end of the church, which is the subject of a very mysterious story.

The wall is 19 feet high, 15 feet wide and 3 feet thick and weighs at least 40 tons. What is so strange about this wall is that it was cleanly sliced at the base and quite clearly sits 3 feet within the outer wall and stands completely upright inside the church.

Local folklore says that way back in 1715 a local mason, who had abandoned the Catholic Church for the Protestant, was found dead one day. It appeared he had fallen from some scaffolding. He was buried at the west end of the church beside the wall. During the night there was a freak storm. In the morning the wall was said to have jumped inwards three feet to exclude the grave of this excommunicated man.

The graveyard is very old and full of interesting old gravestones. Paddy showed me a flat stone in the church grounds marked 1688 and carved with a skull and cross-bones. Paddy explained that a husband and wife were buried there. The skull and crossbones was an odd sight to see on a Christian burial. Nearby was a grave with a stone table over it. It was broken down the middle.

"People were playing cards on the slab back in 1797 when it was struck by lightning as a warning from God," explained Paddy. "The stone was broken in two, but the people weren't hurt."

"What do you know about the story of a six-fingered man?" I asked him.

"Ah! Garrett's Fort," he replied.

He pointed to the distant hills and emphasized the peak of a hill just beyond them. "Buried inside that hill are thousands of Garrett's soldiers who were enchanted by a witch and put to sleep. The fort was buried over with stones and earth and a sword marks the entrance to the cave. They will remain there asleep on horseback until a man with two thumbs on one hand comes and takes the sword. Garrett's men will then awaken from their sleep and ride forth to save Ireland."

Monasterboice

Monasterboice has numerous high crosses and a round tower, and is a hugely popular tourist destination.

Monasterboice (*Mainister Bhuithe*) means "Monastery of Buithe". It was established by St. Buithe in the 6th century. The oldest remains here are three high crosses and a round tower from the 10th century. Beyond the 10th century the settlement is a bit of a mystery, as no written records have been found. The establishment of a 12th-century abbey at nearby Mellifont appears to have spelled the end of the settlement.

The site is surrounded by a stone wall and is hugely popular. The first site I came across was Muiredach's Cross, named after an abbot here. His name is carved into the base. The cross stands just 18 feet high, but it's the sheer thickness of the cross that makes it so compelling. The carvings are still quite visible. The capstone resembles a small church.

Nearby is the taller West Cross. At 21 feet tall it reminded me of the Moone Cross. It's dwarfed by the 110 feet tall round tower that stands nearby. The remains of two churches also stand nearby.

Millmount — Drogheda

Millmount is believed to be the burial place of Amergin, though there is a place in County Kerry that also claims that honor (see pp. 589-590). The round tower on the hill today was meant to repel an invasion from Napoleon that never materialized.

Sitting high above the town of Drogheda, characterized by the Martello Tower (a low, round tower with a conical roof, a common sight along this coast) is Millmount. These towers were built in response to the threat of invasion by Napoleon. The invasion never came.

I then wandered through the archway and found myself in another car park. The tower sits above the car park and the nearby building contains a museum, but this wasn't the reason I was here. I had learned from the guy who gave the astronomy talk at Tara that the mound on which this is built is an ancient burial mound, and believed to be the burial mound of **Amergin**, chief warrior and poet of the Milesians. It has also been suggested that the mound is a large passage mound like Newgrange. The Normans built a Motte here in the 12th century and a castle was built on it later. Whatever it's origins, it certainly commands a superb view of the surrounding bay.

Tuan's Notes

Amergin

Amergin was the Chief Poet of the Milesians, and one of the sons of Mil who led their invasion of Ireland. Amergin was the author of "The Mystery", one of the earliest and most famous poems in Irish history. He also composed many other famous poems, one of which he used to counteract the magic of the Tuatha dé Danann who sought to repel their invasion. Amergin also uttered the first judgment in Ireland in favor of his brother Eremón, whom he prophesied would become the first Milesian High King of Ireland.

Learn more about Amergin and the Milesians in The Mystery: The Invasions (pp. 68-76).

Places to See in Wicklow

⚜ ANCIENT SITES
1. Seefin Passage Cairn
2. The Hollywood Stone 515
3. Athgreany Piper Stones
4. Castleruddery Stone Circle . . 511
5. Moylisha Wedge Cairn
6. Rath Geel Royal Fort
7. Mottee Stone
8. The Devil's Glen 512

✦ CHRISTIAN SITES
9. Glendalough Monastic
Site 511-515
10. Church Mountain
11. Baltinglass Abbey
12. Aghowle Church

⛏ CRYPTID SIGHTINGS
13. The Piast 513

⛰ SCENIC VIEWS
14. The Wicklow
Mountains 511
15. Avoca (Location for the filming of *Ballykissangel* 513

Driving Directions: See pp. 511,
513

Wicklow

Wicklow's geography is dominated by stark mountainous terrain punctuated by large lakes and streams.

riving south from Dublin on the N11 is a marvelous sight. The sign says "The Garden of Ireland", and from the motorway you are treated to a view of grassy peaks soaring majestically into the air. I passed the town of Bray, which takes its name from King Breas, an ancient chieftain of the Tuatha dé Danann.

I turned off the main road and took the back-road into Glendalough, a village in the heart of the Wicklow Mountains. It lies at the bottom of the Wicklow Gap, where a river flows through the deep glacial valley and empties out into two beautifully clear lakes, giving the area its name: Glendalough ("Glen of Two Lakes").

Glendalough

I first came here at the beginning of 2002. Even during the middle of winter in the pouring rain this place is stunningly beautiful. We stayed in the Glendalough Independent hostel, which is just a short walk from the

511

Wicklow
Things to Do & Places to See

Glendalough Monastic Site
Tel: (0404) 45325/45352

St. Kevin's Way
Hollywood to Glendalough, County Wicklow

Castleruddery Stone Circle
Signed off the N81 coming southwards from Hollywood.

Tours
Wild Wicklow Tour
Tel: (01) 4753313
Web: www. discoverdublin.ie

Day Tours Unplugged
1 Fairway Green
Griffith Rd. Dublin 11
Tel: (01) 8340941
Web: www. daytoursunplugged.ie
Email: info@ daytoursunplugged.ie

THE JOURNEY
LEINSTER
COUNTY
WICKLOW

*Eat &
Drink*

Ashford House
Ashford
Tel: (0404) 40481
Web: www.
ashfordhouse.ie
In line with my belief
that the best and
cheapest food is ser-
ved in pubs, the daily
carvery here is excel-
lent with generous
portions. Food is also
available in
Glendalough
Hotel and in
the nearby vil-
lage of Laragh.

*There &
Back Again*

TRAINS
Trains run from
Connolly Station to
Wicklow and Arklow,
on the Dublin to
Rosslare line.

BUSES
Bus Èireann leaves
from Dublin's Central
Bus Station and also
stops at Arklow and
Wicklow. Note that
Bus Èireann only goes
to Glendalough dur-
ing the summer.

THE JOURNEY

LEINSTER

COUNTY
WICKLOW

lakes, but not a short walk to the nearest shop, as the locals might have had us believe. When asked how far the nearest shop is, we were told it was just five minutes down the road. Well, it is five minutes if you drive by car.

The weather was a whole lot better this time around. As well as the stunning landscape, there is also a monastic settlement here very close to the lake, next to the Glendalough Hotel, that grew up around settlements begun by St. Kevin. Just at the start of the village is the Glendalough Visitor Centre, where the bus will drop you off.

I parked up by the river and wandered over to the Visitor Centre first. Before I went in to view the exhibition, the guy at reception told me about a couple of local legends: "There's a place nearby Ashford called 'The Devil's Glen'. The story goes that the Devil was trying to tempt St. Kevin, but got so frustrated at the saint's persistent refusal that he turned himself into a ball of fire and slammed into the nearby mountain, creating what is now known as the Devil's Glen."

He then pointed to a photo of the Wicklow Gap. "At the edge of this mountain is The Giant's Cut.

Glendalough Monastic Site. This monastery grew up around a settlement first established by St. Kevin.

Some of the many beautifully carved high crosses to be found at Glendalough Monastic Site.

The story goes that St. Kevin met Finn McCool here, and told him the story of the crucifixion of Jesus. The giant got so angry that he slammed his sword into the mountain at the Upper Lake." One story that he did not mention is that there once was a *Péist* (**Piast**) living in the lake, a dragon-like water monster that figures prominently in the myths and legends of ancient Ireland. It is said that this particular *Péist*, like all serpents, was driven out by St. Patrick, and will not return again until the time of the end.

Inside the centre I found a fascinating exhibition of St. Kevin's life. I then wandered back out onto the road and headed up to the ruins. Just inside the archway, which marks the entrance, is a stone on the right, fixed inside the wall, that has a cross inscribed upon it. Inside I made my way through the throngs of tour groups hugging the high cross and making a wish. I overheard the tour guide telling them to do this. Fortunately this cross was undecorated.

Inside the site are the remains of a couple of churches from the 10th century. The largest is the cathedral, and a smaller St. Mary's Church. A round tower sits

St. Kevin's Bus Service
Roundwood
Tel: (01) 281 8119
Web: www. glendaloughbus.com
Email: willrosa@eircom.net
Year-round service to Glendalough, Bray and Roundwood from St. Stephen's Green in downtown Dublin.

DRIVING

✠ From Dublin take the N11 south to Ashford and turn off on the R763 through the Devil's Glen to Glendalough.
✠ For the Vale of Avoca drive from Arklow follow the R747 to Woodenbridge and then the R752 to Avoca Village, where *Ballykissangel* was filmed.

Tuan's Notes
The Piast
Learn more about the Piast in The Mystery: Creatures Great & Small (pp. 177-178).

THE JOURNEY
LEINSTER
COUNTY
WICKLOW

"St. Kevin's Kitchen", a unique form of architecture identical to that used in St. Colmcille's house in Kells, Meath.

nearby, and down a small hill is the more interesting St. Kevin's Kitchen, a stone oratory with a small round tower protruding from its roof. The sloping roof is built completely of stone, just like St. Colmcille's house in Kells, County Meath. The Priest's House is just across from this and is a miniature oratory from the 12th century. Only the walls remain, but on the lintel above the doorway there is a representation of a monarch with an abbot either side of him.

From the front of this house was a breathtaking view of lush, green fields backed by verdant mountains glistening in the midday sun. It was easy to see how St. Kevin would have chosen here as a place of solitude. The problem was that the people wouldn't let him have it. There is a story of one woman who became so persistent in her devotion to him that she followed him everywhere, and eventually up to his cave, now known as "St. Kevin's Bed", 30 feet above the lake. He became so infuriated with her that he pushed her away, and she accidentally fell into the lake and drowned.

I wandered back to the van and took a drive along the R756, which takes you on a stunning ride through The Wicklow Gap. I parked at the top and stared down into the valley below. As well as the ruins, this valley is dotted with remains of smaller churches and a number of

514

sites associated with the saint. There is also a 20-mile walking trail known as St. Kevin's Way, which follows the ancient route carved out by the saint himself; up until medieval times it was also a pilgrimage. It runs from Glendalough to a little village now known as Hollywood.

Glendalough also has a round tower of the type that is unique to Ireland

The similarity with L.A.'s Hollywood ends at the name. It's believed that the name actually comes from the place's original name: "Holy Wood". This name came about when the saint himself was walking nearby with some companions when they found themselves blocked by trees. Kevin miraculously parted the trees to allow them through, blessed them, and put a curse on anyone who cuts them down. Thus the wood was considered holy ever after.

HOSTELS
Glendalough International Youth Hostel
Glendalough
Tel: (0404) 45342
Web: www.irelandyha.org
Email: glendaloughyh@ireland.com

CAMPING
Roundwood Caravan and Camping Park
Roundwood
Tel: (01) 281 8163
Web: www.dublin wicklow camping.com
Email: info@dublin wicklowcamping.com

Wolohans
Silver Strand, Dunbur
Tel: (0404) 69404
Web: www.wolohans silverstrand.com
Email: info@wolohans silverstrand.com

For more information visit ireland. mysteriousworld.com/ Journey/Counties/ Wicklow/

THE JOURNEY
LEINSTER
COUNTY WICKLOW

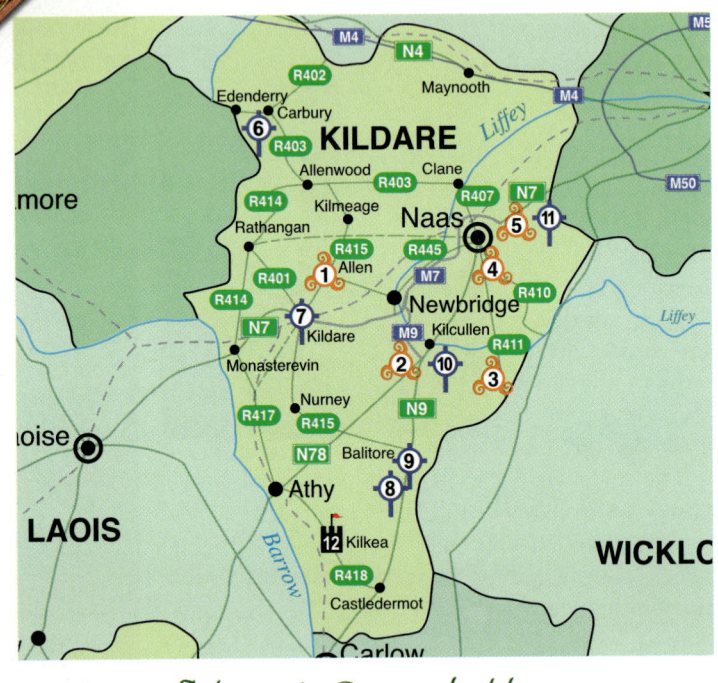

Places to See in Kildare

⚐ Ancient Sites

1. Hill of Allen 518
2. Dún Ailline
3. The Piper's Stones
4. The Longstone
5. Longstone Rath

✙ Christian Sites

6. Trinity Well
(Source of the Boyne) . . . 517-521
7. Cill Dara 517, 522-525
   • St. Brigid's Cathedral
   • St. Brigid's Church
   • St. Brigid's Well
   • The Black Abbey

8. Moone High Cross
& Well 518
9. Ballitore Quaker Village
10. Kilcullen Monastery
11. Kilteel — Knights Hospitaller
Monastery

⚑ Historical Sites

12. Kilkea Castle (Now Kilkea
Castle Hotel) 523

Driving Directions: See pp. 517-518, 521

Kildare
Trinity Well, Source of the Boyne

Trinity Well, the source of the Boyne River, the most historically and mythologically important river in Ireland. Originally associated with the goddess Boann, a festival called The Pattern of the Cross is now held here every first Sunday in June.

o you know anything about a festival here today?" I asked the lady behind the bar.

"No," she replied.

"It's supposed to be held at Trinity Well," I added.

"Ah! You mean the rosary."

"Well, that could be it," I said.

"Yes, it's on today."

"Oh, what time?"

"Two o'clock," she replied.

It was already two. Immediately I canceled the drink I'd ordered, ran back out to the van and sped off back to the well.

I had arrived here in the village of Carbury with high expectations, having read that the annual Pattern of the Cross is still held here every year on the first Sunday in June. I was staying in Trim when I read this, and it suddenly dawned on me that the next day was the first Sunday in June. So I made sure I was there. There were supposed to be huge celebrations with football matches, stalls, music and competitions. But when I arrived in the village, there wasn't a soul around.

St. Brigid's Fire

St. Brigid's Fire
will be kept alive outside the tourist office in Market Square by the time this book is out.

Moone High Cross
Located just south of Timolin, in the village of Moone off the N6 north of Carlow. This magnificent high cross dates from the 8th or 9th century, the carvings depict biblical scenes, including the loaves and fishes, the flight into Egypt and the 12 apostles. It's well-signed from the village, turn right and it's on the right hand side down the road.

Hill of Allen
Beside the crossroads in the village of Allen. Take the R415 north from Kildare through Newbridge. This was once the home of Finn McCool.

THE JOURNEY
LEINSTER
COUNTY
KILDARE

Trinity Well. This small stone structure allows access to the headwaters of the Boyne River.

Trinity Well lies in the grounds of Newberry House. The gates are opposite the turn-off for Edenderry, just outside the village. I had found the well just to the left of a small bridge on the road up to the house. It's small and has a stone canopy built around it. Even the couple who were visiting the well knew nothing about a festival. They filled a plastic bottle with water, and left. The water from this well, the source of the River Boyne, is said to render anyone who drinks it in June a poet. This is because **Boann**, after which the River Boyne is named, is the goddess of poetry. Might be a useful talent to have when my girlfriend is upset with me.

A single car was parked near the well when I arrived. I parked next to it, and got out.

"How's it going?" I said to the man sitting inside.

He simply nodded his head in response.

"Is the rosary here today?" I asked.

He nodded once again. "It'll be starting around 2:30."

I opened the side door of my van and sat down. The man watched me curiously from the corner of his eyes.

"How are ye?" said another man who pulled up on his bicycle.

518

To Christians, the water taken from Trinity Well imparts a blessing. Others believe that drinking the water, especially during the month of June, will make them a poet.

"Not too bad, thanks." I said. "There don't seem to be many people here for the rosary," I added quickly.

"Ah, they'll soon start arriving," he replied.

The Rosary at Trinity Well

As we stood there chatting more cars began pulling up, and soon the field around the well was teeming with local women, some in their best Sunday dresses, and men in their everyday clothes.

"Are you selling things here?" asked the man in the car, who had overcome his shyness and got out when the other man started talking to me.

"No, I'm writing a book on Ireland's ancient history and heard of the Pattern here, so I wanted to come see it."

"Ah, the Pattern of the Cross," said the man with the bike. "It used to be really big here. People set up stalls along the road, games were played and there were all sorts of competitions. That doesn't happen anymore. Nowadays they all go to the turf cutting festival at Ticknevin afterwards."

The priests had arrived by this time and so we all

Eat & Drink
Tyrrells Restaurant
Ballindoolin House & Gardens
Carbury
Tel (046) 9732400
Web: www.ballindoolin.com
Email: nikki@ballindoolin.com
3 miles north of Edenderry near Trinity Well.

Kristiannas Bistro
Market Square
Kildare
Tel: (045) 522985
Email: peterhoffmann@eircom.net

PUBS
Daniel Boland Lounge and Bar
The Square, Kildare
Tel: (045) 521263

Tuan's Notes
Boann
Learn more about Boann in The Mystery: Deities & Demigods (pp. 91-92).

THE JOURNEY
LEINSTER
COUNTY KILDARE

There &
Back
Again

TRAINS
There are regular
trains direct from
Dublin Heuston sta-
tion stopping at
Newbridge, Kildare
(30-40 mins) and
Athy (1 hr.).

BUSES
Bus Èireann
Tel: (01)
8366111
The following
buses stop at
Kildare:
✠ Bus No 8
Dublin to Cork
Bus No 12 Dublin to
Ennis

✠ Bus 126 Dublin to
Kildare stops at
Newbridge also.

✠ Bus 7 Dublin to
Kilkenny & Cork
stops at Athy.

✠ Bus 123 goes twice
a day from
Newbridge to Dublin
and stops on request
at the village of
Allen.

THE JOURNEY
LEINSTER

COUNTY
KILDARE

Though the Pattern of the Cross is a shadow of its former self, true believers still respect the old traditions and keep them alive.

made our way over to the well and joined the crowd. There were two priests. The younger of the two recited the rosary, while the other stood there clutching a cross hanging around his neck. I was amused to see that on the other side of the fence the cows from the neighboring field had gathered in a row to watch the congregation of people.

At the end of the recital the priest thanked everyone for turning up and keeping the old traditions alive. "If you take a drink from the well, then you'll live to attend the rosary next year," he joked.

As everyone began to disperse I got talking to the older priest, Alfie Murphy, who was now retired. I told him what I was doing and asked about the well. Alfie looked down into the glasses that sat on the tip of his nose, bridged his fingers and placed them in front of his chest. He stood there for a moment composing himself, then began to speak. For the next half an hour I listened intently as he told me the fascinating story of the coming of St. Patrick.

Alfie also explained how all the wells of Ireland were considered sacred in the pagan religion, and when Christianity came to Ireland they were blessed and given new names.

"Patrick came here to convert the High King at Tara and while here he blessed this well in the name of the Father, the Son and the Holy Ghost; the Holy Trinity. Thus this well was renamed 'Trinity Well'."

THE ANNUAL TURF CUTTING FESTIVAL

After chatting a bit with Alfie I got in the van and drove to the nearby village of Ticknevin for the annual Turf Cutting Festival. If you've ever watched the episode of *Father Ted* where they hold the annual Craggy Island Fair, then you'll have a mild understanding of how comical this little event was for me. It was held in a field behind a house, and was a way of keeping the old tradition of turf cutting alive. With modern machinery taking over, the old way of cutting by hand has died out.

As I wandered through the brown field to where the cutting was happening, I noticed a small caravan sat at the entrance with a single speaker on a pole beside it. The tinny voice that emitted from it announced upcoming events. Further up the field the competition was in full swing. The cutter used a shovel shaped so it would cut out a single block

Turf, which was once the main source of heat for the ancient Irish, is composed of peat that has become compressed over time. The turf is cut into brick-shaped blocks and burned like coal or wood.

J.J. Kavanagh & Sons Ltd.
Naas Industrial Estate, Naas
Tel: (045) 881400
Web: www.jjkavanagh.ie
Email: info@jjkavanagh.ie

DRIVING
✦ Trinity Well lies in the village of Carbury. Take the R402 west of Edenderry.
✦ Kildare is off the M7 west of Dublin.
✦ Moone is on the N9 north of Carlow.
✦ Allen lies north of Kildare on the R415.
✦ Athy lies on the N78. Take the R415 south of Kildare.

TAXI
Bengy's Cabs
Main St. Newbridge
(045) 434555

Bryan's Cabs
1926, St. Dominics
Newbridge
(045) 436107

AA Cabs
Leinster St., Athy
(059) 8634778

Places to Stay

HOTELS

Kilkea Castle Hotel
Castledermot
Tel: (059) 91 45156
Web:
www.kilkeacastle.ie
E-mail:
info@kilkeacastle.ie
Lying just south of Moone on the N9, this hotel is situated in a castle originally built in 1180. It claims to be the oldest continuously inhabited castle in Ireland, with 36 en-suite rooms, a restaurant and a wealth of outdoor activities.

B & B S

Dara Lodge
The Curragh
Kildare
Tel: (045) 521770
Mob: (087) 2922593
Email: daralodge
bandb@eircom.net
Just a few miles from Kildare town. 4 en-suite rooms.

of turf. He filled a wheelbarrow behind him and a runner took it back to the pile behind.

"The lady on the bike has lost her balloon," announced the voice over the tannoy.

I thought I was hearing things at first, then I spotted a woman with a large hat riding around on her bike. It was easy to see how the writer of *Father Ted* got his inspiration.

It was interesting to watch, for a while. But I couldn't have spent all day there, so I returned to the van and headed south.

Kildare Town

The little town of Kildare (*Cill Dara*) is the location of a monastery established in the 5th century by one-third of Ireland's trinity of best-loved saints, St. Brigid. A Protestant church named after her now takes its place. At 33 meters, the 10th-century round tower in its grounds is the country's second highest. The town's surrounding area also contains many Neolithic sites like standing stones and hill forts.

Stories of Ireland's patroness seem to blend with

St. Brigid's Cathedral stands on the site of the monastery that St. Brigid founded in the 5th century, which was once a major center of culture and learning.

St. Brigid's Tower is the second tallest round tower in Ireland, and one of only two towers in Ireland that can be climbed.

those of the ancient Celtic goddess Brigid, a triple goddess of fertility, healing and poets. Her symbol is fire, and this blends well with the story of how Brigid's Fire was kept alive from the 5th century by vestal virgins in the monastery in Kildare, and protected by the nuns until the twelfth century. The fire was re-lit in 1993 and has been kept alive by the Brigidine Sisters, in their home called *Solas Bhride* ("The Light of Brigid").

When I arrived at the tourist office in the main square, I noticed some construction work going on outside. "They are building a new fire pit so the re-lit St. Brigid's Flame can be put there," said the girl behind the counter. Brigid is said to have come here with her nuns in AD 480. She decided on *Druim Criaig* ("Oak-Covered Ridge") for the place on which to build her abbey. The town takes its name from this: *Cill Dara* ("Church of the Oak").

The legend of the goddess Brigid says she was the daughter of **the Dagda**. The *Dagda mór mac Eladan*, to use his full title, is the chief of the Celtic gods. The Dagda is the greatest of all the gods. A powerful wizard, his special sense was the power of knowledge; knowledge of what was to come or what was hidden. Some accounts also say that Brigid married King Bris

Bella Vista
105 Moorefield Park
Newbridge
Tel: (045) 431047
Email:
belavista@eircom.net
This B&B has 4 en-suite rooms.

Allen Sammax House
Allen Cross Rds.
Allen
Tel: (045) 860089
Mob: (087) 9307790
Email:
sammax2
@eircom.net
Located at the foot of the Hill of Allen.

Bowden
39 Ashville
Athy
Tel: (059) 8631948
I stayed here during my walk and can highly recommend this lovely little B&B.

Ardreigh Lock House
Athy
(059) 8638361
Situated beside the Grand Canal.

St. Brigid's Tower affords an excellent view of the cathedral and grounds including the fire pit in which St. Brigid's Fire once burned.

of the Fomorians, an evil, sea-faring race from the north.

At the rear of the church I came across the round tower and was surprised to learn that you can go inside this one and climb to the top. So I did. After a steep climb up wooden staircases I emerged at the top to a panoramic view of the surrounding landscape. Much of this part of Ireland is simply flat and green. Down below I could see clearly the square fire pit that was once home to Brigid's Fire.

Back down below, the attendant told me that this is one of only two round towers in Ireland where you can go up inside. The other is at St. Canice's Cathedral in Kilkenny. He walked me around the cathedral, showing me the other sites. At the front corner of the cathedral near the gates is a hole in the corner stone called the Wishing Stone. He explained that you must put your arm through the hole and place it on your other shoulder then make a wish. A woman with her young child was standing nearby so I watched as they tried it. Somehow I felt that if I put my arm in there, I might not get it back.

Strangely there is a skull and crossbones carving at the top of a door into the church. Nearby are a couple of medieval burial vaults. I had arrived late and unfortunately the church was closing, so I couldn't go inside. Instead I headed off to St. Brigid's Well, just outside of town.

St. Brigid's Well

From the crossroads I headed out on the Tully road and followed the signs for St. Brigid's Well. I turned

right opposite the Japanese Gardens, and then immediately left.

The well is situated in a grassy clearing, fenced off from the rest of the surrounding fields. A small stream called the Bratog flows into this clearing and to the well at the end. Beside the stream is a concrete crescent

shrine to Brigid, with large crosses on wooden-beaded necklaces hung from various parts of the statues. A stone archway marked the start of the five stones that lead up to the well at the end of the field. These stones mark the *turas*, or pilgrimage, that was once followed every year on St. Brigid's day, 1st February. This is a nice, well-looked-after site and a great place to relax for a while.

Aurora House
Kildare Rd
Athy
Tel: (059) 8633103

The Village Pump
Rathangan
Tel: (045) 524597
Situated in the centre of this quiet village beside the Grand Canal, this is a pub with accommodation upstairs. The rooms are clean and cozy, and extremely well priced.

CAMPING
Forest Farm Camping & Caravan Park
Dublin Rd.. Athy
Tel: (059) 8631231
Web: www.accommodation athy.com
Email: forestfarm@ eircom.net
Only 3 miles from Athy, also does B&B and self catering.

For more information visit ireland. mysteriousworld.com/ Journey/Counties/ Kildare/

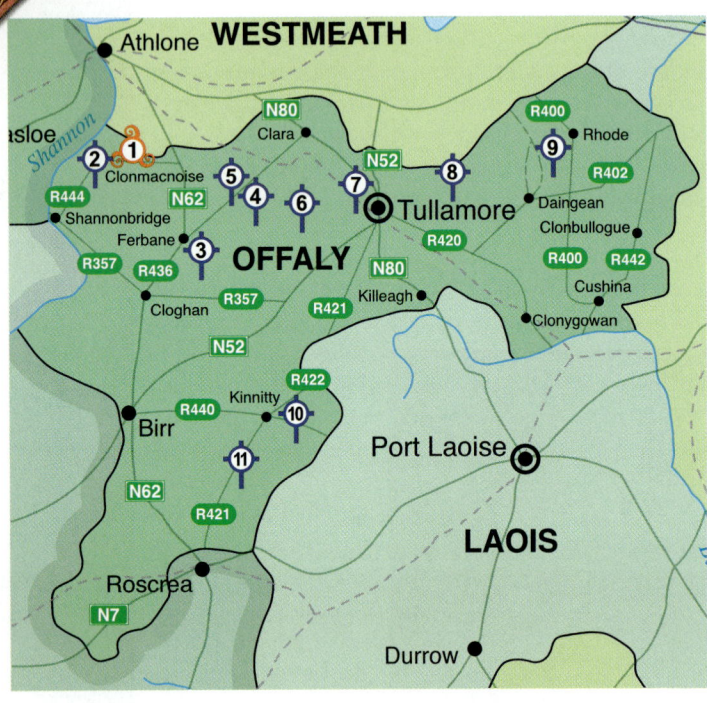

Places to See in Offaly

⚘ ANCIENT SITES
1. Doon Castle Sheela-na-Gig

☦ CHRISTIAN SITES
2. Clonmacnoise 527-529
3. Gallen Priory
4. St. Manchán's Church & Well
5. St. Manchán's Shrine
6. Rahan Monastic Site
7. Tihilly Church & High Cross/
Durrow Monastic Site
8. Rahugh Well & Stone
9. Croghan Hill Cairn

10. Kinnity Cross
11. Seir Kieran

Driving Directions: See pp. 529

Offaly
Clonmacnoise

ying on the southern shores of the mighty River Shannon, at the very western edge of County Offaly, is the incredible monastic settlement of Clonmacnois. The settlement lies on the old Esker road, which was an important road in ancient times. The surrounding bog made much of the landscape impassable, meaning this was the only route through the area, and that everyone had to cross at this point. This is more than likely

The famous Cross of the Scriptures at Clonmacnoise.

why St. Ciarán chose this spot in the 6th century to establish his monastery.

This is a different Ciarán from the one who blessed the holy well outside of Kells, in County Meath. This St. Ciarán was educated under St. Enda on Inishmór, one of the Aran Islands. He came here, after establishing a monastery on an island on nearby Lough Ree, and apparently befriended Prince Diarmuid, who had been exiled by his father King Tual. Ciarán is said to have prophesied that Diarmuid would become king the next day, and sure enough by a twist of fate the king died. Diarmuid was crowned king shortly after.

To show his appreciation King Diarmuid helped Ciarán build the first church here at Clonmacnois. Ciarán is said to have brought with him a dun (gray-

Offaly
Things to Do & Places to See

Clonmacnois
Tel (090) 9674134
Open: Easter to October, Clonmacnois is possibly Ireland's largest and best ancient monastic site.

Festivals
Seachtain Na Gaeilge
Bridge House Hotel
Tullamore
Ireland's biggest indoor festival.
Tel: 057 9325600
Web:
www.bridgehouse.com
Email:
info@bridgehouse.com

Tours
Bus Éireann
Tel: (01) 8366111
Web: www.buseireann.ie

Celtour Ltd.
Phone: (0502) 56157
Web: www.celtour.ie/ireland.htm
Email: celtour@iol.ie
Runs a 1-day tour.

THE JOURNEY
LEINSTER
COUNTY
OFFALY

With numerous high crosses, well preserved ancient ruins, and a place of significance in Irish history, Clonmacnoise is considered to be Ireland's largest and best ancient monastic site.

ish-brown) cow with a never-ending supply of milk. It was from the hide of this cow that the famous *Book of the Dun Cow* was created.

After Ciarán's death the site had grown rapidly. A stone church replaced his wooden structure, and other churches were built along with a round tower. Three high crosses were carved and burial sites were decorated with elaborate grave slabs. The site is so big that it is said to have resembled a small town, rather than just a monastic settlement. Evidence of domestic houses have been found on the site.

The River Shannon sitting beside the site makes it a picturesque and possibly peaceful place, when the crowds are all gone. St. Ciarán is said to be buried in the temple at the rear of the main cathedral that dominates the middle of the site, and was undergoing restoration when I arrived. The three replica crosses sit in front and either side of the 10th-century cathedral, which is the largest building on the site and has a lovely Romanesque doorway. The cathedral was built by Flann Sinna, said to have been the King of Tara.

In the corner is a 10th-century round tower. The

rest of the site is dotted with the remains of other churches. The remains of Temple Finghin on the north side of the site, closest to the river, is an interesting little 12th-century church which has a small round tower built into the edge of it. The site was plundered many times over the centuries by both Vikings and Irish, and was finally reduced to a ruin by the English garrison at Athlone in 1552.

Back inside the visitor centre I walked through the display section where the real crosses sit, along with a selection of carved grave slabs. The Cross of the Scriptures was the centerpiece of the site and is said to be one of the finest surviving examples of a high cross. It was carved from a solid piece of limestone in the 10th century. It stands 14 feet high, and is the most intricately carved of all the three. Depictions of a variety of biblical scenes are carved in every available spot. The South Cross stands 12 feet high and has simple Celtic decorations, while only the shaft of the North Cross remains.

Also on display here are just a few of the 700 decorated grave slabs found in the area. They are inscribed with artistic crosses and the name of the person commemorated.

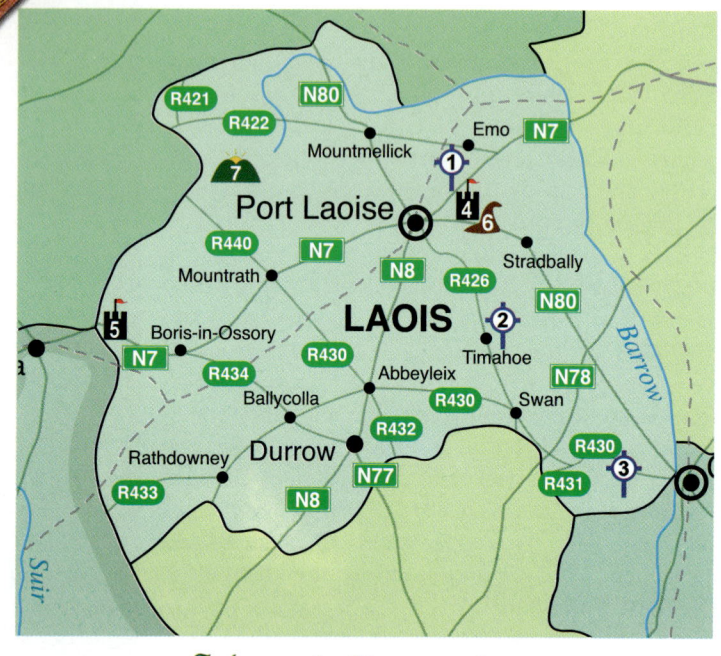

Places to See in Laois

✠ CHRISTIAN SITES
1. St. John's Church
2. Timahoe Monastery & Round Tower
3. Killeshin Church & Monastery

🏛 HISTORICAL SITES
4. The Rock of Dunamase . . . 531
5. Ballaghmore Castle 531

🐾 CRYPTID SIGHTINGS
6. The Bandog 531

🏔 SCENIC VIEWS
7. The Slieve Bloom Mountains 531

Laois

A view from the top of The Rock of Dunamase.†

aois is the small county wedged between Offaly and Kildare. Though possibly the least visited county, it does have the lovely Slieve Bloom Mountains in the west, and in the center is the Rock of Dunamase, a dramatic lump of limestone rising 150 feet high into the air that had been used as a fortification for over 2,000 years. King Laois Ceann Mór of the Milesians used it and also gave his name to the county. It also appeared on a map drawn by Ptolemy in 140AD, which goes to show just how well known this landmark was in ancient times.

The castle, built by the infamous King Diarmuid Mac Murrough, was plundered by the Vikings, later passing into the hands of the Norman Strongbow via marriage. Cromwell later attacked and pretty much destroyed the place. According to *Sacred Ireland* there is a legend that tells of buried treasure inside the rock that is guarded by a fierce dog called the *Bandog*, who breathes flames from his massive jaws at anyone attempting to steal the treasure. I decided to give that one a miss.

Laois
Things to Do & Places to See

Rock of Dunamase
On the N80 east of Portlaoise.

Eat & Drink
Grellan Delaney & Sons, Bar & Bistro
67 Main Street
Portlaoise
Tel: (0502) 22916
Web: www.grellan delaney.com

Places to Stay
Ballaghmore Castle
Dublin Road
Borris-in-Ossory
Tel: (0505) 21453
Fax: (0505) 21195
Web: www. castleballaghmore.com
Email: gracepym@eircom.net

For more information visit ireland. mysteriousworld.com/ Journey/Counties/ Laois/

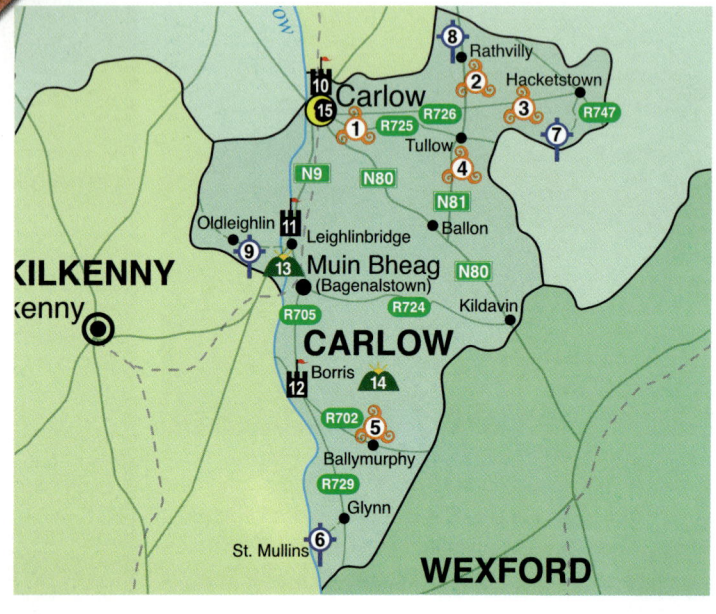

Places to See in Carlow

🚴 ANCIENT SITES
1. Browne's Hill Dolmen 533, 536-537
2. The Six Fingers
3. Haroldstown Dolmen 533
4. The Pillar Stones of N. Carlow
   • Adristan Grooved Pillar Stone
   • Aghade Holed Stone
5. Rathgeran Rock Art

✟ CHRISTIAN SITES
6. St. Mullins 533, 535-536
7. Clonmore
8. Waterstown Monastic Site
9. Old Leighlin Monastery/
St. Molaise's Well

🏛 HISTORICAL SITES
10. Carlow Castle Ruins/
Asylum. 534
11. The Black Castle 539
12. Borris House 538

�︎ SCENIC VIEWS
13. The Barrow Way/Leighlinbridge/
Bagenalstown 533-534
14. Mt. Leinster/The Blackstairs
Mountains

❶ NIGHTLIFE
15. The Dinn Ri Restaurant/
Club 535-536

Driving Directions: See pp. 533, 536-537

Carlow

The River Barrow runs south through Carlow town and east of Waterford before finally emptying into the sea. One can walk the towpaths all the way to the sea along the famous Barrow Way.

On the River Barrow, the town of Carlow tends to be ignored by many people. At first glance it might seem as though there isn't much to see, but the appeal of Carlow is that it is a normal Irish town that doesn't attract many tourists. People had told me before I came here, "Carlow is not a tourist town, it's a college town."

I first came here for the yearly Eigse Arts Festival. I rolled into town in the Scooby Van and went off in search of the Otterholt Riverside Hostel. The Otterholt House is a lovely, whitewashed building with a large, impeccably maintained garden. The beautiful River Barrow runs through the adjacent field. A small sign on the grass bore the words: "Welcome to Otterholt". I was greeted warmly by the staff, and settled in with a cup of tea in the large kitchen before heading off to see the town.

Just beyond Tullow Street, the main shopping cen-

Carlow
Things to Do & Places to See

Brownes Hill Dolmen
On the R726, Tullow Road, just outside Carlow Town

Haroldstown Dolmen
On the R727 continue on to Hacketstown after Brownes Hill Dolmen and it's just at the River Derreen crossing.

Leighlinbridge & Bagenalstown
Lovely villages on the Barrow River.

St. Mullins
Start of the Barrow navigation and home to the monastic settlement established by St. Mullins.

Carlow Tourist Office
Tullow Street.
Tel: (059) 9131554
Web: www. southeastireland.com

THE JOURNEY
LEINSTER
COUNTY
CARLOW

Festivals

Eigse Arts Festival
Over a week's woth of cultural festivities in old Carlow town.
Tel: 059 9140491
Web:
www.eigsecarlow.ie
Email:
eigsecarlo@eircom.net

Bagenalstown Festival

A yearly festival along the River Barrow.
Tel: 05997 21660
Web:
www.bagenals town-festival.com
Email: mims@ eircom.net

Eat & Drink

Dinn Ri
Tullow Street
Carlow
Tel: (059) 9133111
Fax: (0) 59 9134697
Web: www.dinnri.com
Email:
info@dinnri.com
The very popular *Dinn Ri* multistory complex boasts five different venues.

THE JOURNEY

LEINSTER

COUNTY
CARLOW

ter, I found the ruins of an old castle. There wasn't much left, just the front wall flanked by two towers. The guidebook explained that the castle was built by William Marshall in the 12th century. The castle had survived Cromwell's attentions, but the reason for its condition now was due to a Dr. Middleton having turned it into an asylum, then blowing it up in 1814. He must have been a relative. I wandered on and crossed the river. To the left was the Barrow Way, which took me on a nice, scenic walk along the river itself.

Carlow Town

Being as Carlow is a college town it also has a vibrant nightlife. Traditional Irish music might be hard to find — well, it was for me the night I was there anyway. When I did see an advert, it turned out to be two blokes with electric guitars and a very bad PA system. Adding anything electronic somehow seems to kill the atmosphere of a traditional session. After my first trip to Ireland I had fallen in love with the music I had heard in the pubs all across the country. Upon my return home I missed it, and so bought some CDs. Somehow it just wasn't the same. It was good, but it's just impossible to capture the passion and the atmosphere on tape. Nothing can compare to the experience of being in a real Irish pub, with wooden floors and furniture, the smell of freshly poured Guinness and the sight of a row of half-filled pints along the bar, waiting to settle. And a CD cannot recreate the depth of the music being played by the small group of people sitting around the table in the corner, their spirit being encouraged by the crowd of drinkers in the pub tapping their feet on the wooden floor and singing along to their favorite songs.

But please don't let me put you off Carlow's

nightlife. As I said, it has a vibrant and modern music scene. I first experienced this nightlife on a night out with my friend Brendan, who was working in the hostel at the time. We first went looking for music in a pub called *Deveraux*. *Deveraux* is a two-leveled complex with a large pub downstairs and a nightclub upstairs, which unfortunately has a cover charge. From here we went on to *Teach Dolmain*, a much more appealing place. The bar staff here were very friendly, and were sympathetic to our having to suffer the very bad karaoke singers that night. For a very long time I had always believed that every single Irish person was an extremely talented singer. But if you want proof to the contrary, then just go to a karaoke night.

Despite the bad singing, we elected to remain at the *Teach Dolmain* until closing time when we were dragged off by a couple of local girls to the town's most popular nightspot, the *Dinn Ri*. *Dinn Ri* means "The King's Fortress", and has taken its name from the legendary *Dinn Ri* that once lay on the banks of the River Barrow near Leighlinbridge, south of Carlow. We'll get to that story shortly.

Picturesque Leighlinbridge, south of Carlow.

Sean's Lounge
Main St.
Leighlinbridge

Lord Bagenal Inn
Main St.
Leighlinbridge
Tel: (059) 9721668
Web:
www.lordbagenal.com
Email:
info@lordbagenal.com

Teach Dolmain
76 Tullow Rd.
Carlow
Tel: (059) 9131235
Despite the karaoke, this charismatic pub also offers live acts and great Stout.

There & Back Again

TRAINS
The train station is just outside town on station road. It's on the Dublin to Waterford line, and has four trains daily each way.
Tel: (059) 9131633

BUSES
✦ Bus No 4, runs from Dublin starting at 7.15 am and run-

THE JOURNEY
LEINSTER
COUNTY CARLOW

Carlow is on the
Dublin to
Waterford route.
There are several
buses a day. It also
stops at
Leighlinbridge on
request.
♦ There are three
buses a day to and
from Kilkenny (4 &
131).

**J.J. Kavanagh
& Sons Ltd.**
Coach Park
Little Barrack
Street
Carlow Town
Tel: (059) 9143081
Web:
www.jjkavanagh.ie
Email:
info@jjkavanagh.ie
A private bus service
with routes to and
from Carlow to a
variety of places in
the south.

DRIVING
♦ From Wexford take
the N11 north and
just past Enniscorthy,
take the N80 all way
to Carlow. From
Dublin take the N7 to

The modern *Dinn Ri* is a New World nightclub with an Old World flair. It boasts five different bars, each with unique characters.†

The modern *Dinn Ri* is situated in the center of town and is its most prominent landmark, rising high over the main shopping centre. It boasts five different bars each with a different atmosphere, and somewhere in the complex is a nightclub. I can't remember where, I was quite drunk at the time. The *Dinn Ri*'s nightclub is renowned for having one of the best sound systems in Europe. I must admit, if you like clubbing, this is a must-see.

The Irish name for Carlow is *Ceathar Loch* ("Four Lakes"), so named because it was once believed that Carlow was made up of four lakes. Today it marks the meeting point of the Barrow and Burrin Rivers.

Browne's Hill Dolmen
The memories of my previous visit all came flooding back as I drove into town. This time I had no plans to stop, however. I had come here in search of Browne's Hill Dolmen, which lies on the R726 east of town.

Upon arrival I was astounded by the sheer size of the capstone. It's 20 feet square, 5 feet thick and estimated to weight 150 tons. There are four upright stones on one side, but the other side has collapsed. (I would too if I had 150 tons on my shoulders.) This is believed to be the largest capstone in Europe.

The tomb hasn't been excavated so little is known about it. Dolmens, or portal tombs, are characterized by a well-defined entrance with two portal stones and a larger capstone. Other upright stones would prop up the rest of the capstone, but generally the capstone would slope so the rear of the chamber would be lower than the entrance.

Carlow is actually Ireland's second-smallest county. Naturally this means that Carlow is its only major town. But it does have a scattering of attractive little villages. At the far southern end of the county lies St. Mullins, which also signifies the start of the Barrow navigation. From this point not only can you navigate the river right up to Dublin, but you can also walk the towpaths.

Browne's Hill Dolmen, though partially collapsed, still has the distinction of having the largest capstone in Europe.

Naas, then the N9 into Carlow. From Kilkenny follow the N10, then the N9. From Waterford take the N9. The R417 from Athy follows the Barrow River, and is a nice scenic drive.
✤ Scenic drive along the River Barrow from Carlow. For Leighlinbridge and Bagenalstown follow the N9, Kilkenny road and turn off at the signs.
✤ From Bagenalstown take the R705 to Borris, then the R729 to St. Mullins.

TAXI
Carlow Cab Service
20 Woodgrove
Tullow Road
Tel: (059) 9132404

CAR HIRE
Auto Rentals
Carlow Town.
Tel. (059) 9140600
Email:
info@autorentals.ie
Website:
www.autorentals.ie

THE JOURNEY
LEINSTER
COUNTY
CARLOW

Tuan's Notes
*Learn more about The
Legend of King
Labraidh Loingseach in
The Mystery: Folklore
& Mythology (pp. 208-
209).*

St. Mullins

St Mullins' monastery is surrounded by numerous ornate gravestones.

I first made my way to St. Mullins in 2003 as part of my charity walk. Sore and blistered feet had forced a weekend's rest in New Ross, but afterwards I headed off northwards to join the river here. It was only a few miles, some of which were cut off by the hostel owner directing me on a shortcut. Unfortunately he neglected to inform me about the big Doberman and the electric fence.

The town got its name from St. Mullins (also known as "St. Moling") a 7th-century cleric who founded a monastery there, the ruins of which can still be seen. It's said that the ancient kings of south Leinster are buried at the abbey.

The Barrow River snakes its way through the valley between the Blackstairs Mountains and Killeshin Hills, and forms the border between Carlow and Kilkenny. The first major village on the Carlow side is Borris, lying in the woods surrounding Borris House, which is owned by the Kavanagh family who are descendents of the McMurrough-Kavanagh's, ancient kings of Leinster. The most infamous of these chieftains was Art McMurrough who was the most feared and ferocious fighter in the country. He ran rings around the Norman invaders and infuriated King Richard II.

The next major stopover is Bagenalstown, an attractive village founded by Walter Bagenal. The locals here are never short of enthusiasm and ideas. When I arrived here it was just a few days too soon to witness the great rubber duck race for charity. The plan was to place the ducks on the river, then open the lock gates and allow the currents to take them on their journey.

Previous events in the annual Bagenalstown Festival have included such things as rubber duck races down the River Barrow. Visit www.bagenalstown-festival.com for up-to-date information.

A little way north from here I came across Leighlinbridge. This beautiful little village was a pleasant place to rest and soak up the sunny day. It is also the subject of a Carlow legend: **The Legend of King Labhraidh Loingseach**. The *Dinn Ri* (King's Fortress), near present day Leighlinbridge, was once the seat of power for many of south Leinster's kings. But now it seems that the only *Dinn Ri* left in Carlow is just the seat of bad karaoke.

How the mighty have fallen.

"The Black Castle" in Leighlinbridge, originally built to protect the bridge which was a strategic crossing point along the River Barrow.

The Garrison
Leighlinbridge
Tel: (059) 9723956
Web: www.garrison waterside.com
Email: garrison waterside@eircom.net
Just off main street.

Harold & Noreen Ardill
Mulvarra House
St. Mullins
(051) 424936
Email: info@ mulvarra.com
An attractive little B&B situated on a hill overlooking the Barrow Valley.

HOSTELS
Otterholt Riverside Lodge
Kilkenny Rd.
Tel: (059) 9130404
Situated 10 min. walk from the town centre on the main Carlow to Kilkenny road.

For more information visit ireland. mysteriousworld.com/ Journey/Counties/ Carlow/

THE JOURNEY
LEINSTER
COUNTY
CARLOW

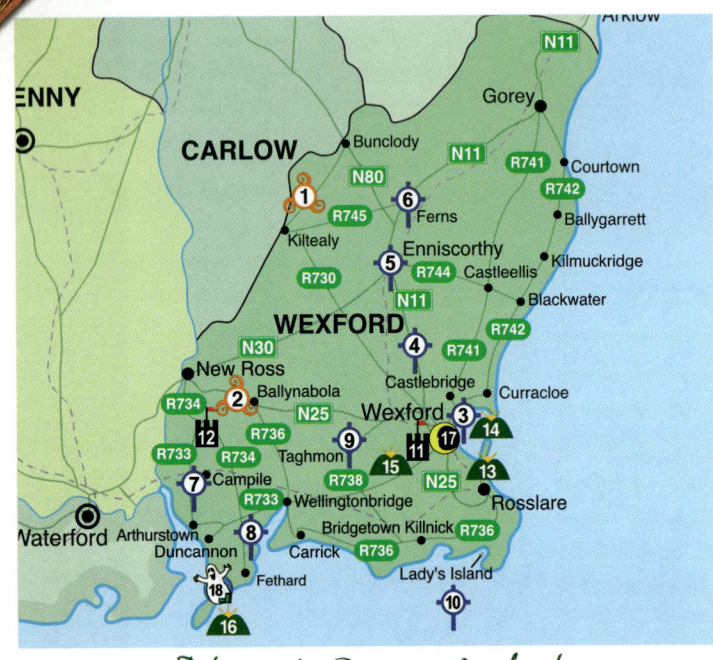

Places to See in Wexford

🔱 Ancient Sites
1. Blackstairs Mountain/
Caher Roe's Den
2. Carrickbryne Hill

✟ Christian Sites
3. Selskar Abbey 542-543
4. St. David's Well
5. St. Aidan's Cathedral
6. Ferns Monastic
Settlement 541-542, 548
7. Dunbrody Abbey
8. Tintern Abbey 542, 549
9. St. Munnu's Cross
10. Lady's Island
   • Holy Well
   • St. Vogue's Monastery

🏛 Historical Sites
11. Irish National Heritage Park
12. John F. Kennedy Park 541

⛰ Scenic Views
13. Sunny Southeast Beaches . . 545
14. Wexford Harbor 542
15. Forth Mountain
16. Hook Peninsula . . 541, 545-546

❶ Nightlife
17. Wexford town 543-544

👻 Haunted Houses
18. Loftus Hall 541, 546-548

Driving Directions: See pp. 541-
542, 546, 547

Wexford
The Last Homely House

Ian outside Kirwan House hostel, the last homely house for many before entering the wild unknown of rural Ireland. Kirwan House has been the starting place for many of Ian's adventures.

he county town of Wexford is the first major town you hit after arriving in Rosslare from Wales or France on the ferry. When I first arrived here back in 1999, I was instantly taken with the place. After much traveling around Ireland my feet bore an uncanny resemblance to the surface of the moon, and I longed for a cozy, homely house in which to rest them. As I walked through Wexford's narrow streets lined with old historic buildings, I knew instantly that I had found that place. This feeling was confirmed upon arrival at Kirwan House tourist hostel, where I received a warm welcome and found a cozy television room inviting me to come in and put my feet up. I decided there and then that I would sling down my backpack and rest for a week. That week turned into a month, for this visit anyway.

Wexford
Things to Do & Places to See

Hook Head Lighthouse
Site of the oldest lighthouse in the world.
Web: www.thehook-wexford.com

Loftus Hall
Believed to be haunted! From the lighthouse, go to the mini roundabout and turn left. The house is just up the road on the left.

Kennedy Homestead
Dunganstown
Tel: (0)51 388264
Web: www.kennedyhomestead.com
Email: info@kennedyhomestead.com
The ancestral home of President Kennedy. South of New Ross on the R733.

Ferns Monastic Settlement
Established by St. Mogue in the village of

Ferns,
north of
Enniscorthy
on the N11.

Tintern Abbey
North of Fethard
on the R734, just
before it crosses the
R733.

**Irish National
Heritage Park**
Ferrycarrig, Wexford
Tel: (053) 20733
Web: www.inhp.com
Email: info@inhp.com

**Wexford
Tourist Office**
Crescent
Quay
Tel: (053)
23111
Web: www.
southeastireland.com

Festivals
**Kilmore Quay
Seafood Festival**
Every July. For more
info, call (053)29922.

For more info on
Festivals in County
Wexford, see Meath,
or go to ireland.
mysteriousworld.com/
ThingsToDo/Festivals/

Wexford Harbor

The river Slaney flows diagonally from northwest to southeast across Wexford into a broad harbor named *Loch Garman* (the original Irish name for Wexford). Vikings sailed into Loch Garman in AD 819 and conquered the area, renaming it "Wexford". There are two harbors at the mouth of the Slaney, an outer and an inner, connected by a "Narrows" on which the town of Wexford is situated.

Wexford's large harbor attracted many races throughout history. The Gaelic name for Wexford is *Loch Garman*, and local legend tells of how one Garman Garbh was drowned on the nearby mudflats by flood waters released by an enchantress. The resultant lake was named Lake of Garman (*Loch Garman*). Much of Wexford harbor is still very shallow, and a large portion of it has been reclaimed to build the front section of the town and the lovely quays that were finished just a couple of years ago. Despite not being the bustling port it once was, Wexford harbor is still a popular fishing port.

Wexford Town

Wexford's skyline is dominated by the spires of its two Catholic churches: Rowe Street and Bride Street churches. One of the town's many attractions is Selskar Abbey, founded by Sir Alexander Roche after a crusade to the Holy Land to recover the Holy Sepulchre. He was

542

forced to go there by his parents in the hope it would prevent him from marrying the local girl he loved, because she was a poor man's daughter. While away the girl was told he had died in battle. Upon his return from Palestine he learned that she had entered a convent. Alexander entered the monastery, took a vow of celibacy and became its first prior, dedicating the monastery to the Holy Sepulchre and decorating it with its relics.

In the old days Wexford's harbor was a bustling port and thus the town has a thriving history as well as an alarming number of pubs, even for an Irish town. I was originally told there are ninety, but later told it was more like sixty. There is no shortage of nightlife, and the main street is awash with bars, restaurants and cafés. I have been living on and off in Wexford over the years, and have sampled this nightlife in great depth. Wexford has a fantastically diverse music scene. Traditional Irish music can be found in many pubs around town, most notably in the Sky and the Ground on South Main Street on Monday, Tuesday and Wednesday night. Some nights the amount of musicians in one setting can fill an entire corner of the pub. On other occasions outsiders might surprise you with a favorite song of theirs. Or you might be coerced into singing a song yourself. The pub has traditional-style décor, and a low-lit ambience. At the weekends there might be a more modern band playing in the beer garden or upstairs. The bar food is excellent, and upstairs you can dine in the Heavens Above Restaurant.

Another must see is Mary's Bar, especially on a Saturday night. Saturday night is traditional music night, and in Mary's this is especially poignant. Mary's is a tiny locals bar. It's the kind of place where you'll be squashed together with local characters who'll make you believe you've been transported into an episode of *Father Ted*. The music could be provided by the usual

Eat & Drink

Cappuccino's Café
25 N. Main St.
Wexford
Highly Recommended
The food is great and the service friendly.

O'Briens Sandwich Bar
41 N. Main St.

PUBS
The Sky and the Ground
112, 113 S. Main St.
Tel: (053) 21273
Eat here in the pub or in the Heavens Above restaurant upstairs. Traditional music sessions are Mon-Wed. with a live band on weekends.

Bar Undertaker (Mackens)
Bullring, N. Main St. Local musicians provide excellent music sessions on Fri, Sat and Sun. Look out for Mocha, a talented guitarist with an amazing voice.

THE JOURNEY
LEINSTER
COUNTY
WEXFORD

Mary's Bar

By the Arts Centre at the end of High Street. A wonderful little locals bar with traditional music on Saturday nights.

Thomas Moore Tavern

Cornmarket
This is a lovely old half-timbered pub reminiscent of an ancient medieval public house. You can just imagine receiving your beer in an old tin tankard as you sit by the open fireplace.

Centenary Stores

Charlotte St.
Possibly the most popular pub in town, it has traditional music sessions some weeknights and on Sunday mornings.

Mooney's Lounge

12 Commerical Quay
Party in the nightclub, or enjoy an ordinary pub atmosphere.

array of traditional instruments, and songs sung by seasoned locals. This is also the one place in town where you'll be guaranteed to hear locals sing acapella when the blinds have gone down at closing time.

Another favorite small pub of mine is Bar Undertaker, on the corner by the Bull Ring (so-named because it was once the center for bull-baiting). Locals mostly refer to this pub as "Mackens". This is after the owner, Eddie Macken. This is very much a locals pub, and at the weekends it gets especially lively with acoustic guitar sessions.

Cafés and coffee houses have come and gone over the years, but one that has remained constantly since I first arrived is Cappuccinos, on the corner of Main Street and Rowe Street. This is fortunate for most backpackers staying at Kirwan House because this is the most likely place in which to find a job. As well as providing work to penniless backpackers, they also provide excellent food. Every time I have been there the place is full. It's a popular place for the locals.

Another good place to eat is O'Brien's Irish Sandwich Bar, one of a chain across Ireland. The sandwiches are well-filled and very tasty. People have been known to question, what is an Irish sandwich? Tom, a local Wexford musician, has the answer: "They're called Irish sandwiches because the filling's on the outside."

The great thing about Wexford town is that the local council has refused permission for large stores to build on the outskirts. This has meant that people come into the town to shop, and many of the small family-run businesses have not been swallowed up by the corporate giants. Even Tesco has had to resign itself to fitting into a moderate unit. Wexford's narrow streets are a reminder of its Viking past and are lined with many old houses.

The Sunny South East

This part of Leinster is known as The Sunny South East. And it's not just a name given to mislead people into coming here, it really does get the most sun of any part of Ireland. In a country noted for its rainy weather, this is a blessed relief. And if this isn't enough, then the county's coastline boasts some of the most stunningly long, golden beaches in the country, rivaled only by County Donegal in the northwest. The difference here is you are more likely to get the weather to enable their enjoyment.

Inland southern County Wexford is extremely remote. A few miles west of the town lies Forth Mountain, where you'll find a hidden lake along the Three Rocks Trail, a waymarked path. Further west is nothing but rural countryside where you'll hardly see a soul, until you reach the Hook Peninsula. Hook houses the oldest lighthouse in the world.

Hook Peninsula

I had lived on and off in Wexford for three years before I finally took a trip to the Hook Peninsula.

Hook Head Lighthouse, the oldest lighthouse in the world. The original is believed to have been built by Dubhán, a 6th-century Welsh monk. The current lighthouse dates to the 12th century.

There & Back Again

FERRIES
Irish Ferries
Tel: (053) 33158 or book online at
www.irishferries.ie

Stena Line
Tel: (053) 61555 or book online at
www.stenaline.ie
Ferries run twice daily to and from Rosslare Europort. Irish Ferries run from Pembroke in Wales, and Stena Line from Fishguard. Both ferries sail to Rosslare once in the afternoon and once during the night. Sailings from Rosslare are in the morning and late evening. Irish Ferries also offers daily sailing to and from France.

For more information on ferry service in Wexford and much more visit ireland.mysteriousworld.com/Counties/Wexford/

TRAINS
O'Hanrahan
Train Station
Tel: 053 22522
is situated at the
north end of town
opposite Redmond
Square. There is
only one train line
running though
Wexford, which
comes from Dublin
and ends at Rosslare
Europort.

BUSES
Bus Èireann
Just outside
the train sta-
tion. Purchase
tickets across the road.

Viking Shuttle Bus
runs services around
the area and to
Kilmore Quay, leav-
ing from Redmond
Square.

**J.J. Kavanagh &
Sons Ltd.**
Main St., Urlingford
Co. Kilkenny
Tel: (056) 8831106
Web:
www.jjkavanagh.ie
Email:
info@jjkavanagh.ie
A private bus service.

THE JOURNEY
LEINSTER
COUNTY
WEXFORD

When I did I wished I hadn't left it for so long. This is the jewel of Wexford county. There are two ways to get to it: the easy way is to drive the R733 (which in the summer is framed with vivid wild-flowers) and the hard way is to cycle there, or walk the Wexford Coastal Path. The Wexford coastal path is part of the Irish Waymarked Trails and takes you from Wexford Town down through Rosslare, the attractive little village of Kilmore Quay (a good time to visit is during the Kilmore Quay Seafood Festival in July) and on through Wellingtonbridge to the Hook Peninsula.

Legend says that Dubhán, a 6th-century Welsh monk established the first light beacon at Hook after his dismay at the sight of shipwrecked bodies along the rugged coastline. It is believed that the first Viking invaders of Ireland were so pleased to have a guiding light that they allowed the monks to live there unharmed, and sailed on to take Waterford.

The current structure was established in the 12th century. The Wexford Coastal Path takes you right through the beauty of this wild and rugged landscape. Entrance to the lighthouse is by guided tour only, and takes you up the 115 steps right to the top where you will have a magnificent view of the entire peninsula. On a good day you can see the Blackstairs Mountains in the north of County Wexford.

Loftus Hall
In the lighthouse restaurant I noticed a plaque on a wall with the headline: Loftus Hall, the most haunt-ed house in Ireland. The story goes that in 1765 a young lady was living there, and that she longed for some romance in her life. The Hook is a bleak and

Loftus Hall is believed to host its very own ghost. The hall is not open to the public, but might still be worth a look-see.

lonely place in the winter, and so life was dull for her. One stormy night a young man arrived on horseback, claiming he was lost and had been guided here by the light from the lighthouse. He needed shelter for the night, and was welcomed in by the owners, much to Anne's delight. He was invited to stay for some time and during the course of his stay romanced the young and lonely Anne, apparently whiling away the long nights with a game of whist. (Must have been one hell of a charmer.) It was during one of these games that Anne was to discover his terrible secret. As she bent down to recover some cards she had dropped, Anne saw that her companion had unmistakably cloven feet. Her screams echoed through the house and made the man aware that his secret was out. Immediately he turned into a ball of fire and exited through the roof. The hole left by his departure apparently resisted all attempts at repair, and remains there as a reminder of the story.

There are many tales of his returning to annoy the residents of Loftus Hall, until he was finally exorcised by a local priest. Anne went insane and

DRIVING
If driving from Dublin take the N11 and follow this straight into Wexford. From Waterford take the N25. The R700 just north of New Ross is the scenic backroad to and from Kilkenny. From Carlow take the N80 south through Bunclody and onto the N11.

Coastal Drive
From Wexford take the N25 southward and turn off onto R736 to Lady's Island, Carnsore Point and onto Kilmore Quay.

TAXI
Wexford Cabs
Tel: (053) 23123

CAR HIRE
Wexford Car Hire
23 Ferrybank
Wexford

Rosslare Harbour Car Hire
Hertz Desk Arrivals
Terminal
Rosslare Harbor

Hotel Curracloe
Curracloe
Tel: (053) 37308
Web: www.
hotelcurracloe.com
Email: hotelcurracloe
@eircom.net
This luxury hotel is
just down the road
from the famous Cur-
racloe Beach, made
famous as the
location for
filming the
award-winning
movie, *Saving
Private Ryan*.

The Talbot Hotel
Trinity St., Wexford
Tel: (053) 9122566
Web:
www.talbothotel.ie
Email:
sales@talbothotel.ie
Has a lovely view of
Wexford Quays and
harbor.

Whites Hotel
 Georges Street
Wexford
Tel: (053) 22311
Web:
www.whiteshotel.ie
Email:
info@whiteshotel.ie

THE JOURNEY

L E I N S T E R

C O U N T Y
W E X F O R D

it is said that her tortured ghost wanders the rooms of the hall to this very day. Unfortunately Loftus Hall isn't open to the public.

Whichever way you go to Hook you will end up in Wellingtonbridge, situated at the start of the peninsula. I first arrived here during my 280-mile walk across Ireland for charity. I'd walked over 15 miles from Wexford town and arrived soaking wet and footsore only to find that the village pub does-n't do accommodation anymore. However, just out-side of town were a couple of B&Bs, so I trudged onwards. Imagine my delight as I came over the brow of the hill to a vacant sign. And imagine my heart sinking when Anne Murphy nodded her head in the negative when she opened the door. Fortunately there was another down the road, so she invited me in and phoned to book me in there. Nell, the owner down the road insisted that she come pick me up, so while we waited a pot of tea and a heater was put on to help warm me up.

The Haven Lodge was a welcome sight, and the

Ferns Monastic Settlement, established by St Mogue in the vil-lage of Ferns, north of Enniscorthy. St Mogue's 18th-century cot-tage has been restored and sits nearby, as does St Mogue's Well.

Just north of Fethard can be found Tintern Abbey, a lovely area featuring the remains of a Cistercian abbey.

cozy little room even more welcome. Being a few miles outside of the village Nell insisted on cooking me dinner and generally pampering my every whim. For €25 this was an absolute bargain, and the friendliness of the family here was just what I needed after a long day walking without hardly a soul to talk to. In the morning Nell saw me off with a hearty breakfast and a packed lunch for the day's walking. I made a point of returning there after the walk and staying another night.

B & B S

Haven Lodge
Rochestown,
Wellingtonbridge
Tel: (051) 561319
Mob: (087) 9732005
Email: ellencolfer
@hotmail.com
Highly recommended

River Valley Farmhouse
Wellingtonbridge
Tel/Fax: (051)561354
Web: www.rivervalley
farmhouse.com
Email:
rivervalley@
oceanfree.net

HOSTELS
Kirwan House
Friary Church View
Mary St.
Wexford
Tel: (053) 21208
Web: homepage.
eircom.net/~kirwan
hostel/
Email: kirwanhostel
@eircom.net
Highly recommended

For more information on places to stay in Wexford and much more visit ireland. mysteriousworld.com/ Journey/Counties/ Wexford/

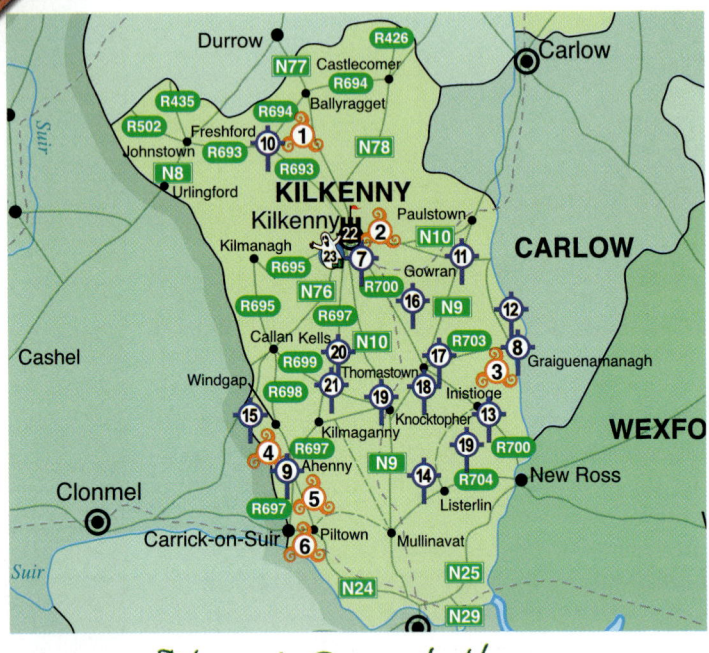

Places to See in Kilkenny

🐚 ANCIENT SITES

1. Rathbeagh Mound
2. Freestone Hill Fort and Cairn
3. Brandon Hill
4. Knockroe Passage Cairn
5. Kilmogue (Harristown)
Dolmen. 551, 556-557
6. Tibberaghny Carved Pillar

☥ CHRISTIAN SITES

7. St. Canice's Cathedral. . 551, 552
8. Graiguenamanagh Abbey . . 551
9. Ahenny High Crosses, Kilkieran
Crosses & Well. 551, 554-555
10. Freshford Church
11. St. Mary's Collegiate Church
12. Ullard High Cross

13. Cloonamery Church
14. Mullennakil Holy Well & Tree
15. Killamery Cross
16. Tullaherin Church & Tower
17. Kilfane Church/Cantwell Fada
18. Jerpoint Abbey
19. Knocktopher Double Effigy
Tomb
20. Kells Priory
21. Kilree Monastic Site

📙 HISTORICAL SITES

22. Kilkenny Castle. 551, 552

🕯 HAUNTED HOUSES

23. Kyteler's Inn 553-554

Driving Directions: See pp. 551-
552, 554-555

Kilkenny

Ahenny High Crosses are distinguished by the addition of a sacred-stone-type "cap" that remembers the old sacred stones of the pagan era.

he road to Kilkenny from Wexford is a particularly attractive one. From Wexford you take the N25 towards New Ross. Just before New Ross you can turn off, or go through New Ross itself. Either way

Kilkenny
Things to Do & Places to See

St. Canice's Cathedral & Round Tower
In Kilkenny at the top of Parliament Street. You can enter the tower.

Kilkenny Castle
There is a charge for entrance, but the gardens are free.

Kilmogue Dolmen
Near the village of Harristown. Follow signs for Harristown Dolmen.

Graiguenamanagh
At the rear of the abbey in the graveyard there are two interesting Celtic crosses.

Ahenny High Crosses, Kilkieran Crosses and Holy Well
In the villages of the same name on the R697 south of Kilkenny

THE JOURNEY
LEINSTER
COUNTY
KILKENNY

M. Doyle's pub in nearby Graiguenamanagh is not only a pub and a grocer, but also a hardware store.

you head for the R700. It takes you along the River Nore and through the little village of Inistioge, where original shop and pub fronts are still prevalent. It's a pity that the bus doesn't go this way.

Once during an interview here on Radio Kilkenny I was berated by the DJ for referring to Kilkenny as a town. Kilkenny is in fact a true city due to its large medieval cathedral, named after St. Canice who founded a monastery here in the 6th century. The round tower on its grounds is one of two in Ireland where you can go inside and climb to the top. This, however, is probably not the first thing that will jump out at you. Instead you will not fail to notice Kilkenny Castle, first built in 1172 and eventually sold to the city in 1967 for the whopping sum of £50. Despite their favorable deal, the council still deem it necessary to charge you to go inside, but a stroll around the castle's lovely gardens is free.

The castle was first established by William the Earl Marshall, son-in-law to the Earl of Pembroke, known as Strongbow. Strongbow was established as pretender heir to the kingdom of Leinster by Diarmuid Mac Murrough, the King of Leinster, in return for helping him regain his kingdom after being banished by the High King for abducting the wife of a local chieftain.

Kilkenny Town

Kilkenny is possibly one of the most attractive towns in Ireland with its narrow streets lined with old-fashioned shop fronts. The Kilkenny Arts Festival in August each year is a particularly good time to visit. The town comes alive with street entertainers, traders and artists from all over Ireland. There are theatres, literature, film and workshops. The festival runs for ten days and you'll find free music every night in many of the pubs. There is also classical, jazz and popular music in various venues around town.

Kilkenny lies upon the River Nore, one of three mighty rivers flowing through the county. The Barrow River runs along the eastern border of the county, and it's possible to walk the river's towpaths from St. Mullins. The river is navigable from this point northwards and so you can also hire canal boats. Graiguenamanagh is a small village lying on a particularly attractive stretch of the river.

The Witch of Kilkenny

In the year 1300 a house was built by the father of Alice Kyteler, a local woman who would eventually be accused of witchcraft.

After her father died, Alice inherited all his wealth and property. She married one of his associates and bore him a son, and afterwards she extended her current house into St. Kieran's Street and developed it into an inn. She was an attractive woman, and the inn soon became the haunt of wealthy men, young and old, who craved her attention.

Alice's first husband died under mysterious circumstances. It is said that he discovered the cupboard of ingredients she used for her satanic witchcraft, and was poisoned shortly after.

Over the years Alice's four husbands all died under

Eat & Drink

Kyteler's Inn
27 St. Kieran's St.
Tel: (056) 7721064
Web:
www.kytelersinn.com
Email:
info@kytelersinn.com
The original home of the Witch of Kilkenny is now a restaurant, bar and nightclub.

PUBS

John Cleere
28, Parliament St., Kilkenny
Highly recommended
The Monday night traditional music session is one of the best I've heard.

The Pump House
26 Parliament St.
Also has traditional sessions Mon., Tues. & Wed. nights.

Byrne (WM)
39, John St.
Great pub up near the train station.

M. Doyles
Graiguenamanagh
This pub is also a grocers and hardware store.

THE JOURNEY
LEINSTER
COUNTY KILKENNY

There & Back Again

TRAINS
McDonagh Train Station
Kilkenny
Tel: (056) 7722024
On Dublin Road, across the river from the main town.

BUSES
Buses operate out of the train station.

J.J. Kavanagh & Sons Ltd.
Main Street
Urlingford
Tel: (056) 8831106
Web:
www.jjkavanagh.ie
Email:
info@jjkavanagh.ie
A private bus service with routes all over the south.

DRIVING
To Kilkenny:
✠ From Wexford take the N25 to New Ross, then follow the R700.
✠ From Carlow take the N9 then N10.
✠ From Dublin, the fastest route from

THE JOURNEY
LEINSTER
COUNTY
KILKENNY

suspicious circumstances, and she was reported to have used her magic to bestow all the town's riches to the house of her son, William Outlawe, from her first marriage. She was eventually charged, along with her sister, son and maid, and ordered to be burned at the stake outside the town hall in 1324, but escaped from her cell under Kilkenny Castle and fled to England. No one knows what happened to the sister. The son bargained for his life by offering to re-roof the St. Canice Cathedral, which collapsed some years later. Only the maid was actually burned at the stake in front of the entire town.

Kyteler's Inn still exists today and is a bar, restaurant and has a nightclub at the back.

Ahenny & Kilkieran Crosses

Just north of Carrick on Suir lie a small cluster of interesting sites. From Kilkenny I took the R697 south through the village of Kells where there is a priory on the site of a 6th-century monastery founded by St. Ciarán. I headed to Ahenny where the old graveyard behind the village had a couple of interesting Celtic crosses, then continued on to the small village of Kilkieran.

Graiguenamanagh, Ahenny and Kilkieran all have large cemeteries with numerous high crosses.

554

The name comes from St. Ciarán, who apparently came this way also and established a monastery here. Nothing really remains of the church, but there are three Celtic crosses at the site. A man was planting flowers in the graveyard as I approached.

"Lovely day, isn't it?" he said.

"Yes it is," I replied.

"What brings you here?" he asked, betraying the fact that not many tourists come anymore.

"I've come to see the crosses, and the holy well."

"Ah, the well is over there in the corner. It's said to cure headaches. I've tried taking some in the past for the wife, but it didn't work."

"Ah well, I guess there are some things even a miracle can't cure," I replied.

I wandered over to the well. A metal lid covers the well, but beside it is a *bullaun* stone filled with water. *Bullauns* are stones with a bowl that has been naturally carved and filled with rainwater. It's traditionally believed that the water that collects in these has curative properties. I took a drink from the stone and headed back to the van, the old man smiling and wishing me good luck. Hopefully mine will be better than his.

Dublin is via the N7 and N78. A more scenic route would be to go via the Wicklow Mountains.

⚜ From Kilkenny, take the R679 through Kells, Ahenny and Kilkieran. Take the N9 to Thomastown, then take R703 to Graiguenamanagh. Take the R705 south along the Barrow River and then the R700 through Inistioge to Kilkenny.

TAXI
Castle Cabs
1 Rose Inn st,
Kilkenny
Tel: (056) 7761188

CAR HIRE
South East Budget
Rent-A-Car
Kilkenny
Tel. (056) 21168

BIKE HIRE
Bikes can be hired from the Tree Grove campsite. See Camping section for more details.

THE JOURNEY
LEINSTER
COUNTY
KILKENNY

<Places to Stay>

HOTELS
Kilkenny River
Court Hotel
The Bridge, John St.
Kilkenny
Tel: (056) 7723388
Web:
www.kilrivercourt.com
Email: reservations
@kilrivercourt.com

B & B S
O'Keeffe B&B
13 John St.
Kilkenny
Tel: (056)
7770219

Teach Èilís
68, Aylesbury
off Freshford Rd.
Tel: (056) 7770339
Mob: (086) 4041574
Email:
kk25@familyhomes.ie

Bellview House
Abbey St.
Tel: (059) 9725917
Overlooks the abbey.

Ballyogan House
Graiguenamanagh
Tel: (059) 9725969
Web: www.
ballyoganhouse.com
Email: info@
ballyoganhouse.com

THE JOURNEY
LEINSTER
COUNTY
KILKENNY

Kilmogue Dolmen

Kilmogue Dolmen, "the Stone of the Ghost". Though partly collapsed, at 15' Kilmogue Dolmen is still the tallest dolmen in Ireland

From here I headed over to Owning to find the Kilmogue Dolmen. I tried to follow the directions I had, but seemed to go around in circles and ended up back at the pub in town. So I asked in the pub for directions.

"Oh! Why did you come here? It's far from here," said the lady behind the bar. She asked the only customer in the pub, an old man wearing a flat cap, sitting in the corner. "It's up near Harristown," he said.

Ironically I'd passed there and seen a sign that read Harristown Dolmen. "I know where that is," I replied. Yet, she still insisted on giving me detailed directions.

A road ran down the side of the pub, with a church on the left. I followed this until I came to a T-junction, where I turned left. Staying on the main road I came to another T-junction where I turned right again. Then I saw a sign pointing left for Harristown Dolmen. I followed this road for 2 miles until I came to a brown sign with Kilmogue Dolmen on it pointing right. A short way down the lane I parked up on the right and found the dolmen.

In Irish its called *Leac an Scáil*, which means, "Stone

of the Ghost". This is the tallest dolmen in Ireland, and quite spectacular. Two 12-foot-high portal stones support a capstone that reaches 15 feet. It has collapsed at the back and the capstone now sits at almost a 45-degree angle. The dolmen lies in pastureland near a tributary of the River Suir, the type of landscape said to have been preferred by the builders of these monuments in the southeast. These tombs were originally surrounded by earth and rocks, but now only the passage stones remain.

Places to See Key for Munster Province

Here is a list of the icons used in the county maps in this section:

☀ Multiple sites near each other

♨ Ancient pagan, pre-Christian sites, often of unknown origin

⚲ Christian sites

📕 Historical sites, heritage centres

🗡 Cryptid sightings (mysterious, unknown and/or legendary creatures)

1 Scenic views and museums

① Nightlife and popular hangouts

👻 Haunted houses and areas

✈ Major airports

🚃 Major train stations

🚌 Major bus stations

Munster Province

Munster province is the southernmost of the four provinces and, like Leinster, contains two very popular counties to visit: Cork and Kerry. Munster was the ancient home of the Tuatha dé Danann and their descendants, the Éoganacht kings, the greatest of which was the famous Brian Boru. Munster is one of the most popular tourist destinations due to its combination of magnificent scenery and exceptional ancient, Christian and historical sites.

County Tipperary boasts The Rock of Cashel, the ancient seat of the Éoganacht kings. County Waterford has excellent scenery and the Ardmore Monastery, believed by some to be the oldest in Ireland. Counties Cork and Kerry are two of the largest and most visited counties in Ireland. Cork features stunning scenery along the Beara Peninsula, as well as the largest ogham stone in Ireland, numerous stone circles, and is also endowed with the Paps of Anu. Kerry has the famous Ring of Kerry, the Dingle Peninsula and the island monastery of Skellig Michael, three of the most popular places to visit in all of Ireland.

County Limerick is the ancient homeland of the Tuatha Dé goddess Áine and the fairy king Donn, with numerous beautiful and mysterious locations associated with each. Not to be outdone, County Clare has Magh Adhair, the ancient inauguration point of the *Dál Cais*, the family of Brian Boru. The Burren is an interesting stretch of rocky terrain stretching for miles all the way to the coast, culminating in the magnificent spectacle of the Cliffs of Moher. Clare also has the Poulnabrone Dolmen, one of the most famous in Ireland.

Munster
General Information

Tourist Information Offices:

✢ **Cork City**
Tel: (021) 4255100
Web:
www.corkkerry.ie
Email: info@
corkkerrytourism.ie

✢ **Glengarriff**
Tel: (027) 63084
Web:
www.bearainfo.com

✢ **Killarney**
Beech Rd.
(064) 31633

✢ **Dingle**
The Quay
(066) 9151188

✢ **Kenmare**
The Square
Tel: (064) 41233

✢ **Waterville**
Tel: (066) 9474646

✢ **Arthurs Quay**
Limerick
Tel: 061 317522

✢ **Adare**
Main Street
Tel: 061 396255

THE JOURNEY
MUNSTER PROVINCE

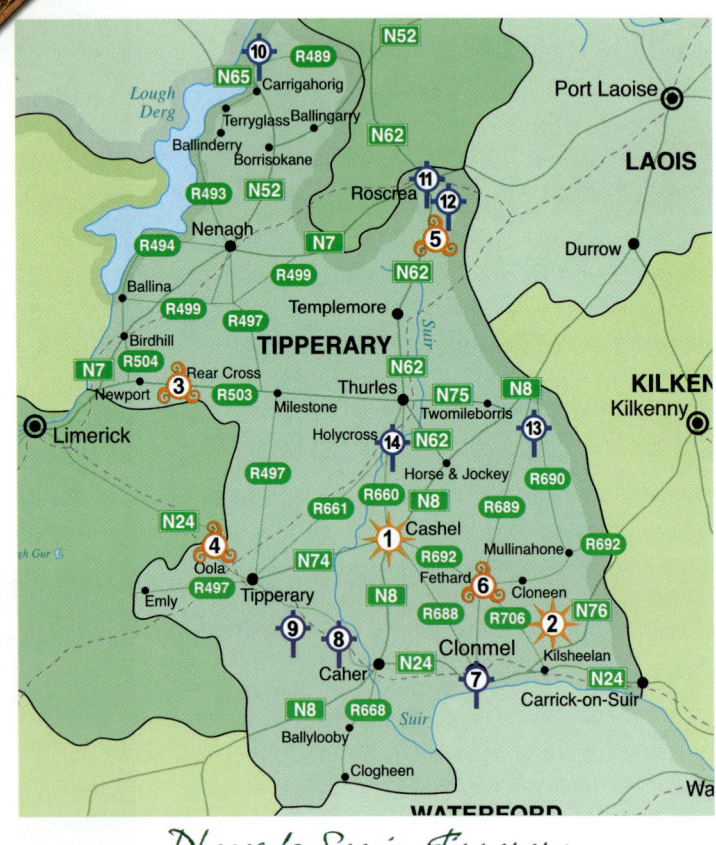

Places to See in Tipperary

☀ MULTI-SITES
1. Rock of Cashel ... 561-564
2. Slievenamon 87, 564

᚛ ANCIENT SITES
3. Baurnadomeeny &
Shanballyedmond Cairns
4. Longstone Rath
5. Timoney Hills Standing Stones
6. Fethard Sheela-na-Gigs

☦ CHRISTIAN SITES
7. St. Patrick's Well
8. Kilpeakan Monastic Site
9. Killberrihert
10. Lorrha Monastery
11. Roscrea/Ross Monasteries
12. Monaincha Retreat
13. Kilcooley Abbey
14. Holy Cross Abbey

Driving Directions: See p. 563

Tipperary
The Rock of Cashel

The Rock of Cashel, the ruling place of the kings of Munster for over 1,500 years.

he small market town of Cashel might otherwise have been overlooked by many if it weren't for its most impressive feature: The Rock of Cashel. The center of Tipperary is little more than a vast, limestone plain. Yet, towering over the village of Cashel, is a 200-foot lump of limestone that is home to over 1,500 years of history.

The small town of Cashel nestles snugly at the foot of the rock.

Tipperary
Things to Do & Places to See

The Rock of Cashel
Lying in the village of Cashel, this was the ancient seat of the kings of Munster.

Tourist Offices:
✠ Tipperary: 062 51457
✠ Cashel: 062 61333

Tours
Bus Éireann offers a 1-day tour from Cork to the Rock of Cashel, Kilkenny City and Lismore.
Tel: (021) 450 8188
Web: www.buseireann.ie

Eat & Drink
Alice's Bistro
105 Main Street
Cashel
Tel: (062) 62170

PUBS
Mulcahys
47 Gladstone Street
Clonmel

THE JOURNEY
MUNSTER
COUNTY
TIPPERARY

THE JOURNEY
MUNSTER
COUNTY
TIPPERARY

In the 5th century the Eóghanacht clan built a fortress here on the rock and ruled for the next 500 years. This was until Brian Boru came and defeated the clan and took the throne of Munster, ruling it from his seat in County Clare.

Of course, like any place of great historical importance, it's also said that St. Patrick came here in the 6th century and

A high cross at Cashel

converted the king to Christianity. The story goes that Patrick accidentally stabbed the king in the foot with his crozier during the ceremony and the king bore the pain,

Cormac's Chapel

St. Patrick's Cross, used in the inauguration of all the kings of Munster.

believing it to be part of the inauguration.

In the 12th century the descendants of Brian Boru handed the rock over to the church, who then built a huge cathedral on it.

The structures on the rock are all enclosed by a wall. In the 15th century the Vicar's Choral was built, and this is where I entered today. A small museum inside holds the remains of St. Patrick's Cross, which is said to have been the sacred cross used at the inauguration of all the Kings of Munster, including Brian Boru. The

The Cathedral of Cashel

Places to Stay

HOTELS
Cashel Palace Hotel
Main Street, Cashel
Tel: (062) 62707
Built in 1731

B & B S
Currabeg B&B
Deer Park, Golden Rd.
Cashel
Tel: (062) 6124
Mob: (087) 2498112
Email: currabeg@
oceanfree.net
On the N74, just
outside of town.

Amberville
Glenconnor Rd.
Clonmel
Tel: (052)
21470
Email:
amberville
@eircom.net
Open Jan-Nov.

HOSTELS
Cashel Holiday Hostel
6 John St., Cashel
Tel: (062) 62330
Web: www.cashel
hostel.com
Email: info@
cashelhostel.com
Open year-round.

The Rock of Cashel also features an 11th-century round tower.

cross is carved from limestone and stands 7 feet high.

I passed through Cormac's Chapel, a fascinating place with medieval furniture, stone head carvings around the ceiling, and a large tapestry with the mural of a king and his queen. To the left of the entrance is a stone sarcophagus, which is believed to hold the remains of King Cormac.

Outside, the cathedral is the centerpiece of the rock. It has an 11th-century round tower built into the side, which stands 28 feet tall. This side was undergoing reconstruction at the time.

Clonmel

"Slievenamon, the Mountain of the Women, is known in local folklore as being the mountain where women would race up the hill, and the first to the top would be the one to marry Finn McCool." I was talking to Niall, the owner of Powers the Pot campsite, in his little bar. I had been here many times before, mostly because it's a nice, peaceful campsite that sits high in the Waterford mountains. But also because of the nice little bar he's created in the old cowsheds beside his house.

The Timulus at Lattin. Tipperary has many mounds, cairns and other archaeological artifacts just waiting to be discovered or rediscovered by the next generation of intrepid explorers.

Powers the Pot campsite not only has an unusual name but, being at 1,200 feet above sea level, also boasts the highest house in Ireland. The campsite actually sits in the region of Clonmel, but is across the river and technically in County Waterford. Because many of the borders are along rivers, many of the border towns actually cross two counties.

Niall explained that there was a cairn on top that can be seen from the campsite on a clear day. There is also a cairn on Knockroe, north of Carrick on Suir. This area is rich in folklore and Neolithic sites. Niall explained that a brand new settlement had been discovered recently and could be the most significant find in years.

I was here a couple of years before when I first learned there was a Magic Road down south. It's in the Comeragh Mountains near to Mahon Falls. Business elsewhere meant that I couldn't go there then, so I returned a few weeks later and ventured further into County Waterford to check it out.

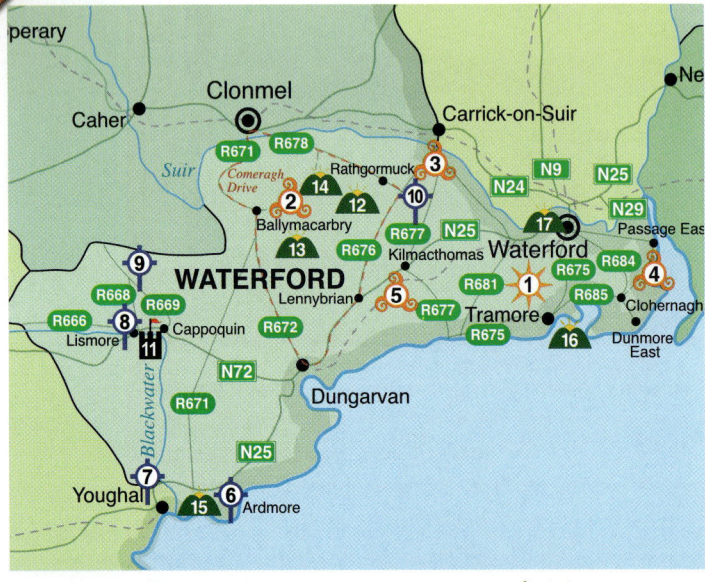

Places to See in Waterford

☀ MULTI-SITES
1. Neolithic Graveyard
   - Carriglong Passage Cairn
   - Knockeen, Gaulstown Dolmens
   - Matthewstown Passage Cairn
   - Ballynageeragh Dolmen

⚐ ANCIENT SITES
2. Magic Hill 567-570
3. Toberchuain Dolmen
4. Harristown Passage Cairn
5. The Ogham Cave of Drumlohan

♱ CHRISTIAN SITES
6. Ardmore Monastery 567, 570-572
7. Molana Abbey
8. Lismore Cathedral . 567, 572-573

9. Mount Melleray Cistercian Monastery
10. Toberchuain Holy Well/ Mothel Abbey

⚑ HISTORICAL SITES
11. Lismore Castle . . 567, 572-573

⛰ SCENIC VIEWS
12. Commeragh Mountains . . 567-570
13. Monavullagh Mountains . . 567
14. Mahon Falls 567-568
15. St. Declan's Way 569, 572
16. Waterford Beaches 567
17. Waterford Crystal Visitor Center 568

Driving Directions: See pp. 567-572

Waterford

Waterford town is a major port town lined with fabulous beaches and scenic coastlines. Image © Richard Cummins/Lonely Planet Images.

The county of Waterford is well known for its fabulous beaches and coastline, scattered with fishing villages and holiday resorts. But as well as this, it also contains beautiful mountainous landscape just a short drive from the coast. The Nire Valley runs between the Comeragh and Monavullagh Mountains. Mahon Falls are located here, and the road that leads to this is known as Magic Road.

(Another) Magic Hill

Magic Hills are not exclusive to Leinster province. Munster also has its own Magic Hill, in Waterford.

From Powers the Pot Campsite I followed the road through Rathgormuck until I reached some crossroads. From here I followed the signs to the right for Mahon Falls and the Comeragh Drive until reaching a little place called Mahon Bridge and turned right at P. Powers and Son food store. I followed the road up

Waterford
Things to Do & Places to See

Ardmore Monastery
Established by St. Declan, before the coming of St. Patrick. To get there take the N25 out of Dungarven towards Cork, and turn left on the R673.

St. Declan's Well
Follow the way-marked path 3 miles from Ardmore up along the cliffs.

Lismore Castle
The Book of Lismore was found here. Lismore lies on the N72 east of Fermoy. Web: www.lismorecastle.com

Lismore Heritage Centre
Just south of the castle, the centre offers excellent exhibits of local history, including *The Book of Lismore*. Educational

THE JOURNEY
MUNSTER
COUNTY
WATERFORD

Scenic Drives
The Comeragh Drive
A lovely drive through the Nire Valley to Mahon Falls and the Magic Road.

The Vee Drive
A lovely drive through the Knockmealdown Mountains. (See *There & Back Again: Driving* for driving directions.)

THE JOURNEY
MUNSTER
COUNTY
WATERFORD

Gorgeous Mahon Falls is one of the scenic highlights of the Waterford countryside. Image © Richard Cummins/Lonely Planet Images.

into the mountains, turned right at another sign for Mahon Falls then followed the road through a small gate. Just past here the road went downhill, at the bottom of which stood a lone tree amid low, thick bushes by the roadside. I stopped here, as I had been instructed.

Behind me were two German backpackers I'd met. Upon learning about what I was doing that day, they decided to follow me. I turned around and indicated that we were here. The driver took his foot off the brake and sure enough his car started rolling back up the hill. I did the same. I chuckled as I watched their faces light up like schoolchildren who had just seen an act of magic for the first time.

I continued on to Mahon Falls. The road twisted through a landscape of green hills dotted with purple heather. The Comeragh Mountains formed a picturesque backdrop. Soon I came upon a car park. From here there is a path where you can walk to the bottom of the falls. Just a short way up the road from the car park, up a steep hill, is another small lay-by. I parked next to a couple who had spent the night here in their camper. From here you get a panoramic view of the surrounding landscape, and, as the family from Leeds had found out, it's a great spot for a picnic.

I had been told that from the start of this Magic Hill it's actually possible to roll all the way back to the shop, which is a good couple of miles. So I decided to test the theory.

I drove to the start of the hill, and then put the van in neutral; leaving the engine running so the brakes would work. Rolling up the hill when facing forward does have the same effect, but it isn't as intense. At the top of the hill I did continue rolling for a while, and then slowed to a painfully slow pace. I was about to give up and put the van in gear when it began to slowly pick up speed again. Soon the pace quickened until I was coasting down a steep hill towards a T-junction. I had no choice but to apply the brakes here because I couldn't see around the corner. Once I had determined nothing was coming I released the brake and once again continued rolling down the giant hill for another mile or so, sweeping through the

A group of hikers on the Seefin Circuit, heading towards Coumshingaum in the picturesque Comeragh Mountains.
Image © Eoin Clarke/Lonely Planet Images.

Scenic Walks

St. Declan's Way
A 60-mile way-marked trail that follows the ancient pilgrimage route from Ardmore, via the Blackwater River, Lismore and through the Knockmealdown Mountains, finally ending in Cashel.

Festivals

Waterford Spraoi
Tel: (051) 841808
Web: www.spraoi.com
Usually held over the August bank holiday weekend.

Tours

Bus Éireann
Runs a tour to Lismore from Cork, taking in the Rock of Cashel and Kilkenny.
Tel: (021) 450 8188
Web: www.buseireann.ie

Tourist Offices
⚘ *Waterford City*
41, The Quay
Tel: (051) 875 823

THE JOURNEY
MUNSTER
COUNTY
WATERFORD

Eat & Drink

Ballyrafter House Hotel & Restaurant
Lismore
Tel: (058) 54002
Web: www.ballyrafterhouse.com
E-mail: info@ballyrafterhouse.com

PUBS

Paddy Mac's Pub
Main Street
Ardmore
Tel: (024) 94166
Also does pub lunches.

Eamon's Place
Main Street, Lismore
Tel: (058) 54025

There & Back Again

AIR

South East Regional Airport
Waterford
Tel: (051) 875589
Web: www.flywaterford.com
E-mail: info@flywaterford.com

TRAINS

Waterford Train Station
Terminus Street

THE JOURNEY

MUNSTER

COUNTY
WATERFORD

narrow country roads until finally parking up beside the shop at the bottom of the hill. So it could be done!

This road is part of the Comeragh Drive, a well signposted drive that circumnavigates the Comeragh Mountains and goes through wooded sections of the Nire Valley. It's a lovely drive and will eventually take you out on the N25, where you can head west for the little seaside village of Ardmore.

Ardmore

The 30-meter-tall round tower and a high cross from St. Declan's original monastery, dating from the 12th century. Image © Richard Cummins/Lonely Planet Images.

The weather was beautiful that day … when I was here two years ago. Today, it was pouring with rain.

Ardmore is well signed off the N25 just south of Dungarvan. It sits tucked into the edge of a promontory close to Ram Head. The first monastery was established here by St. Declan. What's different about this is that St. Declan was said to have come here long before even St. Patrick had begun his journey. This is believed to have been the first-ever monastery established in Ireland.

Ardmore is a lovely little seaside resort with a large, sandy beach. Unfortunately, the rain was lashing down

The ruins of St. Declan's Cathedral date to the 13th century and feature detailed stone carvings.

so fiercely that hardly any of it could be seen today. The streets were empty, and just a few cars were parked in the car park, their owners remaining inside staring out into the mist that had engulfed the entire beach.

I drove up to the hill overlooking the town, where there is a ruined medieval cathedral which now sits upon the site of St. Declan's monastery. I got out and stood under my umbrella in front of the remains of

The cathedral interior still retains many interesting features.

Tel: 051 873401/317899 Trains go to Waterford City only from Rosslare and Dublin.

BUSES
Waterford Bus Station
Merchant's Quay
Tel: (051) 879000

J.J. Kavanagh & Sons Ltd.
Blenheim
Dunmore East Road
Tel: (051) 872777
Web:
www.jjkavanagh.ie
Email: kenneallysbus services@eircom.net
A private bus service.

DRIVING
✦ Waterford is on the N25, 40 miles west of Wexford.
✦ From Waterford take the R675 south through Tramore and along the coast road to Dungarvan. Continue along the N25 and turn off for Ardmore. (Take the N25 all the way for a quicker route).

✦ For Lismore go back to the N25, head towards Youghal and take the immediate right after the bridge. This takes you on a nice country lane along the River Blackwater right into Lismore.
✦ From Lismore take the R668 northwards for a scenic drive through the Knockmealdown Mountains.
✦ For Mahon Falls & the Comeragh Drive take the R676 off the N25 just east of Dungarvan.

CAR HIRE
Europcar
Cork Road
Waterford
Tel. (051) 334808
Web: www.europcar.ie
Email:
sales@europcar.ie
reserve@europcar.ie

Budget
Arrivals Hall
Waterford Airport
Tel: (051) 876127/ 421550

this beautiful building with ornate Roman carvings on what is left of the west wall. A 12th-century round tower sits beside this and is in perfect condition. Every detail remains right up to its conical roof. Inside the cathedral are a couple of ogham stones, and nearby is Declan's Oratory, where the saint was once believed to have been buried.

On the east side of town, high up along the cliffs is St. Declan's Well. Access is via a walking path. There was no way I was going up there in this weather, though. There is also said to be a rock on the beach that is believed to have brought the saint from Wales. This magical rock is said to have healing powers on St. Declan's Day, 24th July, when the pattern is held.

Lismore

I headed back out to the N25 and continued west towards Youghal. There is a large bridge that crosses the River Blackwater just as it empties out into

Lismore Castle. The first castle was built by Prince John in 1185, and was greatly expanded upon over the centuries. The famous *Book of Lismore* and a Bishop's crozier now on display in The National Museum were found hidden in the castle's walls.
Image © Greg Gawlowski/Lonely Planet Images.

Youghal Bay, and is a beautiful sight even in the pouring rain. Just as I reached the other side of the bridge, I found a turn off to the right, which took me on a nice, narrow country road along the Blackwater River and eventually to Lismore. This little town was said to have once boasted 20 churches. Today though, its most striking features are the cathedral and castle. Found hidden in the thick walls of the castle were a bishop's crozier and *The Book of Lismore*, the former currently on display in the National Museum, and the latter currently on display at the Lismore Heritage Centre.

THE BOOK OF LISMORE

The Book of Lismore not only documents the lives of a variety of Ireland's saints, but also tells the story of a legendary meeting between Ossian and St. Patrick. In the legends Ossian, the son of Finn McCool, had gone to live in the land of *Tir nan Óg* with the fairy princess Niamh. A few years later Ossian returned to Ireland to visit his friends, but in the real world several centuries had passed, and Ossian found himself in the 5th century AD, during the early Christian period. There, according to the account in *The Book of Lismore*, he had a series of debates with St. Patrick, where he extolled the virtues of the old order while Patrick praised the new way of Christianity. These stories were of course apocryphal, intended to be didactic in nature, but were quite popular nonetheless.

Unfortunately, entry to the castle is forbidden. It's possible to take a stroll in the gardens, but this really wasn't a day for taking a stroll. The castle is huge, and even driving around it is quite a sight. It was originally built in 1185 by Prince John. Just how these two relics came to be in the walls of this church is a mystery. Perhaps they were hidden there during raids on the castle?

Places to See in Cork

⚜ ANCIENT SITES

1. Rostellan Dolmen
2. Templebryan Stone Circle
3. Callaheenacladdig Cairn & Circle
4. Reanscreena Circle
5. Drombeg Stone Circle... 575-576
6. Skeagh Hilltop Cairn
7. Altar Wedge Cairn
8. Dunbeacon Circle
9. Kealkil Stone Circle
10. Derrintaggart West Circle
11. Faunkill Ogham Stone/
Cailleach Beara 578-580
12. Ardgroom Stone Circle 576
13. Cashelkeelty Circle 576,
580-581
14. Shronebirran Circle ... 576, 581
15. Drombohilly & Uragh Stone
Circles 576, 582
16. Knockraheen Circle
17. Rylane Circle
18. Island Wedge Cairn
19. Carraig Chlíodhna
20. The Hag's Bed

✟ CHRISTIAN SITES

21. St. Mary's Collegiate Church
22. Inchy Doney
23. Timoleague Abbey
24. Templebryan Monastic Site
25. Ballymacrown Killeen & Cross
26. Kilnaruane Cross Pillar
27. Garranes Church Site
28. Gougane Barra
29. St. Gobnait's Well 584-585
30. St. Ólann's Cap Well & Stone
31. St. Laichtean's Well

⚑ HISTORICAL SITES

32. Blarney Castle/Stone 575

⚔ CRYPTID SIGHTINGS

33. The Muircartach.......... 148

⛰ SCENIC VIEWS

34. Beara Peninsula/Way 576-578
35. The Paps of Anu........ 583-585

TRANSPORTATION

✈ Cork International Airport .. 579
⛴ Cork Ferry Terminal 579
Driving Directions: See pp. 575-585

Cork
Drombeg Stone Circle

Drombeg Stone Circle, also known locally as "The Druid's Altar". The circle is perfectly aligned with the setting sun on the winter solstice. © 2005 StonePages.com.

The Drombeg Stone Circle is also known locally as "The Druid's Altar". It lies south of Rosscarbery, near the little coastal village of Glandore. I parked in the car park and wandered out, under my umbrella, to the circle. It was still pouring with rain, and seemed as though it was set in for the day.

This stone circle is in near-perfect condition and sits on a ridge overlooking the sea. Its location is perfect, and of the 17 stones the axial stone is perfectly aligned with the setting sun at the winter solstice. Directly opposite the axial stone are the two tallest stones marking the entrance to the circle. In the center is a flat-topped rock. People had left coins, flowers and, oddly enough, an orange. Perhaps someone thought the gods were lacking in Vitamin C?

Cobh
A picturesque and colorful village south of Cork city.

Blarney Stone
North of Cork City Lies at the top of Blarney Castle in Blarney Village. Legend says that if you kiss this stone you will receive the gift of the gab.

Drombeg Stone Circle
It's on the R597 between Rosscarbery and Glandore. Turn off the N71 at Rosscarbery, just after the bridge east of town, and follow this road until you see a sign for the stone circle pointing left.

Ballycrovane Ogham Stone, Hag of Beara
On the coast road between Eyeries & Ardgroom.

The site was excavated in 1957 and the cremated remains of a youth were found underneath an upturned piece of pottery. It makes you wonder whether this was a sacrifice, or a burial ceremony. Interestingly, nearby were the foundations of a hut and some cooking sites, suggesting that perhaps people lived here as well.

This area sits beside Rosscarbery Bay, linked to a story about an ancient goddess known as Clíodhna, who was a lover of Manannan mac Lir, the god of the sea. Clíodhna fell in love with a mortal and ran away with him. It's said that they arrived here at Glandore. The journey had been long and tiring, so her lover went off in search of food. While he was away Clíodhna went to sleep, and was swept back into the ocean by a great tidal wave sent to shore by Manannan, who then retrieved her and took her back to live with him forever.

Beara Peninsula

West Cork is comprised of a series of peninsulas: Mizen Head, Sheep's Head and Beara. Unlike the lush, green Dingle Peninsula and the Ring of Kerry,

The Beara Peninsula offers superior views of the Atlantic Ocean.

both of which are swarming with busloads of tourists, West Cork's peninsulas are both rugged and less visited. The roads are too small to allow buses, and so large tour groups do not infest the area. It's a much more agreeable part of the country to visit. Beara is my favorite, a true wilderness speckled with historical monuments and archaeological sites. So far, over 600 have been identified.

GLENGARRIFF

The tiny village of Glengarriff lies wedged into the corner of Bantry Bay, and indicates the start of the Beara Peninsula. Glengarriff is simply one road with more accommodation than shops. I stayed in the Murphy's Village Hostel, run by the very friendly and helpful Tony and Susan Murphy, with a little help from their children. It was here that I learned all about the Beara Way, a 197-kilometre network of walking trails that link Glengarriff with Dursey Island and Kenmare via the entire length of the peninsula, Kenmare being in actuality just 20 kilometers north, and Dursey Island lying at the tip 48 kilometers from Glengarriff. Beara is dominated by the Caha Mountains, which run from end to end down the center of the peninsula.

Tony is a fountain of information when it comes to walking in the area. As well as being the start of the Beara Way, Glengarriff is also host to its own network of walking trails on its outskirts. Behind the hostel is the Blue Pool Amenity Area. Inland from the village lies the 300-hectare oak and pine Glengarriff Woods. I drove into the village and was thankful to find a room available in the hostel.

The next morning I headed out onto the R572, Ring of Beara, through Adrigole and Castletownbere, then north to Eyeries, a lovely, colorful little

Blueloo Bar
Glengarriff
Tel: (027) 63167
My personal favorite at the end of the village. A cozy, homely pub.

Glenbrook Bar
Adrigole
Just in front of the Hungry Hill Lodge. During the summer months it also does bar food.

MacCarthy's Bar
Main St.
Castletownbere
Great little Irish pub that is also a grocer's shop.

Murphy's Bar and Restaurant
Main St.
Castletownbere
An excellent selection of seafood and grills.

Causkey's Bar
Eyeries
Lovely village pub with a spectacular bay-window view.

village overlooking Ballycrovane Harbor. I took the time to stop in for a drink in Causkey's Bar, where I'd been years before. It has a large bay window at the rear which frames the spectacular view outside. The last time I was here was by bicycle. We cycled around the tip of the peninsula, right to the crossing point for Dursey Island. From here you can take a cable car over to the island, a trip that will serve as a stark reminder that you are deep in the countryside: on this cable car, the cattle get precedence over humans.

FAUNKILL —
THE LARGEST OGHAM STONE IN IRELAND

Faunkill, towering over 17 feet tall, is the largest ogham stone in Ireland. Ogham is comprised of a series of parallel slash marks, which can be seen here running up the side of the stone. The stone is also sometimes referred to as "The Ballycrovane Ogham Stone".

I drove east along the coast road towards the village of Ardgroom, and turned off on the coast road, following this until I reached Ballycrovane Harbor. Behind a little house here is Faunkill, the largest ogham stone in Ireland.

"We charge €2 entry now because of the Public Liability Insurance that we have to pay," said the old lady who came out of the house, notified of my arrival by her barking dog.

She handed me a leaflet, which confirmed that this is the tallest ogham stone in the world. It dates between 700-800 BC and stands 17.5 feet high. I was then directed through a gate behind the house and over a field. From the gate the stone didn't look all that big, but as I got closer the reality of its size became ever more apparent.

As I stood at the base of the stone it seemed to reach for the sky. The base is a few feet wide but tapers to a rounded point at the top. The stone sits on a small rocky hill overlooking Kilcatherine Point. Despite the sunny day, the wind was strong, as it often is along this peninsula. The clouds rolled over at an accelerated rate, casting moving shadows across the landscape. The ogham inscriptions are quite clear on this stone. They take the form of lines carved along the edge. According to the little leaflet I had, this one reads: "Macci son of Deccadis descendant of Torani".

The Cailleach Beara

From Kilcatherine Point I continued east on the coast road until I came across the sign beside the road for the Hag of Beara (*Cailleách Beara*). She is described as a goddess turned to stone and waiting for her lover Manannan mac Lir, the god of the sea (seems as though he's a bit of a lady's man). But I also wondered if this is the same *Cailleách Beara* as in the legends of Loughcrew.

A gate opens onto a cliff where you can walk along a ledge leading to the stone, which lies entrenched into the hillside. It's a strange sight, not like any other I'd seen until now. Its odd, erratic shape seemed to perfectly reflect this wild and rugged coastline; battered and ravaged by the elements. Encircling its diameter are sharp ledges where coins of all nationalities have been placed. Most have gone rusty. I guess

There & Back Again

AIR
Cork International Airport
Tel: (021) 4313131 (General enquiries)
Web: www.cork-airport.com
Located on the south side on the N27.

FERRIES
Cork Ferry Terminal
Ringaskiddy
Tel: (021) 427 1166
Web: www.swansea-cork.ie
Lies at the end of the N28 out of the city. Swansea-Cork ferries run a daily service from Cork and nightly from Swansea.

TRAINS
Trains run as far as Cork from Rosslare and Dublin. There are also trains to Killarney, which is close to the Cork border, and to Cobh regularly from Cork train station, Lower Glanmire Road.

THE JOURNEY
MUNSTER
COUNTY CORK

BUSES
Cork Bus Station
Merchants Quay
Tel: (021) 4508188

Bus Èireann
Tel: (01) 8366111
Web:
www.buseireann.ie
Daily summer service.

Bantry Rural Transport
5, Main St, Bantry.
Tel: (027) 52727
Weekdays only.

Donoughue's Mini-Bus & Coach Service
Castletownbere
Tel: (027) 70007

DRIVING
From Cork take the N27 and R600 south to the lovely village of Kinsale.

✤ Cross the bridge in Kinsale and take the R600 coast road to Clonakilty.

✤ Take the N71 to Bantry & Glengarriff. From here you can tour each peninsula.

THE JOURNEY
MUNSTER
COUNTY
CORK

The *Cailleách Beara* waiting for her lover to return.

the goddess doesn't want money, she just yearns for the return of her lover. The *Cailleách* has a commanding view of the bay entrance over which she is poised. It does indeed look as if she is waiting and watching for someone's return.

CASHELKEELTY STONE CIRCLE

I returned to the main road. The northern section beyond here is part of County Kerry, but I feel it best to include it in this chapter, to make things easier. The funny thing is that soon after you cross the border, the landscape changes from wind-beaten, treeless terrain to a lush green forest. Just as I entered this I spotted a sign pointing to the right for Cashelkeelty Stone Circle. I parked in a small lay-by nearby.

A stony path led up beside a small river to a waterfall. Over the fence, I followed a sign to the right for the stones. I was now on the old green road between Lauragh and Ardgroom. I walked for ages uphill, and just as I was about to give up and return I came to the summit and found two sets of stone circles. The sun

Cashelkeelty Stone Circle enjoys exceptional views.

was going down and the stones were silhouetted against the light. The tallest stone in among a set of three looks like a giant hand with an extended finger. Just before this is a set of five stones, not as tall but wide and thick like giant teeth protruding from the ground. But what's really special about this place is its location, high up on the hill with a wonderful view of the sea to the north and the steep, sloping valley to the east.

SHRONEBIRRAN STONE CIRCLE

The sights here never seem to end. Further up the road, past the village of Lauragh, I spotted another sign for Shronebirran Stone Circle. I followed it onto a narrow country lane that seemed to go on forever into a beautiful valley, before finally ending at a small house at the end of this valley.

The circle was in the garden next to the house. There are five stones in all, the tallest is about 5-6 feet tall. A sign indicated the walking trail leading up into the hills. It was then that I realized that I was down in the valley that I had been looking into from the Cashelkeelty Stones.

⊕ Take the R572 Ring of Beara to Kenmare.

⊕ From Kenmare take the R569 east and join the N22 for the Paps of Anu and holy wells.

CAR HIRE
Great Island Car Rentals
47 McCurtain Street
Cork City
Tel. (021) 4503536
There are several car rental desks at Cork airport.

BIKE HIRE
Glengarriff Bicycle Hire
Jem Creations
Tel: (027) 63113
In the art gallery around the corner from O'Shea's. Bikes can also be hired at **The Hungry Hill Lodge** in Adrigole.

WALKING
The Beara Way is a 197 km waymarked trail that circumnavigates the entire peninsula.

Ireland's moist climate and hilly terrain provide exceptional opportunities to view nature at its finest. Uragh Stone Circle is the ancient treasure that this rainbow reveals.

I was all set to head into Kenmare, when once again I passed a sign for yet another stone circle. This turning took me into an outstanding valley of shimmering lakes and lush, green hills. The road twisted around these lakes until I came across a sign pointing right. At the end of the road I parked by a gate, and continued on foot along a gushing stream. I traversed a sodden field and emerged upon the brow of a hill. This circle is known as Uragh, and stands on a high ledge overlooking a large lake glistening in the evening sun, backed by the sparsely-lit Caha Mountains. As I watched, a rainbow rose from a black cloud above the mountains and fell into the lake right behind the stone circle. This is the kind of scenery you only dream of.

The circle was small, consisting of 4 stones with a tall stone standing on the outside. The circle diameter is 8 feet. The center contained the remains of a recent fire. Perhaps there had been a modern pagan ceremony here not so long ago. Either that, or it was just a group of lads gathered around with a few beers.

The Paps of Anu

The Paps of Anu grace the skyline of western County Cork along the way to County Kerry.

As I drove over the brow of the hill, my eyes were treated to the sight of a massive pair of mountains endowing the horizon. It seemed I had found what I was looking for: the magnificent twin peaks known as the Paps of Anu.

It was early morning (well, early by my standards), and I had driven from Kenmare to a point just across the border into Cork once again in search of the Paps of Anu. There is a ridge near this border called the

The *omphalos* of Anu, believed by the ancients to have been an oracle, or means of communication, with the goddess.

Maureen's B&B
Glengarriff
Tel: (027) 63201
Web:
www.maureens
glengarriff.com
Email:
info@maureens
glengarriff.com

H O S T E L S
Evergreen House
The Strand
Youghal
Tel: (024) 92877
Web: www.
evergreenireland.com
Email: info@
evergreenireland.com
En-suite dorms and private rooms, with a cozy TV room upstairs.

Kinlay House
Bob & Joan's
Walk
Shandon,
Cork
Tel: (021) 4508966
Web: www.
kinlayhousecork.ie
Email: info@
kinlayhousecork.ie
This huge hostel has 171 beds in spacious dorms, and is a short walk from the city centre.

THE JOURNEY
M U N S T E R
C O U N T Y
C O R K

Derrynasaggart Mountains. According to my map, the Paps lay just north of this mountain range near the village of Cloonken. I had found this easily by following the R569 straight over to the N22 and across. It wasn't really a village, just a scattering of houses within the valley, so I headed south to Ballyvourney, where there is a holy well associated with St. Gobnait.

St. Gobnait's Well

Water from St. Gobnait's Well is still believed to help heal the sick, and people still hang clooties from the tree shading the well, hoping for cures for the afflicted.

St. Gobnait was born in County Clare and fled to the Aran Islands. It was here that she encountered an angel who instructed her to go on a journey. When she came upon a place with nine white deer, that was to be where she should build her church. That place turned out to be Ballyvourney.

Her well and the remains of the church she built are across a bridge and up the hill on the right. I made my way through an archway and down a gravel lane to the well, which was shaded by large trees. Cups were hung from a small shelf with a tap fitted to it, where water is piped from the well. Concrete steps lead down to the well where a lit candle sat at the entrance, illustrating that people regularly visit the place. Clooties hung from a tree shading the well, and even photos of children were pinned to its branches. I wondered whether this was to ensure their health, or because they were sick. St. Gobnait was revered as a great healer of the sick, and apparently kept the plague out of Ballyvourney by simply designating it consecrated ground. Behind the well in the churchyard is a statue of the saint.

The Paps of Anu from a distance really did look magnificent. These hills are traditionally associated with Anu, the ancestor goddess of the Celts — specifically, of the Tuatha dé Danaan. Anu was also known as Aíne, Danu or Dana, from which the Tuatha Dé Danaan, "the Tribe of Dana", had derived their name. She was their patron goddess, goddess of fertility, and goddess of plenty. I would certainly agree with the latter.

I continued on to the village of Cullen, to visit the well of St. Latiaran. She is one of three sisters who lived here. Her story is of course linked to Anu, as saints were typically used by Christian missionaries to replace local gods and goddesses.

I had also read about something called a Curtsey Stone. It's a heart-shaped stone where women would traditionally curtsey on her saint's day, 25th July, which is also the Celtic festival of *Lughnasa*. I couldn't see anything like it in the churchyard, so I returned to the main road and asked in the pub.

"It's on the grass in front of the house, just past the statue," said the barman.

I frowned. "What statue?"

He looked at me as if I was quite mad. "It's right out front as you go down to the graveyard."

He marched me out to the front door and pointed left. There it stood, as big as day. I had actually walked past this statue about three times, and not even noticed it. Well, I did have two other things on my mind.

Hungry Hill Lodge
Adrigole, Beara
Tel: (027) 60228
Web: www. hungryhilllodge.com
Email: info@ hungryhilllodge.com
Highly recommended
Dorms, private rooms and camping are available, and there is a pub just outside. Bikes can also be hired.

Shiplake Mountain Hostel
Dunmanway
Tel: (023) 45750
Web: www.shiplake mountainhostel.com
Email: info@shiplake mountain hostel.com
There are dorms, camping and you can even stay in a gypsy caravan.

C A M P I N G
Camping is available at the Hungry Hill Lodge. (Hostels)

For more information visit ireland. mysteriousworld.com/ Journey/Counties/ Cork/

THE JOURNEY
M U N S T E R
C O U N T Y
C O R K

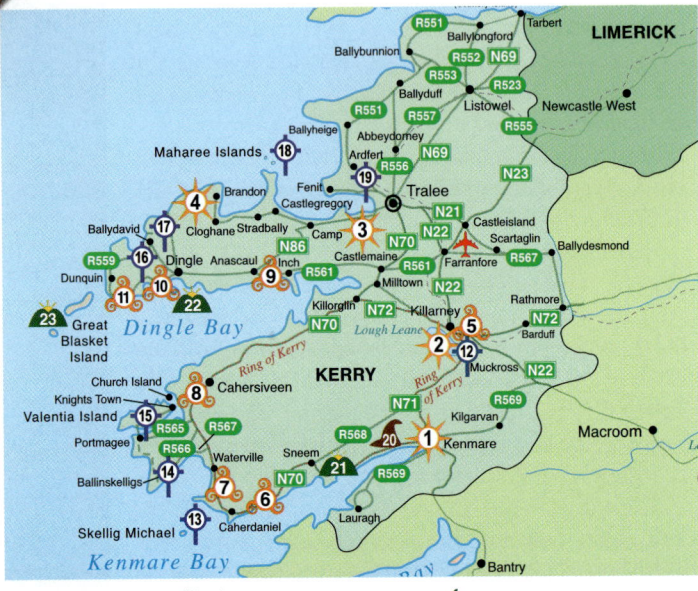

Places to See in Kerry

Kerry
The Ring of Kerry

The Ring of Kerry on the southern coast of Ireland offers spectacular views of golden, sandy beaches wedged between rocky outcrops and coves.

The town of Killarney is one of Ireland's most famous and heavily touristed, but not my favorite, because it *is* so unashamedly touristy. However, its one redeeming feature is that it is the start of "the Ring of Kerry", a 170 kilometer circular road journey from Killarney around the Iveragh and Dingle peninsulas that contains some of the most spectacular views and archaeological remains to be found anywhere in the country.

The N71 south out of Killarney twists and turns through unrivaled beauty and over stunning mountain passes. The Lakes of Killarney make up Killarney National Park, and the largest, at 8 square miles, is Lough Leane. It is here while hunting with the Fianna that Finn McCool and his son **Oisín** encountered **Níamh**, the beautiful fairy princess.

587

The Ring of Kerry
Web: www.ring ofkerrytourism.com
The Ring of Kerry is a 170 km circular road journey from Killarney around the Iveragh Peninsula. There are also special walking and biking trails available, as well as varying routes that also cover St. Finian's Bay and Valentia Island. The Ring of Kerry Tourist Office recommends that drivers drive counterclockwise to minimize traffic problems.

Tuan's Notes
Oisín and Níamh
Learn more about the tale of Oisín and Níamh in The Mystery: Folklore & Mythology (p. 204).

THE JOURNEY
MUNSTER
COUNTY
KERRY

You climb over two great viewpoints, Ladies View and Molls Gap, before descending into Kenmare. It was here at Kenmare Bay that the Milesians came ashore and faced the Tuatha dé Danann, and where Amergin uttered the magical words that thwarted the Tuatha Dé's magic.

THE IVERAGH PENINSULA

It was pouring with rain the first time I ever came here. Today, however, the weather was gorgeous. The light was incredible, and I saw a whole new side to the peninsula. It was easy to see why it attracts such a huge swarm of tourists — so much so that big tour companies now pile them into gigantic coaches and whisk them at breakneck speeds through the narrow road that circumnavigates the coastline.

It isn't really until you reach Sneem that the scenery really becomes dramatic. The road takes you over high cliffs with spectacular views of golden, sandy beaches wedged between rocky outcrops and coves. At Castlecove I pulled over at the visitor's centre for Staigue Fort.

STAIGUE FORT

Inside I viewed the exhibition before driving up the narrow road to where the fort lies perched on a hill overlooking the valley.

Staigue Fort is the largest stone ring fort ever built in Ireland.

This is the largest stone ring fort ever built in Ireland, and it is an incredible sight. It was built entirely from stones placed on top of one another. No mortar was used at all. The walls are four meters thick and stand up to six meters high. The enclosure is thirty meters in diameter, with small chambers built into the wall. It's believed that this was either a military fortification, or a protected home for an important chieftain. Whatever its use, it's an amazing sight and the views from here are fantastic.

EIGHTERCUA STONE CIRCLE

I continued on towards the town of Waterville, outside of which is a stone circle known as Eightercua. The sun was going down as I arrived, so I found a bed for the night at Peter's Place, an eco-friendly hostel with turf fires, animals painted on the walls and a little café next door.

I made my way up to the stone circle for the sunset, which unfortunately, due to the absence of cloud, wasn't as spectacular as I'd hoped. The circle contains four large stones standing ten feet tall,

Eightercua Stone Circle is believed to be the burial place of Amergin, King of the Milesians, whose poem defeated the magic of the Tuatha Dé and allowed the Milesians to land safely.

in Ireland. There are several daily boats to the island leaving from Ballinskellig Pier and Portmagee:

✠ **Casey's**
Portmagee
Tel: (066) 9472437/ 9472069
Mob: (087) 2395470/ 2287519
Web: www. skelligislands.com

✠ **Feehans Boats**
Ballinskellig
Tel: (066) 9479182
Web: www.skelligs boats.com

Dunbeg Fort
A spectacular ring fort on a high cliff's edge.

Blasket Islands
Tel: (066) 9151344
Web: www. greatblasketisland.com
Email: info@ greatblasketisland.com

Mount Brandon
Once associated with the Dagda, now with St. Brendan the Navigator.

Killorglin Puck Fair
Web:
www.puckfair.ie
Every year in August, revolves around adorning a billy goat.

The Rose of Tralee
Tel: (0)66 7121322
Web:
www.roseoftralee.ie
A world-famous beauty pageant held every August.

Dingle Wren Festival
Held every Dec. 26.
Web: www.
dingle-peninsula.ie/
wren.html

Tours
Finnegan's Tours
Kenmare
Tel: (064) 41491
Web: www.kenmare
coachandcab.com
Small bus tours around the Ring of Kerry & Beara.

Boat Trip to Fungie
Dingle
Tel: (066) 9152626
Boat trips to see Fungie the dolphin.

and the remnants of other stones around what looks to be an earthern enclosure. Local folklore credits this mound as the burial place of **Amergin**, King and Poet of the Milesians. This is the same Amergin who is also said to be buried at Millmount, in Drogheda, County Louth. So which is true, we'll never know.

If Amergin is buried here he couldn't have chosen a better spot. The mound overlooks the ocean to the west, and the large and very beautiful Lough Currane to the east. As the sun set over the mountains the other side of town, it cast elongated shadows of the tall stones across the enclosure. A perfect end to a perfect day.

Waterville was very quiet for the time of year. It was the end of June and I expected the area to be a lot busier. I was thankful for this, as it meant I could sit on the wall overlooking the sea, smoking my cigarette and enjoying the sound of the ocean washing up on the beach. I'd had two days of fantastic weather, and I hoped it would remain for the next day. It didn't.

The shadows of Eightercua reach out to beautiful Lough Currane and the hills beyond.

Skellig Michael

The pilgrims' trail up to the monastery on the island of Skellig Michael, where one can view the famous "beehive huts" once used to shelter monks and those on pilgrimage.†

As I drove out of Waterville I took the R567 around the Ring of Skellig to Ballinskelligs, the departure point for Skellig Michael. However, the sea was too rough and the sailing was cancelled when I was there, so keep the weather in mind when planning your trip.

Skellig Michael is an island containing a monastic settlement that has been raved about by travelers I'd met along the way. The site is built 700 feet above the sea and contains two small oratories and six beehive huts. It's the most remote monastic settlement in Ireland and was believed to have been inhabited by the monks until the 12th century. Legend also says that the Viking King Olaf was converted to Christianity here on the island. Skellig Michael is considered to be one of the top three "must see" spots in Ireland.

Eat & Drink

Skellig Mist Coffee Shop
Portmagee
Tel: (066) 77250
A lovely little place with cakes and sandwiches and a view out back of the harbor.

Fisherman's Bar & Skellig Restaurant
Portmagee
Has tables with a view of the harbor.

Harrington's Restaurant & Snack Bar
Strand St., Dingle
Tel: (066) 9151985
Mob: (086) 8299834
A nice family-run seafood restaurant.

Tuan's Notes
Amergin
Learn more about Amergin and his mysterious poem in The Mystery: The Mystery (pp. 21-22, 68-76).

PUBS
**The
Wander Inn**
2, Henry St.
Kenmare
Tel: (064) 42700
Traditional music
sessions most nights.

Foley's
Henry Street
Tel: 064 42162
Web: www.
foleyskenmare.com
Email: info@
foleyskenmare.com
Food and hotel also.

O'Donnabhain's Pub
Henry Street
Tel: (064) 42106
Web: www.
odonnabhain
-kenmare.com
E-mail: info@
odonnabhain
-kenmare.com

**John Benny
Moriarty's Pub**
Strand Street
Dingle
Tel: (066) 9151215
Web: www.
johnbennyspub.com
Email:
jbenny@eircom.net
Excellent pub with
great music on a reg-
ular basis.

THE JOURNEY
MUNSTER
COUNTY
KERRY

The Dingle Peninsula

Disappointed but undaunted, I headed back out onto the Ring of Kerry to check out the Dingle Peninsula. At Castlemaine I branched off onto the R561, which goes along the southern coast of the peninsula and past Inch, a huge, sandy beach on which you can drive your car. The road eventually joins the N86, which whisks you right into the town of Dingle.

GALLARUS ORATORY

On the western outskirts of Dingle is a small round-about. I took the left road here and began my journey along the Slea Head Drive. I took the next right turn for Gallarus and followed the signs.

The Gallarus Oratory is possibly the most amazing and well-preserved stone structure in Ireland, and the most famous. Access is now via the visitor center. It's a small house shaped like the upturned keel of a boat. It's built entirely from carved stones, and has a corbelled roof with nine capstones. The entrance is topped by two long lintel stones each with a hole that may have been used to attach a door upon. Inside is a single window at

Gallarus Oratory, similar in construction style to St. Colmcille's House in Meath and St. Kevin's kitchen in Wicklow, is one of the most famous structures in Ireland.

the rear. The actual hole itself is quite small, but then splays at a 45 degree angle on the inside. The large stones used have been perfectly cut to create this effect.

The oratory was built around the 7th century. It's so solid that it has withstood 1,400 years of being ravaged by the elements. The Dingle Peninsula is constantly exposed to the Atlantic storms, so it is a true testament to the engineering ability of a supposedly primitive people.

But I wondered what its builders would have thought had they known that 1,400 years later it would have to withstand exposure to silly tourists who seem to think it really funny to hang on the rear window and grin while someone takes their photo?

"Most of the people here don't really know what it is they've come to look at," said the guy in the visitor center, who shared my dismay at this. He directed me towards Kilmalkedar Church, where an ogham stone and an ancient sundial lie in the graveyard. Both could be seen from the oratory. There are said to be as many as sixty ogham stones in the Dingle Peninsula alone.

DUNBEG FORT

I returned to the southern half of the drive and continued along the loop road that took me past Dunbeg Fort. Although not as well preserved as Staigue Fort, it is sited in a far more dramatic location right on the edge of a high cliff. There are also a number of beehive huts on the hills along this road.

THE BLASKET ISLANDS

At Slea Head I parked the van beside a stone commemorating the filming of *Ryan's Daughter* here on Slea Head. I sat inside as the ferocious wind battered and rocked the van so hard I feared it would turn over. I watched with amusement as the seagulls attempted to land without success. The Blasket Islands were barely visible in the distant mist. These six islands

There & Back Again

AIR
Kerry International Airport
Farranfore
Tel: (066) 9764644
Web: www.
kerryairport.ie
North on the N22.

TRAINS
KillarneyStation
East Avenue Road
Tel: (064) 31067

Tralee Station
JohnJo Sheehy Rd.
Tel: (066) 7123522

BUSES
Corcorans Tours
Kerry Airport
to Killarney.
Tel: (064)
36666
Web: www.
corcorantours.com
Email: corcorantours
@eircom.net

KillarneyStation
Killarney Outlet
Centre, Park Road
Tel: (064) 34777

Tralee Bus Station
(Next to train)
Tel: (066) 7123566

CAR HIRE

Europcar
Muckross Rd.
Killarney
Tel. (064) 31237

Budget Car Rental
The International
Hotel, Kenmare Place
Killarney
Tel: (064) 34341

DRIVING

From Killarney take
the N71 through the
Lakes of Killarney to
Kenmare. Then join
the N70 around the
Ring of Kerry.

BIKE HIRE

**Paddy's Bike
Shop**
Dykegate
Lane, Dingle
Tel: (066)
9152311
Available
March to October.

Tuan's Notes
*Learn more about St.
Brendan and his mys-
terious journey in The
History: The Saints
(pp. 242-247).*

were once home to a number of famous Irish writers, and in ancient times, by monks, who left behind numerous beehive huts, a church and three stone crosses. Nowadays they are uninhabited.

I continued along the road, following signs for Brandon Creek and arrived in the remote region of Tiduff, where a hidden inlet is the starting point for the incredible journey of St. Brendan the Navigator, the patron saint of Kerry. I stood in the wind staring at the statue of a man in a small sailing boat facing out west towards the ocean. It is believed that Brendan had embarked upon a journey west, discovering America 1,000 years before Columbus.

Brandon Mountain

The nearby Brandon (Brendan) Mountain, at over 3,000 feet, is an imposing sight from here. It's Ireland's second-highest mountain. Some accounts say that Brendan climbed alone to the top of this mountain and fasted for forty days. It was here an angel came to him in a dream and promised to guide him to a beautiful island.

Legend says that Brendan built a small, sturdy wooden boat and set sail with a company of monks in search

A memorial of St. Brendan's voyage into the West.

of this land. Seven years later he arrived on the shores of America. In 1976 his journey was successfully recreated by Tim Severin, explorer and Oxford graduate. He used the exact kind of boat described in the *Navigatio*, a 9th-century literary account of the voyage. This proved that such a voyage was possible, but no one really knows just whether he really did reach America.

Mount Brandon was known before this as *Slieve Dagda*, linking it to the father god of the Tuatha dé Danann. Long before the coming of St. Brendan, this had been a sacred mountain where *Lughnasa* festivals were often celebrated at its summit. There is a pilgrimage trail that starts at Kilmalkedar Church and ends at an oratory on the summit where the saint was said to have had his dream.

It was late evening by this time and I had no intention of climbing the hill in the dwindling light, so I headed off in search of the Mount Brandon Hostel. But to get there I had to go all the way back to Dingle and then take the Connor Pass, Ireland's highest road. And though I had to go out of my way to get there, it was definitely worthwhile as it is a fantastic drive with a viewpoint at the top where you can see for miles on either side.

Places to Stay

H O T E L S

Park Hotel Kenmare
Phone (064) 41200
Web:
www.parkkenmare.com
E-mail: info@ parkkenmare.com
Dating from 1897 this luxury hotel has 46 rooms and overlooks Kenmare Bay.

B & B S

Doyles Townhouse & Seafood Restaurant
John Street, Dingle
Tel: (066) 9151174
Web: www. doylesof dingle.com
Email: cdoyles@iol.ie
Originally a small shop and pub built in 1790, it's now a four star guesthouse and world famous restaurant.

For much more information on B&B's, hostels, camping and more visit ireland. mysteriousworld.com/ Journey/Counties/ Kerry/

THE JOURNEY

M U N S T E R

**C O U N T Y
K E R R Y**

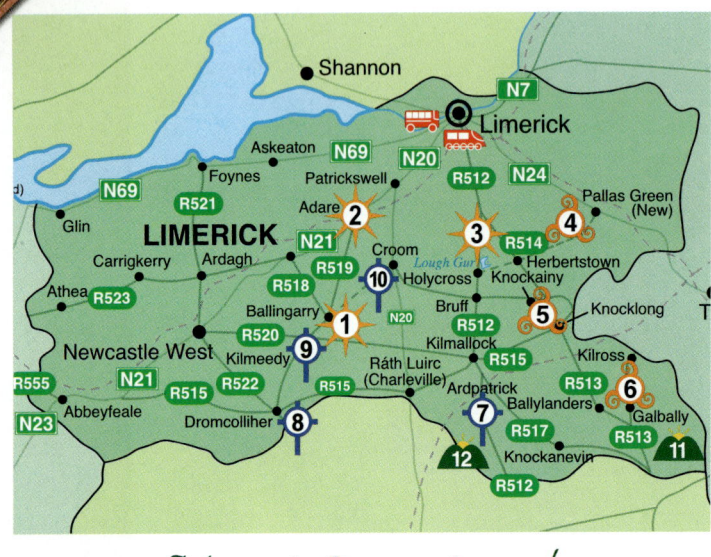

Places to See in Limerick

☀ Multi-Sites

1. Knockfierna
   - Legend of the Fairy King Donn Fírinne 587-599
   - Dolmen. 597, 599
   - Cairn 599
   - Fairy Cave 597, 599
2. Adare
   - Dunaman Castle Sheela-na-Gig
   - Franciscan Friary
   - Augustinian Friary
   - Adare Manor
3. Lough Gur
   - Home of Áine/Entrance to the Otherworld 597, 601-603
   - Knockadoon. 602
   - Interpretive Centre 602
   - Wedge Grave 602-603
   - Grange Stone Circle 603

⚶ Ancient Sites

4. Cnoc Gráinne
5. Cnoc Áine/Knockainy . . 600-601
6. Duntryleague Cairns

♀ Christian Sites

7. Killeedy Church & Holy Well
8. Tullylease Monastic Site
9. Killmallek Priory & Church
10. Disert Oenghusa Church & Round Tower

⛰ Scenic Views

11. Glen of Aherlow/Galty Mtns.
12. Ballyhoura Mountains

Transportation

🚐 Limerick Train Station. . . 600
🚌 Limerick Bus Station. 601

Driving Directions: See pp. 597, 600-603

Limerick
Knockfierna

Limerick
Things to Do & Places to See

Knockfierna
Home to the Fairy King Donn.

Knockainy
Sacred mountain and home to the goddess Áine. Go through village to crossroads, turn left and go past the two houses until you come to a double gate on the left.

Lough Gur
An ancient settlement going back 5,000 years. Follow signs from Holycross. Web: www.shannon heritage.com/ LoughGur.htm

Tourist Offices:
✢ **Arthurs Quay**
Limerick
Tel: 061 317522
✢ **Adare Heritage Centre**
Main Street
Adare
Tel: 061 396255

"he locals call it The Hill of Truth, because it's always a good indication of how the weather will be," said John, as the rain poured down outside the van. I was huddled in the back of my van to escape the rain with a local man called John, whose ruddy features and grinning face matched his jolly personality. I had been directed to John by local people who said that he is a wealth of knowledge regarding the hill, and had found him waiting outside his little house with his dog. He had insisted that we get into my van immediately, for reasons that were now apparent.

"What do you know about the hill being the home of the Fairy King Donn?" I asked.

John stared at me incredulously. "I wouldn't know anything about that," he replied. "But there is a dolmen on the north side of the hill."

"Well, I've heard there is a cave on the hill that is the entrance to his fairy palace."

"There is a cave on the south side of the hill," he

Festivals

**Lough Gur
Halloween
Storytelling
Festival**
Tel: 061 385386
Web: www.
shannonheritage.com
Held at the lake over
the Halloween week-
end.

Eat & Drink

The Arches
Main Street
Adare
Tel: (061) 396246
A family-run restau-
rant serving home-
cooked food.

**The Inn
Between**
Main Street
Adare
Tel: (061)
396633

PUBS

Reardon's
Holycross Bruff
Lough Gur
Tel: (061) 382208
At the crossroads
near the lake.

Red Cellar Bar
Lough Gur
Tel: (061) 382298

THE JOURNEY
MUNSTER
COUNTY
LIMERICK

Knockfierna offers a magnificent view of the Limerick countryside.

replied, cautiously.

"What's the best route to take to the top?"

"Ah well, there are several. But the closest is via the farmhouse just up the road from the petrol station."

I had already seen that. So I thanked John for the information, and he headed back to his little house, while I continued on to the farmhouse. At the farmhouse, a little old lady came out to quieten her snarling dog, who upon my arrival had leapt at the gate.

"Can I get to the top of the hill up here?" I asked, pointing up the muddy road beside her house.

"Yes. Just follow the track."

I've never been one to do as I'm told, and thinking it would be a short cut I turned off the track further up and went along a narrow lane. It wasn't long before I was clambering my way through thick, wet grass and hacking away the bushes to get through. At least it had stopped raining.

I finally made it to the summit, where there is a large cross erected next to a tall antenna, either for a radio or a mobile phone. The hill lies at an altitude of 948 feet. The view from the top is of a vast, green plain with hills on the distant horizon.

THE FAIRY KING DONN FÍRINNE

There is an interesting story associated with Knockfierna called The Curse of the Quicken Trees. Tradition also has it that the hill is the dwelling of the Fairy King **Donn Fírinne**, the Celtic god of death. Donn lives inside the hill, and it is said that anyone trying to investigate the entrance to his palace will not come away unscathed, and might even be kidnapped.

Somewhere on the hill are the remains of a cairn, and I could see a dolmen in a nearby field. The southern field was fenced off, as it was part of the farm I had come through. I climbed the fence and investigated. The south side was completely covered with thick bushes and trees. I was about to dismiss it when I thought I saw something rocky behind a big tree. I followed an old wall up and then scrambled over loose stones to a muddy path. From here I could quite clearly see a small cave entrance hidden behind the bushes and shaded by an overhanging tree. I had found the entrance to Donn's palace.

Unfortunately, the cave was small and tapered off into the hill, and I was too big to fit into the tiny cave entrance. Donn was holding on to his secret.

Knockfierna features a fairy cave believed by some to be the entrance to the Fairy King Donn's palace in the Underworld.

Next to the lake.

The Swans Bar
Longford Bridge
Grange, Bruff
Lough Gur
Tel: (061) 385332
1 mile south of Lough Gur. Has regular music sessions.

Lena's
Main St. Adare
Has traditional Irish music every Wednesday night and served home cooked bar food.

Tuan's Notes

Donn Fírinne
Donn Fírinne is the king of the fairies of Munster province, and is also believed to have been one of the six chiefs of the Tuatha dé Danann. *Learn more about The Fairy King Donn Fírinne in The Mystery: Creatures Great & Small (pp. 161-162).*

THE JOURNEY
MUNSTER
COUNTY
LIMERICK

AIR
Shannon Airport
Tel: (061) 712000
Web: www.
shannonairport.com
The airport lies
halfway between
Limerick & Ennis,
off the N18, and has
international and
domestic flights.

TRAINS
Limerick Station
Parnell St.
Limerick
Tel: (061) 315555
Trains run regularly
to the city of
Limerick from
Dublin
Heuston &
Cork. There
are also sever-
al trains running to
and from Ennis.

Tuan's Notes
Áine
*Learn more about the
goddess Áine in The
Mystery: Deities &
Demigods (pp. 82-83).*

Knockainy

Áine's sacred mound is believed to be a major doorway to the
Underworld. Legend has it that the sound of bells emanating from
the Underworld will lead one to the secret entrance.

From Ballingary I went southeast on the R518 to
Killmallock, north on the R512 to Bruff, and then
took a right onto R516 though to the little town of
Knockainy. Beside this lies the sacred hill associated
with the goddess **Áine**. I had been directed through
the village by a local to some crossroads and told to
turn left, follow this narrow lane up until I came to
some farm gates with a lay-by where I could park. I
climbed the gate and followed a track up the hill,
veered off to the left and made my way up through an
opening in the tree beyond. Many of the low fences
were electrified, so I made sure I was careful when
stepping over.

As I climbed the hill I thought I could hear bells
over to the right. I looked over and saw a stone pillar
on the hill, and headed for it. Here I found the burial
mound, said to be the entrance to the Otherworld and
Aine's palace.

This was also the inauguration site of the
Eóganacht kings, who held the fortress at Cashel in
Tipperary. The ceremony would be a way of keeping

in harmony with the spirits of the Otherworld. It is also said that King Ailill became known as the king with one ear, after having come here on the eve of Samhain under the advice of his druidess to seek the wisdom of Áine in solving a problem. But the king fell asleep, and in the night he awoke to see a beautiful woman appear from the mound with her father. Overcome with desire for this woman he lost control and raped her. Angered by this, the woman bit off the king's ear, thus maiming him for life. As a king could not rule if he had a blemish, he lost his kingdom.

There are several Iron Age barrows nearby and, interestingly, there is a lone tree sitting on the edge of a trench beside the mound. I wondered if this was Áine's fairy tree.

Lough Gur

Lough Gur is another place sacred to Áine, and is also believed to be a portal to the Underworld. This region is rife with legend.

Beside Holycross, north of Bruff, lies an ancient settlement known as Lough Gur. Excavations here have determined the site was first occupied 5,000 years ago, and evidence of round huts have been found. I took the right at the crossroads and followed the road around until I came to the Lough Gur visitor center.

B U S E S
Limerick
Bus Station
(In train station)
Tel: (061) 313333
Limerick is a major hub for Bus Èireann and has services to all major towns in Ireland.

D R I V I N G
☩ For Knockfierna take R519 off N21 west of Adare to Ballingarry.
☩ For Knockainy take R518 to Kilmallock then R512 to Bruff, then R516 east to the village of Knockainy.
☩ For Lough Gur go to Bruff and continue on the R512 north to Holycross. Lough Gur is east of the road.

T A X I
Adare Taxi
Tel: (087) 9911675

City Cabs & Minibus Hire
74 Henry St.
Limerick
Tel: (061) 452880

THE JOURNEY
M U N S T E R
C O U N T Y
LIMERICK

Places to Stay
H O T E L S
Dunraven Arms Hotel
Adare
Tel: (0) 61 396633
Web: www. dunravenhotel.com

Email: reservations@ dunraven hotel.com
A four-star hotel established in 1792.

Adare Manor Hotel & Golf Resort
Adare
Tel: (061) 396566
Web: www.adaremanor.ie
Email: reservations @adaremanor.com
A top-class hotel with 74 rooms.

The local interpretive center is housed in roundhouse-style huts designed to closely approximate the ancient originals.

I had arrived late and the center was closed, so I couldn't get the map of the area they give out. It was housed in two replicas of round huts. The weather had settled a bit, but it was still overcast. The lake was still, and the ducks swam happily along while people sat in cars or walked their dogs. Along the left edge was Bolin Island, a *crannog* (artificial lake). Behind this was Knockadoon, the third sacred hill in the area. Legend has it that Áine created all of this, and appears here in different forms.

The lake is believed to be a portal to the Otherworld, and every seven years is said to dry up and reveal a sacred tree at the bottom which is covered with a green sheet. An old woman keeps watch from under the sheet. Knockadoon is said to be inhabited by Áine's son who can be seen gliding across the lake every seven years on a horse wearing silver shoes.

I got back in the van and drove out towards Holycross. On the way I passed a wedge grave. Apparently the grave was excavated in 1938 and the bones of at least eight adults and four children were found. The entrance is aligned to the setting sun, and this makes you wonder if the builders believed that the spirit of the dead would be taken to the Otherworld with the setting sun. According to *Sacred Ireland* when the bones of the dead were removed every banshee in Ireland could be heard wailing.

The plaque said that a guy called Samuel Hall visited the grave in the 19th century and wrote that an old woman had lived inside it for many years. This could well have been Áine, who is said to appear as a hag guarding the sacred places around the lake.

GRANGE STONE CIRCLE

Back at the crossroads I headed towards Limerick, and on the right came across Grange Stone Circle. This incredible stone circle is 150 feet in diameter and the largest in Ireland. There are 113 stones that encircle the area, entrenched in a 3-foot high bank. It lies close to the lake, and the massive stone at the lakeside is known as *Crom Dubh*, the god of the harvest.

It was getting late and I wanted to get to County Clare before sundown, so I headed northwards through the city of Limerick and on towards Ennis.

At 150 feet wide, Grange Stone Circle in County Limerick is the largest stone circle in Ireland.

B & B S
Hillgare House
Uregare
Kilmallock
Tel: (061) 382275
Web:
homepage.tinet.ie/
~clairepower
Email: clairepower
@eircom.net
Situated on the R512.

Clonunion House
Limerick Road, Adare
Tel: (061) 396657

H O S T E L S
Trainor's Hostel
Ballingarry Village
Tel: (069) 68164
Email: trainorhostel
@eircom.net
Close to
Knockfierna.

C A M P I N G
Adare Camping & Caravan Park
Tel: (061) 395276
Email: dohertycamping
adare@eircom.net
Open March-Sept.

For more information
visit ireland.
mysteriousworld.com/
Journey/Counties/
Limerick/

Places to See in Clare

Clare
The Fairy Tree of Clare

The Fairy Tree of Clare is still believed by locals to be a source of powerful fairy magic.

"id you know there's a fairy tree along the Limerick to Ennis road," Brian said unexpectedly.

"I did hear something about that on the news last year," I replied. "Didn't someone cut the branches off it?"

"Well, a group of lads vandalized it, but that's only part of the story. When they were expanding that section of the road they came to the fairy tree, and needed to cut it down to make room for the road. The problem was that this tree is the traditional meeting place of the Munster fairies before they go off to do battle with the Connaught fairies. Therefore none of the locals would cut it down."

"What did they do then?"

"Well, they brought over a fella from Dublin to do the job. He wasn't so superstitious and gladly

Clare
Things to Do & Places to See

The Fairy Tree of Clare
Beside Limerick to Ennis road, this tree is still believed to be a haunt of the fairies.

Magh Adhair
Inauguration point for the kings of the Dál Cais, the most famous of which is Brian Boru. It is signed on the right from the village of Quin. Follow this road until you come to a right turn with two roads branching off from it. Take the left road, and follow this until you cross a small bridge and see the mound on the left.

Killaloe Cathedral
In the village of Killaloe on the southern shore of Lough Derg.

agreed to cut down the tree. But as he drove towards it, his JCB tipped over completely. After that, he wouldn't go anywhere near the tree. In the end they had to build a bypass road and it cost the government €2.5 million."

"I know that section of road. It's by the Clare Inn Hotel. I thought it was weird at the time. The road diverts off to a roundabout and then rejoins it straight after the bridge."

"That's it. If you look down just beyond the bridge, you'll see the tree. A wooden fence has been built around it. Vandals cut off the branches, but they are growing back. No one ever found out who did it."

"That's an expensive tree."

"Sure is."

I was in the Abbey Tourist Hostel in Ennis, talking to the owner Brian. Brian was a fountain of knowledge when it came to legends and folklore about the area. He had given me a map of the county, and filled my head with all sorts of information. "Since I moved here with my girlfriend and started this place, I've become more interested in it all," he said.

Later that evening I headed out to grab a well-deserved pint of Guinness. It was Saturday night, and Ennis was simply swarming with partygoers. There are so many pubs to choose from, but in the end I popped into the interestingly named Poet's Corner. Inside I found a seat by the bar, and spent the evening listening to the group playing Irish music, one of whom was an American staying at the hostel. It often amazes me how the spirit of Irish music has spilled over into other cultures. People come from all walks of life to play in the pubs here, and the wonderful thing is that they are always welcome to join in.

Magh Adhair

Magh Adair was once the inauguration mound for the kings of the Dál Cais, including their most prominent son, Brian Boru.

I headed south on the Limerick road for a look at the fairy tree first. It lay just past the bridge on the Ennis side, down in a ditch beside the section of road that was now closed. I found it hard to believe that this little tree had been the cause of so much trouble. It just goes to show how deeply entrenched this folklore still is in the lives of the Irish people.

I continued on the to the village of Quin, where I followed a sign out to Magh Adhair. This flat-topped hill was the inauguration mound of the kings of the Dál Cais, and also of Ireland's most famous king, Brian Boru.

"There is a stone pillar with a round depression in it. When Brian Boru was inaugurated there, a child's throat was slit. He said that under his leadership this would be the last time this sort of sacrifice would occur," Brian had said back in Ennis.

I found the stone pillar the other side of the mound. It was a large bullaun stone, about 3 feet high, said to have healing water collected inside it. This was the first I'd heard of it being used as a sacrificial stone.

**Caherconnell
Visitor Centre**
Carron
Tel: (065)7089999
Web:
www.burrenforts.ie
Email:
info@burrenforts.ie
Located just south of
the Poulnabroune
Dolmen.

Tours
**The Abbey Tourist
Hostel**
Runs daily small
group tours to the
Burren, Poulnabrone
and the Cliffs of
Moher. (See Hostel
section for
contact
details)

Bus Èireann
Runs a tour
every Thursday
to Bunratty Castle,
Burren, Lisdoonvarna
& the Cliffs of Moher
from Cork.
Tel: (021) 4508188
Also runs a daily tour
from Galway to the
Burren & Cliffs of
Moher.
Tel: (091) 562000

**THE JOURNEY
MUNSTER
COUNTY
CLARE**

Eat & Drink

Paudie Macs
O'Connell St.
Ennis
Tel: (065) 6845888
A popular bar and
restaurant.

Sizzlers Restaurant
Parnell Street
Ennis
Tel: (065) 6868826

**Bunratty Medieval
Castle Banquet**
South of Ennis
(*Reservations essential*)
Tel: (061) 360788
Free: 1800 269811
A medieval-style
feast with fine wines
and entertain-
ment.

PUBS

**Brogans Bar
& Restaurant**
24 O'Connell Street
Ennis
Tel: (065) 6829480
Traditional Irish music
three times a week.

McDermott's Pub
Upper Village
Doolin
An old world atmos-
phere with fantastic
Irish music sessions.

At only 3 meters, the mound is quite low. But this is a lovely place, situated beside a little stream (unfortunately named Hell River). It's considered by many to be an unusual setting for a king's inauguration, due to being set among low hills. Traditionally these inauguration sites are set on high ground with distant views all around.

Killaloe Cathedral

I drove west to the village of Killaloe, which lies on the southern shore of Lough Derg. The cathedral at the bottom of the hill here is dedicated to St. Flannan, who was an 8th-century prince of the Dál Cais clan. St. Flannan's oratory sits in the graveyard beside the cathedral, which unfortunately was locked. A Sunday service was taking place in the church, so I didn't want to disturb it by trying to find access through the cathedral. After my experience at St. Patrick's Cathedral in Dublin, I felt it unwise to upset any more priests. Instead I went across the road to the AIB bank in the grounds of which lies the saint's well.

Beal Boru

This area is Brian Boru's homeland. The R463 runs along the shore of Lough Derg. I followed this north-ward for a mile until I came to a sign on the right for Beal Boru, where I parked up and followed a grassy lane until I came upon this huge ring fort nestled among the trees. It was excavated in the 1960s and determined that there was a fort here around the time Brian Boru was alive and living in the area. However, there is little information as to its use and if the king himself actually had a fort here. It now lies surround-ed by mature beech and fir trees and has a steep inner bank. The sun filtered through the trees and scattered patches of light across the grassy center. I couldn't help thinking it would be a perfect place for a picnic.

Carriag Liath

The Clare Way walking trail comes along here and another mile further north is Two Mile Gate, where a section of the trail leads up into Cragg Wood. To the left as you hike up the path is the Hill of Craglea, *Carriag Liath* (The Grey Rock). It's 40-feet high and legendary home of Aoibheal, the Banshee of the Dál Cais. It was from here that she set out and flew across Ireland to Clontarf to warn Brian Boru of his impending death at the hands of the Vikings.

The Burren

My mouth dropped open at the very first sight of the Burren landscape. Signs tell you that you are in the Burren, but for long periods all you see is a landscape of grassy fields similar to everywhere else and you begin to think, what's so special about it? Many of the inland roads avoid the most dramatic sections.

I had returned to Ennis and then taken the R476 northward towards Corrofin. My intention was to get to Doolin, but on the way I wanted to see a couple of sights. Brian had told me there was a church in

The Burren is a hilly landscape in western Clare punctuated by stark cliffs and rocky outcrops.

Poet's Corner
The Old Ground Hotel
O'Connell St.
Ennis
Tel: (065) 6828127
Web: www.flynn hotels.com/oldground
Great hotel bar with regular music sessions.

There & Back Again
AIR
Shannon Airport
Tel: (061) 712000
Web: www. shannonairport.com
Halfway between Limerick & Ennis, off the N18. Has international and domestic flights.

FERRIES
Doolin Ferries
The Pier
Doolin
Tel: (065) 7074455/7074466
After hours: (065) 7071710/7074189
Web: www. doolinferries.com
Several sailings per day to and from Inisheer and 2 per day to Inishmor.

THE JOURNEY
MUNSTER
COUNTY CLARE

TRAINS
Train Station
Quinn Road
Ennis
Tel: (065) 6840444
Trains run regularly
from Dublin &
Cork via Limerick.

BUSES

The bus station is in
the train station.
Tel: (065) 6824177
There are regular
services from Dublin
& Cork to Ennis.
✢ Bus 15 runs twice
a day from Ennis to
Doolin.
✢ Bus 50 from Tralee
to Galway stops for 1
hour at the
Cliffs of
Moher & at
Doolin.
✢ Buses 323
& 345 run
from Limerick
to Killaloe.
✢ There is a local
bus service from
Ennis to
Lisdoonvarna stop-
ping at Kilfenora &
Doolin.
✢ Bus 50 runs from
Doolin to Bally-
vaughan June to
Sept.

THE JOURNEY

MUNSTER

COUNTY CLARE

Kilnaboy with a Sheela-na-Gig entrenched into the
wall above the doorway.

Like many small villages in Ireland you can often
drive straight through without realizing. They are
never signed. I had begun to suspect this when I
passed a couple hitchhiking.

"Where are you heading?" I asked, as I approached.

"Well, we want to get to Doolin, but we would
appreciate you taking us as far as you can," said the
man.

"I'm going to Doolin, eventually. I could take you
there if you aren't in a hurry. I want to see a couple of
churches nearby."

"Oh that would be great," he replied.

I opened up the van and he got in the back, and
the girl got in the front.

"I apologize for the noisy exhaust. It's blown a gas-
ket and I have to get it repaired," I shouted.

Actually it had been like this since I left England,
I just had to keep sealing it up with gum to quieten
the noise, and every so often the seal broke.

The girl looked a bit nervous. I couldn't figure out
if she thought I was dodgy-looking and was secretly
cursing her boyfriend for taking the comfy seat in the
back and leaving her to talk to the potential psycho
in the noisy, beat-up van, or her English wasn't very
good. The noise didn't help matters much.

We arrived in Kilnaboy shortly after. The church
was by the roadside, so how I missed it I'll never know.
On the side above the arch doorway is a very worn
Sheela-na-Gig. Brian had told me that these statues
were traditionally placed upon pilgrimage routes to
ward off lust. Somehow I couldn't help thinking that
such a figure, with legs spread and hands clutching
her genitalia, would have the opposite effect. I imagine it made the confession box very popular.

The church apparently stands on a much earlier settlement dedicated to St. Inghean Bhaoth, whose name translates as "the foolish daughter". Perhaps she was the one depicted by the Sheela-na-Gig. A number of interesting crosses and statues are in and around the church. I also read that there is a Tau Cross in the heritage centre in Corrofin, but it was too late to go there. There are only two such crosses in Ireland, and the other is on Tory Island, in Donegal — a place I knew very well, and was looking forward to seeing again.

The doorway arch of Killnaboy Church features the image of a naked woman called a "Sheela-na-Gig" that was intended to ward off lust

"Well, this is the best hitchhiking we've ever done," said my traveling companion above the noise of the van. He was now sitting in the front seat, after his girlfriend's quiet insistence. "We also get our own personal travel writer as a tour guide with it."

"It's all part of the service," I replied. "Where were you coming from anyway?"

"We walked the Burren Way walking trail from Doolin, and were trying to hitch our way back."

"I bet that was beautiful, wasn't it?"

"Oh, yes," he replied. "It's a stunning landscape."

They were from the Czech Republic, and towards the end of a two-week holiday.

DRIVING
⚜ The R469 from Ennis to Quin. Follow signs to Magh Adhair.
⚜ The drive from Killaloe to Scarriff takes you along the shore of Lough Derg.
⚜ From Ennis take the N85 north and then R476 through Kilnaboy, Killfenora and onto to Doolin.
⚜ Scenic drive from Doolin: go to Lisdoonvarna and pick up the R477 coast road to Ballyvaughan, then R480 south for Poulnabrone Dolmen.
⚜ The Cliffs of Moher are south of Doolin on the R478.

TAXI
Dial A Cab
Doolin
Tel: (086) 8127049/(087) 2902060

Peter Mooney
Lisdoonvarna
Tel: (065) 7074663
Mob: (087) 2069019

CAR HIRE
There are several car rental offices at Shannon airport.

BIKE HIRE
Bikes can be hired at the Doolin Bike Store, in front of the Aille River Hostel.
Tel: (065) 7074282

WALKING
The Clare Way goes along Lough Derg and also through the heart of the Burren.

Burren Hill Walks Ltd.
Corkscrew Hill
Ballyvaughan
Tel: (065) 7077168
Web: home page.eircom .net/~burren hillwalks
Email: burrenhillwalks @eircom.net
Guided walks through the Burren region with an experienced local guide. Choose from a selection of tailor-made walks, or design your own to your requirements.

THE JOURNEY
MUNSTER
COUNTY CLARE

After stopping off at the church in Kilfenora to look at the high cross, we chugged our way into Doolin and I managed to camp in my van behind the Aille River Hostel, and patch up the exhaust again.

The next morning I took the R477 coastal road, awed by the stark, grey limestone hills and coastline that covered the landscape. I followed the coastal road right around past Black Head to Ballyvaughan. Here I turned inland along the R480 and drove into the heart of the limestone region. There are over 70 identified Neolithic tombs in the Burren region, but I was looking for Poulnabrone, the most photographed dolmen in Ireland.

Poulnabrone Dolmen

The dolmen stands on a low cairn about 30 feet in diameter. The capstone looks like a solid stone table sitting on four upright stones. The backstone has collapsed. The capstone is traditionally sloping towards the back, and this gives it the dramatic look that has attracted so many photographers.

The grave was excavated in 1968 and found to contain the remains of 22 adults and six children, one a newborn baby. Radiocarbon dating suggests that they were buried around 3800 BC. What

612

helps makes this monument so dramatic is the landscape surrounding it. The cairn is set around cracked limestone sheets with scattered rocks all around and the Aillwee Mountain sitting on the horizon.

Gleninsheen Wedge Grave

Just over a mile up the road towards Ballyvaughan is the Gleninsheen Wedge Grave. It's more easily spotted if coming from Ballyvaughan, as it sits about the height of the nearby wall, and isn't signed. The other problem is that the stile originally used for climbing over to it had been blocked off by the landowner, so I had to walk further up to the gate and climb over that, hoping the farmer didn't catch me.

It was the most magnificent wedge grave I'd seen yet. Its capstone is supported by one long stone either side, and it almost looks like a little house. The front is open, and the back is obscured by bushes, yet the rest of it remains completely visible. A solid gold collar was found here, and is now in the National Museum of Ireland. There is also another wedge grave nearby, but this had been badly displaced and only one stone remains standing.

Places to Stay

H O T E L S

Gregans Castle Hotel
Ballyvaughan
Tel: (065) 7077005
Web: www.gregans.ie
Email: stay@gregans.ie
Although not in the castle itself, this hotel does have a fantastic view of the Burren Mountains. Situated a few miles south of Ballyvaughan on the N67, the castle is just across the road but is only open for viewing in June. The original castle was built by the O'Loughlen clan in the 10th century.

Dromoland Castle
Newmarket-on-Fergus
Tel: (061) 368144
Web: www.dromoland.ie
8 miles from Shannon airport on the Ennis road. Formerly owned by Conor O'Brien, a direct descendent of Brian Boru. This castle is now a top range hotel and golf course.

The Cliffs of Moher

I got to view these by complete surprise five years ago when my bus from Tralee to Doolin stopped unexpectedly at the Cliffs of Moher for an hour. I had come down this way today in search of St. Brigid's Well, and had stopped off at the cliffs along the way.

Stretching 8 kilometers up the coast and soaring to a height of over 200 meters, these cliffs have earned a place among the most famous landmarks of Ireland. To this end, they are also one of the most visited. So being able to experience this without the crowds is next to impossible.

These cliffs drop off at sheer ninety-degree angles. There is a solid concrete ledge where you can lay down flat on your stomach and crawl to the edge to look over. This is the best way to view the cliffs, so long as your stomach can take it. You can hear the waves crash against sharp rocky outcrops far below and see just how it has eaten into the base of the cliffs, forming craggy recesses and caves. The cliffs are made of soft shale and sandstone, and large sections quite often fall away. But it didn't seem to stop the crowds around me.

A pathway leads up along the cliffs to its highest point, where a small castle was built in 1835 by Cornelius O'Brien, a descendant of Brian Boru. County

Clare has a wealth of castles. From here I could just see the outline of Inisheer, the smallest of the three Aran Islands.

St. Brigid's Well

I left the car park and turned right towards Liscannor. At a junction on the right is St. Brigid's Well. Acidic rain falling on the region eats away into the limestone sheets creating underground caves and rivers. The well here flows underground from the hills and dips into the stone basin here. This well is clearly popular. A statue of the saint sits in a courtyard outside, and entrance to the well is through a short tunnel which is lined with statues and all manner of trinkets, gifts and offerings to the saint.

I headed back northward for another journey around the Burren coastline. I was fascinated by it. A strange phenomenon exists here called "turloughs", which are disappearing lakes said in folklore to be magical portals to *Tír nan Óg*. My girlfriend is investigating these as part of her geography thesis, and so I just happen to know that, geologically speaking, they disappear because the limestone is porous. The lakes usually dry up about this time of year, and they are identified by a white residue. But personally, I preferred to believe the former.

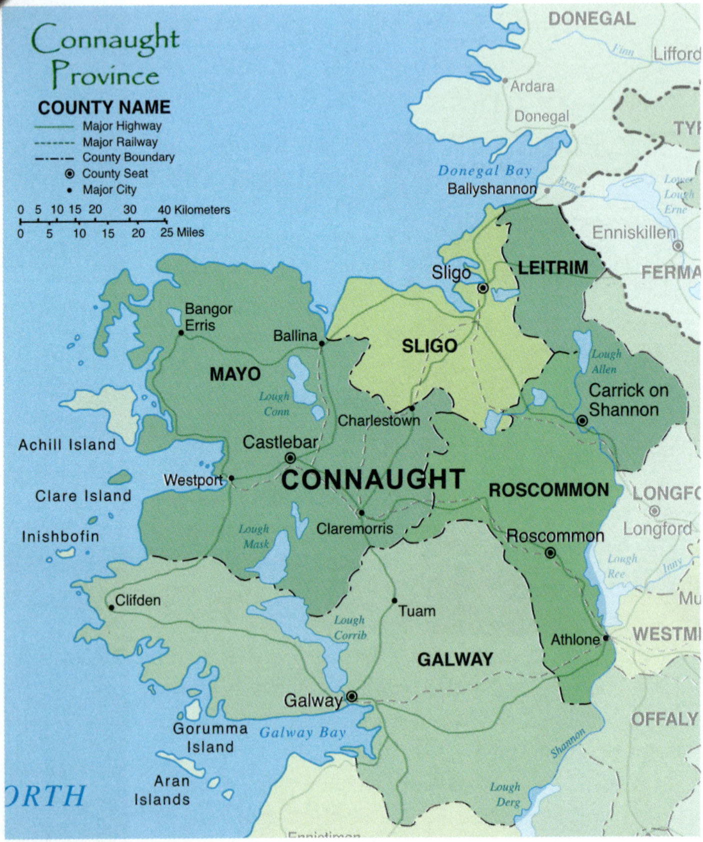

Connaught Province

COUNTY NAME
— Major Highway
---- Major Railway
-·-·- County Boundary
◉ County Seat
• Major City

0 5 10 15 20   30   40 Kilometers
0   5   10   15   20   25 Miles

DONEGAL

Ardara

Donegal

Donegal Bay
Ballyshannon

Enniskillen

TYR

FERMA

Lough Allen

Sligo

LEITRIM

Bangor Erris

Ballina

SLIGO

Carrick on Shannon

MAYO

Lough Conn

Charlestown

Castlebar

Achill Island

Westport

CONNAUGHT

ROSCOMMON

LONGF

Longford

Clare Island

Claremorris

Roscommon

Inishbofin

Lough Mask

Lough Ree

Mu

Clifden

Tuam

Athlone

WESTMI

Lough Corrib

GALWAY

OFFALY

Galway

Gorumma Island

Galway Bay

Shannon

Aran Islands

Lough Derg

ORTH

Places to See Key for Connaught Province

Here is a list of the icons used in the county maps in this section:

☼ Multiple sites near each other

⚸ Ancient pagan, pre-Christian sites, often of unknown origin

☥ Christian sites

🛡 Historical sites, heritage centres

🗡 Cryptid sightings (mysterious, unknown and/or legendary creatures)

▲ Scenic views and museums

❶ Nightlife and popular hangouts

👻 Haunted houses and areas

Connaught Province

onnaught province is the westernmost of the four provinces, and the ancient stronghold of the Fir Bolg. It is best known as the homeland of the infamous Queen Maeve, and as the setting of *The Táin*. It also played host to both battles of Moy Tura, the first between the Fir Bolg and the Tuatha dé Danann in County Mayo, and the second between the Tuatha dé Danann and the Fomorians in County Sligo.

Off the coast of County Galway are the famous Aran Islands, homeland of the even more famous Aran sweater. Inishmór, the largest of the three Aran islands, boasts perhaps the widest variety of ancient and Christian sites to be found on any island in Ireland. Galway also features Clonfert Cathedral, founded by the famous St. Brendan, as well as Mám Ean, a sacred hill with shrines dedicated to St. Patrick.

Speaking of St. Patrick, County Mayo contains the most sacred mountain in Ireland: Eagle Mountain, better known as Croagh Patrick, or simply, "The 'Reek". County Roscommon is best known for Cruachan Aí, the capitol seat of ancient Connaught, that is filled with over 60 ancient monuments, many of which are featured prominently in *The Táin*. Nearby County Sligo was the favorite of famed Irish poet W.B. Yeats, who loved the myths and legends associated with the area, particularly with the Second Battle of Moy Tura fought between the Fomorians and the Tuatha dé Danann.

And last but not least is County Leitrim. Though it is indeed least in size, being the smallest county in Connaught, it too has its fair share of hidden treasures.

Connaught General Information

Tourist Information Offices:

⚜ **Galway**
Tel: (091) 537700

⚜ **Mayo (Cong)**
Tel: 094 9546542
Web: www.quietman-cong.com

⚜ **Roscommon**
Harrison Hall
Roscommon
Tel: (090) 6626342
Web: www.visitroscommon.ie

⚜ **Sligo**
Tel: (071) 9161201
Web: www.irelandnorthwest.ie
Email: info@irelandnorthwest.ie

⚜ **Leitrim**
Bridge St.
Carrick-on-Shannon
Tel: (071) 9620170
Web: www.leitrimtourism.com

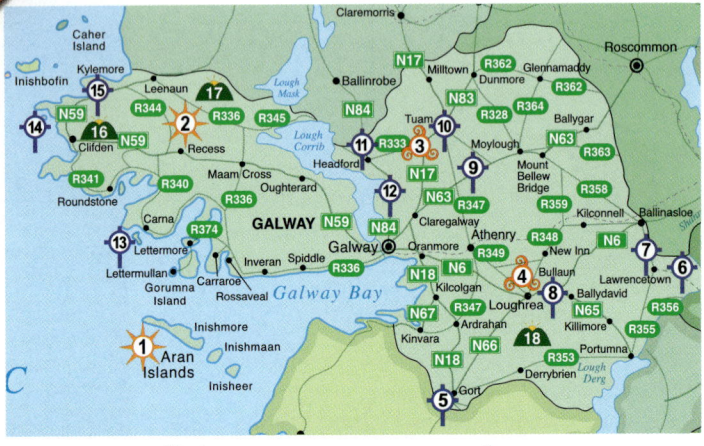

Places to See in Galway

Galway
The Aran Islands

The coast road is a convenient way to get around Inishmór, the largest and most visited of Galway's Aran Islands.

Inishmór is the largest of the three Aran Islands, and the most visited island in the country. Five years ago I'd intended to come here, but enjoyed my time on Inisheer so much I stayed there for the two nights I had on the islands.

The Aran Islands are an extension of the Burren landscape found in County Clare. Here the limestone rises dramatically out of the ocean and forms three islands: Inisheer, Inishmaan and Inishmór. Inisheer was where I first experienced a true awakening when it came to the Irish people's passion for music. Danny, who worked at the hostel in Doolin, had come over for the night and was playing his guitar and singing songs all evening in the pub, his payment simply to be supplied with beer for the duration. The pubs there stay open for as long as they want because there are no police on the island.

Galway
Things to Do & Places to See

The Aran Islands
Inishmór contains a wealth of ancient sites such as the spectacular *Dun Aonghasa*, The Seven Churches and The Church of St. Enda.

Connemara National Park
Letterfrack
Tel: (095) 41054/41006
Situated just outside the little village of Letterfrack, there is an exhibition and audio-visual on the Connemara landscape, as well as picnic areas and a tearoom and self-guided nature trails.

Kylemore Abbey & Garden
Connemara
Tel: (095) 41146
Web: www. kylemoreabbey.com
Email: info@kylemoreabbey.ie

THE JOURNEY
CONNAUGHT
COUNTY
GALWAY

Situated beside a beautiful lake, this is the home of the Irish Benedictine Nuns. There is a visitor center and a restaurant and craft shop.

Mám Ean
Sacred hill blessed by St. Patrick and now containing a shrine and church in his honor. It's signed on the right about 8 miles west of Maam Cross.

Turoe Stone & Pet Farm
Bullaun, nr Loughrea
Tel: (091) 841580
Web: www.esatclear.ie/~turoefarm/
Email: turoefarm@esatclear.ie
In the little village of Bullaun, just a few kms. north of Loughrea, lies the ornately carved Turoe Stone within the Turoe pet farm and leisure centre. Entrance to the stone is free, but the rest holds an

In fact, a newspaper article framed on the wall was testament to this. A few years before, the police had sent over an officer from the mainland disguised as a backpacker, who had noted the closing time of the pub and had promptly fined them for serving out of hours. The newspaper headline had read: "The Landlord that Time Forgot".

Next to this newspaper clipping was a framed illustration depicting a country pub with images of people partying inside, and drunks stumbling about and slumped against the wall outside. Crawling along the roof and watching furtively from behind wails were figures wearing backpacks. The caption read: "Everyone knows there are no police on Inisheer."

And they still don't close on time.

It was three o'clock in the morning and I was just

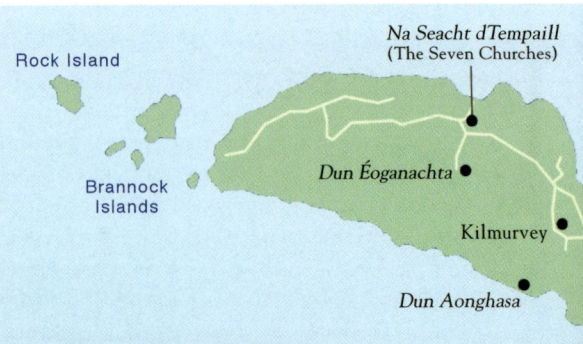

Rock Island

Na Seacht dTempaill
(The Seven Churches)

Brannock Islands

Dun Éoganachta

Kilmurvey

Dun Aonghasa

Inishmór
(Largest of the Aran Islands)

about to light a cigarette when I suddenly became aware that the entire room had fallen deathly silent. I then became aware of a female voice singing, and wandered towards the rear of the pub to find it was a local girl, singing without music. For the next hour I sat and listened intently as each of the locals took it in turn to sing a favorite song of theirs. The songs came from the heart. They weren't singing for money, or for fame. They were singing because they simply loved the songs, and loved to sing them. And I liked that.

Inishmór

The reason I came to Inishmór today was because it is home to a wealth of ancient churches and ring forts. I caught the ferry from Rossaveal, which drops you at the pier in the main village of Kilronan, and was now puffing my way along the coast road on a bike I'd hired from

Teampall an Ceathrar Álainn
(The Church of the Four Comely Saints)

Teampall Ciarán

Fort na Capall

Dun Eochla

Cill Ronain
(Kilronan)

Diarmuid & Gráinne's Bed

Pier

Straw Island

Dun Dubchathair
(The Black Fort)

Cill Einne
(Killeany)

Teaghlach Èinne
(The Household of Enda)

entrance fee. From the village take a left turn, following the signs to the farm.

Clonfert Cathedral
Cathedral established by St. Brendan the Navigator, and also his burial place.

Tourist Information:
☩ Forster Street
Galway City
Tel: (091) 537700

☩ Bridge Street
Ballinasloe
Tel: (090) 9742604

☩ Galway Road
Clifden
Tel: (095) 21163

☩ Tuam
Tel: (093) 25486

Tours
There are many mini tour buses waiting at the pier when you arrive on Inishmór:
☩ **Bus Èireann**
runs a daily tour through the Connemara from

Galway
May–Sept.
Tel: (091)
562000

✝ **Killary Cruises**
Cruise Ireland's
only fjord.
Nancy's Point
Leenane Connemara
Tel: (091) 566736
Web: www.
killarycruises.com
Killary Cruises offer
a 90-minute cruise to
see Ireland's only
fjord. There are four
sailings per day plus
an evening dinner
cruise April–Sept.

Eat & Drink
RESTAURANTS
**Aran Fisherman
Restaurant & Bar**
Kilronan, Inishmór
Tel: (099) 61104
Web: www.
aranfisherman.com
Email: info@
aranfisherman
.com
Good selec-
tion of seafood
and pizzas.

Fogerty's Restaurant
Market St.
Clifden
Tel: (095) 21427

the pier. I had with me a map from the tourist office, and an excellent little pocket guide called *Legends in the Landscape* by Dara Ó Maoildhia. The island is just 9 miles wide and 2.5 at its widest point. Naturally the road network isn't that extensive, but there are two roads to the next major village of Kilmurvey. From Kilronan the road climbs up the hill out of town and then you have the choice of continuing along the high road, or taking the coast road. I took the coast road.

St. Ciarán's Church

St. Ciaran's Church. Ciaran dreamt of a great tree that sprouted in the middle of Ireland that eventually grew to encompass all of Ireland. This tree was interpreted by St. Enda to represent Ciaran's life's work in spreading the Gospel.

For such a small place the island is littered with ancient monuments. St. Ciarán came here and studied under St. Enda before going off to establish his monastery at Clonmacnois. Just outside of Kilronan, which was the first site I came across, are the remains of a small church dedicated to him. It's here in the island where he dreamed of a tree in the middle of Ireland. This dream was interpreted by St. Enda, who said that it represented his life's work. The church sits on a hill with a lovely view of the coast.

THE SEVEN CHURCHES

The Seven Churches complex actually contains the ruins of only two churches, the other five structures being living spaces. These seven buildings were likely called "The Seven Churches" in reference to the seven churches of Asia mentioned in Revelation 1:4.

When I first arrived at Rossaveal, the rain was coming down in sheets. Today the sun illuminated the entire island. I continued on past Kilmurvey and followed a sign to the right for *Na Seacht Teampaill* (The Seven Churches). The Aran Islands are **Gaeltacht** areas, thus all signs are in Irish. These islands contain schools where the Irish language is taught. They are strict, and no English must be spoken or the student will be sent home. The everyday language for the islanders is Irish. It's nice to know that these places exist, but it also means that you need to know the Irish names for the places you want to visit.

According to my pocket guide there were only ever two churches here, and the others are the remains of domestic houses. The largest church at the centre is *Teampall Bhreacáin* (Church of St. Breacán). It seems that around the 6th century the island was divided into two major monastic settlements. This half was controlled by St. Breacán, and the other half by St. Enda, at the other end of the island near Killeany.

CAFÈS
An Tsean Celb
Kilronan
Inishmór
Nice little café serving fresh fish.

Walsh's Coffee Shop & Bakery
Market St., Clifden
Lovely little café with nice cakes.

Tuan's Notes
The Gaeltacht
Learn more about the Gaeltacht in The History: Ireland Today (p. 322).

PUBS
Mannion's Pub
Market St., Clifden
Good lively locals pub with regular Irish music sessions.

Lowry's Pub
Market St.
Clifden
Good family-run pub.

SHOPPING
Aran Sweater Market
Kilronan
A great place to buy the famous Aran knitwear.

THE JOURNEY
CONNAUGHT
COUNTY
GALWAY

*There &
Back Again*

A I R
Galway Airport
Carnmore
Tel: (091) 755569
Web: www.
galwayairport.com
Email: info@
galwayairport.com
A regional airport
located just outside
Galway City.

Aer Arann
Inverin
Tel: (091) 593034
Web: www.
aerarannislands.ie
Email: aerarann@iol.ie
25 flights a day to
each of the Aran Isl-
ands w/a taxi service
from Galway City.

F E R R I E S
Island Ferries
Victoria Place
Galway City
Tel: (091)
568903
After hours
Tel: (091)
572273
Web: www.
aranislandferries.com
Email: island@iol.ie
Daily departures to all
three islands from

THE JOURNEY
CONNAUGHT
COUNTY
GALWAY

THE BED OF THE HOLY SPIRITS

When St. Breacán came here he destroyed a pagan
idol on this site and took his name from it. He then
turned the site into a Christian settlement. In front of
the main church is The Bed of the Holy Spirits (*Leaba
An Spioraid Naoimh*). This is one of the prayer stations. The shaft of a cross sits at the edge. Next to this
is the saint's grave, which contains the broken grave
slab of St. Breacán.

DUN AONGHASA

Dun Aonghasa takes its name from Aenghus Óg, the son of the
Dagda in the myths of the Tuatha de Danann. This fort was likely
the last redoubt of the Fir Bolg after their crippling defeat at the
hands of the Tuatha Dé.

Back out on the road I popped up the opposite hill to
see Dun Eóganachta, a fort established by the
Eóganacht clan from Munster. But the most magnificent fort on the island is Dun Aonghasa. This is the
prime attraction. From the village of Kilmurvey I rode
up to the visitor center and began the long climb to
the high cliff where it sits.

Dun Aonghasa probably takes its name from
Aenghus Óg, the Celtic god of love and son of the
Dagda. Aenghus Óg was also said to be a leader of the
Fir Bolg, who fled to various points around the country

Dun Aonghasa is built on the edge of a sheer cliff with a thrilling view that rivals that of the Cliffs of Moher in County Clare.

after their defeat by the Tuatha dé Danann. Inishmór is believed to have been the last outpost of the Fir Bolg, and this was probably their fort.

The fort is semi-circular and built on-to the cliff edge. It's not until you go through the 20-foot thick walls and into the middle that you really get a feel for the place. In the mid-dle is a raised lime-stone platform. I climbed upon it and walked to the edge.

"Oh my God!!" I exclaimed.

The limestone cliffs dropped away at breathtaking-ly sharp angles. The ledge I was standing on actually protrudes beyond the edge, and from here it tapers inwards until reaching the sea 300 feet below. It was a sight that sent my heart racing.

The platform sits in the center of the fort, and was possibly used for rituals. Once inside here, there was no other way in but via the front. There are actually three ringed walls to enter before you arrive here in the middle, making this place virtually impenetrable. And the views across the island are spectacular. I lay down on the ledge and peered downwards at the giant waves crashing against the rocks all along the coast-line. I actually thought this was far more dramatic than the Cliffs of Moher.

Rossaveal, 20 miles west of Galway City.

Inishboffin Island Ferries
Cleggan
Tel: (095) 44750
Web: www. inishbofinferry.com
Email: inishbofinferry @eircom.net
2-3 sailings a day to this lovely, tranquil island. Cleggan lies just north of Clifden.

T R A I N S
Station Road
Galway
Tel: (091) 562730
Located in the city centre just off Ayre Square. There are several direct trains a day to Galway from Dublin Heuston.

B U S E S
The bus station is next to the train station.

Michael Nee Coaches
Tel: (095) 51082
Runs services to Galway, Letterfrack and Cleggan from Clifden.

THE JOURNEY
CONNAUGHT
COUNTY
GALWAY

Feda O'Donnell Coaches
Tel: (074) 9548114
Web: www. fedaodonnell.com
Email: busfeda@eircom.net
Runs a twice-daily service from Galway to Sligo & Letterkenny, stopping at Tuam.

Inishmór
A local bus service runs between Kilronan and Bungabhla 3-4 times a day, and to Killeany and *Iar Áirne* once a day.
✢ Bus Èireann 424 runs several times a day from Galway and stops at Rossaveal for the ferry.
✢ There are regular buses from Galway to Clifden, going through Maam Cross.
✢ Bus 64 Galway to Sligo stops at Tuam.
✢ Bus 70 Galway to Athlone stops in Loughrea and Ballinasloe.

THE FOUR COMELY SAINTS

Back down below I followed the overland road back towards Kilronan. Time was running short and the ferry back was going at seven, so I had a lot of ground to cover. I also had to return the bike.

Along the way I took a signed turn-off for *An Ceathrar Álainn* (The Four Comely Saints). This is a church with the graves of four revered saints. I was more interested in a dolmen called Diarmuid and Gráinne's Bed. Further on the road leveled out and a grassy path continued up the hill. When I came to a narrow path branching off right I took this as instructed by the guidebook, and as I reached the brow of the hill I could see Dun Aonghasa silhouetted against the distant sun. To the left I could also see the dolmen.

DIARMUID & GRÁINNE'S BED

I made my way across a couple of fields to get there. It's actually a wedge grave that has collapsed. Only two of its capstones remained in place, the other was lying with one side on the ground. The side and backstones were made of several slabs of varying sizes, and the

Diarmuid and Gráinne's Bed is but one of numerous ancient sites scattered throughout Ireland believed to have once been a place of hiding for the famous Diarmuid and Gráinne of legend.

The huge wall of Dun Eóghanacta provides a rocky pathway from which to view the rolling countryside of Inishmór.

whole thing looked like it had cracked and split over the years just like all the limestone pavements on the island. Its position on the hill here meant I got a great panoramic view, and I was alone because I think not many people knew of its existence. According to local folklore, Diarmuid and Gráinne slept here one night whilst on the run from Finn McCool. A similar bed can apparently be found on Inishmaan.

The Household of Enda

Back down on the road I returned to Kilronan and continued on through to the village of Killeany. Just beyond the airstrip is a graveyard sitting beside a shallow inlet with lovely views right across a field of sand to Kilronan pier. In the middle of this graveyard is the sunken church of St. Enda. *Teaghlach Èinne* literally means "The Household of Enda". It lies half buried in the sand and is said to contain the saint's body along with 120 other saints. The graveyard is 1,500 years old and is still used today. The guidebook suggests that he is buried under the altar. It's a small church and inside it are a couple of bullaun stones and parts of a Celtic cross.

DRIVING
⚜ From Galway City take the R336 towards Spiddal and into Rossaveal for the ferry to the Aran Islands.
⚜ Continue west on the R336 to Maam Cross and then head west on the N59, turning right at sign for Mám Ean.
⚜ Go back to N59 and follow this to Clifden for a scenic drive through the Connemara.
⚜ The Sky road outside Clifden is a particularly nice drive.
⚜ Tuam lies on the N17 north of Galway.
⚜ For Turoe Stone take the N6 east out of Galway to Loughrea, then north to the village of Bullaun.
⚜ Clonfert lies south of Ballinasloe. Take the R355 towards Lawrencetown and follow signs.

THE JOURNEY
CONNAUGHT
COUNTY GALWAY

"The Household of Enda" was a cozy church that now serves as a burial place for St. Enda, who is believed to be buried under the altar.

Like St. Breacán, Enda was the son of a king. Through the marriage of his sister to the king of Cashel, he was able to come to Árainn (the original name for Inishmór) and establish his monasteries. He came to the island with 150 monks and began his lifetime's work, building a huge settlement where people like St. Ciarán came to study.

THE BLACK FORT

This corner of the island is littered with churches and sites. Up on the nearby cliffs is *Dun Dubhchathair* (The Black Fort). I came to the disused electricity station where I was supposed to turn off for the climb to the fort. But unfortunately my time had run out. I had to return to Kilronan and return the bike.

"It's a pity you didn't go there," said the guy at the bike hire. "The Black Fort is even more spectacular than Dun Aonghasa."

Oh well, I figured I'd just have to return one day. After all it's not going anywhere, is it? Well, except for about half a centimeter per 1,000 years.

Mám Ean

Back on the mainland, and after a night of singing and bad jokes at Mannion's Pub in Clifden, the next morning I headed back east on the N59 and turned left at the sign for Mám Ean, about 8 miles before Maam Cross. I followed the road until I came to a car park on the right. From here I went through a metal gate with Mám Ean and a Celtic cross on it, and started walking up a rough gravel path.

The weather had taken a turn for the worse once again, but this time I had thought to bring my raincoat. The trail takes you up over a pass between the Maamturk Mountains. The wind was blowing fiercely from the south and actually aided my climb up the hill. At the highest point, 1,200 feet, I came across a statue of St. Patrick seemingly guarding the entrance to a shrine that overlooks a lake in the valley below. There is also a small church that was built into the cliff, as well as a shelter with an altar inside.

This pass is now dedicated to St. Patrick, but before then it was the site of *Lughnasa* celebrations on the last

Email:info@ abbeyglen.ie
The castle was built built in 1832 is also a four-star hotel with open fires and luxurious rooms.

HOSTELS
Kilronan Hostel
Inishmór
Tel: (099) 61255
Email: kilronan hostel@ireland.com
On the hill overlooking the pier. Includes a free breakfast.

Artist's Hostel
Kilronan
Inishmór
Tel (099) 61456
Located just outside of town in a nice quiet corner by the sea.

Bru Radharc na Mara
West Village
Inisheer
Tel: (099) 75024
Email: maire.searraigh @oceanfree.net
Nice hostel and an excellent pub next door.

Mám Ean also hosts a holy well and shrine marking the spot where St. Patrick had come and blessed the land.

Sunday in July, which is known as Mám Ean Sunday. Here they worshiped *Crom Dubh*, the dark god of the harvest (*op. cit.*). Traditionally he would return to the Otherworld with the fruits of the new harvest.

It's said that St. Patrick came here and blessed the land. He spent the night, and a rectangular wall surrounding a gravel bed is said to be the place where he slept. Since then pilgrims have been coming here to the holy well to pray. Lots of Celtic crosses and stone cairns dot the area.

The amazing thing about the Connemara region is that when all around you is gloomy, the dark clouds looming overhead and the wind and the rain blowing against you, generally making you feel totally wretched, a gap will appear in the clouds and illuminate the peak of a distant mountain. This happened as I was walking back down the mountain to the car park. The rocky peak glowed silver, and I wondered if this is what inspired people to place these holy shrines upon the hills, and why they believed them to be sacred. Were they guided here by a similar sign?

Knockmaa

"Queen Maeve is buried there," said the guy in the tourist office in Tuam, after giving me directions.

"Oh, I thought she was buried on Knocknarea," I replied.

"Oh no, she is buried on Knockmaa."

I had read otherwise, but who was I to argue.

I headed south out of town on the N17 and took the right turn for Headford, then followed the road through Belclare and turned left just before an s-bend, where a narrow lane led up to a small car park. From here a forest path led up to and around the hill. The farmer painting a nearby gate told me that when I came to the ruins of an old house by the path, I was to follow the trail up beside it and over the wall, then climb up into a clearing where I'd find Finvarra's Castle.

FINVARRA'S CASTLE

The trail circumnavigates the hill. In keeping with tradition I took the clockwise direction and, half an hour later, came across the house. I soon emerged from the dark forest onto a limestone outcrop with the remains

"Finvarra's Castle" is the name given to the remains of a ruined cairn on Knockmaa believed in local legend to be the palace of Finvarra, the King of the Connaught fairies.

lounge where you are welcomed with tea and cakes.

The Pier House Guest House
Kilronan
Inishmór
Tel: (099) 61416/61417
Web: www.galway.net/pages/pierhouse
Situated right on the pier, open Feb-Nov.

Ard Mhuiris
Kilronan, Inishmór
Tel: (099) 61208
Email: ardmhuiris@eircom.net
Close to the village and ferry, and has 6 en-suite rooms.

Man of Aran Cottages
Kilmurvey
Inishmór
Tel: (099) 61301
Web: homepage.eircom.net/~manofaran
Email: manofaran@eircom.net
Built for the movie.

Bali Lodge B&B
Bridge St., Clifden
Connemara

Tel: (095) 22923
Web: www.bali
lodge-clifden.com
Email: info@bali
lodge-clifden.com
Highly recommended

Rossfield House
Westport Rd., Clifden
Tel: (095) 21392
Email: rossfieldhouse
@eircom.net

Tuan's Notes
Mermaids
*Learn more about
mermaids and other
mysterious sea crea-
tures of Ireland in The
Mystery: Creatures
Great & Small (p.
182).*

Winnowing Hill
Ballyconneely
Rd.
Clifden
Tel: (095)
21281
Web: www.
winnowinghill.com
Email: winnowinghill
@eircom.net

of a burial cairn. A section of it had been rebuilt into a mini fort. I guessed this was Finvarra's Castle.

Finvarra is king of the Connaught fairies and this hill is said to be his abode. There is another interesting story that says this hill is the burial place of Princess Cesair, who was the granddaughter of Noah, as in Noah's ark. When warned of impending flood she came here with her father, two other men and 50 maidens. They were said to have been the first to come to Ireland, but all died not long after.

I could see another cairn from this hill but couldn't find a route up to it, so I continued on around the path while thunder warned of an impending storm.

The Turoe Stone

The Turoe Stone is a superb example of Celtic artwork from the La Téne Period.

North of Loughrea on the R350 in the village of Bullaun is the Turoe Stone. The stone is over 2,000 years old and was originally sited at an ancient rath a few miles from where it is now. It's a 4-foot-high rounded granite stone with ornate carvings from the La Téne period. It now lies in the Turoe House pet farm, in the middle of a field where children play. It's a beautiful example of ancient Celtic art, and it's a miracle it's still in one piece.

Clonfert Cathedral

I headed back to Ballinasloe and took the R355 south to Clonfert. In this village there is a cathedral here said to have been established by St. Brendan the Navigator, whose epic journey to America 1,000 years before Columbus earned him a place in Irish legend. He died in Annaghdown, north of Galway city, and his body was brought here and buried in this cathedral.

It was undergoing repairs when I arrived, and the intricately carved Romanesque doorway was obscured by scaffolding. But I was able to go inside. There are a number of interesting sculptures inside, including a 1,500-year-old stone figure found by builders in the 1980s and carved stones set into the wall. On the walls of the chancel are carvings of saints and angels and, interestingly, a dragon, and a **mermaid**.

The entryway to the cathedral is decorated with several small reliefs, including this playful mermaid holding a small copy of the Bible. This is probably Liban (see Mermaids, p. 182). Parishioners habitually rubbed the image of this mermaid on the way in for good luck.

THE JOURNEY
CONNAUGHT
COUNTY
GALWAY

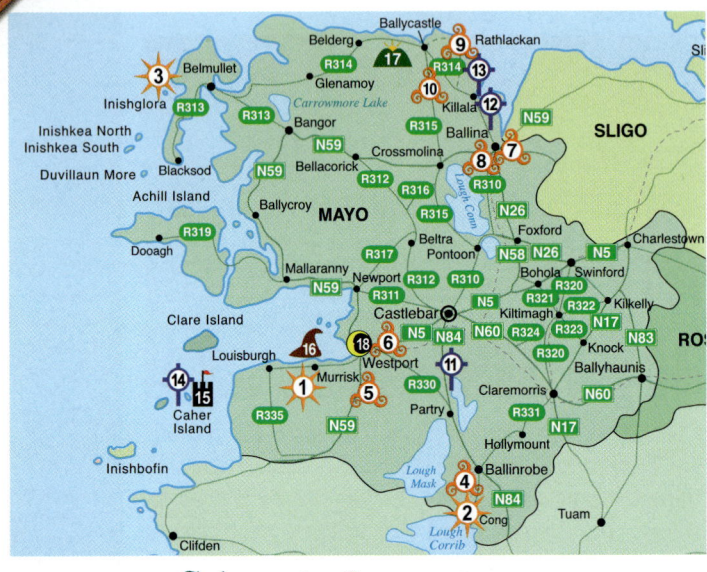

Places to See in Mayo

Mayo
Croagh Patrick

re you ready to climb 'The 'Reek'?" asked Edel as she came in from work.

"Ready when you are," I replied.

It was late Sunday morning and I was staying with my friends Paul and Edel in Ballina, and had managed to convince them and Stephen (Edel's son) to join me on a hike up Croagh Patrick — or, as they call it, "The 'Reek". First Edel prepared a picnic, and then we all jumped into the van and sped off to Westport.

Paul and I had first met each other in Australia whilst working at the same place. After a failed attempt to meet up again during my first trip to Ireland, we finally managed it a couple of years back. Paul had since met Edel, got married, and settled down.

I love Westport. I'd stopped here many times before. It's an attractive, colorful town with a vibrant nightlife. Despite it being a major tourist destination, I feel it still

Mayo
Things to Do & Places to See

Murrisk Abbey & Croagh Patrick Visitor Centre
Murrisk
Web: www. croagh-patrick.com
Start of the ascent of the holy mountain.

Ballintubber Abbey & Celtic Furrow Cultural Centre
Ballintubber
Claremorris
Tel: (094) 9030934
Web: www. museumsofmayo.com/ ballintubber.htm
Email: btubabbey@eircom.net
Situated on the N84, south of Castlebar.

Clare Island
Home of Granuaile, the infamous female pirate.

Ballymacgibbon Cairn
On the R346 between Cross & Cong.

THE JOURNEY
CONNAUGHT
COUNTY
MAYO

retains the charm and character of a small town. It's never dirty. Everytime I come here I find the clean streets lined with flower boxes, and all of the colorful shop-fronts impeccably maintained.

The first time I came here I was blissfully ignorant of this majestic mountain on the outskirts of town. When I returned years later I was promoting one

St. Patrick greets the penitent who seeks to climb his mountain.

of my books and didn't have time to climb it. Instead I left my girlfriend and an American girl hitching with us at the car park and returned to town while they had the "fun" of hiking up.

As we approached Westport we got our first view of Croagh Patrick. Its distinctive conical shape is the most prominent feature on the horizon. In pre-Christian times this was the sacred mountain *Cruáchan Aigh* ("The Mountain of the Eagle"), associated with Lugh. *Lughnasa* assemblies occurred here every year on the last Friday of July. When St. Patrick came here, he is said to have climbed to the summit and fasted for 40 days in order to win some concessions from God, which he apparently succeeded in doing. Whilst up there, it's claimed that he banished all the snakes from Ireland. I'd noted that all the druids at Tara had snakes carved upon their staffs and deduced that this banishment was symbolic of banishing paganism from Ireland.

The mountain was thus renamed Croagh Patrick, and now the annual Christian pilgrimage replaces the *Lughnasa*, and is held on the last Sunday of July ("Reek Sunday", as it's affectionately named). On this day the pilgrims gather at Murrisk Abbey, and start their ascent there. They do this barefoot. The 'Reek can be climbed at all other times of the year for religious purposes, or simply for the sheer enjoyment of it. But it can be very dangerous.

"It's traditional to climb the 'Reek three times," said Edel. "It's dangerous though. A woman died not too long ago after climbing to help her sick son."

The weather can make the hike quite treacherous. Today it was sunny and clear, and the peak was clearly visible. But at 2,500 feet it can often be enshrouded in mist and cloud, making visibility virtually zero.

It was around mid-afternoon when we set foot on the trail. It can take 1-2 hours to reach the top, depending on your level of fitness. In our case, two hours. Steps mark the beginning of the ascent, with a statue of St. Patrick guiding the way. The trail can get

Croagh Patrick takes 1-2 hours to climb, depending upon your level of fitness. Care should be taken to assure a safe climb.

The Quiet Man Coffee Shop
Main St.
Cong
Tel: (094) 9546034
Named after the movie, *The Quiet Man*, this lovely little homely café with a wooden-beamed ceiling, old pine furniture and a nice view of the river and garden out back. Serves drinks, sandwiches and a selection of cakes.

Hungry Monk Café & Internet
Abbey St.
Cong
Tel: 094 9546866
Mob: 086 2756680
Offers a small selection of pasta meals, paninis & homemade burgers. Also has Internet access.

The Bard
Garden St.
Ballina
Tel: 096 21894
Pub & restaurant, well priced with a great selection. Children friendly.

very busy, but thankfully today the crowds had kept away. We began our climb along a small stream where the terrain was quite soft. The trail narrowed and steepened as we veered away from the water. The path had been carved out by millions of people over the past 3,000 years, and was clearly defined.

"Jesus, however did you convince me to do this?" puffed Paul. Ironically, I was the one who was puffing along behind him. Paul and I didn't have a history of hiking mountains together; we had a history of drinking copious amounts of alcohol together. And we had been doing so for the past few nights. Meanwhile, Edel and her ten-year old son looked down in sympathy from the distant rock where they were sitting. Paul wiped the sweat from his brow, and we soldiered on.

We were about a quarter of the way up when I looked back and was stunned at the view of Clew Bay, spreading out before us like an architect's model. The trail tapered off into the distance, and people looked like ants swarming around below. A man hiked his

Croagh Patrick offers stunning views for miles around, including Clew Bay to the north.

Views of distant hills and mountains give a sense of both majesty and humility appropriate for one seeking penance.

Gaughans Pub
O'Rahilly St.
Ballina
Tel: (096) 70096
A nice locals pub with excellent home-cooked food served all day.

The Garden Inn
Garden St.
Ballina
Has good traditional music.

Danagher's Hotel & Bar
Abbey St.
Cong
Tel: 092 46028
Main courses and sandwiches served all day at the bar.

Matt Molloy's
Bridge Street
Westport
Tel: (098) 26655
This excellent pub is deservedly popular. The regular traditional music sessions are not to be missed. Matt Molloy is a member of the Irish group, The Chieftains.

way down past us with a little girl on his back. Fluffy clouds were scattered across the sky, and hazy mountains lined the opposing coastline. It was a beautiful sight, and we were certainly blessed with the weather.

"It's easy to see how people could dream up stories of fantasy and legend when you look at the world from this perspective," Paul said. He was right. Standing up here you feel like you are on top of the world. You feel like you could lean over and pick up the distant mountain between your fingers. The pain it took to get here is all forgotten, and as you breathe in the cleanest air your lungs have ever known you stand in awe of the magnificence of nature and all Creation.

On 'Reek Sunday the pilgrims walk this route barefoot. For the life of me I cannot see how anyone could do that. The trail is mostly gravel and mud with lots of big, sharp rocks just waiting to cut your feet to shreds. As we started the final ascent to the cone, which for the most part was almost a forty-five degree slant, the mud disappeared and gave way to loose scree. It was more a case of scrambling up from here, rather than hiking.

*There &
Back Again*

A I R
Knock Airport
Nr. Charlestown
Tel: (094) 9368100
Lo Call: 1850 672222
Web: <u>www.</u>
<u>knockairport.com</u>
Email: <u>info@ireland</u>
<u>westairport.com</u>
Located south of
Sligo on the N17.
Served by a number
of airlines flying to
Dublin and destina-
tions in the UK.

F E R R I E S
Clare Island Ferry
"The Pirate Queen"
Tickets available
from the Tourist
Office, James St,
Westport.
Tel: (098) 28288.
Mob: (086) 8515003
Web: <u>www.</u>
<u>clareisland</u>
<u>ferry.com</u>
Email:
<u>clareislandferry</u>
<u>@anu.ie</u>
Departs from
Roonagh Quay and
takes 15 minutes.

THE JOURNEY
CONNAUGHT
COUNTY
MAYO

The well-defined path was carved out by the feet of millions of pilgrims over at least 3,000 years, some of whom walked over its often jagged rocks barefoot.

It's here that I was able to get my revenge on Edel and scramble ahead of her as she struggled with the change in terrain. Edel had bought a stick at the base to aid her hiking. I've always found sticks to be more of a hindrance than a help when climbing mountains. Especially on terrains like this where quite often the best thing to do is virtually crawl up like an ape.

Everything seemed so dramatic from there. As I fought to stand still on the loose slate that threatened to fall away at any given moment into a steep valley below, I could easily understand why so many people have been injured or even died on this mountain. Many of the people who climb aren't really hikers. I watched as people came past me in flimsy shoes and shorts. The religious significance of climbing the 'Reek draws many elderly people, who really aren't up to the rigors of such a climb. I can understand how many feel close to God when they are up here, but the sad fact is that they might end up being closer to God than they intended.

Upon reaching the ridge further back a thin layer of cloud had hovered over and obscured the

Loose scree marks the final and most dangerous leg of the journey to the peak of Croagh Patrick.

sun. This cloud had remained ever since. By now we didn't need the sun to keep us warm, and the shade was quite welcoming. Paul and I were now ahead of Edel and Stephen.

Quite often when hiking up mountains, you often question why it is you like to punish yourself in this way. The answer always lies at the top, and it always hits you right when you least expect it.

Paul and I stepped onto the summit almost simultaneously. Suddenly, as though the Lord above was blessing us, the clouds parted and a ray of sunshine burst through, illuminating the ground around us like a floodlight.

"Hallelujah!" I cried.

"God be praised!" yelled Paul.

To some this may have been seen as a moment of divine intervention — a message from God that we had arrived at the holy land. I had to admit it did seem rather poignant, but for us non-believers it felt more like a bit from a Monty Python movie.

For the God-fearing public this wasn't the end. As if climbing up here wasn't enough, they then had to

O'Malleys
Ferries
Tickets available from portacabin at Roonagh Pier.
Tel: (098) 25045.
Mob: (086) 6000204/8870814

T R A I N S
Westport Train Station
Altamont Street
Tel: (098) 25253/25329

Ballina Train Station
Station Road
Tel: 096-71820

Castlebar Train Station
Station Road
Tel: 094-21222
There are direct trains to Castlebar & Westport from Dublin Heuston. Regular services run from Cork and Galway.

B U S E S
Bus Èireann
Tel: (098) 25711
For updated information on bus and other services, see <u>ireland.mysteriousworld.com/Counties/Mayo/</u>

THE JOURNEY
CONNAUGHT
COUNTY
MAYO

THE JOURNEY
CONNAUGHT
COUNTY
MAYO

St. Patrick's Bed and other ancient artifacts have patterns, or ritual paths that penitents walk around them as a demonstration of piety. Note the clockwise direction of the path.

perform many other acts of contrition. Signs everywhere explained what was to be done. I watched as many people encircled St. Patrick's Bed and the church several times while reciting prayers.

Croagh Patrick is made up of white quartzite, like many other mountains in the west of Ireland. This is why they tend to glow when sunlight hits them. I couldn't help thinking that this is why these mountains were often considered sacred or magical. And as had occurred at Mám Ean, a shaft of light amid the bleakness of the cloudy day can break through, and if it happens to hit the mountain it can look like a guiding beacon in the doom and gloom of the weather. It's no wonder many believed this to be a sign from God.

"We climbed the 'Reek!" cried Paul and Edel.

Stephen had collapsed against the wall of the big white church here. A statue of the Virgin Mary sat next to him.

Paul and Edel were cuddling each other and staring out to Clew Bay 2,500 feet below.

"I'm so glad I didn't give up back there," said Paul.

I couldn't agree more.

Along with the gorgeous view, the patient seeker is rewarded at the summit with the sight of the gleaming white Teampall Pádraig.

It had taken us two hours to climb up, and it took another two to get back down. We had left the picnic in the van, so once down we put the kettle on and tucked hungrily into a huge pile of sandwiches and bags of crisps, giving other hikers a sight they would have had to pay good money for at the zoo.

Paul, Edel and Stephen enjoying the view from atop Croagh Patrick. A climb up the 'Reek makes for an ideal family outing.

THE JOURNEY

CONNAUGHT

COUNTY
MAYO

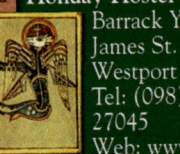
Cong

Cong is a lovely village set along the Cong River, which connects Lough Corrib in the south with Lough Mask in the north.

In the south of the county, bordering Galway on the shore of Lough Corrib, lies the little village of Cong. It was here on the plains north of the village that one of the two most legendary battles of Ireland took place: The First Battle of Moy Tura. There, the Tuatha dé Danann arrived on the shores of Galway Bay, and a fierce battle ensued between them and the Fir Bolg. The battle is said to have taken place here. Over 100,000 of the Fir Bolg were killed before victory for the Tuatha dé Danann was achieved.

CONG ABBEY

Cong sits on a river running between Lough Mask and Lough Corrib. It's a lovely little waterside village with one main street, a couple of pubs and cafés and its most distinctive feature, Cong Abbey.

The first-ever monastic settlement was established by St. Feichin on an island near here, before he went off to establish the settlement at Fore in Westmeath. The first abbey was built in the 7th century, and rebuilt several times after being destroyed by fire and looting. The remains you see today are 13th century. Not much remains of the abbey, but the Romanesque doorways still exist and lead through to the gardens behind.

The abbey sits beside the river, and sitting on its banks, on a stone platform jutting out into the river, are the remains of a small stone house. Experts suggest that this was used by the monks for fishing the river. A bridge in the plat-

Cong Abbey was the location of the famous Cross of Cong that now resides in the National Museum.

form allows water to run underneath, and it's possible that a trapdoor was built in the floor to enable fishing from inside, while being kept warm by the fireplace. Across the main bridge is a walkway through the forest.

It was here at Cong Abbey that the famous Cross of Cong was kept for several centuries in an iron reliquary, brought out for display only on Christmas and Easter. It was later purchased by the Royal Irish Academy and eventually sold to the National Museum, where it resides today as one of the prime artifacts of Ireland's Christian history.

THE QUIET MAN

The Quiet Man is one of the most popular movies about traditional Irish culture and customs ever made. Set in Cong, and starring John Wayne and Maureen O'Hara, this movie has inspired many to visit Ireland. It is still remembered in the names of several local establishments, and even a website: www.quietman-cong.com.

B & B S

The Tighbeag B&B
Glaspatrick
Murrisk, Westport
Tel (098) 64988
Web:
www.anu.ie/tighbeag
E-mail:
tighbeag@anu.ie

Copperfield B&B
Knockranny
Castlebar Rd.
Westport
Tel: (098) 25247
Email:
amhoban@anu.ie

SELF-CATERING
Holiday Apartments
Cong
Tel: (094) 9546068
Behind the Quiet
Man Heritage Centre

CAMPING
Westport House and Country Park
Tel: (098) 27766
Web: www.
westport
house.ie
Email:
camping@west
porthouse.ie

For more information
visit ireland.
mysteriousworld.com/
Journey/Counties/
Mayo/

THE JOURNEY
CONNAUGHT
COUNTY
MAYO

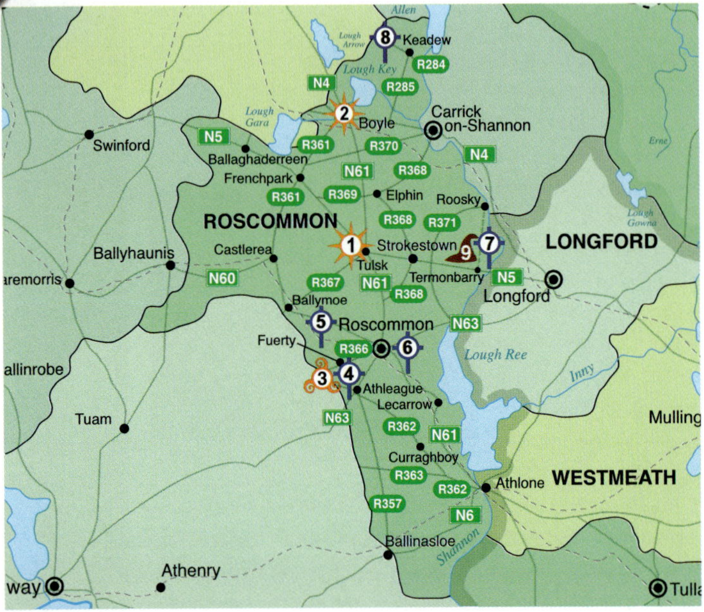

Places to See in Roscommon

☀ Multi-Sites

1. Cruachan Aí  647-651
   - Map of Cruachan Aí 648
   - Rathcrogan Mound 649
   - Maeve's Mound 649
   - Maeve's Lump 649
   - Rathmore.............. 649
   - The Fort of the Bulls..... 650
   - *Oweynagat* – Entrance to the Otherworld.............. 650
   - Daithí's Mound 651
   - Carnfree Inauguration Mound 651
   - *Reilig na Rí* (the Graveyard of the Kings)
   - The Long Stone of Carn
   - The Mound of the Hunt

2. Boyle
   - Drumanone Dolmen
   - St. Attracta's Well
   - Boyle Abbey

⚒ Ancient Sites
3. The Castlestrange Stone

✟ Christian Sites
4. Fuerty Old Church
5. St. Patrick's Holy Well
6. St. Brigid's Well .. 647, 652-653
7. Tobar Barry
8. St. Lassair's Well

⚔ Cryptid Sightings
9. The Great Serpent of Slieve Badhan (Tobar Barry)

Driving Directions: See pp. 647-651

Roscommon

Cruachan Aí
ANCIENT ROYAL SEAT OF CONNAUGHT

Rathcroghan Mound forms the center of the vast *Cruachan Aí* complex of mounds and other important ritual structures that form the setting for the *Taín*.

ruachan Aí is the setting for the beginning of what is generally considered to be the greatest story of pre-Christian Ireland: the *Taín Bó Cuailgne*, or "The Cattle Raid of Cooley". *The Taín* is a semi-historical legend wherein the story is told of how one day King Ailill and Queen Maeve of Connaught had decided to compare their personal wealth in order to see who was the richer. Both went through their entire personal inventories right down to the last goat and found that they matched each other perfectly — except for one thing. It was found that the one thing that the king owned that Maeve could not match was a great white bull named *Finnbennach*, "The White Bull of Connaught".

Desperate to best her husband, Maeve searched far and wide for a bull that was better, and found that

Roscommon

Things to Do & Places to See

Cruachan Aí Heritage Centre
In the village of Tulsk on the N5
Tel: (0)71 9639268
Web:
www.cruachanai.com
Email:
cruachanai@esatclear.ie
Over 60 ancient monuments make up the site of the royal capitol of Connaught, the setting for the *Taín* saga.

St Brigid's Well
Northeast of Roscommon town. The water from this well is said to make the ugly beautiful. From Circular Road, take the road called "the walk" out of town, at the sign for the Gardens B&B. At T-junction turn left then take the 2nd right.

THE JOURNEY
CONNAUGHT
COUNTY
ROSCOMMON

Stop at the first house on the left and ask there. The well is two fields opposite.

Roscommon County Museum
The Square, behind the tourist office.

Tourist Offices
⚜ *Roscommon Office*
Harrison Hall, the Square
Tel: (090) 6626342
Web: www. visitroscommon.ie

Tuan's Notes
Learn more about The Táin in The Mystery: Folklore & Mythology (pp. 193-195).

Tours
Group tours can be booked at the Cruachan Aí Heritage Centre, but must be arranged in advance.
Tel: (0)71 9639268
Web: www.cruachanai.com

the only bull in Ireland that was mightier than her husband's was *Donn Cuailnge*, "The Brown Bull of Cooley", in Ulster province. After a failed attempt with the King of Ulster to bargain for the bull, she decided to take it by force. And it was here, at Cruachan, where **Maeve** rallied her army and rode out towards Cooley.

Lying just to the west of Tulsk, *Cruachan Aí* is the site of Maeve's royal palace, the royal residence of the kings and queens of the province, entrance to the Otherworld, the home to a wealth of ancient raths, burial mounds and monuments and, most importantly, the setting for the beginning of *The Táin*.

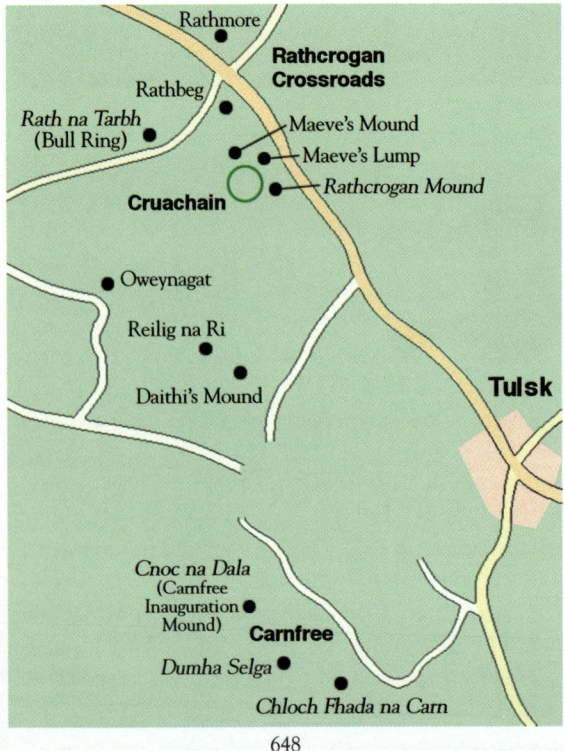

Cruachan and the area around it contains 60 monuments in all, and the main one is on the left before Rathcroghan crossroads. I pulled up in the car park and read the sign:

RATHCROGHAN

The largest mound in the complex, Rathcroghan lies at the center of the entire complex. This large, circular mound is 88 meters in diameter on average at its base and about 4 meters in height on its northern side. It most likely sat at the center of the ancient royal ceremonies, used for both the installment of kings and queens and for their entombment. Recent studies have show that there was once a large enclosure surrounding both the mound and other nearby archaeological features which, at 380 meters in diameter, was the largest of its type in the country.

MAEVE'S MOUND

Maeve's Mound is ten feet high and one of twenty ring forts and burial mounds in the area. It was probably here that the *Táin* saga began.

MAEVE'S LUMP

In front of the mound is a fallen standing stone called *Misgaun Meva* (Maeve's Lump). I wandered over to the mound and could see it has five ridges on it. It's been suggested that this mound was built upon several times over. It's 400 feet in diameter.

RATHMORE

Surrounding this are several other mounds. Some of them are hard to make out, but some are clearly marked. Rathmore, "The Big Fort", is on the right just beyond the crossroads, which are small country roads and easy to miss. The mound is clearly marked though, and there is a small lay-by. The mound is clearly defined and smaller than Rathcroghan at 100 feet in diameter.

Tuan's Notes
Queen Maeve
Maeve (lit., "she who intoxicates"), was the warrior queen of Connaught as portrayed in The Ulster Cycle of Irish mythology, and perhaps the most powerful female figure in all of Irish history and myth. Though there actually may have been a Queen Maeve at one time, it is likely that the legends we have of her are greatly elaborated, possibly the accretions of several different regional, fertility and sovereignty goddesses. To top it off, Maeve was also described in some legends as a queen of the fairies.
Learn more about Queen Maeve in The Mystery: Deities & Demigods (pp. 122-123).

Eat & Drink

Sambos
Main St.
Roscommon
Nice little café with
soups, Irish breakfast
& sandwiches.
Opposite AIB bank.

Tuan's Notes
The Otherworld
*Learn more about the
Otherworld in The
Mystery: Creatures
Great & Small (pp.
151-152).*

**La Trattoria
Italian Café**
The Stone Court
The Square
Tel: (090) 6637904
Nice place overlook-
ing main square.

PUBS
Most of the
cafés and pubs
in Roscom-
mon are along
Castle St.

JC Doorly
Castle St.
Traditional music
sessions some nights.

THE FORT OF THE BULLS

Back at the crossroads I headed south, where *Rathbeg* ("the Little Fort") was signed on the left, and further down on the right is *Rath na dTarbh* ("Fort of the Bulls"). This is supposed to be where the *Táin* reached its bloody conclusion. Inside this rath, the two bulls begin a fight to the death. The mound is 280 feet in diameter and a high bank encircles the inner ditch. It almost looks like a bullring, especially designed for bullfights.

OWEYNAGAT: ENTRANCE TO THE OTHERWORLD

I continued down the road and took the first left. At the end of the road, beside a house, was a metal stile leading into a field. Just down on the left I found Oweynagat, the entrance to **the Otherworld**.

The front of the cave is very deceptive in that it doesn't look that big. But the cave actually runs for 150 feet and a short way along the passage is another chamber to the left. According to a brochure I picked up at the visitor center, this entrance was actually manmade, but further into the cave it's a natural fissure in the limestone. The entrance contains a number of ogham inscriptions, and the entrance lintel bears the words, VRACCI MAQI MEDDVI, "Fraech, son of Medb (or Maeve)".

This little cave is steeped in legend. One of the most famous references is in the tale of Nera, servant to King Aillil, Maeve's husband. In the tale, Nera sees a vision of the palace at Rathcroghan being burned down, and chases the illusory perpetrators into the cave. Once in the cave, he realizes that he has entered the Otherworld, where he remains and marries a beautiful fairy woman. His fairy wife later confides in him that what he thought had been the burning of the palace was actually a premonition, and that Rathcroghan would actually be attacked at the next Samhain. Nera then returns to warn the king, who assembles his armies and goes to war against the Otherworld.

DAITHÍ'S MOUND

I returned to the crossroads and headed back towards Tulsk, taking the next right turn down a country lane. I followed this road until I came across a large barn on the right and a stone stile leading over a wall. In the distance I could see a standing stone on a small mound, and headed over. It lay in a field full of bulls, who became instantly inquisitive at my arrival. I picked up a stick, as Tom had done in Ardagh, and made my way through without incident. The mound is said to be the burial place of Daithí, the last pagan king of Ireland. He was the son of Niall of the Nine Hostages and died in the 5th century. The stone sits on a low, artificial mound and was excavated, with nothing found. It stands six feet tall and is probably there to commemorate the king's life.

CARNFREE INAUGURATION MOUND

I headed back to the crossroads of Tulsk and turned right onto the N61 towards Roscommon. I took the first right and then branched immediately left and followed this until I spotted a standing stone in a field on the left at the top of a hill. In the next field is *Cnoc na Dála* ("Carnfree Inauguration Mound"). It was here that the inauguration ceremonies of the O'Connor kings were held right up until 1641. Traditionally it is also the burial site of Fraech, a hero of Connaught who was killed by Cú Chulainn in *The Táin*. This mound sits on a hill 400 meters in altitude, and has a commanding view of the ancient capital of Connaught.

There are so many more interesting sites to visit in and around Cruachan that I just did not have enough time to visit them all. So I wrapped up my visit to Roscommon with yet another visit with St. Brigid.

There & Back Again

TRAINS
Roscommon Train Station
Abbeytown
Tel: (090) 6626201
Just west of the town centre. Regular services run to and from Dublin, Galway, Westport & Ballina.

BUSES
Buses stop at the square in Roscommon. Services running between Athlone to Sligo & Westport stop in Roscommon. Bus 22 Longford to Ballina stops at Tulsk.

DRIVING
Roscommon lies on N63 east of Galway. N61 north of Athlone. N63 west of Longford. Tulsk lies on N61 north of Roscommon.

TAXIS
Kilduff Thos Taxi Service
5 Circular Rd. Roscommon
Tel: (086) 2544662

St. Brigid's Well

"How did you manage to get this close?" asked Tom.

"I have a guidebook with good directions," I replied. "Am I close then?"

"You are. It's over there in that field."

I was standing next to a house talking to two old farmers, Tom and Ciarán. St Brigid's Well lies near here, and I had stopped to ask directions at this house.

"Are your boots waterproof?" asked Ciarán.

"No. Don't worry though, I'm used to getting wet."

He tipped his cap and looked at Tom. "We'll take him in the tractor, shall we?"

"Sure," replied Tom.

And so before I knew it, I was climbing onto the back of a refurbished 1969 red tractor, bouncing across a field and ducking through trees on my way to the well.

"I've heard a story about two sisters who lived here and used the water from the well to keep themselves beautiful," I shouted over the noise of the tractor.

Tom and Ciarán sport their vintage 1969 red tractor on the the the way to St. Brigid's Well.

St. Brigid's Well, Roscommon in its entlike setting. One wonders if J.R.R. Tolkien derived many of his ideas from a vacation in Ireland.

"Ah, the Gunning sisters!" replied Tom. "Their house used to be near here, but it was demolished a while ago. It's a shame that the government aren't helping to preserve these old houses."

We arrived at the well, which sits shaded among a grove of trees. A low circular wall surrounded it.

"The wall was built around it in the '50s," said Tom.

"So is this your land?"

"That's right. We tried to clean up the well not too long ago, but the pump just kept getting blocked. It's not really used that much anymore, as everyone gets water piped to their homes."

"It looks cleaner than some of the others I've seen," I said, and knelt down to take a drink. "Now I'll no longer be ugly."

They both laughed.

The story of the Gunning sisters is that they were very ugly, and the water from the well transformed them into beautiful women. I just hoped the same wouldn't happen to me.

THE JOURNEY
CONNAUGHT
COUNTY
ROSCOMMON

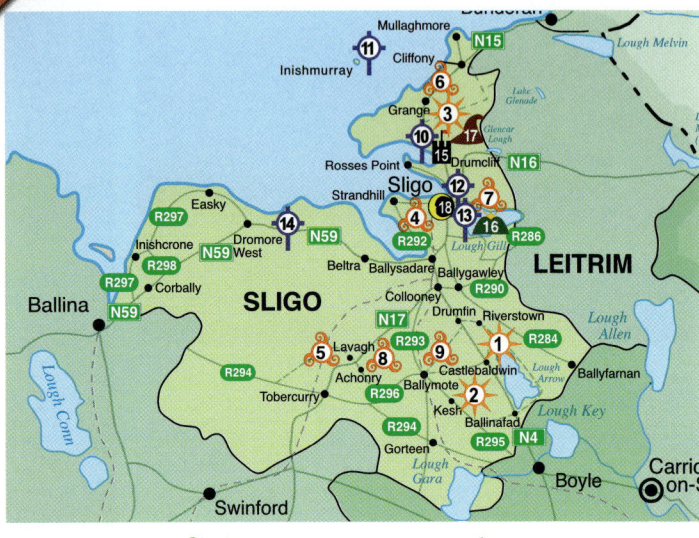

Places to See in Sligo

Sligo
The Plain of Moy Tura

The broad, rolling plains in the foothills of the Bricklieve Mountains are generally believed to be the scene of the Second Battle of Moy Tura, where the Tuatha dé Danann successfully defended Ireland from the Fomorian invaders.
Image © Reggie Thomson, www.reggie.net.

I was standing on the brow of a hill overlooking The Plain of *Maigh Tuireadh* (Moy Tura). According to folklore, this is where the great battle was fought between the Fomorians and the Tuatha dé Danann. Under the leadership of their savior, Lugh of the Long Hand, the Tuatha Dé defeated the evil Fomorian invaders and kept the rulership of Ireland. As a result, this area is littered with megalithic sites from both the first battle against the Fir Bolg, and the second battle against the Fomorians (though — as we have seen — some scholars place the location of the First Battle of Moy Tura just to the south in Cong, County Mayo, and the second battle where I was now, near Lough Arrow in County Sligo).

Sligo
Things to Do & Places to See

The Plain of Moy Tura
A broad, rolling plain in the hills above the eastern shore of Lough Arrow near the Bricklieve Mountains is the generally accepted location of the Second Battle of Moy Tura, where the Tuatha dé Danann successfully defended Ireland from the Fomorians. (This is to be distinguished from the first battle, which is believed by some to have taken place in County Mayo, near Cong.) The plain is one of the most important archaeological, historical and mythological sites in all of Ireland. For more information on the history and mystery behind the plain, see The Mystery: The Invasions (pp. 58-67).

THE JOURNEY
CONNAUGHT
COUNTY SLIGO

Heapstown Cairn is believed to mark the site of "The Well of Healing" used by the Tuatha Dé healer Dian Cécht to heal wounded warriors during the Second Battle of Moy Tura. This heap of stones was placed over it by the Fomorians to make the well unusable.

Heapstown Cairn

Signed just before Heapstown crossroads & Bow and Arrow pub. From the N4 take the road for Riverstown from Drumfin and head south, following signs for Lough Arrow.

Carrickglass Dolmen

In a field behind Cromlech Lodge Hotel. Follow signs from Heapstown to the hotel and park in car park. From here follow the Sligo Way walking signs through the forest.

Barroe North Round Cairn

Visible on a hill from the dolmen. You can continue along the Sligo Way or, from the hotel, take the next left and go until you come to where the trail crosses the road. Follow signs up the hill from here.

To get here I had followed the signs to Riverstown, which lies just northwest of Lough Arrow, and headed south to the crossroads at Heapstown. Just before the pub at the crossroads there is a sign pointing left into the field for Heapstown Cairn. I pulled over at the gate, and made my way across the field to where a clump of trees hid this massive cairn.

You could be forgiven for dismissing this as just a great pile of rocks. It has been ruined by builders over the years, and the kerbstones that do remain are covered in moss. There is also no evidence of a chamber. However, there is a really interesting story linked to this pile of rocks.

Legend has it that at this site was a magical well called "The Well of Healing", where the Tuatha dé Danann's chief healer, Dian Cécht, brought wounded and dead warriors during the great battle against the Fomorians. The healer would immerse the soldiers in the well, whereupon they would be fully healed and able to return to battle. The Fomorians soon learned of this well, and took control of the area. However, instead of using the well to heal their own people, the Fomors threw rock upon rock into the water until finally this huge cairn of rocks was formed, completely blocking access to the well and its magical properties.

From the crossroads I continued on straight and followed the signs for Cromlech Lodge Hotel. The hotel sits on a ridge with a lovely view of Lough Arrow down below, and the remains of what looked like a church. In a field behind the car park was a sign indicating a walking trail. This led me on through a thick forest of pine trees. Suddenly I went from light to dark, as the forest concealed all but the faintest light until I emerged the other side.

"The Tuatha Dé Assemble" — © 1979, Jim Fitzpatrick.

Lake of the Eye
Continue on down the road until you come to a T-junction. Turn right here and the lake is down the road on the right as you near the crossroads.

Keshcorran
Complex of limestone caves set into the side of this dominating hill south of Kesh & Ballymote on the R295.

Carrowmore
Largest and oldest megalithic cemetery in Ireland. Off the R292 west of Sligo.

Carrowkeel
Magnificent complex of passage cairns set on remote hills. From Castlebaldwin on the N4 south from Sligo, turn right and follow signs. Web: www. carrowkeel.com

Knocknarea
Burial place of Warrior Queen Maeve.

THE JOURNEY
CONNAUGHT
COUNTY
SLIGO

CARRICKGLASS DOLMEN

After a short passage through the murky woods I spotted Carrickglass Dolmen. It is a magnificent sight with its gigantic, solid, square capstone perched on a number of supporting stones that are slowly collapsing under its colossal weight. Thick clumps of shrubbery had grown on the top of the capstone, giving it the resemblance of having a very bad hairstyle.

It's also known as Labby Rock (*Leába*), which comes from the Diarmuid and Gráinne story and refers to places they slept during their seven years on the run from Finn McCool. This must have been one of the last places they slept, because it was here in Sligo that the story finally came to its sad conclusion.

"Mirkwood Forest" in Sligo — could this thick stand of trees, through which almost no light penetrates, have been the inspiration for Tolkien's Mirkwood Forest as featured in his seminal work, *The Hobbit?*

Carrickglass Dolmen's weathered top marks the sad end of the story of Diarmuid and Gráinne.

658

BARROE NORTH ROUND CAIRN

Barroe North Round Cairn is believed to be the place from where Lugh directed the armies of the Tuatha dé Danaan during the Second Battle of Moy Tura.

I had turned left out of the Cromlech Lodge and then taken the next left. A short way along this road I pulled up beside a sign for the Sligo Way walking trail (a wooden post with a painted image of a yellow man walking). To the right the trail led up over a hill to where I was standing now, Barroe North Round Cairn.

It's a small, grassy cairn that sits on a ridge 745 feet above sea level, and is identified by an ordinance survey triangulation pillar. Legend says it was from this spot that Lugh directed the battle against the Fomorians. It's easy to see how. From this point you get a commanding view of the whole of Sligo county. I could see Knocknarea to the north, and could also quite clearly make out the giant cairn that sits atop it. It looks like a hill upon a hill. To the west I could make out Keshcorran, and in the farthest distance I could even see the outline of Croagh Patrick with its distinctive cone — a lonely mountain, separate from the rest.

Tours

The Wild Rose Tourboat
Lough Gill Cruises
Tel: (071) 9164266
Mob: (087) 2598869
Email: wildrosewaterbus@eircom.net
Leaves from the pier outside Parkes Castle. An excellent 45-min. cruise around the lake with entertaining stories and poems about Sligo and W.B. Yeats.

Martin Byrne
runs *Bord Fáilte*-approved *Sacred Ireland* tours around Sligo County. A variety of tours are available.
Tel: (071) 9666241
Web: www.carrowkeel.com
E-mail: murt@carrowkeel.com

Discover Sligo
Loughanelton
Sligo
Tel: (071) 9147488
Web: www.discoversligo.com
Email: info@discoversligo.com

THE JOURNEY
CONNAUGHT
COUNTY
SLIGO

Eat &
Drink

Bistro Bianconi
O' Connell St.
Sligo
Restaurant Tel:
(071) 9141744
Takeaway &
Delivery: Tel: (071)
9147000
Web:
www.bistrobianconi.ie
Highly recommended
An excellent Italian
restaurant in the
center of town, serv-
ing fresh pasta and
gourmet pizzas baked
in traditional wood-
burning ovens. The
food and service is
excellent, and good
value for money.

**Murphy's Bar and
Restaurant**
Markievicz St.
Tel: (071) 9147561
Nice place
overlooking
the Garavogue
River.

**Grappa Wine
& Tapas Bar**
Rockwood Parade
Tel: (071) 9147734
Beside the river and
serves a selection of
Spanish tapas.

THE LAKE OF THE EYE

The Lake of the Eye is so named after the great eye of Balor, which
fell and created a great crater after Balor was slain by Lugh.

Lough Arrow was clearly visible below, and just north of
this I could see a small, perfectly round lake. This is The
Lake of the Eye. According to legend, this small, round
lake was formed after Lugh slew the evil Fomorian
leader, Balor of the Evil Eye. Lugh fired a single shot to
Balor's eye and it struck with such force that the eye was
pushed through to the back of his head, falling onto the
ground behind where it burned a great crater that later
filled with water and formed this lake. So critical was
this battle that clear influences can be seen even in modern literature. For example, the Great Eye of Sauron in
The Lord of the Rings was clearly inspired by the evil eye
of Balor. The link with *Star Wars* is even clearer, where
the hero of that tale is also named Luke, and the great
destroying eye appeared as the "Death Star".

The lake is said to dry up periodically and reveal a
large crater with a hole at the bottom. It's happened
twice this century, in 1965 & 1985. If the cycle continues like this then the next time will be 2005. With
a bit of luck I might get back here to see it. It may be
that important secrets about our ancient history still
lay buried there.

Keshkorran

The magnificent caves of Keshcorran are said to be home to the Morrigan, and powerful entrances to the Otherworld.

There wasn't a cloud to be seen anywhere. The sky was deep blue and the sun shone vividly down, illuminating the mountain of Keshcorran as I drove towards it on the R295 from Ballymote, where *The Book of Ballymote* had been compiled. A passage cairn was clearly visible on the top. As I rounded the corner a row of seventeen spectacular limestone caves came into view on the side of this imposing hill.

This vast collection of caves lining the entire side of the hill is home to the *sídhe* (fairy folk), and is believed to be the place where the Mórrigan lives. The Mórrigan, who holds a powerful place in Irish myth and legend, is a fierce protector of this dwelling and of Corran, chief harpist of the Tuatha dé Danann.

When the road became closest to the hill, I turned off left up a country lane that circled back and ran along the base of the hill. I found a small, grassy lay-by on the right and climbed over a brown gate. A muddy path led up through a small row of trees and climbed up the hill to the caves. Most of the caves are small and narrow crevasses in the chunk of exposed limestone. But the caves

THE JOURNEY
CONNAUGHT
COUNTY
SLIGO

Furey's
(*Sheela na Gig's*)
Bridge St.
Sligo
*Highly recom-
mended* A very
popular pub in town
near the river. The
landlady is married to
the guitarist of the
popular Irish band
Dervish, who regularly
play there. Also has
Irish music Sun.-Tues.,
and more contempo-
rary music other days
of the week.

McGarrigles &
Cavanagh Pub are
among a few on
O'Connell Street
that are very good.

The Garavogue
15-16 Rear Stephen
Street, Sligo
Tel: (071) 9140100
Web: www.
cafebardeli.ie
Email: sligo@
cafebardeli.ie
Situated right
on the river-
bank, this
deservedly popular
modern place is a
bar, café and restau-
rant with a water-
front terrace.

on the left are the largest. Shortly after the trees, the trail gave way to a sloping, grassy bank. A lone tree sat just below the large cave, and as I approached I noticed a couple of rabbits staring down at me from a ridge. I chuckled as it put me in mind of the scene from *Monty Python and the Holy Grail*, when they faced the vicious bunny guarding the cave of Caerbannog.

I approached with caution. The Mórrigan is said to be a shape-shifter, and she could well be guarding this entrance in the form of a foul and cruel rabbit with nasty big pointy teeth. Inside the cave was even bigger than it looked. The smaller entrance beside actually joined and the whole thing became one gigantic fissure.

These caves were also home to Diarmuid and Gráinne, when they finally got fed up with being on the run. Gráinne's father, Cormac Mac Art, owned the land around here and so they settled and made this place home. They invited Finn to come and stay with them, and such was the custom that a guest must never harm his host; Finn was powerless to take his revenge.

CORMAC'S WELL

Just up the road, south of the village of Kesh, is a holy well on the left hand side. It is signed on the right as you head back from Keshcorran. A small lane leads up to an ancient churchyard, in the grounds of which is Kingstone Well, also known as The Grave of the Kings. The well is dried up now, but there is a small stone wall at the back of the ditch with the remains of a carved grave slab. According to *Sacred Ireland* this is the place where Ètaín, while travelling to the home of the druid Lugna, gave birth to Cormac Mac Art. During the night the baby was abducted by a she-wolf and a few years later the child was found by Lugna, playing outside the caves of Keshcorran with other wolf cubs. I couldn't help wondering if *The Jungle Book* was inspired by this story.

Carrowkeel

Carrowkeel is a collection of 14 Neolithic cairns atop beautiful hills with dramatic views, referred to locally as "The Pinnacles". There is even the remains of a Neolithic village on the easternmost ridge.

Breathless. This is the only word I can think of to describe how I felt when I turned the corner into this valley in the Bricklieve Mountains, where the megalithic cemetery of Carrowkeel lies. The evening sun cast a soft light over the towering hills, and on the right-hand side was a single passage cairn perched on the edge of the hill, its doorway facing outwards almost as if it were guarding the entrance to the valley.

There are around 14 cairns in this region, each designated with a letter. Two had completely collapsed. Cairn G had a collapsed roof, but the other two were accessible. One had partly collapsed, but I was able to crawl through the entrance on my hands and knees and scramble through the passage to the chamber, where I could stand up. Unfortunately, I didn't have a torch on me so I was unable to get a good look at the recesses. All I could do was use the flash on my camera to get a quick look. There looked to be three, and the back chamber was partially lit by the setting sun. Interestingly, this cairn had a light-box over the main door, just like the

There & Back Again

AIR

Sligo Airport
Strandhill
Tel: (071) 9168280
Web:
www.sligoairport.com
Email:
info@sligoairport.com
A national airport just a few miles from Sligo town with flights to and from Dublin.

TRAINS

Sligo Station
Lord Edward St.
Sligo
Tel: (071) 9169888

Collooney Station
(Not staffed)

Ballymote Station
Tel: (071) 9183311
There are four trains a day from Dublin Connolly station to the above stations. From Galway & Cork you have to go back to Dublin.

BUSES
The Sligo bus station is also in Lord Edward St.
Tel: (071) 9160066

Feda O'Donnell Coaches
Tel: (074) 9548114
Web: www.fedaodonnell.com
Email: busfeda@eircom.net
Arrives and departs from outside Connolly's Pub and runs between Galway, Sligo, Donegal Town and Letterkenny.

DRIVING
✠ For Rosses Point take the R281 off the N15 north of Sligo.
✠ Take the R292 west towards Standhill for Knocknarea and Carrowmore.
✠ Head south on the N4 to Castlebaldwin and turn right at signs for Carrowkeel.
✠ From Ballymote take the R295 south through Kesh for

Newgrange mound. Apparently this light-box was designed to trap the light, rather than allow it through to the chamber, like Newgrange does.

I spent the night in a fantastic camp-site at Rosses Point overlooking Sligo Bay and Coney Island. The outline of the cairn on top of Knocknarea was clearly visible across the bay. I had passed

Numerous dark passages and secret chambers await the intrepid explorer at Carrowkeel.

through a sudden, heavy storm on the road in from Sligo, and emerged the other side to blue sky and a brilliant sunset with thick black clouds rolling off to the east, casting a rainbow that fell across the other side of the bay. Boats bobbed about gently in the after-ripple of the storm.

On the other side of the campsite was a long, sandy beach with Ben Bulben Mountain in the background. Ben Bulben is a distinctive presence on the Sligo horizon, with its long, rectangular shape stretching across the horizon and then sloping off at the end at a near right angle. It was on this mountain where the Diarmuid and Gráinne story reached its terrible conclusion. There was a prophesy that Diarmuid would be killed by a wild boar on the slopes of Ben Bulben, and for this reason he went to great lengths to stay away from this mountain. Finn knew of this prophecy, and used trickery to lure Diarmuid out there one day. The prophecy was realized, and Diarmuid was killed.

Carrowmore

Carrowmore is Ireland's largest megalithic cemetery, with 33 tombs remaining in the form of dolmens and stone circles.

The next morning I took the R292 from Sligo towards Strandhill and followed the signs to Carrowmore, just a mile or so from Knocknarea. Covering an area of 1.5 square miles, this is Ireland's largest megalithic cemetery, and it was recently agreed that it's also the oldest and predates the complex at Newgrange. An archaeological conference in Sligo recently agreed that Ireland's megalithic period boomed between 4200-2500 BC. These findings were significantly characterized by excavation at Carrowmore. Entrance is via the visitor center, where the guide will take you on an interesting tour around the main complex.

Back in 1837 there were as many as 66 tombs here, but now only around 33 remain. These are mostly dolmens and a few stone circles. The weather was beautiful once again, and the cemetery is backed by a ring of mountains. Our guide pointed out Knocknarea, and explained the story:

"Queen Maeve was a very scary woman who had a particular interest in bulls. The story of Maeve was passed down through the centuries and finally writ-

Keshcorran.
⚜ Go back to Castlebaldwin and take the road to Lough Arrow for Heapstown Cairn & Dolmen.
⚜ Go back north of Sligo and take the N16 then the R286 to Parkes Castle for Lough Gill.

CAR HIRE
Hertz Desk
Arrivals Terminal
Sligo Airport
Tel: (071) 9144068

Europcar
Sligo Airport
Tel: (071) 9168400
Web: www.europcar.ie

BIKE HIRE
Flanagan's Cycles
Market Yard, Sligo
Tel: (071) 9144477
Web:
www.cygo.ie/flanagans

WALKING
The Sligo Way Map Guide
by EastWest Mapping
Web: homepage.eircom.net/~eastwest/sligoway.html

THE JOURNEY

CONNAUGHT

COUNTY SLIGO

ten down by the monks in the 11th or 12th century. Their pens were trembling as they wrote down the salacious details of her love life. She had a lot of different husbands, a lot of different wars. Eventually she ran into a bit of bad luck and was killed by a lump of cheese. One of the first known murders with a dairy product."

He waited a while for the chuckling to subside.

"It appears that Queen Maeve got into a dispute with her sister, who had gotten pregnant by her deadly enemy, the king of Ulster. The sister was murdered by Queen Maeve. Eventually the son of that sister came, and he was the cheese merchant, and he dropped, presumably from a great height, this lump of cheese which killed the queen."

He then went on to give a detailed and interesting description of all the different tombs and their possible purposes. He pointed out another hill in the distance known as Knocknashee (Hill of the Fairies). It lies in the village of Collooney and also has a passage tomb on its summit.

After the tour I took the map obtained from the visitor center and wandered across the road to where a number of interesting graves lie surrounded by yellow wildflowers and backed by Knocknarea. Interestingly, one dolmen was surrounded by a stone circle. I hadn't seen that before.

Knocknarea

Knocknarea has traditionally been held to be the tomb of Queen Maeve, who is said to have been buried standing up, spear in hand, facing towards Ulster.

I continued on to Knocknarea, where I parked in a car park and walked the 30-minute trail up to the summit. At the top I could see just why this cairn is so clearly visible from all over the county. It's 200 feet in diameter and stands 35 feet high. There is over 40,000 tons of rock making up the cairn, which is 6,000 years old. It's a mountain on top of a mountain.

The top of the cairn is flat with a smaller pile of rocks on top. From the top the views across Sligo Bay are spectacular. In the fields around the cairn archaeologists have discovered twenty-seven hut sites, suggesting that people lived here on the hill long after the cairn was built.

Although the cairn has never been excavated, legend says that Queen Maeve was buried here standing up, spear in hand and facing Ulster. She never really forgave Ulster for refusing to give in to her demands during the *Táin* saga, and is still waiting for the day when she will have her revenge. The story says that Maeve is buried in a chamber inside the cairn, which

B & B S

Pearse Lodge B&B
Pearse Rd.
Sligo
Tel: (071) 9161090
Mob: (086) 8535416
Email: pearselodge @eircom.net
Just a few minutes walk from the center of town. Open all year and has 4 en-suite rooms.

Tree Tops
Cleveragh Rd.
Sligo
Tel: (071) 9160160
Web: www.sligobandb.com
Email: treetops@iol.ie
Has 5 en-suite rooms

Coral Reef B&B
Rosses Point
Tel: (071) 9177245
Web: www.rossespoint .net/coralreef guesthouse/
E-mail: coralreef@ eircom.net
Perfect location, next to Waterfront bar, and overlooking Sligo Bay.

Hillcrest B&B
Ballindoon
Castlebaldwin
(via Boyle)
Lough Arrow
Tel: (071) 9165559
Web: homepage
.eircom.net/~
hillcrestbandb
Email: hillcrest
farm@eircom.net
Open March-Sept.
and just up the road
from Cromlech lodge.
Has 4 en-suite rooms.

Millhouse
Keenaghan
Ballymote
Tel: (071) 9183449
Web: www.sligo-
accommodation.com
Email: millhouse
bb@eircom.net
Has 5 en-suite rooms
and is close to Kesh-
corran and Carrow-
keel.

HOSTELS
The IHH
White House
Hostel
Markievicz Rd.
Sligo
Tel: (071) 9145160
An excellent place
in the heart of town
overlooking the river.

was then sealed off completely. As I'd already discovered, it's a dominating presence from most other sacred mountains in the county, and most of the other cairns are facing this one. It's quite clear that this was intended to be the focal point of the huge complex that is present in this county.

Sligo Town

That evening I ventured into Sligo town and checked into the White House Hostel, which is a favorite place of mine overlooking the Garavogue River right in the heart of town. I like Sligo. The first time I ever came here it was just to change buses. At the time I didn't think there was much to keep me here, but that was soon proven to be very wrong.

My friend Anne, with whom I had traveled up the west coast first time around, had loved Sligo so much that she moved there a year later, and has been there ever since. Also, to my surprise, my friend Paul was also living there, having moved from Tramore, County Waterford. So I too was returning now, for a reunion with some old friends.

I phoned Anne and we went for a drink.

"I can't believe you are still here," I said.

"I love it. There's a real buzz in this town," she replied as we fought to find a space among the throng of people in Furey's pub (also known as "Sheela na Gig's"). "They say that Sligo lies directly on one of the ley lines, which gives it a real energy."

There was certainly a buzz here tonight, and it was only a weekday. During past visits I had drunk in a number of pubs around town. Many of them, like Shoot the Crows, McLaughlins and the one we were now standing in, are cozy pubs with old wooden décor and dim lighting. Others are more modern, trendy places.

W. B. Yeats

Sligo's most famous son is the poet W.B. Yeats. Although he was born in Dublin, his mother was from here, and so Yeats spent much of his childhood in this area. Many of his poems are linked to this part of Ireland. There is a sculpture outside the Ulster Bank that has his poetry inscribed all over his body. Yeats claimed that Sligo was the place that most affected his life, and inspired his poetry. He was especially taken with a little island in Lough Gill, called the Lake Isle of Innisfree.

On the north side of Sligo, on the N15 in the village of Drumcliff, is a 10th-century high cross opposite the remains of a round tower. The rain was back this morning and the misty bulk of Ben Bulben looked almost haunting in the background of this graveyard. Inside, right in front of the church, is the grave of Yeats. He died in France and, in compliance with his wishes, was brought back here to be buried with a simple grave that held the epitaph:

> Cast a cold eye
> On life, on death
> Horseman pass by

Much of Yeats' poetry was inspired by the legends and folklore of Sligo, which is possibly more prolific here than anywhere else. Because modern development didn't affect Sligo County until recently, much of the old traditions and folklore still survive, along with its prolific amount of ancient sites. What I had seen was just the tip of the iceberg. It seems that Sligo is absolutely littered with remnants of its ancient past. I only wished I had more time. Perhaps in a second coming, I'll learn more.

Eden Hill Holiday Hostel
Ashbrook Pearse Rd., Sligo
Tel: (071) 9143204
Web: homepage .eircom.net/~edenhill
Email: edenhillhostel @eircom.net

CAMPING
Greenlands Caravan and Camping Park
Rosses Point
Tel: (071) 9177113
Highly recommended
On a hill with views of Sligo Bay, Knocknarea and Ben Bulben.

Lough Arrow Touring Park
Ballynary
Castlebaldwin
Lough Arrow
Tel: (071) 9666018
Mob: (086) 8891679
Near Heapstown Cairn, overlooking the lake.

For more information visit ireland. mysteriousworld.com/ Journey/Counties/ Sligo/

THE JOURNEY
CONNAUGHT
COUNTY
SLIGO

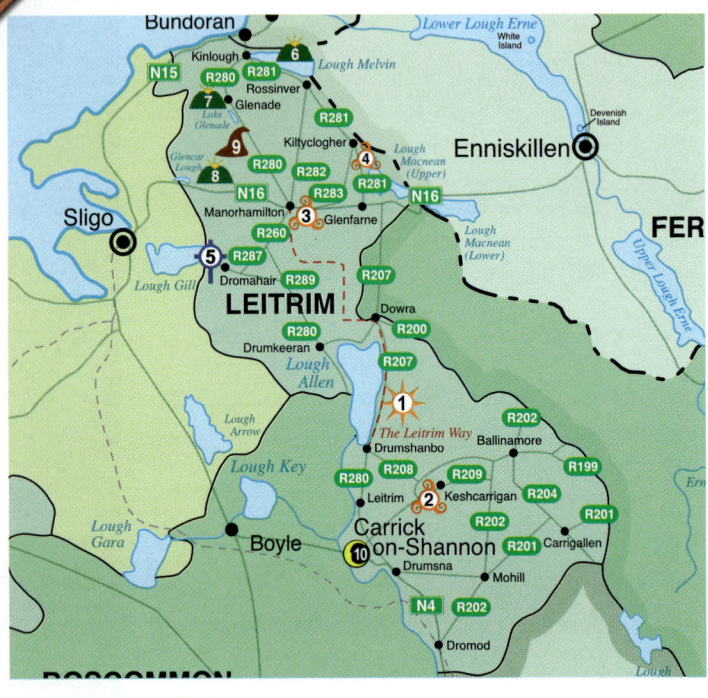

Places to See in Leitrim

☀ MULTI-SITES
1. Slieve Anierin 🔨 ⚚ ⛰ 671, 673
   - Landing Place of the Tuatha dé Danann 46-47, 671
   - Lough Allen 671
   - The Leitrim Way 671

⚒ ANCIENT SITES
2. Sheebeg/Sheemore 671-673
3. Tullyskeherny Megalith
   - The Giant's Grave
   - Fairy Thorn
4. Corracloona Court Cairn

⚚ CHRISTIAN SITES
5. Creevalea Abbey/Killery Churchyard

⛰ SCENIC VIEWS
6. Lough Melvin
7. Glenade Mountains
8. Glencar Waterfall

⚔ CRYPTID SIGHTINGS
9. Dobhar Chú 179

❿ NIGHTLIFE
10. Carrick-on-Shannon 671

Driving Directions: See pp. 671-673

Leitrim
The Leitrim Way

The Leitrim Way is a popular walking trail that encompasses Lough Allen. Image © Gareth McCormack/Lonely Planet Images.

riving into Carrick-on-Shannon brought back a flood of memories. This was one of the resting points on my charity hike, and it's quite a busy little town. Situated on the mighty river Shannon, it's the main town in County Leitrim. It has a number of lively pubs, with boats peppering the marina.

I drove out on the R280 towards the village of Leitrim which, despite being the county's namesake town, is more like a village. My walking route years ago had taken me through here and on to Drumshanbo where I had picked up the Leitrim Way walking trail northwards along Lough Allen to Dowra, the intersection point for three waymarked trails: the Leitrim, Miners and Cavan ways. The walk to Dowra also had taken me along the edge of Slieve Anierin. One legend says that when the Tuatha dé Danann arrived in Ireland, they came from the clouds and landed on this mountain in their cloud ships.

Leitrim
Things to Do & Places to See

The Leitrim Way
A popular 30-mile walking trail around Lough Allen.
Web: www. leitrimtourism.com/ walking.cfm

Sheebeg (Sí Beag)
Burial mound of Finn McCool and Gráinne. Take the R209 towards Keshcarrigan and turn right just before the village. Follow the road around to the left and up the hill to the crossroads. Turn left and go to the top of the hill. The mound is on the left.

Carrick on Shannon Tourist Office
The Old Barrel Store
Tel: (071) 9622045
Web: www. leitrimtourism.com
Web: info@ leitrimtourism.com

THE JOURNEY
CONNAUGHT
COUNTY
LEITRIM

Eat & Drink

Waterside Restaurant
13 Céis Lawns
Keshcarrigan
Tel: (071) 9642111
Italian/Irish food.

Coffee Dock
(two doors down)
Tel: (071) 9642777

Glancy's Bar & Restaurant
Bridge St.
Carrick on Shannon
Tel: (071) 9621500
Asian cuisine.

Coffee Shop and Restaurant
Church Street
Drumshanbo
Tel: (071) 9641992

Riverside Coffee Shop
Leitrim Village
Tel: (071) 9622170

PUBS
Joe Lowes Pub
Main St.
Carrick on Shannon

Cryans Pub and Restaurant
Bridge St.
Carrick on Shannon
Tel: (071) 9620409
Excellent trad. music.

THE JOURNEY
CONNAUGHT
COUNTY LEITRIM

Sheebeg & Sheemore

Sheebeg is believed to be the burial place of Finn McCool and Gráinne. The name means "The Little Fairy Mound".

This time around I turned off before Leitrim on the R209 to Keshcarrigan. Just before I reached the village, I turned right at the sign for Sheebeg, and followed the road around to the left. Sheebeg (*Sí Beag*) means "The Little Fairy Mound". From here it is supposed to be signed, but I couldn't see it. So I drove up to a nearby house and asked, and I found a woman inside the barn giving a dog a bath. "It's up on the hill there," she said, in a strong Northern English accent. "Just follow the road and turn left at the crossroads. Follow this until you reach the top of the hill and it's in a field on the left." After chatting a bit, I found out that she had moved here from England and had started a pet grooming service.

Shortly after setting out to find the mound I realized that I was being stealthily followed by a herd of cows. Suspicious, I stopped and looked back, but the herd had also stopped and were swinging their heads in a variety of directions in an oddly human attempt to appear disinterested. This sort of thing has been happening to me ever since I did my charity walk across

Curious cows follow Ian wherever he goes...

Ireland a few years back, but now I felt as if I was being carefully watched over more than ever.

According to folklore, this little fairy mound is the burial spot of Finn McCool and Gráinne. After luring Diarmuid to his death on Ben Bulben, Finn persuaded Gráinne to marry him after all, and she returned home with him. It obviously wasn't a happy marriage and a year later Gráinne threw herself from his speeding chariot. She was buried here under this mound, and it's also said that Finn was buried next to her when he died. Interestingly, the mound was excavated and two skeletons were found. Although the mound itself is not that spectacular, the view across Leitrim is. Sheemore ("Big Fairy Hill") can also be seen nearby.

I headed back down towards the village of Keshcarrigan and spotted a collapsed dolmen sitting on the shore of the lake. It was sparsely surrounded by trees, and Slieve Anierin formed the backdrop to the lake. This county is nicknamed Lovely Leitrim, and it certainly lived up to its name. I decided to sit there beside the dolmen for a while and soak up the view before venturing off into my favorite northern county: Donegal.

There & Back Again

TRAINS
Carrick-on-Shannon Station
Tel: (071) 9620036

BUSES
Bus Éireann stops by the bridge in Carrick-on-Shannon.

Places to Stay
HOTELS
Bush Hotel, Main St.
Carrick-on-Shannon
Tel: (071) 9671000
Web:
www.bushhotel.com
Email:
info@bushhotel.com

B & B S
Primrose House B&B
Letterfine
Keshcarrigan
Tel: (071) 9642960
Email:
primrosehouse
@hotmail.com
Highly recommended

For more information visit ireland.mysteriousworld.com/Journey/Counties/Leitrim/

THE JOURNEY
CONNAUGHT
COUNTY LEITRIM

Ulster Province

COUNTY NAME
— Major Highway
········ Major Railway
– · – International Boundary
– · · – County Boundary
◉ County Seat
• Major City

0 5 10 15 20   30   40 Kilometers
0   5   10   15   20   25 Miles

Rathlin Island

North Channel

Tory Island

Lough Foyle

Coleraine

Aran Island

Creeslough

Londonderry

DERRY

ANTRIM

Letterkenny

Ballymena

Larne

DONEGAL

Lifford

Strabane

ULSTER

Antrim

Ardara

TYRONE

Bangor

Donegal

Omagh

Lough Neagh

Belfast

Donegal Bay

Lower Lough Erne

Ballyshannon

Portadown

Strangford Lough

Sligo

Enniskillen

DOWN

LEITRIM

FERMANAGH

Monaghan

Armagh

Banbridge

Downpatrick

Upper Lough Erne

ARMAGH

SLIGO

MONAGHAN

Newry

Lough Allen

Carrick on Shannon

Cavan

Dundalk

Dundalk Bay

CAVAN

Lough Sheelin

LOUTH

…GHT

ROSCOMMON

LONGFORD

MEATH

Drogheda

Irish

Roscommon

Longford

Places to See Key for Ulster Province

Here is a list of the icons used in the county maps in this section:

☀ Multiple sites near each other

♵ Ancient pagan, pre-Christian sites, often of unknown origin

⚲ Christian sites

▮ Historical sites, heritage centres

◢ Cryptid sightings (mysterious, unknown and/or legendary creatures)

▲ Scenic views and museums

❶ Nightlife and popular hangouts

♨ Haunted houses and areas

✈ Major airports

🚌 Major bus stations

Ulster Province

Ulster province is the northernmost of the four provinces. It was under the control of the Uí Neill kings during the time of St. Patrick, and was also the province which Patrick made his ecclesiastical seat, in County Armagh. Ulster province also contains Northern Ireland, which includes Counties Derry, Antrim, Down, Armagh, Tyrone and Fermanagh, Counties Donegal, Cavan and Monaghan being part of the Republic of Ireland.

County Donegal is the largest of the northern counties and has fantastic scenery such as Slieve League, ancient sites such as Doon Fort and the Grianán of Aileach, and important Christian sites such as St. Patrick's Purgatory and the Turas Colmcille. Nearby Tory Island also overflows with ancient history and mystery, including its very own king! Neighboring County Derry has St. Columb's Stone & Well and The Giant's Grave, believed to be cursed by an evil dwarf. Country Antrim of course has the world famous Giant's Causeway, and is also believed to host the mysterious sea serpent known as the *Lig na Baste*.

County Down features The Giant's Ring, the largest megalithic ring in Ireland, and Downpatrick Cathedral, where Sts. Patrick, Brigid and Colmcille are believed to be buried. County Armagh has Emain Macha, ancient seat of the kings of Ulster and The Knights of the Red Branch, and also hosts the beautiful Church of Ireland Cathedral and St. Patrick's Roman Catholic Cathedral. And of course Counties Tyrone, Fermanagh, Cavan and Monaghan also have plenty more for the adventurous traveler to discover — or rediscover.

Ulster
General Information

Tourist Offices:

⚜ **Donegal**
The Quay
Donegal town
Tel: (074) 9721148
Web: www.donegaldirect.com

⚜ **Derry**
44 Foyle St.
Tel: (028) 7126 7284
Web: www.derryvisitor.com

⚜ **Antrim**
16 High St.
Antrim Town
Tel: (028) 9442 8331
Web: www.antrim.gov.uk

⚜ **Down**
53a Market St.
Downpatrick
Tel: (028) 4461 2233
Web: www.downdc.gov.uk

⚜ **Armagh**
40 English St.
Armagh
Tel: (028) 3752 1800
Web: www.visit armagh.com

THE JOURNEY
U L S T E R
P R O V I N C E

Places to See in Donegal

Donegal
(A Forgotten County and a Forgotten King)

Donegal's extensive coastline offers stunning views, including Slieve League, at 2,000 feet the highest sea cliffs in Europe.

Donegal
Things to Do & Places to See

Slieve League
At 2,000 feet, the highest sea cliffs in Europe and a magnificent view. From Carrick turn off opposite the Central Bar towards Teelin. Follow signs for Bunglas and park in the car park outside the gate.

St. Patrick's Purgatory
Lough Derg
For bookings:
Tel: (071) 9861518
Web: www.loughderg.org
Email: info@loughderg.org
Take the R233 from Pettigo north where the road ends at the lake. Three-day & one-day pilgrimages are available. Please check their website, call or email ahead to confirm availability before visiting.

ollowing the stunning scenery, I drove northwards into County Donegal. Although technically still part of the Republic, this large county, which occupies the entire northwest corner of Ireland, is still part of the traditional northern province of Ulster, though that province,

Glencolmcille
Absolutely covered with 5,000 years of history and mystery.

Kilclooney Dolmen
On the R261 in the village of Kilclooney, north of Ardara. Stop at the big modern church. Walk up the left side of the church and ask at the house for permission. The dolmen is in a field behind this house.

The Dolmen Centre
Opposite church.
Tel: (074) 9545010

Doon Fort
This ancient stone fort lies camouflaged on a lake island near Kilclooney. Continue on through Portnoo and turn left after the lake. A mile down the road is a sign on the right for boat hire. Follow lane to a white house and knock there. Take the boat and row out into the lake, where the mystery will be revealed.

like the other three, exists now in name only. Since the division of the country, any mention of Northern Ireland causes most tourists to instantly think of the six counties. I've even heard many people refer to Donegal as "Southern Ireland". Yet ironically, this county actually boasts the northernmost point in Ireland: Malin Head.

Just across the border with County Fermanagh lies Lough Derg. A small island just off its shore is home to a pilgrimage that has been going on for centuries. It's said that St. Patrick was lured here by the goddess Corra who, in her form as a giant serpent, lay coiled in the water waiting. As he approached she swallowed him whole, and it took two days for him to cut himself free. The lake ran red with the serpent's blood and when Patrick emerged from inside, her body turned to stone. Rocks jutting out from the lake are believed to be her remains.

St. Patrick's Purgatory

St. Patrick established a monastery on the island here, and pilgrims have been coming ever since. The tradition was to fast and pray before entering a cave for 24

St. Patrick's Purgatory was originally a monastery actually founded by St. Patrick. It remains as a popular place of Christian pilgrimage.

hours to emulate the experience of being trapped inside the belly of the beast, the coming out afterwards emulating your spiritual "rebirth". During this whole time the pilgrim has to remain awake.

Nowadays, the entire island is covered with modern ecclesiastical buildings housing the thousands that come here for a three-day pilgrimage. It was a strange sight to see people wandering around fully dressed, but barefoot. Everyone must remove their footwear upon arrival and then they are given a leaflet outlining their order of services. At midnight on the first day they begin their fast, which ends at midnight on the third day. During this time they are kept busy with a number of stations to perform.

The cave was sealed up years ago, and the vigil is now held in a newly built basilica. Sean, my guide, pointed out the penitential beds sitting on a hill where the cave was said to have once been.

"We don't know for sure," he whispered. "But it's traditionally believed to have been there."

There is a bell tower on the hill now, and the seven penitential beds each represent a saint who was associated with the area. These beds are reconstructed from old monastic cells or oratories, where the monks would pray. There's also a number of crosses on the island, but the oldest to survive is dated from the 6th or 7th century. The stone head is gone, but the metal stem of the cross remains, giving it quite a unique look.

Sean pointed out *Oileán na Noamh*, the island on which the pilgrimage was originally held until being closed by Papal Decree in 1497. It was then moved here to Station Island. It's not possible to visit the island, unless you take part in the 3-day pilgrimage, which you can simply turn up to and join. There is a special one-day retreat available on dates throughout May, August and September, but these must be booked in advance.

Doon Well & Rock of Doon
The rock is where the O'Donnell kings were inaugurated, plus there are marvelous views from the hill on which the rock sits. Take the R251 through the Derryveagh Mountains, either from Gweedore or take the N56 north of Letterkenny and turn off onto the R251. About halfway along this road you'll see a turning signposted Doon Well.

Dunlewey Lakeside Centre
(*Ionad Cois Locha*)
Tel: (074) 9531699
Web: www. dunleweycentre.com
Email: dunlewey centre@eircom.net
There is a storytelling boat trip that runs from the centre, along with a restaurant and craft shop.
Turn right opposite the pub.

Dunlewey & The Poisoned Glen
Sits in the shadow of the mighty Mt. Errigal, where Lugh established his fort in the heart of the Derryveagh Mountains, and slew his grandfather, the evil Balor.

Glenveagh National Park
Tel: (074) 9137090
Signed off the R251 through the Derryveagh Mountains. Comprised of 16,000 acres of mountains, lakes and woods, with an exhibition of the park and a 19th-century castle.

Colmcille Heritage Centre
Gartan
Church Hill
Tel: (074) 9137306
Open May-Sept., contains an interpretive exhibition of the life of St. Colmcille. From the Abbey continue down the road and follow signs.

THE JOURNEY
U L S T E R
COUNTY
DONEGAL

Glencolmcille

The view from Dooey Hostel has a dramatic view of Glencolmcille's valley and bay area that would cost a fortune in a hotel.

"You know, I think the manufacturers of socks should be made to produce three instead of two, to make up for the one you always lose in the washing machine," said Mary.

I was in the Dooey Hostel, perched high upon a cliff with dramatic views of Glencolmcille's valley and bay area. This is the flagship of the IHO chain and run by Mary, a little old lady with wild hair, a wry grin and a mischievous twinkle in her eyes. Whenever anyone arrives here they are welcomed with a tray of tea and biscuits, and entertained by Mary's wonderful expressions and quirky ways. The last time I was here she placed oranges on a small bush out front.

"What are you doing?" I asked.

"Well, I thought I'd at least try to give the impression that we are in a nice warm, sunny place, even if we aren't," she replied.

The hostel has a large kitchen, and along the corridor are dorms, each of which has its own bathroom, shower and kitchen. Upstairs is the common room, a long, spacious room with dining tables, a fireplace and a couple of sofas in the far corner. Running the length of the room to these sofas is a set of large bay windows looking out across the mountains, ocean and down into the valley where a long, golden beach forms a crescent between the mountains. The view is breathtaking — the sort of view you would pay a fortune for in a hotel.

Glencolmcille is a popular haunt for musicians, artists and students of the Irish language. There is a school down in the village where Irish courses are given, and the pubs in town have regular live **music**. My favorite is *Teach Biddy* on the corner as you enter town. It's the oldest pub in Glencolmcille and a cozy little place where you sit next to the musicians as they play. Upon arrival I had got talking to Martin from Derry. Martin plays the violin and said he would be doing so in Biddy's Bar tonight, so I ventured down there and spent the evening drinking good Guinness and listening to Martin and a few others play some of the finest music I've ever heard.

Local pubs such as *Teach Biddy* in Glencolmcille are the best places to sample authentic Irish culture and music.

Irish Music
Just as Ireland's plethora of historical and mythological traditions reflects the island's history of invasions, so too does its music. Scholars who have studied the roots of modern Irish music have revealed a panoply of varying traditions coming not only from Ireland's ancient invaders, but also from cultural contacts from numerous other countries, forming a musical heritage that is truly a melting pot of Western tradition. In many ways, just as Ireland was the savior of Christendom and of the written word, so too it has served as the repository of musical traditions from all over the Western world.

Learn more about Irish music and culture in The History: Ireland Today (pp. 330-339).

THE JOURNEY
U L S T E R
COUNTY
DONEGAL

Tuan's Notes
Turas & Patterns
Turas are religious pilgrimages that the Irish have undertaken since the advent of Christianity. They involve traveling to a holy place, such as Croagh Patrick or the Turas Colmcille, and moving through a series of "stations". At each station, the pilgrim says various prayers according to a predetermined pattern. These turas used to be followed by festivals called "patterns" that involved feasting, games, singing, dancing, and even courtship. These patterns in many ways were the central social event in Irish society until the latter half of the twentieth century.

Learn more about Celtic Christianity in The History: The Coming of Christianity (pp. 219-227).

The Turas Colmcille

St. Colmcille was born in County Donegal. He is said to have banished the demons that fled here after being ousted by St. Patrick from Croagh Patrick. Colmcille drove them out into the sea, where he ordered them to live as red fish with one eye so no fisherman would inadvertently capture and eat them.

Long before Colmcille came here the Neolithic people left their indelible mark upon the land. There are approximately 80 documented pagan and Christian sites on this peninsula spanning 5,000 years, and the peninsula is littered with dolmens and standing stones. Many of the standing stones were Christianized by Colmcille who, rather than invoke the wrath of the people by destroying them, engraved Christian emblems upon them and encouraged the people to make a pilgrimage there to atone for their sins. These stones now make the 3½ mile turas which is taken on the saint's feast day, 9th June, or the Sunday preceding it. After 1,500 years this is still carried out.

STATION 1

Station 1 of the Turas Colmcille starts at the present-day Church of Ireland, which is believed to have been built on the same site where Colmcille's original church was located.

The next day, the clouds had cleared and the sun now illuminated the mountain where I was heading to begin the **Turas**. It starts at the present day Church of Ireland where the original church established by Colmcille was possibly located. There is a souterrain in front of the church in the graveyard. A metal lid covers the entrance but can be removed. I climbed down inside and crawled around, and found a large chamber leading to other narrow passages. I wondered how far they went, but couldn't investigate without a torch.

STATION 2

Station 2 of the Turas Colmcille is a magnificent standing stone with Christian symbols carved on it by St. Colmcille.

Further down the road is a magnificent standing stone perched high upon a rocky ledge overlooking the distant mountain. This is the second station in the Turas. The Christian carvings were still quite well defined.

STATION 3

I drove on across a bridge and as the road turned left I took the right turn down a lane that led to a small house on a hill. The third is down the road to the left

Church Hill
Home and birthplace of St. Colmcille. Near to Doon Rock. Take the same turning off the R251 and follow signs for Colmcille's Abbey.

Tuan's Notes
St. Colmcille
Learn more about St. Colmcille and other Christian saints in The History: The Saints (pp. 228-248).

Grianán of Aileach
South off the N13 just west of Derry. The inauguration point for the Uí Neill clan.

St. Patrick's Cross
In the village of Cardonagh on the Inishowen peninsula.

Donegal Castle
Donegal town
Tel: (074) 9722405
Built by an O'Donnell chieftain in the 15th century.

THE JOURNEY
U L S T E R
COUNTY
DONEGAL

Cloghacorra
Turn off just
before the
Glencolmcille
Hotel for Clogha-
corra and the
Malinmore dolmens.
Down a country lane
in a field on the right
is a collection of six
dolmens in a line.
Most are collapsed,
but are interesting
none the same. All
others I'd seen had
been lone dolmens,
never in a group.

Tory Island
The last outpost of
the Fomorian giants,
this tiny island off the
north coast of Done-
gal is steeped in myth
and legend. Balor of
the Evil Eye and St.
Colmcille both left
their indelible mark
on the island's folk-
lore, as well as a num-
ber of ancient ruins.
The island is also
home to the last re-
maining king in
Ireland, Patsy
Dan Rodgers,
the King of
Tory.

THE JOURNEY
U L S T E R

C O U N T Y
D O N E G A L

Station 3 of the Turas Colmcille is a small cairn with a round
stone (right) that is believed to be useful for healing.

just beside a fence. It's a small cairn with a round
healing stone, which is supposed to be passed around
the body for healing.

STATIONS 4 & 5
I got a bit confused as to where the next station was.
My guide said it was a little further on the right, but I
couldn't see it. On the hill I spotted an old couple sitting in front of their house, and wandered up and

Stations 4 & 5 of the Turas Colmcille are Colmcille's Chapel &
Bed (left) and the remains of a cairn (right).

asked for directions. It turned out to be up on the hill behind the house.

They said I could walk up through, but I decided to return to the van and drive around to the other side where I parked at the base of the mountain, and the start of a stony path that leads up to the summit. This was the end of the road, and a sign by the farmhouse emphasized this.

Stations four and five are behind this house. The first is another **cairn**, and the other the remains of a small rectangular house called Colmcille's Chapel with a rectangular stone box known as Colmcille's Bed. The pilgrim must circle this three times, then lay down on the bed and turn around three times.

STATION 6

Back up on the road I joined the start of the trail up the hill. A sign for Colmcille's Well pointed to the right up by the farmhouse fence, where I found station six, a large boulder entrenched into the hillside. It's traditional to stand on this stone, face west and make three wishes.

Station 6 of the Turas Colmcille is a large boulder entrenched in the hillside, which you are meant to stand on, face west, and make three wishes.

Tours
Rib Boat Rides
Bunbeg Harbour
Tel: (075) 9531305
Web: www. bunbeghouse.com
Email: bunbeg house@eircom.net
Andy Carr offers rib boat rides from Bunbeg House at the harbor to all the islands around the bay. These are fantastic fun. Weather permitting he will also take you on a tour of Tory Island and all the places associated with Balor of the Evil Eye.

Tuan's Notes
Cairns
Learn more about cairns and other neolithic structures in The History: Ancient Irish Culture (p. 255).

Siob Teo provides guided tours of Tory Island from the pier. Tel: (087) 6748449

THE JOURNEY
ULSTER
COUNTY DONEGAL

STATION 7

Station 7 of the Turas Colmcille is a holy well surrounded by a huge cairn of rocks adorned with Latin crosses and statuary.

I continued up to the right and found the well hidden behind a small rise on the hill. Station seven is a well surrounded by a huge cairn of rocks spreading wide in each direction and separated by a narrow path leading to the well. Lying either side of the entrance is a couple of slabs with Latin crosses inscribed upon them. The tradition here is to carry three rocks up and place them one at a time beside the well after each circuit, then take three sips of the water.

STATION 8

Station eight was the most difficult to get to. I had to walk back down towards the farmhouse fence and turn left. There was no discernable trail and I had to walk down the rocky hill through thick vegetation; every step taken with an enhanced sense of trepidation. Any minute I expected to lose my footing and be sent plummeting down the hill like a tumbleweed.

Thankfully that didn't happen. Instead I fought an ongoing battle with the midges. I consider myself a patient man, sometimes. But when it comes to midges

I just can't help myself. Anyone looking on would see a crazed man swinging his fists and backpack in a vain attempt to kill them. The problem is that you kill one, and another fifty come to the funeral. They really are the most irritating creatures created by Mother Nature, or considering what I was doing, I should say God. But whoever created them liked to make people suffer, and I suppose I was being made to atone for not performing the pilgrimage properly.

When I was first in this country I learnt a very harsh lesson. These interesting stone walls that decorate the rural landscape from Cork to Donegal are not built using mortar. I found walking on them a dangerous pastime, which almost put the future of any little Ians in jeopardy.

I passed a couple of ruined buildings and found station eight in a field over one of these walls. There was no stile or gap in the wall, so I had to scramble over. I just hoped the landowner didn't see me as I almost collapsed his wall. I imagine it took a long time to build.

Station 8 of the Turas Colmcille is comprised of 3 round cairns with a standing stone in the middle of each. This was the end of the original 6th-century pilgrimage, though several more stations have been added since then.

THE JOURNEY
ULSTER
COUNTY DONEGAL

Tuan's Notes
Standing Stones
Standing, or "sacred" stones are essentially idols in the form of tall standing stones, often covered with sacred carvings.
Learn more about standing stones in The History: Ancient Irish Culture (p. 259)

Here in a small field are three round cairns, each with a carved **standing stone** in the middle. Once again you must circle each of these three times whilst praying. I just prayed I could get back out of here with my bones intact.

According to *Sacred Ireland*, this marks the end of the original 6th-century pilgrimage. There are actually 15 stations in all, but the rest were added on in more recent years. On the saint's day this is done barefoot. I was having enough trouble with boots on. The next stages were way beyond these hills, and it looked impossible to make the journey on foot. Instead I returned to the van and drove to one or two of the latter ones, which are back in the churchyard and just along the road.

Kilclooney Dolmen

The direct route to Ardara from Glencolmcille takes you over the Glengesh Pass that winds down into a deep valley with dramatically sloping green hills, looking like they have been neatly sliced by a bread-knife. It was still daylight when I arrived in town, so I headed north on the R261 to the little village of Kilclooney.

Kilclooney Dolmen has a 20-foot capstone that appears from one side to emulate the profile of a great eagle.

688

A **dolmen** lies in a field behind the house next to the big modern church. I knocked on the house door and the landowner allowed me access, and didn't charge. The sun was going down behind the nearby hill when I arrived. It stands 6 feet tall and has a 20-foot capstone that gives the appearance of a giant eagle in flight. From the rear it gave the less poetic appearance of a stealth bomber. As the sun went down the dolmen turned deep orange. Apparently if you kiss the capstone and make a wish, it will come true. I wasn't about to find out.

Doon Fort

I spent the night in Ardara, and in the morning headed back out on the R261 through Kilclooney and onto Portnoo. Just the other side of town I turned left just after a lake and drove down a country road. Pond Lake was to my left, and over the hills to the right I could just make out another lake. After about a mile I spotted a small white sign that said, "boat hire".

I pulled in and drove down the lane to a small white house perched on a hill overlooking a small harbor on the lake. My knock was answered by an old man wearing a suit. He directed me down to the lake and told me to take the blue rowing boat.

Doon Fort is enshrouded in mystery. "It keeps its secret until the very end," I'd been told by a guy in Ardara. And he was right. The lake had been barely visible until now. And as I rowed out along the edge of the cliff that sheltered the harbor, I still couldn't see any fort. The water was still, and the splash and subsequent rush of water as I rowed out into the lake was deafening in the surrounding silence. Suddenly, as I cleared the shelter of the hill and the currents became stronger, it appeared like a ghost on the horizon.

This stone ring fort stands 16 feet high and com-

Tuan's Notes
Dolmens
Also known as "cromlechs", dolmens are monuments that are composed of two upright "portal" stones that support a third, usually very large, flat, "capstone". Dolmens, like many forms of ancient architecture, were believed to be portals to the Otherworld, doorways from the world of the physical to the world of the spiritual. They remain today as some of the most spectacular of ancient monuments, and can be found throughout Ireland.
Learn more about dolmens in The History: Ancient Irish Culture (pp. 255).

Charlie's West End Café
Ardara
Good Irish breakfast and well-priced meals.

Doon Fort is a huge stone ring fort that completely covers a small island in Pond Lake as if it were a lake town.

pletely covers a small island just off the shore. Moss covering the walls camouflages the fort and helps keep it hidden until the very last moment. I struggled to negotiate my way through the rocks and dock at the makeshift pier by the fort, pulling the boat well up onto the rocks for fear of losing it.

At 13 feet, the walls of the fort are almost as thick as they are tall. At the entrance are a number of passages inside the walls, one leading out to the top. The construction is very much the same as the others. This was a fortress of the O'Boyles, and Connor O'Boyle was slain here in 1530. It's unusual to find a fort hidden away here in the middle of the lake.

Northern Donegal

After visiting the major sites in the south of Donegal, I continued driving north. Though southern Donegal is a lush, green wonderland dominated by the Bluestacks Mountains, the scenery in northern Donegal, the area north of Ardara, changes dramatically. As you cross the bridge here on the N56, the scenery changes from lush green to a stark, treeless, weather-beaten wilderness.

690

Dún Lúiche (Lugh's Fort)

From the N56, I turned right at the sign for the Glenveagh National Park onto the R251. Dunlewey (*Dún Lúiche*) sits in the shadow of Mount Errigal. This is where Lugh built his fort when he came of age. The village now houses a lakeside visitor center and the Errigal Hostel. A walking trail starts from the back of the hostel and leads to the summit of Mount Errigal, the tallest mountain in County Donegal. There is also another, shorter trail that starts from the road further east of town. I've stayed here a few times in the past, and the walking around this area is great. The Ulster Way leads through here and goes through The Poisoned Glen, just a short walk from the village.

One version of the death of Balor, Wizard-King of the Fomorians, tells how he came to Dunlewey one day and boasted of how he, in fear of the prophecy that he would die at the hand of one of his grandchildren, had slain all of them. However, he was unaware that Lugh, who had overheard his boast, was also one of his grandchildren — one that he did not know about. Upon learning of Balor's crime, Lugh flew into a rage, grabbed a red-hot metal rod from the furnace and thrust it through Balor's eye, fulfilling the prophecy. The land ran red with Balor's blood, and the poison from his evil eye ran into the lake, forming The Poisoned Glen.

Colmcille's Home

I continued along the R251, past the Glenveagh National Park and turned right at a sign for Church Hill and then took the next right signed Colmcille's Abbey. The roads here are diabolical. I bumped and bounced my way over undulating fields until I emerged on the brow of a hill with Lough Gartan down on the left. A sign pointed right for the abbey.

The Reveller
The Square
Donegal
Good live rock music gigs performed here.

Corner House
The Diamond
Ardara
Best place in town for Irish music.

Hudibeag
Bunbeg
This pub has fantastic Irish music sessions.

Foreland Heights
Gweedore
Tel: (074) 9531785
Email: foreland
heights@hotmail.com
On the Bloody Foreland road between Bunbeg and Magheroarty. Superb views, food and accommodation.

Central Bar
Upper Main St.
Letterkenny
Traditional music sessions every Wed. and a nightclub upstairs.

AIR
Donegal Airport
Carrickfin
Kincasslagh
Tel: (074) 9548284
Web:
www.donegalairport.ie
Email: info@
donegalairport.ie
A regional airport
located 15 minutes
from Dungloe. There
are regular flights to
Dublin & Glasgow.
Aer Arann
Flights from Dublin
to Donegal (45 mins)
Tel: (01) 844 7700
Web:
www.aerarann.com

FERRIES
Tory Island Ferry
Bunbeg Pier Office:
Tel: (074) 9531320
*Magheroarty Pier
Office:*
Tel: (074) 9135061
Web: www.toryisland
ferry.com
Email: eolas@
toryisland
ferry.com
First sailing
from Bunbeg
then from
Magheroarty.

THE JOURNEY

ULSTER

COUNTY
DONEGAL

The abbey sits on the site of an ancient fortification. Colmcille was born into the royal O'Donnell clan, and this site was given to him to build his church upon. The current remains were built by one of his descendants. A well is just outside the entrance, and a number of other stations mark the turas that is performed here yearly. I continued down the road and turned right at the sign for Colmcille's birthplace. I parked beside an abandoned house and walked down a lane until I came across a tall, Celtic cross on the left, built to commemorate the saint.

The saint's mother, Eithne, was heading home with her kinsman one day when she sat down beside a stream to rest. Her water broke, and Colmcille was born here on this spot. There is a large, flat stone nearby riddled with potholes which gather rain water. According to *Sacred Ireland*, this is called "The Flagstone of Loneliness". Tradition has it that Colmcille came here to lay down for the night before leaving Ireland. The tradition has been repeated over the years by many people before leaving Ireland. It's said drinking the water from the hollows and spending the night on the stone will cure homesickness.

The Flagstone of Loneliness, upon which Colmcille is believed to have been born, and where he spent his last night before his self-imposed exile from Ireland in AD 563.

692

Grianán of Aileach

Grianán of Aileach, though it appears to be a ring fort, may have actually been an amphitheater.

I drove on through Letterkenny and took the N13 towards Derry. Just before crossing the border I turned right at the sign for Grianán of Aileach. The road led up onto Grianán Mountain, where a huge, circular stone enclosure sits on a flattened section of the hill surrounded by three earthen embankments. Although it looks like a ring fort, experts believe it was an amphitheater rather than a defensive structure.

It was rebuilt in the 1800s, and scaffolding around the fort suggested that more reconstruction was going on. The inner diameter is 76 feet, and the outer wall stands 17 feet high and 13 feet thick. Local legend says that it was built by the Dagda in 1700 BC as a temple of the sun, but this probably refers to the original earthen structure it's built upon. From the 5th to 12th century this was the inauguration point of the Uí Neill clan.

I wandered inside and climbed the steps to the terraces around the outer wall from which there was a magnificent view of the Innishowen Peninsula. This peninsula stretches up to Malin Head, the northernmost point in Ireland.

Arranmore Ferry
Leabgarrow
Arranmore
Tel: (074) 9520532
Web: www.arainnmhor.com/ferry
Leaves from Burtonport and goes several times a day to Arranmore Island.

TRAINS
The closest you can get to Donegal by train is Sligo or Derry. There are three trains a day from Dublin to Sligo, passing through Mullingar. There are several trains from Belfast to Derry.

BUSES
Letterkenny Bus Station
Tel: (074) 9121309
Beside the round-about at the bottom of town on the Derry Road.

Bus Èireann
⚜ 64 runs services from Galway through Sligo, Donegal Town, Letterkenny and on to Derry.

● Bus 490
runs several
times a day
from Donegal
Town to
Glencolmcille.
● Bus 30 Dublin to
Donegal
● Bus 32 Dublin to
Letterkenny.

Feda O'Donnell
Tel: (074) 9548114
Web: www.
fedaodonnell.com
Email:
busfeda@eircom.net
Runs a service be-
tween Gweedore and
Letterkenny. Also
runs services to Done-
gal Town, Sligo, Gal-
way, Derry & Belfast.

McGeehan
Fintown
Tel: 074-9546150
Web: www.
mcgeehancoaches.com
Email: coaches@iol.ie
Runs services all
around the county.

**SITT — Community
Bus Service**
Tel: (074) 9738913
Runs between
Killybegs &
Malinbeg Tues
& Fri.

Tory Island

I might never have come here way back in 1999, if it wasn't for a book I was reading telling me about a king who lives on a tiny, barren island just a few miles off the northwestern corner of this forgotten county. In ancient Ireland there were three levels of kingship: the High King, the provincial king and the petty king. The petty king ruled over small agricul-

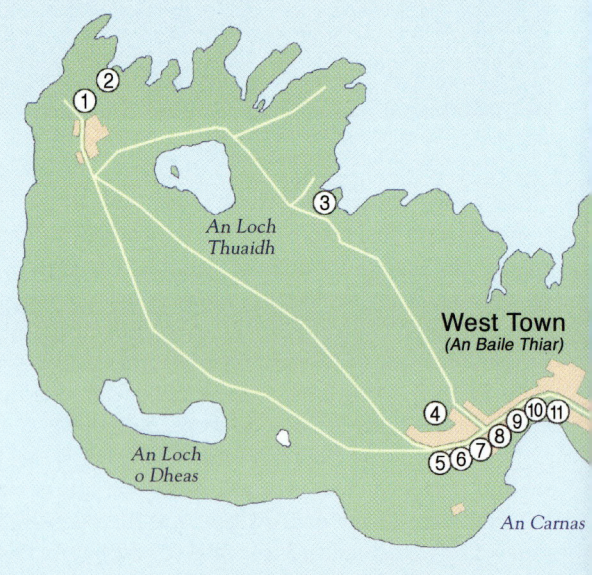

An Loch
Thuaidh

West Town
(An Baile Thiar)

An Loch
o Dheas

An Carnas

Tory Island

1. Light House
2. Cleft of the Seven
3. Port of the Grey Cow
4. The King's Palace
5. The Grave of the Seven
6. St. Brigid's Altar
7. Bell Tower
8. St. John's Altar
9. Old Graveyard
10. Tau Cross
11. Main Pier
12. MacGearra's Rock
13. *Port an Deilig* (Where Balor threw the triplets)
14. Balor's Prison
15. Balor's Fort
16. Wishing Stone
17. Balor's Soldiers

tural communities and was effectively a tribal chieftain, kind of like a town mayor. The King of Tory is a petty king, and the only remaining king in the country.

The moment I read this I knew I had to meet this man. After all, how many people could say that they've journeyed to a barren, desolate island in the north Atlantic, and met a king?

East Town
(An Baile Thoir)

An Loch o Thoir

Port Challa

Port an Duin

⑬ ⑭ ⑮ ⑯ ⑰

Lough Swilly Bus Company
Tel: (074) 9122863
With depots at Derry, Letterkenny and Buncrana this company services Derry, Inishowen and north /northwest Donegal. For Tory Island ferry ask driver to stop at turn-off just past Gortahork. It's a 2-mile walk from there.

DRIVING
⚜ From Northern Ireland you can cross into Donegal at Derry or Strabane. From the south take the N15 from Sligo, or for a more attractive route follow the A46 from Enniskillen. It takes you along Lower Lough Erne.

⚜ R257: A must-see. Just past the village of Gortahork is a turn off for Magheroarty. If you follow this road through it leads over the Bloody Foreland and onto Bunbeg.

✦ N56: This main road leaves from Letterkenny and takes a circular route along the northern coast, round through all the major towns to Donegal town.

✦ R251: This road takes you through the stark wilderness of the Derryveagh Mountains, past the Glenveagh National Park and along high ridges with spectacular views of Lough Dunlewey, the Poisoned Glen and Mt Errigal.

✦ R259: Takes you from Crolly to Dungloe via the Rosses. It leads through rugged coastline and giant inlets with sand as far as the eye can see.

✦ From Donegal town take the N56 west and turn off on the R263 towards Killybegs. Go through this to Carrick, where you can turn left opposite the pub for Teelin and

Getting there could have been a lot easier had I not been so pig-headed and decided to make it an adventure. Bus Èireann took me as far as Letterkenny, where I could simply have gotten on the Swilly Bus to the turn-off for Magheroarty and walked the 2 miles to the ferry port. Instead, I decided to drag my poor traveling partner, Anne, along on a hitchhiking adventure. We did manage to get a lift, after over an hour waiting, from a greasy, rotten-toothed man in soiled clothing driving a beat-up transit van; the sort of decision that would have given my mum many sleepless nights. Fortunately he turned out not to be a serial killer but in fact an extremely funny and nice guy. He dropped us seven miles up the road where, until the bus came along, we stood in the rain watching other drivers ignore our pleas for a lift.

We only just made the ferry, and then clung to the side as gigantic waves churned up by Tory Sound — a notoriously rough strait in the North Atlantic — tossed the little boat across the sea like a piece of flotsam. And this was during the relatively calm period that takes place at the height of summer — in winter, the strait is effectively unnavigable, and the island can be cut off from the mainland for months. It is for this reason, and the fierce independence of the islanders, that Tory's culture has remained so entrenched.

As we stood on the pier at the other side, drenched from the waves that had crashed over the side of the boat, we watched as the dark clouds crept over the island like an impending blanket of doom. A battered caravan stood in the middle of an empty field. The wind howled across the open landscape, and rain was beginning to follow. And so far every guesthouse we'd been to was empty. All this, just to meet a king!

At three miles long, and half a mile at its widest point, Tory Island (*Oileán Toraigh*) could well be just

The exceptionally rough seas of Tory Sound have enhanced its cultural isolation, and can still make travel to the island difficult.

another little island among many around this coastline. But Tory is possibly the most significant and holds a pivotal place in ancient Irish history and folklore. Its situation in the Tory Sound, a treacherous section of ocean, makes it extremely vulnerable to bad weather. Overall, it is best described as a bleak and inhospitable place. Nevertheless, it has a population of 170 living in four towns, imaginatively titled East Town, Middletown, Newtown and West Town. The island is also noted for its school of painters whose work has been displayed throughout Europe and even in New York. The king is one of the best known.

THE KING OF TORY

The presence of a king on Tory goes back to ancient times, and the current reigning monarch is Patsy Dan Rodgers. The king lives in a modest, yellow house on the hill, just outside town. After my fervent attempts to accidentally bump into him on the island had been unsuccessful, I decided to take matters into my own hands and go call for him at his royal palace.

Now I've never called on a king before, and was quite unsure of what to say as I knocked on the front

Slieve League, then back to Carrick and on to Glencolmcille.

✠ From Glencolmcille take a left out of town by Biddy Bar and follow the back road to Ardara. This takes you on a stunning drive over the Glengesh Pass.

✠ From Ardara take R261 for Kilclooney Dolmen and on through Portnoo for Doon Fort.

SCENIC DRIVES
✠ *The Horn Head* Drive north from Dunfanaghy.
✠ *Inishowen Peninsula* Turn off from the N13 just west of Derry for St. Patrick's Cross and Malin Head.

CAR HIRE
Euromobil
• Canal Rd.
Letterkenny
Tel: (074)9122333
• Killybegs Rd.
Donegal town
Tel: (074)
9723484

THE JOURNEY
ULSTER
COUNTY
DONEGAL

TAXIS

Brennan's Cabs
Ardara
Tel: (087) 6675555

Letterkenny Cabs
Letterkenny
Tel: (074) 917000

Doherty's Taxi
Glencolmcille
Tel: (074) 9730174
Mob: (086) 1051231

Roarty Cabs
Derrybeg, Gweedore
Tel: (087) 2497333

BIKE HIRE

Glencolmcille
Bikes can be hired from Biddy's Bar.
Tel: (074) 9730016
Mob: (086) 8277957

Don Byrnes Bikes
West End
Ardara
Tel: (074) 9541658
Mob: (087)6386435
Email:
donbyrne@indigo.ie

Tory Island
Bikes can be hired from Patrick Rodgers, at the house just up from the Bell Tower.

door. After a moment, a little old lady opened the door.

"Hi, is the king there?"

Now I know with the utmost certainty that I will never again utter such a sentence for as long as I live. As it turned out, he wasn't in.

The king is also a renowned artist whose paintings have been exhibited around the world. At the pier on the mainland I was also informed that he had released a CD of his own music, which was on sale at the ferry ticket office.

A king with many talents, it seemed.

Eventually I spotted a man walking past the pier. He wore Wellington boots and a blue raincoat. He saw us coming down the hill and waved, then came over. Under his black fisherman's cap his features were rugged and weathered — the look of a man who had lived a hard life.

"Are you the King of Tory?" asked Anne.

"That I am!" he replied, smiling warmly and shaking our hands.

Patsy apologized for not coming into the pub the night before. (I know, first-name terms! Well, he is a very down-to-earth king.) He was working on preparation for an upcoming exhibition. Usually, he comes to the pub and entertains the tourists with his music.

Patsy explained how the role of king had changed a lot over the years. With the deterioration of agriculture, governing of the island's crop plantations has become redundant. Nowadays the king's role is one of promoting the island as a tourist destination. Patsy expressed his deep love for Tory, and his sadness at the decline of the number of visitors.

"A few years ago Tory would be dotted with tents pitched anywhere and everywhere. People would flock here in the summer to see the island's vast array of bird life and soak up the 4,000 years of history on the island. But in the last few years the numbers have decreased," he said.

Access to the island has always been precarious. Storms could render Tory inaccessible for months. A trip to Tory was only for the hardiest of travelers. But modern boats soon made getting there easier and when the ferry service began, it opened the island to tourism, which was a much-needed boost for its flagging economy.

The independent spirit of the islanders is reflected in a story I read involving a British gunship that wrecked off the eastern side of the island. In 1884 the *HMS Wasp* was on its way to collect taxes from the islanders. Paddy Heggerty, then King of Tory, assembled a group of islanders at the cursing stone and cursed the ship and all its crew. The *HMS Wasp* was engulfed in a ferocious storm and sank just off Tory's lighthouse.

I can't help thinking there was a sort of poetic justice there.

The king came down to the pier and saw all the visitors off with a hearty handshake and a royal wave. The ferry then bounced its way across the tumultuous ocean until it rounded the corner of the mainland and entered the sheltered bay of Bunbeg, whereupon the howling winds and waves subsided, the clouds parted and the whole area was bathed in the orange glow of the evening sun. The transformation was so sudden that I had to shake my head to ensure I wasn't imagining things.

BUNBEG HARBOR

Next to Wexford, Bunbeg Harbor is a place where I always enjoy coming back. Andy, the owner of Bunbeg House, has become a good friend since that first day we arrived. This harbor is a small, sheltered

WALKING
Donegal International Walking Festival
(October)
Tel: (074) 9735967
Web: www.northwest walkingguides.com
Email: info@walkingireland.ie

Hills of Donegal Walking Festival
(April)
Tel: (074) 9153736

Ardara Walking Festival
(March)
Tel: (074) 9541830

The Bluestacks Way is a 110km-long marked trail from Pettigo to Ardara, taking you through the lakes and over the mountains of southern Donegal.
Tel: (074) 9736076/ 9722651
From Malinbeg Hostel there is a trail across Slieve League which ends at Kilcar hostel.

THE JOURNEY
U L S T E R
COUNTY
DONEGAL

Bealach na Gaeltachta
(Gaeltacht Way)
A set of way-marked trails, 50-70kms., taking you through some of Donegal's wildest and most beautiful landscape.
Tel: (066) 9152423/ (074) 9121160
Web:
www.gaelsaoire.ie
Email:
info@gaelsaoire.ie

Tuan's Notes
Ireland's Giants
Learn more about Ireland's giants in The Mystery: Creatures Great & Small (pp. 143-148).

SHOPPING
Triona Design Store
Ardara
One of the best places to buy the famous Donegal Tweed.

THE JOURNEY
U L S T E R
COUNTY
DONEGAL

place and is very peaceful, even in the summer. Bunbeg House sits right at the harbor's edge and is a welcoming sight indeed. I parked up alongside the water. It was quite late by this time and so I knew exactly where to find Andy — in his bar. I entered, and found him sitting in his usual spot.

"Ian, 'owe are yer?" he said in his distinctive Cockney accent.

Andy's bar, although attached to the guesthouse, is open to everyone. There is usually a good crowd and good *craic* there, and I enjoyed the rest of the evening drinking Guinness and catching up.

THERE AND BACK AGAIN

A couple of years later, I returned to Tory for another audience with the king. The road from Bunbeg to Magheroarty, from where the ferry for Tory leaves, is known as The Bloody Foreland. This is a dramatic place where the reddish-brown coastline lies like a serrated knife overlooked by wild and untamed hills. I never tire of driving along here.

This time the king had come to the pier to meet the boat and welcome visitors to his island, as he usually does.

"Patsy, nice to see you again," I said as I stepped off the boat and shook his outstretched hand.

He looked at me inquisitively. "Oh my God, 'tis yourself back again!" He actually remembered me.

Nursing the after-effects of a vigorous handshake, I headed off and found a room in the newly refurbished *Teach Bhillie*, and went straight back out for a walk. A new visitor guide was available on the island, and I picked up a copy in the café at the edge of town. I found the king out at the western side of the island, where he graciously pointed out a few historic landmarks for me.

In Irish folklore the north was always associated

with darkness and evil. **Ireland's giants** of the north, the demonic and malevolent Fomorians, once held a stronghold here. The promontory at the eastern side of the island was once the home of their leader, Balor of the Evil Eye.

The first group of Fomorians to occupy the island did so under the leadership of Conan, who built a great tower here known as *Túr Rí* (Tower of the King). It's believed that Tory's name is derived from this. They were driven out by the Nemedians, but returned under the leadership of Balor. The Druids had prophesied that Balor would be killed by his own grandson, so to avoid this Balor imprisoned his only daughter in a tower on the island so she would never bear any children.

THE PORT OF THE GREY COW

The Fomorians were sea pirates who used Tory as a base from which to plunder the mainland. During one of these raids their leader, Balor, stole a precious grey cow belonging to three brothers of the Tuatha dé Danann and brought it back to Tory. Patsy pointed out *Poirtín Ghlais* (Port of the Grey Cow) where he landed with this cow.

The Port of the Grey Cow is named for a legend of how Balor of the Evil Eye once had stolen a grey cow belonging to the Tuatha dé Danann, bringing it back via this port.

Tuan's Notes
The Fomorians
The Fomorians were a race of giant, brutal barbarians based in what is now central and northern Europe that routinely invaded and plundered not only Ireland, but all of the British Isles. Though the Fomorians had in fact invaded and occupied Ireland several times, they were not given the same status of the other invaders that are listed in the *Lebor Gabala Èrenn*, instead being denigrated to the level of a dark, dangerous, almost demonic infestation that seems to have been considered to be the very antithesis of life, light and civilization.

Learn more about the Fomorians in The Mystery: The Mystery *(pp. 27-30).*

THE JOURNEY
U L S T E R
COUNTY
DONEGAL

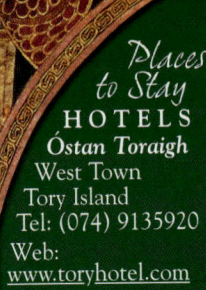

Places to Stay

HOTELS

Óstan Toraigh
West Town
Tory Island
Tel: (074) 9135920
Web:
www.toryhotel.com
Email:
info@toryhotel.com

Glencolmcille Hotel
Glencolmcille
Tel: (074) 9730003
Web:
www.glenhotel.com
Email:
info@glenhotel.com

Fort Royal
Rathmullen
Letterkenny
Tel: (074) 9158100
A 3-star hotel built
in 1819 and set in 18
acres of woodland on
Lough Swilly.

**Gweedore Court
Hotel & Heritage
Centre** (*An Chúirt*)
Tel: (074) 9532900
Web: www.
ostan-gweedore.com
Email: anchuirt
@eircom.net
On the N56
with views of
Mt Errigal and
Dunlewey lake.

One of the brothers, Cian, was sent over to recover the cow, and he paid a visit to Balor's daughter along the way. Nine months later, Balor's daughter gave birth to triplets, and the fearful Balor cast them into the sea. But the eldest of the triplets, Lugh, was rescued by Manannán mac Lir. Lugh later killed Balor, fulfilling the prophecy.

Mac Gearra's Rock

As we wandered back towards town, Patsy also pointed out a set of three rocks on the north side of West Town. The largest of the three, on the left, is known as *Cloch Mac Gearra* (Mac Gearra's Rock). The story goes that when St. Colmcille came to the island he turned a local fisherman to stone for fishing on a Sunday. A jagged outcrop on the right hand side of this rock is said to be the fisherman climbing with his bag of fish.

The Grave of the Seven

Beside the road just down from the king's palace are the remains of a small oratory that is known locally as The Grave of the Seven. These were six men and a woman whose boat had washed up on the eastern shore. Colmcille arranged for them to be buried here and a small oratory built around the grave. The next day the woman's body was found lying above the grave, as it was the following day after being reburied. Colmcille realized that this woman must have been a saint, and ordered the people to bury her separately. Her shrine is just behind.

"The clay from the grave has special powers to ward off vermin," said Patsy. "There are no rats on Tory, and it's attributed to this. Only the oldest member of the local O'Dubhagáin (Duggan) family can lift it from the grave. If you want some you must have a good reason for it, and go to his house the other side of the pier and ask."

The Grave of the Seven actually includes two graves: one for the six men who died, and one for the seventh, a woman, whom Colmcille believed was a saint after finding her body above her original grave. She was then given her own grave (above) to commemorate her sainthood.

I bade farewell to the king as he returned to his palace for lunch, and ventured off to my favorite part of the island: the eastern promontory.

Colmcille's Crater

Tory is a *Gaeltacht* area. All signs are in Gaelic. One road runs the length of the island that, I was amused to see, runs to a small dirt roundabout on the western edge of town. I headed out on the road that runs to East Town, and left it soon after to hike up to the northern cliffs. The eastern side of Tory is characterized by soaring cliffs and jutting promontories overlooking jagged rocks rising precariously out of the choppy seas below. The cliff-faces form an array of erratic shapes, and the rough sea has carved out many deep caves. One section, known as Colmcille's Crater, is where the sea has carved out such a deep cave that the surface of the cliff has completely collapsed, forming a crater that leads out to the sea.

B & B S
Donegal House
Ballyshannon Rd.
Donegal Town
Tel: (074) 9721159
Email: donegal housebedandbreakfast @eircom.net
Open all year with 4 en-suite rooms.

Bunbeg House
The Harbour
Bunbeg
Gweedore
Tel: (074) 9531305
Web: www. bunbeghouse.com
Email: bunbeghouse @eircom.net
Highly recommended
This lovely 3-star guesthouse sits in the tranquil Bunbeg harbor and is a perfect base to explore the coastline. Tory Ferry also leaves from just around the corner. The house has 14 en-suite rooms, and a cozy little bar serving bar snacks (I highly recommend Jean's cooking) where Andy will entertain you with his many stories.

THE JOURNEY
U L S T E R
COUNTY
DONEGAL

BALOR'S FORT

The very eastern edge of the island is known as Balor's Fort. It's an impenetrable plateau nearly 100 meters high with sheer cliffs on three sides. The only access is via a narrow isthmus with ports either side. On the southern side, just before this, is *Port an Deilg*, where **Balor** threw the triplets.

BALOR'S PRISON

Once across the isthmus I made my way up past a series of manmade defensive earthworks facing the entrance. I headed up onto the plateau and ventured over the southern side where the cliff drops off at a frighteningly steep angle into a deep cleft, where a

Balor's Prison — stay well away from the treacherous edge.

pool of water is surrounded by jagged rocks. This is Balor's Prison (*Príosún Bhaloir*) where the giant is said to have thrown his captives. Seeing as anyone thrown down there would have met certain death, I wouldn't have called it a prison.

BALOR'S SOLDIERS

The rocky crags of Balor's Soldiers do indeed look like soldiers standing guard over this long, narrow spur of land.

Behind this is a long, narrow spur jutting out from the cliffs. It's topped by towering pinnacles known as Balor's Soldiers. At the start of it was a flat ledge where I could lay down and stare into the rocky cove below.

THE WISHING STONE

I continued on along the cliffs until I reached the easternmost point where it drops off to a rock inhabited by puffins — one of the many types of bird life on the island, and best viewed from this point. At the edge of the cliff here is the wishing stone, a solid, square bolder perched precariously on top of two other boulders with a narrow, crumbling neck of rock separating it from the main section of the cliff. The tradition is to jump onto the stone, turn around three times and make

Tuan's Notes
Balor of the Evil Eye
Balor "of the Evil Eye" was the Witch-King of the Fomorians, and the arch-enemy of Nuada, King of the Tuatha dé Danann. He was an evil wizard of terrible power who, the legends say, lived in a tower of glass on what is now Tory Island. It was from here that he attempted to enslave the Tuatha dé Danann. Though not actually of Irish ancestry, he was considered in some myths to be the grandson of the Celtic war god Néit, and he also figured prominently in the myths and legends of ancient Ireland as the antagonist *par excellence*.

Learn more about Balor in The Mystery: Wizards, Druids & Poets (pp. 126-127).

Brae House
Front Street
Ardara
Tel: (074)
9541296
In town with 4 en-
suite rooms.

Tory Island
There are many
B&Bs on Tory
Island, the best thing
to do is simply ask
the locals, as none of
them will be signed.

H O S T E L S
Dooey Hostel
Glencolmcille
Tel: (074) 9730130
Web:
www.dooeyhostel.com
Email: dooeyhostel
@holidayhound.com
Highly recommended
Superb hostel with
great facilities, com-
ical owner and
views you would
normally pay a for-
tune for in a hotel.
The welcome with
tea and biscuits
makes you feel right
at home.
Also has
group house
and camping
available.

The Wishing Stone is perched precariously on the edge of a cliff, so please
throw stones instead of climbing.

a wish — or, succeed in throwing three stones on top of it. The latter is by far the better option, as the former would be suicidal. This boulder is balanced on a crumbling ledge that falls away 100 meters onto jagged rocks being pounded by huge waves below. Even if the rock sustained your weight, you could easily lose your balance and end up impaled upon one of those nasty-looking rocks below, making a hearty meal for the prolific bird life nestled on their ledges.

With that thought in mind, I headed back to town for a bite to eat.

DOWNTOWN TORY

Most of Tory has survived the onslaught of modern tourist exploitation, and aside from the newly built *Óstan Toraigh* (Tory Hotel), and a few new houses, much of the island remains just as it has been for years. It's like a land locked in time, and that is its appeal. Being cut off from the mainland has allowed the island to evolve in its own unique way, uninfluenced, for the most part, by the outside world.

Tory Island has one pub, one café, one shop and a hotel bar. The café is at the top of a hill on the edge of town, where I sat and tucked hungrily into my meal and watched as the sun went down outside. I remembered the first time Anne and I sat here five years back, watching as the wind howled past the window and the weather grew steadily worse. In the fading light we could see a small fishing boat riding out into the giant waves that seemed to dwarf the little boat. Teenage girls sat in the corner of the café speaking in Gaelic. Today it was exactly the same. Gaelic is spoken as an everyday language, and the people can switch back and forth with relative ease. But when among themselves they always revert to their native tongue. It was refreshing to see this.

The island pub is called *Club Soisialta* (Social Club), and is the place to go in the evening. The social club contradicts all that is stereotypical of Irish culture. It's a simple building at the top of town, with a bar and a large, wood-floored dance area. At the end of the room is a small, wooden stage where the bands play. But this is what I like about it — it's real. This wasn't built to entertain the

Donegal Town Independent Hostel
Doonan, Donegal
Tel: (074) 9722805
Email: lincunn8@eircom.net
Excellent, cozy hostel on Killybegs Rd. 10 min. walk from town.

Malinbeg Hostel
Malinbeg
Tel: (074) 9730006
Web: www.malinbeghostel.com
Email: malinbeghostel@oceanfree.net
Brand new hostel in Malinbeg, a few miles from Glencolmcille. Beautiful pinewood dorms and private rooms.

Derrylahan Hostel
Kilcar
Glencolmcille
Tel: (074)9738079
Web: homepage.eircom.net/~derrylahan
Email: derrylahan@eircom.net
Located close to Slieve League, this friendly and clean hostel has dorms and private rooms.

Downtown Tory is simple, neat and attractively decorated.

tourists, it was built for the islanders to entertain themselves on the long, dark and stormy nights. It's also the place where you will more than likely find yourself engaged in conversation with the locals. As it was the middle of the week, there wasn't a lot going on. Yet this still didn't stop an old fella from sinking back pints, chatting to us and teaching the girls to do a local dance. What better way to get to know the islanders?

HOUND'S ROCK

"And how are you this morning?" asked the king, as he sat revving the engine on his little red moped.

"Fine thanks," I replied. "I'm looking for the Hound's Rock, which is said to have the imprint of Colmcille's foot when he landed on the island. Do you know where it is?"

"Ah well, I have heard of it. But I'm not sure where it is now. Are you leaving today?"

Though the king wasn't sure, this may be Hound's Rock, now moved next to The Grave of the Seven (*op. cit.*) for easier access. The foot-shaped imprint may be that of St. Colmcille, from when he first stepped on the island.

"Yes, but not until five o clock. I'm catching the last ferry."

"Well you see, I'll ask my father who is very old. He will most definitely know. But I think he will be asleep still. Leave it with me and I'll see what I can do." I watched as he sped off down the road, a king with an earring and a flat cap, riding a motor-cycle. I guess even on Tory royalty has to modern-ize.

The story of St. Colmcille is an interesting one. It's said that he arrived on the shores of northern Donegal with three other saints. Each of them agreed that whomever should cast his staff onto the island from the mainland (7 miles across the sea) would be the one to take Christianity to Tory. Colmcille won. But when he stepped foot on shore, beside the modern-day pier, he was refused entry by the king.

Colmcille said that all he needed was a space the size of his cloak to build a church upon. The king agreed, but when the cloak was lain upon the ground it magically grew and engulfed the entire island. The king was enraged and set a savage hound on the saint. Colmcille stood upon a rock and made the sign of a holy cross. The dog dropped dead. Awed by this man's supernatural powers, the king allowed the saint to come on to the island. According to the visitor guide I had, this rock with the imprint of a foot can still be seen somewhere down along the pier.

Fortunately, the weather had slightly improved. The last time I had come here the weather had been beautiful, and the island had been totally trans-formed. Yet I actually like it when the weather is bad. The bleak, inhospitable feeling that the stormy weather brings makes you feel like you are in a remote place on the edge of the world — which, in a sense, you are. The stormy weather is characteris-tic of the island's dramatic landscape. I could see why **Tory** was a haven for painters, and how it had inspired the exquisite work that is on display in the island gallery.

Greenes Holiday Hostel
Greenes Corner, Carnmore Rd. Dungloe
Tel: (074) 9521943
Nice hostel with camping out back.

Errigal Hostel
Dunlewy
Tel: (074) 9531180
Web: www.errigalhostel.com
Part of the An Óige group, this nice little hostel sits in the imposing shadow of Mt Errigal. The war-den and his dog are very friendly. A walk-ing trail up Errigal starts from the back of this hostel, or you can drive further up the road for a shorter walk. (Open all year.) This hostel is also available to rent out of season.

CAMPING
Tory Island
Wild camping is allowed. Just ask local people for permission on where to camp.

THE JOURNEY
ULSTER
COUNTY
DONEGAL

THE JOURNEY
U L S T E R
COUNTY DONEGAL

THE RETURN OF THE KING

West Town is dominated by the remains of an old bell tower, beside which is St. John's Altar. These are the only remains of an ancient oratory. Fragments of the altar are piled on top of a stone table. Behind the tower, just down an alleyway beside a sign advertising bike hire, is St. Brigid's Altar. There was a stone chalice here once, said to have been used by Colmcille. It is now in the National Museum.

As I wandered through these ancient fragments of Tory's history, the king swung by again on his moped.

"I'm terribly sorry, I couldn't get the information for you," said the king, his rugged features contorted in a look of disappointment.

"No problem," I replied. "I've seen plenty already."

"Well, you give me your address and I'll get the information when my father wakes and send it to you."

It was five in the afternoon.

I gave Patsy my card and he shook my hand warmly. "Thank you for what you are doing," he said. "We need people like yourself to help us in our struggle to

St. Brigid's Altar - note the bullaun stones used to collect water. The stone chalice once used here is now in the National Museum.

Patsy Dan Rodgers, The King of Tory

show others the wonders of our little island."

I boarded the boat and watched as Patsy said good-bye to all the visitors, including the day visitors. I felt sorry for the people who had only come over for the day. All they had seen is an island that looks pretty. They hadn't spent the night and experienced what it can really be like. As the boat chugged slowly out of the harbor, I watched as the king waved and **the Tau Cross** shrank off into the distance. This cross sits at the top of the pier and is an image that has become synonymous with Tory. It's one of only two in Ireland.

I always feel a sense of sadness at leaving here, and I always feel compelled to return. As we headed out into what was possibly the roughest crossing yet, the way the skipper swept the boat in and out of these gigantic waves was a testament to his skill and to the safety of his boat. I stood at the back as the waves crashed over the edge and the boat rolled from side to side. As I stood there enjoying the ride, I made a mental note that next time I came, it would be for much longer than one night.

Tuan's Notes
The Tau Cross
The Tau Cross is named after the Hebrew letter *tav*, which translates into the Greek letter "T". The Tau Cross is a very ancient symbol, stretching all the way back to ancient Egypt, where it was a symbol of Osiris, and to ancient Sumer, where it was the symbol of the god Tammuz. As such, the Tau Cross may indicate a cultural — or possibly even ethnic — link between the Fomorians and ancient Egypt and/or Sumer. Another possible origin may be via Coptic Christians fleeing religious persecution in Egypt. In either case, it now stands transformed as a symbol of Christ.

Learn more about the history of Christianity in Ireland in The History: The Coming of Christianity (pp. 219-227).

THE JOURNEY
U L S T E R
COUNTY
DONEGAL

Places to See in Derry

☀ MULTI-SITES

1. Derry Town
   - St. Columb's Stone . . 713-715
   - St. Columb's Well . . 713, 715
   - Ancient fortifications . . . 714
   - Marko's Stones 715
2. Haunted Dolmens
   - Slaghtaverty Dolmen (The Giant's Grave) . 714, 717-719
   - Fairy Thorn 718-719
   - Ghost of Evil Dwarf 719
   - Tirnony Dolmen. . . . 713, 717
   - Tamnyrankin & Knockoneill Single Court Cairns (nearby)
3. Slieve Gallion
   - Ballybriest Dual Court Cairn. 713, 716

⚚ ANCIENT SITES

4. Boviel Wedge Cairn
5. Dunalis Souterrain/Ogham Stone

✟ CHRISTIAN SITES

6. Eglinton Holy Well
7. Bovevagh Old Church
8. Dungiven Priory
9. Banagher Old Church
10. St. Lurach's Church

⛰ SCENIC VIEWS

11. Sperrin Mountains

TRANSPORTATION

✈ City of Derry Int'l Airport . . 716
🚌 Derry Bus Station 717

Driving Directions: See pp. 713-718

Derry

St. Columb's Stone is set in attractive statuary wherein St. Columb is depicted pointing towards the crucified Christ.

Derry
Things to Do & Places to See

St. Columb's Stone and Well
Derry City
The stone is located in the grounds of the Long Tower Church. Exit the walled city via Bishop's Street, and take the lane down to the right. The well is down to the left of the main road.

Ballybriest Dual Court Cairn
From Draperstown take the B47 towards Omagh, turn left onto B162 to Cookstown. When you cross a bridge at the waterworks, turn left up Ballybriest Road. The cairn is on the right at the top of the hill.

Tirnony Dolmen
From Maghera take Tirkane Rd. and turn right up Tirnony Road. It's on the right.

Politically, crossing into Northern Ireland you are effectively crossing into another country. But there is no border crossing. The only indications that you are in a different country are the color of the road signs, and the road numbers. Car number plates are different, and

Slaghtaverty Dolmen
From Garvagh head south and turn right onto B64 for Dungiven. Take the immediate left and follow road until you come to a left turn for Slaghtaverty Lane. It is behind a green-roofed barn on the right.

Tours
City Tours
11 Carlisle Rd
Derry City
Tel: (027) 7127 1996
Mob: (077) 12937997
Web: www.
irishtourguides.com
Email: derrycitytours
@aol.com

Festivals
Celtic European Festival of the Sea
A celebration of Celtic maritime heritage with ships from all over the world, including tall ships.
Tel: (028) 2076 8813
Web: www.maritime festival.net

also you have to change your money into Sterling. Other than this, things are pretty much the same.

I found it ironic that in Irish folklore the north was always associated with evil. It's true that for a long time the Troubles here may have frightened people off, but that is, for the most part, a thing of the past. The first time I ever ventured up into the north, Donegal included, I found the people to be equally, if not more, friendly and welcoming than the Irish down south. I like it here. The only thing I didn't like was the fact that I now had to pay UK petrol prices, which were a lot higher. Thankfully I'd filled up before leaving County Donegal.

Derry sits beside the River Foyle and is an ancient walled city. The wall was built around the old city in the 1600s as a defence against cannon fire. Derry the city is the major city of Derry the county, and is also the site of several interesting artifacts. Included among these are several artifacts from St. Columba. Columba, also known as St. Colmcille or just "St. Columb", founded a monastery in Derry around AD 560, part of which still survives today.

St. Columb's Stone

A closeup of St. Columb's Stone reveals many centuries of use.

714

I headed up into town to the Diamond, then up Bishop Street through Bishop's Gate to the Long Tower Church just down a lane on the right. In a corner beside the entrance are a series of bronze statues, depicting Christ on the crucifix surrounded by his worshipers. Underneath these statues is St. Columb's stone, with two large depressions in it. This is all that remains of the ancient monastery established by St. Columb in the 6th century.

St. Columb's Well

St. Columb's Well has a pump that may only be ornamental in function.

I had heard that there was also a holy well dedicated to Columb, so I headed back down the side of the wall to the main road below, and found the site of the well on the grass outside a house. It was clearly visible from the main road, directly opposite the Bogside Inn pub.

Nearby are three tall, concrete pillars with artistic swirling carved on their faces, standing a few feet apart. Just to the right I found an old green water pump commemorating the spot where St. Columb's Well once was. According to Slovenian artist Marko Pogacnik, whose "Lithopuncture Project" has raised local awareness about the spiritual nature of these ancient monuments, this well is the "key" to the landscape.

Eat & Drink

Claudes
4, Shipquay St.
Nr Diamond
Derry City
Tel: (028) 7127 9379
Nice little sandwich bar/café with all-day breakfasts and Internet access.

O'Brien's American Steakhouse & Grill
59, Strand Rd.
Tel: (028) 7136 1527

Fitzroys
2-4 Bridge Street.
Tel: 028 7126 6211
E-mail:
fitzroys@lineone.net
Very popular.

PUBS
Peadar O'Donnell
Waterloo St.
Excellent pub with nightly Irish music sessions.

Tracy's Bar
Waterloo St.
Nice, relaxed pub with Irish music during the week.

Most pubs are along Waterloo St.

TRANSLINK

Translink has integrated Citybus, Northern Ireland Railways and Ulsterbus together to provide comprehensive service to the Ulster region: www.translink.co.uk

AIR
City of Derry Int'l Airport
Airport Rd.
Eglinton
Tel: (028) 7181 0784
Web: www. cityofderryairport.com
Email: info@ cityofderryairport.com
7 miles NE of the city.

TRAINS
Derry Train Station
Duke St.
Tel: (028) 7134 2228

Colraine Station
Railway Rd.
Tel: (028) 7032 5400
Regular daily services between Derry & Belfast via Coleraine.

Ballybriest Dual Court Cairn

Two gallery graves remain from a substantial tomb on Slieve Gallion.

From Derry I took the A6 out of town towards Belfast. Just past Dungiven I turned right for Draperstown and then headed out on the B47 towards Omagh. A few miles out of town I turned left onto the B162 for Cookstown. A few miles down the road I crossed a bridge and took the immediate left up Ballybriest Rd. and found the cairn signed on the right over a wooden stile.

There are remains of two gallery graves sitting here on the slopes of Slieve Gallion, overlooking Lough Fea in the distance. This was once a substantial tomb, but it has been badly damaged over the years by farming. There are a number of tombs and passage cairns spread around the surrounding hills. There are two cairns on the 527-meter summit of Slieve Gallion, where, until the mid-1900s *Lughnasa* assemblies were held every year at the end of July.

An interesting story about how the mountain got its name tells of a giant called Callann Mór, who lived in the cairn on the summit. His sister lived nearby and wanted the mountain removed so she could see her friend over in Tyrone. She sent her minions over to remove it, but as they did so their hands became infested with giant, red sores. Legend says that if you try to dig on the mountain, you will suffer the same fate.

Tirnony Dolmen

At five feet tall, Tirnony Dolmen is actually smaller than the Mystery Machine, though not so small that it is in danger of being crushed by a dwarf.

I headed over to the A29 and drove northward to Maghera. I took the Tirkane Road out of town and after about a mile turned right up Tirnony Road. One of the things that I like about Northern Ireland is that their roads have signs indicating the place names, making it easier to find all the old relics scattered across the countryside.

I found the dolmen beside the road on the right. It is unusual in that it is shorter than most others I'd seen. The portal stones were only five feet high, and although the capstone slopes dramatically, the whole thing still seemed dwarfed in comparison to others like Poulenabrone.

Slaghtaverty Dolmen

I drove northward to Garvagh. After obtaining directions in town, I headed back out and took the right turn south of town for the B64 towards Dungiven. As instructed I turned immediately left after this and followed the road until I came to a left turn directly after

BUSES
Derry Bus Station
Foyle St.
Tel: (028) 7126 2261
Derry is a major hub for buses into northwest Ireland and on to Belfast and the north Antrim coast.

DRIVING
Derry lies just across the border with Donegal. See map for more information.

TAXI
Delta Cabs
141b Strand Rd.
Derry City
Tel: (028) 7127 9999

Derry Taxi Association also does tours.

CAR HIRE
Europcar has an office at the airport.
Tel: (028) 7181 2773
Web: www.europcar.ie

BIKE HIRE
Northwest Cycle Hire
13, Magazine St.
Derry City
Tel: (028) 7136 2234
Mob: (077) 3987 7279

THE JOURNEY
U L S T E R
COUNTY DERRY

Slaghtaverty Dolmen, locally referred to as "The Giant's Grave", is comprised of one large rock and two smaller rocks under a fairy hawthorn. Legend has it that Finn McCool had killed an evil dwarf that had been terrorizing the locals and had buried it next to this tree. To this day, grass will not grow here.

the farmhouse gables. The road was signed Slaghtaverty Lane. I continued up this road looking for a dolmen, but couldn't see anything.

"I'm looking for Slaghtaverty Dolmen," I said to a nearby farmer.

"The Giant's Grave?" he asked.

"That could well be it."

"It's back that way, in a field beside a farmhouse with a green roof. You'll see a lone tree in a field down below."

I thanked him and headed back. Sure enough, there was a lone hawthorn tree in the middle of the field.

All day long the sun had been shining. As I climbed the gate and headed across the field to the tree, a thick blanket of cloud rolled eerily over and blocked the sunlight. The field turned from vivid green to dark and gloomy. The wind suddenly picked up and a scattered herd of bulls stopped what they were doing, gathered together and began walking towards me. A wave of unease came over me as I stood beside the tree.

According to *Sacred Ireland*, this is the burial place of an evil dwarf who terrorized the local people with his magical powers and enchanted music. He was killed by Finn McCool and buried upside down beside this tree. A large rock with two smaller ones beside it lay on the ground under the tree, probably the remains of the dolmen. A circle of red mud surrounded its trunk, the exact diameter of the tree. The grass had stopped growing here. I shivered as I looked on. I'm not superstitious, but there really was something sinister about the place. As I took photos the bulls approached and fairly soon I found myself flanked on three sides by them, my only opening towards the gate. Two black bulls stood under the tree staring at me with their small, baleful eyes. The one nearest the tree suddenly began snorting and scraping its foot along the ground.

It was time for me to leave.

I made a hasty exit, closely followed by my four-legged foes. Evil dwarf 1, Ian 0.

Arkle House
2, Coshquin Rd.
Derry City
Tel: (028)71271157
Mob: (077)10299682
Email: arklehse
@tinyonline.co.uk

H O S T E L S
**Derry City
Independent Hostel**
44 Great James St.
Derry City
Tel: (028) 71280542
Web:
www.derryhostel.com
Email: derryhostels
@hotmail.com

Dungiven Castle
Main St., Dungiven
Tel: (028) 7774 2428
Web: www.
dungivencastle.com
Email: enquiries@
dungivencastle.com

C A M P I N G
Benone Caravan Park
5, Benone Ave.
Limavady
Tel: (028) 7775 0557

For more information
visit ireland.
mysterious
world.com/
Journey/
Counties/
Derry/

THE JOURNEY
U L S T E R
COUNTY
DERRY

Places to See in Antrim

Antrim
The Giant's Causeway

Giant's Causeway is made up of volcanic basalt that had cooled rapidly into hexagonal columns, forming what appear to be steps.

After parking up my van, I stepped out and wandered to the edge of the cliff. What lay out before me was astounding. The Giant's Causeway is just one section of the Antrim coastline, which consists of mile upon mile of soaring cliff tops, rugged inlets and

Antrim
Things to Do & Places to See

The Giant's Causeway
A stunning and unusual landscape set amid the soaring Antrim coastline. Said to have been built by Finn McCool. On the A2 NE of Coleraine. Web: www. giantscausewayofficial guide.com/home.htm

Lisanduff Circles
A series of raths on the coast in Portballintrae. Signed off the A2 north of Bushmills.

Dunseverick Castle
On the left as you travel from the Giant's Causeway on the coast road on a sheer rocky ledge overlooking the sea.

Ballintoy Harbor & Carrick-a-Rede Rope Bridge
Near the village of Ballintoy, on the A2 east of Giant's Causeway.

THE JOURNEY
ULSTER
COUNTY
ANTRIM

Ossian's Grave
On the A2 north of Cushendell, take the turn off for Ballymoney. A short way on the left is a small road, opposite a white house. Park and walk up the lane to a gate. The grave is in a field to the right.

Layd Church
From the crossroads in Cushendall take the road for Cross and turn left at the fork for Layd Church. Has an interesting holed stone, known locally as *Cross na Naghan*.

The White Lady
Beside the A2, north of Carnlough.

Slemish Mountain
On the left as you travel from Carnlough to Ballymena on the A42. St. Patrick lived here in his youth.

Doagh Hole Stone
B59 north from Doagh and right onto Holestone Road, on the right.

The columns descend rapidly into the sea, giving the appearance of a "causeway" which reappears on the island of Staffa.

sheltered coves. Looking at the size of the landscape it was clear to me how a giant could be well at home here.

I wandered down the pathway that takes you to the actual causeway. Every step I took brought me closer to the most unusual terrain I've ever seen. The ocean waves crashed against large, hexagonal blocks that spread out before me like a huge array of stepping-stones, each about the size of a giant's foot. The bulk of the Causeway stretches out into the ocean like a collapsed bridge.

It is said that across the ocean, on the Scottish island of Staffa, there is a similar causeway. This has given rise to the legend that Finn McCool built the causeway with his own hands in order to walk across and challenge the Scottish giant, Benandonner. But after the incredibly tiresome feat of building the bridge, Finn went home and fell asleep. Benandonner soon made his way across the bridge to Finn's home. Seeing him coming, Finn's wife dressed her sleeping husband as a baby, and warned Benandonner not to wake her child. Once Benandonner saw the size of Finn's child, he gulped at the prospect that if the child was this big, then Finn himself must be ten times bigger than him. So before

Finn returned, his Scottish opponent ran back to his lair on Staffa, tearing up the causeway as he went.

The walkway extended beyond the main part of the causeway, so I followed as it zig-zagged upwards and took me on a walk along the cliff edge. There is a pathway that leads from the Causeway right up to the town of Ballycastle, ten miles away.

The geological explanation for the Causeway is that it was formed by the volcanic eruption that formed the Antrim plateau. Upon hitting the cool seawater, the molten lava rapidly cooled and shrank, creating these basalt hexagonal blocks. There are over 40,000 blocks — some are black, and others are more reddish-brown. I must admit I found this theory a bit hard to believe. If it was caused by a volcanic eruption, why does it stretch all the way to Staffa Island? I guess I was getting too much into these legends, and preferred to believe it was built by a giant.

At the base of the mountain the main causeway stretches from a high ledge and runs off into the sea. A bit further along the path is a great rock shaped like a boot, which has been named "The Giant's Boot". On the cliffs further up is "The Giant's Organ". This is a 40-foot high series of hexagonal columns sitting in the middle of the cliffside, much resembling a gigantic pipe-organ.

"The Giant's Boot" may be a rock that has been carved into a boot, may have been naturally shaped, or may even have been part of a larger statue.

Tours
Old Bushmills Distillery
Distillery Rd.
Bushmills
Tel:
(028) 207 33218
Web: www.
bushmills.com
The oldest distillery in the world and the only source of the famous whiskey. Visitor centre is across the road. Tours are available daily.

Ulsterbus Tours
The Travelcentre
Europa Buscentre
Glengall Street,
Belfast
Tel: (028) 9033 7004
Runs a variety of tours around Northern Ireland.

Festivals
Viking Boat Challenge
Lough Shore Park
Antrim
Held in August.
Tel: (028) 7032 6868
Viking boat races and battle displays.

THE JOURNEY
U L S T E R
COUNTY
ANTRIM

The Lig na Baste

Ancient legends say that the caves on the coast around Ballintoy were once inhabited by a giant sea serpent sent by God to punish the locals.

I drove my van on to Ballintoy and down to Ballintoy Harbor, and basked in the sun. Even this little harbor is littered with folklore. The oldest is the legend of the *Lig na Baste*. Said to have existed in the time of the druids, the *Lig na Baste* is a giant sea serpent which is believed to inhabit the caves in and around Ballintoy. The story tells of how the harbor was once an ancient prehistoric maritime city, but its inhabitants worshiped pagan gods and because of this they were punished by God. A great sea snake was released into the area, and then the city and all its inhabitants were turned to stone. Around the 1500s there were reports of a great sea monster attacking and sinking ships off the area. Could this have been the *Lig na Baste*?

The jagged and quite haunting rock formations along this entire coast certainly add fuel to these stories. The giant caves and hidden coves could well hide such a monster.

CARRICK-A-REDE ROPE BRIDGE

I drove on through the village and turned left into the car park for Carrick-a-Rede Rope Bridge. This is a precarious rope bridge erected over a 24-meter-deep and 18-

meter-wide chasm between the mainland and Rock Island. If you dare to cross, then you are rewarded with views of a number of deep caves along the coast, which could well be the abode of the *Lig na Baste*. The bridge was built by salmon fishermen who have a small house sitting on a low ledge on the island.

Carrick-a-RedeRope Bridge will add a thrill to your Antrim adventure.

Ossian's Grave

I continued on the coast road to Ballycastle, then on to the A2 for a while before branching off to Torr Head. This road took me on a lovely drive that weaved up and along this attractive part of Antrim

Ossian's Grave is a semi-circular court cairn around 16 feet in diameter with a dramatic view of the Antrim Mountains.

There & Back Again

TRANSLINK
Complete service to the Ulster region.
www.translink.co.uk

AIR
Belfast Int'l Airport
Belfast
Tel: (028) 9448 4848
Web: www.bial.co.uk
Located 18 miles NW of Belfast.

George Best Belfast City Airport
Tel: (028) 9093 9093
Web: www.belfastcityairport.com
Email info@belfastcityairport.com
Closer to the city.

FERRIES
P&O Irish Sea
The Terminal, Larne
Tel: (0870) 242 4777
Web: www.poirishsea.com
Daily from Cairnryan, Scotland to Larne.

Victoria Terminal
Belfast
A few miles north of the city centre.

THE JOURNEY
ULSTER
COUNTY
ANTRIM

Norse Merchant Ferries
To and from Liverpool
Web: www.norse merchant.com

Stena Line
To and from Stranraer, Scotland
Web: www.stenaline.com

TRAINS

Antrim Rail Station
Railway St.
Antrim Town
Tel: (028) 9442 9185

BUSES

Antrim Bus Station
Station Rd.
Antrim town
Tel: (028) 9442 8729

Ballymena Station
Tel: (028) 25652214

Larne Station
Tel: (028) 2827 2345

DRIVING

✢ For Giant's Causeway take the B146 off A2.
✢ Re-join the A2 and turn right at sign for Ballymoney, turning left opposite white house for Ossian's Grave.

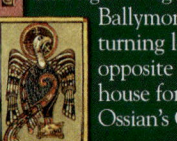

known as The Nine Glens of Antrim, now enshrouded in mist by the sudden change in weather. It was a narrow road and slow going when tractors and big camper vans met. It finally re-joined the A2, where I headed south towards Cushendall. Just before I reached town I took the right turn for Ballymoney and headed up the road in search of a court cairn called Ossian's Grave.

"Excuse me, could you tell me how I get to Ossian's Grave?" I asked the old man walking his dog up the road.

"You've passed it," he said. He paused for a moment to think. "I'll go get my car and show you."

"Well, why don't I give you a lift?"

He looked at his dog, soaking wet and jumping up at him with muddy paws. "No, I'll get the car."

I drove up and turned around. When I came back

down I found him waiting in his car, the dog sitting faithfully in the passenger seat. He took me back down the road and parked by a turning on the right, opposite a white house.

"It's up there about a mile," he said pointing up the road. "The road is bad, but you can park in a car park and walk the rest of the way."

I thanked him, and parked in the car park. As I stepped

Collies and terriers are among the most popular breeds kept by the Irish, so it is likely you will meet some on your journey.

out of the van I was greeted by a tri-color border collie and a little terrier, who proceeded to follow me as I trudged up the road under my umbrella. The collie ran into a shed and re-emerged with a brick of turf in its mouth.

After about three-quarters of a mile I found the grave in a field on the right. It's a semi-circular court cairn about 16 feet in diameter and sits on a hill with a view of the Antrim Mountains. According to folklore, it's the burial place of Ossian, son of Finn McCool.

Lough Neagh

Lying virtually in the center of the six counties, Lough Neagh is the largest lake in the British Isles. I arrived here quite late in the evening with the intention of spending the night, but the swarms of midges immediately put an end to that line of thought. These weren't just a few though; this was an invasion. I stepped out of the van and was engulfed by the nearest battalion. It was like something out of a bad horror movie. I had no choice but to dive back in the van and then kill any that had followed. In the end I decided that a B&B was in order, and found one in the little village of Ahoghill, a few miles north on the road to Ballymena.

A high cross at Layd Church, just north of Cushendall.

⚜ From Cushendall follow A2 south to Carnlough, turn right onto A42 to Ballymena. Follow signs for Slemish Mountain.

TAXI
Causeway Coast Taxis
3, Coleraine Rd, Portrush
Tel: (028) 7082 3421

1st Antrim Taxis
90 Church St, Antrim.
Tel: (028) 9446 6661

CAR HIRE
Direct Car Van & Minibus Rentals
78 Steeple Road, Antrim.
Tel: 028 9446 7975 / 07710 902229
Email:
maggie.montgomery@btopenworld.com

BIKE HIRE
Bushmills Bike Hire
140 Main St.
Bushmills
Tel: (028) 2073 0262
Mob: (079) 6691 3682

THE JOURNEY
U L S T E R
COUNTY ANTRIM

Places to Stay

HOTELS

Causeway Hotel
40 Causeway Rd.
Bushmills
Tel: (028) 2073
1210/2073 1226
Web: www.
giants-causeway-
hotel.com
Email: reception@
giants-causeway-
hotel.com
On the cliff over-
looking the Giant's
Causeway coastline.

The Bushmills Inn
9 Dunluce Road
Bushmills
Tel: (028) 2073 3000
Web: www.
bushmillsinn.com
Email: mail@
bushmillsinn.com

B & B S

Portcampley B&B
8 Harbour Road
Ballintoy
Tel: (028) 2076 8200
Web: www.
portcampley.8k.com
Email: m.donnelly@
btconnect.com
Overlooking
Ballintoy
Harbor.

THE JOURNEY

U L S T E R

COUNTY
ANTRIM

The White Lady is an unusually human-looking rock that can be seen along the A2 overlooking the sea.

I returned the next morning to find that the swarms had dwindled. There were still a few about, but at least the few were bearable. I was in the Lough Neagh Forum, a leisure complex just outside Antrim. Fred, who worked at the caravan park, kindly handed me a pile of leaflets about the area, and also informed me that the midges come out on hot days, and only live for 24 hours. Unfortunately just as many are born the next day.

Lough Neagh is the subject of a few legends. The one that had brought me here was of Finn McCool. It is said that during one of his battles with the Scottish giant Benandonner, Finn scooped up a chunk of land and threw it at his adversary. But Finn grossly underestimated his own strength, and threw the clump of land so far that it missed its target and landed in the middle of the Irish Sea, to become known as the Isle of Man.

The Lough Neagh Forum is located at the northeast tip of the lake where the Sixmilewater River runs into it. The Legend of the Overflowing Well tells of how the crater formed by Finn McCool became a lake. At the bottom of the crater was a magical well, whose keeper was believed locally to be a witch. Her job was to close the gate after the visitors came. One day she forgot, and the well overflowed, forming the lake. It's said that there was a city around the well, and that the waters had actually risen to punish the people for their greed. On clear days it's said that the towers from this city can still be seen under the surface of the lake.

Doagh Hole Stone

The village of Doagh lies east of Antrim Town, where the B95 joins the B59. I took the B59 towards Ballymena and after a couple of miles turned right into Holestone Road. At the top of a hill I found a sign just inside a field gate to the right advertising Doagh Hole Stone. The stone itself sits on a small mound, and was obscured by thick bushes. I found an entrance behind the mound which led up to this very unusual standing stone.

Standing 1.5 metres high, the stone tapers off at the top. What is unusual is the perfectly round hole carved through it. The hole has a perfectly smooth and round taper either side. According to the sign, there has long been a tradition here that lovers would perform a ceremony to bind themselves together. The hole will only allow a female hand to be placed through it. She must then clasp her lover's hand and the two must pledge themselves to each other for life. The power of the stone is unlocked and the magic binds them together, and can never be broken. Apparently lovers still come here today to perform this ancient ceremony.

A closeup of the Doagh Hole Stone shows the narrowness of the hole and how only a small hand could fit.

HOSTELS
Sheep Island View
42A Main St,
Ballintoy
Tel: (028) 2076 9391
Web: www.
sheepislandview.com
Email: info@
sheepislandview.com

Castle Hostel
62 Quay Road
Ballycastle
Tel: (028) 2076 2337/2076 2299
Web:
www.castlehostel.com
Email: info@
castlehostel.com

CAMPING
Sixmilewater Camping & Caravanning Park
Antrim Forum
Leisure Complex
Lough Rd., Antrim
Tel: (028) 94464131
Email:
forum@antrim.gov.uk

For more information visit ireland.
mysterious
world.com/
Journey/
Counties/
Antrim/

THE JOURNEY
ULSTER
COUNTY
ANTRIM

Places to See in Down

Down
The Giant's Ring

Despite the relatively small dolmen at its center the Giant's Ring, at 600 feet in diameter, is the largest ritual enclosure in Ireland

rom the heart of Belfast city I got on the A55 ring road southwards and turned off at the sign for the Giant's Ring. I followed the signs until I arrived at the car park. Through a gate I found myself standing in a huge, grassy enclosure, 600 feet in diameter, ringed by an earthen bank. The bank was 12 feet high. Sitting in the middle, looking tiny in its huge surroundings, was a dolmen.

The dolmen itself is not that impressive, standing about five feet high with a single capstone and five upright stones. The purpose of the ring is a total mystery, as there is no written or oral history surrounding it. Archaeologists have suggested it's a ritual enclosure, and this makes it the largest ritual enclosure in the country.

The site is away from the hustle and bustle of the city, and didn't appear to be overly visited. All that could be heard was the whistling of the breeze and the singing of the birds. I quite liked it here, it was very peaceful.

Down
Things to Do & Places to See

The Giant's Ring
From Belfast City take the A55 outer ring southward and follow signs. From Lisburn follow B23 to Belfast and you'll see a big sign pointing left.

Downpatrick Cathedral and **Mound of Down**
Burial place of St. Patrick and ancient rath of the Red Branch Knights.

The St. Patrick Centre
53a Lower Market St. Downpatrick
Tel: (028) 4461 9000
Web: www.saint patrickcentre.com
Email: director@saint patrickcentre.com
An interpretive centre telling the story of Ireland's patron saint. Charge for entry.

THE JOURNEY
ULSTER
COUNTY DOWN

Old Gaol Museum
English St.
Downpatrick
Tel: (028) 4461
5218
Web: www.down
countymuseum.com
Email: mail@down
countymuseum.com

Tuan's Notes
Red Branch Knights
Learn more about The Knights of the Red Branch in The Mystery: Deities & Demigods (pp. 111-113).

Legananny Dolmen
From Castlewellan take A50 Banbridge road north. Turn right at Leitrim Rd., then right onto Legananny Rd.

Dundrum Castle
Built by the Norman John de Courcy. Legend says a monster inhabits the bay.

Slieve Donard
The cairn on the summit is the burial place of Slánga, a Partholónian prince.

THE JOURNEY
U L S T E R
COUNTY DOWN

The Mound of Down was the headquarters of the Dál Fiatach family of Red Branch Knights who ruled eastern Ulster.

The Mound of Down

Behind a school in Downpatrick, enclosed in a ring of trees, is the Mound of Down. This was said to have been the headquarters of the Dál Fiatach family of **Red Branch Knights** who ruled eastern Ulster in the 11th century. The outer mound is 1,000 years old, and many more mounds were added over the years.

I entered via a gate and followed a grassy path which split into two, so I followed the left path. It took me around the enclosure until I came upon a grassy lane leading up onto the mound. Inside I found a motte, just off-center. It was more like three mottes joined into one with a path going up the middle.

Downpatrick sits at the southern tip of the huge Strangford Lough, which stretches 15 miles northward. The Mound sits beside the Quoile Marshes, and from the top of the Motte I got a great view of the lake and nearby hills.

The Hill of Down

Visible from the hill was Downpatrick's other mound, the Hill of Down. I made my way back to the van and drove over to where the present Church of Ireland Cathedral now sits. Originally the hill was a hill fort, until St. Patrick came along and established a monastery there, believed to be his first. At the time the hill was under the control of Celtchair, a knight of Emain Macha. It is now home to Downpatrick Cathedral.

Downpatrick Cathedral

Downpatrick Cathedral is believed by some to be not only the first monastery established in Ireland by St. Patrick, but also the place of his burial.

Dominating the landscape of Downpatrick is Downpatrick Cathedral, high atop a hill. In front of the cathedral is a very worn Celtic cross dated to around the 9th century. Not only is it claimed that St. Patrick established his first monastery here, it is also claimed that he is buried here. From the front of the cathedral I headed up the left side and into the graveyard. A path led directly to a large stone in the shape of a battle-shield, said to mark his grave. According to legend Patrick died in nearby Saul, just east of town, and was buried here next to the church. Other stories also credit this as the burial place for Saints Colmcille and Brigid.

Tours

Mourne Cycle Tours
13, Spelga Ave.
Newcastle
Tel: (028)43724348

Bus Èireann Mountains of Mourne Tour
Tour from Dublin runs Tues, Thurs. & Sat., July-Aug.

Festivals

St. Patrick's Festival & Cross Community Carnival Parade
Downpatrick, Co. Down & Armagh, Co. Armagh
Tel: 028 4461 9000
Web:
www.st-patricks dayfestival.com
When: Week of March 17.

All Ireland Busking Festival
Dundrum
Street circus, children's shows, Viking longboats and a prize for the best buskers.
Tel: (028) 4375 1528
Web: www.all irelandbusking competition .com
When: Every August.

THE JOURNEY
ULSTER
COUNTY DOWN

Eat & Drink

Justine's Restaurant & Steakhouse
English St.
Downpatrick
Tel: (028) 4461 7886

Denvers Restaurant & Guesthouse
English St.
Downpatrick
Tel: (028) 4461 2012

The Maple Leaf Cottage Tea Room
149, Bryansford Road
Newcastle
Tel: (028) 4372 3500

Stone Boat Restaurant
4 South Promenade
Tel: (028) 4372 3445
Web: www.stoneboatrestaurant.com
Email: info@stoneboatrestaurant.com

PUBS

Mullens Bar
Church St.
Downpatrick

The Anchor Bar
9-11 Bryansford Road
Newcastle
Serves pub food also.

Struell Wells

Struell Wells is comprised of four wells that were channeled into various uses, such as drinking and bathing. The women's bathing well (above) is the only one that is still usable.

I followed the signs out of town for Ardglass and soon came to signs for the wells. St. Patrick came here regularly to bathe. I doubt he would have done so had he been alive today.

The area is beautiful, situated in a small, green valley, and from the outside the wells look quite inviting. There are four wells here, all coming from the same stream, but rising up at different points. The first two, drinking well and eye well, have small beehive huts built around them. The other two are the bathing wells where stone houses have been erected, creating separate bathing sections for men and women.

Beside the drinking well are the remains of a church. I looked through the gate to the drinking well and was shocked to see it littered with fizzy drink bottles and sweet wrappers. The eye well was the same. I wandered down to the bathing wells. The women's bath house was nice and clean, and the water entered through a hole in the wall and filled a long, rectangular trough on the floor. It looked like it was more for bathing your feet in, rather than your body. The men's bath house, however, was not fit for use.

Legananny Dolmen

From Downpatrick I headed west on the A25 to Castlewellan, then took the A50 towards Banbridge. A short way up the road I turned right onto Leitrim Road, and drove along this for what seemed like ages until I came across more signs finally directing me to Legananny Dolmen, the most amazing dolmen in Ireland.

I say amazing because I'm amazed it's still standing. The huge capstone, a solid square lump of granite, sits precariously on three upright stones. This gives it the appearance of a giant, three-legged table. The entrance stones are two meters high, and the backstone is lower but tapers to a point where it holds the capstone up barely by its edge. Sitting on this small hill it commands a view surrounded by an array of mountains, the most notable being Slieve Croob, formerly a Lughnasa site.

This surrounding townland took its name from this dolmen. In Irish it's *Liagán Áine*, which means "The Pillar Stone of Anya". This seems to refer to the goddess Áine from Limerick, or "Anu" as she's known in Kerry. It seems that this goddess of fertility got around a bit.

Legananny Dolmen is dedicated to the goddess Áine of the Tuatha dé Danann, which may indicate their influence in this region.

There & Back Again

FERRIES
Strangford Ferry
The Slip
Tel: (028) 4488 1637

TRAINS
Newry Train Station
Newry
Tel: (028) 3026 9271

BUSES
Downpatrick Bus Station
Market St.
Tel: (028) 4461 2384

Newcastle Bus Station
Railway St., Newcastle
Tel: (028) 4372 2296

CAR HIRE
C. McKeown
53 Killough Rd.
Downpatrick
Tel: (028) 4461 3055

McKibben Motors
19, The Square
Clough
Tel: (028) 4481 1679

BIKE HIRE
Discount Cycles
Church St.
Downpatrick
Tel: (028) 4461 4990

THE JOURNEY
ULSTER
COUNTY DOWN

Places to Stay

HOTELS

Enniskeen House Hotel
98 Bryansford Rd. Newcastle
Tel: (028) 4372 2392
E-Mail:
breaks@enniskeen-hotel.demon.co.uk
Located about a few minutes outside of Newcastle and also serves home-cooked food.

B & B S

Swan Lodge B&B
30 St. Patrick's Road Saul, Downpatrick
Tel: (028) 4461 5542
Mob: (077) 39267939
Situated on a hill overlooking Strangford Lough and close to Struell Wells. Has four rooms.

Tyrella House
Tyrella, Downpatrick
Tel: (028) 4485 1422
Web: www.hidden-ireland.com/tyrella.html

South of Clough on the A2 towards Ardglass. Has 3 rooms, dinner and a private beach.

THE JOURNEY

ULSTER

COUNTY DOWN

Dundrum Castle & Bay

Dundrum Castle and city is associated with the ancient Partholónians, one of the earliest invaders of Ireland.

Just north of Newcastle I stopped in the lovely village of Dundrum, which sits beside a small inlet known as Dundrum Bay. On the hill behind the village is Dundrum Castle, which I drove up to.

The castle was established by John de Courcy after taking Downpatrick to the north. I wandered into the grounds, and was able to walk up to the top of the surviving keep and marvel at the views across the bay. The original name for the bay was *Loch Rudhraighe*, who was a son of Partholón, the leader of the first race to invade Ireland. Legend says that he was drowned in the bay by the waters rising up against him in anger.

There is also a legend of a great monster that lives in the bay. When King Fearghus mac Léide lived here he came across this monster one day, and it was so hideous that his mouth twisted and contorted in fear. As a king couldn't reign if he had a blemish, he had to hide it. But one day a local girl discovered his secret, and he was forced to step down as king. In order to redeem himself, he went into the bay to kill the monster, where he unfortunately met his doom.

Slieve Donard

Slieve Donard is a dominating presence just to the south of Newcastle, one of the biggest towns along this coastline. The mountain sits on the edge of the magnif-icent Mourne Mountains, and is said in folklore to be the burial place of Slánga, another son of Partholón. He is supposed to be buried in a cairn on the summit. The best viewing point is at the unfortunately named Bloody Bridge. You can access it via a car park on the left as you travel south from Newcastle. This point also marks the start of a hiking trail that leads up to the cairn on the 2,800-foot summit.

Oakleigh House
30, Middle Tollymore Rd.
Newcastle
Tel: (028) 4372 3353 / 4372 6816
Web: www.oakleigh-ireland.com
Email: enquiries@oakleigh-ireland.com

HOSTELS
Newcastle Youth Hostel
30 Downs Rd.
Newcastle
Tel: (028) 4372 2133
Email: info@hini.org.uk
Open Mar-Dec.

CAMPING
The Camping and Caravanning Club Site
Delamont Ctry. Club
Downpatrick Rd.
Tel: (028) 4482 1833
Web: www.campingand caravanningclub.co.uk
Just off the A22 between Downpatrick and Killyleagh.

For more information visit ireland.mysterious world.com/Journey/Counties/Down/

THE JOURNEY
ULSTER
COUNTY DOWN

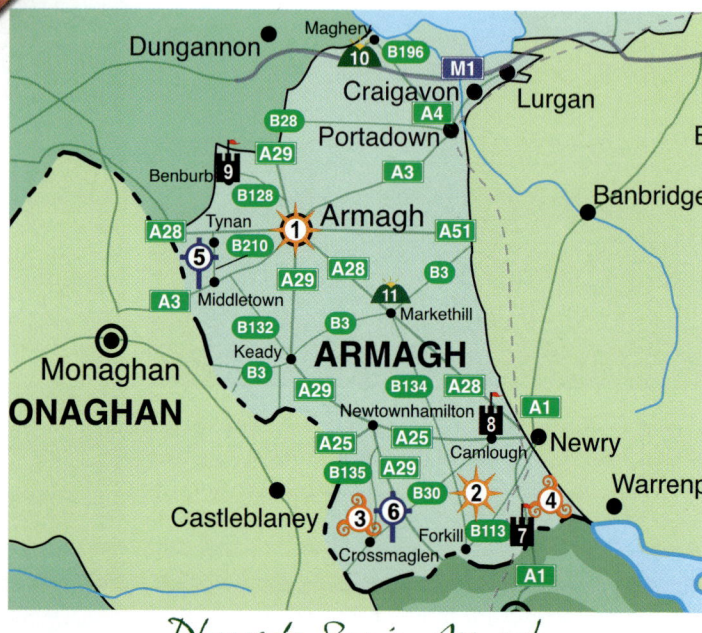

Places to See in Armagh

☀ Multi-Sites

1. Armagh
   - Emain Macha 739-740
   - The Church of Ireland
     Cathedral 739, 741-742
   - St. Patrick's Roman Catholic
     Cathedral 739, 743
   - Armagh Friary
   - St. Patrick's Trian 740
   - The Pilgrim's Trail
2. Slieve Gullion . . 740, 745
   - Ballykeel Dolmen . 740, 744-45
   - Ballymacdermot Court Cairn
   - Kileavy Monastic Church
   - Ti Chulainn Cultural Centre
   - Kilnasaggart Monastic Site

⚜ Ancient Sites

3. Annaghmare Court Cairn
4. Clontygorra Court Cairn

☥ Christian Sites

5. Tynan Cross 739, 744
6. Cardinal O'Fiach Centre

🏰 Historical Sites

7. Moyry Castle
8. Derrymore House
9. Benburb Castle

🏞 Scenic Views

10. The Ulster Way
11. Gosford Forest Park

Driving Directions: See pp. 739-740, 744-745

Armagh
Emain Macha

The ancient mound of Emain Macha is the traditional Royal Seat of Ulster. It is also where the twins of Macha were born, and where the goddess Macha uttered the infamous Curse of the Ulstermen.

he oldest and most interesting feature of this landscape is *Emain Macha*, or Navan Fort as it is also called. This artificial mound lies about a mile outside of Armagh City. I took the A28 out of town turned right at the sign for Navan Fort. I turned left again and found the mound signed on the right side of the road. Emain Macha means 'Twins of Macha", and takes its name from the legend of the goddess Macha.

One day a local nobleman, Crunnchu, was visited by a strange and beautiful woman. The mysterious lady remained with him, and soon they were married and she became pregnant. As the hour of the child's birth drew near, Crunnchu went into town where a festival of horseracing was taking place. He got drunk and began to boast to the king that his wife could run faster than any of his horses. The king became angry and demanded that this woman be brought before

Emain Macha
Royal seat of the Ulster Kings. Located a mile outside of Armagh City and signed off the A28.

The Church of Ireland Cathedral
Abbey St., Armagh
Contains the grave of Brian Boru and an array of interesting ancient carvings and statues.
Web: www.stpatricks-cathedral.org

St. Patrick's Roman Catholic Cathedral
Cathedral Rd.
Armagh
On the other side of the city, the wonderfully ornate interior is truly moving.

Tynan Cross
The village of Tynan lies west of Armagh. Take a right in front of the church and the cross is beside a car park.

St.
Patrick's
Trian
40 English St.
Armagh
Tel:
(028)37521801
Web: www.saint
patrickstrian.com
Email: info@saint
patrickstrian.com
Exhibitions on St.
Patrick and *The Book
of Armagh*.

Tuan's Notes
Macha
*Learn more about
Macha in The Mystery:
Deities & Demigods
(pp. 94-95).*

Ballykeel Dolmen
From Newry take the
road west to Cam-
lough, and then fol-
low signs for Slieve
Gullion until you are
on the B134 towards
Forkhill. Turn right
onto Ballykeel road.

Slieve Gullion
Along the B134 there
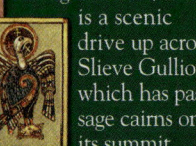
is a scenic
drive up across
Slieve Gullion,
which has pas-
sage cairns on
its summit.

him, or else he would cut off Crunnchu's head.

Macha had no choice but to race the horses. She beat the horses, and at the end fell down here in this spot where I was standing and gave birth to twin babies. She looked up in fury at all the men around her and uttered the following **curse**: "You men of Ulster," she said, pointing her finger around, "for nine generations, at a time when Ulster needs you to defend it, you will know the pain of childbirth, and be rendered weak and helpless in your hour of need." This is the reason why Ulster was defenseless when Queen Maeve attacked during the *Táin Bó Cuailnge* — Cú Chulainn, being part god, was the only man immune from this curse. Cú was thus left to defend Ulster alone, as the other Knights of the Red Branch, and all of the other warriors of Ulster, had been rendered helpless by the birth pangs.

THE KNIGHTS OF THE RED BRANCH
The name of the assembly hall in Emain Macha was called *Craebh Ruadh*, which in English translates literally as "Red Branch". The Knights of the Red Branch was a military order similar to the Fianna that protected the province of Ulster, specifically Emain, which was traditionally known as the Royal Seat of Ulster. This place is home to many ancient stories.

A path led up a hill from the road and onto the spot where the main mound had been built. This was possibly where the royal palace would have sat. The mound stands high over the landscape, and it is believed to have been more of a ritual site rather than a defensive fortification. Nearby Loughnashade was where the trumpet I saw in the National Museum of Ireland was found, along with many other musical instruments. A smaller mound lay nearby, and the main mound here was fringed with large trees where two lovers had taken shelter from the incessant drizzle.

Armagh City

Two cathedrals dedicated to St. Patrick are the dominating features of this town. *The Book of Armagh* was written here in the 9th century, and contains a copy of his own *Confessio*.

THE CHURCH OF IRELAND CATHEDRAL

The Church of Ireland Cathedral was built on the site of the original church, where Brian Boru had been buried.

On a hill just above the center of town is the Church of Ireland Cathedral, built on the site of the first church that had been built in the 5th century. This is a most important historical place that contains many interesting relics, and is also the traditional burial place of Brian Boru, who had died

Tours
Conducted tours of the Church of Ireland Cathedral are available June-August. Contact the Dean at:
Tel: (028) 3752 3142
Email: dean@armagh.anglican.org

Tuan's Notes
The Curse of Macha
Learn more about The Curse of the Ulstermen in The Mystery: Folklore & Mythology (pp. 191-192).

Armagh Guided Tours
with Barbara Ferguson
Beechlodge Farm
Coolmillish Rd.
Markethill
Tel: (028) 3755 1119
Mob: (077) 40511442
Web: www.armagh guidedtours.com
Email: info@armarh guidedtours.com
A wide range of tours tailored to suit individual or group needs. City or country tours available.

THE JOURNEY
U L S T E R

COUNTY
ARMAGH

Eat
& Drink

Bagel Bean
60 Lwr English St.
Armagh City
Tel: (028)3751 5251

Fat Sams
13, Lwr English St.
Armagh City
Tel: (028) 3752 5555

**The Shambles Bar
& Restaurant**
9, Lower English St.
Armagh City
Tel: (028) 3752 4107

C A F È S
**Café Papa Deli Bar
and Bistro**
15, Thomas St.
Armagh City
Tel: (028) 3751 1205

P U B S
The Gas Lamp
Thomas St., Armagh
A small yellow front,
but once inside it's
like being in the
Tardis. Has traditional
music on Wed. nights.

**Charlemont Arms
Hotel Bar**
57-65 English
St.
Armagh City
Tel: (028)
3752 2028

A bas relief of the legendary King Labhraidh Loingseach, showing off his donkeylike ears.

during the Battle of Clontarf, in Dublin. A plaque on the front wall commemorates his burial spot.

Inside the cathedral I found a row of ancient stone statues along the wall. Two of the most interesting are the Tandragee Man (so named because it was found in Tandragee Gardens) and a carving of a man holding his donkey-sized ears. The latter is assumed to be King Labhraidh Loingseach. "Tandragee Man", also known as "The Tandragee Idol", is believed actually to be an image of Nuada of the Silver Arm, ancient King of the Tuatha dé Danann. It shows him clutching his arm, the arm that had been severed at the end of The First Battle of Moy Tura by Streng, the champion of the Fir Bolg.

However, not only did Nuada lose one of his arms, but also the kingship, as one of the requirements of kingship at that time was that the king had to be physically whole. A silver arm that worked perfectly was created for him, however, and he won back the kingship.

The Tandragee Man is most likely King Nuada, shown clutching his silver arm.

St. Patrick's Roman Catholic Cathedral

Also known as The National Cathedral of St. Patrick, St. Patrick's Roman Catholic Cathedral was built on the site that Patrick had prophesied would one day be a place where God would be given great glory. His prophecy finally was fulfilled in 1904.

At the other side of town I found St. Patrick's Roman Catholic Cathedral, its tall, twin spires rising majestically over the city. Although not old, having been built in the 1800s, I found the inside of this cathedral to be truly magnificent. I'm not a religious man, but I couldn't help being moved by the ornate carvings, beautifully decorated walls and ceilings and the circular, decorated plaques commemorating all the saints of Ireland. This was possibly the most beautiful cathedral I had ever been in.

There & Back Again

TRAINS
The nearest you can get by train is Newry.

BUSES
Armagh Bus Station
Lonsdale Rd.
Armagh City
Tel: (028) 3752 2266

TAXI
Eurocabs
Tel: (028) 3751 1900

Central Taxis
Tel: (028) 3752 6999

BIKE HIRE
Browne's Bikes
32, Cormeen Rd.
Killylea
Tel: (028) 3752 2782
4 miles west of the city off the A28.

WALKING
The Pilgrim's Trail is a self-guided walking tour of the city taking in all the history. It starts at the tourist office and a leaflet with information and a map is available there.

THE JOURNEY
ULSTER
COUNTY
ARMAGH

Places to Stay

HOTELS

Charlemont Arms Hotel Bar
57-65 English St.
Armagh
Tel: (028) 3752 2028
Located in the heart of the city.

B & B S

Ballinahinch House
47, Ballygroobany
Rd., Richhill
Armagh
Tel: (028) 38870081
Web: www.ballina
hinchhouse.com
Email: info@ballina
hinchhouse.com
Located in the village of Richhill a few miles east of Armagh, this lovely Victorian residence has 3 rooms.

Hillview Lodge
33, Newtownhamilton
Armagh
Tel: (028) 3752 2000
Web: www.
hillviewlodge.com
Email: info@hill
viewlodge.com
About 1 mile south of town with 6 en-suite rooms.

Tynan Cross is actually made up of two different crosses.

Before leaving Armagh I drove out west to the little village of Tynan, where an interesting **Celtic cross** is all that remains of an ancient church dedicated to St. Vindic. The cross is actually made up of two crosses and stands on a raised concrete table beside the current church. It's an interesting-looking cross.

Ballykeel Dolmen

Forget everything I said about Leganany being the most amazing dolmen in Ireland. Ballykeel Dolmen could easily rival that. It's proportionately similar, with its three, 7-foot-high upright stones and the

Ballykeel Dolmen is a large, well-preserved dolmen that is still surrounded by its large court cairn

huge capstone resting gracefully on top. (It also made a great shelter from the rain.) A ring of stone entrenched into the ground surrounded the dolmen, the only evidence of the cairn that once surrounded the portal.

Ballykeel Dolmen lies close to Slieve Gullion, which marks the other side of the Gap of the North. This ancient passage leads up over a pass into County Louth, coming out at Forkhill, the birthplace of St. Brigid.

Slieve Gullion

Slieve Gullion, seen in the distance with Ballymacdermott Court Cairn in the foreground, sits on one side of "The Gap of the North", a strategically important mountain pass between Ulster and Leinster provinces in ancient times. Slieve Gullion hosts several passage cairns, and is also a popular hiking and climbing destination. Image courtesy Assignments Plus Publications, www.assignmentsplus.com.

I headed back out onto the B134 and followed a sign for a scenic drive up across Slieve Gullion. There are supposed to be two passage cairns here on the mountain, but as I headed upwards the narrow, pitted road became barely discernable in the ensuing mist. So I headed back down to safety and popped across the border to fill up with cheaper petrol, before heading north again into County Tyrone.

HOSTELS
Armagh City Youth Hostel
39 Abbey Street
Tel: (028) 9032 4733
Web: www.hini.org.uk
Email:
info@hini.org.uk
Situated in the city center near the Church of Ireland.

Tuan's Notes
Celtic Crosses
Learn more about Celtic Christianity in The History: The Coming of Christianity (pp. 219-227).

CAMPING
Clare Glen Caravan Park
Markethill Rd.
Tandragee
Tel: (028) 3884 1110
Email:
trc@armagh.gov.uk

For more information visit ireland. mysterious world.com/ Journey/ Counties/ Armagh/

THE JOURNEY
U L S T E R
COUNTY ARMAGH

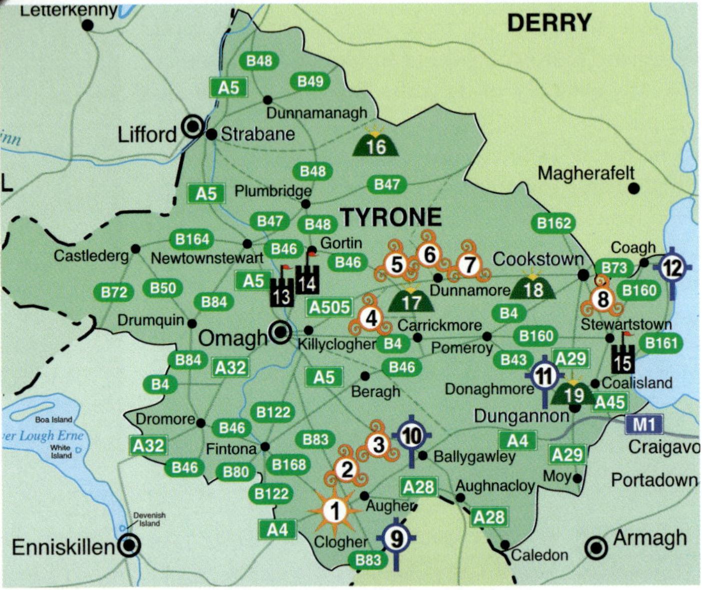

Places to See in Tyrone

☀ Multi-Sites

1. Clogher 🐾 ⚓ 🏛
   - Rathmore 747-750
   - The Clogh Oír 750-751
   - Clogher Cathedral . . 747, 750-1

🐾 Ancient Sites

2. Knockmany Passage Cairn . . 748
3. Sess Kilgreen Passage Cairn
4. Loughmacrory Wedge Cairn/
   Altdrumman Portal Dolmen
5. Dun Ruadh/Aghascrebagh
   Ogham Stone
6. Beaghmore Stone Circle . . 747-49
7. Cregganconroe Passage Cairn/
   Creggandevesky Court Cairn
8. Tullahogue Fort 747-748

⚓ Christian Sites

9. St. Patrick's Chair & Well . 748
752-753
10. Errigal Kerrogue Church & Well
11. Donaghmore High Cross
12. Ardboe Cross & Abbey

🏛 Historical Sites

13. Ulster American Folk Park
14. Ulster History Park
15. Mountjoy Castle

⚓ Scenic Views

16. The Sperrin Mountains
17. An Creagan Visitor Centre
18. Drum Manor Forest Park
19. Tyrone Crystal

Driving Directions: See pp. 747-750, 752

Tyrone
Tullahogue Fort

A view of Tullahogue Fort in the midground, with Slieve Gallion in the distance. The fort is a 100-foot-wide, circular enclosure surrounded by two high banks separated by a large trench.

I spent the night in a nice, friendly campsite in Dungannon Park. From here I headed north to Cookstown and took the road south towards Tullahogue. Just as I rounded a sharp left turn, there was a sign pointing left to the fort.

A country lane led up the hill and through a gate where I found myself standing high up on the hill with lovely views to the north of Slieve Gallion across the border in County Derry, and rolling green hills to the south. The fort itself was enclosed by trees and inside I found a wide, circular enclosure surrounded by two high banks with a large trench separating them. The trench was so wide that I thought for a moment that it might have been a moat. At the center the diameter is 100 feet and the surrounding bank looks down upon it. I wandered around the outer ditch, closely

Tullahogue Fort
Inauguration point of the Uí Neills. From Cookstown take the B520 south towards Tullahogue, and as the road bends sharply to the left, look for a turning into a car park. The fort is up on the hill.

Beaghmore Stone Circle
Fantastic site with seven stone circles and a number of cairns. Take the A505 west from Cookstown, turn right for Dunnamore and follow signs.

Rathmore & Clogher Cathedral
In the village of Clogher on the A4 west of Dungannon. The church contains the *Clogh Óir*, one of the three magical stones of Ireland. If the

THE JOURNEY
ULSTER
COUNTY
TYRONE

church is locked, telephone the Deanery at (028) 8554 8235.

St. Patrick's Chair & Well

A pagan site Christianized by St. Patrick. From Augher, east of Clogher, take the A28 towards Aughnacloy. Turn right at sign and follow road until you come to a signed car park on the right.

Knockmany Passage Cairn

Just outside of Clogher. Take the B83 towards Omagh and follow signs. At the crossroads go straight ahead until you come to a sign pointing right. From the car park follow the forest path to the right and keep left as it spirals up onto the summit. Note: Access may be limited.

THE JOURNEY
U L S T E R
COUNTY
TYRONE

followed by a stray cat. It was at that point that I realized that animals in one form or another had been shadowing me throughout my journey.

Tullahoge Fort was the inauguration point for the Uí Neill's, and the O'Hagans were guardians of the site for the clan. It's said that there was an ancient stone chair in the middle used as a throne for the king's inauguration. The chair was marked on a 17th-century map of the area, but was broken up a few years later during the English invasion.

Beaghmore Stone Circle

Beagmore Stone Circle is actually made up of seven circles in total, interspersed with cairns and stone rows.

Lying just north of the village of Dunnamore is the largest concentration of stone circles I've ever seen in one small area. There are seven circles in total, with a number of cairns and stone rows in-between. This must have been the location for some very important rituals, and it invoked images of huge pagan ceremonies and festivals. Many of the circles are quite wide, with soft, green grass in the interior. But one circle differs from the rest. It is filled with 800 smaller stones entrenched into the ground, known as "The Dragon's Teeth".

This field of ancient monuments is a fantastic place, with low hills surrounding the horizon that seemed a million miles away from this wide plain. The light was consistently changing in the open landscape, illuminating the stones one minute then casting shadows across them the next. One of the theories is that this site was intended as an astronomical observatory. Or maybe it was intended as a site for ritual celebrations. We may never know for sure.

Rathmore

Rathmore sits on a hill behind Clogher Cathedral and has a great view of both village and countryside.

The village of Clogher lies on the A4. To get to it from the A505 meant going into Omagh and heading back southeast on the A5. I have this problem that I always like to take the smaller roads if I can. So, instead of going into Omagh, I decided to cut across on the B46. But inexplicably, I ended up in Omagh, so I had to take the main road.

This little village is home to another ancient hillfort known as *Rathmore* ("Big Fort"). It's a dominating presence from the village, and sits behind Clogher

Ulster American Folk Park
2 Mellon Road,
Castletown
Omagh
Tel: (028) 8224 3292
Web:
www.folkpark.com

Tourist Information
⊕ *Killymaddy Tourist Information*
190, Ballygawley Rd.
Dungannon
Tel: (028) 8776 7259
Email: killymaddy@freeuk.com
⊕ *Cookstown Tourist Information*
Burnavon Centre,
Burn Rd.
Tel: (028) 8676 6727
Email: tic@cookstown.gov.uk

Festivals
Folk in the Park
Tel: (028) 8224 3292
Web:
www.folkpark.com
Musicians, singers and dancers will gather to provide entertainment within the unique setting of the outdoor museum.

Eat &
Drink

The Country Café
4 Scotch Street
Dungannon
Tel: (028) 87727207

Castle Bay Restaurant
187 Mountjoy Rd.
Dungannon
Tel: (028) 8773 8916

Strangmore Country House
65 Moy Rd.
Dungannon
Tel: (028) 8772 5600

Rosamunds Coffee Shop
Station Road
Clogher
Tel: (028) 8554 8601

PUBS
Dungannon is the best place to find traditional Irish music. Monday night: **The Bailey**, Lower Scotch St.
Tuesday night: **Ropers Bar**, 80 Scotch St.
Saturday night: **McGrath's Bar**, 55 Irish St.

THE JOURNEY
U L S T E R
COUNTY
TYRONE

Cathedral. I followed signs up a road after the cathedral and parked in a car park at the base of the hill. A grassy pathway led up to the top of the hill, where I found myself shaded by tall trees. The hill has a great view across the town, and it would be a great spot for a picnic.

To the south is Slieve Beagh, which has a passage cairn on its summit that is said to be the burial place of Bith, Noah's son. Bith was also the father of Princess Cessair, who is believed by some to be buried in Knockmaa, in County Galway. Rathmore was built around 100 BC, but was said to have been an inauguration point for the Oriel kings of Ulster, who were driven this way after the burning of Emain Macha.

Clogher Cathedral

Clogher Cathedral's grounds include a sizable cemetary complete with high crosses.

In the village I found the cathedral locked. Inside there is said to be one of the three magical stones of Ireland, the *Clogh Óir* (Golden Stone). The town of Clogher derived its name from this. *Sacred Ireland* lists a number to phone if the cathedral is closed, so I did. The lady who answered informed me that the vicar was already on his way over to open up.

The *Clogh Óir* (above), along with the *Lia Fáil* of Tara and the *Crom Cruach* (*q.v.*) of Cavan, comprise the "Three Magical Stones" of ancient Ireland. The *Clogh Óir* was known as "The Chief Idol of the North"

The vicar was a jovial man with silver hair swept into a side parting with strands running down his forehead in a 1980s New Romantic style. He looked like an aging Brian Ferry. He explained the history of the church.

"St. Patrick came this way and established a church on this spot. But during their travels the servant had become tired of moving around and wanted to stay somewhere. So Patrick sent him back here to Clogher and made him bishop. He said to his servant, 'You'll be close enough to be my friend, but far enough away not to interfere.'"

He led me to the hallway where the *Clogh Óir* was standing against the wall. This tall, rectangular stone was once adorned with silver and gold. Like the *Lia Fáil* of Tara, this may have been used in the inauguration ceremonies for the kings of Ulster. There is a tradition that King Conchobar consulted it. It was once known as "The Chief Idol of the North". Like the *Lia Fáil*, some say that this isn't the original stone. But, considering it's been around for 2,000 years, we'll never know for sure. The third magical stone is the *Crom Cruach*, "The Chief Idol of Ireland", which now lies south of here in the Cavan County Museum.

There & Back Again

TRAINS
There are no trains to anywhere in Tyrone.

BUSES
Dungannon Station
Scotch St.
Tel: (028) 8772 2251

Cookstown Station
Molesworth St.
Tel: (028) 8676 6440

Omagh Station
Mountjoy Rd.
Tel: (028) 8224 2711

CAR HIRE
Lakeside Self Drive Car Hire Ltd.
Ballybrack Rd.
Sixmilecross, Omagh
Tel: (028)8076 1060
Web: www.grugan.com
Email: f.grugan@grugan.com

BIKE HIRE
Clogher Valley Cycles
Augher
Tel: (028) 8554 9802

WALKING
The Ulster Way and **Slieve Beagh** pass by St. Patrick's Chair.

THE JOURNEY
U L S T E R

COUNTY
TYRONE

Places to Stay

HOTELS

Erganagh House
21 Glenpark Road Omagh
Tel: (028) 82252852
Built in the 18th century, this former rectory is open all year except Christmas.

B & B S

Clanabogan House
85 Clanabogan Rd. Omagh
Tel: (028) 8224 1171
Web: www. clanaboganhouse. freeserve.co.uk
Email: m@ clanaboganhouse. freeserve.co.uk

Park View B&B
3, Victoria Rd. Dungannon
Tel: (028)87725291

Corick Country House
20 Corick Rd. Clogher.
Tel: (028) 8554 8216
A 3-star guesthouse in a 17th-century country house.

St. Patrick's Chair & Well

St. Patrick's Chair is probably an old druid's chair that was repurposed by St. Patrick as a pulpit for preaching.

I drove to Augher, just east of Clogher, and then took the A28 towards Aughnacloy. Soon I came across signs directing me to the site.

I pulled up next to a car and followed a couple of old fellas into the forest. The trail led up some forest steps onto a rocky ledge surrounded by thick forest. I couldn't fail to miss the huge stone seat that sits on the ledge overlooking the well. It's a large, square boulder curiously shaped like a big chair. The story is that St. Patrick passed this way after leaving Clogher and came across this pagan site, which he proceeded to Christianize. He sat in this chair and preached to the people, then commanded water to appear from the rock so he could baptize them.

The well is not actually a well, but a bullaun in a large table of rock. It sits below the chair in a dip, where clooties had been hung by the hundreds on the branches of an overhanging tree.

Being in the forest I was once again relentlessly attacked by midges. This had been a common problem lately, so I decided to invoke the powers of the chair to deal with this.

St. Patrick's Well is set in a beautiful sylvan setting accented by hundreds of colorful clooties.

Tradition says that if you sit in the chair and make a wish, it will come true. So I headed back up to the ledge, climbed the solid, square rock the chair is perched upon, and sat down in it. I felt like a dwarf in an armchair. This was more than likely a druid's chair,

like the one I had seen in South Dublin, that had been around before St. Patrick came along. But this druid must have been a giant. I made my wish:

"I wish these pesky midges would all stay away from me from now on!"

It is said that in order for the wish to come true, you mustn't tell anyone. So I didn't. Except you, of course. ;)

The well is actually a bullaun, a natural depression in the rock that collects rainwater over time.

THE JOURNEY
ULSTER
COUNTY
TYRONE

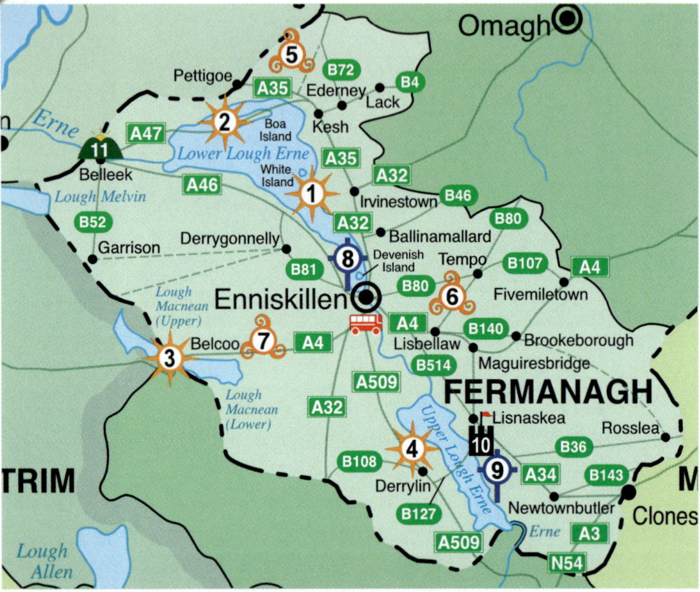

![map of Fermanagh]

Places to See in Fermanagh

☀ MULTI-SITES
1. White Island ♿ ⚑ ⛰ . . 755-57
2. Boa Island ♿ ⛰
   - Janus Figure. . . . 755, 758-759
   - The Lusty Man. 759
3. Belcoo ♿ ⚑ ⛰
   - Crom Cruach Standing Stone
   - Aghlanack Dual Court Cairn
   - Templerushin 761
   - Bullaun Stones 761
   - St. Patrick's Well . . . 755, 761
   - Templenaffrin
4. Knockninny ♿ ⚑ ⛰
   - Knockninny Court Cairn
   - Shehinny Cave
   - St. Ninnidh's Well

♲ ANCIENT SITES
5. Drumskinny Circle . . . 755, 760
6. Topped Mountain Cairn
7. Belmore Mountain Passsage Cairn

⚑ CHRISTIAN SITES
8. Devenish Island. 755-756
9. Aghalurcher Church

⛪ HISTORICAL SITES
10. Castle Belfour

⛰ SCENIC VIEWS
11. Belleek Pottery Tour 756

🚌 TRANSPORTATION
Enniskillen Bus Station

Driving Directions: See pp. 755-756, 758, 760-761

Fermanagh

Lower Lough Erne, at 50 miles long, is one of the largest lakes in Ireland. Lower Lough Erne, in the northwest of County Fermanagh, is connected via the River Erne to the slightly smaller Upper Lough Erne in the southeast. Image © Kersten Bastian, 2004.

County Fermanagh is one of the smallest counties in Ireland, yet it has one of the largest lakes in Ireland. Lower Lough Erne is 50 miles long and narrows into a river running south through the county's major town of Enniskillen, widening once again to form Upper Lough Erne.

White Island

I drove into the Castle Archdale Marina and parked amongst the flurry of activity in the area. Boats lined the marina, families swarmed about with ice creams and people in wetsuits were preparing to go jet skiing. I wandered into the boat hire hut and learned of a little island just off shore that contains one of the area's most interesting attractions. A regular ferry runs on the hour and I caught it just in time. The journey took about 15 minutes, and on the way I picked up a book titled: *White Island: History & Mystery* by Richard Chambers. I leafed

Fermanagh
Things to Do & Places to See

White Island Church
Tiny island with mysterious stone carvings in the wall of a ruined church. Access via ferry from Castle Archdale Marina.

Janus Figure
Mysterious stone idol in the ancient Caldragh cemetery resembling a bug-eyed alien. From Kesh go north on A35 and head west on A47 onto Boa Island.

Drumskinny Stone Circle
Off to the right of the A35 north of Kesh.

St Patrick's Well
In the village of Belcoo.

Devenish Island
The remains of the monastery here are of a 12th-century Romanesque

style, including a round tower. Access is via ferry, 2 miles north of Enniskillen on the A32.

Tours

White Island Ferry
Castle Archdale Marina
Irvinestown
Tel: (028) 6862 1892 / 6862 1156
Every hour daily in July & August. Weekends only, April-May & Sept. Pony trekking, boat & bike hire and horse and carriage rides also available.

Erne Heritage Tour Guides
Commons, Belleek
Tel: (028) 6865 8327
Web: www.erneheritagetours.com
Email: adam4eves@aol.com

Belleek Pottery Tour
Belleek
Tel: (028) 6865 9300
Web: www.belleek.ie
Email: visitorcentre @belleek.ie

Though the 12th-century monastery on White Island is in ruins, the doorway and its magnificent archway are intact.

through it as we chugged across the lake in the little boat, unaware at the time that the rugged sailor-type at the wheel was also the author.

White Island is tiny and uninhabited. We pulled up at the wooden pier and I made my way up to where the ruins of a 12th-century monastery lay not far from the water's edge. The walls remain, along with the Ro-

The White Island figures have been the subject of various theories, including the idea that they were originally used as caryatid columns to support a pulpit in the original wooden church that stood on this site, or even as a means of illustrating a story about how St. Patrick had once healed a local king. The individual stat-

manesque doorway. But the most interesting feature is inside. Built into the rear wall are seven stone statues and a single stone head. Among these is a Sheela-na-Gig. The others are various Celtic Christian figures. The statues are actually around 300 years older than the church and are all depicted in a seated position. According to the book, this was common practice in the early Christian church. Richard believes that the builders found them and were too superstitious to destroy them. They therefore used them as building blocks, facing inwards so they wouldn't be seen. The deterioration of the building has revealed them once again for all to see.

The figures are obviously Christian, but have definite pagan undertones. The Celts believed that the head contained the soul, and this explains the heads being larger than the bodies. The book mentioned another famous figure that lies in the Caldragh Cemetery on Boa Island. So, once back on the mainland I headed there.

ues represent, from left to right: 1) a Sheela-na-Gig, intended to ward off lust; 2) Christ, similar to a representation in *The Book of Kells*; 3) St. Patrick, or perhaps Constans, builder of the abbey; 4) possibly King David, with his harp; 5&6) probably two more representations of Christ 7&8) unknown.

BUSES
**Enniskillen Bus
Station**
Shore Rd.
Enniskillen is a
major hub for desti-
nations all over
Ireland.

DRIVING
For Enniskillen take
the A4 west of
Dungannon or the
A32 west from
Omagh.

TAXI
Eurocabs
Irvinestown (near
Kesh)
Tel: (028) 6638 9777

County Cabs
22 Sedan Terrace
Enniskillen
Tel: (028) 6632 8888

CAR HIRE
Donnelly Self Drive
101 Irvinestown Rd.
Enniskillen
Tel: (028)6632 4712

Email:
donnelly
citreon
@dealer.
citreon.co.uk

Boa Island

The famous Boa Island Janus Figure. Photo courtesy PDPhoto.org.

Boa Island stretches across the northern shore of the lake, and is connected to the mainland via two bridges. I headed to the village of Kesh and turned left just north of here onto the A47 which takes you straight through the island. I pulled over on the left next to a sign for the cemetery and found it just around the corner hidden behind some trees.

THE JANUS FIGURE

The Janus Figure is named after the two-faced Roman god Janus. On both sides the figure appears to be holding its stomach in pain, though only the reverse side (right) shows a look of pain on its face. This statue may be linked to the story of the twins of Macha.

This is an ancient graveyard, and most of the graves are simply designated with ordinary, unmarked stones. In the middle stands the 2,000-year-old, three-foot-high Janus Figure. This fascinating statue is a total mystery. It's a double-sided carving of a figure with a large, oval-shaped head whose chin tapers to a point. It has huge bug-eyes, a long nose and a wide, narrow mouth. Its arms are folded across its torso.

THE LUSTY MAN

Though the man depicted in this figure may indeed have been "lusty", The Lusty Man takes its name from the island on which it originally resided, Lusty Beg. Now it sits beside the Janus figure and, like the Janus figure, people still throw coins on it for good luck.

Nearby is a smaller figure known as The Lusty Man. It was brought here from the nearby island of Lusty Beg. It's a lot more faded than the Janus figure, but does look as though it's holding its genitalia, just like the Sheela-na-Gig.

Or, instead of holding his genitals, perhaps the man depicted is in pain, suffering the "birth-pains" that the men of Ulster suffered whenever danger approached, as recounted in the story of "The Twins of Macha". Could it be that the Janus figure and The Lusty Man were meant to symbolize the "twins" of the legend? Or perhaps the Janus figure incorporates both of the twins into one? Another mystery to solve.

Drumskinny Stone Circle

I drove back towards Kesh and turned off at the sign for Drumskinny Stone Circle. The sign indicated it was another 3 miles. A short way up the road I turned right again at a sign that said "Drumskinny Stone Circle: 4½ miles". It's always been the old joke that the Irish do things backwards, and it seemed that here in Fermanagh they had taken that literally.

Whether it was three or four miles, it was a long way. The road dipped and peaked until I finally reached a sign pointing right, which led me to a car park. In the field is a single ring of stones measuring 43 feet in diameter. A cairn sits beside the circle and a row of stones run from the cairn down beside the circle.

It was discovered in 1934 buried in the bog. Many of the 39 stones are missing and have been replaced with replicas marked "MOF". The cairn is surrounded by a number of kerbstones. This is a nice, cleanly located site — I couldn't help thinking that it looked too perfect. The area around the stones had been dug out and filled with gravel, and the rest was raised grass. It seemed unnatural, and I much preferred the site at Beaghmore for that reason.

(Another) St. Patrick's Well

I headed back down through Enniskillen and took the A4 west to the border town of Belcoo. I was in the last of the six counties, and here I would cross over to County Cavan for the last two of the Ulster counties.

Before I crossed the bridge though, I followed the signs for St Patrick's Well and arrived at the Templerushin Church. Inside the graveyard was a large bullaun stone, deeply entrenched into the ground. I crossed the road and walked down by the forked road which led to the well.

It looks more like a pool of water from a stream that trickles down from the hill and runs off along the side of the road. But in fact it is the water bubbling up from the ground that is running off to create the streams. The well apparently yields up to 600 gallons of water per minute. It's also said to be the coldest water in Ireland, and a cure for nervous disorders and stomach complaints.

The well has long been an old **Lughnasa** site, traditionally visited from the last Sunday in July until the 15th August. St. Patrick blessed the well and thus the Lughnasa was replaced with a Christian pilgrimage. Among the stations was the bullaun across the road.

Tuan's Notes
Lughnasa
Learn more about Lughnasa and other ancient festivals in The History: Ancient Irish Culture (pp. 263-264).

THE JOURNEY
U L S T E R
C O U N T Y FERMANAGH

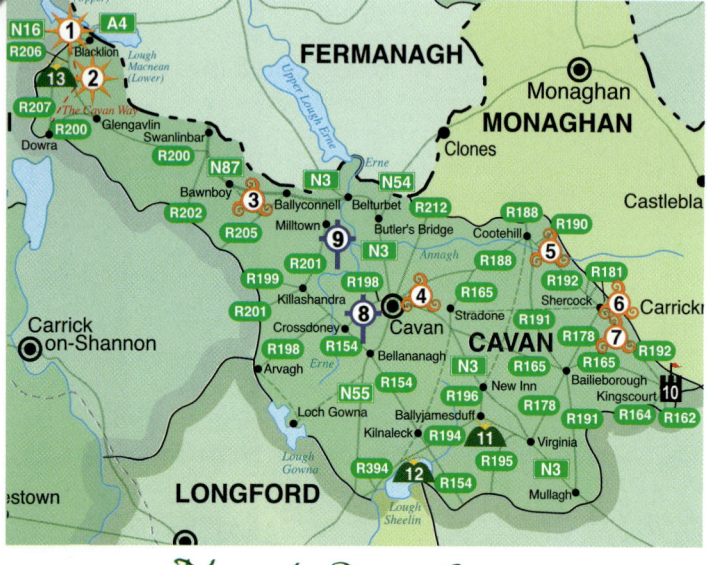

Places to See in Cavan

☀ Multi-Sites

1. St. Brigid's Stones 🛡 ⚲ ⛰
   - Killinagh Church 763
   - Lough Macnean 763
2. The Burren 🛡 ⛰ . . . 764-765
   - The Dolmen
   - The Giant's Grave . . 763-765
   - Moneygashel Sweat House
   - Shannon Pot 763, 766

🛡 Ancient Sites

3. The Crom Cruach (replica)
4. Finn McCool's Fingers
5. Cohaw Giant's Grave 764
6. The Giant's Bed
   (Labbyfirmore)
7. The Lughnasa Assemblies
   - Loughanleah Hill

- Taghart Hill
- Corleck Hill

⚲ Christian Sites

8. Kilmore Cathedral
9. Drumlane Abbey

⛏ Historical Sites

10. Cabra Castle Hotel 766

⛰ Scenic Views

11. Cavan County Museum . . 764
    - The Crom Cruach
      (original) 767
    - The Corleck Triple Head
    - Sheela na Gigs
12. Lough Sheelin
13. The Cavan Way 765

Driving Directions: See pp. 763-767

Cavan
St. Brigid's Stones

According to tradition, St. Brigid's Stones, though generally called "cursing stones", can be used to invoke either a blessing or a curse.

nce again I was back in the Republic. The border town of Blacklion lies just across the bridge from Belcoo. It's more of a village than a town.

I headed west on the N16 towards Sligo, and pulled over on the right just outside of town where Killinagh Church lay just across a field. I waded through the soaking wet long grass to get there. It wasn't actually the church I was interested in, but what lay behind. I climbed over the gate and wandered across a large, open field sitting beside Lough Macnean. It was a lovely spot, and would have been better if it weren't raining.

At the back of the field sitting beside a row of bushes I found a large boulder with a number of rounded depressions on the top. The difference between these and all the other bullauns I'd seen is that each depression holds a rounded stone. These are called "cursing stones".

Cavan
Things to Do & Places to See

St. Brigid's Stones
Located behind the ruins of Killinagh church. Take the N16 west out of Blacklion and stop at sign on right.

The Giant's Grave
From Blacklion take the first left off the Sligo road, then the next left signed "Cornagee Lookout". Follow this road until you come to a forestry entrance on the left. Take the right hand trail at the dolmen through the fallen trees to the grave.

Shannon Pot
From Blacklion take the first left off the Sligo road and then the second left. Follow this until you come to a sign pointing left up to a car park.

THE JOURNEY
ULSTER
COUNTY
CAVAN

The term is a little misleading because although they can be used for cursing, they are primarily used to invoke a blessing. The stone must be turned clockwise in order to invoke a blessing. To invoke a curse, the stone must be turned anti-clockwise.

I considered myself fortunate to have come this far, considering the dire state of the Scooby Van. So I decided to invoke a blessing to ensure its continuing good fortune: "Blessed art thou Scooby for having brought me thus far, despite your age and ailments. May you continue to ride smoothly until this adventure is at an end."

I was tempted to turn the stone back the other way and invoke a curse upon these pesky midges, seeing as St. Patrick's Chair hadn't granted me my wish. But I'd read that if a curse is unjust, then it will come back upon the perpetrator.

The Giant's Grave

You can imagine how confused I was when the woman in the garage told me to head for the Burren in order to find The Giant's Grave. Just on the outskirts of Blacklion there is a sign pointing left for it.

The Giant's Grave is a massive wedge grave that is possibly the largest and best preserved of its type in Ireland.

The word burren actually means "rocky place". Obviously the burren here is not the famous burren of County Clare. I took the first left out of Blacklion and then the next left, which was signed for Cornagee Lookout. The road was a rough, narrow country lane which eventually passed by a forestry entrance signed "Burren". I pulled over beside the gate and walked from there.

Following the forest road I headed up beside lush, green woods with moss-covered walkways and stones. Wooden signs pointed into the forest indicating ancient round enclosures and hut sites. I continued on along the path until it emerged at the start of a clearing, where deforestation had taken away a large chunk of these beautiful woods. To the left I found the remains of a dolmen inside the ruins of a house. The dolmen itself has been destroyed by whoever built the house. The 16-foot limestone capstone lies half on the floor, and is supported by the side wall of the house.

Directly opposite the house a sign pointed across the field of fallen trees to The Giant's Grave. I followed the path until it went up into the forest again. The narrow, muddy trail emerged at the top of a hill to a massive wedge grave, far more noteworthy of the name "Giant's Grave" than any others I'd seen.

There are three chambers, the largest being 17 feet long. The whole thing is about 4 feet wide. Five solid limestone capstones cover the chambers, and it really looks like it could contain the body of a giant. There is supposed to be a gully nearby called "The Giant's Leap" where, according to local folklore, the giant is said to have met his death. He was then buried here in this grave.

From the grave there was the familiar sight of the waymarked poles, so I followed them through the forest and back out onto the path.

Donaghue's Pub
Upper Main St.
Cavan Town

Farnham Arms Hotel
Main St.
Cavan Town
Tel: (049) 4332577
Has Irish music on Wednesday nights.

There & Back Again
B U S E S
Bus Éireann
Farnham St.
Cavan
Tel: (049)
4331353/4332533

C A R H I R E
Enterprise Rent-a-Car
Ballinagh Rd.
Cavan Town
Tel: (049) 4365000

B I K E H I R E
Fitzpatrick's Bicycle Hire
Belturbet
Tel: (049) 9522866

W A L K I N G
The Cavan Way starts at Blacklion and ends in Dowra, beside Lough Allen.

THE JOURNEY
U L S T E R
COUNTY CAVAN

Places to Stay

HOTELS

Cabra Castle Hotel
Kingscourt
Tel: (042) 966 7030
Web:
www.cabracastle.com
Email:
sales@cabracastle.com
The castle has a history going back as far as the 1700s. A massive place with 80 rooms.

B & B S

The Beeches
Station Rd.
Cootehill
Tel: (049) 5552307
A nice friendly place in town with 3 rooms.

Glendown
33 Cathedral Rd.
Cavan
Tel: (049) 4332257
Email:
glendown@eircom.net
In town with 4 en-suite rooms.

Rockwood House

Cloverhill
Belturbet
Tel: (047) 55351

THE JOURNEY

ULSTER

COUNTY CAVAN

Shannon Pot

Shannon Pot is a natural spring fed by rainwater from the Cuilcagh Mountains that forms the headwaters of the River Shannon.

I returned to the van and headed back down to the first turning I'd taken. I turned left and then took the next left for Glengelvin. I followed this road for a while until I came to another left turn that led up to a car park.

At the end of a footpath I found the large pool of water that is the source of the mighty River Shannon. At 240 miles long this is the longest river in Ireland, and longer than any in the UK. Rainwater from the nearby Cuilcagh Mountains trickles through a number of limestone caverns and rises up here at this 50-foot-wide spring. This is a beautiful spot with a bench beside the pool. The water is clear and shaded by large, overhanging trees.

There is a similar story here to the birth of the Boyne. Legend has it that Sinnann, grand-daughter of Manannán mac Lir, came here in search of the Salmon of Wisdom. It's said that when she caught the fish, it was so angry that it lashed its tail so furiously that the well rose up and gushed forth across the land, carving out a route across Ireland until it emptied into the sea.

The Crom Cruach

The bottom half of the *Crom Cruach* idol that had been broken by St. Patrick. The top half is also on display in the museum.

South of Cavan town, in the village of Ballyjamesduff, is the Cavan County Museum. I was here in order to see the third of "The Three Magical Stones of Ireland", the *Crom Cruach*. It is also known as "The Killycluggin Stone", as it was originally sited in the townland of Killycluggin. According to legend, the stone was broken in half by St. Patrick. It has since been removed to the museum and a replica sits in its place at Killycluggin.

Whereas the other two magical stones of Ireland were uncarved, I found it interesting that this stone is completely covered with Celtic artwork from the *La Téne* period. It looks a lot like the Turoe Stone in Galway, only it is larger, barrel-shaped and has a flat top. The stone is associated with the dark god of the harvest, *Crom Cruach (op. cit.)*. It was found outside a stone circle, which can still be seen at Killycluggin. The story of St. Patrick breaking the stone may be symbolic of his attempt to destroy the power of the pagan god, and establish Christianity as the more powerful religion. Whatever happened, the stone was definitely broken at some point, as the original top half lay on a stand next to it.

THE JOURNEY
ULSTER
COUNTY CAVAN

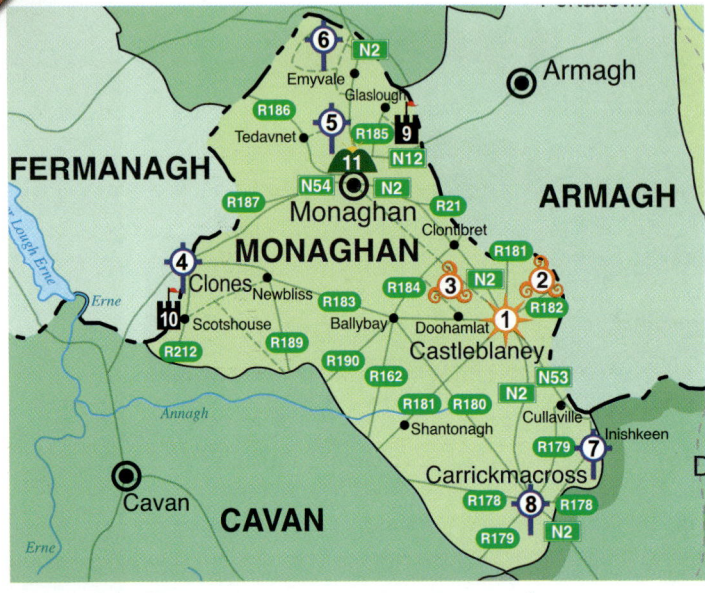

Places to See in Monaghan

☀ MULTI-SITES

1. Hope Castle 🏚 🔥 ⚓ 🏕 . . . 770
   - The Curse of the Hope Diamond
   - Remains of Blaney Castle
   - Former convent
   - View of Lough Muckno

🚲 ANCIENT SITES

2. Mullyash Hill
   - Hilltop cairn
   - The Long Stone
   - Old Lughnasa site
3. Lennan Dolmen/Corlealackagh Giant's Grave

⚓ CHRISTIAN SITES

🏚 HISTORICAL SITES

⚓ SCENIC VIEWS

Driving Directions: See pp. 770-771

Monaghan

Downtown Clones still preserves a beautiful high cross and a round tower from the original monastic settlement.

y journey was at an end. I couldn't believe I'd been on the road for 2 months now searching out these places. I had actually found things of interest in every county in Ireland. I'd been traveling in this country on and off for five years now, and people often said to me, "I expect you've been all over Ireland by now."

Well, now I had.

There was just one more place to visit: Clones.

Clones

In the center of this little village is a beautiful 10th-century high cross, standing 15 feet high. *Sacred Ireland* describes it as being quite worn, but I thought in comparison to others I'd seen the carvings were quite discernable. Sitting in the center of the Diamond, it's backed by St. Tighernach's Church of Ireland.

Clones town dates back to the 1600s, and many of

Clones
A high cross and round tower remain from the monastic settlement.

Monaghan County Museum
1-2 Hill Street
Monaghan
Tel: (047) 82928
Email: comuseum@monaghancoco.ie

Eat & Drink
The Round Tower Bar
Cara St.
Clones
Tel: (047) 51158
Bar food is served and B&B is also available.

There & Back Again
B U S E S
Monaghan Station
North Rd., Monaghan
Tel: (047) 82377
Buses stop at the Diamond in Clones.

THE JOURNEY
U L S T E R
C O U N T Y
M O N A G H A N

its Georgian townhouses are well preserved. The area behind the church is believed to have been the site of the first monastery established here in the 6th century by St. Tighernach. The book said you can access the hill behind the church via a small lane beside it, but I ended up at a dead end. So I asked a man pushing a rubbish bin along the road. Tommy was his name.

"It's up by the Diamond," he said.

"Yes, but I couldn't get up there."

"Wait here a moment," he said.

When he had finished moving his bin he then sped off up the road, beckoning me with his hand to follow.

"What are you looking for?" he asked.

"Well, according to this book there is a hill fort behind the church."

A look of comprehension entered his eyes and he sped off once again. I hurried along behind as he led me down Cara Street to the left of the Diamond. Opposite the Round Tower Pub he turned and went up a small alley.

"Just through that archway there," he said, pointing to the pub, "is access to the round tower and the graveyard."

We continued up the lane, along a field of allotments and snarling dogs, then went through a wooden gate which led us up onto the top of the hill.

"There it is," said Tommy. "It was a fort once, but you can't get in there now because of all the bushes."

The view was magnificent though. It's possible that this was an ancient fort before the saint came and built his church. I thanked Tommy for bringing me here, and he scurried back down the hill to return to the job that he had forsaken so he could help me.

I tried to find an entrance to the fort, but it was completely blocked, so I headed back down to the street and went through the archway. The path led to the round tower, which is all that remains of the church established here in the 10th century. Inside the graveyard I found a fascinating shrine to St. Tighernach. It was a mini church, carved from a solid lump of rock. A simple gravestone with a Celtic cross sat in front of the little church, with the following inscription:

Here lie the remains of St. Tighernach,
of the Royal House of Oriel.
First Abbot of Clones & Bishop of Clogher
500 AD to 4th April 548.

Though I was glad to have finally found this interesting place, I thought it unfortunate that something so historically important should be so hard to access. Throughout my journey I had noticed that many of Ireland's ancient treasures were either in a sorry state of repair, or simply inaccessible. Many people I had met were working hard to protect what remained of their legacy. Like the Druid's Chair in Killiney, in some places where the local government refused to fund their upkeep, the local people contributed their own time to care for these monuments. Hopefully the Irish government and more of the Irish people will realize the value of the treasures that they have buried in their own backyards, and take the necessary steps to keep them safe.

I understand now why that mysterious little guard back in the National Museum had been so zealous in his protection of the ancient artifacts on display there — it was his own history that he was protecting. Perhaps that was the lesson that I needed to learn on this journey — how our past is sacred, and that without it, we are incomplete.

THE JOURNEY
U L S T E R
COUNTY
MONAGHAN

Journey's End

here I was, at the end of my journey to rediscover mysterious Ireland. Though I had read many books on Irish mythology, history and travel in Ireland, had traveled throughout much of Ireland, and had even written a book and numerous articles about Ireland, before now I hadn't realized how much Ireland truly has to offer. The memories of interesting places, fascinating legends, wonderful music and good times with good friends I had had on my journey will be mine to treasure forever. Here, at journey's end, I realized that I had come of age, that I had truly been there and back again.

Though Ireland's respect for its past is less than it once was, it still stands out among the nations of the West as one of the countries that has kept its ancient heritage the most intact. In fact, many of the Irish still reject Modernism, Post-Modernism and secular humanism to varying degrees, instead holding to the old ways — to a belief in God, in the fairies and/or in the supernatural in general. As a result, many look with growing concern at the increasing modernization of Ireland, and feel a growing fear that the abandonment of the old ways will inevitably lead to retribution from the divine realm.

To quote from Yeats' poem, "The Second Coming", "turning and turning in the widening gyre", modern society seems to be drifting farther and farther away from its ancient heritage. Rootless and wandering, "the best lack all convictions, while the worst are full of passionate intensity".

Surely, some revelation is at hand.

I decided to end my journey by returning to Meath, whose role as the spiritual heart of Ireland I now understood. I headed east to Monaghan town, and then took the N2 straight south to Slane, where I checked into the welcoming atmosphere of the Slane Farm Hostel. After filling my ever-expanding stomach with food, I decided I'd give the pub a miss that night and instead sit out front, under the stars, and contemplate my journey. I got chatting with a guy from New Zealand who had an interest in ancient legends, and he was quite interested to hear about my journey. He was fascinated to learn that there were so many ancient sites to visit here in Ireland, and also told me of some in New Zealand. What I had seen in this country over the last two months was just the tip of the iceberg — there is so much more in this mysterious world of ours to see and experience — so much ancient history to rediscover that has either been sadly neglected, purposely buried or forgotten altogether.

The ash tray slowly filled up with cigarette butts as we swapped stories and information, until we finally admitted we were tired and called it a night — him with a new itinerary for his journey around Ireland, and me with the idea of going to New Zealand for my next adventure.

It seemed that my journey wasn't at an end after all. It was only just beginning.

TRAVEL INFORMATION
AT · A · GLANCE

Calling Ireland

When calling from outside Ireland, type in your country's international code, followed by 353, then remove the "0" before the listed number. For Northern Ireland, dial 44.

COUNTRY	CODE	EXAMPLE
U.S.	011	011 353 1234 5678
U.K.	00	00 353 1234 5678
Canada	011	011 353 1234 5678
Australia	0011	0011 353 1234 5678
N.Z.	00	00 353 1234 5678

See ireland.mysteriousworld.com/Journey/ for more contact information.

Important Phone Numbers

Use these numbers when calling from within Ireland:

Official Tourist Board .. (01) 850 230 330
Met Éireann Weather .... (01) 806 4200
Emergencies (Republic and North) . . . 999

AIRLINES:
Aer Lingus . . . . (0818) 365 000
RyanAir. . . . . (0818) 30 30 30
Air Coach . . . .(01) 844 7118

MAJOR AIRPORTS:
Dublin . . . . (01) 814 1111
Cork . . . . (021) 431 3131
Shannon. . . . . (061) 712 000

FERRIES:
Stena Line . . . . (01) 204 7777
IrishFerries.com . . . . (0818) 300 400

TRAINS:
Irish Rail . . . . (01) 850 366 222
DART . . . . (01) 850 366 222
Translink (N. Ireland) . (028) 90 66 66 30

BUSES:
Bus Éireann . . . . (01) 836 6111
J.J. Kavanagh & Sons . . . (056) 883 1106

CAR RENTAL:
Irish Car Rentals: . . . . . . (01) 850 206 088
Budget Car Rental. . . . . . . (090) 66 27 711

Handy Travel Tips

• Purchase quality luggage and include your identification on the inside and outside.
• Do not pack weapons, tools, or anything that could be considered dangerous.
• Avoid bringing electrical equipment. If you must, then use the correct converter.
• Bring personal ID, necessary medicines, some extra cash, and traveler's checks.
• You can purchase a special SIM card for your cell phone, or rent a cell phone.
• Dress for cool, wet weather with layers that can easily be added or removed.
• The best time to visit is during the summer, when it is warmest and there is less rain. To avoid the crowds, visit in late spring or early fall, though some activities only take place during the summer.
• Festivals are usually the best time to visit, when the best of Ireland is on display. See. pp. 445-473 for more festival information, and pp. 340-351 for more travel tips.

Common Gaelic Terms

• *Dia dhuit* ("dee-ah gwit"): Hello
• *Slán agat* ("slawn ah-got"): Goodbye
• *Slán* ("slawn"): Bye
• *Fortan leat* ("fort-on le-ott"): Good luck!
• *Le do thoil* ("leh duh thall"): Please
• *Go riabh maith agat* ("Go reav mah ahgat"): Thank you
• *Fàilte oirbh* ("falt-sha eorv"): You're welcome.
• *Cead mìle fàilte!* ("Kayd meal falt-sha"): One thousand welcomes!
• *Slán abhaile* ("slawn awail-eh"): Have a safe trip
• *Sláinte* ("slawnt-sha"): Cheers!
• *Ta me are meisce* ("taw may air mesh-keh"): I am very drunk
• *An léprechaun ghoid sé mo leabhar* ("On leprechaun geed say mo leave-ar"): A leprechaun has stolen my book!